TEXTBOOK ON

MEDICAL LAW

DR M.D. MACLEOD MBChB MRCGP
The Health Centre
Wellington Avenue
Aldershot
Hants
GU11 1PA
Tel: 01252 324577
Fax: 01252 324861
e.mail:mdmacleod@librykim.demon.co.uk

TEXTBOOK ON

MEDICAL LAW

Second Edition

Michael Davies
BSc (Econ) (Wales), LLM (Reading)

BLACKSTONE
PRESS LIMITED

First published in Great Britain 1996 by Blackstone Press Limited, Aldine Place, London W12 8AA. Telephone: 0181-740 2277

© M. Davies, 1996

First edition, 1996
Second edition, 1998

ISBN: 1 85431 842 X

British Library Cataloguing in Publication Data
A CIP catalogue for this book is available from the British Library

Typeset by Style Photosetting Limited, Mayfield, East Sussex
Printed by Ashford Colour Press, Gosport, Hants

Contents

1 The nature of medical law   1

1.1 The scope of medical law   1.2 Medical law and the general law
1.3 Medical law and medical ethics   1.3.1 Introduction   1.3.2 Deontological theory of absolutes   1.3.3 Moral theory of cost and benefit   1.3.4 A
moral theory of clinical intuition?   1.4 From medical ethics to medical law
1.5 Medical law and human rights   1.6 A brief history of medicine
1.7 Modern structure of the Health Service   1.7.1 Introduction
1.7.2 Development of the National Health Service market   1.7.3 NHS
trusts and service provision   1.8 Modern control of medical practice
1.8.1 General Medical Council: complaints against a general practitioner
1.8.2 Complaints in the NHS   1.8.3 Clinical and non-clinical complaints
against hospitals   1.9 Structure of the book

2 Confidentiality and access to medical information   29

2.1 Introduction   2.2 Ethics of confidence   2.3 Legal recognition of
confidence   2.4 Place of confidentiality in general law   2.5 Modifying the
duty in the public interest   2.6 Confidentiality and the legally incompetent
2.7 Consent to communicate information   2.8 Statutory control of confidential information   2.8.1 Abortion Regulations 1991 (SI 1991/499)
2.8.2 Public Health (Control of Disease) Act 1984   2.8.3 National Health
Service (Venereal Diseases) Regulations 1974 (SI 1974/29)   2.8.4 Police and
Criminal Evidence Act 1984   2.9 Remedies for breach of a medical

12   Abortion and the law   266

13   Sterilisation and the mentally handicapped   260

14   Neonaticide   317

Preface

While medical law is still to some extent in its infancy, there is now a developing pattern of judicial and legislative control over medical practice. The notion that there was no such thing as medical law, merely an amalgam of doctrines from criminal law, contract, tort and property, for example, is now of historical interest only. This book aims to reveal the uncertainties which still pervade medical law as well as these developing underlying themes. The core of medical law remains the dynamic of the doctor–patient relationship. In 1998 the relationship is increasingly studded with the conflict between patient's demands that their human rights be acknowledged and medical paternalism. Medical law at the millenium is marked by the final recognition in this country that core human rights demands need to be contained within a legislative framework of protection. The Human Rights Act 1998, which will soon become law, is likely to prove the next crucial phase for medical law.

As with the first edition of this book, the focus remains on the ethical and human rights context of medical law, but tempered with a recognition that there are still significant moral and practical pressures on the medical profession. It will be seen that the key to an understanding and most importantly analysis of medical law is to consider whether the decisions of medicine still lie with the doctor, or whether the patient has the right to control this decision-making process. Of increasing significance too is the question of whether the medical profession rather than the law should remain a judge of its own profession, particularly where there are allegations that a professional colleague has been negligent in the practice of medicine. The House of Lords decision in *Bolitho* v *City and Hackney Health Authority* [1997] 3 WLR 115 has been considered by some to be a slight shift back in favour of the law. In contrast, the enduring power of the medical as opposed to legal test of the standard of care in medical practice from the case of *Bolam* v *Friern Hospital Management Committee* [1957] 1 WLR 582 is also apparent in the 1990s, and has equally still been considered as the mainstay of judging the vast majority of medical practice, not just medical negligence and consent.

It will be seen during the course of this book that there are a number of extra-judicial bodies being set up to oversee medicine. The pace of scientific breakthrough is incredible, and the law is suffering from the inevitable problem of trying to react to novel, and to some bizarre, developments. The cloning of Dolly the sheep will be seen as opening up the possibility of cloning humans. It does not take a great deal of thought to recognise that this has the most fundamental ramifications, not just for medical law and ethics, but for the human race itself. The transplantation of organs from animals into humans has attracted similarly profound debate, and has forced the government to create a body of experts to oversee this crucial development. The image of joy that a family may gain from a loved one able to live because of such transplantation is confronted with the spectre of a human population ravaged by disease passed from animal to human.

Medical legislation has also developed, as has the interpretation that has been placed on it by the courts. The Mental Health Act 1983 has been increasingly used to treat patients without their consent not only for their mental disorder, but also for other physical ailments which have been considered to be at best ancillary to the mental condition which requires formal control under the Act itself. Cases such as *B* v *Croydon Health Authority* [1995] Fam 133 and *Tameside and Glossop Acute Services Trust* v *CH* [1996] 1 FLR 762 have been criticised as interpreting the 1983 Act in a way not envisaged by the drafters.

Consent remains a crucial element of medical law in determining who can control whether members of the medical profession intervene to save life or maintain health. Recent case law has had to consider whether the patient with a phobia is rational enough to have his or her refusal to accept medical treatment acknowledged. The courts have decided that the fear of the needle which led one patient to refuse an operation which may well have resulted in the death of her unborn child made her unable to balance the information that was given her; she was declared incapable of consent and was treated against her wishes (*Re MB (Medical Treatment)* [1997] 2 FLR 426). The House of Lords decision in the case of Tony Bland (*Airedale NHS Trust* v *Bland* [1993] AC 789) paved the way for a number of applications to be made that medical law should allow people who are not necessarily in a persistent vegetative state, but are in a low state of awareness, to die with dignity rather than live by means of modern medical technology. The courts now have an awareness of the significance of these decisions, but still appear willing to sanction a clinical regime that will lead to death in a broader set of circumstances than considered by the House of Lords in 1993.

The above are just some of the examples of a subject which invites daily debate in the media. The changes that take place in medicine and the law affect us all and it is hoped that this book makes the debates which take place informed ones.

Throughout this book the document 'Promotion of the Rights of Patients in Europe: Proceedings of a WHO Consultation' (Kluwer, 1995) has been referred to. While it is by no means the only document which sets a human rights agenda for medico-legal decision-making, it is considered here as it is an influential and thoughtful template for the design of a medical law system. It is also hoped that this book seeks to put some flesh on the bones of what are often 'open-textured' documents produced by such important bodies.

I should like to express my thanks to everyone at Blackstone Press, to Professor Robin White for information on the Human Rights Bill and Evita Catselli for valuable assistance at the proof stage (Good luck at the Bar!).

Michael Davies
September 1998

Table of Cases

Table of Statutes

Table of Statutory Instruments

ONE
The nature of medical law

1.1 THE SCOPE OF MEDICAL LAW

Every day there is news of a scientific development that it is hoped will lead to the saving of life. Equally every day there is a poignant story of a patient who is terminally ill, awaiting a transplant, or a child suffering from a defect handed down from generation to generation. Medicine provides one of the means by which humans can overcome the perils of life: disease, accident, genetic defect, even the natural process of ageing. The medical practitioner in every culture has traditionally been an honoured citizen, in recognition of the skill of the art of healing and of the mystique which surrounds the ability to cure ills.

Medicine is not a stagnant science, far from it. The dynamics of medicine allow it to focus on a vast array of challenges, both perpetual and modern in origin. There are few who do not still await the cure for the common cold, and those who long for the development of 'wonder drugs' that will eliminate cancer or the ravages of AIDS.

Medicine is neither stagnant nor exact. Whether it is the performance of an operation, the development or prescription of a drug or the diagnosis of the particular illness suffered, things can go wrong. The adverse result can be due to human error, negligent or not, or the particular physical reaction of the patient to the treatment correctly given. The human body can react in any number of ways to impacts upon it. Medical law concerns itself partly with the responsibility of the medical practitioner for that impact. I might react badly to an injection of an anaesthetic and go into shock. This might be due to the fact that the anaesthetist has injected too much or has failed to make a preliminary test of my reaction to a full dose of the drug; it might be an idiosyncratic reaction of my body to the drug, or even a psycho-physiological reaction to having an injection – hating the sight of the needle. Medical law is concerned with the responsibility of members of the medical profession for their actions. It is also about human rights, moral viewpoints, ethical concepts, economic demands on society and duties owed. The newspapers may be full of the scientific developments that it is hoped will treat the patient with Alzheimer's disease, the negligent doctor who has left a swab inside a patient or has conducted an abortion without the patient's consent during the course of another operation. They will also contain the tragic story of the accident victim in a persistent vegetative state (PVS), unable to communicate, rationalise, see, hear, eat, drink or perform many other bodily functions, but kept 'alive' by means of modern medical technology. Medical law is a forum for debating whether the machinery should be switched off. Medical law is literally about life or death issues. More often, however, the courtroom or Parliament sees the conclusion of the debate and is the site where the mechanism of enforcement of an ethical decision is designed and activated. The law may decide that the doctor can turn off the artificial life-support mechanism, but not allow the doctor to accelerate the process of death by injecting a lethal drug into the PVS patient. The various members of the judiciary may present many of the contentious elements of the debate about whether the ending of life of such a patient should be actively accelerated or passively allowed to end, indeed whether it should be allowed to end at all; but this is not the sole forum.

Medical law is not simply about decisions of the courts or legislation enacted by Parliament. Medical law, which leads from medical ethics, is the mechanism for 'doing the right thing' in a vast array of medical circumstances. A good medical law is an ethical law. This book, as well as being a description of medical law, is an analysis of whether the various laws are 'good' ones. One must therefore decide what it means to be ethical. Before that, however, there needs to be an awareness of the place of medical law in the scheme of law as a whole.

1.2 MEDICAL LAW AND THE GENERAL LAW

There appears to have been a growing presumption that there is a distinct branch of law called 'medical law'. It will be seen in chapter 2 that the courts have *assumed* a duty of confidence to rest on the doctor, without any real attempt at justifying the existence of this general duty. Similarly, writers in the broad area of law in relation to medical practice have tended to pass through justifying the existence of the separate discipline, and gone on to describe and analyse this assumed 'medical law'. Does medical law exist? The mere fact of writing a book entitled *Medical Law* is scant, if any, justification; the rest of chapter 1 will, it is suggested and hoped, provide this justification.

A 'one-line' definition of 'medical law' may be desired by some, but it is not easy to devise one, and should not unduly deter from developing analysis of individual issues. Too often students and academics alike have agonised over the precise meaning and place of 'tort' or 'crime' to the exclusion of analysing their constituent elements. The definitions available, like definitions of many subjects, suffer from being over-inclusive or exclusive. For example, to define medical law as the law relating to the doctor–patient relationship would be to exclude the issue of the manufacture of defective drugs. To define medical law as the law relating to health care within society would necessitate consideration of the legal regulation of pollutants and so forth, as these affect the health of society. Nevertheless, for those desiring a convenient starting point, the definition of Kennedy and Grubb, from the first edition of their *Medical Law* (London: Butterworths, 1989), p. 3 may be apposite:

> Medical law does not respect the traditional compartments with which lawyers have become familiar, such as torts, contracts, criminal law, family law and public law. Instead medical law cuts across all of these subjects and today must be regarded as a subject in its own right. . . . It is a discrete area concerned with the law governing the interactions between doctors and patients and the organisation of health care.

Medical law is recognised too by the emerging underlying ethical themes that will be seen throughout this work, and analysed in this chapter: the pre-eminence of the moral, ethical and legal doctrine of the autonomy of the individual, respect, telling the truth, doing good and not doing harm. The link between medical ethics and its practical expression through the law is the essence of defining medical law.

Criminal law, the law of torts, property, contract, family law and public law may at times apply in the medical context, but the traditional rules of those branches of law have been strained and bent, if not at times broken, where medicine is in issue. One has only to follow the development of the apparently simple rule formulated in *Bolam* v *Friern Hospital Management Committee* [1957] 1 WLR 582: that a medical practitioner has come up to the standard of care expected at law when acting in accordance with a responsible body of medical opinion. The courts have elevated this simple proposition of negligence law into a broad theory of medical law to be applied equally (if not uncontroversially) to the issues of euthanasia, selective non-treatment of the newborn and the sterilisation of the mentally handicapped. Contract law may traditionally be typified by offer, acceptance, consideration and intention to create legal relations, but how can it apply where the contract may be to perform a successful operation where the results can be virtually impossible to guarantee? The difficulties of this have already confronted the courts (see 8.2). Consider too the distortions that were painfully obvious in considering the issue of criminal causation in terminating the life-support regime of Anthony Bland (see 15.6.4). As Lord Mustill pointed out when the issue went to the House of Lords:

> One argument in support of the conclusion that if the proposed conduct is carried out and Anthony Bland then dies the doctors will nevertheless be guilty of no offence depends upon a very special application of the doctrine of causation. . . . Professor Skegg frankly accepts that some manipulation of the law of causation will be needed to produce the desired result. I am bound to say that the argument seems to me to require not manipulation of the law so much as its application in an entirely new and illogical way. (*Airedale NHS Trust* v *Bland* [1993] AC 789 at p. 895)

Family law will obviously be important, as medicine involves treating children as well as adults, and, as is emerging, the conflict between a child's decisions about medical treatment and those of the parent(s). The development of medical law in relation to the minor has shown a broadening of the recognition of the independence that can exist within minority, but at the same time a broadening of the concept of 'best interests' by the family law court in the exercise of its wardship jurisdiction to control the clinical decision-making of the child. The issue of minors refusing to consent to treatment is a potent example of the adaptations of family law in the medical context (see 6.3).

Such distortions of traditional legal concepts are not isolated events.

A number of cases together consider numerous issues of law from these different branches. This has often been noted, for example, in relation to the famous medical law case of *Gillick* v *West Norfolk and Wisbech Area Health Authority* [1986] AC 112, HL. Mrs Gillick sought declarations on a number of legal matters in relation to the prescribing to her 15-year-old daughter, without Mrs Gillick's prior knowledge, of contraceptives and contraceptive advice. As a matter of the *criminal law* there was debate about whether the doctor was aiding and abetting the criminal offence of under-age sexual intercourse. There was a *public law* debate in relation to a DHSS circular that appeared to support the doctor's actions. There was thus a potential challenge by way of judicial review of the actions of the executive arm of government. There was the issue, both of *public policy* and *private law* of the relative legal rights of parents and children to consent to medical treatment, one of the most enduring debates in medical law, as well as the legal duty of confidentiality and its scope for the doctor.

The cloth of medical law, which is fashioned from the traditional principled patterns of these branches of law, will be seen to be at present a patchwork. This chapter (and really the whole book) is an attempt to create a theoretical framework whereby the existence and success of the medical law described can be evaluated. But first the significance of medical ethics to medical law needs to be briefly considered.

1.3 MEDICAL LAW AND MEDICAL ETHICS

1.3.1 Introduction

The Hippocratic oath was formerly sworn by every doctor upon qualification, and is still of practical relevance to the medical profession. The oath is about helping others and not doing harm – beneficence and non-maleficence. It is a moral code. One cannot, therefore, consider the nature and scope of medical law without some notion of medical ethics and human rights. The link between law and medical ethics is a vital starting point:

> With the establishment of medical law in the health care context there is a tendency to conflate legal and ethical analyses and to fail to distinguish legal questions from moral or ethical questions. Clearly, law and ethics

share many common concerns. However, laws can fail to receive ethical sanction, and ethical points of view are not always reflected in legislation or court decisions. More problematic still is the fact that judges and legislators may avoid examining the moral principles presupposed in requirements established by law. Whatever confusions occur at the law/ethics interface, one thing is certain; a legal analysis of particular problems is and should be open to philosophical exploration and critique. (H. Engelhardt and S. Spicker, *The Law–Medicine Relation: A Philosophical Exploration* (Dordrecht: Reidel Publishing, 1978), p. xv)

While this book will be primarily concerned with the legal analysis, it will also recognise the crucial place of ethical debate in that analysis. To ignore medical ethics is to place medical law in a moral and social vacuum.

The crucial ethical issues facing medicine are those that have faced ethics generally: doing good, not doing harm, telling the truth, treating equally and respecting autonomy. They have all taxed moral philosophy at one time or another, but have tended not to be overtly considered by professional codes of ethics. As an example, autonomy is rarely referred to. It is certainly not explicitly referred to in the Hippocratic oath. Accepting this, it is nevertheless the case that the issue of autonomy – respecting the individual – has come to dominate the debate in modern medicine. It also acts as a bridge between two apparently irreconcilable views of morality – utilitarianism and deontology – which in essence are answers to the first question for the medical lawyer: What ought to be done? What ought to be done is the right thing, that which is moral. Morality in a situation where one is considering turning off a life-support machine of an individual in a persistent vegetative state depends on whether one accepts the former or the latter philosophical tradition. Whether one accepts the former or latter is dependent on the myriad personal influences on one's life. Medical law will be seen to have reflections of both philosophical traditions. Gorovitz (*Doctors' Dilemmas* (New York: Macmillan 1982)), an entertaining and accessible writer on this area of medicine, took it for granted that everyone wanted to see the doctor 'do the right thing' and proceeded to discover how this could be achieved.

1.3.2 Deontological theory of absolutes

The deontological philosopher would hold that one should 'take rights seriously'. We all have an innate sense of right and wrong (which is not the same as saying we always *do* the 'right' thing). Those who act morally are those who obey what the philosopher Immanuel Kant termed the 'categorical imperative'. An action is moral if it treats others never simply as a means but always as an end in themselves. It has been described as a moral theory of absolutes. An example of a deontological view is 'Thou shalt not kill'. Kant was a philosopher who wanted to be able to discover a principle by which the moral character of actions could be judged scientifically. This 'categorical imperative' was designed to enable actions to accord to a maxim that could be universal in application.

In addition Kant devoted considerable efforts to distinguishing between law and ethics. Law was seen as a system of commands which regulate social relations in order that no individual's freedom is hampered more than is necessary to maintain the freedom of all. Ethics concerns the duties of individuals. Law is really a system of duties encompassing the categorical imperative and the principle of autonomy. Ethics will require an individual to act from an intrinsic sense of duty; law will require that individual to act according to duty, even though that person's motives go against it. An ethical law therefore is one which accords with that individual's intrinsic sense of duty. A doctor might consider it a duty never to end the life of a patient. The law might provide that it is a duty of the doctor never to end the life of a patient. According to Kantian deontology this is an ethical law. But what of the doctor who considers that there are circumstances where the life of the patient should be brought to an end? The answer for Kant would be that the doctor must act according to the duty prescribed by law, which itself would accord with the categorical imperative. The rational side of nature – the moral action – dominates through the law. So, an act is moral if it conforms with how we would wish others to act towards us. 'Do as you would be done by' is the crux of deontology. To obtain a system of moral ends through the law is the ultimate goal of all moral action.

Deontology then is very much a system of sharp dividing lines. An action is either right or wrong. *Do not* kill, *never* tell lies, *always* respect the dignity of another. Kantian deontology provides no answers for the moral dilemmas of medicine, but is one of the landmarks of the Western philosophical tradition. Consider how the deontologist would answer the following problem.

Dr Jones has just prescribed contraceptives to Jane, aged 15. He promises her that the prescription will remain confidential. Helen, Jane's mother, arrives later and asks what her daughter wanted of the doctor. Dr Jones replies, 'That is confidential'. Helen then asks, 'Did you prescribe Jane with contraceptives?' Dr Jones replies, 'No'.

The doctor has respected Jane's autonomy and dignity by keeping the confidence, but lied to Helen. The deontologist misses a dimension of debate frequently crucial in the context of medical law (see, for example, the conflict apparent in *W* v *Egdell* [1990] Ch 359 discussed in 2.5). The missing dimension is provided by looking at the consequences of the doctor's actions and is the focus of the philosophical analysis of utilitarianism.

1.3.3 Moral theory of cost and benefit

Utilitarianism can be broadly identified with the following phrases which, while essentially correct, rather oversimplify matters: 'the maximisation of welfare', 'the greatest happiness of the greatest number' or 'consequentialism'. One of the main supporters and contributors to utilitarian thought was John Stuart Mill. The template for this philosophical theory was provided by the work *On Liberty*.

Utilitarianism, like deontology, is based on the maximisation of the freedom of the individual. It is a theory that will be seen in a number of areas

of medical law. Of preliminary significance is that utilitarianism was considered to apply only to those with the ability to rationalise and reflect on their
actions – the mentally competent. This will be seen to have potentially wide
repercussions where the issue of consent of the mentally handicapped to
treatment is in issue.

To the utilitarian freedom is good of itself, while restraint of that freedom
is burdensome and evil. All laws are therefore evil of themselves because they
impose restraints. Such 'evils' can only be justified by the greater good they
do for society as a whole. A utilitarian would hold that there are circumstances where humans would be less free but happier. The essential issue then is
to balance the moral character of an act with its consequences. An individual
should be able to have complete freedom of action where that action does not
harm or impact on any other member of society. Such 'self-regarding' actions
are allowed. If a person who has been diagnosed as being terminally ill wishes
to commit suicide, and this does not adversely affect others, then the act is
ethically justifiable. The difficulty is that there are few acts that do not impact
on others.

Mill and other writers in the liberal tradition felt that the 'pain and
pleasure' or 'cost-benefit' principle could reduce consideration of the morality
of an act to a simple calculation. To take the example of embryo research: the
'pain' or 'cost' is the interference with or destruction of the embryo, the
'pleasure' or 'benefit' is the developments that can be made in the diagnosis
of congenital defects in unborn children and the treatment of infertile women
(amongst other things). If the benefit of such developments outweighs the
burden of interference or destruction, the act is ethically justifiable. The
answer to the calculation tells society what it ought to do and what it shall
do. The writers in this tradition felt that there was no proposed action which
could fail to be calculated according to this principle. To writers such as
Jeremy Bentham (*Principles of the Morals of Legislation*) it was the place of
legislation to provide the link between ethics and the law. The law provides
the means by which human activity can be controlled while maintaining the
maximum utility. Human activity needs to be controlled because everyone
who receives the protection of society owes a return for that benefit, and the
fact that living in a society is seen as indispensable means that each should
be bound to observe a certain line of conduct towards the rest. The
individual's freedom is that which is compatible with the freedom of others.

While also being a fundamental philosophical posture in Western civilisation, utilitariansim too suffers from serious defects, the main one being the
difficulties of calculating the costs and benefits of actions and consequences,
particularly in medicine. Consider the following situation.

There are five patients on a transplant ward, and all require a different
organ to survive. The doctor treating them has no organs available. Suddenly
that doctor is rushed to treat a sixth patient, who has been in a car accident. If
treatment of this new patient is started immediately, there are very good
prospects of a successful outcome. The doctor realises too that if this patient is
deliberately not treated properly, he will die, but provide the organs necessary
to save the five patients awaiting transplants. What should the doctor do?

Obviously one must temporarily suspend knowledge of the legal minefield the doctor is entering. The utilitarian surely would applaud the doctor saving the lives of the five at the cost of the one. But is the utilitarian happy that the doctor has done the 'right thing'? Measuring the moral quality of acts through their consequences is not always as easy as those in the utilitarian tradition make out.

The significance of knowing of these two lines of moral philosophy is that both will be seen in existence in all chapters of this book. Indeed you may well see reflections of the two philosophical traditions in your own analysis of the ethical arguments in favour of and against a particular practice of medicine considered at the start of each chapter.

1.3.4 A moral theory of clinical intuition?

Does our intuition have any place in a debate about medical ethics? Mason and McCall Smith are not alone in arguing that:

> For many doctors, the first practical guide to morality is likely to be 'conscience' which is a somewhat vague concept but one which roughly accords with what the moral philosopher terms 'moral intuition'. Intuition has a limited appeal as a basis for moral philosophy but it should not be wholly discounted. (*Law and Medical Ethics*, 4th ed. (London: Butterworths, 1994), p. 7)

It might be worth attempting to increase the appeal of intuition to the medical lawyer considering the moral basis of a particular law. It should be noted, however, that this view may not sit comfortably with those about to embark on a study of medical law considering the autonomy of the patient to be paramount, particularly where the issues of refusal of treatment and euthanasia are concerned.

Clinical intuition can be a valuable arbiter of action where it has broadly based principles which can be articulated. One can look behind to the rationalisation of the doctor who acts or refrains from acting because 'it felt right'. Two effective writers on clinical intuition, Siegler and Goldblatt ('Clinical Intuition' in Spicker et al., op. cit., pp. 5–31), consider that intuition must primarily be based on an acknowledgement (one which will be seen to be crucial to starting to understand modern medical law) that the doctor–patient relationship is now one of balancing rights and responsibilities: the rights of the patient and the responsibilities of the medical profession. The 'two-way street' typified by the Canadian and US patient-oriented doctrine of informed consent (see chapters 6 and 7) recognises this change. Medical law in Britain is in a state of flux because the basis of any decision is confused. Does the doctor–patient relationship exist in a paternalist or a libertarian environment? If it is the former, clinical intuition will be based on the pre-eminence of the doctor in the decision-making processes of medicine and treatment. If it is the latter, the patient has the power. Siegler and Goldblatt have some suspicions of a fully libertarian model of this relationship:

> The recent tendency to move toward a patient-oriented model of medicine, led by medical ethicists and philosophers, and more recently by lawyers, is probably unworkable. We suspect that the implications of this movement are unacceptable to many patients. (p. 9)

It still needs to be borne in mind that the patient will often rely on the clinical intuition of the doctor during a period of weakness, anxiety and isolation. It is unrealistic that the doctor's intuition of the right thing to do should be predicated on the pre-eminence of the patient's autonomy at a time when that patient needs help, sometimes as much with decision-making as anything else.

Intuition, particularly in the area of patient refusal of treatment, can be based on a slightly altered view of patient autonomy and doctor responsibility. Eric Cassell (*The Function of Medicine* 1977, Hastings Centre Report 7, 16–19) argued that the true function of medicine was to restore the autonomy of the patient, even if this meant overriding a patient's rational refusal. Illness can render a patient's decisions 'unauthentic', and Gerald Dworkin ('Paternalism' (1972) 56 The Monist 64) described autonomy as 'authenticity plus independence'. Clinical intuition should be based on a consideration of the patient's ability to make choices. In the absence of this there exists a dominant ethical and legal duty to preserve life. The next basis of clinical intuition is to consider whether the decision (or rather refusal) of the patient is 'authentic'. 'Is it consistent with the "kind of person" this patient is?' (Siegler and Goldblatt, op. cit., p. 14). This can be established by antecedent conduct, membership of a particular religious group, the writing of a 'living will' or the appointment of a surrogate decision-maker. While all this may be valuable it has to coexist with a recognition that people can and do change their minds.

Another matter that could be the basis of clinical intuition is the nature of the particular illness. If the prognosis of successful treatment is good, then intuition directs towards treatment; if terminal illness, then it does not. The age of the patient may also weigh in the intuitive balance.

Siegler and Goldblatt see all of the above as having an advantage as a basis for clinical intuition for doctors because 'their actual decisions in individual cases have a potentially coherent procedure which can be applied, explained and subjected to public scrutiny.' (p. 16).

Perhaps more realistically there is also a recognition of the need for the courts and legislature to be involved in the compilation of a list of factors to articulate or even 'guide' that intuition. The recent *Practice Note (Sterilisation: Minors and Mental Health Patients)* [1993] 3 All ER 222, which has been replaced by *Practice Note (Official Solicitor: Sterilisation)* [1996] 2 FLR 111, in relation to sterilisation of the mentally handicapped is evidence of the development of such a list to guide or perhaps rationalise clinical intuition (see 13.7).

Siegler and Goldblatt conclude their analysis of the moral value of clinical intuition with a fairly stinging rebuke to those championing unfettered autonomy of the patient:

Notwithstanding the celebration of unlimited patient autonomy by some commentators on the medical scene, it is usually difficult to convince those more directly involved that the curable do not want to be cured, that the decision to refuse treatment, made in the midst of extreme pain, fear and anxiety, was authentic. (p. 19)

Consider this matter when encountering the case law concerning those who have actually refused treatment. Is a rationalised and articulated regime of clinical intuition a sufficient basis upon which the law can 'do the right thing'?

1.4 FROM MEDICAL ETHICS TO MEDICAL LAW

So far then, we have been concerned with finding out how one calculates the 'right thing' to do in a given situation, and have considered three different forms of calculation. Does the fact that we know what the right thing is automatically mean that the law should be invoked? The Warnock Report (Department of Health and Social Security, *Report of the Committee of Inquiry into Human Fertilisation and Embryology* (Cmnd 9314) (London: HMSO, 1984)), which concerned the ethical and legal dilemmas posed by the developments in artificial reproduction (test-tube babies and so forth), had to go through a two-stage process of analysis:

(a) Is the proposed action right or wrong?
(b) If the proposed action is wrong, should the law be invoked to stop it?

On considering this briefly one is tempted to answer, 'If something is wrong of course you invoke the law to stop it happening', but matters are rarely so simple. It is the backdrop to one of the most contentious of modern ethico-legal debates, which has been encapsulated by terming it the 'Hart–Devlin' debate. This surfaced in the late 50s and early 60s over the morality and legality of homosexual acts between consenting males.

Lord Devlin in his work, *The Enforcement of Morals* (Oxford: Oxford University Press, 1965), considered that in relation to certain issues there is a social agreement (discovered by finding out what the 'man on the Clapham omnibus' would think) that the matter under consideration will undermine the moral fabric which binds us together, if allowed to take place. The law should intervene to stop what is seen by society as wrong and destructive. There is one moral view on an issue confronting society, and dependent on that view the law will be invoked to stop it.

The obvious criticism made of Lord Devlin's thesis has been that we live in a society of diversity. There is less and less credence in considering our pluralist society capable of having one shared moral view. All well and good, but if there is no shared morality, how do we decide that the law should intervene in a particular area?

H. L. A. Hart (*Law, Liberty and Morality* (Oxford: Oxford University Press, 1963) approached the matter somewhat differently from Lord Devlin, and this latter view is arguably the most pertinent in considering the contentious subjects in this book. The approach is essentially the two-point process seen above. Consider whether the action is right or wrong. Then consider whether the limitations on personal liberty that any law would necessarily impose would be right or wrong.

The Warnock Report had to consider (amongst other subjects) the concept of surrogacy, which is, essentially, where one woman goes through the process of pregnancy (usually initiated by the artificial insemination of the sperm of the male partner of a woman who cannot go through a pregnancy herself) with the intention of giving the child born to this 'commissioning' couple. The Committee answered what its chair, then Dame Mary Warnock, termed the 'primary' question: Is the practice of surrogacy morally wrong? The short answer was yes. The Committee were against the practice of surrogacy. Then the second or 'critical' question: Should the law be invoked to stop the practice? The short answer was no. While surrogacy may be wrong, any law which sought to criminalise the conduct would be intrusive. The infringement of liberty by enforcement agencies 'snooping' into an intimate aspect of personal life and the fact that any law would be difficult to enforce outweighed any benefit that might accrue from criminalisation. The practical advantage of the Hart formulation was that it allowed the Warnock Report to ask the questions again in relation to surrogacy: Is commercial surrogacy (the use of agencies) wrong? If so, should the law be invoked to stop it? The Report answered yes to both questions. The enforcement of the law would not be too intrusive because it would only attack the agents who arranged the surrogacies, not the private lives of the individuals more intimately involved.

It can thus be seen that while law and morality often march hand in hand, there is no automatic requirement that they do so. The reader might feel that a certain act is immoral but would find any law to be disproportionate to that feeling of immorality. I might consider that it is immoral to remove feeding and hydration from a patient in a persistent vegetative state, but would not have the doctor who removed the apparatus incarcerated for murder.

An allied point of significance arises from looking at the Hart–Devlin debate. Even if the law should be invoked to control a particular aspect of medicine, who should make it? At present obviously medical law is made by either the courts or Parliament. Is either particularly well qualified to consider legal regulation of this often most complex of areas? The judiciary certainly do not feel at all comfortable in the role of medical lawmaker. *Airedale NHS Trust* v *Bland* [1993] AC 789 provided the opportunity for the judiciary to voice this discomfort. Lord Browne-Wilkinson, at p. 880, perfectly captures the practical and constitutional unease:

Where a case raises wholly new moral and social issues, in my judgment it is not for the judges to seek new, all-embracing principles of law in a way which reflects the individual judges' moral stance when society as a whole is substantially divided on the relevant moral issues. Moreover, it is not legitimate for a judge in reaching a view as to what is for the benefit of the one individual whose life is in issue to take into account the wider practical issues as to allocation of limited financial resources or the impact on third parties of altering the time at which death occurs.

For these reasons, it seems to me imperative that the moral, social and legal issues raised by this case should be considered by Parliament. The judges' function in this area of the law should be to apply the principles which society, through the democratic process, adopts, not to impose their standards on society. If Parliament fails to act, then judge-made law will of necessity through a gradual and uncertain process provide a legal answer to each new question as it arises. But in my judgment that is not the best way to proceed.

So, the common law should react and interpret what the people dictate through their Parliamentary representatives. It is not the role of the judges to be proactive and create law, particularly where such weighty societal matters hang in the balance. Will Parliament do any better at responding to the legal challenges thrown down by developments in medicine? The Warnock Report will be seen to give scant comfort for those who hope that a committee of 'specialists' can accomplish a great deal. The difficulties of compromise apparent in the report have broader repercussions. It is political necessity to perfect the art of compromise, but where issues of medicine are concerned there is often no consensus. A politician who seeks legislation to outlaw all abortion will gain support from a particular interest group, but lose it from another. This was one of the reasons why the Human Fertilisation and Embryology Act, which represented the legislative expressions of the Warnock recommendations, was not enacted until 1990, though the Warnock Report was presented in 1984. There is scant political mileage in antagonising a particular group of society, so things are left in limbo.

Can some other 'body' consider and recommend authoritatively on the major issues that will confront medicine in the future? In 1980, US President Carter set up the President's Commission for the Study of Ethical Problems in Medicine and Biomedical and Behavioral Research. The reports that were produced were well-considered, accessible documents combining medical law and ethics. Nevertheless even this useful innovation was subject to political whim and was 'defunded' by President Reagan in 1985 (see Kennedy and Grubb, *Medical Law*, 2nd ed. (London: Butterworths, 1994), pp. 24–30).

Recently, an apolitical and apolitically funded body called the Nuffield Council of Bioethics was set up by the Trustees of the Nuffield Foundation. The ambit of this body is described as:

   (a)   to identify and define ethical questions raised by recent advances in biological and medical research in order to respond to, and to anticipate public concern;
   (b)   to make arrangements for examining and reporting on such questions with a view to promoting public understanding and discussion; this may lead, where needed, to the formulation of new guidelines by the appropriate regulatory or other body; and
   (c)   in the light of the outcome of its work, to publish reports; and to make representations, as the Council may judge appropriate. (Kennedy and Grubb, op. cit., p. 31.)

In relation to consent to treatment and the mentally incapacitated adult patient, the Law Commission has produced a number of papers (see chapter 5). It is hoped that, unlike worthwhile and well-considered recommendations of the Law Commission in other areas of law, these will not be swept under the political carpet of compromise.

Recently the British government has been more proactive in setting up bodies made up of a number of experts, medical, ethical and legal, to discuss and propose solutions to crucial questions thrown up by medical technological advancement. One example is the Advisory Group on Xenotransplantation (the transplantation of organs from one species to another) under the chairmanship of Professor Ian Kennedy. Such groups have the obvious advantage of being able to canvass a wide range of opinion on matters which can impact on a number of aspects of medicine. (For more information on the aspects of this debate see 16.6 and also M. Fox and J. McHale, 'Regulating xenotransplantation' (1997) 147 NLJ 139.) The House of Lords Select Committee on Science and Technology has also been increasingly active in the area of the Human Genome Initiative (HGI) and cloning. In addition there have been other specialist bodies set up and even combining to pool expertise. In January 1998 the Human Genetics Advisory Commission combined with the Human Fertilisation and Embryology Authority to publish a consultation document, *Cloning Issues in Reproduction, Science and Medicine*, on the scientific, ethical and legal implications of developments in cloning (for more detail on this debate see chapter 16).

1.5 MEDICAL LAW AND HUMAN RIGHTS

As well as a description and analysis of the law as it applies to medical practice, this is a book of rights and duties, ethical and moral as well as legal. All of the traditional ways of looking at how to act ethically (deontological, utilitarian or intuitive) have their failings, but are agreed that a fundamental aspect of doing the right thing is to respect the individual. Modern medicine has increasingly been seen in terms of human rights. A vast array of literature has grown up and continues to grow which analyses the existence, scope and enforceability of these human rights.

> It has become fashionable to talk about 'rights' for everyone, and patients and their providers are no exception. While there are many groups in society that desperately need to have their rights recognised and enforced . . . perhaps none is as vulnerable as the desperately ill patient. This vulnerability and the potential abuses it permits have led many to suggest that the provider–patient relationship should be made more equitable, and that the status of the patient should be improved with this goal in mind. (George Annas, 'The Function of Legal Rights in the Health Care Setting' in Spicker et al., op. cit., at p. 265)

Where issues of medical law and practice are concerned, human rights issues abound. It is worth very briefly reviewing two views of the meaning and importance of human rights to the lawyer.

John Rawls, in his seminal work *A Theory of Justice* (Oxford: Clarendon Press, 1972) considers that society is a collection of individuals under a form of social contract. The contract consists of reciprocal notions that all would abide by. Effectively these notions can be reduced to the principles that:

(a) Everyone should enjoy the maximum amount of liberty which is compatible with the liberty of all.

(b) Where there are inequalities, whether of wealth or power, they should only be allowed to exist to the extent that they work towards the benefit of the 'worst-off' members of that society.

George Annas (op. cit., at p. 267) has argued that a whole system of health care could be based on these two broad premises. It would be one which recognised the freedom of the individual and that the patient is the 'worst-off' one whom society should use its power and influence to assist.

Ronald Dworkin, in the equally well-known tract *Taking Rights Seriously* (London: Duckworth, 1978) sees legal rights as a way of helping those weakest amongst us:

The bulk of the law – that part which defines and implements social, economic, and foreign policy – cannot be neutral. It must state, in its greatest part, the majority's view of the common good. The institution of rights is therefore crucial, because it represents the majority's promise to the minorities that their dignity and equality will be respected. When the divisions among the groups are most violent, then this gesture, if law is to work, must be most sincere. . . . [Taking individual rights seriously is] the one feature that distinguishes law from ordered brutality.

In 1995 the World Health Organisation (WHO) published a document, entitled *Promotion of the Rights of Patients in Europe: Proceedings of a WHO Consultation* (Kluwer, 1995), which is a significant modern piece of work for the study of medical law and human rights. It indicates that there are certain international unifying rights themes for medical law.

The foreword to the report sets the scene:

During the last decades there has been a progressive acceptance of human rights as expressed in the United Nations human rights instruments and those of the Council of Europe. One of its effects has been a very positive international trend in the consideration and definition of patients' rights. (p. vii)

The document notes the common concern that States have with the health of the nation. It may be that the primary focal point should be the common concern with the vulnerability and fear that surround ill health. There is danger in national policy treating a disease rather than a person. The trend to compartmentalise people by the nature of their illness is itself an unhealthy one within which to fashion human rights objectives. The WHO also acknowledges the fact that people are more willing to ask questions of the medical profession. 'Absolute faith in the medical profession is more and more a thing of the past' (p. 2).

Perhaps the most significant point made by the WHO for present purposes notes the changes in the doctor–patient relationship:

> Until the beginning of the 1970s [it] was defined primarily by the rules of medical ethics. During the last two decades, an approach to this relationship focusing more on legal provisions has emerged. With the introduction of the concepts of autonomy and self-determination, the relationship was gradually redefined in terms of a contract. The regulation of the patients' rights underlines the importance and meaning of negotiation and patient participation. (p. 8)

The principles of patients' rights which emerged focused more than ever before on a beneficial doctor–patient relationship which encouraged the participation of and respect for the patient and protected the patient's dignity and integrity. Further, it would allow patients to obtain the fullest possible benefit from the health care system and would encourage a wider dialogue between societal pressure groups, doctors and patients.

The document makes a number of important points which are considered to be general guiding principles for the fullest expression of human rights in health care (p. 38):

(a) Everyone has the right to respect of his or her person as a human being.

(b) Everyone has the right to self-determination.

(c) Everyone has the right to physical and mental integrity and to the security of his or her person.

(d) Everyone has the right to respect for his or her privacy.

(e) Everyone has the right to have his or her moral and cultural values and religious and philosophical traditions respected.

(f) Everyone has the right to such protection of health as is afforded by appropriate measures for disease prevention and health care, and to the opportunity to pursue his or her own highest attainable level of health.

The document then goes on to describe specific rights. These will be referred to in each chapter of this book, where relevant, so that as well as the ethical and legal evaluation of the current state of medicine and the doctor–patient relationship, medical law can be evaluated in its approximation to the human rights goals of the WHO. This can be based on these specific principles and perhaps more fundamentally analysed according to the ideals expressed above. A good medical law will be a law that is ethical and respects fundamental human rights.

A number of chapters of this book reveal that often medicine, and thereafter medical law, are called upon to consider the rights of those who are either temporarily (minors, for example) or permanently (the severely mentally handicapped patient) unable to articulate demands. The issue of the human rights of such individuals would appear paramount. Both Rawls and Dworkin recognise the respect to be paid to, and guarantees of rights to be given to, such patients. Case law in the medical arena has, however, only recently started to make decisions in 'rights' terms. In one of the most important recent decisions in medical law, the House of Lords in *Airedale NHS Trust v Bland* [1993] AC 789 considered the rights of patients in a persistent vegetative state. Overtly or covertly the right to life, the right to die and the right to the utmost dignity at the end of life and in memory were considered relevant. The House of Lords linked patient and doctor together in *Airedale NHS Trust v Bland* perhaps more strongly than ever before by considering the *rights* of patients and the *duties* of doctors.

In the United States and other jurisdictions the rights of patients have been more clearly articulated in the courtroom because of the existence of a written constitution. Cases such as the famous *Roe v Wade* (1973) 410 US 113, which held that a woman has a constitutional right to an abortion, free of any State interference during the first three months of pregnancy, have set the scene for further rights-based demands to enter the courtroom. In English common law, there is an innate conservatism that does not allow for such clarity of human-rights-based decision-making. Some of the most important cases in this book show judicial recognition that the common law is a clumsy tool to use where the dynamics of medicine are concerned, but may also indicate that times are changing, and the judiciary will question whether the 'rights' of patients have been respected.

Kennedy and Grubb see a slightly different significance for human rights in the medical law context. Their opinion is that, in the absence of persistent views expressed by legislation or common law on autonomy, respect for dignity, truth telling and consent, human rights currently is the glue that binds together apparently disparate elements of law. It may be that, in time, respect for articulated human rights will lead to the creation of a more coherent framework that will explain medical law and act as a guide to actions that may be proposed in medicine in the future. English medical law is not yet at that stage.

During the last decade there have been an increasing number of cases before the courts in which human rights pleas have been taken directly from the European Convention for the Protection of Human Rights and Funda-mental Freedoms, drawn up in 1950, and the European Charter (1961). An individual who feels that one of these numerous rights has been infringed and that all national remedies have been exhausted can petition the European Commission on Human Rights. Aside from articles of the Convention which deal with the prevention of disease and matters such as access to health care, there are very few articles expressly referring to health upon which a disgruntled patient can petition. However, there are also articles that are sufficiently 'open textured' to be potentially applicable. Claims could be made that art. 8 of the Convention that 'everyone should be able to establish details of their own identity as individual meetings' enables a child born as the result of artificial insemination by donor sperm (AID) to know who the anonymous donor is. An unsuccessful claim has been made that article 2 of the Convention, that 'Everyone's right to life shall be protected by law', means that a father could prevent his partner from having an abortion. The very important case of *Airedale NHS Trust v Bland* [1993] AC 789 considered the impact of art. 2 where the issue was the termination of life support for the patient in a persistent vegetative state. It seems that petitions under the Convention where medical matters are concerned will only increase in England and Wales. In addition there are new human rights documents on medico-legal matters of significance being published. The Council of Europe has produced recently a Convention on Human Rights and Biomedicine (Council of Europe, Convention for the Protection of Human Rights and Dignity of the Human Being with regard to the Application of Biology and Medicine: Convention on Human Rights and Biomedicine (DIR/JUR (96) 14)) and UNESCO has issued the Universal Declaration on the Human Genome and Human Rights (1997).

Perhaps the most significant future development of medical law in this country will come with the enactment in 1998 of the Human Rights Act. The Bill currently under consideration will mean that case law which comes from the European Court and the Commission will be directly applicable. While the Act will see a fundamental general shift in the balance of power between the arms of government and the law, the 'open-textured' rights in the European Convention articles are extremely likely to be a focus of renewed attacks on issues such as abortion and access to infertility treatment. There are, however, some limitations on the nature of litigants with the proposed s. 7(3) and (4) not allowing third parties to bring what can be termed 'public interest' actions (for further debate on the proposed legislation see S. Greer, 'The Human Rights Act 1998' (1998) 23 EL Rev hRS).

1.6 A BRIEF HISTORY OF MEDICINE

An introduction to the issues that will be explored in greater depth in the succeeding chapters would be incomplete without a basic understanding of how medicine, and particularly the doctor–patient relationship, has changed. There has been a change in this relationship from one of trust and dependency by the patient, and control by the doctor, to a more bilateral relationship of increasing equality. The more cynical may see the modern doctor–patient relationship as one based on mutual distrust; with the patient more willing to make demands, ask questions and scrutinise replies, and the doctor feeling the dagger of litigation should any mistake be made. How have things changed?

As already noted, the medical practitioner historically had been revered and maybe a little feared too. The hands of the healer were seen as extensions of some supernatural power. As Mason and McCall Smith confirm:

Very early medicine was, of course, a matter of mystery; there being no apparent natural reason why disease struck one person rather than another, the answer had to be found in the supernatural and, supernatural powers being sparingly distributed, healing became a prerogative of a few whose power depended largely on the ignorance of others. (*Law and Medical Ethics*, 4th ed. (London: Butterworths, 1994), p. 3)

Those with this 'power', as well as protecting their own mystique, also drew the gifted, and took on the role of educators as well as practitioners.

Perhaps rather cynically, some 2,000 years ago, Philemon the Younger wrote:

Only physicians and lawyers can commit murder without being put to death for it.

Behind this comment lies an important historical fact, that of the regulation of the medical profession. The remark appears to presume that doctors (and one must not forget lawyers) were above the control of the law or society. That this was not necessarily the case has been recognised by Darrel Amundsen:

As long as there have been those in Western civilisation who call themselves physicians or doctors or surgeons and undertake to cure, alleviate or correct abnormalities, or provide prophylaxis, certain standards of competence, etiquette and responsibility have been assumed, if not always precisely defined in legal terms.('Physician, Patient and Malpractice: An Historical Perspective' in Spicker et al., op. cit., p. 255)

In Roman law, the standard of the *bonus paterfamilias* (who essentially equates to the 'reasonable man' in English common law) was applied to the medical profession in judging the correctness of actions taken in relation to the patient. Licensing of the medical profession in the Middle Ages came either from a guild of practitioners seeking a monopoly over medical services in a particular area, or was imposed by ecclesiastical authority. Whatever the source of the authority to practise, the guild would need to argue that the monopoly was based on expertise. It would protect from the charlatans who roamed the countryside. The medical profession had to be regulated because of the serious harms that could flow from incompetent medical practice.

When considering the existence of the litigation explosion in England in section 3.2 below, and the difficulties of establishing negligence in chapter 4, consider how times have changed from the following:

In communities where licensure had been imposed and in those where guilds had achieved a protective closed shop, malpractice litigation continued and, in the case of the latter, the guilds more often than not appear to have *sided with the aggrieved patient* against the incompetent or negligent guild member. (Amundsen, op. cit., p. 256)

There is little evidence now that the 'closed shop' that is the medical profession would be quite as likely to side with a patient over a fellow professional. This has become a crucial element in the continuing difficulty in maintaining a negligence action against a doctor.

Nevertheless, even before the Middle Ages, there had grown up a number of codes or oaths, which, while having dubious legal status, had a force over the profession itself. There is evidence of a Code of Hammurabi at around 1900 BC, but the most familiar has to be the Hippocratic oath, created around 1400 years after the Babylonian Hammurabi Code. To swear such an oath was to join a brotherhood of like-minded and dedicated individuals, thus maintaining the separation of the medical profession from other professions.

Echoes of the Hippocratic oath will be heard throughout this book, so what, in essence, does it say? Without quoting it chapter and verse the main points of the oath (in its orginal formulation rather than the updated version in the Declaration of Geneva, Sydney, 1968) are as follows:

(a) To respect the educator in medicine.
(b) To be prepared to teach others medicine.
(c) To strive to the best of one's ability to do good for the patient, and to not do harm.
(d) Never give advice or drugs that will cause death, even if asked.
(e) Never procure an abortion.
(f) To leave specialist medicine to those able to practise it.
(g) Never use the position of trust as a means for seduction.
(h) To keep relevant matters confidential.

Although the Hippocratic oath has been considered a potent force of regulation during the development of medical practice, its scope is rather limited. Alternatively (but far less likely), the individual elements of the oath itself could be considered to be 'open-textured', i.e., a broad statement of principle that can be applied equally to a number of different factual situations. Nevertheless there would be few doctors who did not, in the practice of everyday medicine, hold to at least one of these tenets. Indeed, where confidentiality is concerned, for example, medical law requires that they abide by the relevant sentiment of the oath (see 2.2).

There is evidence that doctors have lost a substantial part of their professional independence in modern times. John Ladd (in Spicker et al., op. cit., p. 39) sees two reasons for this. First, the increase in biomedical technology has forced the doctor to rely more on others less and less intimately linked with the 'traditional' medical profession. Secondly, the growth of hospitals and other medical institutions has rendered the doctor more and more an employee, subject to the professional whim of others. This will be seen as clearly evident in the growth of the vicarious liability of the hospital for the negligence of the doctor (see 3.6).

A useful point Ladd makes, not considered that often, is the success of the medical profession. This has changed the way in which doctors are evaluated by society. Doctors are now judged on a product. This product of the practice of medicine is the 'saved' patient. Such success is visible and easily understood. We can all judge success (or of course failure) in these terms; it does not require a medical qualification. Ladd leads on from this to state sardonically:

> When, therefore, physicians bemoan the meddling of lay people in the evaluation of their services, the intervention of patients, families, lawyers and administrators, they are simply suffering from the symptoms of their own success. (p. 40)

Patients now expect more, and are disappointed when it does not happen. This could be one of the reasons for the steep rise in the number of claims against doctors in the civil courts (see chapter 3)

Up to, and during the course of the twentieth century, there has been an increasingly secular view of the medical profession, and increasing regulation has been developed by legislation and by the medical profession itself, as a means of voluntary internal regulation. Before the form of modern regulation of the medical profession is introduced, it is necessary to consider briefly the motivation for such imposed forms of legal regulation. Not all of its forms are the product of the altruism of medicine wishing to regulate itself.

In the twentieth century, regulation of those involved in research has largely come from the horrors of Nazi experimentation during the Second World War. The Nuremberg trials, the Nuremberg Code and the supplement provided by the Helsinki Declaration (World Medical Association, 1964) recognised that horror, regulated as far as possible against its repetition and untangled the fundamental ethical issue of the use of the results of this terrible research. Also the events focused attention again on the central nature of free consent of the patient to treatment or research, which has remained a focal element for the medical lawyer.

The Nuremberg Code, which was basically the 10 main points made in sentencing those convicted of these war crimes, is the first systematic attempt to regulate research on humans. It marked the point in modern times at which the medical profession as a whole were looked at afresh, and, ethically at least, found somewhat wanting. Society appeared ill-prepared for the revelation that qualified doctors could kill in the name of medical science.

It is useful to describe briefly the contents of the Code and to consider the deontological and utilitarian methodology involved. Some absolutes are contained within it as well as judgments based on the consequences of the research.

(a)   The voluntary consent of the human subject is absolutely essential.

(b)   The research conducted should be for the good of society. It should be systematic and necessary, but not able to be carried out by other means.

(c)   There should be preliminary experimentation which indicates a justification for stepping up to research on human subjects.

(d)   The conduct of any experiment should be such that all unnecessary pain and suffering is avoided.

(e)   Experiments should not be conducted where there is a priori reason to suppose disabling injury or death may occur. It may be that such experimentation can be carried out where the subjects of the research are the research scientists themselves.

(f)   The risk of the experiment must be outweighed by the humanitarian importance of the research.

(g)   Precautions must be taken to protect the human subject against the dangers of injury, disability or death.

(h)   Only those scientifically qualified should carry out such experiments, and they should act with the utmost skill and care.

(i)   A research subject who finds it impossible to continue participation in the experiment should be at liberty to bring the research to an end.

(j)   A research scientist who considers that there is a risk of injury, disability or death in continuing the experiment must be prepared to terminate the experiment.

This Code, and the supplements that came after as refining documents, illustrated that the self-regulation of the profession was no longer to be considered necessarily sufficient; the courts or Parliament could regulate the professions too. This takes us to the basic structure of the modern health service and the present regulatory framework of the medical profession.

1.7 MODERN STRUCTURE OF THE HEALTH SERVICE

1.7.1 Introduction

There are numerous works which explore the complex structure of the modern Health Service in considerable detail (see, for example, C. Newdick, *Who Should We Treat?* (Oxford: Clarendon Press, 1995) and J. Montgomery, *Health Care Law* (Oxford: OUP, 1997), ch. 4). These works embrace matters such as employment and dismissal of the myriad staff involved in modern medical practice, central administrative planning and control, the economic structure of the National Health Service and the 'contracting' system. Here it is not necessary to go into as much detail, but there would be a considerable gap in one's knowledge of the nature of medical law were there no basic knowledge of the set-up. The significance of this knowledge is bolstered by the fact that there have been increasing attempts to use medical law to attack the current structures, at least where they have been perceived to result in a delay in the treatment of the individual patient, or, in the case of one patient, a refusal to treat at all (see 3.3.7).

1.7.2 Development of the National Health Service market

The National Health Service (NHS) was created by the National Health Service Act 1946. The essential structure which undertook to provide the facilities to carry out the wide duties imposed by this act came into existence in 1948. The basic planning of services was given at that time to regional boards and management committees. The structure itself was found to lead to unnecessary levels of bureaucracy and these regional boards were replaced by regional health authorities divided into area health authorities. However, there was dissatisfaction with the breadth of work undertaken by these area health auithorities and there was further sizing down of the system to district health authorities in 1982.

The current system came into being in 1996, when the Health Authorities Act 1995 took effect. Between the 1970s and the 1990s there had been fairly consistent criticism that the systems imposed had been overly bureaucratic and in essence had not provided value for money because of numerous inefficiencies. The primary motive of the 1995 Act was to make the system simpler. There had been a confusion of roles between the regional health authorities, family health service authorities and district health authorities, particularly in terms of the 'purchasing' of services. There is now in existence what Jonathan Montgomery describes as 'an integrated purchasing authority, responsible for securing health services for their local populations' (*Health Care Law* (Oxford: OUP, 1997) at p. 83).

The legislation passed in 1946 placed duties on the Secretary of State for Health. Elsewhere in this book the fact that the essence of the duty has always been to provide 'a comprehensive health service' (see 3.3.7 and the National Health Service Act 1977, s. 1) has been noted. It goes without saying that the Secretary of State delegates responsibility for such an enormous task to the Department of Health, that body itself looks to the more specialist NHS Executive to consider control of health care matters (amongst other things such as public health and other what may be termed 'social matters'). While such a body has not been created by statute it is effectively the core of the Department of Health as it is the central focus of strategic planning and policy with regard to the NHS. Another of the key strategic roles is to advise the Secretary of State directly on both short and long-term strategic economic planning within a 'contract and purchasing' regime. One of the more commonly encountered products of such strategic review has been the publication of the (non-legally binding) aspirational *Patient's Charter* (London: Department of Health, 1995). The National Health Service Executive also has a great deal of influence over local NHS spending by health authorities.

One of the key debating points surrounding this (and for that matter any other) national health service has been the issue of cost. The previous government had considered that there needed to be a form of market system to make the NHS more economically efficient. While this is not the place to debate the success of the market system in any detail one can feel safe in stating that it did not provide the real level of competition and the subsequent driving down in pricing of the system that was envisaged. The essence of the 'purchasing system' is succinctly introduced by Montgomery:

> Since 1991, the principal functions of health authorities have been to operate the NHS market system, in which services are procured for patients through a system of contracting. . . . Since April 1996, the responsibility for monitoring the operation of the NHS market, both purchasing and providing, has lain with the NHS Executive. The main responsibilities of

the new health authorities are to deal with the purchasing of services. (*Health Care Law* at pp. 86–7)

Health authorities have essentially the same duty as the Secretary of State, it is just that this task is undertaken at a local level. The health authority achieves this through a system of statutory contracts. In addition GPs themselves could choose to purchase community services as well as local hospital services through becoming fundholders. Obviously again these GPs only have a duty to purchase services for 'their' patients (that is patients on that GP's or practice's list). Not every practice can choose to become a fundholding one as there would be logistical, managerial and most importantly economic efficiency, problems. The main limitation is that there needs to be a patient list of 5,000 or more. The GP provides medical expertise through a statutory contract with the health authority, but the significance of fundholding is that this practice would buy other health and community services for its patients, and clearly that service is purchased with money from the fund. There is the danger that the GP may overspend on the fund or be unable to 'afford' to purchase a particular medical service. This is partially alleviated by the fact that the district health authority itself pays for individual treatments over £6,000. If the DHA did not pay this then there would be a danger of a doctor either not becoming a fundholder or a patient finding difficulty in securing a place on a patient list.

What of the GP who, or practice which, overspends? The Secretary of State has numerous powers to halt the activities of a practice which misapplies funds. There can be an order of immediate effect that the practice is no longer a fundholder (see the National Health Service (Fund-holding Practices) Regulations 1996 (SI 1996/706), regs 15 and 16). Alternatively, what of the practice which makes a saving? The practice itself can utilise this saving, but must spend it for matters on which it would spend its normal budget. One example would be to use the extra funds to provide a play area for the children of patients visiting the practice, or even to update the computer system which monitors patient records.

1.7.3 NHS trusts and service provision

These bodies are independent of health authorities which can nevertheless still provide a direct medical service. These trusts are formed by specific statutory instrument, but the overarching structure comes from the National Health Service and Community Care Act 1990. The duties incumbent upon the Secretary of State for Health are delegated to each trust. NHS trusts are not under the direct control of health authorities, but because of the delegation of power they remain responsible to the Secretary of State (although in actual fact the monitoring of each trust will be a matter for the NHS Executive itself). These trusts exist in a regime which might be described as 'managed freedom'. They are allowed to do a number of things, such as provide NHS patients with private care if the patient is willing to pay for it. They have the power, in certain circumstances, to compulsorily purchase land, and can hold various assets. The best example of an NHS trust having this managed freedom is the employment of staff. Technically these trusts can have their own terms and conditions of employment, whereas 'traditional' NHS staff had a nationally agreed pay and employment structure (called the 'Whitley' scale). The reality for the trust is somewhat different. Under s. 6 of the National Health Service and Community Care Act 1990 staff transferring into an NHS trust could keep their previous terms and conditions. Therefore the trust could not drive down pay scales, and in fact has had to improve on those offered by the non-trust health authorities. Freedom is further limited where the trust makes a profit. It may not utilise this profit other than for statutorily approved projects. Indeed profits can be utilised by the Secretary of State for the NHS as a whole, at least where the profit is surplus to the trust's reasonably foreseeable requirements.

Overall there are many issues concerning NHS structure, such as the governing and management of the various bodies outlined. These are important for medicine, but do not directly impact on the vast majority of issues encountered in this work. One aspect of importance to this book is, however, the disciplinary mechanisms for members of the medical profession.

1.8   MODERN CONTROL OF MEDICAL PRACTICE

As well as the many legal controls that have been placed on the practice of medicine and which will be outlined in this book, the medical profession has now developed internal regulation of its members, whether it is by the 'trade union' that is the British Medical Association (BMA) or the rather more broadly based and impartial General Medical Council (GMC), set up as long ago as 1858 by the Medical Act. Other professions within medicine, such as nursing, also have their own bodies controlling professional practice.

There has been criticism of the 'closed shop' and peer-group regulation provided through such bodies as the GMC and the BMA, which itself is indicative of a growing public recognition that the medical professions are less than perfect. The phrase 'doctor knows best' is becoming more and more of historical interest only.

1.8.1   General Medical Council: complaints against a general practitioner

The key issue as far as the medical lawyer is concerned, as well as the public, is that the medical profession are 'internally' accountable for their actions. A doctor who, for example, is found wanting in the performance of some medical procedure will, as well as being liable in damages to the injured party, possibly face professional discipline by the GMC. While accountability lies at the heart of public satisfaction with medical regulation, there is strong criticism of the nature and effectiveness of these disciplinary and complaints procedures. The basic problem is revealed by Chris Newdick:

> An aggrieved patient wishing to pursue a complaint against a doctor faces a procedural maze of considerable complexity; first, in the varied

institutional structure of the NHS, covering general practice and community health as well as hospitals; second, in the distinction which has to be made between clinical and non-clinical complaints. (*Who Should We Treat?* (Oxford: Oxford University Press, 1995))

The GMC has a potentially wide power over a doctor's career. Consider s. 36 of the Medical Act 1983, which sets out the statutory powers of the GMC:

(1)   Where a fully registered person—
    (a)   is found by the Professional Conduct Committee [the PCC] to have been convicted in the British Islands of a criminal offence, whether while so registered or not; or
    (b)   is judged by the Professional Conduct Committee to have been guilty of serious professional misconduct, whether while so registered or not; the Committee may, if they think fit, direct—
        (i)   that his name shall be erased from the register;
        (ii)   that his registration in the register shall be suspended (that is to say, shall not have effect) during such period not exceeding 12 months as may be specified in the direction; or
        (iii)   that his registration shall be conditional on his compliance, during such period not exceeding three years as may be specified in the direction, with such requirements so specified as the Committee think fit to impose for the protection of members of the public or in his interests.

Dr Cox (*R* v *Cox* (1992) 12 BMLR 38), who injected a substance with no pain killing effect into a terminally ill patient, Lillian Boyes, knowing that this injection would shorten her life, was made subject to sanction by the GMC as well as receiving a suspended sentence of imprisonment for attempted murder. There does then appear to be effective professional sanction to bolster the sanctions of the general law.

What does 'serious professional conduct' mean? Given the potentially career-ending consequences for the doctor, this phrase needs accurate interpretation; case law has not really provided it. Consider the following case, which although not involving the GMC, required a definition of the term. In *Doughty* v *General Dental Council* [1988] AC 164, PC (approved in *McCandless* v *General Medical Council* [1996] 1 WLR 168), a dentist had been charged with various forms of misconduct, amongst them an allegation that he had not exercised reasonable care and skill in treating six patients, and also another four treated later. When the matter first came for consideration by the relevant PCC, the decision was made to remove the dentist's name from the register, making it illegal for him to practise dentistry. In the Privy Council, the dentist's counsel sought to argue that in relation to the latter four patients, to be guilty of 'serious professional misconduct' the dentist had to have formed a view on treatment that could not have been honestly held by him or any other dentist. Counsel then was seeking to equate 'serious professional misconduct' with dishonest conduct. Lord Mackay of Clashfern responded that the test of serious professional misconduct is a simple one:

(a)   Did the dentist's conduct fall short, by act or omission, of the standard expected among dentists? If yes, then:

(b)   Was this 'falling short' serious?

There was no need to seek to refine the test to one which denoted dishonesty. This case has left us with a definition so open-textured as to be valueless in predicting the disciplinary consequences of certain conduct. Earlier in *Sloan* v *General Medical Council* [1970] 1 WLR 1130 the Privy Council had considered that the boundaries of misconduct could never be closely defined and it would be a matter for the relevant professional committee, made up of the appellant's own profession, to decide whether alleged facts amount to sufficient misconduct, or indeed misconduct at all (see also *Fox* v *General Medical Council* [1960] 1 WLR 1017). Does the profession itself have a view of what amounts to 'serious professional misconduct'? Is their view one that would be shared by many of us? The so-called 'Blue Book' (General Medical Council, *Professional Conduct and Discipline: Fitness to Practise* (1993)), which has now been updated to a certain extent by the GMC guidance contained in the first of the four codes (namely *Good Medical Practice, Confidentiality, HIV and AIDS: The Ethical Considerations* and *Advertising* (1995)), lists some of the matters considered to come into this category:

(a)   neglect or disregard of personal responsibilities to patients for their care and treatment;

(b)   abuse of professional privileges or skills;

(c)   personal behaviour which is derogatory to the reputation of the medical profession;

(d)   self-promotion, advertising and canvassing.

These appear overly broad, and depend on the GMC itself for interpretation. However, they indicate the possibility of the profession disciplining itself alongside the general medical law.

As is often the case the workings of particular disciplinary committees become the focus of an allegation that there has been a breach of one or more of the principles of natural justice. The allegation is not necessarily that the wrong decision was reached, but that it was the process of the hearing or preparations for it which were detrimental to the aggrieved party. For example, natural justice dictates that where the complaint from a patient is followed by a disciplinary hearing a considerable period later it would not always be fair to hold such a hearing. So even were no particular statutory time limit in place, there could still be a ruling that effectively the hearing is 'out of time' (but see the case of *R* v *General Medical Council, ex parte Shaikh* (3 July 1998 unreported) where a court decided that a hearing could proceed where there had been an allegation of rape made four and a half years earlier).

1.8.2   Complaints in the NHS

Anecdotal evidence indicates that many medical negligence actions are undertaken because there has been inadequate explanation of, or complete failure to explain, what happened when the patient was in hospital; no explanation or evidence that some complaints procedure has been initiated; no apology. As well as actions based on medical law, there needs, in any system of the complexity in terms of size and subject matter of the NHS, to be a procedure by which complaints can be transparently and effectively dealt with. Otherwise patients will go to court.

Various regulations aside from the disciplinary powers of the GMC have defined the types of conduct that can begin the complaints process in the NHS (see, for example, National Health Service (Service Committees and Tribunal) Regulations 1992 (SI 1992/664)). The Family Health Service Authority (FHSA), when it receives a complaint, has a number of things it can do. Obviously it can seek to satisfy the complainant informally. If this does not work, the formal procedure has to be instituted. A particular service committee, depending on the clinical area of the complaint, will decide whether there has been evidence of clinical failure. If there is a formal hearing, the complainant can attend with someone to assist, but cannot have legal aid to pay for that assistance. After that the matter goes back to the FHSA, which can warn the doctor that further failure to abide by the terms of service imposed could lead to withholding of payment, or limit the number of patients the doctor is allowed to treat. The complainant, however, can receive no compensation. This is obviously a less than adequate complaints procedure, and one that has been subject to fairly trenchant and consistent criticism.

1.8.3   Clinical and non-clinical complaints against hospitals

A Department of Health circular (*Health Service Management Hospital Complaints Procedure* (HC (88) 37)) ensures that there is what is termed a 'designated officer' to receive complaints and act on them. The procedure appears largely to have been left up to that individual officer, at least in relation to non-clinical complaints (for example, about inefficient administrative procedures).

There is a more precise, but still inadequate system, introduced in 1981 (*Memorandum of an Agreement for Dealing with Complaints Relating to the Exercise of Clinical Judgment by Hospital Medical and Dental Staff* (Department of Health Circular, (HC (81) 5)) to deal with clinical matters. Upon receipt of a complaint.

(a)   The consultant involved should deal with the issue directly, either in person or in writing, 'in a matter of days'.

(b)   If the oral or written explanation does not prove satisfactory for the complainant, the complaint goes to the district health authority, back to the consultant, but in any event to the regional medical officer.

(c)   An independent review is then set up, though only where court action is unlikely. In any event, the regional medical officer will get a second opinion on the clinical management of the case provided by two independent specialists in the field.

Amazingly to some the person who makes the complaint has no right to see the findings of the review and the medical staff involved in the complaint have no duty to cooperate with the review. What can justify inaction in the face of litigation? The answer was given ﹏﹏ R v *Thanet District Health Authority, ex parte F* (1994) Med LR 132. The review is designed to get a second opinion on the case with a view to improving clinical practice where necessary. If there is to be litigation, it would be unreasonable to expect the consultant to cooperate in a voluntary exercise. The litigation, it was argued, would provide its own searching enquiry.

The patent inadequacies of the complaints procedure, and the continued perception of the professional regulatory bodies as insufficiently disinterested to be necessarily fair are compounded by this last procedure. As Margaret Brazier succinctly points out:

> It is a strange situation where an employer cannot require his employee to explain conduct that has resulted in injury to the clients of the business. (*Medicine, Patients and the Law*, 2nd ed. (London: Penguin, 1992), p. 207)

While such procedures remain, the medical lawyer will spend a vast amount of time and energy pursuing the consultant by way of the medical negligence action.

1.9   STRUCTURE OF THE BOOK

This textbook is a description of medical law *and* an evaluation of it. The succeeding chapters will consider how each element of medical practice and law has followed the pathway from moral analysis to legal sanction, regulation, prohibition or even legal non-involvement. This will be seen through the ethical and legal debates that have been fuelled by developments in medical practice and technology. There is a need to be aware of the moral, ethical and human rights aspects of the legal debate. To help this, and to stimulate further debate between readers, a number of examples of the dilemmas which can and sometimes have faced medical law will be given. It is worthwhile, when considering debate on an aspect of medical law to look at one of these fictitious situations and consider first how you think the law might react. Secondly, having considered the development and current state of the law, ask whether medical law provides an answer to the dilemma, and thirdly, whether, if it does provide an answer it is a satisfactory one morally and in terms of human rights as well as traditional legal concepts.

Medical law focuses debate on profound issues and evokes strong emotions. In the conclusions to each chapter there is a brief and very personal evaluation of the state of medical law and its approximation to the moral aspirations that have been expressed in this chapter. If the author has opinions then they have been stated. It is hoped that these elements, indeed the work as a whole, will stimulate further the fierce debates that are already apparent in medicine.

TWO
Confidentiality and access to medical information

2.1 INTRODUCTION

Most, if not all, will need to consult a medical practitioner at some time or another. It may well be routine, such as treatment for 'flu, or it may be for some matter more serious, or more intimate. It may be a time when a patient will not want the information to be known to others, and may be a time when the patient is vulnerable to suggestion and pressure. The doctor will be told something secret: the 15-year-old girl seeking contraceptive advice without her parents' approval, or knowing that the parents will never approve of such a thing; the patient who suspects infection with the AIDS virus and wants to be tested for the disease. That many other examples could be (and will be) given of an equally contentious nature shows the fundamental practical nature of the concept of confidentiality. A patient may be embarrassed by a particular illness and simply not want anyone to know about it. The condition may mean the patient could become the subject of narrow-minded social stigma. It might have a detrimental effect on current or prospective employment or the gaining of insurance cover. These are just a few of the practical impacts of the doctor not keeping a secret.

There are also potential detrimental effects in the doctor keeping all information on the patient strictly confidential: the doctor who does not inform the police, when asked, that a particular patient, suspected of rape, has recently received treatment for deep facial scratches; the doctor who tells no one that an AIDS-infected patient has just left the surgery vowing to 'infect the world' by injecting strangers with contaminated blood; the doctor who refuses to release information on a patient to a medical specialist called in to diagnose that patient's mysterious but life-threatening illness. These are the practical dilemmas that can be faced. But what of the ethical justification for the existence of confidentiality?

2.2 ETHICS OF CONFIDENCE

The practical necessity of maintaining a medical confidence is bolstered by the ethical imperative placed on the medical profession by the Hippocratic oath:

Whatsoever things I see or hear concerning the life of men, in my attendance on the sick or even apart therefrom, which ought not to be noised abroad, I will keep silence thereon, counting such things to be as sacred secrets.

This part of the original oath recognises, but does not state, the circumstances where a confidence is not absolute by the phrase 'which ought not to be noised abroad', but the amended version in the Declaration of Geneva does appear to be absolute:

I will respect the secrets which are confided in me, even if the patient has died.

The first issue to be considered is the basis of this ethical obligation and the human rights that are respected by keeping the confidences given by the patient to the doctor. A basic starting point for any consideration of confidentiality is a simple one: the duty to maintain a confidence as a matter of ethics, human rights and law is an exceedingly strict one. Why?

Raanan Gillon in his influential work *Philosophical Medical Ethics* (Chichester Wiley, 1986) accepts this innate importance, but goes on to ask:

Is it morally valuable in itself, or, if not, why is it morally important? Is it an absolute requirement? How does it relate to other obligations? (p. 107)

For a moral duty to arise for the doctor, there needs to be a promise to keep the matter secret, and the matter must in fact be a secret. The ethical significance of keeping a confidence is consequentialist. The telling of a secret will simply result in less happiness for the patient. The absolutism of deontology would accept confidentiality on the fundamental ethical basis of the respect for the individual – autonomy. Perhaps even the ethical concept of privacy.

Gillon, amongst others, recognises how unrealistic an absolute obligation to keep a medical secret would be, but notes the paucity of justifications that have been forthcoming for the exceptions to the moral rule. Forcefully it is argued that:

Such cynicism could be reduced – without much if any harm to patient care – by admitting openly that medical confidentiality is not absolute and then justifying, rather than simply stating, the sorts of exception approved by the profession, with a view to achieving a sort of social contract between the profession and society about the categories of exception that would and would not be acceptable. (p. 110)

It is important ethically and legally to be able to point to these justifications for breaching the ethical underpinning of medical law – the autonomy of the patient. Consider the ethical dimension of the legal debate surrounding alleged breaches of this obligation, and consider when looking at the medical law of confidence how ethics and medical law would respond to the following situations faced by the patient or doctor.

(a) John is a taxi driver who has been feeling unwell at work for some time. He consults Dr Thomas who diagnoses John as an epileptic. The condition can be partially controlled by medication, but is prone to occur unexpectedly, perhaps while in a taxi containing passengers. John says to the doctor, 'Don't tell my employer, I'll lose my licence and my job'.

(b) Steve has just been diagnosed as being HIV positive. Dr Jones asks whether Steve has a current sexual partner. Steve replies, 'Yes, but don't tell her, she would leave me'. He maintains this stance when told by the doctor that his partner could become infected.

(c) Joan has just had an operation to remove an unsightly blemish on her arm. As she is leaving the hospital she walks past a lecture theatre and sees a doctor discussing the technical aspects of Joan's operation with medical students and analysing her full medical history, as well as watching a video of the operation. She was never previously informed that any of this was going to happen, and would never have agreed to it if she had been.

(d) Dr Edwards has just seen a patient in a disturbed mental state saying that he is going to kill his wife and child because he believes they are plotting to poison him. During the course of the consultation, the patient pulls out a length of rope and says 'This is what I'm going to use on them'.

The above scenarios indicate that there are ethical as well as practical pressures on both patient and doctor. Where do the ethical and legal rights, duties and responsibilities lie?

The WHO, when considering the issue of confidence, made specific recommendations for medical law to maximise its respect for human rights in this context. Remember first the relevant broad human rights principles: that everyone has the right to respect as a human being, to self-determination, to physical and mental integrity and to privacy. Specifically, the WHO states:

(a) All information must be kept confidential, even after death.

(b) Information can only be disclosed if the patient gives explicit consent, or if the law specifically provides. Consent may be presumed where disclosure is to other health care providers involved in that patient's treatment.

(c) All identifiable patient data must be protected.

(d) Patients have the right of access to their medical files and so forth which pertain to diagnosis, treatment and care.

(e) Patients have the right to require the correction, completion, deletion, clarification and/or updating of personal and medical data concerning them which are inaccurate, incomplete, ambiguous or outdated, or which are not relevant to the purposes of diagnosis, treatment and care.

(f)   There can be no intrusion into a patient's private and family life unless and only if, in addition to the patient consenting to it, it can be justified as necessary to the patient's diagnosis, treatment and care.

(g)   Medical interventions may only be carried out when there is proper respect shown for the privacy of the individual. This means that the only persons who may be present when an intervention is carried out are persons who are necessary for the intervention unless the patient consents or requests otherwise.

(h)   Patients admitted to health care establishments have the right to expect physical facilities which ensure privacy, particularly when health care providers are offering them personal care or carrying out examinations or treatment.

So, does medical law accord with the ethical imperative to respect autonomy and the human rights aspirations of the WHO? Or is acting in accordance with such demands practically and legally impossible?

2.3   LEGAL RECOGNITION OF CONFIDENCE

The common law has recognised that the notion of confidence does exist, but never really sought a sound justification for its existence. The seminal case which established in forthright terms that confidentiality does exist, as well as setting out the general features of the duty, has become known as the *Spycatcher* case (*Attorney-General* v *Guardian Newspapers Ltd (No. 2)* [1990] 1 AC 109). It is worth considering the analysis of the relevant law detailed by Lord Goff:

> . . . a duty of confidence arises when confidential information comes to the knowledge of a person (the confidant) in *circumstances* where he has *notice*, or is held to have agreed, that the information is confidential, with the effect that it would be just in all the circumstances that he should be precluded from disclosing the information to others. I have use the word 'notice' advisedly, in order to avoid the . . . question of the extent to which actual knowledge is necessary; though I of course understand knowledge to include circumstances where the confidant has deliberately closed his eyes to the obvious. The extent of this broad general principle reflects the fact that there is such a public interest in the maintenance of confidences, that the law will provide remedies for their protection. (emphasis added)

There seems little doubt that such circumstances are commonly encountered in the practice of medicine.

Some important points arise out of this summary. It is essential as a matter of law to declare which 'circumstances' can be considered to create a situation of confidence. With a doctor–patient, solicitor–client or banker–customer scenario this would on surface inspection appear obvious. Consider, however, the number of medical professionals that can be concerned with a person who complains of a medical condition: the receptionist who makes an appointment to see the doctor, the doctor who does the examination, possibly the medical trainee who sits in on the examination, the secretary who types up the referral letter to the specialist, the colleague in the doctor's partnership who discusses the case over the telephone to provide a second informal opinion. If the matter requires medical intervention in a hospital then it is not difficult to imagine the increase in the number of personnel who will have intimate knowledge of the patient's medical history and current condition. It is a complex matter for the courts to consider whether all of these individuals can be regarded as receiving factual information in a circumstance of confidence. An important initial point for medical law comes from considering the increasing numbers of medical and allied staff knowing of the patient's condition. Gillon (*Philosophical Medical Ethics* (Chichester: Wiley, 1986), pp. 109–10) describes a US doctor who has viewed modern medical confidentiality in less than favourable terms (M. Siegler, 'Confidentiality in Medicine: A Decrepit Concept' (1982) 307 New Eng J Med 1518–21):

> He had looked into the matter after a patient complained that all sorts of people whom he (the patient) had not authorised were looking at his notes. On investigation Dr Siegler was 'astonished to learn that at least 25 and possibly as many as 100 health professionals and administrative personnel at our university hospital had access to the patient's record and that all of them had a legitimate need, indeed a professional responsibility, to open and use that chart'.

In the context of medicine one therefore has to treat the prerequisites of Lord Goff with some caution. There appear, according to Dr Siegler's experience, to be a potentially vast range of personnel who can claim a legal right to view confidential information. The more who see it the less confidential it becomes.

The response of medical law to the issue of confidence could take a number of forms. It could adopt a strict theory of confidence, whereby there is a limited group of those who, as a matter of law, can receive medical or allied information on a person. They will thereafter be prima facie regarded as being in a position of confidence at law and therefore liable if that confidence is not kept.

The difficulties caused by such an idea would be considerable. There would most obviously be problems concerning the transfer of information between medical professionals and therefore the patient's effective treatment may be jeopardised. The student doctor would be more difficult to train without full access to patient information to help in gaining the ability to diagnose effectively. There is increasing pressure on the medical profession to train and research. A strict duty could undermine this. Nevertheless a strict delineation of medical personnel allowed to view patient records, allied to a specific and articulated justification for each of these having such access is a possibility.

There may be a modified theory of confidence based on the status of the medical individual involved, with a class of such professionals having a

protective mechanism which enables limited amounts of confidential information to be disclosed to a similar class, but where such disclosure is in the
interests of the patient. It is this notion of 'the interest of the patient' that could
provide the justification for both the duty of confidence and the duty to access
that confidential information. It is a patient-oriented view of confidence which
would appear to accord with the modern view of the rights-based and bilateral
doctor–patient relationship. It could be argued in response that in practical
terms this would only improve matters slightly. It would certainly not appear to
help the trainee doctor or the researcher. How could the student or the
academic researcher justify access as being in that particular patient's interest?
It does still have to be recognised that there is a broader danger in always
keeping any of these 'in the dark' about details concerning the patient.

The other possibility would be to have a liberal regime of information
circulation, with the control mechanism being a matter of clinical judgment.
The difficulties of this would be that, like other areas of medical law, there
would be given to the medical profession discretion in what is not always a
strictly clinical environment, absolved from the ethical responsibilities exemplified by the strictures of the Hippocratic oath and a broad theory of patient
autonomy. The changing face of the doctor–patient relationship makes
clinical dominance over the access to information decision less and less
tenable. In the past there may have been free flow of confidential medical
information between fellow professionals, but the new patient-oriented
language of legal rights in medicine would appear to preclude such a thing.

The main determinant of the breadth of exception to the duty of confidence comes from the phrase 'public interest'. The law recognises here that
while a patient might have a personal (or more accurately here *private*)
interest in the non-disclosure of medical information, there is the more
ethical, and for our purposes legal, interest for society as a whole in the
maintenance of confidence. Go back to the examples given at the start of the
chapter. To complete three of the scenarios:

(a) John goes to work the next day, and while driving a couple to the
airport has an epileptic fit, and crashes the car. He and the couple are killed.

(b) Steve continues to have unprotected sexual intercourse with his
partner, and she becomes HIV positive.

(c) Dr Edwards's patient returns home and kills his wife and child.

There can be pressure on the doctor to keep a medical secret, but there
may be danger to others in doing so.

This major aspect of the law will be considered a little later.

2.4 PLACE OF CONFIDENTIALITY IN GENERAL LAW

Before a consideration of any of the case law, one must consider the form the
action for a breach of confidence could take. After all the doctor–patient
relationship can have implications in the realms of contract, tort, equity,
property and even the criminal law. This can have significant impacts for the

patient, particularly in terms of the sort of legal remedies that will be available. It is of some small matter to the doctor, whose form of liability could impact financially, professionally and, if the criminal law were to be invoked, in terms of liberty. Which branch of law covers confidence between the parties?

One can do little better than examine the general law in this area as discussed by Francis Gurry (*Breach of Confidence* (Oxford: Clarendon Press, 1984)). Gurry points out that an analysis of the law generally in relation to confidence leads one to the conclusion that the courts have been both 'pragmatic' and 'flexible' in developing the concepts underlying the action. It is apparent that the courts have not felt hamstrung and bound to one branch of law in deciding the relevant principles to use. As he comments:

. . . the courts have relied on principles freely drawn from the fields of contract, equity and property, and . . . the liberal use of these principles points to the existence of a *sui generis* action which has, in terms of conventional categories, a composite jurisdictional basis.

The pragmatism can be seen in the principle that a remedy will be given to a plaintiff in a matter alleging breach of confidence if it is just in all the circumstances. Explicitly or implicitly it will be seen that in medical confidence cases courts are required to carry out a balancing act of interests. Despite the flexibility of judicial response to the dilemmas of alleged breaches of medical confidence, Gurry asserts that there is an underlying policy which permeates this whole area: 'The policy of holding confidence sacrosanct'. So, some flexibility, but with an eye to the ethical importance of keeping the patient's secret.

The crux of the matter is shown by the factors Gurry considers go to make up a position of trust which may be enforceable at law:

(a)   The information conveyed must have been done so in circumstances which give rise to a position of trust.

(b)   A disclosure by a doctor will not betray a confidence where the matter concerned was already in the public domain.

(c)   Information is of a confidential nature where it is such that the confider wishes it to be kept secret.

(d)   The use of the confidential information must be unauthorised, and must cause a detriment to the confider.

It is important, before one moves on to consider how wide the obligation is, to bear in mind that, as Gurry confirms, the overriding policy of maintaining confidence is one which still *unites* contract, equity and property concepts. One needs also to be aware of the fact that the courts, in the medical context, have not felt the need to discuss in any great detail whether the duty of confidence exists, there being a long-held presumption that it does (see *Hunter* v *Mann* [1974] QB 767 below at p. 32). The central matter that has concerned the courts and Parliament has been the scope of that recognised duty.

While it is apparent that confidentiality is something of a stew of a number of parts of the general law, the equitable nature of the action seems to predominate, with the courts, at least in other jurisdictions, declaring the doctor's duty a fiduciary one – one of trust. An example from the US shows what this means.

In *Morris* v *Consolidation Coal Co.* (1994) 444 SE 2d 648, Mr Morris had sought benefit for a work-related disability from a workers' fund. A doctor had supported the claim. Some time later a representative of the defendant company visited the doctor and showed him videos of Mr Morris digging at a time when he had said he was too injured to work. Thereafter the doctor refused to certify that Morris was unfit for work. Morris brought a claim for breach of medical confidence. Aspects of his case had been discussed between the company representative and the doctor.

In the Supreme Court some general principles relating to medical confidence were established or reiterated, some of which at least are immediately relevant to England and Wales:

(a)   The doctor–patient relationship is a fiduciary one.

(b)   This relationship of trust prohibits *ex parte* communications between the employer and the physician treating a claimant, notwithstanding the need to investigate fraud.

(c)   The interest in resolving claims expeditiously demands a communication between employer and treating physician. This will be legitimate provided legislation authorises release of the records.

(d)   A cause of action for breach of confidentiality will lie against a third party who induces a doctor to breach this fiduciary duty if:

(i)   the third party knew or reasonably should have known of the doctor–patient relationship.

(ii)   the third party intended to induce a wrongful disclosure, or reasonably should have anticipated that actions would have that effect;

(iii)   the third party did not reasonably believe that the doctor could disclose the information without violating the duty of confidence;

(iv)   the information was actually disclosed to the third party.

Of course, in the unlikely event that the plaintiff is harmed physically by the unwarranted diclosure of personal medical information, he or she could use the traditional medical negligence action.

Consider the New Zealand case of *Furniss* v *Fitchett* [1958] NZLR 396. The plaintiff's husband asked the couple's doctor to write a letter detailing the doctor's observations regarding the plaintiff. He obliged and wrote the following revealing letter which the husband later used in separation proceedings:

Mrs Phyllis C. L. Furniss
32 Mornington Road

The above has been attending me for some time and during this period I have observed several things:

(1)   Deluded that her husband is doping her.

(2)   Accuses her husband of cruelty and even occasional violence.

(3)   Considers that her husband is insane and states that it is a family failing.

On the basis of the above I consider she exhibits symptoms of paranoia and should be given treatment for same if possible. An examination by a psychiatrist would be needed to fully diagnose her case and its requirements.

Your faithfully
A. J. Fitchett.

The doctor admitted that he knew the disclosure of such information could be harmful to the patient. Barrowclough CJ confirmed that the court would need to be satisfied that the doctor ought to have contemplated that Mrs Furniss would be physically harmed by his revelations. If so, she would be a legal 'neighbour' for the purposes of the law of negligence and owed a duty of care. That was mainfestly the case on the evidence. The letter was not even marked 'confidential'. Nevertheless the court did note that while this duty of care would be a relatively strict one, it would be unrealistic to make it an absolute one. Disclosure would be dependent on the public interest and reasonable professional practice.

2.5 MODIFYING THE DUTY IN THE PUBLIC INTEREST

The 'Blue Book' (General Medical Council, *Professional Conduct and Discipline: Fitness to Practise* (1993)) introduces the concept of the competition between public interests:

> Rarely, cases may arise in which disclosure in the public interest may be justified, for example, a situation in which the failure to disclose appropriate information would expose the patient, or someone else, to a risk of death or serious harm. (para. 86)

The more recent code, appropriately entitled *Confidentiality* (London: GMC, 1995) repeats in similar terms this significant obligation. It retains the notion that the medical profession need to keep in mind the fact that maintaining confidence is the key. Aside from patient authorisation being an exception there is this limited exception based on danger of death or serious harm. The GMC has also now extended the list of exceptions to the obligation of confidence. To many these extensions are warranted, but there is equally a worry that as the list gets longer the obligation to maintain confidence appears to be rather less of an imperative to the medical profession. The GMC now acknowledges for example, that where there is a statutory order that a certain type of disclosure take place then this creates an exception to the obligation.

Of more significance is the GMC's consideration of the place of the patient's consent in all this, which is a matter which will be considered separately later (see 2.7). There is also now an obligation on the medical profession to breach patient confidence to the Driver and Vehicle Licensing Authority. A doctor who considers that a patient is unfit to drive should seek to persuade the patient to inform the DVLA of that fact, but if the patient refuses to do so, a confidential note should be sent to the medical adviser to the DVLA.

It will also be recalled that the law has recognised that there is a public interest in maintaining confidences. The above comment also notes the existence of a possible competitor, the public interest in the protection of members of society. Note that where there is a *private* interest versus a *public* interest, invariably at law the private interest comes second. If the duty of keeping a confidence were regarded as an interest private to the confider, then, as the law has long recognised, it would invariably lose out to a wider societal interest – the public interest – therefore leading to the erosion in the apparently relatively strict duty on the medical profession to protect confidential information. The law has decided that it would be incorrect to call an individual patient's demand that information be kept secret a private interest. Instead medical law has declared that the need to have a medical matter remain confidential is something that we would all wish – it is a public interest. Here then we have the possibility of a competition, or as will more accurately reflect the law's position, a balancing exercise, between the two interests: protection of the public and protection of the medical secret.

The issue of public interest was the central to the main case discussed in this chapter of *W* v *Egdell* [1990] Ch 359 (CA). In the medical context also, the case of *Hunter* v *Mann* [1974] QB 767 indicated that interests are themselves based on the fact that:

> In common with other professional men . . . the doctor is under a duty not to disclose [voluntarily] without the consent of his patient information which he, the doctor, has obtained in his professional capacity, save in very exceptional circumstances. (p. 772)

There appears no better example of the attitude of the courts than the case of *W* v *Egdell*. Another one of significance is *X* v *Y* [1988] 2 All ER 648, and is of some importance to those stigmatised with public knowledge that they are HIV positive or have developed full blown AIDS. *W* v *Egdell* will be the main focus here. But, one should note at this point that given the pragmatic, partially equitable nature of the confidence action, the facts of the particular case take on a special importance.

W was detained as a patient in a secure hospital for reasons of public safety after he had killed five people and wounded two others. As was his right, he applied some time after his detention for review by a mental health review tribunal for discharge, or transfer with a view to discharge. The Secretary of State opposed the application, whereas W's responsible medical officer felt that W's schizophrenia could be successfully controlled by drugs. W's solicitors instructed Dr Egdell to review W and to produce a report to use in the substantive application.

Dr Egdell's report opposed transfer, drawing attention to a number of matters, including the patient's long-standing interest in firearms and explosives. The report was sent to W's solicitors with a view to its consideration by the tribunal. As a result of viewing the contents of this report, W, through his solicitors, withdrew the application. Dr Egdell discovered that neither the Tribunal nor the medical establishment charged with W's current care had seen the report. He therefore sent a copy to the medical director of the hospital where W was being kept. A copy was also forwarded by the hospital to the Secretary of State. W brought actions in contract and equity alleging a breach of the duty of confidence. At the trial stage Scott J argued that the core of the matter:

> is not whether Dr Egdell was under a duty of confidence; he plainly was. The question is as to the breadth of that duty. Did the duty extend so as to bar disclosure of the report to the medical director of the hospital? Did it bar disclosure to the Home Office? ([1990] Ch 359 at p. 389)

Counsel for both sides agreed that the duty existed, but the central question was to balance the two public interests promulgated here. W, as a patient, deserved as a matter of public interest to have the report, produced in an environment of confidence, kept confidential. The other public interest was that publication should take place to those who currently had access to the report on the grounds of the maintenance of public safety from death or serious injury. At both the trial and the subsequent appeal, weight was given to the disciplinary rules for doctors contained in the then applicable professional guidance, the Blue Book, while recognising that they did not have statutory authority.

These rules confirmed that a doctor has a strict duty to maintain the patient's confidence (Blue Book, r. 80), but that this is made subject to a number of exceptions. The doctor may share confidential information with other health care professionals who assist or take over in the clinical management of a patient. This can extend to other people who are helping in such clinical management, but only to the extent that it is necessary for that purpose (r. 81 (b)). More importantly here the rules also state that there may be circumstances where it is in the public interest to disclose what would otherwise be confidential information. The rules give as an example the investigation of a serious crime requiring information to be given to the police (r. 81(g)).

While not agreeing totally with the implication of Scott J at trial that the matter of disclosure was one of clinical judgment to be decided exclusively by the doctor, there was agreement by the Court of Appeal that a balance had to be struck. There was a recognition by Bingham LJ that while W had a private interest in keeping information confidential in that this would serve his private interest in gaining freedom, there was also the wider public interest in keeping confidences.

Apart from some very specific issues, counsel for W's main contention was that maintaining confidences itself would be in the public interest of safety. Patients, if they felt assured that their conditions and comments would not be publicised, would be more open in discussing matters with doctors.

On the other side, counsel for Dr Egdell obviously argued that disclosure was in the public interest as W might be a danger to the public in future. It was this that tipped the balance, and the Court of Appeal found that the doctor's conduct was in the interests of public safety and therefore not unlawful. It was further decided that:

(a)   Disclosure should be limited to those regarded as vitally in need of the information. There would be no justification, for example, in disclosing information for financial profit to a national newspaper.

(b)   The risk, if the material is not disclosed, must be real rather than fanciful. It is unclear what a real as opposed to an unsubstantiated threat would be. It is submitted that this was clear in *W* v *Egdell*, but in any event would be something to be considered individually as part of the circumstances of the case.

(c)   Rather more specifically this real threat needs to be of physical, as opposed to some other form of, harm.

While there may be disquiet that this case represents serious inroads into the doctor–patient relationship and the trust a patient can have in the doctor keeping the confidence, there needs to be an acknowledgement of the fact that this is a confidentiality case which has the features of the general law of confidentiality. One of its main features, one should recall, is flexibility. There seems no reason to suspect that a general legal notion that a doctor, on hearing any material which may be detrimental to certain members of society, can inform a wide spectrum of individuals. The control factors in *W* v *Egdell* are merely specific examples of a minimalist approach to the release of information. If the public interest requires disclosure, it should only be done to the extent that it is absolutely necessary to counter a *specific* threat.

An equally dramatic case, which has a wider societal significance in the context of HIV and AIDS as well as providing another effective example of the judicial approach to balancing public interests, is that of *X* v *Y* [1988] 2 All ER 648. One or more of the employees of the plaintiff health authority supplied information to a reporter (defendant 1) of a national newspaper (defendant 2) identifying two doctors who had AIDS, yet were still practising medicine. This information was obtained from confidential medical records held by the hospital. The plaintiffs subsequently obtained an order restraining publication or other use of the information received. Despite the existence of the order, the second defendant published an article written by defendant 1 entitled 'Scandal of Docs with AIDS'. It was clear that the follow-up article intended to publish the names of the doctors. The plaintiffs applied to the court for an injunction restraining publication of anything which purported to name the doctors, and for the defendants to disclose their sources. The question was whether the second defendants had a public interest in publication.

Rose J was forceful in viewing the public interest in maintaining confidence in the circumstance of AIDS as a significant and fundamental one. The judge was clear about the implications of allowing such breaches of confidence as contemplated here. Patients who knew or feared that their condition would become known would be afraid to come forward for treatment and advice that might alleviate the risk of the spread of the disease. Against this had to be weighed the public interest in the freedom of the press. Rose J went further, and agreed that there would be a public interest in knowing what was sought to be published. The judge found, however, that the public interests in publication were 'substantially outweighed' by confidentiality in the medical context generally, and with the medical records of the AIDS patient in particular. Usefully Rose J pointed out that the public interest in debating the AIDS issue would not be substantially affected by the granting of an injunction. There was already a public debate on many aspects of the disease. The injunction was granted, but the application for the defendants to reveal the names of the sources was not made out here. Rose J did, however, make it clear that an informer in future might not be so fortunate and a custodial sentence would ensue:

The public in general and patients in particular are entitled to expect hospital records to be confidential and it is not for any individual to take it upon himself or herself to breach that confidence whether induced by a journalist or otherwise. ([1988] 2 All ER 648 at p. 665)

X v *Y* is also a relevant introduction to a wider consideration of the particular problems of confidentiality where AIDS and HIV are concerned. Difficulties can be acute here, and the balancing act, which largely rests on the shoulders of the medical profession, can be near impossible of satisfactory resolution. The General Medical Council has issued guidelines to supplement the National Health Service (Venereal Diseases) Regulations 1974 (SI 1974/29), which themselves recognise, much as Rose J did, the importance of keeping confidences here. The GMC guidelines consider the myriad of factual situations that can confront the doctor. The backbone of the guidelines is the need for the doctor to have open and honest discussion of the implications of the disease to the AIDS and HIV-infected patient. The GMC perhaps puts the matter higher than that in stating:

. . . any doctor who discovers that a patient is HIV positive or suffering from AIDS has a *duty* to discuss these matters fully with the patient. (emphasis added)

We will return to the matter of duty in a moment, given its potentially wide-ranging legal significance to the doctor.

Paragraph 16 of the original GMC guidance gives the first practical situation that can arise. A patient is diagnosed by a specialist as suffering from one or other of the conditions, but the patient refuses to let the specialist inform the relevant general practitioner. The guidance sees two sets of obligations as arising. The obvious one is the obligation to keep a patient's confidence. The other obligation is to protect other health care workers from unnecessary risk. The paragraph emphasises counselling of the patient, but emphasises that in the face of a refusal that confidence must be respected, unless the doctor decides that there is a serious risk that a health worker or health care team will be put at risk. Where the Secretary of State considers it necessary, one should note, a person infected with the AIDS virus can be detained under the Public Health (Infectious Diseases) Regulations 1988 (SI 1988/1546, reg. 5).

Of particular difficulty is the situation where a patient who is informed of having contracted AIDS or being HIV positive has a current spouse or sexual partner whom the patient refuses to inform of the illness. The obligations on the doctor should be obvious. Paragraph 19 provides that in most cases counselling will solve the problem, but on the rare occasions that it does not, it is suggested that the doctor may be considered to be under a duty to inform this partner of the risk of what is, after all, an invariably fatal illness.

Of importance as far as medical law is concerned is whether the doctor who decides not to inform the partner of the risk can be found liable as a matter of law or professional discipline. Can the duty suggested in the GMC guidance be seen to be a legal one, so that failure to observe it can found an action in negligence? A US case which might provide some guidance to English law if such a matter were to confront the courts is that of *Tarasoff* v *Regents of the University of California* (1976) 551 P 2d 334. The case also raises wider issues of medical law. How specific is the danger in keeping the medical secret? In *W* v *Egdell* it appeared to be the determinative factor, at least for the Court of Appeal. *Tarasoff*, while a leading case, is not the only one to consider the danger concept. The case law also reveals a difficulty seen in many aspects of medical law, that of duty. Here the difficulty is the duty of the doctor towards third parties who may be injured by the doctor keeping patient confidence.

The plaintiffs were the parents of a woman killed by a mentally disturbed patient. The allegation specifically was that a psychologist employed by the defendants was told by the patient, Prosenjit Poddar, that he intended to kill Tatiana Tarasoff because she had rejected his advances. The parents framed the action in negligence. It was argued that the death was a proximate result of the defendant's failure to warn the deceased, or others who could have communicated the danger to her. The California Supreme Court decided that there is a duty to inform a specific individual of a threat where the danger of death or serious injury is foreseeable.

While in the USA this decision has been elevated to the status of a proposition of general law (see, for example, *Davis* v *Lhim* (1983) 335 NW 2d 481), as a pointer to the possible development of English law it needs to be treated with caution. Michael Jones (*Medical Negligence* (London: Sweet & Maxwell, 1991)) and others have cast considerable doubt on the possibility of this duty existing here. It is appreciated that English case law has approximated to the US duty to others in danger from patients (see *Holgate* v *Lancashire Mental Hospitals Board* [1937] 4 All ER 19 where the defendants were found liable in negligence where a dangerous patient was let out on licence and assaulted the plaintiff), but only to the extent that such decisions have been made on the issue of control of the patient, rather than the duty not to maintain patient confidence where there is an identifiable risk. The real difficulty lies with the proximity of the doctor and the person endangered by the failure to communicate the confidential information.

The more foreseeable the harm the more likely it is that a court will find the relationship between the parties to be proximate. Thus, if a patient made genuine threats of serious injury to an identified third person and there was a real risk that the threats would be carried out, it is arguable that a doctor would come under a duty of care to the potential victim. The duty, if any, arises from the defendant's knowledge of the foreseeable danger of serious physical harm to the third party. (Jones, *Medical Negligence*, 2.64)

Any likelihood of this being the case is diminished by the strong line of authority in English law that there is no duty to prevent harm from befalling an individual; in short there is no duty to rescue. This may be offset to a limited degree by the possibility of founding an action where the person identified as at risk from the transmission of HIV is also the patient of the doctor treating the already infected partner. There would appear to be a proximate relationship here.

The decision in *Tarasoff* has not been without its critics. In *Taylor* v *United States* 221 2d 398 at p. 401 Edgerton J noted:

The psychiatric patient confides more utterly than anyone in the world. He exposes to the therapist not only what his words express, he lays bare his entire self, his dreams, his fantasies, his sins and his shame.

The broad duty that arises from *Tarasoff* might deter the mentally ill from seeking help, or truly confiding all. The doctor could be seen as some sort of 'double agent'. Doctors could fear liability for a failure to tell an intended victim or the police. This makes it more likely that the doctor will view it as a duty to breach a confidence where the course of action is legally unclear. *Tarasoff*, it should be noted, elevated what was a permissible disclosure in limited circumstances into a potentially wide legal duty.

In response to this, de Haan ('My Patient's Keeper: The Liability of Medical Practitioners for Negligent Injury to Third Parties' (1986) 2 PN 86) cites *Brady* v *Hopper* (1983) 570 F Supp 1333 as authority for a somewhat narrower rule. William Hinckley Jr had tried to kill Ronald Reagan, and had shot the plaintiff, a presidential aide. The defendant psychiatrist had been treating Hinckley. The plaintiff alleged the doctor knew that the would-be assassin collected books on assassination and had access to guns and ammunition. Hinckley's parents had also suggested to the doctor that their son needed hospitalisation. The claim failed. Hinckley had never made a specific threat. The court found that a duty might arise once a patient had made specific threats and made them against identifiable potential victims.

The possibility of harm then became foreseeable. This was described during the course of the judgment as a 'workable rule'.

Underlying it all is once more the inexact nature of medical science. When will a patient's directed violent fantasies be turned into reality and destructive action?

There being a general rule of English medical law that there is no liability for the acts of third parties, the courts could perceive that such is the risk of fatal infection or threats of violence becoming actual violence, and so simple its avoidance by the actions of the doctor, that these limited circumstances may warrant an exception to the general law. This does not, however, solve the very real dilemma that faces the doctor. Margaret Brazier holds that the chances of third-party success are slim:

> The courts in England are reluctant in effect to make A liable for a wrong committed by B. So the injured individual would have to satisfy the court that the doctor's knowledge of the risk to him was sufficient to make it 'just and reasonable' for the doctor to be required to protect him. (*Medicine, Patients and the Law*, 2nd ed. (London: Penguin, 1992), p. 58)

There is another possibility for liability on the part of the doctor, and relates directly to the situation of John the taxi driver in the example at the start of the chapter. It relates the issue of liability to the level of discrimination used in imparting confidential information in the public interest. The issue is set out clearly by de Haan:

> To disclose the details of certain illnesses to a patient's employer or to the authorities may lead to the loss of some privilege such as a driving licence or of the ability to earn a living by operating machinery. In the result some individuals might be reluctant to seek medical advice or be tempted to conceal potentially dangerous symptoms from the doctor. ((1986) 2 PN 86 at p. 88)

How can medical law solve this very real dilemma? A potential answer is to see it as another public interest issue. An example comes from the New Zealand case of *Duncan* v *Medical Practitioners Disciplinary Committee* [1986] 1 NZLR 513. Mr Henry, a bus driver, complained to Dr Duncan's professional disciplinary body. Mr Henry had undergone a triple heart by-pass operation having suffered a number of heart attacks. A surgeon thereafter certified that he was fit to drive. Dr Duncan, Mr Henry's GP, asked that the bus driving licence be withdrawn, and went so far as to warn potential passengers of his condition. Initially the Medical Practitioners Disciplinary Committee found him:

> guilty of professional misconduct in that he breached professional confidence in informing lay people of his patient's personal medical history. The Committee takes the view that professional confidence can only be breached in most exceptional circumstances and then only if the public interest is paramount.

On judicial review of the findings, the New Zealand High Court found that there may indeed be circumstances where the public interest merited disclosure, but the doctor had a duty when so doing to ensure that there was some discrimination in who received that information. Only those in a position of 'responsible authority' should receive it. Dr Duncan did not show this discrimination.

2.6 CONFIDENTIALITY AND THE LEGALLY INCOMPETENT

The individuals under discussion here are those who are undergoing treatment or receiving advice, yet are not regarded at law as having the ability to control the dissemination or otherwise of their confidential medical records. The candidates for control may be the parent(s) of a minor, the person legally designated as acting in the interests of a mentally incompetent adult or the doctor using clinical judgment in the best interests of the patient. The later chapters on consent and mental health will discuss in detail the ability of the mentally incompetent generally to make decisions about themselves, but a few general points should be noted here.

The case of *Gillick* v *West Norfolk and Wisbech Area Health Authority* [1986] AC 112, HL, while essentially a matter of consent, has still enunciated a principle of general application to minors in medical law. Where confidentiality is in issue, note the pressures that exist. The parents are naturally concerned to know what is happening to their child. The child wants to keep more and more secrets. The choice in *Gillick* was between a status and a capacity approach. The status approach has the advantage of certainty. There would be a single cut-off point. A child under the age of 16 would not be regarded in law as competent to make decisions about medical treatment. The alternative view canvassed, and the one which is accepted and permeates medical law as it relates to minors, is the capacity approach. A child is competent to make decisions on treatment independently of the wishes of the parents. This can only take place, however, where the child is regarded, whatever his or her age, as capable of understanding the contents and implications of the choices which can be made. This applies equally to the situation where the parent or another requests or demands confidential medical information on the child. This is not to blind oneself to the conflicting pressures that can exist in this situation. The welfare of the child is of paramount importance, and it would be anticipated that the doctor would base the assessment of understanding with regard to the welfare issue alongside the simple application of the *Gillick* formula. The doctor has a duty to promote the best interests of the child. If there is evidence of sexual abuse, for example, then there is the public interest in the detection of crime and the best interests of the child's mental and physical welfare and protection.

Where the incompetent adult is concerned it will be discovered that there is no longer a *parens patriae* (really the court acting as the protector of those who cannot protect themselves) jurisdiction to allow for judicial pronouncement on information disclosure. Aside from the mental health legislation that exists at present, there appears to be scant structure to organise a decision-making process on releasing information relating to the mentally incompetent adult. There are difficulties in medical law viewing this as a 'typical' bilateral doctor–patient relationship. The adult patient cannot in practice enter a relationship of confidence by mere reason of the incapacity. The matter at present is rather ad hoc. The development of case law on the sterilisation of the mentally handicapped (see chapter 13) indicates a form of development, denoting another common law 'best interests of the patient' test, but one which, it might be suggested, is a less than ideal template.

2.7 CONSENT TO COMMUNICATE INFORMATION

Obtaining the patient's consent is the most obvious way of communicating information regarding a patient's medical condition to others without attracting legal sanction. As Kennedy and Grubb correctly indicate, the existence of consent is not an exception to the rule of confidence; it simply means that the information is not confidential (Kennedy and Grubb, *Medical Law*, 2nd ed. (London: Butterworths, 1994, p. 644). The original 1993 guidance for the medical profession also indicates that the communication of the information should accord with the nature of the consent:

> Where a patient, or a person authorised to act on a patient's behalf, consents to disclosure, information to which the consent refers may be disclosed in accordance with that consent. (para. 77)

It has been suggested that consent, as well as being express, can also be implied. This should be treated with caution. In the absence of an express and detailed consent to what may be disclosed and to whom, there is some difficulty in assuming the level and breadth of information which it is legitimate to disclose. Doctors would be prudent in limiting dissemination of patient information on the basis of carefully considered clinical need. To some extent the 1993 guidance also recognises that caution is needed:

> Most doctors in hospital and general practice are working in health care teams, some of whose members may need access to information, given or obtained in confidence about individuals, in order to perform their duties. It is for doctors who lead such teams to judge when it is appropriate for information to be disclosed for that purpose. They must leave those whom they authorise to receive such information in no doubt that it is given to them in professional confidence. The doctor also has a responsibility to ensure that arrangements exist to inform patients of the circumstances in which information about them is likely to be shared and to give the patients the opportunity to state any objection to this. (para. 79)

For there to be consent as a matter of ethics as well as law, it needs to be as informed as possible and also voluntary. As already indicated, the patient consulting the doctor is in a vulnerable position. How many, on having a pre-operative examination in hospital would refuse the surgeon who asks 'You don't mind if these 15 medical students watch me examine you, do you?'? The situation is fraught with potential anxiety for the patient and ripe for seldom-questioned breaches of medical confidence. Medical law in this instance should provide for a recognition of the tension of this situation and require an explicit form of request to release the confidential information. One would surely feel more in control were the form of question demanded at law to be something like, 'These are medical students. As part of their training they need to see this form of pre-operative examination. I need your consent for that to happen, but you needn't give it if you feel uncomfortable. Do you understand?' Aside from the very important question of whether the patient is competent to decide whether information regarding an aspect of his or her treatment should be released (and here the 1995 code encourages the medical profession to persuade the incompetent party to involve another person in the decision-making process, and if not, to breach confidence only in that patient's 'best interests'), the 1995 GMC code now seems to be adding worryingly vague exceptions to the need to gain patient consent. The code states that there may be 'medical reasons' why the doctor may not be able to gain such consent without articulating in any form what is meant by 'medical reasons'. It may simply be that the GMC code envisages that there needs to be information given to another medical team where the patient is unconscious. Equally it may be interpreted broadly to encompass any situation where the doctor feels that disclosure would be of medical assistance to that patient. A second situation is that encountered in relation to Joan (see the scenario at the start of the chapter) involving issues of research and education. The 1995 code recognises that the patient should be informed that information from which the patient could be identified may be used for education or research. Where the patient refuses then the information should not be used. But what if the patient cannot be recognised? There may well be an argument that there can be no breach of confidentiality as the patient is never identified. One needs though to be slightly wary of the term 'identification'. Is it to be interpreted as meaning identified as a specific individual? Or is identification to be predicated on the issue of potential harm to the patient? Is the matter merely that the patient considers that he or she has been 'seen'? It may be that Joan did not want to have her personal details read out to the class, but what if none of the students had ever heard of or seen her as an identifiable individual? If she were to refuse beforehand, should that be respected because of the danger of recognition, or is it based on the broader notion of respect for the individual's privacy? There seems once more to be an acknowledgement without a justification.

2.8 STATUTORY CONTROL OF CONFIDENTIAL INFORMATION

The numerous statutory measures that have been enacted are designed with differing objectives in mind. The statutes may confirm the strict nature of the duty of confidentiality on those holding patient information. They may also empower modifications to the duty of confidentiality in a given set of circumstances. Finally the statutes may make it a duty at law to disclose certain confidential information.

2.8.1 Abortion Regulations 1991 (SI 1991/499)

Paragraph 5 of the Abortion Regulations 1991 allows for limited disclosure
by the Chief Medical Officer of matters which may be of concern to the
Director of Public Prosecutions. The main matter envisaged is an investigation into whether there has been a breach of the abortion legislation (see
chapter 12). Disclosure of information may also be authorised where it is for
the purposes of bona fide research, to the practitioner who carried out the
particular termination, or to a practitioner who, with the consent of the
woman whose pregnancy was terminated, or when the President of the GMC
requests information as part of an investigation into whether there has been
some serious professional misconduct on the part of a registered medical
practitioner.

2.8.2 Public Health (Control of Disease) Act 1984

Section 10 of the Act defines notifiable diseases as 'cholera, plague, relapsing
fever, smallpox and typhus'. Section 11(1) provides that:

> If a registered medical practitioner becomes aware, or suspects, that a
> patient whom he is attending within the district of a local authority is
> suffering from a notifiable disease or from food poisoning, he shall, unless
> he believes, and has reasonable grounds for believing, that some other
> medical practitioner has complied with this subsection with respect to the
> patient, forthwith send to the proper officer of the local authority for that
> district a certificate stating—
>
> (a)   the name, age and sex of the patient and the address of the premises
> where the patient is,
>
> (b)   the disease or, as the case may be, particulars of the poisoning from
> which the patient is, or is suspected to be, suffering and the date, or
> approximate date, of its onset, and
>
> (c)   if the premises are a hospital, the day on which the patient was
> admitted, the address of the premises from which he came there and
> whether or not, in the opinion of the person giving the certificate, the
> disease or poisoning from which the patient is, or is suspected to be,
> suffering was contracted in the hospital.

Failure to do so will lead to summary conviction.

This legislation has been supplemented by the Public Health (Infectious
Diseases) Regulations 1988 (SI 1988/1546) which greatly extend the list of
notifiable diseases in line with international health regulations.

2.8.3 National Health Service (Venereal Diseases) Regulations 1974 (SI 1974/29)

Regulation 2 sets out the simple objective of the legislation:

Every regional health authority and every district health authority shall take all necessary steps to secure that any information capable of identifying an individual obtained by officers of the authority with respect to persons examined or treated for any sexually transmitted disease shall not be disclosed except—

(a) for the purpose of communicating that information to a medical practitioner, or to a person employed under the direction of a medical practitioner in connection with the treatment of persons suffering from such disease or the prevention of the spread thereof, and

(b) for the purpose of such treatment or prevention.

In *X* v *Y* [1988] 2 All ER 648, Rose J placed emphasis on this piece of legislation as an illustration of the legislature's concern that the public interest in confidence be upheld in this context.

Of some concern is the fact that the legislation, as it affects the HIV-positive patient, only covers diseases sexually transmitted. It should be remembered that this is only one way in which this virus can be communicated. It appears that the haemophiliac who contracts the illness through contaminated blood will have to look to the general common law on confidence (with the assistance of the GMC guidelines rehearsed earlier).

2.8.4 Police and Criminal Evidence Act 1984

It has to be regarded as essential that there is access by the police to significant levels of information to tackle crime effectively. Section 9 of the Police and Criminal Evidence Act 1984 allows for special access to what is termed 'excluded material' for the purposes of a criminal investigation. Section 11 defines 'excluded material' as, amongst other things, 'human tissue or tissue fluid which has been taken for the purposes of diagnosis or medical treatment and which a person holds in confidence'. Section 12 allows for access to personal records which relate to an individual's physical or mental health.

2.9 REMEDIES FOR BREACH OF A MEDICAL CONFIDENCE

It will be recalled that the action for breach of confidence has a 'composite jurisdictional base', therefore one needs to decide the most pertinent remedy at law. If the patient suffers physical injury, then *Furniss* v *Fitchett* [1958] NZLR 396 indicated that damages are available as a remedy in a negligence action. The one remedy which would seem the most relevant to the aggrieved patient would be an injunction to prevent publication of the confidential material. Where the information has already been released, though, an injunction is largely useless. It will stop a repeat, but now the information has lost some of its confidential character. Can a patient who is harmed emotionally or even financially claim damages for this breach? *W* v *Egdell* [1990] Ch 359 considered the issue and came to the conclusion that contractual authority was against such an award. Scott J pointed out that it had long been the view of the courts that in contract actions general damages were not to be awarded for frustration, mental distress or annoyance suffered through breach. The law of tort has developed along similar lines. The judge then went on to use the well-worn phrase that 'equity follows the law' and thus would preclude damages in what was essentially a breach of an implied contractual term.

This is not to suggest that if there was some form of economic loss, for example, by the patient losing a job, then damages would not be recoverable. There are obviously professional sanctions against a doctor who breaches a patient's confidence, but this does not greatly assist the aggrieved patient. Note, however, the important broad point made by Mason and McCall Smith:

> The GMC, at present, fills a gap in constraining such conduct as is not actionable yet which would not be expected of the ethical practitioner. Thus, the law on medical confidentiality is in many ways unclear but few doctors would wish to tangle with the GMC on the issue of professional secrecy. (*Law and Medical Ethics*, 4th ed. (London: Butterworths, 1994), p. 11)

In *Attorney-General* v *Guardian Newspapers Ltd (No. 2)* [1990] 1 AC 109, it was considered that there should be damages for disclosure of health information, even where there was no resultant economic loss. It was considered a possibility (although insufficient on the facts of the case) in *X* v *Y* [1988] 2 All ER 648. The overall possibility of gaining damages remains, but is highly unlikely on the facts and consequences of many breaches of confidence. In terms of remedy, if the breach of confidence were successfully framed as being the breach of a property right then circumstances might be more conducive to a range of remedies in that branch of law (see Stuckey 'The Equitable Action for Breach of Confidence: Is Information Ever Property?' (1981) 9 Syd LR 402). A property analysis is more pertinent to issues of commercial exploitation than unethical medical practice.

2.10 CONFIDENCE AND DEATH

A brief mention should be made of confidences that endure after death. Why? Simply because of the ethical notion of respecting the memory of the deceased, but also because medical revelations can harm the living. The declaration of Geneva, it will be recalled, could not be clearer on the matter. Strangely, there is little confidential about the death itself, because the death certificate itself is a public document. Mason and McCall Smith pertinently note the stigma of AIDS following victims to the grave. To be strictly accurate on the death certificate, the doctor should correctly indicate the cause of death. If 'AIDS' is placed on the certificate, then ill-informed rumour might well attach to living partners, friends and relatives. The key to the issue of death and confidentiality in medical law takes one back to the beginning: upon what is it based? If it is the reciprocity of the doctor–patient relationship, then that has ceased to exist. If it is the doctor's duty to society as a whole, then this 'public' duty might include an enduring duty of overall medical confidence.

2.11   ACCESS TO INFORMATION

This chapter is really about two matters which resolve into one issue: the control of information. Part of the control issue is whether there is control in terms of access to personal medical information held by others. The available candidates here are limited. Does the patient have unfettered access to what is after all intimate information, or is it the case that the possessor of the physical information is the one who controls through limiting access?

Before that is answered, consider once more how a human rights analysis would approach the matter. The WHO document, *Promotion of the Rights of Patients in Europe: Proceedings of a WHO Consultation* (Kluwer, 1995), is quite specific about rights of information access, in addition to those noted at the start of the chapter. The following are of particular relevance:

(a)   Patients have the right to be fully informed about their health status, including the medical facts about their condition.

(b)   Information may only be withheld from patients exceptionally where there is good reason to believe that this information would without any expectation of obvious positive effects cause them serious harm.

Once more an evaluation of medical law needs to consider whether there is an approximation to all the relevant human rights objectives that have been expressed.

Matters of access are now largely governed by statute, but a basic question still needs to be answered. Who owns the information?

2.11.1   Ownership

The issue of ownership would appear to be a clear one. If the patient 'owns' the information then there should be no legal limit to the access to be afforded. If ownership is basically a matter of who 'owns' the paper containing the information then this would point away from unfettered access. While nothing between patient and doctor or hospital is likely to be express it would appear likely for reasons of clinical management and necessity that were it called on to do so, the law would vest ownership in the 'treating institution'.

In relation to National Health Service patients both general practitioners (National Health Service (General Medical Services) Regulations 1992 (SI 1992/635), sch. 2, para. 36) and NHS hospitals own medical records, whether through the use of FHSA forms or by making records at a hospital.

The general result is that the patient has no automatic right of access to personal medical records and needs to look to either the common law or statute to provide exceptions to this exclusion.

An example of a rather vaguely articulated common law exception is provided by the case of *C* v *C* [1946] 1 All ER 562. This case concerned access by a patient to information relating to her venereal disease infection for use in matrimonial proceedings. It was questioned whether a doctor who is asked by a patient to give particulars of information to be used in court could refuse to so provide until subpoenaed. Here in the particular circumstances of the case, while recognising that confidentiality is often vital to the continued effectiveness of a particular service, the doctor should divulge the information sought. It has to be doubted whether this could be regarded as a continuing effective statement of law, however, as it was decided on its particular facts. The reasoning of the court justifying access to the information was scant to say the least.

A case of potentially broader implication is *R v Mid-Glamorgan FHSA, ex parte Martin* (1993) *The Times*, 2 June 1993. It concerned a patient suffering from a number of severe psychiatric problems. The patient had been receiving psychotherapy as well as support from a social worker, Miss B. During the course of his treatment the patient formed an emotional attachment to Miss B. It was therefore decided, as part of the clinical management of the case, to remove Miss B from participation. Since that time the patient had sought sight of the notes on the case, particularly that relating to the decision to remove Miss B.

The legal claim was made in the realm of public as opposed to contract law. The respondents contended that there was a right to refuse access and this was confirmed by statutes providing rights of access, which themselves make it clear by their existence that there is no corresponding common law right. Primarily, the respondents relied on the existence of the Access to Health Records Act 1990, which is 'An act to establish a right of access to health records by the individuals to whom they relate and other persons'. The word 'establish' was argued as being the key to the denial of the common law right. The statute became the sole determinant of access in such circumstances.

Popplewell J decided that the above, along with the existence of other statutory access rights '. . . seem to me to be an almost insuperable obstacle to the submission made on the applicant's behalf that there is a common law right'.

2.11.2 Statutory access to information

2.11.2.1 Data Protection Act 1984 The general basis of the Act is to allow a 'data subject' to have knowledge of the existence and nature of electronically stored information held by the 'data user' (s. 21(1)). Nevertheless where health care matters are concerned the Data Protection (Subject Access Modification) (Health) Order 1987 (SI 1987/1903) regulates. This allows for modification of the provisions of the Data Protection Act 1984 'in relation to personal data consisting of information as to the physical or mental health of the data subject'. By art. 4(2), the access provisions do not apply where application of them:

(a) would be likely to cause serious harm to the physical or mental health of the data subject; or

(b)   would be likely to disclose to the data subject the identity of another individual (who has not consented to the disclosure of the information) either as a person to whom the information or part of it relates or as the source of the information or enable that identity to be deduced by the data subject either from the information itself or from a combination of that information and other information which the data subject has or is likely to have.

2.11.2.2   Access to Health Records Act 1990   This Act provides largely the same regime for manually stored information as exists for electronically stored information under the Data Protection Act 1984.

Under s. 3(1), an application for access can be made by:

(a)   the patient,
(b)   a person authorised to apply on the patient's behalf,
(c)   the person who has parental responsibility for a child,
(d)   where the person is incompetent at law to manage his or her affairs, the person lawfully appointed to manage them,
(e)   the personal representative of a deceased person where the information is needed to substantiate a claim arising out of the death.

The Act only applies to records created after 1 November 1991. Access to earlier records must be given where in the opinion of the holder of the record it would be necessary to make the subsequent reports intelligible. According to s. 4 a holder does not have to allow access where the records concern a child, unless the holder is satisfied that the child is capable of understanding the nature of the application. By virtue of s. 4(2), where a parent or someone with parental responsibility applies for access to a child's records, the holder needs to be satisfied that the child has consented or that the child is incapable of consenting, and access would be in the child's best interests.

Section 5(1) places a familiar discretionary limitation on access. The holder need not give access where in the holder's opinion such access would be likely to cause serious harm to the physical or mental health of the patient or any other individual. This is also the case where the access to information would identify someone other than the patient.

Non-compliance with the Act is not a ground for the payment of damages, but application can be made to the High Court for an order requiring the relevant party to comply with the Act.

2.11.2.3   Access to Medical Reports Act 1988   This Act creates a right for a patient to have access to reports prepared for insurance or employment purposes. The general principles are covered in s. 1:

It shall be the right of an individual to have access, in accordance with the provisions of this Act, to any medical report relating to the individual which is to be, or has been, supplied by a medical practitioner for employment purposes or insurance purposes.

An individual may specify personal access to the records as a condition of consenting to these other parties' access. Even where this is not done, s. 4(3) allows the individual to receive the report before it is supplied to the commissioner of that report, as long as it is done by giving notice to the examining doctor.

Section 7 limits access in a manner typical in this area. A doctor may not grant access where:

(a)   it would cause harm to the physical or mental health of the patient;
(b)   it 'would indicate the intentions of the practitioner in respect of the individual';
(c)   the information would, or would be likely to, identify another.

The loophole in the legislation is that a doctor is obliged to divulge information under the Act only if he is regarded as being or having been responsible for the clinical care of the patient (s. 2(1)). Therefore it is open to the employer or insurer to employ a medical practitioner solely for the purposes of compiling such a report and that person could be outside s. 2(1) so that the access measures would not apply and one would need to look to the general law on confidentiality and access.

2.11.3   Access and disclosure during the process of litigation

Disclosure of medical reports and records is obviously vital during the course of litigation, particularly medical negligence actions. No evidence no case. Early sight of the information upon which the allegation is to be made can save money. It could reveal that there was no negligence and so end the matter there. If that information was not expeditiously available, there could be a great deal of fruitless legal 'fencing' based on suspicion and intuition rather than fact. Modern litigation works using what may be termed a 'cards on the table' approach. It improves the efficiency of litigation by allowing both plaintiff and defendant access to the majority of the evidence which goes to the dispute between the parties. Issues of causation and damage can only be fully considered where there is full information. The Supreme Court Act 1981 facilitates such efficiency.

By s. 33 a person who is likely to be a party to proceedings can seek a High Court order for the disclosure of information from another who is likely to be a party to the proceedings. Section 34 provides for the production of documents from someone who is likely to be in possession of relevant material even though they are not a party to the action. This is usually utilised in medical negligence actions to get the GP's notes, or notes held by another health authority. Section 35 cuts down the access somewhat in stating that the High Court does not have jurisdiction to make such an order where it would not be in the public interest.

The power to order 'discovery' of medical documents applies to a person who is 'likely' to be a party to a personal injury action. However, as far as medical records are concerned, it is more and more the case that the Access to Health Records Act 1990, which gives the patient largely unfettered access to records created after October 1991, will be utilised to get the information.

A prospective defendant can always claim that certain documents are privileged (see Rules of the Supreme Court 1965, ord. 24, r. 7A(6)). One relevant class of document that is privileged is one that is prepared with the anticipated legal action as its main purpose.

2.12   CONCLUSION

The modern law of medical confidence lacks coherence. There is the primary difficulty of justifying the existence of the obligation as a matter of law. Human rights, moral philosophy and medical ethics justify its existence in terms of respect for self-determination, autonomy and privacy rights. Medical law, if it attempts it at all, bases it on the duty of the doctor in the context of the overall doctor–patient relationship. Again it is worth emphasising that the relative strengths of the two parties to this relationship are in the process of re-forming. English medical law, unlike the medical confidence law of the USA, or the other common law jurisdictions, still does not know whether to frame the matter in terms of clinical judgment, best interests or rights. Until it does, confidentiality will continue to be a hotchpotch of common law and isolated legislation without the rights-based theoretical underpinning it requires.

There is a general acknowledgement that the obligation as a matter of law needs to be strict. It is further acknowledged that it would be legally foolish and practically dangerous to make it absolute. Any legal reform should, as well as justifying the existence of medical confidences, specifically articulate exceptions to that obligation. To invite the courts to undertake a balancing exercise of public interests is too vague, and is likely to be something that the judges themselves would not be happy to continue to do.

Further reading

Jones, M. A., 'Medical Confidentiality and the Public Interest' (1990) 6 PN 16.
McConnell, T., 'Confidentiality and the Law' (1994) 20 J Med Ethics 47.

THREE

Medical negligence I: duties in medicine

3.1 INTRODUCTION

3.1.1 The breadth of the duty issue

Modern medical law has begun to take on the language of rights. It has also taken on the concurrent language of duties. Duties pervade the whole study of medical law. Here the duty of care incumbent on the medical practitioner as a matter of negligence, contract and public law will be considered. The vast majority of duty of care cases in medicine are medical negligence actions. In general terms, where there is an allegation of negligence against a doctor, the patient has to show, on the balance of probabilities, that the particular defendant owed the patient a duty of care, has breached that duty by acting below the standard prescribed by law and that this breach has caused legally recognised damage. Beneath this seemingly straightforward line of proof lie significant difficulties for the patient plaintiff. The difficulties lie in the particular rigours of negligence actions as a whole, but more significantly for the disgruntled patient, by the historical dominance of the medical professional in the doctor–judge as well as the doctor–patient relationship. Margaret Brazier sums up the problem well:

> The judges in England defer in most part to the views of the doctors. Unlike their American brethren, English judges will rarely challenge the accepted views of the medical profession. (*Medicine, Patients and the Law* (London: Penguin, 1992), p. 21)

Through the developing recognition of human rights demands, the tide may be slowly turning toward 'patient power'. This may in future have a knock-on effect and in turn encourage the judiciary to question the existence and scope of a duty of care in the particular circumstances of a medical negligence case. As already noted in 1.5, this process is well under way in the

USA, as well as the broadly comparable common law jurisdictions of Canada and Australia.

This chapter will consider the following duty issues. The first is highly relevant to the other chapters on standards of care, causation and damage, defective drugs and medical products, consent and wrongful conception, birth and life.

(a) The growth of medical litigation in Britain.
(b) The formation of the duty of care.
(c) Duties and emergencies.
(d) Duties in private medicine.
(e) Duty of care and the hospital.
(f) Vicarious duty of the hospital.
(g) Duty and the Secretary of State.
(h) Duty to keep up with professional developments.
(i) Duty to patients who may harm themselves or others.
(j) Duty to inform the patient of adverse results.
(k) Duty to write prescriptions clearly.

When considering these specific elements of the duty of care, ask the following simple, but important, questions:

(a) Should such a duty exist as a matter of law?
(b) If so, what should be the scope of that duty?

Before these separate elements are considered, there needs to be an understanding of two primary issues which create the theoretical and legal backdrop to the modern duty in medical law: the place of human rights in the duty context and the changes that have taken place in the duty of care in tort law as a whole.

3.1.2 Duties and rights

It seems strange to consider relevant human rights issues where one is analysing such a solid, substantive matter of negligence law. Remind yourself, though, what is behind this debate: the changing face of the doctor–patient relationship. There are duties, but they are increasingly based on 'rights' that have been demanded.

In the latter part of the nineteenth century and the beginning of the twentieth, the scope of doctor duties owed would have been of much smaller range than it is now possible to discuss in this chapter. The doctor decided what duties existed toward the patient, no one else. Those days are gone. This is not to say that historically a doctor could not be called to account for failing to exercise reasonable care. It is just that the circumstances were extremely limited.

The WHO document, *Promotion of the Rights of Patients in Europe: Proceedings of a WHO Consultation* (Kluwer, 1995), is studded with a variety of articulated rights. These seek to impose general and particular duties on the medical profession. As well as general rights to information, there are specific demands for information. One example should indicate the potential relevance for the duty issue:

> Patients have the right to be fully informed about their health status, including the medical facts about their condition; about the proposed medical procedures, together with the potential risks and benefits of each procedure; about alternatives to the proposed procedures, including the effect of no treatment and about the diagnosis, prognosis and progress of treatment.

To accord with the aspirations of this human rights document, there would appear to be a wide range of duties on the medical profession. According to this one example, the doctor appears to have a duty to keep the patient fully informed of the patient's condition, what treatment options are available, and indeed the consequences of the no-treatment option. The doctor would appear basically to have the duty to tell the patient everything the patient can possibly need to know about his or her treatment. The practical impact of this will be considered when looking at the growth of medical litigation.

3.1.3 Medical duty of care and the general law

Primarily the issue is about medical negligence law. One needs, however, to be aware of the point made by Harvey Teff (*Reasonable Care: Legal Perspectives on the Doctor–Patient Relationship* (Oxford: Clarendon Press, 1994)):

> There is no rational justification for regarding medical negligence as somehow conceptually different from negligence in general. (p. 175)

What is happening to duty of care in negligence as a whole has a bearing on duty of care in the medical context. So what has been happening? To establish a duty of care as a matter of the general law of negligence there needs to be the foreseeability of harm to the plaintiff, and a proximate relationship between plaintiff and defendant. Finally, as a matter of policy, it needs to be just and reasonable that a duty of care be owed in the circumstances of the case (see *Caparo Industries plc v Dickman* [1990] 2 AC 605). There has been, in the law of negligence, an increasing awareness of the influence that policy can have. The policy aspect means that what is 'just and reasonable' will be swayed in part by the impact the legal imposition of duty of care would have on professional practice as a whole. The policy aspect is further concerned with the economic impact of finding duties. It is with these two factors in mind that the courts have developed the notion that duties of care in new situations will only be considered applicable where they are analogous to existing lines of legal duty. Negligence law at present is not expansive. Recently this has been seen clearly in medical negligence case law, and is evidenced by the comments of the Court of Appeal in the case of

Goodwill v *British Pregnancy Advisory Service* [1996] 1 WLR 1397 in relation to duties of care owed to third parties (see 3.2).

3.2 GROWTH OF LITIGATION

The historical growth of the action against the doctor is revealed by the fact that:

In the late nineteenth and early twentieth century it was very unusual for patients to sue their doctors. Conventionally considered an almost presumptious thing to do, it was in any event beyond the means of all but a tiny minority. Reporting in 1978, the Pearson Commission observed that whereas 50 or 60 years previously claims against doctors had been rare, this had changed since the introduction of the NHS, reaching some 500 claims a year against doctors in the mid-1970s. (Teff, *Reasonable Care* (Oxford: Clarendon Press, 1994), p. 17)

Since the 1970s the number of claims has increased rapidly. Doctors have had to increase subscriptions to medical defence organisations, damages paid out have increased in individual cases, as has the amount paid out overall for medical negligence. According to a number of sources (see, for example, *The Economist*, 13 November 1993) the NHS will spend well over £100 million on medical negligence cases, and in 1994/5 the annual figure given was £125 million. Why has this change taken place? Many explanations have been offered, and it appears that all have some validity. In general they focus on the increased expectations of patients, knowledge of access to the law, assistance in bringing a claim and increased pressures on the health care system.

Medical science, as stated at the start of this book, is not stagnant. The developments in diagnostics, drugs and replacement organs are coming thick and fast. With such developments come two things. More complexity means that more can go wrong. In addition, the faster developments occur the more is expected of the doctor in putting them to effective use. Doctors can use technology to attempt things that only a few years ago would have invariably proved incapable of improvement through medicine, but such attempts do entail risks. A patient who sees a new drug that is experimental, but holds out hope of curing a form of cancer, may now be less disposed simply to wait, and may use the law to demand that the doctor has a duty to use it. That same patient, in the unlikely event of the medical profession acquiescing in the face of the demand, or the law enforcing that demand, may now be well disposed to sue when the injection results in paralysis.

There may be an increase in medical litigation because the public are more informed about legal matters. There is less likelihood of the English 'stiff upper lip' and abstention from legal action where the injured patient has read of a similar case where the patient received £100,000. Partially in response to the rise in litigation, and partially assisting in that rise have been the growth of patient plaintiff pressure and information groups. Such bodies provide support mechanisms for those entering the arena of medical negligence litigation. They also provide inside knowledge of the difficulties that remain for the plaintiff (see, for example, the Association for the Victims of Medical Accidents (AVMA) who, amongst other things, provide advice on finding an expert medical witness to consider the clinical management of a plaintiff's case).

The growth in litigation may be partially due to the increased pressures placed on doctors. The judicial recognition of such pressure was underscored by the case of *Johnstone* v *Bloomsbury Health Authority* [1992] QB 333 (for a further analysis and the facts of this case see 3.3.5). As Teff notes:

In some settings it can almost seem as if the ingredients for negligent treatment have been consciously built into the system. The combination of budgetary constraints, overworked and sometimes inexperienced medical staff under pressure to cut waiting lists, and continued growth in the number of referrals is a recipe for litigation. (*Reasonable Care*, p. 19)

There appears then to be ample and incontrovertible evidence that there are more patients suing doctors for ever-increasing sums of money for a number of reasons. What is the potential impact of this?

The USA has proved a popular example of the disasters that can befall a health-care system when there is a 'litigation explosion'. The main potential for medical practice in Britain is based around the side-effect of medical negligence litigation: the practice of defensive medicine.

It is suggested that a doctor, aware of the risks of litigation arising from the performance of a particular medical procedure, will have that risk in mind rather than the primary concern, the health and welfare of patients. There is ample evidence that in the USA, the cost of insurance has meant that fewer doctors are willing to practise certain 'well litigated' areas of medical practice, such as gynaecology. The shadow of litigation may also have a detrimental effect on the development of innovative forms of treatment.

There are those, however, who believe that the practice of defensive medicine, if it really exists at all, is actually only evidence of a correctly cautious approach to the practice of medicine. The individual patient, the arguments goes, cannot suffer unduly in a regime of 'careful' medicine. If the doctor has an awareness of the prospect of litigation, this may lead to a clearer understanding of the need for the patient to be fully and accurately informed of the need for surgery, the risks involved in it and the alternative forms of treatment that might be available. In response to this it is contended that to have such a 'cautious' approach to each patient would be practically impossible and economically disastrous. Modern medicine exists in a society where resources are limited, the population is ageing and the demands on the health-care system as a whole difficult to withstand. To devote such time to each patient would invariably mean that there was less time for someone else. To have a clinical regime based on the chances of being sued could ultimately destroy the system.

At the moment there is increasing litigation based on the perceived inability of the system to maintain a 'just' service. Many of the most contentious modern duty cases are those which argue that the hospital or even the Secretary of State are not abiding by their respective duties to have a safe system of treatment in operation or a comprehensive health service. Limited success at present appears unlikely to stop those stuck on the waiting list from going to law to get treatment.

Against this tide of evidence of a 'malpractice crisis' one has to weigh a very important point that will become clear in this, and even more so in the next, chapter: it is very difficult for the plaintiff to succeed in a medical negligence action. While there are essentially logistical difficulties of maintaining an action – getting legal aid and gathering evidence – the true stumbling blocks are contained in the substantive law. The existing culture of the medical profession being a 'closed shop', when combined with the almost insurmountable difficulties of proving that the conduct caused the damage, might not stifle attempts to sue, but does stifle plaintiff success. The medical profession are felt to see an attack on one of their number as an attack on their profession as a whole. The reaction of the whole profession is then one of mutual protection and defence. When threatened, 'close ranks' is still the order of the day.

One should consider how the cost of medical litigation in this county has taxed recent governments. There has been something of a sea change of attitude from the medical and the legal profession which may have profound repercussions for litigation. The cost of the system to the NHS has recently led to the development of contingency fees (Court and Legal Services Act 1990, s. 58). The solicitors preparing certain cases will work on a 'no win no fee' basis, but on successful completion of the case for the plaintiff, their costs will be uprated by an agreed percentage. This has sparked a fierce debate, with opponents of the system arguing that it will deter both potential plaintiffs coming forward with claims, solicitors being unprepared to handle anything other than a cast-iron case, and even the successful plaintiff being undercompensated. There has further been a debate whether the drain on the legal aid system from medical negligence litigation is in reality much of a drain at all. Strangely opponents of the system alternatively argue that the contingency fee system will lead to the image of a US-inspired situation of 'ambulance chasing' lawyers keen to discover a case of certain liability, and an increase in litigants who previously did not qualify for legal aid but were not wealthy enough to afford to fund the action themselves. Proponents of the contingency fee scheme argue that it helps to weed out hopeless cases quickly, as the solicitor will make a more rigorous early test of the merits of the case before committing the firm's time and expertise to it. The contingency scheme was also felt to give plaintiffs in a 'black hole' of litigation (not qualifying for legal aid but unable to fund the case themselves) the chance to pursue a claim. There is still much jockeying for position on this matter, with the medical profession seeking, it has been suggested, a tightening up of the legal aid scheme as another form of protection for themselves. The legal profession, it has also been suggested, oppose the system as it represents a reduction in their legal aid portfolio, and simply reduces what has always been a lucrative income for many firms.

All the above pressures, difficulties and changes in the doctor–patient relationship need to be borne in mind when considering the duty of care as a matter of medical law.

3.3 DUTIES OF CARE

3.3.1 Formation of the duty of care

The duty of care needs to be clearly established, otherwise the action fails without any further consideration. It is the first hurdle for the disgruntled plaintiff patient to overcome. Of course, one then needs to move on to the sometimes difficult question in medicine of the proper scope of that duty of care. In terms of medical negligence the term 'duty of care' has become synonymous with the concept of the 'undertaking' towards the patient. This concept of undertaking and the essence of the medical negligence action was most effectively put, strangely, in a manslaughter case, *R* v *Bateman* (1925) 94 LJ KB 791:

> If a doctor holds himself out as possessing special skill and knowledge, and he is consulted, as possessing such skill and knowledge, by or on behalf of the patient, he owes a duty to the patient to use due caution in undertaking the treatment. If he accepts the responsibility and undertakes the treatment and the patient submits to his discretion and treatment accordingly, he owes a duty to the patient to use diligence, care, knowledge, skill and caution in administering the treatment. No contractual relation is necessary, nor is it necessary that the service be rendered for reward.

The key notions underlying the establishment of the duty of care appear then to be the assumption of responsibility of the patient: an undertaking to use best skill and endeavours for that patient.

This is fine, but does not articulate the factual circumstances where the undertaking becomes a legal one. Is it when the patient requires treatment? The first communication with a doctor, nurse or ambulanceman? The specific statement of undertaking by one of these parties? The first laying on of hands to initiate treatment? The official registration (in whatever form) that the patient now 'belongs' to a particular doctor or hospital? That there is no simple answer to these questions would appear to indicate that Margaret Brazier is somewhat over-optimistic when she asserts that:

> A patient claiming against *his* doctor . . . usually has little difficulty in establishing that the doctor owes him a duty of care. (*Medicine, Patients and the Law*, 2nd ed. (London: Penguin, 1992) pp. 117–18)

The problem for medical law is when does the patient 'have' a doctor?

Two lines of argument may be considered on where to draw the duty line in terms of the medical practitioner. The first is that the duty of care does not arise until a regulated and definite undertaking procedure has been complied with. An example of this would be when the general practitioner registers the individual as his patient, or when the hospital admissions procedure has been completed and the patient has been allocated a bed. While this idea might have the advantage of certainty, that certainty might equally be described as inflexibility, and unable to take account of the myriad complexities encountered in the practice of medicine. The other argument would be that a hospital or doctor would have an implicit automatic responsibility to treat those who present themselves, whatever the situation, to the best of their ability in the particular circumstances encountered. That this will create enormous pressures on the medical profession is obvious, as is the limitation on their freedom of movement! The other problem is that English law in general terms is uncomfortable with the concept of the Good Samaritan (see R. Lee, 'Hospital Admissions – Duty of Care' (1979) 129 NLJ 567). The general law does not make it a necessity to rescue a stranger. Negligence law requires a proximate relationship between the parties; this would not exist in the doctor–stranger situation.

Of course legislation could impose a duty of care in emergency circumstances. The general practitioner at present, for example, does have a statutory duty to treat all those patients on the practice list (National Health Service (General Medical and Pharmaceutical) Regulations 1974 (SI 1989/1897)).

The duty of care of the doctor for the patient thus exists somewhere along this line, but the law has not yet made an authoritative determination of where to attach it.

Recently difficulties over the formation of the duty of care have confronted the courts where medical practitioners have carried out some form of pre-employment examination of a prospective employee. The two decisions of *Baker* v *Kaye* (1996) *The Times*, 13 December 1996 and *Kapfunde* v *Abbey National plc and Another* (1998) *The Times*, 6 April 1998 indicate something of a conflict over whether such practitioners are under a duty, or perhaps more fundamentally whether this prospective employee is indeed a patient of the practitioner. In *Baker* v *Kaye* the prospective employee sued a doctor for such an examination. The doctor in evidence considered himself to be under a duty to tell the plaintiff if this examination had revealed any illness. To the High Court this denoted both a relationship of sufficient proximity and that it was fair, just and reasonable to impose a duty of care. The matter however failed on breach of duty.

The opposite conclusion was reached, albeit in slightly different circumstances in the Court of Appeal decision in *Kapfunde*. The plaintiff here was looking for work with Abbey National and was required to fill in a medical questionnaire, which amongst other things required the plaintiff to complete a section on previous absences due to illness. An occupational health adviser, Dr Daniel, advised Abbey National that the plaintiff was likely to have a higher than average potential for absences; therefore she was not appointed. At first instance her negligence claim failed, so she appealed. In terms of whether the doctor owed a duty here, the fact that there was no physical examination was crucial to the finding that there was no duty owed. The Court of Appeal went on to state that while Baker was correctly decided as a matter of the breach issue, it should also have failed on the preliminary duty of care issue. In analysing the case along the traditional lines of proximity and whether there was an assumption of responsibility the Court found there to be no special relationship. One must doubt the wisdom of basing such a finding largely on the presence or absence of physical examination, particularly where cases such as the crucial *Barnett* (see section 3.3.3) found there to be sufficient proximity where the negligent 'act' was insufficient advice over the telephone. With the increasing use of computer diagnosis there needs to be a rather more careful consideration of (at least in terms of duty of care) when the doctor-patient relationship begins.

Before considering the different circumstances where the duty issue may become significant it should be noted that this issue extends beyond the doctor–patient relationship to the duty incumbent on the hospital itself or even the State, with the latter moving the focus away from duty in the context of medical negligence and into the realm of public law, and specifically, judicial review of administrative action.

3.3.2 Duties and third parties

Bear in mind first of all the essence of the duty of care:

> The duty of care adheres to any person who holds himself out as a medical practitioner and is owed not only to patients but also to certain classes of third parties recognised by the law as being so closely and directly affected by treatment or advice that the doctor or other practitioner ought to have them in mind and it is just and reasonable to do so. (Nelson-Jones and Burton, *Medical Negligence Case Law* (Fourmat Publishing) p. 43)

The issue is how far this duty to third parties extends in medical law within the generally limited scope available in current negligence law as a whole. The issue then is as much about policy as anything else. (For an early consideration of the third-party issue see *Evans* v *Liverpool Corporation* [1906] 1 KB 160.) Bear in mind that the US case of *Tarasoff* v *Regents of the University of California* (1976) 551 P 2d 334 found a duty of care to identifiable third parties in the context of confidentiality (see 2.5). The English case of *W* v *Egdell* [1990] 1 All ER 835 (see 2.5) would appear to enable the courts to find a duty of care owed to third parties where the threat was specific and of physical violence. There would not appear to be any sustainable public policy objections to this, other than a further legal debate about balancing public interests.

The issue of duties of care to third parties in the medical context is potentially a significant one in the area of nervous shock; an issue of general negligence law that has seen stark policy lines drawn. The case law appears to suggest the possibility of a third party claiming damages for nervous shock where the negligence of a doctor has confronted a husband, wife or parent with the horrific consequences of medical negligence. The case of *Taylor* v *Somerset Health Authority* (1993) 4 Med LR 34, however, shows the difficulties of succeeding. The defendant hospital had failed to diagnose correctly and treat Mr Taylor's heart disease. A year later he died of a heart attack while at work. Shortly after he had been pronounced dead, his wife (the plaintiff) was told that her husband was ill. She arrived at the hospital just after he had been pronounced dead, and she was informed a little after her arrival of the death. Due partially to instructions, and partly to disbelief, she identified the body. As a result of all of this she suffered a psychiatric illness.

While accepting responsibility for the diagnostic failure which resulted in Mr Taylor's death, the health authority denied the nervous shock. Auld J held that the events had not constituted an external traumatic event, as required by law. The law in addition requires that the plaintiff be present at the time and place of the accident or its immediate aftermath. Being told by the doctor, even within an hour of the death would not be 'the immediate aftermath'. That also applied to the viewing of the body, as it bore no marks to conjure up images of the heart attack, and was undertaken to settle her disbelief.

This clearly shows how difficult it is for plaintiff third parties to claim nervous shock. The possibility of a claim nevertheless exists because of *Tredget* v *Bexley Health Authority* (1994) 5 Med LR 178. The plaintiff parents here suffered psychiatric illness, having seen their new-born son deteriorate and die after the negligent delivery of the child by the defendant hospital. The following important points of the judgment indicate the broad rules of nervous shock, the duties to third parties and sadly the anguish and confusion that can occur in medical practice:

(a) As the plaintiffs were the parents of the child, the requirement of proximity between the parties was clearly satisfied.

(b) The requirement of reasonable foreseeability was also satisfied. Neo-natal death is a potent cause of psychiatric disturbance of the kind suffered by the plaintiffs.

(c) Each suffered a form of psychiatric illness. This was more than mere grief, distress or sorrow.

(d) The actual birth with its chaos or pandemonium, the difficulties that the mother had on delivery, the sense in the room that something was wrong on the arrival of the child in a distressed condition requiring immediate resuscitation was extremely frightening for the parents. It constituted a horrifying external event.

(e) What happened was in full sight of the father. It would be unrealistic to distinguish the mother because she was in labour, in pain, sedated and suffering from exhaustion, and was not fully conscious of what was happening about her. It would also be unrealistic to separate out and isolate the delivery as an event, from the other sequence of happenings from the onset of labour to (the child's) death two days later.

(f) Therefore the plaintiffs were liable to pay damages to the parents for their psychiatric illnesses and consequential loss.

In the end the parents received £300,000.

Recently there was a rather exotic attempt to develop the duty of care owed to third parties in the context of pre-operative medical advice. The case of *Goodwill* v *British Pregnancy Advisory Service* [1996] 1 WLR 1397 is one that has relevance for issues of wrongful conception and birth (see 8.3.2), but is worth mentioning here because an attempt was made to extend incrementally a third-party duty of care. Mrs Goodwill met a Mr Mackinley a few years after he had been vasectomised. Mrs Goodwill knew of the vasectomy, and, having sought further assurance of the fact that it had made Mr Mackinley sterile, she stopped using contraceptives. She became pregnant later because the man's operation had undergone a natural reversal. Her allegation against the clinic offering reassurance to Mackinley and his then partner that the operation had been a success was that:

> the law of negligence allows for the incremental extension of the duty of care. Where a doctor provides a service to a patient one of the duties is to give informed advice of the nature, effects and implications of surgery or other forms of therapy. Where, as here, there is an operation aimed to make that patient sterile then it is reasonably foreseeable that the doctor owes a duty to a current partner. As an incremental extension this duty could bind the advising doctor to the future sexual partner. Such a move would be to recognise the common law's arguable goal of reacting to societal change. ('Reliance on Medical Advice by Third Parties: The Limits of *Goodwill*' (1996) 12 PN 2, 54 at p. 55)

The Court of Appeal realised that to allow a duty of care to be placed on the doctor to future partners would be simply too wide, unprincipled and unwieldy. The doctor, albeit possibly negligent, cannot be expected to foresee such a large and indeterminate class of possible plaintiffs. In cases such as *Thake* v *Maurice* [1986] QB 644 (for the facts and judgment see 8.2), the third-party reliance was based on presence or at least knowledge of the existence of the third party at the time of giving the advice. A doctor could expect to owe, for example, a duty of care to the existing partner of a man given negligent advice about the reversibility of the sterilisation operation, but not all those he might encounter in the future.

It is therefore the case that the doctor can owe a duty of care to third parties, albeit in strictly limited circumstances (on a duty of care to third parties concerning the violent acts of discharged mental patients see F. Morris and G. Adshead, 'The Liability of Psychiatrists for The Violent Acts of Their Patients' (1997) 147 NLJ 558 and 3.4.2).

3.3.3 Duties and emergencies: the basic structure of duty in medicine

The key case to consider on the requirement of proving a duty of care in a medical negligence action is *Barnett* v *Chelsea and Kensington Hospital Management Committee* [1969] 1 QB 428. It applies beyond the emergency situation, and is a general (if rather inadequate) statement of the applicable law. Three nightwatchmen who had been drinking tea at work became ill and started vomiting. At around 8.00 a.m. they walked into the casualty department of the defendant's hospital, which was open at that time. One of the three (the deceased) appeared ill at that time and lay on some chairs in the casualty department. One of the other men told the nurse on duty at reception of their common symptoms. The nurse telephoned the casualty doctor and relayed these symptoms. The casualty doctor, himself unwell, told the nurse by telephone that they should all go home and see their doctors, and did not personally examine the deceased. The men did go home, and the deceased died some time later from what was shown to have been arsenic poisoning.

Nield J, giving judgment, cited with approval the sentiments of Denning LJ in *Cassidy* v *Ministry of Health* [1951] 2 KB 343 that, with regard to hospital authorities: 'Once they undertake the task they come under a duty to use care in the doing of it, and that is so whether they do it for reward or not'. What was also found in *Cassidy* v *Ministry of Health*, however, was that a duty would arise once the hospital had accepted the patient for treatment. Acceptance implies undertaking and therefore duty.

The question for Nield J was whether, on the facts, there was a relationship as a matter of law between the three nightwatchmen and the hospital staff. The court found there to be such a duty of care, which was breached by the failure of the doctor to attend the poisoned patient. The casualty doctor should have arranged to see them personally, or at least for some other medical practitioner to attend and make a proper diagnosis. The action, however, failed on causation (see 4.3.1).

Nield J has been cited with approval, but in actual fact did not articulate in general terms *when* such an undertaking can be said to come into existence. One would hesitate to dispute the existence of the duty of care on the facts of *Barnett*, but Nield J gave only a vague indication of factors during the course of his judgment. The court seemed to suggest that, because casualty departments can be abused from time to time there would be no automatic duty on casualty staff to treat all who presented themselves. Some examples cited were where the visitor comes for a second opinion, having seen his or her own doctor, or the injury is such that the nurse can treat it without recourse to the casualty officer. One might accept that the duty to treat any who present themselves would prove unduly onerous and financially disastrous, but some further indication of when the duty comes into existence would have been useful as a guidance for the medical profession and indeed the medical lawyer here.

Some small assistance may be found in the unusual case of *Barnes* v *Crabtree* [1955] 2 BMJ 1213. This was an action for assault and battery. The plaintiff claimed that on Christmas Day as a result of feeling unwell she attended at the doctor's surgery where she believed she was registered. The doctor informed her that there was no surgery on this day, and anyway, she was not on his list. The result of this refusal was that she lay down on the doorstep of the surgery until the police were called to remove her. Some of this evidence was disputed, with the doctor admitting openly she was on his list, that he had informed her she was well and if she disagreed she should consult another doctor, and had then closed the door. The judge directed the jury on the relevant points of law:

> In a case of real acute emergency a doctor under the National Health Service scheme was under an obligation to treat any patient who was acutely ill; for example if there was a motor accident and someone was lying seriously injured. The obligation of a doctor under the health scheme to a patient on his list was to render all necessary and proper care he had to exercise reasonable skill in diagnosis. But in a case of chronic illness when he had been seeing the patient frequently that did not mean that he was required to make a full clinical examination every time the patient asked for it.

Counsel for the doctor nevertheless admitted that an undertaking might be made where a doctor starts to treat a patient. The jury found that on the evidence the doctor had no case to answer.

In general, the duty of care will be a matter of fact in each case, but with the decision on its existence based on the general common law idea of an undertaking of responsibility, which to some extent may give some credence to the view that, at least as far as the hospital doctor and the GP are concerned, it should be fairly easy to see on the facts of a particular case.

3.3.4 Duty of care and private medicine

This is really a residual area for the medical lawyer. The duty of care in contract and tort is for all practical purposes identical. Most patients are still treated under the National Health Service. There is no true contractual relationship between the patient and the NHS employee. The relationship in duty terms will be statutory or tortious (see *Pfizer Corporation* v *Ministry of Health* [1965] AC 512). The general practitioner, however, when placing a patient on the practice list sees more money come into the practice. The patient might 'offer' to become the patient of the doctor, the doctor might 'accept' the patient by placing him or her on the list and the consideration will be treatment of the patient and the payment for that treatment by effectively claiming remuneration. The doctor, however, does not get money directly from the patient but from the State (through the FHSA). The patient 'pays' for the treatment by taxation. This view does not lend itself to seeing the relationship as contractual. There are nevertheless sufficient differences that remain in using contract law in the medical context to warrant a brief analysis of contractual duty.

The prime focus of the duty here is the nature of the doctor–patient contract. Where the issue revolves around an allegation of negligence, the contractual establishment of the duty of care will accord with the tenor of *Barnett* v *Chelsea and Kensington Hospital Management Committee* [1969] 1 QB 428. However, the question of whether there has been an undertaking of responsibility in contract should be capable of resolution by simply looking at what this contract states. The essence of contract obviously being the offer, acceptance and consideration, it will be created by the doctor offering to treat the patient, or the patient who offers to pay the doctor if the treatment is undertaken. In addition the express terms of these contracts in private medicine will be contained in the consent form that the patient has to sign before treatment can begin.

Difficulties arise, in contracts for medical treatment as in many other kinds of contract, where there is the question, not so much of the existence of the duty of care, but of its scope. The difficulty of what is implied into a contract is more severe for the medical lawyer because medicine is not an exact science, and specific results and occurrences are difficult to guarantee in many forms of treatment. The classic case which indicates the attitude of the courts to implied terms in 'treatment contracts' is *Thake* v *Maurice* [1986] QB 644 (see also 8.2). The plaintiffs decided that they did not wish to have any more children. The first plaintiff informed a doctor of this fact, and decided to have a vasectomy. He signed a consent form to effect this operation. The contract was thus to perform a vasectomy for a sum of money. Matters, however, did not remain as simple as this. Two years after the operation, the second plaintiff became pregnant. By the time the pregnancy was discovered it was too late for an abortion, so the couple ended up with an unplanned child. An action was brought in contract and tort. The primary allegation was that the contract was to sterilise, and that had been breached by its obvious lack of success. An alternative allegation was that the plaintiffs had both been induced to enter into a contract by the use of a false warranty or innocent misrepresentation that the operation would sterilise. The defendant was found to have breached the contract, but appealed to the Court of Appeal.

As a matter of evidence, it was accepted that the defendant never used the actual word 'guarantee' of sterilisation. The plaintiffs had contended that the actions of the consultant here would have led a reasonable man to conclude that the operation would result in sterility. The consultant did, however, use the term 'irreversible' a number of times when describing what was going to happen. While casting doubt on the expectation that it would be 100 per cent successful, given the inexactitude of medicine, the Court of Appeal found that the failure to warn was a breach of contractual and tortious duty of care.

There is likely to be continuing litigation on the basis of the scope of the duty of care in contractual terms in private medicine, given the increasing popularity of elective or more specifically cosmetic surgery in the private sector of medical practice. Elective surgery may be the most fertile ground.

The Canadian case of *La Fleur* v *Cornelis* (1979) 28 NBR (2d) 569 would appear to indicate that the courts may well see a distinct difference between cosmetic surgery and therapeutic surgery. Barry J described the doctor in the former context as 'more akin to a businessman' and felt that a failure to inform of a 10 per cent risk of deformity after surgery to reduce the size of the plaintiff's nose was different 'from the ordinary malpractice case'. Notwithstanding that in medicine his lordship felt that there can never be complete guarantees of success, it was decided that, in basic terms, the plaintiff did not get exactly what she contracted for, so the doctor was liable for breach of contract.

It will be interesting to see if a view that separates the nature of contractual duties depending on whether the surgery is elective or not will prove popular with the courts in England and Wales.

3.3.5 Duty of care and the hospital

The development of the direct duty of care of the hospital itself can be towards patients, visitors or even its own employees. Historically there were few duties incumbent on the hospital or hospital authority. As Teff explains:

> For hundreds of years the hospital was essentially the location where surgeons came to train and practise their skills. Well into the twentieth century, the most that was required of the hospital authority was to provide a properly equipped facility. (*Reasonable Care* (Oxford: Clarendon Press, 1994), p. 25)

The existence and scope of the direct duty of care of the hospital is generally as follows. There is a duty to employ those who are suitably qualified for the desired task and are competent to perfom that task in the hospital. Allied to this there is a duty for the hospital to make arrangements to see that these staff are effectively supervised in what they do. These senior employees should also instruct in relevant areas. There is a primary duty on the hospital to provide a system of operation that is safe in terms of its employees and the patients who enter it (see, for example, *Ogden v Airedale Health Authority* (1996) 7 Med LR 153). Finally, the hospital has a duty to provide proper facilities and equipment in the hospital (see E. Picard, 'The Liability of Hospitals in Common Law Canada' (1981) 26 McGill LJ 997).

Recently there has been a great deal of debate about the extent of these duties in a regime where there are finite resources available to fund medical care. While a consideration of this politically sensitive and complex debate is the subject of the recent work by Chris Newdick (*Who Shall We Treat?* (Oxford: Clarendon Press, 1995), one should be aware that the primary duty of the hospital to provide for arrangements, in a regime of limited funding, to be in place in a particular hospital has been, and increasingly is being, questioned in the courts. The focus of this legal debate has been delay or absence of a particular form of treatment alleged to create an unsafe operational system in a hospital. The reply of the hospital authority in turn has been that the level of service is the best that the available money can buy.

The law has shown a clear reluctance to find there to be any breadth to the primary duty of the hospital (but now it is more accurate to term the umbrella organisation, the common defendant in such actions, 'the health authority') itself, but the possibility of proceeding with an allegation was clearly recognised by Browne-Wilkinson V-C in the important medical negligence case of *Wilsher v Essex Area Heath Authority* [1987] QB 730, CA.

I agree with the comments of Mustill LJ as to the confusion which has been caused in this case . . . which blurred the distinction between the vicarious liability of the health authority for the negligence of its doctors and the direct liability of the health authority for negligently failing to provide skilled treatment of the kind that it was offering to the public. In my judgment, a health authority which so conducts its hospital that it fails to provide doctors of sufficient skill and experience to give the treatment offered at the hospital may be directly liable in negligence to the patient. Although we are told in argument that no case has ever been decided on this ground and that it is not the practice to formulate claims in this way, I can see no reason why, in principle, the health authority should not be so liable if its organisation is at fault.

Academic discussion appears unsure whether there is a primary duty on the health authority to provide for a reasonably safe and effective care regime, notwithstanding the limited funds available (see M. Jones, *Medical Negligence* (1991), p. 283), but the case of *Bull* v *Devon Area Health Authority* (1993) 4 Med LR 117 appears to accept its existence quite emphatically. Mrs Bull brought an action in negligence against the health authority both on her own behalf and on behalf of her disabled son. It was claimed that the decision of the health authority to operate a split-site service at the local hospital led to a breakdown in the system. The allegation was that her son's brain damage had been caused by asphyxia, which in turn was caused by the delay in summoning the doctor from the other site.

Slade LJ was clear that the health authority were under a duty to provide pregnant women with a reasonable standard of gynaecological and obstetric care, in terms of providing for the safe delivery of the baby and the health of the mother and baby. In this particular circumstance Slade LJ felt that the most likely explanation for the failure to attend the mother at this critical time was either due to inefficiency of the call-out system at the two-site hospital or the negligence of a particular person or persons working in that system.

Commonwealth authority points to an equivocal attitude to the breadth of the primary duty of the health authority or hospital (compare the Australian case of *Ellis* v *Wallsend District Hospital* (1989) 17 NSWLR 553 where there was a fairly expansive view of primary liability, at least to the extent of those going directly to hospital, and the Canadian case of *Yepremian* v *Scarborough General Hospital* (1980) 110 DLR (3d) 513, where this primary duty only went as far as employing competent staff). However, *Bull* v *Devon Area Health Authority* and the increasingly direct reliance people place on the local hospital will mean that the perceived judicial reluctance to find such duties will further decrease.

There has recently been a growing dissatisfaction among, particularly, junior doctors concerning the amount of work they are required to do, suggesting it represents an unsafe system of work. The doctor is becoming physically and emotionally harmed by the pressures of long hours and the patient endangered or actually harmed by the exhausted doctor giving the wrong dose of a potentially lethal drug. This basically was the argument of the plaintiff in *Johnstone* v *Bloomsbury Health Authority* [1992] QB 333. The plaintiff's contract of employment provided that his basic hours would be 40 per week, but he was required to be on call for a further 48 hours per week, a grand total of a potential 88-hour week. Notwithstanding the contractual hours of work, the plaintiff said in evidence that he could end up some weeks working over 100 hours. He argued he was suffering from stress and depression, could not eat or sleep when not on duty, and at times had felt suicidal. Stuart-Smith LJ noted counsel for the Authority's point that 'if you can't stand the heat get out of the kitchen', but responded:

> Although the principle that if you cannot stand the heat in the kitchen you should get out, or not go in, may be a sound one, it would have serious implications if applied in these circumstances.

It was noted that the NHS was in effect a monopoly employer. There was too much scope for the NHS to make any contractual provision it wanted, no matter how unreasonable. Every junior doctor needs to have a year as a house officer. If they do not accept the contract of employment, they do not qualify for any promotion. The contract of employment had to be viewed then in the light of the duty of the hospital authority to take reasonable care not to injure the health of the employee. The doctor therefore was entitled to a declaration that the contract of employment as it stood was unlawful.

3.3.6 Duty of care: vicarious liability of the hospital

The direct or primary duty of the hospital authority was considered in 3.3.5. In contrast this section is concerned with the liability of the hospital for the negligent acts of its 'employees', even though the authority itself is not at fault. In 1990 something called 'Crown indemnity' came into force (Department of Health Circular HC (89) 34, HC (FP) 22). This replaced the informal arrangement that used to exist between health authorities and private medical defence societies. They used to arrange to pay an agreed proportion of the damages in a medical negligence case. The post-1990 scheme requires the health authorities to assume all responsibility for the conduct of their employees for negligent actions during the course of their employment.

The general law on vicarious liability is based on the theory of 'control' of the employee's activities by the employer. The employee is the individual who is engaged upon a contract *of* service. There is no vicarious liability for the activities of an independent contractor (under a contract *for* services). To make an employer vicariously liable for an employee's negligence it must be shown that the allegedly negligent activity was performed within the course of the employment. Such matters will usually be clear from the evidence.

Of relevance too is the place of vicarious liability in the increase in medical negligence litigation:

> A central element in the growth of medical litigation is the altered conception of the hospital as an institution and the legal changes this has

prompted. In this respect, too, one might reasonably anticipate an increasing disposition to sue. As the relationship of patients and the NHS is redefined in terms of 'value for money', patients are in effect encouraged by government to use market remedies, of which recourse to the law is a prime example. (Teff, *Reasonable Care* (Oxford: Clarendon Press, 1994), p. 24)

The hospital used to be merely the physical structure in which doctors practised the healing art. Now it is the focal site where treatment is situated as a whole. As Teff points out, the hospital is no longer a 'venue *for* treatment' but 'a provider *of* treatment'. As such a provider it has become the focus of the medical negligence action.

Historically the hospital–employee situation proved unsuitable for a control-based analysis. In *Evans* v *Liverpool Corporation* [1906] 1 KB 160, and *Hillyer* v *St Bartholomew's Hospital* [1909] 2 KB 820 the courts found that the lack of control the hospital had over the clinical (as opposed to administrative) activities of the employee doctors meant that the employer would not be vicariously liable.

This judicial attitude of splitting up responsibility for administrative and clinical activities was discarded in *Gold* v *Essex County Council* [1942] 2 KB 293. This change was confirmed by Denning LJ's recognition in *Cassidy* v *Minister of Health* [1951] 2 KB 343 that an employer's power to employ a doctor and terminate that employment was indicative of the existence of broad-based control. Later, in *Razzel* v *Snowball* [1954] 1 WLR 1382, in debunking too the argument that the consultant was not an employee, Denning LJ was forceful in stating:

. . . whatever may have been the position of a consultant in former times, nowadays, since the National Health Service Act 1946, the term 'consultant' does not denote a particular relationship between a doctor and a hospital. It is simply a title denoting his place in the hierarchy of the hospital staff. He is a senior member of the staff, and is just as much a member of the staff as the house surgeon is. Whether he is called specialist or consultant makes no difference.

This is now accepted as an end to the issue.

3.3.7 Duty and the Secretary of State

Although not strictly a matter of medical negligence this issue is relevant here as it is important to place issues of duty in the general medical law context. A doctor can be found to have a duty of care in general terms to those designated as his or her patients. The health authority can be found to be under a duty to ensure that the hospitals in the authority area run a 'safe system', or can have vicarious reponsibility for the negligent actions of its employees. Can the Secretary of State for Health be under a duty for the provision of health care? The implications of the discovery of such a duty would be significant to say the least.

The National Health Service Act 1977 imposes on the Secretary of State a duty to make provision for 'a comprehensive health service' (s. 1). This provision should be for the physical and mental health of the people of England and Wales, to prevent, diagnose and treat illness and with that in mind to make provision for the effective provision of services. Section 3(1) of the Act sets out in some detail the duties of the Secretary of State:

It is the Secretary of State's *duty* to provide throughout England and Wales, to such extent as he considers necessary to meet all reasonable requirements—

(a)   hospital accommodation;

(b)   other accommodation for the purpose of any service provided under this Act;

(c)   medical, dental, nursing and ambulance services;

(d)   such other facilities for the care of expectant and nursing mothers and young children as he considers are appropriate as part of the health service;

(e)   such facilities for the prevention of illness, the care of persons suffering from illness and the after-care of persons who have suffered from illness as he considers appropriate as part of the health service;

(f)   such other services as are required for the diagnosis and treatment of illness. (emphasis added)

There have been a number of attempts, some of them well publicised, to set the parameters of this statutory duty as a matter of law, and thereby to make them enforceable ones, to date without any notable success.

The first case to consider the scope of the duty under s. 3(1) was that of *R v Secretary of State for Social Services, ex parte Hincks* (1980) 1 BMLR 93. The applicants were orthopaedic patients who had been waiting for a potentially medically hazardous period. This delay was due to a shortage of the required facilities, itself a result of financial constraints. The allegation against the regional health authority, the area health authority and the Secretary of State was of a failure to provide a comprehensive health service, as required by s. 1, by a failure to provide the facilities for such a service as required by s. 3. In response the Secretary of State accepted that there was a local need for an increase in orthopaedic services, but those increases could not be initiated in the near future because of financial priority going to other types of patient and facility. Lord Denning MR crystallised the form of the action as being based on the fact that:

If the Secretary of State needs money to do it, then he must see that Parliament gives it to him. Alternatively if Parliament does not give it to him, then a provision should be put in the statute to excuse him from his duty.

The patients failed in their action against the Secretary of State. At first instance, Wien J appeared to regard the phrase 'as he considers necessary' in the legislation as providing the Secretary of State with an excuse. As Wien J argued, the issue is one of financial resources, which is not a matter for the courts but is one for Parliament. 'If the money is not there then the services cannot be met in one particular place.'

On appeal, Lord Denning MR focused more on the concept of 'reasonable' and read it as meaning reasonable within the range of available resources. The Court of Appeal did, however, raise the possibility that in the future such a decision may be actionable if it could be regarded as so 'unreasonable' that no Minister directing his mind to the issue properly would have come to such a decision. Therefore the action would take place as a matter of public law. There could be judicial review of the reasonableness of administrative action.

The next case, *R v Central Birmingham Health Authority, ex parte Walker* (1987) 3 BMLR 32, was as unsuccessful. The reason that an operation could not be performed on a baby was due once more to financial constraints, which led to a lack of intensive care beds and specially trained nurses. The tenor of the judgment of Macpherson J revealed the dilemma:

> I find it impossible to say that there is any decision made by the health authority or by the surgeons who act on their behalf, any illegality nor any procedural defect, nor any such unreasonableness. The fact that the decision is unfortunate, disturbing and in human terms distressing, simply cannot lead to a conclusion that the court should interfere in a case of this kind.

While he refused to allow the action to proceed in the Court of Appeal, Donaldson MR referred directly to the public law concept of *Wednesbury* unreasonableness (*Associated Provincial Picture Houses Ltd v Wednesbury Corporation* [1948] 1 KB 223). The essence of 'unreasonableness' relates to:

> . . . a decision which is so outrageous in its defiance of logic or of accepted moral standards that no sensible person who had applied his mind to the question to be decided could have arrived at it. Whether a decision falls within this category is a question that judges by their training and experience would be well equipped to answer, or else there would be something wrong with our system. (*Council of Civil Service Unions v Minister for the Civil Service* [1985] AC 374 at p. 410 per Lord Diplock)

In the next attempt, *R v Central Birmingham Health Authority, ex parte Collier* (6 January 1988 unreported), a four-year-old child was suffering from a hole in the heart. The consultant involved in the clinical management of the child described him as 'desperately needing surgery'. This child was then placed on top of the waiting list. Some five months later the operation had been cancelled a number of times. It was clear that unless an intensive care bed was found the child would die. The Court of Appeal was clear in its view that:

> . . . even assuming that [medical evidence] does establish that there is immediate danger to health, it seems to me that the legal principles to be

applied do not differ from *R* v *Central Birmingham Health Authority, ex parte Walker*. This court is in no position to judge the allocation of resources by this particular health authority. . . . there is no suggestion here that the hospital authority have behaved in a way that is deserving of condemnation or criticism. What is suggested is that somehow more resources should be made available to enable the hospital authorities to ensure that the treatment is immediately given.

This list of abortive attempts to invoke the concept of *Wednesbury* unreasonableness to achieve treatment where the refusal results from limited resources was added to and given a wealth of publicity by the ultimately tragic case of *R* v *Cambridge Health Authority, ex parte B* [1995] 1 WLR 898. This case was an emotionally charged one as it concerned a 10-year-old girl (later named in the press with the father's agreement as Jaymee Bowen) with leukaemia. The child had been in the care of the Cambridge Health Authority since 1990. By 1995 the child's condition had become grave and she was expected to die within months without treatment. The health authority refused, apparently on clinical grounds, to fund this treatment, deciding instead that the child's chances of survival were so poor that she should only receive palliative treatment (to relieve suffering rather than cure) to make the last months of her life comfortable. There was some difference of medical opinion as to the effectiveness of the treatment, so the matter went to court to question this refusal. At first instance Laws J significantly found that the health authority should reconsider the reasons and evidence for the refusal to treat. In doing so his lordship may have been swayed by the fact that, while the responsible person had written to B's father stating that the grounds for the refusal were purely clinical ones, affidavit evidence before the court itself indicated that one of the reasons for the refusal was the issue of where to allocate scant resources. Laws J indicated to the authority in direct terms that:

> . . . merely to point to the fact of finite resources tells us nothing about the wisdom, or . . . the legality of the decision to withhold funding in the particular case. . . . Where a question is whether the life of a 10-year-old child might be saved, by however slim a chance, the responsible authority must do more than toll the bell of tight resources. They must explain the priorities that have led them to decline to fund the treatment.

On the same day the Court of Appeal overturned the order of mandamus. It appeared that there was sufficient consideration given to the clinical desirability of the treatment given by the health authority.

It would seem then that while there appears to be a statutory duty to provide a comprehensive health service under the 1977 Act, there is considerable difficulty in enforcing that duty through public law.

An attempt has been made to enforce a duty on the Secretary of State in negligence. The litigation was based on the importing of a blood concentrate for haemophiliacs called Factor VIII, contaminated with HIV from the USA (*Re HIV Haemophiliac Litigation* (1990) 140 NLJ 1349). Nine hundred and sixty-two haemophiliacs had developed AIDS as a result of using this concentrate. The allegation against the Secretary of State was that there had been a failure to ensure that the country was self-sufficient in blood supplies. The failure in this duty had caused the plaintiffs to develop AIDS.

The plaintiffs had applied to the court for an order that certain government documents which related to the possible benefits of being self-sufficient in blood supplies be released. The government argued that these documents attracted public interest immunity because they related to the formulation of government policy. The essential issue, as far as duty was concerned, and which went to the Court of Appeal, was whether 'the rejection of the claim for breach of statutory duty must of itself negative any coterminous claim in negligence' (per Ralph Gibson LJ). The court went on to find that it would be difficult to maintain an action concerning the existence and breadth of the duties of the Secretary of State under the 1977 Act, mainly because the legislation allowed for the exercising of discretion on the Minister's part. This would also allow for discretion in the allocation of resources. This did not mean, however, that there could never be a claim in negligence, although the matter was not tested here.

In general, then, as a matter of medical law, the Secretary of State is under a statutory duty of care according to ss. 1 and 3 of the National Health Service Act 1977, and this duty is potentially enforceable in a court of law through judicial review or even possibly common law negligence. There has as yet been little sign of either proving successful.

3.4 SPECIFIC DUTIES OF MEDICAL CARE

3.4.1 Duty to keep up with professional developments

There is substantial evidence from the specialist press and from popular science on television that medicine is advancing apace. As well as technological advances, theories and new techniques are expounded and debated in almost every edition of the *British Medical Journal* and *The Lancet* (to name just two). The obvious question is what is the extent (if one exists at all) of the duty of the doctor to keep up with professional developments in the field of medicine as a whole or in a specialist field of medical practice. First of all, there needs to be established a base level of duty of knowledge. The case of *Crawford* v *Board of Governors of Charing Cross Hospital* (1953) *The Times*, 8 December 1953 provides an ideal starting point. The plaintiff had been admitted to hospital for the removal of his bladder. This operation required a blood transfusion. The left arm of the plaintiff was extended away from the body to facilitate this. After the operation had taken place, the plaintiff was found to have a paralysed left arm. Seven months earlier there had been an article in *The Lancet* which cast doubt on this method of performing a transfusion. The allegation was that those performing the operation should have been aware of the contents of this article and acted according to its findings. On appeal against the finding that there was a duty to keep up to date, and specifically here, a duty to read and act on this particular article,

Denning LJ felt that it would place an intolerable burden on the medical profession if they had to read every article in the medical press.

With respect, Denning LJ was somewhat flippant in asserting that a finding of negligence here would in effect mean that doctors would have to subscribe to and read every medical book and journal. What is expected is that medical practitioners maintain a reasonable professional standard in their continuing education and take on board those findings and theories that other professionals in the same specialist area would keep abreast of (on the standard of care see chapter 4). Denning LJ recognised that there may be difficulties of demarcation. When is a theory proved so that it should be adopted, and when is a theory merely a theory? What such a difficulty should not do is deflect attention from the need to maintain a level of vigilance commensurate with a professional standard. That the view of the Court of Appeal is now regarded as something of an anomaly is confirmed by the fact that:

> The practice of modern medicine has . . . become increasingly based on principles of scientific elucidation and report and the pressure on doctors to keep abreast of current developments is now considerable. It is no longer possible for a doctor to coast along on the basis of long experience; as in many professions and callings, such an attitude has been firmly discredited. (Mason and McCall Smith, *Law and Medical Ethics*, 4th ed. (London: Butterworths, 1994), p. 202)

3.4.2 Duty to patients who may harm themselves or others

It is a sad truth that modern hospitals have to deal with an increasing variety of patients, including those who may be mentally disturbed as well as presenting physical symptoms needing treatment. The case law that has developed indicates that a duty to care for patients one may loosely term 'at risk' of harming themselves or others is clearly established. What is not so consistently apparent from these cases is the scope of that duty, which can take in a range of factually differing circumstances and dangers. A case which is indicative of a tragic problem for nursing staff is *Thorne v Northern Group Hospital Management Committee* (1964) 108 SJ 484. A husband informed the ward sister at a hospital that his wife, while attending the hospital, had been threatening suicide. With this danger in mind the patient was placed in a convalescent ward. She was due to be moved again for treatment in a neurosis unit as her condition had been perplexing medical staff. The nurse and the ward sister left the ward temporarily. The wife took the opportunity to walk out of the hospital, went home and committed suicide.

Evidence indicated that the ward sister had not communicated the information about the threat to the other medical staff. The defendants sought to respond that threats were always communicated to medical staff so that a stricter regime of supervision could be put in place.

In a less than clear judgment for the defendants, Edmund Davies J argued that while the duty of medical staff was higher in the case of suicidal patients than 'ordinary' patients, that duty could not amount to keeping a constant vigil. Here:

As later events showed, the patient was set upon making her escape for the purpose of self-destruction, and it was highly conceivable that she kept a wary eye on the nurses and seized her opportunity immediately their backs were turned and they had absented themselves temporarily. That did not connote negligence on the part of the nurses.

The next case, *Selfe v Ilford and District Hospital Management Committee* (1970) 4 BMJ 754, when compared with that of *Thorn*, indicates the scope of the duty of care when confronted with a patient exhibiting suicidal tendencies. The three nurses monitoring this 'at risk' patient who had taken a drug overdose, placed him in a ward containing 27 other patients, four of whom were also suicide risks, so the monitoring would be easier. For differing reasons, but without informing each other of the fact, all three nurses left the ward. The plaintiff climbed through the ground-floor window of the ward, climbed up to a roof and threw himself off. His injuries were such that he was reduced to a paraplegic state.

The court found that the duty of care with such patients was dependent on the magnitude of risk and harm in the particular case. Here the ratio of nursing staff to patient was inadequate given the particular patient's risk of attempting suicide again. As Hinchcliffe J simply argued: 'To leave unobserved a youth of 17 with suicidal tendencies and an unlocked window behind his bed was asking for trouble'.

The pendulum swung back away from a broad-based duty of care on such staff in the case of *Hyde v Tameside Area Health Authority* [1981] CLY 1854, where Lord Denning had to consider an attempted suicide of a patient convinced he had incurable cancer. He had climbed on to a parapet having smashed a window in the ward at night to escape. The case appeared to turn on the difficulty of the nursing and medical staff considering him either depressed because of pain or determined to commit suicide. In finding for the defendants, Lord Denning based his decision to an extent on a matter that gives the case some distinct importance to medical law in general: public policy.

Lord Denning reviewed all the cases that had been concerned with 'successful' or attempted suicides while a hospital patient. While it was admitted that suicide was no longer a criminal offence, as a result of the passing of the Suicide Act 1961, s. 1, it was still an offence as a matter of ecclesiastical law. Lord Denning admitted that this view of the immorality of suicide might appear outdated, but felt that there was something distasteful about claiming in negligence for self-inflicted injury as a result of which 'he has made himself a burden on the whole community'. He concluded that such cases should be disallowed from the outset. Whatever the merits of this somewhat outmoded and ill-considered argument, there seems little chance that medical staff will be able to argue that they owe no duty of care to those at risk to themselves on the basis that to attempt to kill oneself is immoral and 'unfitting'. (But note the recent case where a GP was found liable in negligence for underestimating the seriousness of the plaintiff's depression, which resulted in an attempt at suicide. It was held that the patient would have been unlikely to suffer such injuries if supported and treated properly. See also *Mahmood* v *Siggins* (1996) 7 Med LR 76 QBD.)

There is also established a duty as a matter of medical law on the medical profession to protect others from a patient who is considered to be a danger to others. That patient should be contained in a secure environment. (The duty to inform the authorities of the existence of a patient threatening to commit a violent offence against a specific individual, or informing the authorities where there is evidence of child abuse is dealt with in chapter 2.) Two examples here should suffice to indicate the difficulties of establishing a duty of care in this context. In *Holgate* v *Lancashire Mental Hospitals Board* [1937] 4 All ER 19, a dangerous prisoner who had been released on licence assaulted the plaintiff. The central issue in the case was the level of control, and the duty of care issue in the medical context was found to be difficult to define accurately for all cases, but could be analogous to the prisoner–prison officer situation. The difficulty of such cases in duty terms would really appear to centre around the proximity of plaintiff and defendant, particularly if the patient has not uttered a specific threat prior to escape. In recent years there has been a great deal of publicity surrounding discharged mental patients who have killed or severely injured. Two notorious instances, those involving Christopher Clunis and Martin Mursell, have focused attention on whether there should be damages awarded on the basis that members of the medical profession owe a duty to the victims (and families of victims) of crimes. The traditional view of the House of Lords in the case of *Hill* v *Chief Constable of West Yorkshire* [1989] AC 53 was that there was insufficient proximity between the police and a class of persons, here potential victims of the Yorkshire Ripper, to impose a duty of care. This view would lend itself to not imposing liability on the medical profession in cases such as that of Clunis. In another significant decision, however, that of *Osman* v *Ferguson* [1993] 4 All ER 344, there was found to be sufficient proximity where the potential victim of crime was within a small range of individuals (here a man shot the father of a boy who had been 'stalked' by the defendant, who had indicated to police that he might do something insane) yet there was no liability imposed because of the second phase involved in considering the duty issue. Behind these cases is this strong second element of public policy. In *Hill* v *Chief Constable of West Yorkshire* there was a fear that flood of litigation would result from the imposition of a duty of care to these third parties and this would lead to defensive police practices. In *Osman* v *Ferguson* this fear was also expressed. Now *Clunis* v *Camden and Islington Health Authority* (1996) *The Times*, 27 December 1996 has decided that there is nothing in principle to exclude liability where a medical practitioner fails properly to treat a mentally disordered patient who subsequently harms himself or others. This could have profound implications for the practice of psychiatric medicine, as this area is fraught with difficulties of accurate diagnosis and subsequent treatment.

3.4.3 Duty to write prescriptions clearly

The poorly written prescription, while something of a standing joke against the medical profession, can have serious, even fatal, consequences. In

Prendergast v *Sam and Dee Ltd* (1988) *The Times*, 24 March 1988 it was held that a handwritten prescription has to be sufficiently legible to allow for the mistakes that might be made by those who will process it. Allied to this, the case is also authority for a principle that where a prescription is of sufficient clarity that the pharmacist should suspect that it may be wrong, and the pharmacist fails to spot that error, there could be a breach of the duty of vigilance on the part of that pharmacist (see also J. Finch, 'A Costly Oversight' (1982) 132 NLJ 176 on *Dwyer* v *Roderick*).

3.4.4 Duty to inform of adverse results

Here the focus of the allegation of negligence lies not in the treatment given, or even pre-operative advice and warnings (for which see chapter 7). Negligence may be alleged where there has been a failure to inform the patient of what has gone wrong with the treatment, even if the failure is due to a non-negligent cause.

In *Gerber* v *Pines* (1934) 79 SJ 13 the doctor had given the plaintiff a series of injections as treatment for rheumatism. While giving the last injection, the patient had a muscle spasm in the area of the injection and the needle broke. The doctor found himself unable to get the needle out of the patient's body. Some days later it was removed by operation. It was found that there had been no negligence in the performance of the injection. The question then was whether the doctor should have told the patient of the accident as soon as it occurred. As a general rule Du Parcq J found that where there was a foreign substance left in the body of a patient, the doctor had a duty to inform the patient of that fact. His lordship seemed to be prepared to admit exceptions to this general rule. It may be that a doctor would not be under such a duty where the adverse result is minor, can be easily alleviated and disclosure of it might cause undue anxiety to the patient. However, where the modern state of medical law begins to turn towards the recognition of autonomy and a patient's right to full information, even this situation might call for a duty to inform to be placed on the doctor by the law.

In the factually similar case of *Daniels* v *Heskin* [1954] IR 73 the court found that there was no negligence in breaking the needle, or in the decision to defer operating to remove the needle while advising a midwife to look for unusual symptoms. Kingsmill Moore J admitted the problems of enunciating a general duty of care. The reason being:

> All depends on the circumstances – the character of the patient, her health, her social position, her intelligence, the nature of the tissue in which the needle is embedded, the possibility of subsequent infection, the arrangements made for future observation and care, and innumerable other considerations.

As later chapters will indicate, this view tends to run counter to a strong line of authority in medical law that the doctor is under a duty to keep the patient effectively informed. Contrary to what the court argued in *Daniels* v

Heskin, it could have quite simply said that there is a duty to inform the patient of the general nature of the adverse medical result which has taken place.

More recent cases have sought to be more realistic in considering that the general duty to keep a patient informed includes the duty to inform of the less successful aspects of the treatment (see *Lee v South West Thames Regional Health Authority* [1985] 1 WLR 845). In *Naylor v Preston Area Health Authority* [1987] 1 WLR 958, Donaldson MR effectively put an end to any controversy over the existence of such a duty by saying:

> ... in professional negligence cases, and in particular in medical negligence cases, there is a duty of candour resting upon the professional man. This is recognised by the legal professions in their ethical rules requiring their members to refer the client to other advisers, if it appears that the client has a valid claim for negligence. This also appears to be recognised by the Medical Defence Union, whose view is that 'the patient is entitled to a prompt, sympathetic and above all truthful account of what has occurred' (*Journal of the Medical Defence Union*, Spring 1987, p. 23).

3.5 CONCLUSION

It should be apparent that with the complexity of modern medical practice, the issue of the duty of care is always likely to remain a little vague. The common law courts are likely to be asked (as they were in *Goodwill v British Pregnancy Advisory Service* [1996] 1 WLR 1397) to make incremental extensions to the ambit of the duty of care that exists. In keeping with the general law relating to the duty of care it also appears likely that such demands will not be met.

The circumstances in which a duty of care will be held to exist will have to remain fluid, but there needs to be some more specific formulation of when the duty of care is undertaken by doctor, nurse or dentist. How is the doctor at the theatre to respond to the call, 'Is there a doctor in the house?'? The fact that there is no duty of care toward a stranger and no duty to rescue may not deter the doctor from going forward to help. There need to be some more clearly articulated legal rules which encourage the doctor, or at least give advanced warning that to step forward is to assume a duty of care toward the patient.

It seems inevitable too that the vicarious liability of the hospital will remain the main focus for litigation, but may be joined by increased litigation based on the direct liability of the hospital for the regime of care and its availability. The limited success of the actions directly against the health authorities or the incumbent Secretary of State is not likely to deter. Is the possibility of legal success going to continue to be the sole motivation for starting such actions? It may well be that the publicity which surrounds cases such as that of Jaymee Bowen may achieve politically what cannot at present be achieved in medical law by calling on those involved with health care to do their duty.

Further reading

Davies, M., 'Resource Allocation in Medicine and Professional Liability – The Final Nail?' (1996) 12 PN 15.
Lee, R., 'Hospital Admissions and Duty of Care' (1979) 129 NLJ 567.
Morris, F., and Adshead, G., 'The Liability of Psychiatrists for the Violent Acts of their Patients' (1997) 147 NLJ 558.
Picard, E., 'The Liability of Hospitals in Common Law Canada' (1981) 26 McGill LJ 997.

FOUR

Medical negligence II: standards of care, causation and damage

4.1 INTRODUCTION

In chapter 3 examples of the specific duties of care which may arise were considered, along with the need to establish that in a particular medical context an 'undertaking' has been made to treat the patient. While the margins of the duty of care in terms of existence and extent can appear blurred at times, on the facts of many medical negligence cases the existence of the duty of care will be obvious and admitted. Thus the duty of care is reasonably easy to establish, but the same could not be said about showing that the duty has been breached by falling below a legally recognised standard of 'performance' of medicine, or showing the causative link between that failing and the subsequent legally recognised damage.

The growth in medical negligence litigation has already been considered, as has the continuing general difficulty of the plaintiff succceeding in a medical negligence claim. The need to establish breach of care and causation is the main culprit for this continued lack of success. It is rare to be able to point to one case which, as well as being the focal analysis of the breach issue, has grown beyond its relatively humble beginnings to overshadow the vast majority of medical law, but *Bolam* v *Friern Hospital Management Committee* [1957] 1 WLR 582 is such a case. A consideration of medical negligence, indeed medical law as a whole, would be sadly lacking without complete awareness of the nature and impact of 'the *Bolam* test'. Harvey Teff admitted that much of his book, *Reasonable Care* (Oxford: Clarendon Press, 1994), was 'about how [the *Bolam* test's] application and influence in the medical sphere have served to buttress the paternalist tradition in medical practice' (p. 34).

The test is of the professional standard of the doctor, which must accord with a 'responsible body of medical opinion'. The standard is that of professional colleagues. Therefore the legal test becomes a matter of medical professional opinion. *Bolam*, perhaps more than any other single piece of common law, shows medical law to be a discrete area. Lord Scarman described it as 'a totally medical proposition erected into a working rule of law' ('Law and Medical Practice' in P. Byrne (ed.), *Medicine in Contemporary Society* (London: King Edwards, 1987), p. 134). It is safe to say that, since the *Bolam* test was formulated, it has been the medical profession that has largely dictated the direction that medical law has taken.

As far as the medical negligence allegation is concerned, the advantage of the defendant doctor over the plaintiff patient (because of *Bolam*) will be clear. Consider this comment from an expert in the field:

My experience in trauma and orthopaedic negligence claims for which I receive instructions in over 300 cases a year, leads me to believe that the *Bolam* test strongly favours the defence. It may well have been appropriate when medicine and particularly surgery was much less complex and sophisticated than it is today.

There is good evidence from experienced medical experts that deserving plaintiffs lose their claims – not so much on the facts and their interpretation, but because unfortunately there is a minority of expert witnesses who are willing to say that they would support the doctor's action and that what was done is accepted practice. Enquiry will often indicate that the expert's evidence is not supported by his own clinical practice; nevertheless his evidence is generally accepted by the court without question. (N. Harris, 'Medical Negligence Litigation: The Need for Reform' (1992) 60 Medico-Legal Journal 205 at p. 206)

The numerous impacts, criticisms and reform proposals surrounding *Bolam* will be considered below.

The vast array of case law to consider in terms of the standard of care in medical negligence actions indicates both the complexities of the concepts under discussion and the frequency with which the matter is a live issue in the cases themselves. The case law development reveals that establishing that the doctor or other health-care professional has fallen below the legal standard of care expected is one of the most difficult aspects of the medical negligence claim and a stark illustration of the underlying protective ethic of the medical profession toward fellow professionals.

4.2 GENERAL PRINCIPLES OF THE STANDARD OF CARE

Works on negligence generally tend to open consideration of the standard of care with the seminal case of the learner driver in *Nettleship* v *Weston* [1971] 2 QB 691. The medical law text can do little better than open with a consideration of what has already been described as the most important case in terms of medical law as a whole, *Bolam* v *Friern Hospital Management Committee* [1957] 1 WLR 582.

The plaintiff in this case was suffering from mental illness. A decision was made that this patient should undergo electroconvulsive therapy (ECT). During the course of the administration of this, no relaxant drugs were used and the plaintiff was largely unrestrained, apart from some manual control of the lower jaw. At the time of this treatment, there were two contrary bodies of medical opinion in existence. One school of thought considered that some sort of control, whether manual or by way of administration of drugs, should be used. The other school of thought found that such an approach was potentially dangerous. Debate also surrounded whether, if relaxant drugs were not used, there should still be manual control of the patient's convulsive movements caused by the therapy. During the course of the therapy the convulsive movements were such that the patient received dislocation of both hip joints and fractures of the pelvis.

In finding that the doctors had not breached their duty in deciding against restraining the patient, or informing the patient of the risks associated with ECT, McNair J made a number of comments that have been repeated with approval on a number of occasions, both in the broad context of medical law and in terms of negligence actions as a whole.

As those who have considered negligence generally will be all too well aware, the standard of care in general is that of the reasonable man, the 'man on the Clapham omnibus'. McNair J reasoned why this figure was inapplicable in the context of this issue of professional liability:

. . . where you get a situation which involves the use of some special skill or competence, then the test as to whether there has been negligence or not is not the test of the man on the top of a Clapham omnibus, because he has not got this special skill. The test is the standard of the ordinary skilled man exercising and professing to have that special skill. A man need not possess the highest expert skill; it is well established law that it is sufficient if he exercises the ordinary skill of an ordinary competent man exercising that particular art. . . .

[A doctor] is not guilty of negligence if he has acted in accordance with a practice accepted as proper by a responsible body of medical men skilled in that particular art.

This apparently straightforward test has proved over time to be a popular one with the courts, but unpopular with plaintiffs, academics and increasingly with judges in other jurisdictions. Potentially the test can be used to cover a vast array of professional activity in medicine (see further R. B. M. Howie, 'The Standard of Care in Medical Negligence' [1983] JR 193).

4.2.1 Professionally approved practice

Under the '*Bolam*' test there is no negligence where the doctor complies with practices that a competent body of colleagues would regard as correct. The first controversial issue is: Who decides whether what the doctor has done complies with that standard practice? One would confidently expect that the establishment of the standard of care would be a matter for the judge to rule on as one of law. It would then be a matter of fact whether the doctor in the particular circumstances of the case measured up to that prescribed standard, to be discovered through medical evidence. The alternative would be that the peer group of the defendant doctor would declare what standard they would expect to see in a particular case. The implication of this latter idea would be that the doctors would be deciding what doctors ought to do. The development of the case law in the medical context reveals that it is the latter approach that has been adopted, and the medical profession are now deciding both factual and legal issues.

This control by the medical profession can be combined with the fact that there may be some sympathy with the plight of a professional colleague who faces an allegation of negligence, and therefore a closing of the professional ranks. This would reduce the possibility that the act will be declared to be one which the profession would not condone. The plaintiff seems to be at a profound disadvantage.

Against this there appears now to be slim evidence that the courts may be willing to question the wisdom of a standard of conduct accepted by the responsible body. This is particularly evident where the issue is the level of disclosure of information about risks prior to treatment, and is certainly growing in popularity as a reaction against the all-encompassing *Bolam* test in other common law jurisdictions (this will be fully considered in chapter 7, but see now evidence of a possible reaction against *Bolam* in the Court of Appeal decision in *Joyce* v *Merton, Sutton and Wandsworth Health Authority* (1996) 7 Med LR 1) and also the House of Lords in *Bolitho* v *City and Hackney Health Authority* [1997] 3 WLR 1151).

In *Marshall* v *Lindsey County Council* [1935] 1 KB 516 Maugham LJ anticipated the *Bolam* test when he stated that the act could not be considered negligent if it accorded to professional practice. What this and a number of other cases have ignored (at least until recently) is the fact that the practice of a whole body may be consistent, but it can be consistently wrong. The change becoming apparent is that the court is seeking to distinguish between a professional practice adopted by the doctors in the particular area under dispute and the correctness of that professional practice as a whole. The doctor who is alleged to have been negligent may say 'I was doing what my colleagues would do' and be backed up by those colleagues. The court may be seeking to reply, 'Yes, you did act according to how your colleagues would have, but you are negligent in what you have done, and they are potentially negligent in what they are all doing'.

As early as 1950, case law indicated that standard professional practice as a whole could be regarded as negligent. In *Clarke* v *Adams* (1950) 94 SJ 599 it was found that the information given to a patient to notify the doctor if a form of heat treatment got too warm was inadequate. This was despite the fact that it was indicated in evidence that the standard warning for such a treatment had been used. In much the same vein, in *Hucks* v *Cole* (1968) 4 Med LR 393 a doctor who failed to treat a patient with penicillin in circumstances which accorded to professional practice was nevertheless found to be negligent. The comments of Sachs LJ are useful in finding the roots of the development of a change of attitude apparent in the minds of at least some of the judiciary, and on a broader front in terms of the danger of allowing a professional body to hold sway in deciding the legal parameters of the standard of care:

> . . . the fact that other practitioners would have done the same thing as the defendant practitioner is a very weighty matter to be put in the scales on his behalf; but it is not . . . conclusive. The court must be vigilant to see whether the reasons given for putting a patient at risk are valid in the light of any well-known advance in medical knowledge, or whether they stem from a residual adherence to out-of-date ideas – a tendency which in the present case may well have affected the views of at any rate one of the defendant's witnesses, who, at a considerable age, seemed not to have any particular respect for laboratory results.

Such comments appear to suggest that there is some concrete evidence that not all judges are intimidated by the complexities of medical practice and thus leave the issues of law to the profession itself. Such a view is bolstered by the views of both the Court of Appeal and House of Lords in *Sidaway* v *Board of Governors of the Bethlem Royal Hospital* [1984] QB 493, CA; [1985] AC 871, HL, which suggested that the professional medical view (at least as far as disclosure of information is concerned) that is held has to be 'rightly' held (for a full discussion of the facts and judgment in *Sidaway* see 7.3).

Recently the ability and willingness of the courts to consider the correctness of a professional view has extended beyond disclosure of information and into the traditional home of *Bolam*, treatment. *Bolitho* v *City and Hackney Health Authority* [1997] 3 WLR 1151 concerned the failure of a doctor to attend a patient in hospital, leading to brain damage through asphyxia. The Court of Appeal accepted to a limited extent the sentiments expressed in *Hucks* v *Cole* and appeared to formulate a test which brought principles of public law into the realm of medical negligence (although the House of Lords distanced itself from such an overt view). Dillon LJ explained, albeit in tentative fashion, that:

> In my judgment, the court could only adopt the approach of Sachs LJ and reject medical opinion on the ground that the reasons of one group of doctors do not really stand up to analysis, if the court, fully conscious of its own lack of medical knowledge and clinical experience, was nonetheless clearly satisfied that the views of that group of doctors were *Wednesbury* unreasonable, i.e. views such as no reasonable body of doctors could have held.

More recently, in *De Freitas* v *O'Brien* (1993) 4 Med LR 281, a first-instance decision, Byrt J also went against the unquestioning acquiescence of other members of the judiciary in finding that the court can choose between different schools of medical opinion, finding one to be flawed. Before one sees this as a considerable step away from *Bolam* as it has traditionally been understood, it should be emphasised that it will still be particularly difficult to show such unreasonableness where there is apparently only one body holding one opinion on standard practice in a particular sphere of medicine.

It remains unlikely that judges would question the accepted views of the medical profession where the whole weight of the evidence of that profession regards the conduct of the defendant as 'standard practice' (for further discussion of recent challenges, see section 4.2.7).

4.2.2   Differences of medical opinion

In *Bolam v Friern Hospital Management Committee* [1957] 1 WLR 582 there were clearly differences of opinion over what should be done during the course of the therapy. McNair J quoted from the Scottish case of *Hunter v Hanley* (1955) SC 200:

> In the realm of diagnosis and treatment there is ample scope for genuine difference of opinion and one man clearly is not negligent merely because his conclusion differs from that of other professional men, nor because he has displayed less skill or knowledge than others would have shown. The true test for establishing negligence in diagnosis or treatment on the part of a doctor is whether he has been proved to be guilty of such failure as *no* doctor of ordinary skill would be guilty of if acting with ordinary care. (emphasis added)

The apparent consistency with which the courts have endorsed the view that they will not decide between different expert opinions is a further illustration of the judicial unease in such a complex area of medical law. In the early case of *Chapman v Rix* (1958) *The Times*, 19 November 1958, Romer LJ felt able to argue that he was 'aware of no case in which a medical man has been guilty in negligence when eminent members of his own profession have expressed on oath their approval of what he has done'.

Perhaps the clearest example of the House of Lords distancing itself from having to decide between conflicting schools of medical thought is *Maynard v West Midlands Regional Health Authority* [1984] 1 WLR 634, where the trial judge's preference of one body of medical opinion over another was regarded by the House of Lords as an unsatisfactory way to approach the issue of negligence in the case. The argument was really that the *Bolam* test simply states that the doctor has to act in accordance with a practice which is accepted by a responsible body of medical opinion, the test is not that the doctor has to act in accordance with all medical opinion; that would be virtually impossible.

In *Bolam* itself, McNair J, as well as formulating the test of the standard of care, concluded his consideration of general issues by arguing that while it may not be essential to a consideration of the standard of care to decide if one medical opinion is to be preferred over another:

> . . . as long as you accept that what the defendants did was in accordance with a practice accepted by responsible persons; *if the result of the evidence is that you are satisfied that his practice is better than the practice spoken of on the other side, then it is really a stronger case.* (emphasis added)

That this matter has been largely overlooked in considerations of medical negligence is rather strange. McNair J is clearly arguing that the court can decide that one body of professional opinion is to be preferred over another where there is dispute. If this is accepted, it has major repercussions. The medical profession will not be exclusively deciding what the standard of care is. Where division of opinion exists the courts can sift the evidence and conclude that a body of opinion is incorrect, as happened in *De Freitas* v *O'Brien*.

That this element of *Bolam* has not been considered in other cases may be evidence that the court may still see the *Bolam* test as unassailable. In the context of differences of opinion where levels of disclosure of information have been in issue, the courts have shown a willingness to have an eye to the common practice in the particular matter, but not to the exclusion of the court having to consider that this view of the responsible body of medical opinion is 'rightly held' (*Sidaway* v *Board of Governors of the Bethlem Royal Hospital* [1984] QB 493). This has been even more forcefully put in the Australian High Court (*Rogers* v *Whitaker* (1992) 175 CLR 479) where it was felt that:

> . . . it has been accepted that the standard of care to be observed by a person with some special skill or competence is that of the ordinary skilled person exercising and professing to have that special skill. But, that standard is not determined solely or even primarily by reference to the practice followed or supported by a responsible body of opinion in the relevant profession or trade. (p. 487)

While to some such a view is to be welcomed, it is still apparent that as a matter of English medical law such a strident reassertion of the respective roles of the court and the medical profession within the realm of diagnosis and treatment appears unlikely (but for a tentative attempt to establish a 'New Bolam' see the recent Court of Appeal decision in *Joyce* v *Merton, Sutton and Wandsworth Health Authority* (1996) 2 Med LR 1; see also 4.2.7 and the House of Lords decision in *Bolitho* v *City and Hackney Health Authority* [1997] 3 WLR 1151).

4.2.3 Departure from established practice and innovative treatment

The case of *Hunter* v *Hanley* (1955) SC 200 provided Lord President Clyde with the opportunity to deal with the test of establishing negligence where the doctor has deviated from the norm. A departure from normal practice will not, of itself, be necessarily negligent. In order to find it negligent, it has to be shown on the evidence that there is in fact a standard practice in relation to the activity under discussion, that the defendant has not adopted this standard approach, and (reminding one of *Bolam*), that the deviation from the standard is one which no person of ordinary skill would have undertaken if acting with ordinary care.

The more recent case of *Clark* v *MacLennan* [1983] 1 All ER 416 proves an effective example of the operation of the rules laid down in *Hunter* v

Hanley. The plaintiff was admitted to hospital for the delivery of her child. After the child was born it was discovered that the mother was suffering from a not uncommon post-natal condition of stress incontinence. With this plaintiff the condition was described as acute. The condition persisted after the conventional treatment had been undertaken, so the defendant gynaecologist decided to perform what is known as an anterior colporrhaphy operation. Practice at that time indicated that such an operation should not be performed until three months after birth because of the risk of a haemorrhage. In the case of the plaintiff this eventuality occurred resulting in the operation breaking down and the condition of incontinence becoming a chronic one. Peter Pain J considered the nature of the plaintiff's submissions, and found that:

> . . . if the plaintiff could show (1) that there was a general practice not to perform an anterior colporrhaphy until at least three months after birth, (2) that one of the reasons for this practice was to protect the patient from the risk of haemorrhage and a breakdown of the repair, (3) that an operation was performed within four weeks and (4) that the haemorrhage occurred and the repair broke down, then the burden of showing that he was not in breach of duty shifted to the defendants.

This was a recognition that where the precise damage which the operation was designed to prevent or alleviate occurs, then, along with the other requirements detailed by Peter Pain J, the plaintiff has made out a prima facie case that will have to be rebutted. *Wilsher* v *Essex Area Health Authority* [1987] QB 730 appears to cast some doubt on the legitimacy of such a judicial exercise, as it appears to shift the burden of proof from plaintiff to defendant. It would be more accurate to suggest that the plaintiff has established the case of negligence on the balance of probabilities if no rebuttal evidence is forthcoming (see also the recent case of *Waters* v *West Sussex Health Authority* (1995) 6 Med LR 362 per Buxton J which involved an allegation that a neurosurgeon has been negligent in undertaking a unique form of back operation. In finding against negligence here, the Court found that there was no material or body of professional opinion existing which could confirm the operation had been performed negligently).

4.2.4 Levels of skill

The factual circumstances of the practice of medicine and the variety of sub-professions practising medicine, from the junior doctor to the highly specialist neurosurgeon, mean that a single standard of care might prove ridiculously easy for the specialist to conform with and extremely difficult for the newly qualified doctor to attain. The *Bolam* standard would need to be particular enough to cover the full variety of medical expertise or broad enough to provide a general statement of the standards of care expected. It should be apparent that in assessing the standard of the ordinary skilful doctor or other medical professional it is necessary to recognise the real pressures of training on the job and the existence of emergency situations. The major cases have all encountered this dilemma of general standard or particular standards and have opted for the general statement of standard of care, under the umbrella of the *Bolam* formulation.

Wilsher v *Essex Area Health Authority* [1987] QB 730, CA; [1988] AC 1074, HL is indicative of the judicial response to the standard of care applied in a complex professional scenario, involving, as many operative procedures now do, a number of medical professionals with different designations, different tasks and different abilities.

Martin Wilsher had been born prematurely and was suffering from a number of conditions, the most significant of which for present purposes was oxygen deficiency. The child's prognosis was grave enough to warrant transfer to a special baby care unit. The medical team in the unit consisted of a senior registrar, two consultants, several doctors and trained nurses. The plaintiff was being monitored by a number of the team and at one time by a doctor described in evidence as 'junior and inexperienced'. The doctor placed a catheter in a vein rather than an artery. This doctor then asked the senior registrar to check that the correct procedure had been undertaken, but the registrar failed to spot the mistake. The failure led to incorrect oxygen readings and the child was given excess oxygen. The plaintiff was later diagnosed as being blind through a condition known as retrolental fibroplasia (RLF). One of the possible causes of this was the administration of excess oxygen. The allegation was that the failure of the employees of the hospital resulted in the blindness. The major question aside from what caused the blindness was the standard of care required of the members of the special baby care unit.

There were a number of possible ways to approach the question, and most of the possible answers were canvassed by Mustill LJ, who recognised the complexities for the court in such circumstances:

(a)   *The team standard.* Plaintiff counsel's assertion here was that 'each of the members of the unit held themselves out as capable of performing the specialised operations of the unit as a whole'. Mustill LJ rejected this approach as it would prove disastrous to the less experienced members of this 'team'. The nurse would be judged by the same standard as the consultant.

(b)   *The individualised standard.* A doctor's standard of treatment would be judged by his or her *actual* qualifications and experience. This would be virtually a subjective standard. Mustill LJ noted that this would mean for the patient that the standard of care which could be expected would depend on who was on duty at the time. If the doctor is on the first week in the particular unit or area of specialisation, the standard would be of the inexperienced doctor on the first week in the unit, the standard of the consultant of 20 years' standing that of the particular consultant of 20 years and so forth. Against this, Mustill LJ was firm in acknowledging that:

> . . . this notion of a duty tailored to the actor, rather than to the act which he elects to perform, has no place in the law of tort. . . . Public hospital

medicine has always been organised so that young doctors and nurses learn on the job. . . . The longer term interests of patients as a whole are best served by maintaining the present system, even if this may diminish the legal rights of the individual patient: for, after all, medicine is about curing, not litigation. ([1987] QB 730 at p. 750)

(c)   *The environment or 'post' standard.* The standard of care to be expected of the junior doctor in *Wilsher* v *Essex Area Health Authority* was regarded by the Court of Appeal as the standard of the reasonable junior doctor acting in a special baby care unit. The standard in general then takes something from both of the above options. The doctor's inexperience in the practice of medicine is acknowledged by the first part of the test, as is the fact that notwithstanding that inexperience, the doctor is still working in a specialist environment – the second part of the test. Patients should be able to expect a minimum standard of expertise in a particular area, but should also recognise the reality that experience is often best obtained on the job itself. Glidewell LJ responded to the contention that this was unduly harsh as a test for the junior doctor, by arguing that to do otherwise would lead to the frequent plea of inexperience in an allegation of medical negligence. The strictures of the test were also eased by Glidewell LJ's acknowledgement that the junior doctor who consults a superior for confirmation of a procedure's correctness will have come up to the standard expected.

It is worth noting the dissenting comments of Browne-Wilkinson V-C, that the burden of the test would be unfair on the doctors who are seeking to acquire the necessary skills needed in the unit. There is an implicit recognition that the threat to the doctor posed by the imposition of such a standard may lead to specialisms being unpopular training grounds, or prove the focus for the overly cautious and uneconomical practice of specialist medicine. Allied to this is Browne-Wilkinson V-C's strongly voiced view that negligence could be apportioned to a doctor without personal fault on that doctor's part.

Frequently acknowledged as a continuing problem with the inexperienced doctor is the lack of knowledge that there is even a risk involved. A doctor may well only feel suitably 'protected' where in any case of doubt a more experienced colleague is questioned. The implication of this might be that the junior doctor, if aware of the dangers of litigation, will, when in the slightest doubt, contact a senior colleague, and thus may unduly delay important treatment. This might allow the danger of litigation to arise 'by the back door'. Senior members of medical staff may feel pestered by constant inquiries and neglect their own patients as a result. That this is a little speculative should not detract from the possibility.

With regard to the specialist a number of issues arise as to the standard of care to be expected. Does the standard depend on whether the doctor is in fact a specialist? Does it depend on the patient's knowledge of the doctor's specialism? *Ashcroft* v *Mersey Regional Health Authority* [1985] 2 All ER 96 is authority for the view that the specialist is to be similarly judged, i.e., by the standard of general expertise in the particular post being occupied or the particular procedure being undertaken.

4.2.5   Errors of clinical judgment

This discredited debate on the standard of care in medicine is important as clear evidence of the existence of a policy of judicial protection of the medical profession. It was one, however, which swiftly eroded as an attempt at further refining the standard of care applicable in relation to, and for the protection of, the medical profession. The existence of the broad defensive theory of the error of clinical judgment arose amongst others in the judgment of Lord Denning MR in another important case for medical negligence, *Whitehouse* v *Jordan* [1980] 1 All ER 650, CA; [1981] 1 WLR 246, HL. A child was due to be delivered by the defendant, a senior registrar, after the mother had been through a high-risk pregnancy. She had been in labour for 22 hours when the defendant decided to carry out a test to see if the child could be delivered by the use of forceps. This trial of forceps involved the defendant pulling five or six times with the forceps around the baby's head. This did not work, and the defendant, worried for the health of the mother, delivered the child by Caesarean section. The child was found to be suffering from cerebral palsy through asphyxiation, itself alleged to have been caused by the defendant pulling too long and too hard on the forceps.

Lord Denning approved of his own previous pronouncements when he stated:

> We must say, and say firmly, that, in a professional man, an error of judgment is not negligent. To test it, I would suggest that you ask the average competent and careful practitioner: 'Is this the sort of mistake that you yourself might have made?' If he says: 'Yes, even doing the best I could, it might have happened to me', then it is not negligent. In saying this, I am only reaffirming what I said in *Hatcher* v *Black* (1954) *The Times*, 2 July 1954, . . . *Roe* v *Ministry of Health* [1954] 2 QB 66 and *Hucks* v *Cole* (8 May 1968 unreported). ([1980] 1 All ER 650 at p. 658)

The reason for such a strong view, that an error of clinical judgment can never be negligent, was based on a perception voiced by Denning LJ (as he was then) in one of the cases mentioned above, *Hatcher* v *Black* (1954) *The Times*, 2 July 1954, that the uncertainties inherent in the practice of medicine were such that a doctor, aware of a law which regards errors of clinical judgment as negligent, would sense this as a 'dagger at his back' when undertaking treatment. Even more fundamentally, in all the cases of his which he cited, Lord Denning considered that the medical profession should be held in special regard and interfered with by the law as little as possible (see Sheila Maclean, 'Negligence – A Dagger at the Doctor's Back?' in Robson and Watchman (eds), *Justice, Lord Denning and the Constitution*). His lordship had also made his views clear in *Roe* v *Minister of Health* [1954] 2 QB 66 at pp. 86–7. Consider their accuracy:

> These two men [the injured plaintiffs] have suffered such terrible conse-
> quences that there is a natural feeling that they should be compensated.

But we should be doing a disservice to the community at large if we were to impose liability on hospitals and doctors for everything that happens to go wrong. Doctors would be led to think more of their own safety than of the good of their patients. Initiative would be stifled and confidence shaken. . . . We must insist on due care for the patient at every point, but we must not condemn as negligence that which is only a misadventure.

In the House of Lords in *Whitehouse* v *Jordan* [1981] 1 WLR 246, Lord Fraser of Tullybelton confirmed Donaldson LJ's rejection of Lord Denning MR's view in the Court of Appeal:

> . . . I think that the learned Master of the Rolls must have meant to say that an error of judgment 'is not *necessarily* negligent'. But in my respectful opinion, the statement as it stands is not an accurate statement of the law. Merely to describe something as an error of judgment tells us nothing about whether it is negligent or not. The true position is that an error of judgment may, or may not, be negligent; it depends on the nature of the error. If it is one that would not have been made by a reasonably competent professional man professing to have the standard and type of skill that the defendant held himself out as having, and acting with ordinary care, then it is negligent. If, on the other hand, it is an error that such a man, acting with ordinary care, might have made, then it is not negligent.

This criticism of Lord Denning was confirmed by the comments of Lord Edmund-Davies. Gerald Robertson ('Medical Negligence Retried' (1981) 44 MLR 457) echoes the opinions of many medical law writers in arguing that the protectionist views of Lord Denning evident in his various expressions with regard to the standard of care, causation and proof are unacceptable. There is a distortion of the 'dispassionate' role of the judge in considering evidence in such cases. Lord Denning seemed to place the medical profession on a pedestal, to the extent of attempting (but ultimately failing) to rewrite medical negligence to accommodate this elevated status.

4.2.6 Deficiencies of the *Bolam* test

While some jurisdictions are willing to question the legal correctness and ethical propriety of the medical profession deciding its own legal standard of performance (particularly in relation to levels of information disclosure and the theory of informed consent evident in Canada and Australia), one has to strain to find any forthright denunciation of professional governing of legal standards from English judges. The *Bolam* test is the main reason why Margaret Brazier (*Medicine, Patients and the Law* (London: Penguin, 1992)) saw English judges as unique in their acquiescence before the views of the medical profession. Similarly Harvey Teff (*Reasonable Care* (Oxford: Clarendon Press, 1994)) has said:

> In England, at the highest levels of judicial decision-making, the general picture has been one of increasing involvement in medical conduct, but

with few signs of a desire to shape it. The three leading medical negligence cases of the 1980s to reach the House of Lords – between them covering the three functions of diagnosis, treatment and advice [respectively, *Maynard* v *West Midlands Regional Health Authority* [1984] 1 WLR 634; *Whitehouse* v *Jordan* [1981] 1 WLR 246, and *Sidaway* v *Board of Governors of the Bethlem Royal Hospital* [1985] AC 871] – left medical standards all but immune from judicial control, by their obeisance to the *Bolam* principle of 'accepted medical practice'. (p. 63)

The new language of medical law, that of rights and duties, can be an impetus to move away from *Bolam*. The emerging culture of patients' rights demands a 'professional service' from doctors. The doctor has the duty to act to a standard just and reasonable in the particular circumstances because the patient demands that right. There could be a more equitable evaluation of the standard of care in a particular case, with the professional standard of the doctor being judged according, at least to some extent, to the expectations of the patient. Combine with this the development of a more interventionist stance of the judges towards medical law questions and it may be possible to change the focus of the standard of care issue.

The *Bolam* test in part survives because it is ambiguous. Was McNair J advocating a normative or descriptive analysis of the professional standard of doctors at law? Where does the court have an articulated role in the evaluation of the professional standard of care in a particular case? (For an analysis of the risks of ambiguity in *Bolam* see J. Montrose, 'Is Negligence an Ethical or a Sociological Concept?' (1958) 21 MLR 259.) There are no ready answers to these or many other questions of what *Bolam* really means. It would seem strange, however, for McNair J to have judicially renounced the court's power to make decisions on the standard of medical care. Remember McNair J described the standard as one 'accepted as proper by a *responsible* body of opinion'. Obviously this means that there is scope for the court to declare that a practice is accepted as proper by an *irresponsible* body of medical opinion, and therefore there is a breach of duty. This would mean that the courts would have to question expert evidence (see the discussion of the House of Lords decision in *Bolitho* v *City and Hackney Health Authority* [1997] 3 WLR 1151 and *Hucks* v *Cole* (1968) 4 Med LR 393 in 4.2.1). In more forthright terms, Hirst J argued in *Hills* v *Potter* [1984] 1 WLR 641:

I do not accept the argument that by adopting the *Bolam* principle, the court in effect abdicates its power of decision to the doctors. In every case the court must be satisfied that the standard contended for on their behalf accords with that upheld by a substantial body of medical opinion, and that this body of medical opinion is both respectable and responsible, and experienced in this particular field of medicine. (p. 653)

Looking back on the development of *Bolam* in the courts, the true meaning of the test may be clouded, but the impact is all too clear – in medical negligence actions the doctor has inordinate power to influence results and the patient little if any such power. *Bolam* is still a mainstay of medical law and its continuing influence in realms of medical practice that appear far distant from the 'usual' medical negligence case will be referred to often, and reveal its enduring, if highly controversial, power.

4.2.7   Challenges to *Bolam*?

As indicated earlier in this chapter, *Hucks* v *Cole* (1968) 4 Med LR 393 and a few other cases have been interpreted as challenges to the principle contained in *Bolam* v *Friern Hospital Management Committee* [1957] 1 WLR 582 and confirmed in *Whitehouse* v *Jordan* [1981] 1 WLR 246 and *Maynard* v *West Midlands Regional Health Authority* [1984] 1 WLR 634. Now the House of Lords have considered a strong challenge to *Bolam* in *Bolitho* v *City and Hackney Health Authority* [1997] 3 WLR 1151 to add to the cases of *Smith* v *Tunbridge Wells Health Authority* (1994) 5 Med LR 334, *Joyce* v *Merton, Sutton and Wandsworth Health Authority* (1996) 7 Med LR 1, and *Lybert* v *Warrington Health Authority* (1995) 7 Med LR 71 (CA) (for more detail on these cases see M. Davies, 'The New *Bolam*: Another False Dawn for Medical Negligence?' (1996) 12 PN 120). Is this case (indeed are any of these cases) a real change in judicial attitude to received medical wisdom?

It will be recalled that *Bolitho* concerned issues of breach of duty and causation after Patrick Bolitho 'suffered catastrophic brain damage as a result of cardiac arrest induced by respiratory failure'. The boy had suffered three episodes where he had difficulty breathing and at none of these times did the senior paediatric registrar or her deputy attend. The third event led to cardiac arrest and the brain damage, and the child died before the issue came before the court. The defendant health authority accepted that the registrar was in breach of her duty of care having not attended or arranged for a deputy to attend after being informed of each episode by a nurse. The question to be decided then was that of causation. As a matter of fact it was accepted that the insertion of a tube to provide Patrick with an airway would have meant there would not have been cardiac failure. The questions appeared relatively straightforward to the trial judge:

> . . . the issue was what would Dr Horn or another competent doctor sent in her place have done had they attended. . . . the real question was what would Dr Horn or that other doctor have done or what should they have done. As it seems to me, if Dr Horn would have intubated, then the plaintiff succeeds, whether or not that is a course which all reasonably competent practitioners would have followed, If, however, Dr Horn would not have intubated, then the plaintiff can only succeed if such failure was contrary to accepted medical practice.

At trial there was a fairly considerable body of evidence presented for both sides. The majority of experts called argued that they would have intubated after the second episode. Nevertheless the trial judge was equally impressed with the evidence of an expert who would not have intubated. It will be recalled that in *Maynard* v *West Midlands Regional Health Authority* [1984] 1 WLR 634 Lord Scarman said, at p. 639:

> . . . I have to say that a judge's 'preference' for one body of professional opinion to another also professionally distinguished is not sufficient to establish negligence in a practitioner whose actions have received the seal of approval of those whose opinions, truthfully expressed, honestly held, were not preferred. If this was the real reason for the judge's finding, he erred in law even though elsewhere in his judgment he stated the law correctly. For in the realm of diagnosis and treatment negligence is not established by preferring one respectable body of professional opinion to another. Failure to exercise the ordinary skill of a doctor is necessary.

It was therefore held at trial that both opinions on intubation were responsible bodies of opinion so it was not proved that the breach of duty of the defendants in not attending had caused the damage suffered by Patrick Bolitho. This was upheld on appeal with a dissent by Simon Brown LJ (for more detail on this issue of causation see 4.3.1). In the House of Lords counsel for the appellants sought again to argue that the *Bolam* formulation had no application to issues of causation (a view accepted by Simon Brown LJ in the Court of Appeal). For present purposes the important part of the appellant's case was that the views of the defendant's experts were not logical and that the House should substitute its own views where this was the case. There was a strong submission made that the trial judge was forced by an unadulterated utilisation of *Bolam* to accept an opinion even though unpersuaded of its logic. It was a matter for the court, not medical opinion, to decide the standard of professional care. This view met with a tentative agreement from Lord Browne-Wilkinson:

> I agree with these submissions to the extent that, in my view, the court is not bound to hold that a defendant doctor escapes liability for negligent treatment or diagnosis just because he leads evidence from a number of medical experts who are genuinely of the opinion that the defendant's treatment or diagnosis accorded with sound medical practice.

The House of Lords went on to note that in *Maynard* there had been reference to a medical opinion being 'respectable', 'reasonable' or 'responsible', and this meant that an opinion had to have a logical basis. There was a reasonably strong approval for the approach adopted in *Hucks* v *Cole* (1968) 4 Med LR 393, which was felt not to conflict with the 'message' of *Bolam*. Indeed it was noted that in *Bolam* itself reference was made to a 'responsible body of medical men'. Nevertheless it was still also acknowledged that such challenges would be rare, and the case of Patrick Bolitho was not such a rare case and the majority view of the Court of Appeal was approved. It appears therefore that *Bolitho* really says nothing that has not been explicit in the 'traditional' *Bolam* cases. There have been some academic comments that this is a major change for medical negligence. It is rather the case that if this case represents any real change at all it is that the courts are being more explicit in publicising their rare and residual power to question medical practice. The slight change is more cultural than substantive.

4.3   PROVING MEDICAL NEGLIGENCE

4.3.1   Causation

It should be apparent that the existence of the *Bolam* test of the standard of care, still leading largely to the medical profession deciding the standards to be expected and applied to their own profession, has meant that there is profound difficulty in establishing that a breach of duty has taken place. Even where there may have been such a breach of duty, more problems arise because of the complexities and inexactitudes of medicine. How does the plaintiff show that the injury has been caused by the doctor falling below the prescribed standard of care as opposed to being a manifestation of the risk inherent in the operation itself? Go back to the example given at the start of the book (see p. 1). Was the anaesthetic itself defective and a cause of the shock? Was the anaesthetic wrongly prescribed by the doctor thinking about his annual holiday rather than the correct dosage? Am I one of the few people in the world who have a 'bad' reaction to the drug, whether negligently prescribed or not? 'Was the breach of duty by the doctor the cause of the damage?' is one of the most difficult questions in medical negligence cases. In looking at the cases that have been mainly or exclusively concerned with matters of causation, there are two questions to be answered:

(a)   Could the breach cause the injury? A question of factual causation.
(b)   Did the breach cause the injury? A question of fact and law.

Medical negligence cases are not like other personal injury cases because:

> Most cases in personal injury litigation pose no factual or conceptual difficulty in relating the injury to a direct consequence of a negligent event. In such cases a simple lineal concept of cause is commonsensically obvious. If a previously healthy plaintiff damages a finger in an unguarded machine he need only prove negligence . . . on the part of the defendant, and the question of causation, the negligence leading to the loss, is self-evident. (Nelson-Jones and Burton *Medical Negligence Case Law* (Fourmat Publishing) at p. 67)

If only things were as simple where the claim is one of medical negligence rather than industrial injury.

As a matter of the general law of negligence, it is for the plaintiff to show that the breach of duty caused or materially contributed to the legally recognised injury on the balance of probabilities. In setting out the general rules on causation the House of Lords in *McGhee* v *National Coal Board* [1973] 1 WLR 1 seemed to be advocating a simple test:

. . . it has often been said that the legal concept of causation is not based on logic or philosophy. It is based on the practical way in which the ordinary man's mind works in the everyday affairs of life. From a broad and practical viewpoint I can see no substantial difference between saying that what the defender did materially increased the risk of injury to the pursuer and saying what the defender did made a material contribution to his injury. (at p. 5 per Lord Reid)

The case of *Barnett* v *Chelsea and Kensington Hospital Management Committee* [1969] 1 QB 428, discussed in 3.3.3, provides an introduction to the application of legal causation to the issue of medical negligence. The deceased, it will be recalled, had been poisoned by arsenic and left untreated by the casualty officer. This was a clear case of 'but for' causation. If the plaintiff could show that 'but for' the defendant's failure to attend her husband he would have lived, on the balance of probabilities, then the breach is the cause of death. If the husband would have died even if there had been proper treatment, then the breach was not the cause of death.

The defendant admitted that there was a duty of care and a breach of that duty but contended that the deceased would have died even if there had been no negligent behaviour. The deceased had entered the defendant casualty department between 8.05 and 8.10 a.m. It was accepted that even if the patient had been admitted at this time, the deceased would not have been on a ward before 11.00 a.m and the drip and consequent discovery of potassium loss, indicative of this type of poisoning not discovered until 12.30 p.m. Nield J concluded consideration of the evidence by stating: 'I find that the plaintiff has failed to establish, on the grounds of probability, that the defendant's negligence caused the death of the deceased' (at p. 439).

Barnett confirms that the questions to be asked are: 'Did the breach of duty cause the damage?' and 'Could the breach cause the injury'?

The questions were raised again in the major case of *Wilsher* v *Essex Area Health Authority* [1988] AC 1074, in which it was also necessary to consider a strand of authority which appeared to suggest that, in certain circumstances, the *defendant* might have to establish that the breach of duty did *not* cause or materially contribute to the injury. A reversal of the burden of proving negligence. The general facts have already been reviewed. It will be remembered that Martin Wilsher was found to be suffering from RLF after (note that I have not said 'because of') the receipt of excess oxygen, itself due to a failure to place a catheter in an artery rather than a vein. It was accepted that the RLF *could* be caused by such an activity. RLF, however, could be caused by a number of other conditions (not caused by breach of duty) from which Martin Wilsher suffered during the early part of his life. It was this matter which was to task all courts considering the case.

At trial, Peter Pain J relied on a principle of law which was derived from *McGhee* v *National Coal Board* [1973] 1 WLR 1 and which had been stated earlier by his lordship in *Clark* v *MacLennan* [1983] 1 All ER 416 at p. 427:

It seems to me that it follows from *McGhee* that where there is a situation in which a general duty of care arises and there is a failure to take a precaution, and that very damage occurs against which the precaution is designed to be a protection, then the burden lies *on the defendant* to show that he was not in breach of duty as well as to show that the damage did not result from his breach of duty. (emphasis added)

From this his lordship found that the authority had failed to show that its breach of duty had not caused or materially contributed to Martin Wilsher's RLF.

By the time the matter had reached the House of Lords, it was accepted that the factual evidence should be reviewed at a retrial (which never in fact took place as the matter was settled out of court). The House of Lords, however, took the opportunity to make a key judgment on the question of causation as a matter of law to be considered in this and other cases. Note that the House of Lords was never required to come to a specific decision on the legal cause of Martin Wilsher's blindness, because of the expected retrial.

Lord Bridge pointed out during his analysis of the facts of the case and the issues of law considered by the trial judge, that there was strong evidence that Peter Pain J had considered the matter as one in which broadly the defendants were being required to disprove the case, on the balance of probabilities, rather than the plaintiff having to prove the case.

The House of Lords, while not overruling the decision in *McGhee* did seek to distinguish it on the basis that in *McGhee* there was only one cause of the illness, whereas in *Wilsher* there were a number of possible factual causes for the RLF, all in existence at one time or another. Lord Bridge found that *McGhee* propounded no new principle of law. The burden lay on the plaintiff to show on the balance of probabilities that the excess oxygen caused or materially contributed to the risk of injury. The negligence increased the number of possible causes of the RLF but could not be shown to have materially contributed to the injury. Lord Bridge felt that in finding for the plaintiff in *McGhee* the majority in the House of Lords had taken 'a robust and pragmatic approach' to the issue, and drawn an inference of fact that the defenders' negligence had materially contributed to the injury.

In essence, the House of Lords decided in *Wilsher* v *Essex Area Health Authority* that the existence of breach and injury could not necessarily raise an inference of negligence. The burden would still be on the plaintiff to establish the link between the two. Subsequently it has been confirmed that the existence of a *possibility* that a certain matter might cause injury was not to be regarded as sufficient to show cause at law (see *Loveday* v *Renton* (1990) 1 Med LR 117).

Suggestions have been made that there should be a higher burden of proof in medical negligence cases, because of the serious financial and professional implications of a finding of negligently caused injury. Mason and McCall Smith (*Law and Medical Ethics*, 4th ed. (London: Butterworths, 1994), p. 198) point out that the success rate in medical negligence actions is 30 to 40 per cent whereas in personal injury actions generally the success rate is 86 per cent, so there seems to be little need for a higher burden of proof in medical cases.

Overall the difficulties of causation and proof are generated by the tension revealed by May LJ in *Dwyer* v *Roderick* (1983) 127 SJ 805. While there is sympathy with the plight of the injured patient, it would be:

> to shut one's eyes to the obvious if one denied that the burden of achieving something more than the mere chance of probabilities was greater when one was investigating the complicated and sophisticated actions of a qualified and experienced doctor than when one was enquiring into the inattention of the driver in a simple running-down action.

There seems little likelihood, then, that the courts will deal more 'leniently' with medical causative issues which are simply often not susceptible to the type of proof which the law requires. The problems of legal and factual causation are compounded by further examples of judicial protection of the medical profession. This protectionism is further emphasised by a recent decision which distances medical causation issues further from *McGhee* and amazingly places *Bolam* in the context of deciding causation. The process of judicial logic needs to be followed carefully in *Bolitho* v *City and Hackney Health Authority* [1997] 3 WLR 1151, the facts of which have been given in some detail in s. 4.2.7. Simply put, the non-attendance at Patrick Bolitho's bedside was a breach of duty, but was not a cause of the cardiac arrest. The Court of Appeal stated that it was for the plaintiffs to prove that had the doctor attended, intubation would have taken place. The doctor involved argued that she would not have intubated. Therefore the plaintiffs also needed to show that the decision not to intubate was one which no responsible doctor would have taken – the *Bolam* test.

Counsel for the plaintiffs made a strong argument that issues of causation were not the place to use the *Bolam* test and that the principles expounded in *McGhee* and *Wilsher* were the exclusive principles of causation. Farquharson and Dillon LJJ felt bound to rely on the evidence of the practice of the medical profession, but in the Court of Appeal Simon Brown LJ dissented, saying that cases such as *Bolam* were:

> forged specifically in the context of liability, of negligence, not of causation. . . . it seems to me that quite different considerations come into play when the issue is one of causation. . . . This case does not involve a doctor adhering to one body of responsible medical opinion rather than another. No doctor in this case ever took a decision whether or not to intubate. The plain fact here is that no doctor ever arrived at Patrick's bedside. (4 Med LR 381, at 388, CA.)

The true question, according to Simon Brown LJ, was simply whether a doctor who attended would probably have intubated or not. In practical terms, a defendant doctor may be willing to admit negligence, but not necessarily causation. *Bolam*, when applied to causation, readily allows the doctor to admit negligence, but rely on colleagues to be able to deny causation. Nevertheless the House of Lords approved the majority view of the Court of Appeal.

4.3.2   Loss of a chance of a better medical result

The significance of the issue as a matter of proof of medical negligence was recognised in succinct terms by Walter Scott ('Causation in Medico-Legal Practice: A Doctor's Approach to the "Lost Opportunity" Cases' (1992) 55 MLR 521).

> Advances in modern medicine increasingly provide patients with opportunities of cure which would hitherto have been impossible. If a patient can show that the doctor's negligence caused him to lose that opportunity, the question arises of how to quantify the damage in a way that is just for both parties.

A court dealing with an allegation that a doctor's negligence has lost the patient the chance of a full recovery from an injury caused by some other incident may choose a proportionate or absolute assessment. The latter can be seen in *Kenyon v Bell* (1953) SC 125. The case is also useful as an introduction to the type of situation where the loss of a chance becomes an active issue for the court's consideration.

A girl suffered an eye injury, and subsequently underwent medical treatment. It was alleged that this treatment was negligent, and had caused the girl to lose the chance of having her sight saved. The evidence indicated that the chances of the sight being saved, even with effective medical treatment, would have been less than 50 per cent. The court adopted the rule that where the chances of the sight being saved were over 50 per cent with effective (non-negligent) treatment, the plaintiff could recover full damages on the basis that the opportunity to have the sight saved existed on the balance of probabilities. It was not achieved here, so damages were not awarded.

The main case to have decided the issue, but not the controversy over the issue itself, is *Hotson v East Berkshire Area Health Authority* [1987] AC 750. A boy had injured his hip in a fall, and was taken to the local hospital for a check-up. His examination was negligent, in that no X-ray was taken, which would have revealed a fracture. This fracture was of a type which could develop into a chronic condition called avascular necrosis. Due to his continued pain, his GP sent him back to the same hospital, which finally made the correct diagnosis, and gave the appropriate treatment. The medical evidence given at the trial indicated that even if the correct diagnosis had been made on the first visit to the hospital, there was still a 75 per cent chance that the necrosis would develop. Stephen Brown J at first instance, decided that because there was a 75 per cent chance that the child would have developed the condition in the absence of negligence, the damages the child would get would be reduced by that percentage; so the child obtained 25 per cent of a full award. Loss of a chance was here reduced to a percentage and converted into damages. The Court of Appeal approved of this decision, and the matter was appealed by the defendant health authority to the House of Lords.

The House of Lords could either approve this percentage reduction idea (the proportional approach) or the idea in *Kenyon v Bell* that the child had failed to show on the balance of probabilities that the necrosis would have developed anyway.

Lord Bridge recognised that there was a basic difficulty of classifying the issue. At first instance (sub nom. *Hotson* v *Fitzgerald* [1985] 1 WLR 1036), Simon Brown J had said that:

> ... the problem comes down to one of classification. Is this on true analysis a case where the plaintiff is concerned to establish causative negligence or is it rather a case where the real question is the proper quantum of damage? Clearly the case hovers near the border. ... If the issue is one of causation then the health authority succeed since the plaintiff will have failed to prove his claim on the balance of probabilities. ... If, however, the issue is one of quantification then the plaintiff succeeds because it is trite law that the quantum of a recognised head of damage must be evaluated according to the chances of the loss occurring.

While the Court of Appeal saw the matter as one of quantification, the House of Lords saw it in the same way as *Kenyon* v *Bell*, and decided that the plaintiff had failed to show, on the balance of probabilities, that the avascular necrosis would develop due to the negligent failure to diagnose.

Scott (1992) 55 MLR 521 sees the absolute approach as unfair to the plaintiff patient with a small chance of recovery lost because of negligence, and is equally unfair to the defendant doctor where the patient may not have recovered even had the treatment been non-negligent. The principal objection to this approach is that it rests on the designation of an event in terms of a percentage. Why is a passenger in a negligently driven car 25 per cent to blame for injuries if he has not worn a seat belt (see *Froom* v *Butcher* [1976] QB 286) as opposed to 30 or 40 per cent? Why is the chance of a condition developing in the absence of negligence 49 per cent not 51 per cent? The danger of using a percentage analysis is that it is not a true reflection of the fact that the decisions, while being expressed in terms of balance of probabilities, are never, at least in the field of medical negligence, capable of such mathematical precision.

4.3.3 Hope for the plaintiff? *Res ipsa loquitur*

It is well known in negligence law generally, and medical negligence in particular, that things can go wrong without there being a full or sufficient explanation for what actually happened. The complexity of modern medical procedures means that the patient who wakes from the anaesthetic with some form of paralysis, for example, may never know the exact cause. It could be the negligent performance of the operation itself, the mistake (negligent or not) of the anaesthetist in monitoring the patient's oxygen intake level or a spontaneous reaction of the body that can never be predicted. It would be unfair on the patient to have to prove negligence where all indications are that there was fault somewhere along the line of care.

One of the classic expositions of the maxim *res ipsa loquitur* which could aid such a patient came in *Cassidy* v *Ministry of Health* [1951] 2 KB 343, where Denning LJ stated:

If the plaintiff had to prove that some particular doctor or nurse was negligent, he would not be able to do it. But he was not put to that impossible task: he says, 'I went into the hospital to be cured of two stiff fingers. I have come out with four stiff fingers and my hand is useless. That should not have happened if due care had been used. Explain it, if you can.'

There have been relatively few cases, however, at least in the field of medical negligence, where the maxim has been utilised. One of the few to consider it, *Mahon* v *Osborne* [1939] 2 KB 14, was a majority decision on facts which to some would cry out for an explanation (see also the comments of Denning LJ in *Garner* v *Morrell* (1953) *The Times*, 31 October 1953).

After an abdominal operation, there was the usual swab count and the surgeon was informed by a theatre nurse that the right number of swabs had been recovered. The patient underwent a further operation some two months later when a swab was found. It was generally accepted that the subsequent death of the patient was due to the fact that the swab was left in the body for that amount of time. The swab count system was explained in court and was found to be a satisfactory one. The plaintiff obviously sought to rely on *res ipsa loquitur*. In the Court of Appeal the doctor's appeal against the award of damages failed.

Scott LJ, in a dissenting judgment, made a clear statement of judicial antipathy toward the widespread utilisation of the doctrine, which his lordship felt would mean that the plaintiff would need little evidence before the defendant was put to proof that the injury was not due to negligence on the defendant's part. Scott LJ appeared to feel that this was releasing the plaintiff from the duty to provide some positive evidence of breach of duty. While criticising its potential application to all 'swab cases', Scott LJ stated that the maxim would apply where:

. . . it is an inference which the reasonable man knowing the facts would naturally draw, and that is in most cases for two reasons (1) because the control over the happening of such an event rested solely with the defendant, and (2) that in the ordinary experience of mankind such an event does not happen unless the person in control has failed to exercise due care.

There was a strong hint of judicial protectionism and professed ignorance in the comment of Scott LJ, that the judge was in no position to consider the complexities of an abdominal operation. There would be dangers to the medical profession in judges making inferences of fact from complex events. McKinnon LJ felt rather more confident that one of the five people involved in the operation must have been negligent. Goddard LJ sought comfort in a more limited application of *res ipsa loquitur* on the ground that the surgeon had been in overall charge, and therefore had control over events.

So, the majority of the Court of Appeal in this case felt that the doctor should be required to provide an explanation for what happened.

More recently there has been some evidence of less antipathy towards utilising the maxim to put the defendant to an explanation. In *Saunders* v

Leeds Western Health Authority (1985) 82 LS Gaz 1491 a four-year-old girl had an operation for a congenitally dislocated hip. During the course of this operation the child's heart stopped and the attempts to start it again only proved successful after 35–40 minutes. The child was found thereafter to be suffering from brain damage, quadriplegia and blindness. Mann J considered that the fact that the plaintiff relied on *res ipsa loquitur* made it unnecessary for her to rely on suggesting a specific cause for the cardiac arrest. 'It is plain from the evidence that the heart of a fit child does not arrest under anaesthesia if proper care is taken in the anaesthetic and surgery processes.' (See also *Glass v Cambridge Health Authority* (1995) 6 Med LR 91.)

The general uneasiness in medical negligence cases towards this plaintiff-friendly doctrine is based on the fact that often the activities undertaken are high-risk. That something has gone wrong should not automatically mean that the plaintiff is bound to provide an explanation. In *Whitehouse v Jordan* [1980] 1 All ER 650 Lord Denning MR responded to the argument that:

> In getting [the head] wedged or stuck, or unwedged and unstuck, Mr Jordan caused asphyxia which in turn caused the cerebral palsy. In this respect Mr Jordan fell below the very high standard of professional competence that the law required of him. The first sentence suggests that, because the baby suffered damage, therefore Mr Jordan was at fault. In other words *res ipsa loquitur*. That would be an error. In a high-risk case, damage during birth is quite possible, even though all care is used. No inference of negligence should be drawn from it.

As most medical procedures and operations are high-risk the maxim will rarely be applied for the benefit of the patient (see *Howard* v *Wessex Regional Health Authority* (1994) 5 Med LR 57).

More recently still there has been an acknowledgement that with the changes underway to reform personal injury litigation as a whole, including the combination of cost-cutting efficiency in the process of litigation with the efficient, and one would argue just, 'cards on the table' pre-trial disclosure of information between plaintiff and defendant, the need for recourse to *res ipsa loquitur* may not be particularly necessary. In *Bull v Devon Area Health Authority* (1993) 4 Med LR 117 there was a suggestion that the length of the delay before the doctor came from the other site to check on the patient was such as to raise an inference of negligence. Mustill LJ replied that there was no need to look deeply into the matter, as there was sufficient evidence before the court to enable it to make a decision without recourse to presumptions (now see also *Fallows v Randle*, 7 May 1996).

There is some confusion about the precise effect of the invocation of the maxim. Does it shift the burden of proof on to the defendant? In *Ng Chun Pui v Lee Chuen Tat* [1988] RTR 298 it was stated that the burden of proving the negligence still rested on the plaintiff. The Privy Council found that 'the so-called doctrine of *res ipsa loquitur* . . . is no more than the use of a Latin maxim to describe the state of the evidence from which it is proper to draw the inference of negligence'.

4.4 LEGALLY RECOGNISED DAMAGE

Although this will frequently be obvious, and therefore no stumbling block for the plaintiff in the medical negligence case who has managed the other legal hurdles, there may be instances where the relatives or friends may suffer emotional or psychiatric damage from the effects of the medical negligence on the primary victim. We have already seen the difficulties of claiming nervous shock resulting from the negligent damage to a partner or child. There is residual suspicion of the authenticity of psychiatric illness allegedly caused by medical negligence. This is not peculiar to medical negligence claims, but is a current problem for the general law of tort.

4.4 CONCLUSION

Any criticism of the current medical negligence aspects of standard of care and causation lead back to the inadequacies of the test in *Bolam* v *Friern Hospital Management Committee* [1957] 1 WLR 582. Montrose ('Is Negligence an Ethical or a Sociological Concept?' (1958) 21 MLR 259) showed the confusion that was possible with the development of the *Bolam* test, and has been proved correct. The test confuses what is done with what ought to be done.

> The question of negligence is one of what *ought* to be done in the circumstances, not what *is* done in similar circumstances by most people or even by all people. In so far as negligence is concerned with what ought to be done, it may be called an ethical concept: in so far as it is concerned with what is done, with practice, it may be said to be a sociological concept. (Montrose, op. cit.)

A good medical law is an ethical law. There needs to be judicial acknowledgement of this ethical dimension of negligence.

Historically issues of professional standards of doctors were predicated on the powerful yet independent status of the doctor. The *Bolam* test is a culmination of the isolation and power of the medical profession. Now medical law is entering a new phase of development, which might be termed 'the rights phase'. In this new era of medical law, within a framework of rights-based autonomy, the *Bolam* test is likely to be increasingly questioned because it is from a previous incarnation of medical law, based on paternalism rather than bilateralism.

It is tempting to make *Bolam* the 'fault' of the medical profession. This would be unfair. The judiciary have offered and re-offered doctors the opportunity to set the legal standard of care of the profession. It has been gratefully accepted. How many professions would do otherwise? Teff considers the place of *Bolam* succinctly:

> All in all, the enormous influence that was to be exerted by *Bolam*, a suspect first-instance decision based on a somewhat confusing jury

direction, remains one of the more remarkable features of medical law. (*Reasonable Care* (Oxford: Clarendon Press, 1994), p. 194)

Bolam was really a 'child of its time'. McNair J, in formulating the test, was acutely aware of the strains that were being placed on the medical profession and the hospitals. Rumours of defensive medicine and the threat of litigation, combined with the increasing availability of legal aid, created an atmosphere within which his lordship saw a need to protect the medical profession, without recognising the potential cost to the plaintiff.

The future of *Bolam* is now uncertain. Other jurisdictions have started to chip away at its applicability to the many areas of medical law that have referred to it. Subsequent chapters will reveal less than wholehearted approval of *Bolam* in the context of disclosure of information and medical risks. In Australia and Canada this has been accelerating, in England rather stalling judicial questioning appears again to be the norm.

The issues of standard of care, causation and also duty of care, considered in chapters 3 and 4, reveal the need for general reform of medical negligence. This reform aspect has received considerable attention. It would be prudent to point to a few of these ideas.

The Pearson Report (Royal Commission on Civil Liability and Compensation for Personal Injury, *Report* Cmnd 7054) (London: HMSO, 1978)) noted that, at the time of reporting, to some 30–40 per cent of medical negligence claims were successful, against an 86 per cent success rate in other personal injury litigation. The main 'culprits' for this lower success rate were the difficulties of proving causation, and the process of evidence gathering. The latter has largely been sorted out (see 2.11.3), but not the former, which, if anything, has become more of a problem after *Bolitho* v *City and Hackney Health Authority* (1993) 4 Med LR 381 (CA); affirmed [1997] 3 WLR 1151 (HL).

Pearson was not well disposed to the proposal that the burden of proof in medical negligence cases be reversed. To make the defendant doctor prove lack of negligence on the balance of probabilities would increase the number of groundless claims, and lead to the practice of defensive medicine.

There was a suggestion that medical negligence be a matter of strict liability. This would avoid the problems of proving negligence, but not of the plaintiff still having to prove that the damage would not have occurred in any event. A regime of strict liability would also lead itself to the practice of defensive medicine. It would: 'imply rigid standards of professional skill beyond those which the present law requires to be exhibited, and beyond those which (in our view) can fairly be expected' (Pearson Report, para. 1338).

An idea popular at the time in Sweden and New Zealand, of no-fault compensation – compensation from the State for the mere fact of medical injury, however caused – was also rejected for many ethical, economic and practical reasons. Significantly, Pearson noted that no-fault compensation would still not solve the problem of causation. Science might be able to establish more causal relationships, but scientific developments reveal and create more complex interactions of events. It will remain difficult to distinguish between a medical accident (which would be compensated) and the natural development of a disease or illness (which would not).

Reform appears difficult to initiate in a drastic form. Medical negligence, it is hoped, will evolve into the new legal culture of patient rights and doctor duties.

Further reading

Harris, N., 'Medical Negligence Litigation: The Need for Reform' (1992) 60 Medico-Legal Journal 205.
Howie, R. B. M., 'The Standard of Care in Medical Negligence' [1983] JR 193.
Jones, M. A., 'Medical Negligence – The Burden of Proof' (1984) 134 NLJ 7.
Price, D. P. T., 'Causation – The Lords' Lost Chance' (1989) 38 ICLQ 735.
Robertson, G., '*Whitehouse* v *Jordan* – Medical Negligence Retried' (1981) 44 MLR 457.
Stapleton, J., 'The Gist of Negligence' (1988) 104 LQR 389.

FIVE

Medical negligence III: defective drugs and medical products

5.1 INTRODUCTION

A vast array of drugs and products is now available for the treatment of patients. The patient who would have died only a few years ago of cancer can now survive with the assistance of powerful pharmaceutical developments. Available drugs range from cough medicines, through those that can lower blood pressure, to life-saving immunosuppressants to protect the body from rejecting a transplant organ (see 16.6 for the importance of this development). A million and one examples of pharmaceutical and medical product breakthroughs can be given. It is, then, one of the most dynamic aspects of medicine. It is also, however an area where patient gains can be great but patient losses equally dramatic. As technology develops, the complex interactions between the human body and the medicine prescribed increase. The ability of the body to deal with a particular biochemical introduction is less easy to predict confidently. The drugs that are able to deal with life-threatening illness also increase the possibility of something else going wrong. One only has to consider the dramatic legal and medical history of Thalidomide – a drug meant to help pregnant women suffering from morning sickness, but which resulted in the birth of physically deformed children – to see that there are burdens in this aspect of medicine, as well as obvious benefits. Allegations have increased over the years that drugs have come on to the market without sufficient testing, poor manufacturing or sufficient warning about possible side-effects. Equally claims have been made in relation to products, such as the intrauterine device (IUD), the Dalcon Shield and even silicone breast implants.

It has been persuasively argued that the increase in such claims is another element in the litigation explosion, considered at the start of chapter 3. The increase in mass drug injury claims has pushed the pharmaceutical companies' activities into the national press. While the existence of this explosive element is no doubt true, medical law relating to defective drugs and products is important as a platform for debating the massive area of consumer protection and the political, economic and philosophical theories of the whole of the law of tort. There is a vast array of literature on consumer protection which considers the issues from a wide spectrum. While these works are more comprehensive analyses than is possible here, it would be rather strange to have no mention of the legal and ethical issues relating to the design and manufacture of medicines in a work on medical law. The law of consent also has a place in consideration of defective drugs law; allegations being as much about not being told enough of the risks to make an assessment on treatment as any defect in the drug.

The Consumer Protection Act 1987, which is the main consideration of this chapter, has been promoted as the third phase of tort law. Before *Donoghue v Stevenson* [1932] AC 562, the common law had been predicated on the privity of contract rule. Prior to that 1932 decision the law of tort had been extremely sympathetic to the industrial and commercial interests of producers of goods. As a strict law of negligence with regard to product development and manufacture would have had an inhibitive effect on economic and industrial expansion, the rights of potential plaintiffs had to take a back seat, in order to secure this development. During this time, allegations of negligence against sellers of goods had to be accompanied by evidence, brought by the injured party, of an undertaking as to the merchantability of those goods. *Donoghue v Stevenson* denoted the start of a phase which did not require this contractual closeness for tortious liability for personal injury. All that was required for liability was fault, and a relationship of legal 'neighbourhood' between manufacturer and consumer. The 1987 Act was contended to produce a new phase of tort law based on strict liability. That it has not done this will become clear. In addition, this area of medical law is a clear indication of the influence and tensions that come from membership of the European Community. David Howarth confirms that:

> the intention of the statute was to go further than to reform the common law and to reintroduce it in statutory form. The intention was to create a different form of liability that plaintiffs would be able to use in addition to their common law rights. The [Act] was enacted to fulfil the United Kingdom's obligations . . . concerning liability for defective products. The Act provides explicitly that it shall be construed so that it complies with the [product liability Directive]. This provision may become very important since . . . the Act diverges in significant detail from the Directive. (*Textbook on Tort* (London: Butterworths, 1995), pp. 392–3)

Before looking at the ethical debate on what should motivate medical law here – the deontological tradition of absolutes, or the utilitarianism of benefits and burdens – consider how medical law might react to the following fictitious situations:

(a) Bio Line Ltd has been developing a drug which it is anticipated will cure the common cold. Research shows that the drug can cause severe vomiting in one in 10,000 people who take it, and prove fatal to one in 100,000. The company decides to manufacture the drug, but with only a warning about the risk of vomiting, not the risk of fatality, because it is believed that advertising the risk of death would destroy sales, and mean that those who would not suffer side-effects would not take the drug.

(b)   Res Tech Ltd, a UK company, has developed a drug which will delay the onset of AIDS for a considerable period. There appears to be no severe side-effect and the drug is cheap to produce. Unknown to the research scientists, an Australian journal has recently produced a controversial article which details tests on laboratory rats with a similar compound, with the rats suffering 90 per cent mortality from taking the drug. Res Tech produces its drug, but six months later the company is referred to the article by one of its scientists. On the same day reports begin to come in about fatalities of AIDS patients who have been put on the drug. There is no conclusive evidence as to the precise cause of each death.

5.2   ETHICAL DIMENSIONS OF DRUG DEVELOPMENT

It is evident, then, that as much as medical law is here concerned with the traditional mainstays of medical negligence – namely duty of care, breach of that duty and the breach causing legally recognised damage – it is about moral theories and ethical concepts too. Where other aspects of medical law focus on the rights of patients and the duties of doctors, here the focus is on the patient's rights as a consumer and the pharmaceutical company's duty as the producer of a potentially or actually defective or dangerous product. One should not, however, forget that doctors are still legally involved; after all a vast majority of drugs are prescribed by the medical profession. The modern state of medicine is one of consumerism. Many doctors are being pulled in different ethical directions by the growing perception that they may be in possession of less than objective information about the efficacy of new drugs from companies promoting their products in the face of ever-increasing competition (for a useful analysis of this issue see J. Collier, 'Conflicts between Pharmaceutical Company Largesse and Patients' Rights' (1992) 60 Medico-Legal Journal 243).

Theories of absolute duty (see 1.3.2) would point the pharmaceutical company toward actions which appear to go against the profit and therapeutic motive of drug development. Those theories argue that there is a duty *never* to produce a drug that may be harmful to a patient, or *always* to inform the consumer of any danger or defect. But the company, in doing the right thing in not producing such a drug, or withdrawing it from the market on discovering a defect or danger, is still caught up in a moral dilemma of medicine. The one in 10,000 patient might be saved from death or injury (itself highly speculative), but what of the countless patients who would have been helped or saved by the manufacture of the drug? The deontological theory of absolutes is seen once more as one-dimensional. A slightly different argument on product liability and moral theory comes from Howarth (*Textbook on Tort* (London: Butterworths, 1995)), and is based on the idea that a moral duty on the pharmaceutical company is itself founded on the fact that to state that someone is under a duty 'implies a belief that it is possible for the person to fulfil that duty – in other words that ought implies can'. The significance of this maturing of the deontological argument is that:

> If the defendant could not possibly have foreseen the harm, it makes no sense to say that he ought to have prevented it. It also points to opposition to liability without causation, since under such a rule it is also possible for defendants to be held liable in circumstances in which the defendant could not have prevented the damage. (p. 403)

It would be unjust to hold a manufacturer of a drug which is later found to be hazardous responsible in the absence of such knowledge when the drug was 'made'. The law cannot, the argument goes, be based on blaming those who are not aware of the morality (or lack) of actions. Res Tech Ltd cannot be regarded as having done the 'wrong' thing, because it did not have full knowledge of the nature of the act. Bio Line Ltd knew whether it was doing the right thing or not because it was in possession of all the relevant factors. There can be no moral sanction where nothing could be done to stop the event happening.

Medical law in relation to defective drugs and products, perhaps more starkly than any other area under consideration, is an example of utilitarianism. The Consumer Protection Act 1987 clearly bases civil liability on the benefits and burdens of the production of particular drugs or products. What needs to be understood is that medical law could utilise the benefits and burdens argument in two contrasting ways. As a purely moral idea the argument has been seen that the 'good' law is one which achieves the correct balance between the rights of the individual and the rights of other members of society. A consumer protection law, to be a good law, should maximise freedom of action, while maintaining the freedom of all. The calculation is the difficult part. Look at example (a) above again. What should the law do? That there may well be no unanimity indicates that the moral theory of benefits and burdens also fails to solve the dilemma.

A different way of looking at the utiliarianism of benefits and burdens, according to Howarth, is to use the well-worn but modern phrase, 'the polluter pays'. The perspective slightly shifts then, and stays on the manufacturer. It is not the benefit and burden to the patient. The pharmaceutical company takes the profits from the product, and should therefore accept the losses that might be occasioned by it. This would be so 'regardless of whether the harm was foreseeable or only preventable at great cost' (at p. 403). Overall, then, the moral arguments once more point in different directions, which themselves here are also frustratingly unclear. It may well be that the moral answer to the above situations depends once more on the other life-influences of the reader. Overall one has to be content to acknowledge again that:

> The principle that ought implies can see morality in terms of individuals doing right or wrong. The benefit and burden principle belongs to a world

of social obligation in which right and wrong consist of acknowledging or not acknowledging debts owed to other people which have been created by the help they have given one because of the same principle. (Howarth, op. cit., p. 404)

A significant ethical and in fact legal factor in drug development is this utilitarianism of cost and benefit. There is in existence in the development of drugs something known as the 'conscious and deliberate design compromise'. The favoured principle here is a form of precarious balancing act between the potential risks presented by a product and the anticipated benefits. The Committee on the Safety of Medicines, a powerful force in the licensing of new drugs (see below for the licensing scheme) exemplified the problem by arguing, 'How does one weigh a slightly increased risk of mortality against the easing of crippling arthritic pain?'

In seeking to understand the issue of liability for defective drugs or medical products, one has to be aware of the common law issues that can surface. There is one key reason for looking at the common law before the changes wrought by the 1987 Act. There is the argument that the Act itself has not really changed the common law that much. For example, it is widely viewed that there now exists a statutory regime of 'watered down strict liability to a point where it adds very little to ordinary principles of liability for negligence under the common law' (Charles Lewis, *Medical Negligence*, 2nd ed. (Croydon: Tolley, 1992), p. 394). A description of medical law relating to defective drugs could just consider the current statutory scheme. An evaluation of that law needs to look at what the Act was supposed to change, and whether it succeeded.

5.3 THE COMMON LAW

Any number of things can happen to a drug or medical product between the idea and the end-use by the patient. The drug could simply have been poorly designed so as to prove an unreasonable hazard to those who would use it. There may have been some failing in the manufacturing process itself. For example, a batch of tablets could have become contaminated by the leaking of lubrication fluid from the processing machine into the tablet mix. The standard expected of the manufacturing process as a matter of the common law would be that of the reasonably competent manufacturer. The third form of potential common law liability is shown by the first example given at the start of the chapter. The pharmaceutical company may be under a duty to inform those who might take the tablets or use the product of the risks associated with it.

Consider how the common law and any future legislation might react to the following situation. This scenario also indicates the complexities of sorting out cause as much as duty or breach issues.

Dav Co. manufactures an inhaler for use by asthmatics which eases the symptoms of breathlessness. There is a small percentage danger that the use of the drug can cause temporary irregular heartbeat. During the process of manufacturing the inhaler, one of Dav Co.'s employees accidently hits a lever with his arm and for two hours inhalers are produced of slightly irregular shape. The Company does not withdraw them.

Meanwhile Org Co. manufactures the capsules which go into the inhaler. They are sealed capsules, which are broken inside the inhaler by the patient just before use. During the sealing process, one of the machines is left untended and does not completely seal the capsules. This is not noticed until all of the week's production has been dispatched across the country and into EC member States. The company decides the risk of harm is virtually non-existent, and does not recall the capsules.

Doug, a pharmacist, on receipt of prescriptions, hands over inhalers and a supply of capsules to a patient. One day he notices stains on his hands after handling the capsules. He dismisses this, and carries on handing out the inhalers and capsules.

Some months later doctors in a number of countries note that asthmatic children are suffering fatal heart attacks. On testing one of the inhalers of a fatality, it is found that the compound inside the capsule is contaminated and that the inhaler shape shatters the capsule and releases small plastic pellets along with the compound.

While the search for a satisfactory legal solution might be difficult, the common law issues should be clear. The classic case for the tort lawyer, *Donoghue v Stevenson* [1932] AC 562, is a useful staging post in considering the common law here, as the 'snail in the ginger beer bottle' case was obviously one of an allegation of product liability causing physical injury. The case involved the broad issues of negligence liability, as well as a matter of particular relevance here, the role of intermediate inspection of goods. The classic statement of Lord Atkin is particularly apposite here:

> . . . a manufacturer of products, which he sells in such a form as to show that he intends them to reach the ultimate consumer in the form in which they left him with no reasonable possibility of intermediate examination, and with the knowledge that the absence of reasonable care in the preparation or putting up of the products will result in an injury to the consumer's life or property, owes a duty to the consumer to take that reasonable care. (p. 599)

It is therefore apparent that when a manufacturer of a product comes voluntarily within a relationship to another, it has a duty to exercise reasonable skill, for example, by placing warnings on medicinal products. There is not just a duty to provide such a warning, there is a duty to have a warning of a sufficient standard to inform of a danger. This is a comparative test, dependent on the level of the danger. The intermediate inspection (in the example above, the pharmacist) has to be reasonably probable, according to Lord Atkin, for the manufacturer to escape liability.

The real difficulty for the common law here is to prove what actually occurred and what should have occurred. Look at the situation again. What caused the fatal heart attacks? Was it the compound? Was it the plastic? Was it the plastic combined with the compound? Was it because of the failure to put a warning on both products? Was it a failure of the pharmacist to check on the medicines that were being handed out? Was it a natural event in each case? The crux of the issue for product liability at common law is: What happened? and Whose fault was it? Sometimes as a matter of evidence the operative cause of the physical damage will be obvious, but particularly where pharmaceuticals are concerned this will not always be the case. According to the line of authority from *Grant* v *Australian Knitting Mills* [1936] AC 85, 'if the plaintiff can show that it is unlikely that anything that happened to the product after it left the manufacturer's control made it dangerous, the court should conclude that the defect must have arisen during manufacture' (Howarth, *Textbook on Tort* (London: Butterworths, 1995), p. 432). If the system is declared to be a foolproof one, the presumption is that there had to be negligence on the part of someone in creating the defect, or failing to spot it. The other line of authority (from *Daniels* v *R. White and Sons Ltd* [1938] 4 All ER 258) holds that where the system is practically foolproof, liability points away from the manufacturing process. This latter approach is the more realistic, as the other points towards a notion of strict liability. This still does not help in answering the basic question of what caused the fatal heart attacks. The common law of causation having already been described (see 4.3), it is only necessary to repeat that causation remains the main stumbling block in many a medical negligence action, whether against a doctor or a pharmaceutical company. The broad language of 'material contribution' and 'material increase of risk of damage' hinders rather than helps.

Common law actions involving defective drugs being something of a rarity in Britain, an example of the general issues that can be involved in such cases comes from the Canadian case of *Buchan* v *Ortho Pharmaceuticals (Canada) Ltd* (1986) 54 OR (2d) 92. The case involved an allegation against Ortho that it should have warned and should have known that there was a link between a particular oral contraceptive and strokes. It is apparent that the Ontario Court of Appeal had high expectations of the manufacturers of pharmaceutical products. Robins JA said that the duty of the company was to keep up with developments in the field of manufacturing particular pharmaceuticals. This duty does not end at manufacture, but is a continuing one. Where subsequent research highlights dangers, there is a duty incumbent on such a manufacturer to warn those who might be affected. The level of warning depends on a number of factors – but essentially it is what is reasonable in the particular circumstances. Some examples of relevant factors might be: the number of people who might be harmed by the drug, the level of the injury that might be suffered or the overall benefit the drug will have to the public as a whole. As Robins JA put it, 'the graver the danger, the higher the duty'. The evidence in the case was that there was a wealth of scientific literature which discussed the contraceptive–stroke link, and should have put the manufacturer on guard. The court, in discussing the level of information required for there to be an effective warning repeated the views of Laskin J in *Lambert* v *Lastoplex Chemicals Co. Ltd* (1972) 25 DLR (3d) 121:

Where manufactured products are put on the market for ultimate purchase and use by the general public and carry danger, . . . although put to the use for which they are intended, the manufacturer, knowing of their hazardous nature, has a duty to specify the attendant dangers, which it must be taken to appreciate in a detail not known to the ordinary consumer or user. A general warning, as for example, that the product is inflammable, will not suffice where the likelihood of fire may be increased according to the surroundings in which it may reasonably be expected that the product will be used. The required explicitness of the warning will, of course, vary with the danger likely to be encountered in the ordinary use of the product. (p. 125)

This fairly onerous duty is tempered by the rule encountered earlier, that with modern distribution of drugs being through GP and pharmacist, there is a duty on those parties to satisfy themselves as to the appropriateness of the particular drug for the patient. The legal place of the GP has been described here as that of the 'learned intermediary', from US product liability case law, whereas, with the pharmaceutical company which supplies direct to the patient (for example, cough medicine) there is a direct duty to that person. Where prescription drugs are concerned, the company has the duty of candour, research and warning to the prescribing doctor. Once more it should be said that although this view is correct as a matter of common law, it must be acknowledged that manufacturers and doctors can find commercial pressure confronting professional duties to patient or ultimate consumer. Modern drug selling is high-pressure, and the common law duty of candour may fall by the wayside, particularly where a company is deciding on what risk ought to be disclosed to the doctor, who will effectively be buying the drug for the patient. In addition it should be noted that there are grey areas for the common law where drugs like contraceptives are in issue. While they are prescription drugs their relative popularity, lack of complexity and the fact that prescriptions run for considerable periods of time without physician input, may mean that the patient is owed a direct duty by the manufacturer. Indeed, this was the decision of the Ontario Court of Appeal in *Buchan v Ortho Pharmaceuticals (Canada) Ltd.*

In general terms, then, the major stumbling block will be for the common law to decide what level of information disclosure is reasonable in the particular circumstances of the pharmaceutical in question. The question of whether the duty owed by the manufacturer is to the GP or directly to the patient is unlikely to prove particularly troublesome. The two major difficulties for a plaintiff alleging negligence have been the fact that the defendant points to the fact that at the time the drug was made, the technology and diagnostic knowledge was not at a level where the risk or defect could have been detected. It simply was not reasonably foreseeable. The common law has decided that in assessing fault the court cannot look backwards, or, as Denning LJ argued in *Roe v Minister of Health* [1954] 2 QB 66, 'We must not look at a 1947 accident with 1954 spectacles'. It was this aspect of the common law that provided some of the motivation for the development of both the product liability Directive and the Consumer Protection Act 1987.

5.4 DRUG LICENSING

After the public outcry over thalidomide, the Medicines Act 1968 bolstered the already established Committee on the Safety of Medicines (CSM) by making it compulsory to test and vet new drugs that were approaching the market place. The Secretary of State for Health holds the reins of licence by reason of s. 6 of the Act, although many of the Secretary of State's enforcement powers under the Act are delegated both to the Committee on the Safety of Medicines (CSM) and the Royal Pharmaceutical Society. The Act controls manufacture, market and import. None of these activities can be undertaken without a licence. The manufacturing process is controlled by s. 7, which requires a clinical trial certificate to be in existence in relation to the particular drug in question. This will allow patient trials. After this stage a product licence is required before the drug can be marketed.

Section 2 of the Act provides for a specialist body, known as the Medicines Commission, to advise the Secretary of State generally on licensing matters. Specialist subcommittees in turn provide the core advice, with the CSM being one of them. Section 4 of the Act gives the CSM a central role in the licensing scheme by providing that it promotes the collection of data on adverse reactions to drugs. The Minister has no right to give a product licence without consultation with the CSM.

The CSM is directed by the legislation to look at matters such as the quality of the drug, particularly in terms of its manufacture and distribution. The CSM also considers the usefulness or efficacy of the drug for the purpose for which it is marketed.

The Secretary of State can revoke a product licence where there is evidence that the drug is no longer efficacious or no longer safe. If the CSM decides that a licence should be revoked, but the Secretary of State disagrees, an independent inquiry can be set up. Any decision of the CSM can also be scrutinised by the Medicines Commission.

There are a number of key phases in the development of new drugs, and the process itself appears to be an arduous one for those involved. The development is regulated by a 'phased' process. Phase I trials are the first tests of the drug on human subjects (animal tests are controlled by the Animals (Scientific Procedures) Act 1986). There are some difficulties involved in this phase. The legislation does not actually cover this phase as the drug is not yet a 'medicine' so as to be caught by the provisions of the 1968 Act. It would seem then that the testing must accord with the general law of consent. Here, as in donation of organs from one patient to another (see 16.6.1.1), the concept that a person cannot consent to a harmful event would preclude a volunteer being able to give the necessary consent, as a phase I trial aims to indicate the maximum tolerance the subject has for the drug; i.e., at some stage the test will prove harmful. As one might expect, this has not been tested in the courts. The next phase (II) checks the medical impact of the drug at the acceptable tolerance level indicated in phase I. If there appear to be uses for the drug, the phase III trials consider the benefits of this drug alongside existing treatments. It is after phase I that a licence will be required to continue with development.

This system appears on the surface to be rigorous, but in reality to have been remarkably ineffective in scrutinising drug development. A great deal of the information to enable the CSM to grant a product licence comes from the manufacturers themselves. To the pharmaceutical companies, the system of licensing is crude yet bureaucratic and is argued to increase the costs of drug production, eventually passed on to the consumer.

5.5 PRODUCT LIABILITY DIRECTIVE

This Directive (85/474) became effective in 1985, but was the product of a great deal of negotiation. There was a strong political element to the debate, but, more importantly for present purposes, was based on a shift of attitude which recognised that the difficulties for a plaintiff suing a pharmaceutical company were virtually insurmountable in a fault-based legal system. According to Howarth (*Textbook on Tort* (London: Butterworths, 1995), pp. 406–9) there was also a strong influence from the USA. The Restatement (Second) of Torts, s. 402A, had established what at first blush looked like strict liability – liability without having to prove that the manufacturer was at fault. The prerequisites were that the product had to be sold in the course of a business, there had to be a defect which made that product unreasonably dangerous to those who used it and it had to have reached the injured person without being substantially changed between manufacture and use. If this was the case, then there would be liability even where the manufacturer could prove that all possible care had been exercised in design and manufacture. The development of US law after this suggested strongly that there was a benefits and burdens calculation going on, and therefore a watering down of the apparent strictness of the rule. Note that the defect has to make the product 'unreasonably dangerous'. This suggests that there are some dangers that the law will regard as acceptable. If a US court had to consider the examples at the beginning of this chapter, it might consider that the 1 in 10,000 risk of vomiting is a 'reasonable danger'. Other developments, such as the 'state of the art' defence, reduced strict liability by reintroducing foreseeability into the liability equation. The US pattern is important to note as unfortunately it has foreshadowed the reaction of the UK government and a number of others in interpreting the attempt as a form of strict liability in the Directive.

Article 1 of the Directive simply states that 'The producer shall be liable for damage caused by a defect in his product'. This certainly appears to be strict liability. The only similarity between this and the common law is that there is still a need to prove that the damage was *caused* by the defect. Of itself no easy matter where complex pharmaceuticals are concerned. The crucial word in art. 1 is 'defect'. This appears a simple enough term. Consider, however, whether a new drug to combat the common cold, with a small percentage risk attached to its use has a 'defect'. Article 6 defines the term by saying that:

A product is defective when it does not provide the safety which a person is entitled to expect, taking all circumstances into account, including:

(a) the presentation of the product;

(b) the use to which it could reasonably be expected that the product would be put;

(c) the time when the product was put into circulation.

It has been noted frequently that the term 'entitled to expect' can mean a number of different things. To go back to the first example. Is a person entitled to expect 100 per cent safety from a new drug to cure the common cold? If not how much safety is one entitled to expect? I might expect such a drug to be safe if there is no risk of death, but a small risk of some temporary discomfort; another might accept the small risk of death. Of course, art. 6 does put some gloss on the notion of defect. Paragraph (b) introduces a rule requiring less than absolute safety. Paragraph (c) shows similarities to the US development that equates liability with foreseeability. This is reinforced by art. 6(2) which states:

A product shall not be considered defective for the sole reason that a better product is subsequently put into circulation.

Therefore if, five years after Bio Line develops its cold cure (with its attendant risks), Cold Co. develops one with no appreciable risk of death and a risk of slight upset stomach of 1 in 100,000, this is not in itself proof that the earlier product is defective.

Perhaps the most significant undermining of the intention that the Directive would usher in a phase of strict liability for defective drugs and medical products comes from art. 7. This provides for a number of defences for the producer of a defective drug:

The producer shall not be liable as a result of this Directive if he proves:

(a) that he did not put the product into circulation; or

(b) that, having regard to the circumstances, it is probable that the defect which caused the damage did not exist at the time when the product was put into circulation by him or that this defect came into being afterwards; or

(c) that the product was neither manufactured by him for sale or any form of distribution for economic purpose nor manufactured or distributed by him in the course of his business; or

(d) that the defect is due to compliance of the product with mandatory regulations issued by the public authorities; or

(e) that the state of scientific and technical knowledge at the time when he put the product into circulation was not such as to enable the defect to be discovered; or

(f) in the case of a manufacturer of a component, that the defect is attributable to the design of the product in which the component has been fitted or to the instructions given by the manufacturer of the product.

While all elements of art. 7 are significant for the producer of pharmaceutical products, the main focus of the Directive and its subsequent reinterpretation in the Consumer Protection Act 1987 is that afforded by para. (e). This has an obvious similarity with the US 'state of the art' defence. Note carefully what is required for this defence to be effective. It is for the producer to prove that the state of scientific and technical knowledge was not in existence. No mention is made of any reasonableness requirement. The producer will not be able to argue that the time and additional expense of discovering a particular defect was such as to make the product unprofitable. In addition art. 7(e) is not expressed in term's of the manufacturer's knowledge. It could be argued that art. 7(e) will not be available where the knowledge to enable the defect to be discovered was available somewhere.

Article 15 permits member States to omit the art. 7(e) defence from their national legislation implementing the Directive, but only Luxembourg has done so. All other EU States have provided the art. 7(e) defence because of the enormous shield it represents to producers of pharmaceuticals. Article 7(e) has been considered by many to be too severe a test for such a producer, and the compromise that is contained in the Consumer Protection Act 1987 has been fashioned with that lobby group very much in mind.

5.6 CONSUMER PROTECTION ACT 1987

Barry Cotter (*Defective and Unsafe Products* (London: Butterworths, 1996)) introduces the relevant issues for medical law:

> Neither the Directive nor the Consumer Protection Act 1987 provides any special provision for pharmaceuticals or other medical products. Arguments were put forward that by the very nature of many 'drugs' damage may be caused to the system and strict liability could induce conservative practices which would in due course be to the disadvantage of the population as a whole. This view did not find favour. The position of such products will however be very different from the vast majority of other products and the questions as to whether a 'defect' existed and also the defence concerning the state of scientific and technical knowledge at the relevant time are likely in some cases to be extremely complicated.

As with the Directive, the important issues are the definition of 'defect' and the 'state of the art' or 'development risk' defence. Interpretation must be tentative because there has been no litigation on the Act concerning allegations of defective pharmaceuticals, and the tenor of the legislation, when compared with the Directive, makes prediction difficult.

5.6.1 'Defect'

The Consumer Protection Act 1987, like the Directive, provides that a product will have a defect where the 'safety of the product is not such as persons generally are entitled to expect' (s. 3(1)). The refinements of art. 6 of the Directive are reproduced in the Act, if phrased a little more acutely in relation to the element of 'presentation' of the product. The use of the term 'marketed' focuses attention more than the Directive on what a reasonable consumer would expect of the product; the benefits that would accrue from use rather than the hazards of that use. Section 3(2)(a) states instead that account is to be taken of:

> the manner in which, and purposes for which, the product has been marketed, its get-up, the use of any mark in relation to the product and any instructions for, or warnings with respect to, doing or refraining from doing anything with or in relation to the product.

As with the Directive, the notion of foreseeability is maintained by not making safety dependent on the fact that no later and safer product comes on to the market (see the final words of s. 3(2)). It does, however, seem to be more liberal than the Directive. The forerunner to s. 3(2) had simply stated that a product must not be regarded as defective just because a better product is later put into circulation. Section 3(2) concludes:

> and nothing in this section shall require a defect to be inferred from the fact alone that the safety of a product which is supplied after [the time when the product was supplied by its producer to another] is greater than the safety of the product in question.

As with the Directive there is no guidance on the term 'persons generally are entitled to expect'. One has to look behind the Act, at its purpose, to put some flesh on the bones of such a phrase. The Act, like the Directive, was designed to ease the burdens on plaintiffs who were hampered by the fault-based common law. The Act is both protective and facilitative. It protects the consumer from poorly designed, manufactured drugs. It facilitates compensation for those harmed by such pharmaceuticals. If that is kept in mind, then 'persons generally' are 'entitled to expect' a high level of safety and a low standard of proof of defect. The main problem with this section, and with the Act as a whole, is that it is not clear what exactly can be taken into account. What does the legislation do about the drug manufacturer who argues that consumers are only entitled to expect a reasonable standard of safety. That reasonable standard has to keep the economics of precautions in mind. The producer would argue that the consumer can only expect safety within a framework of reasonable profitability. The difficulty for the legislation is that it was intended to be consumer led, but is open to an interpretation that is producer led. Howarth inevitably sees the legislation as plotting something of a midway course, and:

> Its stance is that persons generally are entitled to expect that producers will not trade consumer safety off against their own profits, but they may trade off safety for some against benefit for others. (*Textbook on Tort* (London: Butterworths, 1995), p. 416).

5.6.2 Development risk defence

There has been a considerable analysis of this defence, which above all others can protect a producer of pharmaceuticals against extensive liability (see particularly Chris Newdick, 'The Development Risk Defence of the Consumer Protection Act 1987' [1988] CLJ 455). Article 7(e) of the Directive appeared to impose a strict test for the defendant producer to prove. The version of that article in s. 4(1)(e) of the Act looks somewhat different:

> In any civil proceedings by virtue of this Part against any person . . . in respect of a defect in a product it shall be a defence for him to show—
> (e) that the state of scientific and technical knowledge at the relevant time was not such that a producer of products of the same description as the product in question might be expected to have discovered the defect if it had existed in his products while they were under his control.

A comparison of the two shows some marked points of departure in the legislation. There had been considerable Parliamentary debate over what the introduction of the undiluted 'development risk' defence of art. 7(e) would do to the development of new drugs. The Act provides what is essentially a fault-based test of liability. If, at the time of the supply of the product, manufacturers of the same sort of products were not 'expected' to discover the defect because of the state of scientific and technical knowledge, then there is no liability. Making it a comparative exercise – judging the reasonableness of the particular producer's actions against those of colleagues in the same area of expertise – appears to be a legislative introduction of the *Bolam* test. Howarth again gets to the core of the issues in arguing that:

> . . . the state of the art defence allows the defendant to say that even though more investment in research may have pushed the state of knowledge on so far that the defect would have become discoverable, a producer of such products would not have been expected to make such an investment because it would have cost too much. (*Textbook on Tort*, p. 421)

The defence limits the kinds of research required of the manufacturer of pharmaceuticals. The Directive appeared to invoke the idea of a wide-ranging obligation to keep up with scientific and technological developments. The Act makes no such demands. A manufacturer will not be required to scour obscure journals, or even journals where there is a chance that some research might have implications for and applications to a different field.

Overall there is little disputing the fact that the development risk defence of the Consumer Protection Act 1987 has undermined the Directive. The Directive explicitly and knowingly excluded the term 'reasonable' because it preferred a strict approach. The producer should 'scour the planet' for information on the product, and not merely search for some illusory partner in a related industry. Drug monopolies are widespread. Most pharmaceutical companies design a drug, develop it, test it, market it and sell it. Direct comparison with other pharmaceutical companies is rarely possible and then only a theoretical exercise. The alternative view is that the Directive was mistaken in its appreciation about what such a defence was intended to achieve. This view holds that it is ridiculous to expect the producer to search every internal memorandum of any research scientist involved in the pharmaceutical field.

Recently the issue of whether the Consumer Protection Act 1987 properly implemented the Directive led to consideration by the European Court of Justice in infringement proceedings brought by the Commission against the UK (*Commission* v *UK* (case C-300/95) [1997] ECR I-2649; for more detail on this case, see P. Milne, 'Hope for Manufacturers of Defective Products' (1997) 147 NLJ 1437). The decision was that the UK courts were able to construe the section with the spirit of the Directive in mind. As Milne says, the European Court were suggesting that there was indeed a severe test of technical knowledge:

> In order for the relevant scientific and technical knowledge to be successfully pleaded as against the producer, that knowledge must have been accessible at the time when the product in question was put into circulation.

Nevertheless there is acknowledgement that it is still the case that the fact that the knowledge exists somewhere ought not to preclude reliance on the defence.

5.7 CONCLUSION

Throughout the debates on the Bill which became the Consumer Protection Act 1987, it was argued that the development risk defence would be a difficult one to invoke. Lord Lucas of Chilworth in the House of Lords stressed that:

> Only if the producer can prove to the court that he took all the steps that a producer of that kind might reasonably be expected to take, and that the state of scientific and technical knowledge would have allowed him to take, will the defence be of any value. (Hansard, HL 20 January 1987, col. 841)

Such an attempt at reassuring justification of the defence disguises the wider difficulties of it, particularly when combined with the legislation as a whole. If a particular branch of pharmaceuticals has a low research level, the defence is nevertheless available. Even if the producer may have not researched as expected, the plaintiff also has to prove that there was a defect, and that the defect caused the damage complained of. It is difficult to see the Consumer Protection Act 1987 as anything substantially more than legislating on a fault-based tort system for medical products. The allegation continues to be made that medical law in relation to pharmaceutical products invites overseas manufacturers to use Britain as a testing ground for products, with little fear of litigation.

Medical negligence actions are fraught with the difficulties engendered by the fault-based common law system; duty of care may be apparent whether the defendant is a doctor, hospital authority or manufacturer of pharmaceuticals. The standard expected of all these is based on allied professional practice. Inferences of causation are hard to make successfully in the medical law courtroom. To prove whether a drug caused death because of a discoverable fault, unacceptable risk never warned of or the peculiar reaction of the individual's body is often difficult, but medical law gives little assistance, whether by common law or statute. The litigation explosion (whether perceived as good or bad) is still merely apparent. To be real there needs to be an increase, not in claims, but in success. Current medical negligence in Britain country does not lend itself to plaintiff success.

Further reading

Newdick, C., 'The Development Risk Defence of the Consumer Protection Act 1987' [1988] CLJ 455.
Stolker, C. J., 'Objections to the Development Risk Defence' (1990) 9 Med Law 783.

SIX
Ethical and legal basis of consent

6.1 INTRODUCTION: CONSENT, ETHICS AND HUMAN RIGHTS

It is difficult, if not impossible, to understand medical law fully without a consideration and understanding of the breadth and significance of the concept of consent. There are few areas of medical law where the issue of its existence and scope is not of paramount importance. As already seen, a patient can consent to the release of confidential medical information about him- or herself. This consent makes lawful what would otherwise be a legally recognised breach of the confidence between doctor and patient. Whereas the confidential nature of the doctor–patient relationship has been seen as one of the aspects of medical law under pressure from the new language of patient rights and consumer choice, and medical negligence litigation as one of the battlegrounds for the old paternalism and the new liberalism of patient control over care, it would not be unfair to say that the true matter which ties together the whole spectrum of medical law issues is consent. It illustrates the dilemmas of moral philosophy, the place of human rights in medical care, the primary focus for 'doing the right thing' and respecting the patient's philosophical, ethical and intuitive right to self-determination. It is also the place where the dilemmas of modern medicine become most stark.

Consider how you would react, and how medical law would react, to the following circumstances, and then consider them again at the end of the chapter:

(a) Susan, who is 13 years old, has been in a serious car accident. She is rushed to hospital, conscious but in urgent need of a blood transfusion. When she is told of this she says, 'There is nothing for me on this world, I'll wait and see what's on the next one', and refuses the blood transfusion. All attempts to persuade her come to nothing, but all are convinced that Susan is lucid, if weak. The doctors decide to go ahead with the blood transfusion.

(b)   Albert, who appears to have been living on the streets, has been found by a police officer in an alleyway. He is taken to hospital and found to have pneumonia. When told that he needs treatment in hospital says, 'I know the implications of having pneumonia. I am, after all the famous surgeon, Dr Schwartz. Fresh air and good exercise, that's what's needed', and staggers out of the hospital. The doctors make no attempt to stop him.

(c)   Carol has been taken into hospital having been diagnosed as having the eating disorder anorexia nervosa. She is in the advanced stages of malnourishment and dehydration. On being told that she requires fluids immediately replies, 'Not now, let's see how I feel in a couple of days'. The doctors think her condition is reaching a critical phase and decide to force intravenous fluids into Carol against her weak physical and verbal struggles.

(d)   Helen has been rushed into hospital in premature labour. The unborn child is found to be in a 'breech' position and it is decided that there should be a Caesarean section. There will need to be an injection of anaesthetic to help the mother during the birth. Helen agrees to the Caesarean but cannot stand the thought of having a needle put in her; she has a phobia about needles. The doctors seek to persuade her that is in her interests and those of her child. She readily accepts this point, but each time she is approached with a needle she becomes hysterical and struggles. Dr Jones finally decides to have her physically restrained and injects her.

The Western tradition of moral philosophy stressed the freedom of the individual and the maximisation of that freedom of action in any way compatible with the freedom of others. Mill, it will be recalled, qualified that in an important way. Such freedom of action and respect for autonomy only applied to those 'in the maturity of their faculties'. The implication then was that those incapable of rational thought and expression were the 'underclass' who had no rights to equal treatment within society. To enjoy the libertarian regime promoted by utilitarianism made (and continues to make) it vital to be declared rational. Echoes of that need abound in the issue of who can consent as a matter of law to treatment.

The philosophical tradition of utilitarianism, despite having this major limiting facet, is important in the current structuring of the issues of who can consent to treatment. The concept of competence to consent, in practical terms for the doctor and current medical law, is predicated on the consequences of accepting the patient's demand. The doctor and the law will be seen to be more likely to 'accept' that a patient is rational in refusing consent to an intimate examination for the purposes of getting a health insurance certificate, than the patient who refuses a life-saving blood transfusion. It is the consequence which structures the question of rationality to consent.

On the other hand, deontology, the moral philosophy of absolutes, is at once simpler yet more difficult in practical terms. It is simple because the deontologist, respecting freedom, autonomy and the categorical imperative of 'Do unto others', will say, 'Do not treat the patient who refuses'. Another situation shows the practical difficulty:

(e)   John needs a blood transfusion after a car accident. He refuses on the ground that he is a Jehovah's Witness – a member of a religious group who believe that to have blood put into their bodies is a mortal sin against God. Mary, John's wife, pleads with the doctor, saying, 'If he dies the children and I will have no one'.

If John is not treated, there is respect for autonomy, but John's wife has not had moral rights accepted. Once more the deontologist misses the dilemma by ignoring the consequence.

Clinical intuition, it will be noted a number of times, structures consent on medical paternalism and patient welfare. Clinical intuition moves the issue away from the unfettered freedom of the patient to decide, because medicine has as its aim the restoration of patient autonomy, which has been taken away by illness. Illness means that the patient's autonomy, defined as 'authenticity plus independence', no longer exists. Autonomy and clinical intuition do not sit comfortably together (note the comment from Siegler and Goldblatt in 1.3.4).

In the new medical culture of rights, consent becomes a focal point for the changing structure of medical law. The language of human rights documents is of rights and respect. The WHO in its recent document *Promotion of the Rights of Patients in Europe* (Kluwer, 1995) devoted the majority of its time and energy to consent to medical treatment. Once more, you can judge whether medical law at present is 'good' law in measuring up to these human rights aspirations:

(a)   The informed consent of the patient is a prerequisite for any medical intervention.

(b)   A patient has the right to refuse or halt a medical intervention. The implications of doing so must be carefully explained to the patient.

(c)   When a patient is unable to express his or her will, and a medical intervention is urgently needed, the consent of the patient may be presumed, unless it is obvious from a previously declared expression of will that consent would be refused in the situation.

(d)   A doctor can proceed with treatment in the absence of a legal representative or proxy decision-maker if the intervention is too urgent to wait.

(e)   Even where there is a proxy decision-maker, the patient should be allowed to be involved to the extent of his or her capacity.

(f)   If the proxy refuses consent and the physician is of the opinion that the intervention is in the interests of the patient, a court or other form of arbitration should review the decision.

(g)   Where there is no advance declaration or proxy, appropriate measures should be taken to provide for a substitute decision-making process taking account of what is known or can be presumed about the wishes of the patient.

It may be that the philosophical and ethical theories that surround medical law provide useful guidance on the 'right thing to do', but does the fact that it is felt wrong, for example, to let a patient who refuses treatment die, mean that the law should be invoked to make the doctor treat? Devlin might suggest that to condone non-treatment by failing to enact a prohibitory law would undermine the moral fabric of society. Hart might reply that it might indeed be wrong, but a law which forced a doctor to action in the face of imprisonment would be a law which prohibits freedom beyond the value of the morality it protects. Whatever view one takes of the Hart–Devlin debate the practical involvement of the law in consent is clear:

The courts have shown a . . . reluctance to question the judgment as regards the competence of patients to consent to treatment, whether they be under-age children or adults who are either clearly incapable of making decisions about treatment, or whose capacity to do so is in question. In these circumstances, too, medical perceptions of the patient's best interests are often decisive. Despite occasional dicta which might convey a contrary impression, this is one of the underlying themes of [*Gillick* v *West Norfolk and Wisbech Area Health Authority* [1986] AC 112, *Re F (Mental Patient: Sterilisation)* [1990] 2 AC 1], and many other relevant cases to be decided in the last few years. (Teff, *Reasonable Care* (Oxford: Clarendon Press, 1994), p. 38)

A general starting point for the medical lawyer tracing judicial significance attaching to consent, is the now famous phrase of Justice Cardozo in the US case of *Schloendorff* v *Society of New York Hospital* (1914) 105 NE 92:

Every human being of adult years and sound mind has a right to determine what shall be done with his own body; and a surgeon who performs an operation without his patient's consent commits an assault.

This judicial expression of the ethical notion of self-determination has been directly or indirectly repeated on numerous occasions in numerous jurisdictions, and in cases which are of some significance to the medical lawyer (see, for example, *Sidaway* v *Board of Governors of the Bethlem Royal Hospital* [1985] AC 871; *Re F (Mental Patient: Sterilisation)* [1990] 2 AC 1; *Airedale NHS Trust* v *Bland* [1993] AC 789; *Re T (Adult: Refusal of Treatment)* [1993] Fam 95; *St George's Healthcare National Health Service Trust* v *S, Regina v Collins and Others ex parte S* (1998) *The Times*, 8 May 1998).

It is frequently stated by judges that the right of self-determination is a governing force for both medical treatment and other forms of conduct where the individual's physical integrity is compromised. It will also become apparent that both the civil law and the criminal law recognise that there is a broad symbolic importance in the theory that the individual's body is inviolate. In the recesses of legal history the right of personal security was regarded as one of 'the immutable laws of nature' (Sir William Blackstone, *Commentaries on the Law of England*, vol. 3, p. 119).

In modern times the idea of patient autonomy and individual rights, while still being expressed as a fundamental theoretical and legal underpinning of patient treatment, is now becoming more directly in competition with another idea, that of paternalism. While the followers of the sentiments of Cardozo J would uphold the autonomy of the individual and allow the patient to refuse to be treated, the paternalist (a relative of the patient, the doctor, perhaps even the State) would claim to be in a better position to judge what is best for the patient's welfare, and would want that opinion to hold sway at law. Recently attempts have been made to use legislation, such as the Mental Health Act 1983, to place rational patients in a protective environment where there are fears that, for example, an unborn child would be harmed by a mother's decision to have a 'natural' childbirth. The courts, however, made it clear that paternalism must give way to rational expressions of autonomy, even when they place the unborn in danger (*St George's Healthcare National Health Service Trust* v *S* (1998) *The Times*, 8 May 1998).

While one may consider that the development of such paternalism runs in direct contradiction to the oft-repeated legal recognition of autonomy, the development of medical law shows that, at least to a limited extent, there exists a tacit recognition of the fact that 'doctor knows best' or perhaps 'judge knows best', and may treat or authorise treatment without patient consent, or even in the face of a direct refusal. Modern medical case law, it will be argued, may now be paying lip service to the right of the patient to decide on, or more particularly to decline, treatment. The courts may be playing a formal rather than substantive role. The medical profession, bolstered by the law, are utilising alternative grounds, such as those of competence and rationality, to give modern function to the ethical imperative of the Hipp-ocratic oath, which invokes a paternalist stance when saying (emphasis added): 'I will follow that system of regimen which, according to my ability and *judgment*, I consider for the benefit of my patients, and abstain from whatever is deleterious and mischievous'. The doctor might well argue that to accept the refusal of a patient to treatment would be a major conflict with this ethical duty. The doctor, or even the relative, might equally attempt to argue that the patient is not in a position to judge competently the nature of the treatment, or even the nature of the medical condition requiring the treatment; therefore any consent or refusal would be factually and legally useless. The relative might be the mother, father or guardian of a child and declare that the child's request, demand or refusal of treatment is similarly made by a person who, because of youth, is also incapable of understanding what is happening and incapable therefore of deciding for him- or herself. The doctor might be confronted by a patient in an emergency situation and unable to get consent to treatment because the patient is unconscious. In all of the above scenarios the seemingly irreconcilable concepts of autonomy and paternalism suggest different solutions. In addition there is the dilemma of the doctor's clinical intuition, which, in almost all difficult cases, will lean toward treatment. After all it is what the doctor has trained for.

In this chapter all of the above types of scenario will be considered as they not uncommonly confront those involved in medical practice, and very often thereafter come to confront the court. Courts, as well as specific issues within consent as a whole (for example, the decision to sterilise the mentally handicapped), have been given the opportunity to decide whether autonomy is an irreducible ethic or whether, in given circumstances, it can give way to other considerations; whether it is society's role to protect those who cannot protect themselves, maintaining the integrity of the medical profession, or even that an individual's responsibility to society or others within society demands that they 'sacrifice themselves' to treatment.

Following on from the development of legal expression of this ethical debate, the next chapter will consider patients who, while appearing to consent to treatment, allege that they have simply not been told enough about what was going to happen, particularly the risks involved, in order to make an informed choice whether to undergo or decline the treatment. This is a specific example of the medical negligence action, and also of the concept of battery, which, while having surface similarities with the issues considered in chapters 3 and 4, also evidences somewhat different judicial motivations from those expressed and exemplified in *Bolam* v *Friern Hospital Management Committee* [1957] 1 WLR 582.

One element which needs to be understood before beginning with a look at consent and the legally incompetent is that, whatever view one takes of the autonomy–paternalism debate, there is no doubt that there needs to be someone who makes a decision on treatment. One may venture further and state that, because of the continuing symbolic importance of self-determination, there needs to be some 'body' which can and does consent. To have in existence a legal regime where the consent for those incapable of deciding for themselves is unstructured, and those who can consent undefined, would be to put medical law in a dangerous position. It would leave the weakest patients, those without a voice to express their autonomy, outside a regime of rights that we all share.

6.2 COMPETENCE AND CONSENT

6.2.1 Introduction: status and capacity to consent

The mere fact of becoming a patient means that the individual loses some autonomy. The patient will need to disclose personal details to aid in effective diagnosis, as well as rely on the judgment and advice of the doctor on the best course of treatment. The consent of a patient to giving these details appears free in the abstract, but cannot be said to be truly free when the option of refusal closes the door to treatment. Nevertheless consent legitimises what would otherwise be unlawful conduct (whether contrary to the civil or criminal law). A patient has the right to do with his or her body as he or she thinks fit, and (subject to the qualifications which will be outlined later) effect must be given to those decisions.

While having all this in mind, one has to realise that there are individuals who are incapable, for whatever reason, of making decisions affecting their lives, and that includes medical treatment. This lack of competence can be temporary (as in the case of the young child), transient (as in the case of the unconscious emergency patient) or permanent (as in the case of some mentally handicapped patients). The difficult question to address is where the law draws the competence 'line'. The law would be deficient if it did not recognise, and give effect to the fact, that there are members of society who may be in need of medical treatment but who also lack the mental facility to make a decision whether to undergo it or not. There are some members of society who simply cannot be regarded as autonomous. But it should be remembered that a 'good' medical law sees this lack of ability to act autonomously in the context of an overarching respect for individuals' rights. But who should the law recognise is incapable?

There are commonly two pathways that can be followed where legal discovery of the 'competence threshold' is required:

(a)   Status.
(b)   Capacity.

To use the former approach is to determine a single and specific cut-off point. If a patient is declared to be of a competent legal status then patient consent is required, if not of competent status then the treatment decision will be made by another body and decisions made and expressed by the incompetent patient can be ignored. Numerous examples of the status cut-off have been suggested. Of concern here will be the following:

(a)   Mental disorder.
(b)   Minority.

6.2.1.1   Mental disorder; status v capacity   Where the mentally disorder-ed are concerned, this declaration could conceivably be a threshold concept. Those deemed incompetent lack the status to consent. Such an approach would have the benefit of certainty, and, aside from the difficulties of medically defining what is meant by 'mental incompetence', such a blanket definition could be easily applied, arguably without recourse to the courts, with the accompanying saving of expense and time. The argument against this status approach is that it is indiscriminate and overreaching. Just because a person is declared to be mentally incompetent should not automatically mean that this person is incompetent to make any type of decision. The provisions of the Mental Health Act 1983 (see chapter 9) explicitly recognise that a patient who is detained for mental disorder is nevertheless required to consent to certain treatment. For example, ss. 57 and 58 of the Act, relating to surgical removal of brain tissue or that tissue's function, the surgical implantation of hormones to reduce sex drive or electroconvulsive therapy for example, require that there be certification that the patient 'is capable of understanding its nature, purpose and likely effects and has consented to it'. The rationale for the Act is that merely to have mental disorder does not make a person an automatic candidate for non-consensual treatment. The capacity of the patient to consent has to be judged and certified before treatment of the type described above can begin.

The Law Commission has reiterated the desire to pursue this capacity (as opposed to status) objective in two recent Consultation Papers (Nos. 119 and

129; see 6.6 for further details of the proposals). Kennedy and Grubb ('The Law Commission's Proposals: An Introduction' (1994) 2 Med L Rev 1 at p. 4) describe the object of the proposals as:

(1) to enable and encourage individuals to take decisions for themselves where they are able to do so; (2) to ensure that, where it is necessary for others to take decisions, any intervention should be as limited as possible and should seek to achieve what the individuals themselves would want; and (3) to protect incapacitated individuals from exploitation, neglect and abuse.

Given that the consent of the mentally disordered should be based on the capacity of the individual rather than the status of 'mental disorder', there still needs to be some guidance on what amounts to sufficient capacity to make it necessary to recognise autonomy by gaining patient consent. Once more, it would be to close society's eyes to the realities of life if the law failed to have cognisance of the fact that unfortunately there are individuals whose inability to rationalise, reflect and communicate their lifestyle preferences make them candidates for paternalist intervention and decision-making. While most people can think of clear examples of an individual who lacks capacity to consent, as in many areas of debate in medical law, controversy exists at the margins of 'capacity' and the values attached to that term.

The case law which considers the competence of the adult patient where medical treatment is proposed is growing, as is the academic discussion that analyses the judicial consideration of the existence and ambit of a competence test. To a large extent the capacity tests that have been enunciated could arguably be different in emphasis because of the very real urgency of many of the situations, the desire of those concerned with the patient that treatment take place, or simply the factual differences between the cases. The facts also indicate the variety of situations that have been encountered. Alternatively the differences of emphasis could result from the breadth inherent in the term and its potential for flexibility (or for the rather more cynical, manipulation). The Law Commission has itself attempted to propound a test of capacity which takes these many issues into account, without ignoring the rights of the patient.

So, the term 'capacity' is shaped by the consequences of the definition. To declare Susan, Albert and Carol (considered at the start of the chapter) as '*in*-capable' of making decisions regarding treatment takes away that means of manifesting autonomy: refusing. But it potentially saves all three lives. The treatment decision is taken away from them, and the next question has to be, who makes the decision now? First, though, when can the treatment decision be 'taken away'?

An example of the approach of current medical law to the question, and of the problems that abound in attempting to define what amounts to the 'capacity to consent' can be found in the signifcant case of *Re C (Adult: Refusal of Treatment)* [1994] 1 WLR 290. It is also one of the many medical law cases that cause readers to wring their hands with the conflicting dilemmas and emotions involved. As well as considering the legal and practical arguments about capacity, consider whether the decision was the 'right thing to do', either as a matter of philosophical enquiry, ethics or intuition. Consider even whether this was a decision for doctors, and 'none of the law's business'.

C was 68 years old. He had developed gangrene in his foot. Those with clinical management of the patient felt that an operation to amputate below the knee was required to prevent the spread of the gangrene. C was a paranoid schizophrenic; he was convinced, for example, that he was an internationally recognised doctor in practice. He applied for and was granted an injunction preventing the amputation being carried out. This was despite the fact that there was something like an 85 per cent chance that death would result, and that the refusal would soon be irrevocable, because C's mental state was deteriorating. Thorpe J, in allowing C's injunction against treatment, considered the relevant question regarding capacity to be whether 'Mr C's capacity is so reduced by his chronic mental illness that he does not sufficiently understand the *nature, purpose* and *effects* of the proferred amputation' (emphasis added).

Michael Gunn ('The Meaning of Incapacity' (1994) 2 Med L Rev 8 at pp. 10–11) paraphrases an expert witness in the case, a Dr Eastman, in giving a three-stage test of 'capacity', accepted by the court as '(1) comprehending and retaining treatment information; (2) believing it; (3) weighing it in the balance to arrive at a choice'. It will be noticed that it is not enough that the patient understands what is going on. The patient needs to have the ability to make decisions and analyse that information. To put matters more simply, the patient needs to show discretion and discrimination.

The case is useful in that it also discusses the procedure to be adopted by the court where such issues are raised, as well as the possibility of obtaining injunctions preventing doctors from treating. Andrew Grubb's commentary on the decision of Thorpe J ((1994) 2 Med L Rev 93) correctly regards the consideration of the test of competence, however, to be the most important part of the judgment (even accepting the fact that it is a first-instance decision). In deciding that C was competent the court therefore concluded that 'the presumption that C had the right of self-determination had not been displaced'. The fact that C believed that he was a medical practitioner did not affect his ability to comprehend and retain information, believe it and weigh it in the balance to arrive at a decision. But, consider again, was this a 'good' medical law decision? The decision upheld the autonomy of C, but acted contrary to the clinical intuition of where the 'best interest' of the patient lay.

The case indicated that the key element was the 'understanding' of the patient. In this, Grubb confirms, the court was essentially following the line of authority and rationale from *Gillick* v *West Norfolk and Wisbech Area Health Authority* [1986] AC 112. Therefore the test appears to be one equally applicable to the refusal of minors and the question of their competence (but while the competent adult refusal will be fully effective, it will be seen shortly that a 'competent' minor can refuse, but others can consent on his or her behalf).

The case of C also came to a decision on a rather thorny problem which was to tax the Law Commission and a number of academic writers (see Kennedy and Grubb, *Medical Law*, 2nd ed. (London: Butterworths, 1994), pp. 120–2; M. Gunn, 'The Meaning of Incapacity' (1994) 2 Med L Rev at pp. 17–18) of whether there needed to be *actual* understanding of the specific treatment issues at hand or an ability to understand matters *generally*. It might be considered that relying on the actual understanding of a patient has the danger of making competence turn on the level of information given to the particular patient by the doctor. One will see in relation to minors that the patient with what has been termed 'fluctuating lucidity' presents particular difficulties if the test is what the patient actually understands. With this in mind Kennedy and Grubb (at p. 121) decide that:

> It must, therefore, be the law that competence is determined by reference to the unvarying conceptual standard of *capacity* or *ability* to understand. Whether, thereafter a patient who is judged competent because she has the capacity or ability to understand, in fact consented, is a distinct question turning upon the reality of the consent based upon legally adequate information.

Gunn correctly regards the test in *Re C* as a more accurate test than that propounded by Bristow J in *Chatterton* v *Gerson* [1981] QB 432 that the patient need only understand 'in broad terms' what is proposed for the consent to be real.

There is also in existence the Mental Health Act Code of Practice, which sets out a more elaborate test of capacity which could be utilised alongside the *Re C* test. Paragraph 15.10 of the Code provides a checklist. To have capacity (as far as treatment under the provisions of the Mental Health Act 1983 are concerned), a patient must be able:

(a)   to understand what is meant by medical treatment, that it is needed and why it is needed;

(b)   (as in *Re C* and *Chatterton* v *Gerson*) to understand in broad terms the nature of the treatment which is proposed;

(c)   to understand the risks attaching to the treatment as well as the benefits of it;

(d)   to understand what will happen if treatment does not take place;

(e)   to have the capacity to make a choice.

As well as this checklist the Code also issues a few valuable reminders:

(a)   The assessment of capacity according to the above list should be made with a specific proposal of treatment in mind.

(b)   This assessment needs to be made at the time that the treatment is proposed. In many cases lucidity and mental disorder will not be constant.

(c)   There should be full recording of capacity assessments in the patient's notes.

Despite these apparently attractive tests, which combine comprehensive testing and an appreciation that the individual should, as far as is possible, be given the right to consent, other factual situations confronted by the courts have indicated the tensions between a respect for the autonomy of the individual and the desire to treat those whose health (and as was seen in *Re C*, life) is at risk. It may be that the test of competence is being manipulated to facilitate treatment, thus being based on a paternalistic notion of patient welfare, rather than being a true test of the ability of the particular patient to act in an autonomous manner. An example of such a treatment-based 'competence' test, which is useful as an illustration of ethical and practical tension, is the patient suffering from the eating disorder anorexia nervosa.

In *Re W (A Minor) (Medical Treatment: Court's Jurisdiction)* [1993] Fam 64, a 16-year-old girl was suffering from anorexia nervosa. Doctors needed to have the option of force-feeding the girl if her condition deteriorated to an extent that this became necessary. She refused to be treated in this way or be moved to a specialist institution. At first instance it was decided by Thorpe J that W had 'sufficient understanding to make an informed choice'. While the Court of Appeal was mainly concerned with the existence and extent of the court's jurisdiction to treat in the face of a 'competent' refusal (see below), Lord Donaldson of Lymington MR pointed to the fact that a feature of anorexia nervosa was a compulsion to refuse to be treated, or to accept treatment which it is likely would be ineffective. The key element of the judgments of Lord Donaldson MR and Balcombe LJ in the Court of Appeal was the destruction of the ability to make an *informed* choice as part of the condition of anorexia nervosa itself (see also *South West Hertfordshire Health Authority* v *Brady* (1994) 2 Med L Rev 208).

The courts have had other opportunities to consider the impact of the test of capacity which came from *Re C (Adult: Refusal of Medical Treatment)* [1994] 1 WLR 290 and in the examples given here appear to be extending the ambit of this test of competence to cover those with phobic reactions. The law also seems to be interpreting the elements involved in this test of competence exclusively, i.e., a patient who is incapable of satisfying one element can be considered incompetent.

In *Re MB (Medical Treatment)* [1997] 2 FLR 426 there was a comprehensive consideration of many of the key factors for medical law on capacity and consent. The case even extends consideration to the impact of refusals on the unborn and the impact of the Convention on Human Rights in protecting that foetus. Miss MB had during her pregnancy often objected to needle pricks to enable blood samples to be taken. When she was 40 weeks pregnant the foetus was found to be in the breech position, and there was a 50 per cent risk that the child would be harmed, although Miss MB herself was in no significant danger. The problem was that Miss MB's needle phobia made a Caesarean all but impossible. Miss MB agreed to the operation, but her phobia led to panic and objection to the operation each time. There was an application by the health authority for a declaration that it would be lawful to insert a needle for the purposes of the operation and also lawful to use reasonable force to effect that. There was an appeal on the basis that Hollis

J had been incorrect to find on the evidence that Miss MB lacked the capacity to consent or refuse the treatment. On appeal Butler-Sloss LJ began by considering the expert evidence in the case. Dr F gave evidence that MB clearly saw the need for the operation; indeed when asked about it accepted the whole idea of the operation. The doctor expressed the view that she was naive and frightened and had 'the abnormal medical condition of needle phobia'. The doctor went on to explain the difficulties of MB when it came time to operate and was the key to the issue of capacity:

> It seemed to me that at the actual point she was not capable of making a decision at all, in the sense of being able to hold information in the balance and make a choice. At that moment the needle . . . dominated her thinking and made her quite unable to consider anything else.

Butler-Sloss LJ then considered, as had many judges beforehand in such cases, the general principle that a mentally competent person has an absolute right to refuse treatment, and, as stated in cases such as *Re T (Adult: Medical Treatment)* [1993] Fam 95 per Lord Donaldson of Lymington MR, such a refusal can be rational, irrational or for no reason at all. The issue then was how the court tested whether a patient was competent or not. It was acknowledged that the three-stage test from *Re C (Adult Refusal of Treatment)* [1994] 1 WLR 290 had effectively been adopted by the Law Commission in the 1995 document *Mental Incapacity* (Law Com No. 231) in considering that a patient is lacking capacity to consent when:

(a)   that patient is unable to understand or retain the relevant information, including the reasonably foreseeable consequences of that decision, or

(b)   he or she is unable to make a decision based on the information given.

The Court of Appeal also took the opportunity to review some of the more recent case law which had to consider the idea of capacity or otherwise; these were grouped together under the banner of 'the Caesarean cases'. In the first of these, *Tameside and Glossop Acute Services Trust v CH* [1996] 1 FLR 762, the patient was detained under the Mental Health Act 1983, s. 3; her pregnancy was complex and the foetus was in danger if the pregnancy continued. Wall J made the declaration required for the treatment to take place (Mental Health Act 1983, s. 63) after directly applying the three-part test already encountered in *Re C*. In the second case cited, that of *Norfolk and Norwich Healthcare (NHS) Trust v W* [1996] 2 FLR 613, the patient was actually denying that she was pregnant. Her situation required either a Caesarean or a forceps delivery. It appeared, however, that the expert evidence did not strictly accord with the prerequisites of *Re C*. There was uncertainty whether the patient could or could not comprehend and retain the relevant information; there was further uncertainty whether the patient believed the information which was given about the treatment. There did, however, seem to be a firm opinion that the patient was not capable of balancing that information so as to arrive at a choice. Therefore it seemed that only one of the prerequisites from *Re C* was definitely present. Nevertheless the court authorised treatment. The rationale behind this decision was that:

. . . although she was not suffering from a mental disorder within the meaning of the statute, she lacked the mental competence to make a decision about the treatment that was proposed because she was incapable of weighing up the considerations that were involved. She was called upon to make that decision at a time of acute emotional stress and physical pain in the ordinary course of labour made even more difficult because of her own particular mental history. ([1996] 2 FLR 613 at p. 616)

In similar vein Johnson J decided that there should be a Caesarean section performed on a patient who required it as a matter of dire emergency; the patient was in serious risk of injury and the foetus of death. Again *Rochdale Healthcare (NHS) Trust* v *C* (3 July 1996 unreported) appeared to be based on the fact that the patient was not capable within the third element of the *Re C* test, namely balancing the information. Butler-Sloss L:J in *Re MB* expressed some doubt whether on the facts of the case the patient in this latter case was truly incompetent.

Butler-Sloss LJ also had the advantage of an unreported case very similar to the facts of *Re MB*. In *Re L* (5 December 1996 unreported) Kirkwood J applied the *Re C* test and stated:

that her extreme needle phobia amounted to an involuntary compulsion that disabled L from weighing treatment information in the balance to make a choice. Indeed it was an affliction of a psychological nature that compelled L against medical advice with such force that her own life would be in serious peril.

It seems more apparent here than in the other cases Butler-Sloss LJ had for consideration that the test of competence was being predicated not so much on the actual capacity of the patient but rather the consequences of the refusal. Once again it appeared that the more serious the consequences of the refusal the more likely the declaration of incompetence.

From these cases Butler-Sloss LJ, at [1997] 2 FLR pp. 436–7, sought to provide a non-exhaustive list of guiding principles. In terms of the debate on capacity and consent as a whole they are worth listing in full:

(1)   As previously stated the presumption is that the patient has the capacity to make decisions whether to accept or refuse treatment. The presumption can be rebutted.
(2)   A woman with the capacity to decide has the right to make a decision, rational, irrational or for no reason, even though the consequence may be her own death or that of the child she is carrying.

(3)   Irrationality is here used to connote a decision which is so outrageous in its defiance of logic or of accepted moral standards that no sensible person who had applied his mind to the question to be decided it could have arrived at it. As Kennedy and Grubb . . . point out, it might be otherwise if a decision is based on a misperception of reality (e.g., the blood is poisoned because it is red). Such a misperception will be more readily accepted to be a disorder of the mind. Although it might be thought that irrationality sits uneasily with competence to decide, panic, indecisiveness and irrationality in themselves do not as such amount to incompetence, but they may be symptoms or evidence of incompetence. The graver the consequences of the decision, the commensurately greater the level of competence is required to take the decision.

(4)   A patient lacks capacity where they are unable to comprehend the information, particularly the consequences and they cannot weigh it in the balance.

(5)   Temporary factors may erode the capacity to decide. Examples given are confusion, shock and fatigue.

(6)   A significant factor may be panic which is induced by fear, but this needs to be treated with caution when looking at the evidence.

Applying these principles to the case of MB, Butler-Sloss LJ found that the patient was incapable of giving consent or refusal. She was regarded as temporarily incompetent.

It is worth mentioning that the Court of Appeal also looked briefly at the issue of the rights of the unborn child and came to the conclusion long accepted (but not uncontroversial) by medical law that the court does not have the jurisdiction to take the interests of the unborn into account (see also *St George's Healthcare National Health Service Trust* v *S* (1998) *The Times*, 8 May 1998. Even the cases which have come before the European Commission of Human Rights, while not precisely on this issue, have come to the conclusion that the rights of the unborn may only be considered in certain (although not articulated) circumstances (see, for example, *H* v *Norway* (No. 17004/90) (1992) 73 Decisions & Reports 155.

Overall, in terms of competence and consent these cases indicate that the interpretation of *Re C* has broadened, and now seems intimately linked with the consequences of the decision of the patient.

Of increasing significance too for both the doctor and the medical lawyer is where there is a refusal to undergo life-saving treatment based on what may be perceived by many to be irrational religious convictions. Is the patient who refuses life-saving treatment regarded by the law as lacking the capacity to act autonomously and therefore incapable of consenting? It would appear that under the mantle of Lord Donaldson, treatment despite refusal will be justified on any ground that happens to be generally available, whether it is the perceived incapacity of the patient to decide or other parties having the power to override the consent of the patient (see also J. Mason, 'Master of the Balancers; Non-voluntary Therapy under the Mantle of Lord Donaldson' [1993] JR 115).

The issue was addressed by the courts in the 1970s in the context of whether the refusal of a Jehovah's Witness to undergo a blood transfusion required as the result of an assault broke the chain of causation between the assault and the subsequent death of the victim (*R* v *Blaue* [1975] 1 WLR 1411). Counsel for the assailant had sought to argue that the refusal was unreasonable and therefore broke the chain of causation. The fact that the court decided that the deceased had a right to refuse treatment because of religious beliefs made that refusal reasonable and did not break the chain of causation.

A case which led the Court of Appeal to confront the issue of religious beliefs and competence to consent to medical treatment was once more concerned with Jehovah's Witnesses. In *Re T (Adult: Refusal of Treatment)* [1993] Fam 95, T, who was 34 weeks pregnant, was rushed to hospital after a car accident. T was not a Jehovah's Witness but had been raised by her mother, who was. After she had entered hospital she had conversations in private with her mother, and thereafter stated that she held some of the beliefs of Jehovah's Witnesses including the fact that a blood transfusion was a sin. She thus refused consent for one to take place. Soon after this she went into premature labour, and her medical condition after the accident meant that the child needed to be born by Caesarian section. She had signed a form refusing a blood transfusion if one were required, which became the case when T's condition deteriorated. The consultant anaesthetist placed T on a ventilator and administered paralysing drugs even though if consent had been forthcoming a blood transfusion would have immediately taken place. At first instance it was decided that a transfusion would not be unlawful in the absence of consent, because it was obviously in T's best interests. T appealed against this decision.

Lord Donaldson MR paraphrased the main aspects of the decision to authorise treatment. In doing so a number of valuable and general statements concerning consent were made as well as the fact that it was felt that the refusal of treatment was based on the undue influence of the mother. The summary was as follows:

(a) Every adult has the right and capacity to decide whether to accept or decline treatment, even where the refusal would lead to permanent injury or death. Such a refusal can be rational or irrational, unknown or even not in existence. It has equally to be recognised that there is a strong public interest in the preservation of life. With that in mind the presumption that all adults have the capacity to decide for themselves can be rebutted.

(b) A patient may not have the capacity to decide because of long-term mental incapacity or retarded development, or the lack of capacity may be temporary and due to unconsciousness, pain, shock or even the effects of drugs, for example.

(c) Where the patient lacks capacity for whatever reason, doctors have a duty to treat a patient so as to act in that patient's best interests.

(d) There may be cases where the doctor is not faced with a clear issue of capacity or non-capacity, but with reduced capacity. 'What matters is whether at the time the patient's capacity was reduced below the level needed in the case of a refusal of that importance, for refusal can vary in importance. Some may involve a risk to life or of irreparable damage to health. Others may not.'

(e) Doctors in deciding about capacity will need to be aware of the possibility of undue influence. If that is found to be in existence then the refusal is vitiated. It should be borne in mind that some scenarios and relationships lend themselves more readily to undue influence.

(f) Doctors will need to consider the precise scope of the refusal and whether it was meant to cover the situation actually encountered. A refusal may be vitiated where it rests on a false assumption of circumstances.

(g) Patients should be forcibly reminded of the consequences of a refusal.

(h) When in doubt apply to the court for assistance.

In *Re T* the Court of Appeal concluded that the refusal was vitiated, but was clear that if T had been declared to be a 'true' Jehovah's Witness, then the refusal would have made any subsequent administration of blood unlawful. It should be emphasised again that *Re T* is useful both as an example of the tensions that exist in such situations between presumptions of competence and the public interest in the saving of life and as an effective summary of an approach to be adopted, but the case is less effective in its consideration of what is competence. The judgment of Lord Donaldson MR appears at times to invoke the low threshold of competence encountered in *Chatterton* v *Gerson* [1981] QB 432, and may even be interpreted as an assumption that one knows competence or the lack of it when one sees it, without the need to examine what goes into the test. To this extent the case itself, if wholeheartedly adopted, might well lead to an unacceptably subjective approach from doctors and thereby allow for other influences to hold sway in deciding whether to treat.

Lord Donaldson's rather basic understanding of the concept of competence may be due to the fact that 'ignorance is bliss'. To state broadly that there appears to be incapacity really hides a basic and, some might suggest, laudable judicial paternalism (and as will be seen in the context of *Re W (A Minor) (Medical Treatment: Court's Jurisdiction)* [1993] Fam 64 later, medical protectionism). This is more clearly illustrated by *Re S (Adult: Refusal of Treatment)* [1993] Fam 123. Here the patient mother of two was beyond the term with her third pregnancy. She was at the time a 'born-again' Christian. The child was in a transverse position which endangered both the mother and child, and could only be alleviated by a caesarian section. This was a case which had to be decided in a matter of minutes. Lord Donaldson in reacting swiftly authorised the operation to take place despite the woman's religious objection to this happening.

Obviously Lord Donaldson did not base the decision to go ahead with the operation on the incapacity of S to consent or refuse on the grounds of the perceived illogicality of the religious conviction. The basis was the equally legally and ethically dubious rights of the unborn child (see 12.2). There was no question though of S being considered mentally disordered.

The Law Commission has now considered the tests of competence that are available to apply in a judicial setting where consent to medical treatment of the mentally disordered is in issue. The Commission itself would have been unable to tackle the next difficult question of who can consent on behalf of the legally incompetent and what treatment that proxy consent can relate to, without coming to a decision on the 'characteristics' to be identified before the patient is declared to be incapable of making treatment decisions personally.

While there has been extensive academic debate on the available tests of capacity (see, for example, the seminal work by L. H. Roth, A. Meisel and C. W. Lidz, 'Tests of Competency to Consent to Treatment' (1977) 134 American Journal of Psychiatry 279; R. R. Faden and T. Beauchamp, *A History and Theory of Informed Consent* (New York: Oxford University Press, 1986)), the Law Commission has now proposed a test described as 'cognitive and functional':

> A mentally disordered person should be considered unable to take the medical treatment decision in question if he or she is unable to understand an explanation in broad terms and simple language of the basic information relevant to taking it, including information about the reasonably foresee- able consequences of taking or failing to take it, or is unable to retain the information for long enough to take an effective decision. (*Mentally Incapacitated Adults and Decision-making. Medical Treatment and Research* (Consultation Paper No. 129) (London: HMSO, 1993), para. 2.12)

A further recommendation was that:

> A mentally disordered person should be considered unable to take the medical treatment decision in question if he or she can understand the information relevant to taking the decision but is unable because of mental disorder to make a true choice in relation to it. (para. 2.20)

6.2.1.2 Minors: status, capacity and competence   The issue of minors and consent to medical treatment has aroused a considerable level of controversy and media attention with the attempt by Mrs Gillick to have a say in the proposed prescription of contraceptives to her 15-year-old daugh- ter, and to question whether a government circular which sanctioned the giving of such advice and prescription to the under-16 girl was lawful in the absence of parental consent (*Gillick* v *West Norfolk and Wisbech Area Health Authority* [1986] AC 112). The relevant point here is that in the Court of Appeal Fox LJ invoked a status approach to the treatment of those under 16:

> I conclude that as a matter of law a girl under 16 can give no valid consent to anything in the areas under consideration which apart from consent would constitute an assault, whether civil or criminal, and can impose no valid prohibition on a doctor against seeking parental consent.

There is a solid echo of Kantian deontology and absolutism here. A girl under the age of 16 can give *no* valid consent. That is an end to the matter as far as Fox LJ was concerned.

The reason that the Court of Appeal came to such a 'status' decision was mainly because it gave an element of certainty to the law. The decision meant that a doctor could not examine, treat or possibly even advise a person under the age of 16 without parental consent. Overtly, the Court of Appeal announced that it was respecting the fact that the parents of a child have a 'bundle of rights' in relation to that child. Included in this 'bundle' was the right to control elements of the child's life 'subject to the right of the court to override the parental rights in the interests of the child'.

While there is little doubt that certainty would result from such a judicial pronouncement, it could also be perceived as an inflexible tool which did little or nothing to respect the rights of the minor, or the fact that a child's development does not proceed in such an ordered, 'staged' and universal way. As everyone is aware, children mature as individuals in an individual manner which is a manifestation and reflection of physiological, psychological and environmental influences. To state that all children before their 16th birthdays cannot consent, but on the day after that birthday can consent is to ignore the reality of individualism. Reality was, however, reflected in the 'capacity' decision of the House of Lords.

Lord Scarman, in giving the leading judgment of the House of Lords, was well aware that societal developments meant that a great deal of the common law relating to consent of minors, which reflected a society that was uncomfortable with the independence of the young, ignorant of the provision of contraceptives and Draconian in its failure to recognise the rights of women, was incapable of reflecting modern society.

The rights of parents cannot be ignored, but 'parental rights are derived from parental duty and exist only so long as they are needed for the protection of the person and property of the child'.

Lord Scarman considered that the common law would be failing in its own duty to be flexible if it established a fixed threshhold on the ability to consent. In referring to *R v D* [1984] AC 778, which concerned an allegation of kidnapping against a father who had taken away his own child, Lord Scarman in *Gillick* was of the opinion that it had established clearly that:

> . . . save where statute otherwise provides, a minor's capacity to make his or her own decision depends upon the minor having sufficient understanding and intelligence to make the decision and is not to be determined by reference to any judicially fixed age limit.

The most significant aspect of the judgment of the House of Lords in *Gillick* is that it both established the existence of a capacity approach and also (although rather less successfully) attempted to give some flesh to the bones of that concept. Lord Scarman's conclusion is worthy of reproduction:

> I would hold that as a matter of law the parental right to determine whether or not their minor child below the age of 16 will have medical treatment

terminates if and when the child achieves a sufficient understanding and intelligence to enable him or her to understand fully what is proposed. It will be a question of fact whether a child seeking advice has sufficient understanding of what is involved to give a consent valid in law. Until the child achieves the capacity to consent, the parental right to make the decision continues save only in exceptional circumstances. Emergency, parental neglect, abandonment of the child, or inability to find the parent are examples of exceptional situations justifying the doctor proceeding to treat the child without parental knowledge and consent; but there will arise, no doubt, other exceptional situations in which it will be reasonable for the doctor to proceed without the parent's consent.

While the majority decision of the House of Lords has been welcomed, and the capacity approach of Lord Scarman is something of a landmark for children's autonomous rights in health care, consider the doctor's part in all this. Lord Scarman was clear in considering that the treating doctor had to be satisfied that the child was competent. There is thus a potentially powerful voice to control the declaration of capacity or incapacity. As with medical negligence, a court is likely to defer to a doctor declaring that the child does not have the maturity to understand the implications of the treatment (or non-treatment) option. The doctor considering that the decision of the minor, whether based on paternalism or clinical intuition, to be 'damaging' to that child, is likely to make the declaration of incapacity.

Earlier the Law Commission proposals were briefly considered. Those proposals only apply to a patient suffering from mental disorder according to the Mental Health Act 1983 and over the age of 16 (see Consultation Paper No. 129, para. 2.23). Nevertheless it is important to see whether there has been any elaboration on the broad definition of capacity introduced in *Gillick*.

The case which has attempted to place a limit on the applicability of such a definition (and its applicability to the patient with a condition of fluctuating lucidity), as well as containing some less than popular pronouncements on the supposed inviolability of the 'mature minor' refusal of treatment, concerned a 15-year-old girl, R (*Re R (A Minor) (Wardship: Consent to Medical Treatment)* [1992] Fam 11). This emotionally abused child had been suffering from increasingly disturbed behaviour, and amongst other things had been threatening suicide and hearing persecuting voices. At one stage her condition was such that it was considered that she should be 'sectioned' under the Mental Health Act 1983 (for details of the reasons for sectioning and the implications of it, see chapter 9). This child had been sedated from time to time, but this was done with patient consent. As matters progressed concern grew about R's fluctuating mental state. Consideration was given to the use of compulsory medication because, amongst other things, R was to an extent denying her illness. When offered narcoleptics (anti-psychotic drugs), R replied that she did not need them and did not want to take them. One of the experts who gave evidence felt that at times the patient had sufficient understanding to make a choice, but when in a florid, psychotic state could not and was a suicide risk. The question for the court was whether R was competent to refuse to take these drugs, given the fact that her lucidity was variable.

Lord Donaldson MR set out why the test of '*Gillick* competence' was inappropriate here:

> The House of Lords in that case [*Gillick*] was quite clearly considering the staged development of a normal child. . . . What is really being looked at is an assessment of mental and emotional age, as contrasted with chronological age, but even this test needs to be modified in the case of fluctuating mental disability to take account of that misfortune. It should be added that in any event what is involved is not merely an ability to understand the nature of the proposed treatment – in this case compulsory medication – but a full understanding and appreciation of the consequences both of the treatment in terms of intended and possible side effects and, equally important, the anticipated consequences of a failure to treat. (pp. 25–6)

Lord Donaldson went on to say that *Gillick* competence referred to someone with a consistency of patterned development which could not exist in R's fluctuating state. Competence, the argument goes, cannot be judged by a snapshot of the patient's understanding. R needed to have a persistence of ability to understand the nature and effects of the treatment. While one might applaud the general result the process of legal reasoning is less than satisfactory. *Gillick* did apply, but the child, by reason of denying past experiences, was unable to understand the nature and purpose of the treatment. To 'chip away' at the broad applicability and desirability of *Gillick* competence is not to be encouraged.

6.3   CONSENT, REFUSAL AND THE *GILLICK*-COMPETENT MINOR

In 6.2.1.2, *Re R (A Minor) (Wardship: Consent to Treatment)* [1992] Fam 11 was considered in relation to the definition of capacity. But perhaps even more significant and more open to criticism is its consideration of the power of the 'mature minor' to refuse medical treatment. The decision has been vividly described as 'driving a coach and horses through *Gillick*' (see I. Kennedy, 'Consent to Treatment: The Capable Person' in C. Dyer (ed.), *Doctors, Patients and the Law* (1992) ch. 3). This is because, along with the decision in relation to over 16s in *Re W (A Minor) (Medical Treatment: Court's Jurisdiction)* [1993] Fam 64, it decided that while the *Gillick*-competent child's decision to consent to treatment could not be usurped by the parents (or those with a parental responsibility for the minor), a *refusal* to undergo treatment could be. The two cases, when combined, show that the autonomy of the minor, while a valued concept, loses out to judicial paternalism toward the child, and indeed judicial paternalism toward the 'embattled' medical profession.

In both *Re R* and *Re W* the opportunity arose to consider the interrelationship at law between minors, parents and the court. The Court of Appeal was of the view that it had wider powers over a child in wardship than the child's parents had, and that this came from the fact that the court's jurisdiction was independent of parental rights and responsibilities. While this appears logical, it does not follow that since a court can override the decision of a parent in relation to the ward, there is no reason why it cannot override the ward's decision as well (see G. Douglas, 'The Retreat from *Gillick*' (1992) 55 MLR 569).

Staughton LJ in *Re R (A Minor) (Wardship: Consent to Treatment)* [1992] Fam 11 sought to justify this expression of power with a consideration of a number of wardship cases which indicated the right to usurp the decision of the ward, but, as Gillian Douglas points out, they were either decided before *Gillick*, or concerned minors who could by no stretch of the imagination be regarded as mature, or whose views happened to coincide with those of the court itself. Staughton LJ concluded:

> . . . the powers of a wardship judge do indeed include power to consent to medical treatment when the ward has not been asked or has declined. If that means that the wardship judge has wider powers than a natural parent . . . it seems to me to be warranted by the authorities to which I have referrred. (p. 28)

The protest which followed *Re R* was based on the fallacy underlying the right of the wardship court to refuse. The logical consequence of the right of the *Gillick*-competent child to consent to treatment in the face of parental refusal or ignorance is the right of such a child to refuse to be treated. Lord Scarman had noted in *Gillick* that the legally mature minor took over the parental power to approve *or decline* treatment (see [1986] AC 112 at pp. 188–9).

Lord Donaldson MR in *Re R* explored the relative powers of parents and children in treatment decisions. Counsel for the Official Solicitor had sought to argue that once the child gains the right to give consent, the parents' rights to consent decline or cease to exist. As an extension of this, the court, in its wardship capacity has no right to consent or refuse because wardship only enables the court 'to step into the shoes' of the parents. Obviously, counsel argued, this is only the case where the child is first declared incapable of understanding the nature and implications of the treatment proposed. It will be recalled that, according to Lord Scarman, until a child reaches *Gillick* competence, there are only a few exceptional circumstances where the decision rights of the parents will be overruled. Lord Donaldson MR's response has attracted severe criticism. Consent, he declared:

> is merely a key which unlocks a door. Furthermore, whilst in the case of an adult of full capacity there will usually only be one keyholder, namely the patient, in the ordinary family unit where a young child is the patient there will be two keyholders, namely the parents, with a several as well as a joint right to turn the key and unlock the door. (p. 22)

While this may well be an applicable point as regards the very young, where the more mature child is concerned it should not be. To declare the parents of a *Gillick*-competent child to be an independent treatment keyholder is to diminish the consensual rights of that child to a virtual nullity.

Lord Donaldson MR further 'finessed' Lord Scarman's judgment in *Gillick*. Lord Scarman declared that it is the right to *determine* medical treatment which terminates on the child being held competent at law. According to Lord Donaldson, this still allowed the right of the parents to consent in the face of a refusal:

> The parents can only have a right of determination if *either* the child has no right to consent, that is, is not a keyholder, *or* the parents hold a master key which could nullify the child's consent. I do not understand Lord Scarman to be saying that, if a child was '*Gillick* competent'. . . the parents ceased to have an independent right of consent as contrasted with ceasing to have a right of determination, that is, a veto. In a case in which the '*Gillick* competent' child refuses treatment, but the parents consent, that consent *enables* treatment to be undertaken lawfully, but in no way determines that the child shall be so treated. In a case in which the positions are reversed, it is the child's consent which is the enabling factor and again the parents' refusal of consent is not determinative. (p. 23)

If this appears to be a little confused, that is because there is an illogicality which pervades this notion. One cannot split up consensual rights, and indicate that the right to *determine* medical treatment might cease, but the right to *consent* does not. A parent either has the power to overrule the child's refusal of treatment, in which case *Gillick* competence appears to be an abandoned concept, or does not, in which case the concept of the autonomous right of the *Gillick*-competent patient to accept or decline treatment is maintained.

One might consider the judgment of Lord Donaldson MR an isolated one, given that the child was clearly not able to understand the implications of the proposed treatment, i.e., was not competent. In *Re W (A Minor) (Medical Treatment: Court's Jurisdiction)* [1993] Fam 64, however, Lord Donaldson was faced more directly with a similar issue; whether there can be a power, the extent of that power and the source of that power to override the decisions of those over the age of 16. It also gave Lord Donaldson an opportunity to reconsider the application of *Gillick* to legislation, having acknowledged that there had been a welter of criticism of his views in *Re R*. It will be recalled that *Re W* concerned a girl of 16 who was suffering from anorexia nervosa, and was refusing certain treatment.

The common law of *Gillick* applies to persons under 16. The Family Law Reform Act 1969, s.8, applies to medical treatment and those between the age of 16 and majority at 18. It states:

> (1)   The consent of a minor who has attained the age of 16 years to any surgical, medical or dental treatment which, in the absence of consent,

would constitute a trespass to his person, shall be as effective as it would be if he were of full age; and where a minor has by virtue of this section given an effective consent to any treatment it shall not be necessary to obtain any consent for it from his parent or guardian.

(2)   In this section 'surgical, medical or dental treatment' includes any procedure undertaken for the purposes of diagnosis, and this section applies to any procedure (including, in particular, the administration of an anaesthetic) which is ancillary to any treatment as it applies to that treatment.

(3)   Nothing in this section shall be construed as making ineffective any consent which would have been effective if this section had not been enacted.

This section appears to be a clear indication of the exclusive right of the 16-year-old to consent to or decline treatment without recourse to a parent or guardian, yet Lord Donaldson in *Re W* sought to reinterpret s. 8 to read alongside the interpretation he placed on *Gillick* in *Re R*. Lord Donaldson first recognised that:

The most promising argument in favour of W having an exclusive right to consent to treatment and thus, by refusing consent, to attract the protection of the law on trespass to the person, lies in concentrating upon the words 'as effective as it would be if he were of full age'. If she were of full age her ability to consent would have two separate effects. First, her consent would be fully effective as such. Second, a failure or refusal to give consent would be fully effective as a veto, but only *because no one else would be in a position to consent*. (p. 77)

Lord Donaldson (with whom the other members of the Court of Appeal agreed) considered that s. 8 did not relate to the refusal of the 16- or 17-year-old simply because the section does not mention refusal. In any case it was felt that the wide powers of the court in its wardship capacity existed, notwithstanding the provisions of s. 8, and the purpose of consent here was to provide those involved with a:

legal 'flak jacket' which protects the doctor from claims by the litigious whether he acquires it from his patient who may be a minor over the age of 16, or a '*Gillick* competent' child under that age or from another person having parental responsibilities which include a right to consent to treatment of the minor. Anyone who gives him a flak jacket (that is, consent) may take it back, but the doctor only needs one and so long as he continues to have one he has the legal right to proceed. (p. 78)

It is apparent from this last quote that the Court of Appeal may well have been more concerned with protecting the doctor from litigation than with the right of the competent 16- or 17-year-old to refuse treatment. As with *Gillick*, logic dictates that a right to consent from s. 8 must bring with it a right to refuse. Medical law does not appear to follow logic here.

Their lordships were also made aware in argument that to compound the error of interpreting the common law of *Gillick* in *Re R* with such an interpretation of statute in *Re W* would potentially lead, for example, to the performance of an abortion on a 16-year-old who refused such an operation, but which was consented to by the parents. That they were unable to reply other than to regard such a scenario as 'more apparent than real' might suggest that there are broad future dangers in creating a legal culture of compulsion.

In the end Teff is right in saying that 'what Lord Donaldson's view does reveal is a value judgment in which protecting doctors against a relatively remote risk is more highly prized than the autonomy interest of competent patients in not having to submit to invasive treatment' (*Reasonable Care* (Oxford: Clarendon Press, 1994), p. 149). The language of human rights in medicine will only stretch so far in judicial hands. Where there appears a physical hazard in the competent patient refusing treatment, the noble phrases of Cardozo J in *Schloendorff* v *Society of New York Hospital* (1914) 105 NE 92 (see 6.1) are conveniently forgotten.

In addition, Kennedy and Grubb (*Medical Law*, 2nd ed. (London: Butterworths, 1994)) note the numerous jurisdictional, policy and ethical criticisms of the decisions in *Re R* and *Re W*:

(a) The court was exercising a *parens patriae* power by way of wardship or the invocation of the inherent jurisdiction of the court. It has to be accepted that it is a necessary contingency that the jurisdiction of the court once it becomes relevant can be potentially unlimited (or certainly not limited to the powers of the parent). This is not to say, however, that the jurisdiction can be utilised in any circumstance. The court should only have power, indeed the basis of wardship recognises the fact, where the individual concerned is not competent. It would be fallacious indeed to argue that the wardship court, for example, should throw a legal cloak of protection around those who are able to understand the implications of the decisions that they make. It is nonsensical to protect those able to protect themselves.

(b) Once more the fundamental fact for medical law is that in its reinterpretation of the House of Lords' decision in *Gillick*, the Court of Appeal, in *Re R* and *Re W* sought to move the emphasis away from the recognition of the autonomous rights of the competent minor to a stance which was paternalist. It did so in seeking to give the judiciary the power to choose the option which, in its own perceptions, is the right one; one based on the consequences of decision-making. The Court of Appeal also shifted the emphasis away from the rights of the individual to the protection of the doctor. As Mason and McCall Smith suggest 'It is, therefore, possible to criticise the two decisions as concentrating on this aspect and taking insufficient notice of the developing autonomy of adolescence' (*Law and Medical Ethics*, 4th ed. (London: Butterworths, 1994), p. 229).

Overall the case law indicates that the 'original test' of capacity enunciated by Lord Scarman in *Gillick* is incomplete. The capacity of a child is to be judged on ability to understand the implications and consequences of a decision, and the hidden ingredient added by Lord Donaldson, what the consequences of a refusal are for the welfare of the child as perceived by the courts.

6.4 TREATMENT OF INCOMPETENT MINORS

Whatever the controversy over the relative powers of the competent minor, the parents and the courts to consent to treatment, there exist children under the age of majority who are not yet *Gillick* competent, or less fortunately can never be *Gillick* competent because of mental disability. They nevertheless require treatment.

The simple questions one needs to answer are:

(a) Who has the power to intervene and consent on the child's behalf?
(b) On what basis and to what degree can that intervention take place?

In many circumstances there will be no real issue involved; the parents discover that their child is ill, they consult a doctor, who recommends a form of treatment, and that subsequently takes place. It is nevertheless true to say that where the child, whether permanently incompetent through mental disability or temporarily so by reason of immaturity, needs treatment, there must be someone who can consent on that child's behalf. Often it is trite to observe that it will be the parents with the power to consent. Under the Children Act 1989 the parent with 'parental responsibility' will be the one to consent. That 'responsibility' can be removed or restricted and be placed in the hands of others (see s. 33(3) and (4)). Others who, as a matter of fact, may need the power to consent, for example, teachers and childminders, are given it by being considered, in the words of s. 3(5), 'A person who does not have parental responsibility for a particular child; but has care of the child'. Such a person 'may . . . do what is reasonable in all the circumstances of the case for the purpose of safeguarding and promoting the child's welfare'. It should be noted that doing what is reasonable would probably not include consenting to medical treatment without the prior authorisation of the parents, who remain the persons with 'parental responsibility', unless the matter is an emergency, when the doctor could treat without gaining explicit consent in any event (see below for the rationale of treatment in an emergency).

The existence of the proxy consentor is, then, a recognition of the ethical importance of the concept of consent, and a means by which the consent can be given. It may also be the case that a judicial power of consent where a minor is concerned may be predicated on the child's need of protection from the actions or motivations of others. The court (as will be seen in relation to the issue of neonatal treatment in chapter 14 and the sterilisation decision in chapter 13) can act as the ward of the child.

In *Re D (A Minor) (Wardship: Sterilisation)* [1976] Fam 185 (see 13.3.3) Heilbron J referred to the fact that the jurisdiction was a protective one and designed to 'throw care around the ward'. In the more recent case of *Re C (A Minor) (Wardship: Medical Treatment) (No. 2)* [1990] Fam 39 Lord Donaldson MR confirmed that:

> The origin of the wardship jurisdiction is the duty of the Crown to protect its subjects and particularly children who are the generations of the future. It is exercised by the courts on behalf of the Crown. . . . The machinery for its exercise is an application to make the child a ward of court. Thereafter, the court is entitled and bound in appropriate cases to make decisions in the interests of the child which override the rights of its parents. Futhermore, the court is entitled, and bound in appropriate cases, to make orders affecting third parties which the parents could not themselves have made.

The simple protective advantage of wardship is revealed by this succinct description, but not the specific circumstances where it can be used. Aside from the parents and the wardship court, there exist other legislative mechanisms by which proxy decisions can be made to facilitate the medical treatment of the minor.

Under the Children Act 1989, s. 100(2)(c), the wardship jurisdiction cannot be exercised where the child is in the care of a local authority. The court may, however, use its broader based 'inherent jurisdiction' to treat such a child. Under s. 100(3) a local authority may apply to the court to exercise that jurisdiction. The exercise of the inherent jurisdiction would not lead to total control over the child's life, but would be issue (or rather treatment) specific. The 1989 Act has also, by virtue of s. 8(1), given the court other clearly defined powers which can relate to medical consensual issues which could impact on the child:

> In this Act—
> . . .
> 'a prohibited steps order' means an order that no step which could be taken by a parent in meeting his parental responsibility for a child, and which is of a kind specified in the order, shall be taken by any person without the consent of the court;
> . . .
> 'a specific issue order' means an order giving directions for the purpose of determining a specific question which has arisen, or which may arise, in connection with any aspect of parental responsibility for a child.'

Whatever jurisdictional basis is utilised as a matter of procedure, the most significant issue is the breadth of that jurisdiction and its theoretical and practical limits as far as consenting to medical treatment is concerned.

As with a vast number of aspects of medical law and treatment, the breadth of the power rests on the broadly defined and based 'best interests' of the child. Time and again the courts have announced that the best interests of the child lie at the heart of the wardship jurisdiction of the court, and is the 'golden thread' which runs through the exercise of the jurisdiction. Section 1(1) of the Children Act 1989 has now given statutory recognition to that fact, although the legislature has preferred the term 'welfare'. A topical and effective example of the utilisation of the best interests test, and a good example of the type of circumstances likely to be encountered by the court in the exercise of its wardship function can be found in *Re S (A Minor) (Medical Treatment)* [1993] 1 FLR 376.

The child here was some four years old, and was suffering from an extremely serious condition. Part of the treatment required the use of blood and blood products. S's parents were Jehovah's Witnesses. The case report indicates that this fact was acknowledged on the family's medical records. Consultations between the doctors and the parents only confirmed that the parents would not consent to the use of blood or blood products on themselves or their child because of their faith. The local authority had attempted to utilise s. 100 of the Children Act 1989 to invoke the inherent jurisdiction of the court to authorise the doctors to undertake the desired form of treatment. In response the parents also sought to use the 1989 Act to get a prohibited steps order.

In granting the order the local authority required for treatment to take place, Thorpe J declared that '. . . the test must remain the welfare of the child as the paramount consideration'. While there were risks attaching to the procedure the doctors wished to adopt, the chances of success were significantly higher than a treatment regime which did not involve the use of blood or blood products. In acting with the child's welfare in mind Thorpe J was well aware of the argument that the future welfare might be affected by the realisation of the child that his life had been saved by an act which was contrary to God's law as understood by this sect. In answer to that Thorpe J also indicated (in rather unconvincing fashion) the effect of the invocation of the inherent jurisdiction of the court: 'The reality seems to me to be that family reaction will recognise that the responsibility for consent was taken from them and, as a judicial act, absolved their conscience of responsibility'. (See also *Re E (A Minor) (Wardship: Medical Treatment)* [1993] 1 FLR 386.)

Best interests or welfare of the child will invariably be issue-specific and fact-based. In *Re J (A Minor) (Child in Care: Medical Treatment)* [1993] Fam 15 (for more detail on this case see chapter 14) Lord Donaldson MR was concerned with the welfare of a severely handicapped new-born baby. While one might consider it odd for there to be a debate on whether it would be in the best interests of such a child to be treated in such a way that his or her life would come to an end, such a debate becomes clearer where one considers a broad best interests test which can include dignity and the relief of suffering as a form of 'welfare' for the minor. One should also be aware that the court, particularly where the handicapped and incompetent neonate is being considered, is developing a test which reveals values of the sanctity of life, but tempered with a realisation that quality of life issues have a place in a test which is more appropriate when substituting the court's judgment of what the handicapped neonate would wish to happen if in a position to indicate a view of what treatment regime would be in his or her best interests (see 14.6).

6.5 CONSENT AND INCOMPETENT ADULTS

It would appear illogical if there were no jurisdictional or justificatory basis upon which the incompetent adult could be treated. While the justificatory basis is that of the 'best interests' of this incompetent patient, indicating a level of symmetry between the incompetent minor and adult, the courts have struggled in recent years to find a sound jurisdictional base. As already noted there needs to be some 'body' to consent on behalf of those who cannot. Medical law needs to promote effective decision-making here.

As will be indicated in relation to the sterilisation of the incompetent adult, the House of Lords in *Re F (Mental Patient: Sterilisation)* [1990] 2 AC 1 rather clumsily sought and found a jurisdictional basis for making a proxy decision on treatment. The House of Lords had to confront the problem facing Wood J in *T v T* [1988] Fam 52 that the Mental Health Act 1983 only referred to the treatment of those suffering from a recognised form of mental disorder, and then the legislative proxy mechanism could only be invoked to initiate treatment for that mental disorder. Under ss. 7 and 8 of the 1983 Act a guardianship order can be made, but only to give the guardian power to consent to treatment for the mental condition which made the legislation applicable.

Lord Brandon, faced in *Re F* with the proposed sterilisation of a 36-year-old woman, could find no assistance from the ancient prerogative *parens patriae* jurisdiction because the earlier Mental Health Act 1959 could only be read as 'sweep[ing] away the previous statutory and prerogative jurisdiction in lunacy, leaving the law relating to persons of unsound mind to be governed solely, so far as statutory enactments are concerned, by the provisions of that Act'.

The solution found by the House of Lords was to make an advance declaration that the performance by a doctor of some form of treatment would not be unlawful, notwithstanding the absence of consent. This treatment would not be unlawful provided it was undertaken in the 'best interests' of the incompetent patient.

As with the scope and ingredients of the best interests or welfare notion in relation to the immature minor and consent, there is evidence that the best interests test in relation to the mentally handicapped adult is profoundly, perhaps inevitably, vague. As stated earlier, the best interests of the patient can depend on a number of factors, not all of them necessarily related to the patient. The test where the mentally incompetent patient is concerned can easily (and I suggest has) become a means by which the medical profession fashion a decision-making process on paternalism and clinical need which is acquiesced in at law by the application of the *Bolam* test (as utilised in *Re F*). How does the court arrive at a conclusion of what is in the 'best interests' of the patient? It asks the doctor what a responsible body of medical opinion would regard as being in the patient's best interests. This may be supported by many as the true basis on which such decisions have to be made. Even if this is so, concern can be expressed that judges are once more handing over legal questions to the medical profession in circumstances where the issues are not always clinical, but ethical and societal ones to be addressed in a judicial forum (in the continued absence of legislative intervention).

This process of 'medicalising' a judicial process may be in the beginnings of a reversal with the tentative judicial acknowledgement in *Re J (A Minor) (Child in Care: Medical Treatment)* [1993] Fam 15 (applying to incompetent minors) and *Airedale NHS Trust v Bland* [1993] AC 789 (in relation to mentally incompetent adults) of the existence of a 'substituted judgment' test. One needs to be cautious about seeing this test as a sea change in consensual issues in medicine, because it may be that it is only a micro-element of the best interests test established from *Bolam*, and, in relation particularly to the facts and the decision in *Airedale NHS Trust v Bland*, is likely only to work where there is some evidence of prior opinion by the patient before becoming incompetent. The House of Lords acknowledged that they might have been swayed by a clear advance statement of Tony Bland's preferences.

Robertson describes the essence of substituted judgment in the following terms (J. Robertson, 'Organ Donations by Incompetents and the Substituted Judgment Doctrine' (1976) 76 Colum L Rev 48):

> If a person because of age or mental disability cannot select or communicate his preferences, respect for persons requires that the integrity of the person still be maintained. As stated by Rawls [*A Theory of Justice*], maintaining the integrity of the person means that we act toward him 'as we have reason to believe [he] would choose for [himself] if [he] were [capable] of reason and deciding rationally'. It does not provide a licence to impute to him preferences he never had or to ignore previous preferences.

Of course it may be that the law will need to have regard to preferences stated during competence (consider the advance treatment directives proposed by the Law Commission, see 6.6) as a confirmation of autonomy consisting as much about making decisions with regard to one's future as one's present. What of the patient who has never been (or has yet to obtain the capacity to be) able to make such decisions? In *Re J (A Minor) (Wardship: Medical Treatment)* [1991] Fam 33, substituted judgment was nevertheless found to be applicable, even though Taylor LJ's judgment could be interpreted as merely stating that to utilise 'best interests' properly one must consider the circumstances of the individual patient at hand. Substituted judgment is potentially applicable to the patient never able to express a meaningful preference, not as an alternative to the best interests test, but as a recognition that the potential liability of the medical staff and the justification of medical treatment in the absence of consent are not the only considerations. There are broader issues such as respect for dignity and religious culture which require the judicial mind to consider subjective issues as much as objective standards and potential liability. To utilise the culture exemplified by the term substituted judgment is to extend autonomy to its full logical expression.

Nevetheless it would appear that *Re T (Adult: Refusal of Treatment)* [1993] Fam 95 exemplifies the current practice:

Consultation with the next of kin . . . may reveal information as to the personal circumstances of the patient and as to the choice which the patient might have made, if he or she had been in a position to make it. Neither the personal circumstances of the patient nor a speculative answer to the question 'What would the patient have chosen?' can bind the practitioner in his choice of whether or not to treat or how to treat or justify him in acting contrary to a clearly established anticipatory refusal to accept treatment but they are factors to be taken into account by him in forming a clinical judgment as to what is in the best interests of the patient. (p. 103)

In *Airedale NHS Trust v Bland*, Lords Goff and Mustill were equally uncomfortable with substituted judgment because, at least in relation to a patient who had never been capable of expressing preferences, it was a fictitious construct.

In the end it may well be that the substituted judgment test can only apply as far as the patient who has become incompetent and prior to that has expressed precise and rational indications about future events. Alternatively, the substituted judgment test has been misconstrued as a term. It might mean little more than the reality of what takes place. The incompetent person cannot consent, someone must consent on that person's behalf, in so doing that person or body is merely substituting its own judgment for that of the incompetent person. Structured clinical intuition notes that lifestyle preferences expressed or otherwise evident can move the form of that intuition away from treatment, but such preferences need to be visible, and construed in the context that people can have a change of heart (see 1.3.4).

6.6 LAW COMMISSION PROPOSALS

As well as proposing a more comprehensive and accurate test of competence, the Law Commission in Consultation Paper 129, *Mentally Incapacitated Adults and Decision-Making: Medical Treatment and Research*, sought a statutory scheme to replace the rather ad hoc and vague authority and grounds to treat the mentally incompetent over-16 patient exemplified in *Re F (Mental Patient: Sterilisation)* [1990] 2 AC 1. The Law Commission proposed schemes to make advance directives to control treatment in the event of later incapacity, to allow for the existence of what are termed 'treatment providers' to promote the best interests of those declared to be incapable of consenting. The Law Commission, in proposing a statutory authority to treat: 'Proposes that incapacitated people who have not had the foresight to make a legally binding anticipatory decision or appoint a treatment attorney would be treated under the statutory authority to be conferred on treatment providers' (see also P. Fennell, 'Statutory Authority to Treat' (1994) 2 Med L Rev 42).

The definition of treatment provider obviously includes doctors and dentists as well as people providing a broader type of treatment. Fennell gives the example of care workers or even family members prescribing medication. Of importance is the fact that the treatment provider is there to act in the best interests of the patient, but it is apparent that there is a wider definition of best interests than the purely clinical test enunciated in *Bolam v Friern Hospital Management Committee* [1957] 1 WLR 582 and utilised in *Re F*. There appears to be a dawning recognition that the concept of substituted judgment has a place in the list of factors. The treatment provider needs to bear in mind:

(a) Past and present wishes of the patient, as far as they can be ascertained. Those wishes have to be considered in the light of the understanding of the patient when the wishes were expressed.

(b) Whether there is an alternative treatment to the one proposed; that alternative being 'more conservative or less intrusive and restrictive'.

(c) 'The factors the incapacitated person might be expected to consider if able to do so, including the likely effect of the treatment on the person's life expectancy, health, happiness, freedom and dignity' (Law Commission Consultation Paper 129, para. 3.56).

The Law Commission also sought to clarify the position of relatives. While as a matter of clinical practice there has long been a tradition that the views of parents or other available relatives are taken before the intellectually disabled are treated, it was felt that this should not be part of a future decision-making structure, at least as far as making the consultation a duty before treatment. Consultation would still be a duty on the part of the treatment provider, but only in so far as providing information to the 'nearest relative' or other person nominated by the patient before incapacity as a person whose views should be ascertained (paras 3.64–3.65). Those views are not to be binding legally.

The consultation paper attempts to give as wide a power as possible to the incapacitated patient, and where this proves impossible seeks to utilise a 'judicial forum' where there is objection to a form of treatment. When an incapacitated patient objects: 'he should not be forced to comply with it without some independent confirmation that the patient is actually incapacitated and that the benefits of the treatment outweigh the harm which even an incapacitated person may suffer if treatment is forced upon him' (para. 3.44).

If the objection is in the form of an advance declaration as to treatment, the judicial forum needs to consider the ambit and applicability of this declaration, and, where it is sufficiently clear, to give effect to this. Such a development will be seen to have the potential to impact significantly on the law and practice of euthanasia (see chapter 15). A refusal of consent by the treatment proxy would mean that the judicial forum would step in and make an assessment of what the best interests of the patient demand in the particular situation.

The Law Commission's consideration of the issues would have been noticeably incomplete if it did not consider emergency situations. The Law Commission's answer is summarised by Fennell:

Where the treatment is contrary to a valid anticipatory decision by the patient or a refusal of consent by a person with authority to do so (a court-appointed treatment proxy or a patient-appointed treatment attorney) it can only be given if it is necessary to prevent loss of life or irreversible deterioration of health while an issue is referred to the judicial forum. (1994) 2 Med LR 42 at p. 46)

Emergency treatment can take place where there has been no anticipatory refusal, or there is no proxy to consent where the treatment is 'essential to prevent an immediate risk of serious harm to that person or others' (Law Commission Consultation Paper 129, para. 3.45).

6.7   EMERGENCY TREATMENT AND CONSENT

The example of the unconscious casualty arriving in the accident and emergency department of the hospital provides an opportunity to consider two other justificatory theories of treatment without consent, implied consent and necessity.

The first of these can be swiftly disposed of. While it might be said that the patient walking into the same department with a head wound and remaining compliant while the casualty doctor treats impliedly consents to such an activity, to describe an unconscious casualty patient as impliedly consenting to the use of immunosuppressant drugs, blood transfusions and so forth would mean some considerable expansion on the sorts of things which are implied between people within society. It cannot be said to be a true reflection of the rationale for the casualty doctor's treatment, ethically, intuitively or legally. The better question is: How would the doctor rationalise treating the unconscious emergency patient?

A more accurate expression is that the casualty doctor is treating the unconscious patient as a matter of necessity. The doctor is simply saying, 'I had to treat the patient'. One should note here that as a matter of the criminal law the concept of necessity has had something of a chequered history, and concerns about the principle evolving into a legal duty to treat or otherwise act in an emergency situation have meant that the application of the principle of necessity has been limited. The coercive nature of necessity has even led some to call the defence 'duress of circumstances'. The notion here is of being forced by pressure of events to act. Nevertheless, as Lord Goff in *Re F (Mental Patient: Sterilisation)* [1990] 2 AC 1 has indicated, to invoke the doctrine of necessity justifying the activity undertaken without consent in the emergency, 'not only (1) must there be a necessity to act when it is not practicable to communicate with the assisted person, but also (2) the action taken must be such as a reasonable person would in all the circumstances take, acting in the best interests of the assisted person'.

Lord Goff went on to establish that the principle of necessity would not be confined to the emergency situation but was broad enough to encompass the 'mentally disordered person who is disabled from giving consent' and this could extend to routine forms of treatment such as dental work but only in so far as the treatment or activity conformed to the actions of a reasonable person acting in the best interests of the patient. 'Best interests' are indicated where the clinical judgment corresponds with a responsible body of medical opinion – to the *Bolam* test (see also the development of the concept of necessity under common law in *R v Bournewood Community and Mental Health NHS Trust, ex parte L (Secretary of State for Health and others intervening)* [1998] 3 All ER 289 — see Chapter 9 for more detail on this case).

Of importance was the recognition in *Re F* that the doctor operating on a patient rendered temporarily incapable of consenting should do no more than immediately necessary in the patient's best interests. Reference was made to the Canadian cases of *Marshall v Curry* [1933] 3 DLR 260 and *Murray v McMurchy* [1949] 2 DLR 442 where this matter was of central concern.

In *Marshall v Curry* there was an allegation of battery made against a doctor who had removed a diseased testicle during a hernia operation. The defendant doctor claimed that the removal was necessary to protect the patient's life and health, and a delay would have been hazardous. The court agreed.

In *Murray v McMurchy*, on the other hand, the doctor was sucessfully sued in battery where a sterilisation operation had been performed on a woman during a Caesarean section, when the wall of the plaintiff's uterus was found to be such that any future pregnancy would have proved dangerous. It was held to have been merely a convenient as opposed to a necessary operation. It would not have been unreasonable to delay until the patient was again conscious and could come to a personal decision.

What becomes apparent is that to act in the best interests of the patient in such circumstances the doctor should do no more than is immediately necessary for the patient. Mason and McCall Smith make the point (*Law and Medical Ethics*, 4th ed. (London: Butterworths, 1994), p. 221) that the difficulty with modern medicine is that a consent form signed by a competent patient prior to an operation already discussed between doctor and patient can sometimes be couched in terms that make it apparent that the doctor has a discretion to take additional measures during performance of the agreed operation. This may, however, be little more than a reflection of the fact that *post facto* most patients would approve of the additional measures taken by a doctor. The paucity of litigation in England alleging that the doctor 'went too far' appears to be evidence of this. Nevertheless in *Devi v West Midlands Health Authority* [1981] CA Transcript 491 the plaintiff successfully sued a doctor where there was agreement to an operation to repair the uterus, but not to perform a sterilisation as well. Chapter 7 discusses the difficulties patients have in bringing actions against doctors where such consensual issues are concerned.

6.8 CONCLUSION

Judicial and legislative utterances on consent all recognise the symbolic, philosophical, ethical, human-rights and legal importance of autonomy and the free consent of the individual to accept or decline medical treatment. This is not the same thing as saying that, as a matter of legal practice and medical treatment, this autonomy is unfettered or even particularly highly respected.

Modern medical law's conflicts between paternalism and freedom create obvious confusion here. Lord Donaldson, in manipulating *Gillick* v *West Norfolk and Wisbech Area Health Authority* [1986] AC 112 so heavily as virtually to destroy it in *Re R (A Minor) (Wardship: Consent to Treatment)* [1992] Fam 11 and *Re W (A Minor) (Medical Treatment: Court's Jurisdiction)* [1993] Fam 64, placed different weight on factors than many writers on medical law and ethics have done, and has come into conflict with them for that. The judiciary have placed the medical perception of patient welfare above rights and freedoms by distinguishing between a child's accepted right to consent to treatment, and a rejected right to refuse. In addition the right of the patient to consent or refuse treatment has been subordinated to the need for the medical profession to be protected from legal sanction for their actions, even where such a possibility is remote. Once more the medical profession have been allowed to hold all the cards on decision-making by the judiciary's expansion of the notion of common professional practice in medical negligence litigation (*Bolam* v *Friern Hospital Management Committee* [1957] 1 WLR 582) into this broader arena of rights in medical law.

The Law Commission proposals represent a hope for an increasing rights agenda in medical law. The maximisation of freedom within the confines of mental disability through a comprehensive but largely unintrusive definition of 'capacity' is to be welcomed. It only needs now to become part of medical law rather than remain a proposal, and to extend beyond those covered by the provisions of the Mental Health Act 1983.

Further reading

Bainham, A., 'The Judge and the Competent Minor' (1992) 108 LQR 194.
Fennell, P., 'Statutory Authority to Treat' (1994) 2 Med L Rev 42.
Gunn, M., 'The Meaning of Incapacity' (1994) 2 Med L Rev 8.
Kennedy, I., and Grubb, A., 'The Law Commission's Proposals: An Introduction' (1994) 2 Med L Rev 1.

SEVEN
Informed consent to treatment

7.1 INTRODUCTION

While the issue of consent to medical treatment as a potential action in battery (see *R* v *Richardson* (1998) *The Times*, 6 April 1998) or medical negligence does not initially conjure up images of human rights and the ethical dimensions of medical law, they are equally important here. Consider this initial question from the perspective of human rights, the demands of moral philosophy and clinical intuition. Why does the patient need to be informed about his or her medical condition, the proposed treatment of it, the risks, consequences of, and alternatives to, it?

The simplest available answer encompasses all of the moral and ethical demands: patients have a 'right' to know. Why? because it enables individuals to make autonomous choices about what should happen to them. The matter of the freedom of the individual to decide, autonomy, self-determination, whatever one prefers to call it, is once again crucial to medical ethics and therefore medical law. In the last chapter the ethical importance of consent *per se* was stressed, but the importance really lies in medical law respecting autonomy by demanding 'real' consent from the patient. Consent that is made by the competent, but also based on sufficient information beforehand. Harvey Teff notes in the key case on this area of medical law, *Sidaway* v *Board of Governors of the Bethlem Royal Hospital* [1985] AC 871, a lone voice:

Lord Scarman . . . favoured incorporating what he called the 'transatlantic doctrine of informed consent' into English law. He saw the doctrine as embodying the doctor's obligation to satisfy the patient's right to know. (*Reasonable Care* (Oxford: Clarendon Press, 1994), p. 196)

The term 'informed' consent has its transatlantic tag because it was first used in the US case of *Salgo* v *Leland Stanford Jr University Board of Trustees* (1957) 317 P 2d 170. The court used the comments of Cardozo J in

Schloendorff v *Society of New York Hospital* (1914) 105 NE 92 (see 6.1) as a springboard to accepting that a patient needs sufficient information to be informed of risks, benefits and alternatives to make a true choice about treatment. A great deal of former US confusion, similar to current English law in some ways, between patient rights and professional dominance was evidenced by this case. *Salgo* is an early indication of equivocal language in informed consent as a matter of medical law: '. . . in discussing the element of risk a certain amount of discretion must be employed consistent with the full disclosure of facts necessary to an informed consent' (317 P 2d 170 at p. 181). The latter part refers to the right to be fully informed, yet the former suggests that the doctor may decide how much is 'full disclosure'.

Medical law, being in large part comprised of patient rights and doctor duties, has once more discovered the tensions between the right, need, and demand of the patient to have full pre-treatment information, and the doctor's right, whether from motives of paternalism, intuition or fear of litigation, to limit the amount of information the patient gets. Medical law has seen those pressures in the context of 'informed' consent, but once more balked at an outright statement on levels of information disclosure commensurate with human rights. English medical law has instead appeared increasingly internationally isolated in holding the levels of information to be given to the patient to be dependent on the persistent defence mechanism of medical law, the 'reponsible body of medical opinion'. *Bolam v Friern Hospital Management Committee* [1957] 1 WLR 582 yet again dictates the rules and decides the referee.

The language of informed consent can make it prone to a number of interpretations. The various available meanings and their potential applicability need to be noted before the forms of legal action alleging a lack of 'informed' consent are considered. English judges, when they talk of 'informed consent' mean the view confirmed by Lord Scarman and enunciated in *Sidaway* as the 'transatlantic concept' of patient rights. Informed consent does not mean this alone, and is the cause of some confusion in medical law writing on consensual issues. Change the focus and it becomes clear. The analysis is not just whether we do, or should have, this notion from the USA and Canada. It is how 'informed' does a consent need to be as a matter of ethics, rights and law, to prove ethically correct, respect human rights, be legally effective and practically possible?

(a) John walks into the doctor's surgery, and is told by the doctor, 'I require a blood sample of you'. Here John has certainly been informed about an intention on the part of the doctor. If John now says 'OK', is that an informed consent? The answer is an uncomfortable yes. As a matter of fact he has been informed what is intended and has agreed. It does not yet, it is suggested, have the dimension of 'knowledge' or 'comprehension' on the patient's part. The difference for medical law and patient rights is between being notified, and being in possession of information sufficient to make a choice. There is a mechanical feeling to the above case. The 'OK' is based on bare notification, there has been no 'why', 'how', 'when', 'where', 'at what risk?' or even 'who'? Informed consent, to even a base legal level, has to be based on dialogue between doctor and patient.

(b) John is told by the same doctor, 'I wish to take a blood sample for some tests'. John asks, 'What tests?'. The doctor replies, 'Just routine ones'. John says 'OK'. Is this more like 'informed' consent? The information level is higher, but it is still notification of an intention, now combined with a request for more information, and a barely informative reply. Is John yet in a sufficient position to decide whether to agree to the blood sample being taken? Is there enough information to make a choice?

It is not hard to imagine these scenarios developing in complexity. There may be individuals who feel that situation (b) contains sufficient information to come to a decision, others may not. That is the problem for medical law, and indeed for both patient and doctor. How much information is enough for an informed consent?

The legal answer depends on where the question is directed. In the USA and other common law jurisdictions the question for the law has come from the perspective of the patient; the law will ask: How much does the patient need to know? In English medical law the question comes from the medical profession; the law will ask: How much does the doctor think the patient needs to know? The difference is between the rights-based medical law of these other countries and the paternalism and medical protectionism of medical law in England. The legal development of these ethical distinctions will be considered later.

7.2 ACTION FOR BATTERY

There may be circumstances where the patient, while not suffering an apparent physical or economic loss, alleges that there was no consent to treatment at law. In the cases of *Marshall* v *Curry* [1933] 3 DLR 260, *Murray* v *McMurchy* [1949] 2 DLR 442 and *Devi* v *West Midlands Health Authority* [1981] CA Transcript 491, considered in 6.7, the allegation was that there was no consent to the 'extra' operative procedures that were undertaken. The form of the action was a civil action for battery.

One should first be aware of the fact that the criminal courts are concerned with battery, but aside from the instance where the patient's consent to being touched by the doctor is induced by fraud (for example, sexual intercourse with the patient after representing that it was part of a medical examination: *R* v *Williams* [1923] 1 KB 340), there is little realistic prospect of the doctor coming before the criminal courts where the patient alleges lack of consent during the everyday practice of medicine by the doctor. Recently, however, there was an attempt made to convict a member of the medical profession. In *R* v *Richardson* (1998) *The Times*, 6 April 1998, a dentist had been suspended from practice by the General Dental Council. Nevertheless she continued to practice. She was charged with assault occasioning actual bodily harm, convicted and appealed. The prosecution had contended that prac-ticing while suspended constituted a fraud which vitiated the consent of her patients. She admitted that she was in breach of s. 38 of the Dentists Act

1934 (praticing while unqualified) but patients were in no doubt as to the nature and quality of the treatment undertaken or the person carrying it out; therefore consent was valid. The Court of Appeal accepted that there was valid consent and therefore no assault — the conviction was quashed.

The civil action for battery is a significant prospect for the patient alleging lack of consent in that it is a legal recognition of the ethical importance of the autonomy of the patient, and the advantages of framing the action in battery rather than negligence reflect this. The plaintiff merely has to show that there was a non-consensual touching. The mere fact of being touched is sufficient without proof of damage suffered as a consequence. The damage is having one's bodily integrity interfered with. This fact means that one need not overcome the high legal hurdle of causation. As far as damages are concerned, where, in the negligence action, the recoverable damages are those that are foreseeable, in a battery action all direct damages are recoverable whether foreseeable or not.

Cases such as *Collins* v *Wilcock* [1984] 1 WLR 1172 and *Re F (Mental Patient: Sterilisation)* [1990] 2 AC 1 stress time and again the essence of self-determination earlier expressed by Cardozo J (see 6.1). The touching of the patient requires, to avoid liability under the civil and criminal law of battery, the consent of the patient. As in chapter 6, the reality of this ethical commitment, as a matter of modern medical law has to be tested.

While there needs to be a touching of the patient without consent to maintain an action in battery, the courts were for a time unclear whether this touching had to be done with hostile intent. The contact needs to be intentional, that much is clear, and is unlikely to be a contentious issue in any battery action in the medical context (see *Fowler* v *Lanning* [1959] 1 QB 426 on the general issue of intent in battery). The case of *Collins* v *Wilcock* [1984] 1 WLR 1172 established that while 'the least touching of another in anger is battery, it is more common nowadays to treat [cases of battery] as falling within a general exception embracing all physical contact which is a generally accepted conduct of daily life' (per Goff LJ at p. 1177).

So there does not need to be overt hostility to maintain a battery action. For example, in the Canadian case of *Malette* v *Schulman* (1988) 47 DLR (4th) 18, a Jehovah's Witness successfully sued a doctor in battery for a blood transfusion that she did not consent to, and would not have done, as was clear from the card that she carried (see 15.4.3). From the formulation of Goff LJ, there are envisaged circumstances where a battery will be the result of 'unacceptable physical contact'.

Strangely the Court of Appeal appeared to endorse the requirement of hostility in *Wilson* v *Pringle* [1987] QB 237 at p. 253. In *Re F (Mental Patient: Sterilisation)*, Lord Goff regarded that as incorrect, and an unreasonable limitation on the notion of battery. His Lordship also took the opportunity to reiterate the symbolic protective importance of the battery action.

The battery action is thus available where there is an absence of consent, or the consent does not accord with the medical procedure which subsequently takes place.

A question potentially of some significance to a patient is whether the battery action is available where the allegation is not that the patient did not consent as a matter of fact, but that consent was based on inadequate disclosure of pre-operative information by the doctor. While there is controversy over the scope and application of the term for the medical lawyer, the essence of the allegation is that the consent was not 'informed'.

The patient making such an allegation will generally be disappointed if the attempt is made to frame the action in battery. There is distinct judicial antipathy to using the battery action in this sphere, and is typified by the judgment of Bristow J in the important medical law case of *Chatterton* v *Gerson* [1981] QB 432.

Mrs Chatterton had been suffering from chronic pain around an operation scar. She consulted the defendant, who was a specialist in the treatment of such pain. The first attempt to relieve the pain was only partially successful, so a second injection was given. Not only was this attempt unsuccessful in relieving the pain, it had the further impact of numbing Mrs Chatterton's right leg, making it useless. The allegation was that there had been a failure to warn of the risk that this could happen, therefore the consent was legally ineffective and the doctor should be liable for battery. In this claim and the claim for negligence Mrs Chatterton was unsuccessful.

Bristow J felt that, at least as far as the allegation of battery was concerned, the court should ask the simple question: Was the consent real? The answer to his own question has become a common feature of judgments concerning consent and battery in medicine:

. . . once the patient is informed *in broad terms* of the nature of the procedure which is intended, and gives her consent, that consent is real, and the cause of the action on which to base a claim for failure to go into risks and implications is negligence, not trespass. Of course if information is withheld in bad faith, the consent will be vitiated by fraud. . . . it would be very much against the interests of justice if actions which are really based on a failure by the doctor to perform his duty adequately to inform were pleaded in trespass. (emphasis added)

These sentiments have been repeated on a number of occasions, and in more direct terms. In the key modern case on consent and medical treatment in this context (and that of negligence), *Sidaway* v *Board of Governors of the Bethlem Royal Hospital* [1985] AC 871, Lord Scarman repeated the view of Hirst J in *Hills* v *Potter* [1984] 1 WLR 641 that to use such an action in this context would be 'deplorable'. Why such antipathy? Gerald Robertson ('Informed Consent to Medical Treatment' (1981) 97 LQR 102) confirms that the answer to this is based on the serious consequences of the successful battery action on the reputation of the doctor. It may be that such an action against a doctor is seen as a more serious matter than an allegation of negligence. The view is that liability on the part of the doctor for battery carries with it some taint of criminality and brutality. This may be coupled with the fact that there is still a perception that the true place of the battery action is in relation to acts of obvious hostility which would appear anathema to the common practice of medicine. The battery action, if it had the potential for success in the area of information disclosure to the patient, would lead on to a practice of medicine which would be chiefly concerned with the avoidance of liability by the doctor, rather than the interests of the patient, defensive medicine. Case law in a number of jurisdictions recognises that the only place for battery actions in medicine would be where the patient is given different treatment than that discussed beforehand, or there is some type of fraud or misrepresentation practised on the patient in relation to the treatment.

In *Davis* v *Barking, Havering and Brentwood Health Authority* (1993) 2 Med LR 366 the acceptance of the *Chatterton* v *Gerson* level of information disclosure to preclude a battery action was approved, and seems to close the door firmly on using it where there has been a base level of real, if not informed, consent. John, in situation (b) at the beginning of this chapter would not have a battery claim.

In combination with this distinct legal antipathy to the use of battery, is the less considered fact that legal consent, if not to be a battery, has also to be free of duress. This makes sense. It would be rather nonsensical to talk of consent being an expression of autonomy if that consent were 'forced'. If it were coerced in some way, the patient has not acted as an autonomous individual. Someone else has wielded power (note the fact that the consent was found not to be 'free' because of the undue influence of the Jehovah's Witness mother in *Re T (Adult: Refusal of Treatment)* [1993] Fam 95 and could therefore be overridden in the 'best interests' of the patient; see also 6.2.1.1).

In *Freeman* v *Home Office* [1984] 1 WLR 1172 the court found that the fact that a person was a prisoner did not negate the ability of that prisoner to give free consent, even though consent was given in a coercive environment. Nevertheless, coercive elements can exist to negative the practical freedom of the consent, even in the doctor's surgery. Go back to the first situaton involving John, at the beginning of this chapter. The authority of the doctor in 'demanding' the blood sample may well sufficiently intimidate certain patients into submission without true consent. To consider this unlikely is to ignore the continued deference some have towards the demands of the doctor, and the very real fear some people have of entering the surgery. Combined with this is the comment of M. Somerville, *Consent to Medical Care* (Ottawa: Law Reform Commission of Canada, 1980) that:

> . . . coercive factors may be at their most subtle and difficult to detect, and freedom of choice most threatened, in a situation in which the more powerful party believes he is acting for the benefit of the other. (pp. 47–8)

Nevertheless the minimalist approach of *Chatterton* v *Gerson*, and the subsequent medically protective antipathy of English common law to the battery action is clear. What is less clear is how the law can justify not utilising the battery action when the essence of getting consent is the common law maxim of *volenti non fit iniuria*. Consent negates legal injury, but there has to be consent to run a risk. There cannot be consent to run a risk where the patient is not informed of that risk. I walk into the local hospital with severe back pain after a rugby match. The doctor informs me that I require a general anaesthetic, because there is a need for an exploratory operation to see if I have damaged or exposed some nerves. I agree. The doctor has not informed me, either of the small risk of injury through anaesthesia, or of the risk of paralysis in carrying out the operation. How can I have agreed to run those risks? (See also the general tort law cases that would appear to support liability here: *Barrett* v *Ministry of Defence* (1993), *Independent*, 3 June 1993; *Morris* v *Murray* [1991] 2 QB 6). Nevertheless the door is pretty much closed to actions in battery.

One needs, then, to look to the law of negligence, where the allegation is that the patient was insufficiently informed of the risks of the operative procedure and one or more of those risks became a reality and caused the patient damage.

7.3 INFORMED CONSENT AND THE ACTION IN NEGLIGENCE

7.3.1 Introduction

The two central issues once more bring attention to the difficulties of succeeding in a medical negligence action: The questions of the standard of disclosure to be expected of the doctor at law, and the very real difficulty here, the issue of causation. The patient may well claim that the level of information given was insufficient, and the court may agree, but would the patient have refused even knowing this extra information about risk?

The attitude of the English courts in relation to the standard or level of disclosure to be expected as a matter of medical law is now to be seen in the significant case of *Sidaway* v *Board of Governors of the Bethlem Royal Hospital* [1985] AC 871. Although that case represents the current state of the law, it is not without its detractors and in itself does not fit particularly comfortably with the formulation of *Bolam* v *Friern Hospital Management Committee* [1957] 1 WLR 582 when applied in this context.

7.3.2 The facts of *Sidaway*

The plaintiff required an operation on cervical vertebrae to rid herself of recurrent pain. The operation carried a risk of around 2 per cent of damage to the nerve root. There was a 1 per cent risk too of damage to the spinal cord. The latter would have much more serious consequences were it to occur. It did, and the plaintiff suffered from severe disability. It was established at trial that the operation had been performed properly, but the patient had only been informed of the risk of damage to the nerve root and not the risk to the spinal cord itself. Skinner J at first instance also found that the doctor had failed to tell the plaintiff that the operation was one of choice rather than necessity. At trial, Skinner J found that the neurosurgeon had adopted a practice of disclosure that accorded with the actions of a responsible body of neurosurgeons at the time, and, applying the *Bolam* test, had come up to the standard expected at law.

7.3.3   The issues in *Sidaway*

While both the Court of Appeal and the House of Lords endorsed the first-instance decision, there was less than wholehearted support for the simple application of the *Bolam* test to the issue of disclosure of information. Lord Bridge in the House of Lords crystallised the central issue in the following terms:

> The important question which this appeal raises is whether the law imposes any, and if so what, different criterion as the measure of the medical man's duty of care to his patient when giving advice with respect to a proposed course of treatment. It is clearly right to recognise that a conscious adult of sound mind is entitled to decide for himself whether or not he will submit to a particular course of treatment proposed by the doctor, most significantly surgical treatment under general anaesthesia.

Note the two related issues here. Lord Bridge is asking: Does *Bolam* apply here as well as in diagnosis and treatment? The other issue is: Can *Bolam* apply because of the symbolic importance of autonomy and the right to refuse?

The House of Lords appears to endorse the view that the patient, in order to exercise choice, needs to have sufficient information to make a decision about the treatment proposed. The question for medical law is whether noble words have manifested themselves in deeds and laws.

7.3.4   Informed consent

The USA, Canada and Australia have used this ethical backbone of medical law, patient autonomy, to fashion what has become known as the doctrine of 'informed consent'. It is typified by the US case of *Canterbury* v *Spence* (1972) 464 F 2d 772 and accepted by the important Canadian case of *Reibl* v *Hughes* (1980) 114 DLR (3d) 1.

Canterbury v *Spence* was something of a reaction against the equivocal decision in *Salgo* v *Leland Stanford, Jr, University Board of Trustees* (1957) 317 P 2d 170, which (see 7.1) recognised the right to be fully informed, but within a framework of medical discretion. *Canterbury* v *Spence* moved the focus back to the patient, in declaring that:

> respect for the patient's right of self-determination on particular therapy demands a standard set by law for physicians rather than one which physicians may or may not impose upon themselves. (p. 784)

The point could not have been made more clearly. The doctor is to be judged not on what the doctor considered the patient needed, but from the patient's point of view. It has been dubbed since the 'prudent patient' test of informational need. There is a rather important caveat, however, attaching to this test. The court in *Canterbury* v *Spence* decided that there still had to be a sort of therapeutic privilege to withhold certain information from the patient. The objective nature of the 'prudent patient' meant that there could be evidence adduced that certain pre-operative revelations would do more harm than good to the reasonable patient. For example, there is a risk of death or disability in all instances where general anaesthetics are used. The level of risk is dependent on the individual patient obviously, but the overall risk is miniscule. To tell a patient this, even to theorise telling the 'prudent patient' this risk, might distort the patient's perception of the benefits and burdens of the therapy and harm patient welfare. Whatever view one takes of this 'privilege', there is no doubt it chips away at patient autonomy a little more. While it was to prove a popular decision to Lord Scarman in *Sidaway*, *Canterbury* v *Spence* 'promises more than it delivers' (Teff, *Reasonable Care* (Oxford: Clarendon Press, 1994), p. 204). There is evidence that the US medical profession see it as intrusive and an unnecessary undermining of their abilities. In practical terms, question answering and form filling are time-consuming formalities which are seen to detract time and attention from the true task of the doctor, which is to cure the sick. The alternative view is that part of the doctor's job is to cure the sick *and* respect individual rights.

7.3.5 Lord Scarman in *Sidaway*; endorsement of the 'prudent patient'

Lord Scarman in *Sidaway* enunciated what were considered the four key principles of the doctrine of informed consent gleaned from both the US and Canadian positions:

(a)   It is a basic concept that an individual of adult years and sound mind has a right to choose what shall happen to his or her body (from Cardozo J in *Schloendorff* v *Society of New York Hospital* (1914) 105 NE 92, see 6.1).

(b)   'The consent is the informed exercise of a choice, and that entails an opportunity to evaluate knowledgeably the options available and the risks attendant on each.'

(c)   The doctor must, therefore, disclose all 'material risks'; what risks are 'material' is determined by the 'prudent patient' test. This test uses as its template what the reasonable patient, in the plaintiff's position, would attach significance to in coming to a decision on treatment advice given.

(d)   There is however, a 'therapeutic privilege' for the doctor to withhold information which it is considered would prove a 'psychological detriment to the patient'.

7.3.6 Other options for the House of Lords

In addition to the doctrine of informed consent, there were a number of other ways in which the House of Lords could have judged the standard of information disclosure required to absolve the defendant doctor from liability.

The optimum expression of patient autonomy, of the 'right to know', could be achieved by the utilisation of the subjective knowledge of the particular patient. A patient, to be truly informed, would need to know everything about the proposed operation before coming to a decision. Slightly less Utopian might be the duty on the doctor to fully inform and educate the patient on the risks and benefits of the treatment, but subject to a clinical discretion to withhold information that might distort the patient's decision-making. A patient who has to know 'everything' about the operation needs to know as much as the doctor. Despite the practical difficulties of this test, the US courts at one stage came remarkably close to endorsing it. In *Fain* v *Smith* (1985) 479 So 2d 1150, the court, while endorsing the objective standard of the prudent patient test, argued that 'the objective standard requires consideration by the factfinder of what a reasonable person with all of the characterstics of the plaintiff, including his idiosyncracies and religious beliefs, would have under the same circumstances' (pp. 1154–5). In other words the test is subjective. While a virtually pure expression of individual self-determination, *Fain* v *Smith* is an isolated case.

Lord Bridge in *Sidaway* identified another extreme which the courts could adopt, namely, the purely clinical level of information disclosure. This approach would place all the power in the hands of the particular doctor. Having come to the decision that the particular operation is in the best interests of the patient the doctor makes a clinical affirmation of its necessity. There would thereafter be no need to inform the patient of risks, benefits or alternatives. This would be the ultimate expression of paternalism. The doctor has decided what is best for the patient, so why bother to tell the patient anything? While there has never really been an overt acceptance of this as a matter of medical law, one has some suspicions that it is a view that some members of the medical profession might also keep to themselves, but nevertheless hold.

A less drastic variant might be that the doctor would be under no duty to inform of the risks and benefits unless specifically asked about them by the patient. This theoretical option has its own problems. It leaves power in the hands of the doctor, and gives the patient an opportunity to open dialogue. In practical terms, though, matters will come to an impasse. As Kennedy and Grubb appreciate, the time will come when the following will happen:

Dr: 'So that is what happens. Is there anything else you need to know?'
Patient: 'I don't know, is there anything more I can know?'
Dr: 'Yes, the following happens . . . now is there anything else you want to know?'
Patient: 'I'm not sure, is there anything else you can tell me?' (*Medical Law*, 2nd ed. (London: Butterworths, 1994), p. 190)

Requiring the patient to be told everything is an unrealistic expression of autonomous decision-making. Doctors, the argument goes, cannot be expected to fully educate each patient so that they have the optimum amount of information on which to base a choice. It would be practically impossible and in terms of the effective use of the doctor's time, little short of a disaster for any health-care system. The second test, the clinical test, is a simple expression of a theory of paternalism which has within it no respect for the autonomy of the individual. The final option is practically impossible.

The prudent patient test indicated by *Canterbury* v *Spence* (1972) 464 F 2d 772 (see 7.3.4) is a form of decision-making which recognises autonomy through a standard dictated by the needs of the patient rather than the requirements of the doctor.

7.3.7 Rejection of informed consent

Lord Bridge, in an important but controversial statement of principle and practice, *rejected* the prudent patient standard as impractical, and gave the following three reasons why:

> First, it gives insufficient weight to the doctor–patient relationship. A very wide variety of factors must enter into a doctor's clinical judgment not only as to what treatment is appropriate for a particular patient, but also as to how best to communicate to the patient the significant factors necessary to enable the patient to make an informed decision whether to undergo the treatment. The doctor cannot set out to educate the patient to his own standard of medical knowledge of all the relevant factors involved. He may take the view, certainly with some patients, that the very fact of his volunteering, without being asked, information of some remote risk involved in the treatment proposed, even though he describes it as remote, may lead to that risk assuming an undue significance in the patient's calculations. Secondly, it would seem to me quite unrealistic in any medical negligence action to confine the expert medical evidence to an explanation of the primary medical factors involved and to deny the court the benefit of evidence of medical opinion and practice on the particular issue of disclosure which is under consideration. Thirdly, the objective test which *Canterbury* propounds seems to me to be so imprecise as to be almost meaningless. If it is to be left to individual judges to decide for themselves what 'a reasonable person in the patient's position' would consider a risk of sufficient significance that he should be told about it, the outcome of litigation in this field is likely to be quite unpredictable. (*Sidaway* v *Board of Governors of the Bethlem Royal Hospital* [1985] AC 871 at p. 899)

If none of the above tests was applicable, would a simple application of the *Bolam* test to the standard of disclosure of material be any more pertinent? In the Canadian case of *Reibl* v *Hughes* (1980) 114 DLR (3d) 1 at p. 13, Laskin CJC considered that while expert evidence of common practice from the medical profession would obviously be relevant to the issue of the standard of disclosure required, to make it determinative would be 'to hand over to the medical profession the entire question of the scope of the duty of disclosure, including the question whether there has been a breach of that duty'.

7.3.8   *Bolam*, or something else?

In *Sidaway*, Lord Bridge concluded that the issue was still one which was a matter of clinical judgment, while recognising that there was some force in the rights-based view of Laskin CJC in *Reibl* v *Hughes* (see 7.3.7). With those two factors in mind Lord Bridge then said that the test of the level of disclosure was to be decided 'primarily' according to the expert medical evidence, applying the *Bolam* test.

A number of writers have picked up on the term 'primarily' as an indication that where issues of information disclosure are concerned, the House of Lords may be indicating a willingness to question common medical practice in this less technical and therefore less mysterious area. There does not need to be, the argument goes, a discussion of percentage risks or the intricacies of surgery. A judge, like the rest of us, is capable of considering whether a piece of information is one that is 'needed' and should therefore be legally 'demanded' to gain 'informed' consent.

Lord Diplock, however, felt unable to move any distance away from the *Bolam* test here; indicating that the eponymous case was itself partly concerned with levels of disclosure as well as negligent treatment. It would therefore seem illogical to split the practice of medicine into component legal duties, making *Bolam* apply to some areas but not to others.

7.3.9   Deficiencies of *Bolam*

In *Sidaway*, Lord Scarman, in what was effectively a dissenting judgment, actually rejected the application of the *Bolam* test to the disclosure of risk and found the decisions of Skinner J and the Court of Appeal 'disturbing' in implication. Lord Scarman gave voice to the problems caused by *Bolam*:

> The profession . . . should not be judge in its own cause; or, less emotively but more correctly, the courts should not allow medical opinion as to what is best for the patient to override the patient's right to decide for himself whether he will submit to the treatment offered him.

Lord Scarman indicated that *Bolam* suffered from inherent limitations when applied *simpliciter* to the disclosure of information. While the doctor might have clinical reasons for withholding information, which accord with the actions of colleagues, the patient might have wider aspirations and values than the purely medical. The correct balance between clinical decision-making and the rights of the patient is, Lord Scarman felt, to be found in the 'prudent patient' test of *Canterbury* v *Spence* (1972) 464 F 2d 772 (see 7.3.4). It was acknowledged that the purely subjective patient test would be Utopian and unrealistic. However, the prudent patient test, with the protective mechanism of the doctor's therapeutic privilege of withholding potentially distorting or damaging information, does work in practice without the inflexibility it has been thought it might create in clinical decision-making. This has been shown by the development of law in the USA, Canada and now in Australia with *Rogers* v *Whitaker* (1992) 175 CLR 479 (for an effective analysis of this decision see Chalmers and Schwarz, '*Rogers* v *Whitaker* and Informed Consent in Australia: A Fair Dinkum Duty of Disclosure' (1993) 1 Med L Rev 139).

7.3.10   A workable alternative?

Lord Scarman considered appropriate a course which was later described in *Rogers* v *Whitaker* (1992) 175 CLR 479 at p. 490:

> The law should recognise that a doctor has a duty to warn a patient of a material risk inherent in the proposed treatment; a risk is material if, in the circumstances of the particular case, a reasonable person in the patient's position, if warned of the risk, would be likely to attach significance to it or if the medical practitioner is or should reasonably be aware that the particular patient, if warned of the risk, would be likely to attach significance to it.

The patient in *Rogers* v *Whitaker* was advised that scar tissue, which was damaging vision in one eye, could be removed and improve vision. The patient asked a great many questions, and was particularly concerned about the possible risks to her 'good' eye, through an accident, but never whether the operation itself might cause damage. The chance was said to be in the order of 1 in 14,000. Her chances were slightly raised because she had already suffered a penetrating injury to the eye. The operation was properly carried out, but the risk became reality and she became almost blind within a year. Evidence showed that professional practice was not to tell the patient of this risk unless specifically asked. Despite this, and the remote chance of that risk, the failure to warn of it was found to be a breach of the doctor's duty of care.

The real significance of the decision in *Rogers* v *Whitaker* is that it sought to distinguish between duties in diagnosis, treatment and information disclosure. *Bolam* might apply to the former two but not the third. The questions here were 'of a different order altogether'. The essence of the joint judgment is in the following passage:

> In Australia . . . the standard of care . . . is not to be determined solely or even primarily by reference to the practice followed or supported by a responsible body of opinion in the relevant profession or trade. Even in the sphere of diagnosis and treatment, the heartland of the skilled medical practitioner, the *Bolam* principle has not always been applied. Further, and more importantly, particularly in the field of non-disclosure of risk and the provision of advice and information, the *Bolam* principle has been discarded and, instead, the courts have adopted the principle that . . . it is for the courts to adjudicate on what is the appropriate standard of care. (175 CLR 479 at p. 487)

It is really a reassertion of the 'prudent patient plus therapeutic privilege' test of *Canterbury* v *Spence*. It applies to risks which are material to the prudent patient making an informed decision, even when the enquiry is general rather than specific (as was the case on the facts of *Rogers* v *Whitaker*). The focus is fundamentally different for medical law if such a rule is adopted. The court first asks what is required of the patient to express self-determination fully, then the court (not the doctors) decides how much information needs to be given for that expression.

7.3.11   What does *Sidaway* propose?

While Lord Scarman effectively dissented from the decisions of the other Law Lords in *Sidaway* (effectively, in that the applicability of *Bolam* was rejected by Lord Scarman, but the overall decision that the defendant was not liable should remain), Lord Bridge (with whom Lord Keith agreed) propounded a sort of *Bolam* test. In the Court of Appeal, Lord Donaldson MR had also reinterpreted *Bolam* as meaning in this context that: 'The duty is fulfilled if the doctor acts in accordance with a practice *rightly* accepted as proper by a body of skilled and experienced medical men'.

The practice of not disclosing a particular risk inherent in an operation prior to treatment is a clinical matter, but the law nevertheless retains the power to intervene. Medical law can state that while *Bolam* is *primarily* the means by which the standard of disclosure is judged, a common practice might be declared not to be *rightly* accepted; in other words there may be a common practice, but it might be that such common professional practice is wrong.

It could just be that their lordships were phrasing *Bolam* differently, while maintaining an implicit notion of the traditional meaning and comprehensive application of the test. This, aside from Lord Diplock's clear endorsement of *Bolam simpliciter*, does appear hard to sustain. Lords Bridge and Keith modified *Bolam*, but into what is still hard to fathom. Nevertheless the Court of Appeal in *Gold* v *Haringey Health Authority* [1988] QB 481 indicated that *Bolam* in 'unadulterated' form was applicable to diagnosis, treatment *and* disclosure of risk.

Mason and McCall Smith (*Law and Medical Ethics*, 4th ed. (London: Butterworths, 1994), p. 244) consider the undiluted use of *Bolam* in *Gold* v *Haringey Health Authority* in strident terms:

> This attitude is beginning to take on an atmosphere of stubbornness and is becoming almost unique in face of the now universal acceptance of a patient's right to decide on his or her own treatment.

It seems a pity that leave to appeal to the House of Lords was not given in *Gold* v *Haringey Health Authority*.

Lord Bridge in *Sidaway* also considered that there would be circumstances where the provision of information would be 'so obviously necessary to an informed choice that no prudent medical man would fail to make it'. This would be so even if non-disclosure was common professional practice in a particular area of medicine. While Lord Bridge went on to give the example of a 10 per cent risk of a stroke, there is a danger in beginning to play a numbers game in the abstract, particularly in an aspect of medical care that will be dependent on any number of other factors. It might be better if the courts remain with Lord Bridge's general statement that there be 'a substantial risk of grave adverse consequences' which would necessitate disclosure.

If this statement is still thought to beg too many questions, one might consider the utilisation of 'materiality'. A piece of information is 'obviously necessary' if its provision will be material to the decision-making process. As the earlier overseas cases have indicated, materiality of information can be assessed from the effect it would have on the reasonably prudent patient.

There may be circumstances where the patient attempts to alter the duty of disclosure which the doctor might have and even to impinge on therapeutic privilege; the patient may request more information. Lord Bridge in *Sidaway* was succinct, clear and, it is suggested, correct in the view that:

> When questioned specifically by a patient of apparently sound mind about risks involved in a particular treatment proposed, the doctor's duty must, in my opinion, be to answer both truthfully and as fully as the questioner requires.

Despite the clarity of this view, the duty has been made subject to a clinical discretion to withhold certain information (see *Lee* v *South West Thames Regional Health Authority* [1985] 1 WLR 845 and a case which appears to take paternalism to Draconian levels at times, *Blyth* v *Bloomsbury Health Authority* (1993) 4 Med LR 151). In *Blyth*, clinical discretion was held to apply even where the patient asks a specific question. This was a trained nurse asking specific questions! Mrs Blyth claimed that she was not told of the side-effects possible after the injection of the controversial contraceptive Depo-Provera. There were a number of these side-effects, and Mrs Blyth had only been told of one of them. Her claim failed because of the frankly astounding utilisation of *Bolam* to protect a doctor who does not answer a direct question.

It may be, however, that the recent House of Lords decision in *Bolitho* v *City and Hackney Health Authority* [1997] 3 WLR 1151, if it represents a change at all, may be an indication that where the judge is considering a less complex medical issue, such as the level of information disclosure, there may be a willingness to find that a standard medical practice of retaining information does not rest on a logical base and therefore reject it. If this were to happen at all then it would only be in rare cases (for more detail on the impact of *Bolitho* see chapter 4).

7.4 CONSENT AND CAUSATION

A successful allegation that the level of pre-operative disclosure fell below the legal standard expected will mean nothing if the patient cannot show on the balance of probabilities that he or she would *not* have undertaken the treatment if informed of the risk that has become a reality. There are once more a number of ways that the law can tackle this factual issue.

The court could adopt a subjective test of causation, and simply ask: Would *this* plaintiff have gone through with the operation knowing of the risk? The problem with adopting such a simple test is that in reality every plaintiff injured by a risk inherent in the operation that was performed would say, 'If I had known of the risk I would have refused the operation'. This is not to depict such plaintiffs in a cynical light, but to accept that it would be a typical reaction to the distress of injury and their frustration that of all the people who had undergone the operation with a successful outcome theirs was one of the percentage that could and did go wrong. This test does not, and really cannot, represent English medical law.

At the other end of the spectrum, one could adopt a 'reasonable patient' test and ask: Would a reasonably prudent patient have consented to go through with the operation having been informed of the risk? Such a test has as its advantage the fact that the judge can use personal experience, as an actual or potential patient, to consider whether the patient would have gone through with the operation. Allied to this is the fact that there would be some likelihood of the law developing a consistent practice in assessing risk and causation.

The disadvantage lies in the fact that while the reasonable patient might well have still gone through with the operation, the particular plaintiff, because of some personal reason, would not have done so if told. For example, a patient is not informed that there is a small risk that a spinal operation might cause paralysis (as in *Chatterton* v *Gerson* [1981] QB 432). The reasonable patient might consider such a small risk as acceptable (if told), because it relieves a persistent back pain, but the particular patient, because of a strong desire to maintain independence and mobility, with a profound fear of never being able to walk again, would prefer to keep the pain and avoid the risk.

With this inadequacy in mind the courts have come up with a test that amalgamates the two. The test of causation is whether the reasonable patient, sharing such of the particular patient's characteristics as might affect the decision to consent, knowing the risk would have declined the operation on being informed (see *Smith* v *Barking, Havering and Brentwood Health Authority* (unreported 29 July 1989) and the Scottish case of *Goorkani* v *Tayside Health Board* (1991) 3 Med LR 33). This test has as its advantage the relative certainty of objectivity and the personal justice and respect for autonomy in its subjective element.

In *Smith* v *Barking, Havering and Brentwood Health Authority*, the plaintiff suffered from a condition that would have led to paralysis within a year, unless an operation was carried out. There was a 25 per cent risk that the operation would accelerate the paralysis. The defendant doctor negligently failed to tell the plaintiff this fact. It was held that there was a strong possibility that the plaintiff would have taken the risk, and gone ahead with the operation even knowing of the dangers. Damages were therefore limited to the depression and shock caused by the plaintiff discovering herself paralysed without any prior warning of the possibility of it.

The essence of the 'reasonable patient' analysis of causation here is that it is objective, whereas the traditonal test for causation in negligence is subjective. Nevertheless with the dangers of 'denial in hindsight' by the patient there has to be some normative concept in existence.

7.5 CONCLUSION

The power of the medical profession to decide on the level of disclosure of information to patients appears both unassailable as a matter of English medical law at present, and increasingly anomalous. The international recognition in medical law and human rights of the central place of the patient in deciding how much information is enough to make a choice has been put into effect to a large extent in the decisions of the USA, Canada and Australia. As a matter of English medical law, any encouragement that might have been given to patients by the vague analysis of *Bolam* v *Friern Hospital Management Committee* [1957] 1 WLR 582 in *Sidaway* v *Board of Governors of the Bethlem Royal Hospital* [1985] AC 871 has been lost by the re-emphasis of its all-encompassing and undiluted form by the recent cases of *Gold* v *Haringey Health Authority* [1988] QB 481, *Blyth* v *Bloomsbury Health Authority* (1993) 4 Med LR 151 and *Maynard* v *West Midlands Regional Health Authority* [1984] 1 WLR 634. The standard of information disclosure necessary for informed consent on the part of the patient is once more decided by the medical profession, acquiesced in by the judiciary and out of the patient's hands.

In 1954, Denning LJ invoked the principle that the therapeutic lie – the lie that is supposed to protect the patient from worry – was legally permissible. In 1996 that view still predominates in Britain. Medical law relating to the disclosure of information is not 'good' law. It fails to respect the most fundamental tenets of Western moral philosophy, international human rights and respect for persons. A 'good' medical law is one which has this objective of autonomy, it is also one that promotes truth telling. The decisions of the medical law courts in this country do neither.

Further reading

Chalmers, D., and Schwartz, R., '*Rogers* v *Whitaker* and Informed Consent in Australia' (1993) 1 Med L Rev 139.
Kennedy, I., 'The Patient on the Clapham Omnibus' (1984) 47 MLR 454.
Newdick, C., 'The Doctor's Duties of Care under *Sidaway*' (1985) 36 NILQ 243.
Robertson, G., 'Informed Consent to Medical Treatment' (1981) 97 LQR 102.

EIGHT
Wrongful birth, conception and life

8.1 INTRODUCTION

There may be physiological, economic, social or lifestyle reasons why an individual or couple might wish to undertake a medical procedure to render them unable to have children. For the male there is the option of vasectomy, for the female hysterectomy or tubal ligation. As already amply indicated in considering the issue of consent specifically, and medical negligence actions generally, operative procedures either go wrong through the fault of the doctor or risks become realities. There may even be an allegation of inadequacy of advance information disclosure to enable the patient to make a choice between risks. Here there are a number of situations which can affect either parent or child and potentially create liability in tort or contract on the part of a doctor.

The situations of concern here are:

(a) An action by a pregnant woman or couple alleging that the current pregnancy was unintended and unexpected. The sterilisation operation one or other underwent has failed because of the negligence of the operating doctor. This is a typical negligence action which would follow the same general path as encountered in relation to medical negligence actions as a whole. The plaintiff must prove, on the balance of probabilities, that the doctor owed a duty of care, has breached that standard of care by falling below the standard of care expected at law, that this breach of duty caused the damage complained of, and finally that the damage caused was of a legally recognisable type.

(b) An action in contract or tort for a failure to warn that a sterilisation operation can naturally reverse, so that precautionary contraceptive measures were not thought necessary for a time after the sterilisation operation. Alternatively there was a failure to diagnose a pregnancy. The result is:

(i)   a termination of the pregnancy,

(ii)   the birth of a healthy baby,
(iii) the birth of a handicapped baby.

(c)   An action by a child for a handicapped as opposed to a healthy existence due to the pre-natal negligence of the doctor to him or her when a foetus, or negligence to the pregnant mother.

(d)   An action alleging that the negligence of the doctor has meant a handicapped existence for the child which should not have been born at all. It is a claim by the child for a 'wrongful life', which should have been terminated rather than negligently allowed to continue.

The main issues of contention common to all areas is the scope of the duty of the doctor and the type of damages which should be awarded by the court. This issue of medical law is inextricably bound up with the consent debate considered in previous chapters. There are certain public policy issues which are by no means easy to resolve, even though the applicable law is relatively easy to explain.

While the medical law may be relatively easily understood, the ethical dilemmas posed by the above allegations are considerable. There are profound issues of death, life and quality of existence here. The question of the economic value of life, and who should pay for an unexpected 'arrival' has even been brought before the courts in this and other common law jurisdictions. The issue of damages has required some difficult dilemmas to be solved; and the courts appear, at least as far as a particular type of damages claim is concerned, to have a more sympathetic ear to the plea of social and economic costs of the unexpected arrival of a baby. The ethical problem that remains focal is the contention that the medical profession, fearing an extensive level of damages for negligent failures which amount to handicapped or healthy birth, are facing less and less subtle pressure to encourage abortions rather than face the prospect of paying extended damages for the child's upbringing. The image of a medical law culture based on the maxim 'Abort, don't litigate' would appear a real one. The medical law court has also been faced with the intangible possibility of potential psychological harm to the children who result from negligence. There is somewhat flimsy anecdotal evidence that this has taxed the courts, and influenced them for a time.

8.2   CONTRACTS TO STERILISE

Does the doctor give a warranty that the operation will render the patient permanently sterile? Does the doctor have a contractual duty to warn the patient of the risk of natural reversal of the process of sterilisation? Is it a material misrepresentation to use the term 'irreversible' when discussing the operation? These issues were raised, but not necessarily completely solved in *Eyre* v *Measday* [1986] 1 All ER 488 and *Thake* v *Maurice* [1986] QB 644. While difficulties remain as a result of these cases, the problem should now be put into perspective. The potential cost of successful contractual (as well as tortious) claims where there has been a lack of legal consent, has lead the National Health Service and private practice to promote a comprehensive sterilisation consent form. It is there for the avoidance of all doubt about the existence of the small risk of natural reversal of sterilisation, and the need to take contraceptive precautions for some time after the operation (National Health Service Management Executive, *A Guide to Consent for Examination or Treatment*, app. A(2)).

In *Eyre* v *Measday* the plaintiff, having decided with her husband that she did not wish to have any more children, consulted the defendant with a sterilisation in mind. The defendant explained the nature of the operation, emphasising to the plaintiff that the operation would be irreversible. There was a less than 1 per cent risk that the operation could naturally reverse, but the plaintiff was not told of this. This risk became real and the plaintiff gave birth to a child a year or so later. The contractual action was based on the representation that the operation was irreversible, which, combined with the failure to warn of the reversal rate, was a breach of the contract. Alternatively a claim was made that there was an express or contractual warranty of sterility as a result of the operation. The doctor, on this allegation, was argued to have effectively given a contractual guarantee that the operation would be success-ful. The general claim failed, but the plaintiff appealed.

The key element to the judgment was that the court considered the meaning of terms such as 'irreversible' according to what they *objectively* meant, that is, what they could reasonably be considered by the court to encompass. The plaintiff attempted to argue that the contract was to sterilise. While one can see some attraction in the allegation that 'this operation will be irreversible' meant literally that this was an absolute cut-off point (excuse the pun), the Court of Appeal found this to be untenable on the evidence. The contract was to perform a sterilisation *operation*. There can be little doubt that, save in the most unusual circumstances (perhaps elective cosmetic surgery as happened in *La Fleur* v *Cornelis* (1979) 28 NBR (2d) 569; see 3.3.4), it could not be in line with the reality of medical practice to enforce implied guarantees of operative success. Was there in the alternative an express or implied warranty of sterility? The evidence clearly indicated the use of the term 'irreversible' by the doctor. In conversations the defendant advised that the operation 'must be regarded as a permanent procedure'. Slade LJ could not accept that this was a warranty of sterility. 'Irreversible' was found to mean irreversible by way of remedial operation, and did not imply that there could be no natural reversal.

The plaintiff attempted to argue that the parties to this contract would have departed from the conversations that had taken place *reasonably* considering that there was a contractual implication of sterility. It seems rather perverse that the Court of Appeal accepted that the *defendant* also thought that the *plaintiff* would have left with the idea that she would be sterilised. Slade LJ (with whom the other members of the Court of Appeal agreed) unusually interpreted such an admission as different from it being reasonable to consider that a *guarantee* was in place. The warranty, the Court of Appeal found, was to perform the operation with reasonable care and skill. Charles

Lewis is more accurate in reflecting the reality of such doctor–patient discussions and understandings:

> [The surgeon and nurses] use phrases such as 'you know you will never be able to have any more babies . . .'. It is . . . highly arguable that, if no other information is given to the patient which suggests otherwise, she is being given to understand that permanent sterility is the *inevitable* outcome of the operation. It would be easy enough for the surgeon to tell her, and to record his telling her, that the *overwhelming probability* is that she will be rendered permanently sterile, but there nevertheless remains a very small chance that nature could at some later date reverse the effect of the operation. (*Medical Negligence*, 2nd ed. (Croydon: Tolley, 1992), p. 299, emphasis added)

This concept of reasonableness of expectation of the operation was also asserted in *Thake* v *Maurice*. The plaintiff husband sought a vasectomy operation, and signed a consent form, after discussions with the defendant. Two years after this operation was performed, his wife, the second plaintiff, became pregnant. By the time this was discovered it was too late for the performance of an abortion and a healthy child was duly born. Damages were claimed on a number of contractual grounds. First, that the contract was to sterilise, which was obviously breached by the birth. Secondly, that the plaintiffs had been induced to enter into the contract by the use of a false warranty or alternatively an innocent misrepresentation. The defendant was found in breach of contract at first instance and appealed. The plaintiffs alleged that the representations by the defendant doctor would have led a reasonable person to believe that the operation would result in permanent sterility. The defendant's response was that the term 'guarantee' was never used, but the term 'irreversible' was. The defendant in this case admitted that the plaintiffs would have believed the operation to produce permanent sterility. The Court of Appeal was unimpressed by this evidence, and relied on an attitude exemplified clearly by Neill LJ:

> It is the common experience of mankind that the results of medical treatment are to some extent unpredictable and that any treatment may be affected by the special characteristics of the particular patient. It has been well said that 'the dynamics of the human body of each individual are themselves individual'.

Once more it was held that it was not reasonable to expect a guarantee of sterility unless that term was used.

While it thus appears that there would need to be specific written or oral assurances of permanent sterility for an action in contract to succeed, one might consider that where such elective surgery is concerned, and undertaken in the private sector, the courts could take a less 'protective' contractual analysis and adopt that of Barry J in the Canadian case of *La Fleur* v *Cornelis* (1979) 28 NBR (2d) 569. The failure to warn of a 10 per cent risk of scarring during cosmetic nose surgery led the court to conclude that 'There is no law preventing a doctor from contracting to do that which he is paid to do'. It was admitted that there would usually be no implied warranty of success, but the doctor here made an express agreement that the plaintiff would 'be very happy' without warning of the risk. There was thus a breach of contract. This was a case where the court equated the doctor with a 'businessman'. This itself implied that normally the medical law courts would treat the doctor rather differently to the 'common run of business-kind', at least in terms of guarantees of success.

As a matter of current medical law with regard to the contractual action for wrongful conception, on the rare occasion that it will be relevant, the contractual duty of the doctor will reflect the view of duty of care of the law of medical negligence (see also *Worster* v *City and Hackney Health Authority* (1987) *The Times*, 22 June 1987). Contract law can, of course, create a higher duty, where it is expressly provided for in the contract. It is the case that 'this happens infrequently in practice, as doctors are not disposed to guarantee a particular outcome and the courts do not readily infer that they have done so' (Teff, *Reasonable Care* (Oxford: Clarendon Press, 1994), pp. 160–1). *Thake* v *Maurice* and *Eyre* v *Measday* clearly point to this. There may be an image of increased consumerism in the doctor–patient relationship, but it would not extend to therapeutic surgery. There would need to be a sea change in the view of the doctor–patient relationship to encompass such stark contractual principles. Nevertheless Teff sees it as a possibility, which, while extremely doubtful, is worthy of consideration:

> In certain respects the relationship between doctor and patient does have more affinity with contract than with tort, an affinity which tends to be obscured because we naturally associate personal injury claims with tort. To begin with, it is a *relationship*. Medical encounters differ from stock situations in tort in that the parties are seldom total strangers to one another prior to the event precipitating litigation. There is, in principle, scope for negotiation about the terms of the arrangements which they make; the doctor is paid for having undertaken to provide professional services to the patient. (*Reasonable Care*, p. 165)

With respect, this is difficult to apply to the patient entering the modern hospital. The parties are now very likely to be strangers. The market economy would have to move more aggressively into the doctor's surgery before competition would force the doctor to sign a contract indicating a higher standard of care and result than a colleague. Before attempting to be too dogmatic, however, one should accept that the US litigation explosion has rippled to England and Wales. So may the contract-based reformist ideas of medical litigation emanating from the USA travel the Atlantic (see further W. Ginsberg, 'Contractual Revisions to Medical Malpractice Liability' (1986) 49(2) Law and Contemp Probs 253). This issue might tax the medical law courts and medical law writers in the future.

8.3   ACTION FOR NEGLIGENCE

8.3.1   Introduction

The main factual allegation to consider is essentially the same as the contractual action. Here the plaintiff is alleging that there was no disclosure of the failure rate, in circumstances where there was a duty to so disclose. Such a failure was a breach of that duty, which caused the pregnancy, and termination or birth, because of a failure to be made aware of the need to use contraceptives for a period of time. It is easy to see that the wrongful conception and birth actions in negligence are 'typical' medical negligence claims. The same general issues, difficulties and criticisms apply. In addition there are particular problems associated with these types of action. For example, one of the main difficulties is one not usually encountered in other claims. The concept of legally recognised damage. Later one will see the peculiar legal and ethical debate about whether the birth of a healthy, if unexpected, child can be described as 'damage'.

8.3.2   To whom is the duty of care owed

While this is not usually a contentious matter in medical negligence, here the question is to whom the doctor should reasonably be directing his mind when giving pre-operative advice on sterilisation. Normally a couple will be counselled and informed together, or one of the couple will be consulted, but with the doctor knowing that there is an identifiable third party to be considered when doing one's medical duty of informing. Where matters may get a little more difficult for the duty of care issue is where an individual consults the doctor about sterilisation, but has no current sexual partner, a number of them or possibly a prospective one. Until recently this had to be considered itself a prospective issue for medical law in this country, but has recently fallen to be considered by the Court of Appeal in *Goodwill* v *British Pregnancy Advisory Service* [1996] 1 WLR 1397. While in *Thake* v *Maurice* [1986] QB 644 and *Eyre* v *Measday* [1986] 1 All ER 488 the duty to the partner of the party being sterilised was accepted without question, here the relationship was rather more distant to say the least. The case is also a timely reminder to the medical lawyer of the application of the general law of duty of care to the practice of medicine. M had a vasectomy in 1984, and the defendant informed him of its success a year later. He was told he need not take any contraceptive measures. In 1988 when an affair began between M and the plaintiff, M informed her that he had been sterilised. In reliance on that information (despite her own GP telling her there was a 'one-in-a-million chance of natural reversal') she stopped using any contraceptives, but became pregnant and gave birth when the vasectomy underwent a spontaneous reversal in 1989. The plaintiff claimed that there was a duty of care owed to her as a future sexual partner of M by M's original advising doctor.

The claim of a duty of care was predicated on the fact that the law of negligence as a whole 'should develop incrementally by reference to or analogy with established categories of situations where the law has recognised that a duty of care arises and a plaintiff may recover for his loss' (per Peter Gibson LJ at p. 163). This was a duty case which could be decided as an incremental development. The defendants argued instead that this was not an incremental development, but 'an impermissible leap' in the legal categories of duty of care.

Specifically it was argued on behalf of the plaintiff that the purpose of the operation was to render M sterile. It is reasonably foreseeable that M's current partner would rely on such advice. Further, it was contended that in modern society it is foreseeable that the patient could have a sexual relationship with another partner. This is the incremental societal development that was argued as broadening the duty of care and should be recognised by the common law. Counsel sought to argue that the plaintiff's position here was analogous to the duty owed by a solicitor to the intended beneficiaries of a will, financially disappointed by negligent delays in its preparation (*White v Jones* [1995] 2 AC 207). In response his lordship considered *White v Jones* to be a very specific case to overcome a 'rank injustice' which did not exist here. As one might have expected, the plaintiff's claim was struck out. In doing so his lordship quoted with approval Lord Oliver in *Caparo Industries plc v Dickman* [1990] 2 AC 605 at p. 638 that:

> . . . the necessary relationship [to establish a duty of care] between the maker of a statement or giver of advice ('the adviser') and the recipient who acts in reliance upon it ('the advisee') may typically be held to exist where (1) the advice is required for a purpose, whether particularly specified or generally described, which is made known, either actually or inferentially, to the adviser at the time when the advice is given; (2) the adviser knows, either actually or inferentially, that his advice will be communicated to the advisee, either specifically or as a member of an *ascertainable class*, in order that it should be used by the advisee for that purpose; (3) it is known either actually or inferentially, that the advice so communicated is likely to be acted upon by the advisee for that purpose *without independent inquiry*; and (4) it is so acted upon by the advisee to his detriment. (emphasis added)

While Peter Gibson LJ saw the absence of (3) as particularly fatal to the cause of action, it was also doubted whether (2) and (4) existed in the present case. It would indeed seem rather unusual to state that those who may have sexual relations with M in the future are an 'ascertainable class'. In conclusion Peter Gibson LJ said:

> I find it impossible to believe that the policy of the law is or should be to treat so tenuous a relationship between the adviser and advisee as giving rise to a duty of care, and there is no analogous situation recognised as giving rise to that duty. (p. 169)

This case, if read along with *Thake v Maurice*, would indicate that for a person other than the patient who is negligently not informed of the failure rate to maintain an action, she would need to be a current sexual partner, and, if not present at the consultation, would have to prove that the doctor intended the contents of the consultation to be communicated to her (see also *Newell* v *Goldenberg* (1995) 6 Med LR 371).

8.3.3   Extent of the duty to inform

While the law appears clear on the types of plaintiff who may be owed a duty of information, the ambit of the duty of care in giving advice is dictated, as with diagnosis and therapy, by the *Bolam* test. In the context of the action for wrongful conception and birth, this test was interpreted in *Gold* v *Haringey Health Authority* [1988] QB 481. A couple had two children, with the woman being pregnant with a third, when they decided that these three would be enough. They sought advice on sterilisation, but were not given information on the option of the husband having a vasectomy (which had a lower failure rate) or the risk of the woman's sterilisation failing. The sterilisation operation was performed just after the birth of the third child. It was not a success, and the couple ended up with a fourth child. The trial judge found that, in the non-therapeutic circumstances in which the advice was given, the failure to warn of reversal was negligent. The implication of the trial judge was that where an operation is one of choice, and clearly here there was no clinical need for the woman to have a sterilisation (the couple just had enough children), rather than medical necessity, a higher duty of care exists. On appeal, the pre-eminence of the conduct of the doctor having to accord with a responsible body of medical opinion was reasserted. The evidence, which was regarded by the trial judge as not conclusive of the matter, was that there was such a body of opinion which did not warn. The *Bolam* test was extended into the realms of pre-operative advice with regard to voluntary non-therapeutic sterilisation.

The difficulties with regard to the level of information disclosure here are really practical as well as legal. The doctor is pulled in two directions when giving pre-operative advice or counselling about sterilisation. At the same time that the doctor should be giving the patient the fullest possible inform-ation as a matter of good medical practice and good medical ethics, there may be other professional pressures. There is also a duty incumbent on the doctor to stress that, save in the most extreme circumstances, the operation, if successful, will mean that the patient can no longer have children. This is a major step, and there needs to be clarity in the doctor's mind as much as the patient's that this is what is really wanted. To begin to bring issues of reversibility into the consultation carries with it the danger that it will not be taken as the 'final option' which all but terminates the ability to reproduce, but rather as a temporary measure which can be reversed if a change of heart occurs later.

There is once again a tug-of-war between theories of paternalism, and autonomy and human rights. The rights-based focus of medical law should place more power in the hands of the patient here. The doctor should be required to provide the information essential for an informed choice and should not attempt to second-guess the impact of information on the actions of the patient. Clinical intuition would not condone this. The patient's rights may be respected by this level of information disclosure, but not necessarily his or her welfare. Medical law, in using the *Bolam* test, has left the matter really as one for the doctor to weigh up. Welfare may be protected, but at what cost to rights?

8.3.4 Causation

As with consent actions in negligence generally, the question here is what the patient would have done if the information that there was a risk of reversal had been given. If the reasonable patient in the position of the plaintiff would have taken protective measures to counteract the risk of such natural reversal, if warned, then the breach of duty is the cause of the damage, whether it is pregnancy, which is terminated on the instructions of the plaintiff, or birth. The difficulties of proving causation having already been noted in relation to medical negligence generally. An exotic idea might be that the patient who finds she is pregnant after a sterilisation operation can utilise the concept of *res ipsa loquitur* (see 4.3) to indicate that the fact of pregnancy demonstrates the sterilisation has been negligently performed in the absence of rebuttal by the defendant. Charles Lewis (*Medical Negligence*, 2nd ed. (Croydon: Tolley, 1992)) replies that the fact of natural reversal would preclude its utilisation (p. 298). There cannot be a presumption of negligence where a woman becomes pregnant.

The potentially critical issue of *novus actus interveniens* and the failure to mitigate loss was raised and thankfully answered in the important case on both causation and damages in wrongful birth actions, *Emeh* v *Kensington and Chelsea and Westminster Area Health Authority* [1985] QB 1012. In this case, rather than an allegation of lack of information, there was an allegation that the sterilisation itself was negligently performed when done at the same time as a termination of pregnancy. The plaintiff did not discover the pregnancy until 20 weeks' gestation, and decided to go through with it. Sadly, she gave birth to a child with congenital abnormalities. Her claim was for the failure of the operation itself (which was admitted by the defendants) and for damages resulting from the various impacts of the pregnancy, as well as the birth and upbringing of the child. At first instance it was held that the refusal to have the termination of pregnancy was so unreasonable as to be a *novus actus interveniens* (a new intervening act, which eclipses the negligence of the defendant) or otherwise a failure of the defendant's duty to mitigate the damage that had occurred. The plaintiff having an abortion, the argument went, would limit the negligence and damages of the defendants. The award of damages was thus limited to those related to the negligence and impacts up to the time the termination was refused, and not beyond that time. On appeal Slade LJ was succinct in disapproving of such judicial sentiments, saying that:

> By their own negligence, they faced her with the very dilemma which she had sought to avoid by having herself sterilised. . . . they could, and should

have reasonably foreseen that if, as a consequence of the negligent performance of the operation she should find herself pregnant again, particularly
after some months of pregnancy, she might well decide to keep the child.
. . . Save in the most exceptional circumstances, I cannot think it right that
the court should ever declare it unreasonable for a woman to decline to
have an abortion in a case where there is no evidence that there were any
medical or psychiatric grounds for terminating the particular pregnancy.

What would be an 'exceptional circumstance? One that could be tentatively
suggested might involve the following: Sarah goes to the local GP, thinking that
she might have some form of food poisoning, as she is unwell every morning.
The GP, after a cursory examination, prescribes aspirin and a week off work.
Sarah's condition does not improve, and a month later she seeks a second
opinion. This doctor informs her that she is 15 weeks pregnant, and the foetus
is showing an erratic heartbeat. This could be an indication of a congenital
defect that is in Sarah's family. Nevertheless, Sarah does not have a termination and the child is born with the defect everyone feared. The negligent first
doctor might claim *novus actus* or failure to mitigate. The example is tentative,
because one would have to consider so many other factual issues. Did Sarah
have a religious or moral objection to abortion, for example? In reality, and
quite correctly, there seems little prospect of the plaintiff in such a case being
'punished' by a reduction of damages for not having an abortion.

8.3.5 Damages

The unexpected birth of a child might be a moment of joy or sadness. The
child might be healthy or handicapped. The child born as a result of a
sterilisation which was negligently performed or where there was negligent
failure to inform of risk of reversal is the ground for an action to recover
tortious damages, but what damages, and damages for what?
    The development of the wrongful conception and birth actions has in-
dicated a judicial policy which has altered over time, but one which still
reveals tensions over aspects of public policy surrounding such actions. One
of the first reported cases on this area concerned an abortion which failed
through the negligence of the attending doctor (*Scuriaga v Powell* (1979) 123
SJ 406). Damages were awarded for future loss of earnings through having to
look after the child, impairment of marriage prospects and a sum for the pain,
distress and humiliation associated with the Caesarean section that was
performed, and of course for the 'debilitating' effects of the pregnancy as a
whole. The judgments in the High Court and the Court of Appeal (unreported) were indicative of a debate which was to become rather more
heated in cases to follow. Watkins J found that:

Surely no one in these days would argue [that damages were irrecoverable]
if the child were born defective or diseased. The fact that a child born is
healthy cannot give rise to a different conclusion save as to the measure of
damages.

In the Court of Appeal, Waller LJ, while accepting that the plaintiff had not claimed for the upbringing of the child, felt that policy considerations might preclude such an award in the future, as the loss of money from rearing a child was offset by the 'joy of parenthood'.

The key cases which exposed this policy debate most clearly were decided in the early 1980s. In *Udale v Bloomsbury Area Heath Authority* [1983] 1 WLR 1098 at first instance, Jupp J found that it would be against public policy to award damages for the upkeep of a healthy child. The arguments against such an award were listed as follows:

(a)   It is undesirable that a child should grow up to learn that a court has decided that its life is an unwanted mistake or even a disaster. 'Such pronouncements would disrupt families and weaken the structure of society.'

(b)   Where a parent loves and cares for this 'accidental' child, any damages would be offset by the joy of parenting; virtue would go unrewarded. On the other hand, the parent who showed no maternal instincts and remained bitter about the birth would receive more.

(c)   Doctors would come under a psychological pressure to advise abortions where pregnancy results from their negligence, in order to save the expense of damages for the upbringing of the child.

(d)   The birth of a child is culturally seen as a moment of joy and celebration, not for the award of damages.

Subsequently, in *Emeh v Kensington and Chelsea and Westminster Area Health Authority* [1985] QB 1012, the Court of Appeal endorsed the realism of Peter Pain J in *Thake v Maurice* [1986] QB 644 that 'every baby has a belly to be filled and a body to be clothed'. Waller LJ in *Emeh* did not accept the public policy arguments that had been expressed in *Udale*. It was considered that the judiciary should be slow to lay down strong lines of public policy. Legal principle rather than guiding policy should be the objective of the court. The reality was perceived to be that whatever the financial difficulties that flow from this 'unexpected arrival', the child is often welcomed into the family. Nevertheless the raw costs of bringing up the child remain.

The case of *Gold v Haringey Health Authority* [1988] QB 481 confirms the legitimacy of the claim for the upbringing of a healthy child. The recent judgment of Brooke J in *Allen v Bloomsbury Health Authority* [1993] 1 All ER 651 has paraphrased the principles of damages that are relevant:

(a)   The general law of negligence entitles the plaintiff who gives birth to a child as the result of the negligence of the doctor to damages for foreseeable loss and damage suffered as a result of that negligence.

(b)   The general damages recoverable for the continuation of the pregnancy and the delivery of the child must be set off against the benefit that has been gained by avoiding the pain and suffering of a termination (see *Gardiner v Mounfield* (1989) 5 BMLR 1).

(c)   Damages for economic loss unassociated with the physical injury are recoverable of the following type:

    (i)   feeding, clothing, housing and educating the child born until adulthood,

    (ii)   financial loss associated with the mother's loss of earnings because of having to look after the child.

    (d) A woman would foreseeably suffer from wear and tear and tiredness looking after the child, but this will generally be set off against the joy of bringing a child into existence and watching it grow to maturity.

    (e) While the set-off in (d) will exist where the child born is healthy, there will be no corresponding set-off where the child born is handicapped.

In addition Brooke J ventured the view that where the doctor is negligent and a child is born, if the existing children of the family have received education in the private sector, this child, born of negligence, should also receive such an education paid for by the appropriate award of damages. If this was thought to be inappropriate then the matter should be dealt with by Parliament.

Recently the conflict between the idea that the birth of the child could be the subject of a claim for damages and that the birth of a child cannot be considered 'damage' at law has resurfaced with *Crouchman v Burke* (1997) *The Times*, 10 October 1997 and the Scottish case of *McFarlane v Tayside Health Board* (1996) *The Times*, 11 November 1996. The case of *Crouchman* follows the pattern of recent English case law. The parents were awarded £100,000 after the woman was negligently sterilised and subsequently gave birth. In *McFarlane* the couple were wrongly reassured that Mr McFarlane's vasectomy had resulted in sterilisation. As a result they discontinued the use of other contraceptive measures and Mrs McFarlane fell pregnant and gave birth to a daughter. They made the 'usual' claim for the pain and suffering involved in Mrs McFarlane's pregnancy and labour as well as the more significant cost of bringing up this daughter. The trial judge utilised a number of overseas precedents to justify the conclusion that there should be no award of damages (see *Public Health Trust v Brown* (1980) 388 So 2d 1084; *Cockrum v Baumgartner* (1983) 477 NE 2d 385). Essentially the objections to the award of damages were amalgams of those already encountered, namely:

    (a) That one cannot place a monetary value on the joy of parenthood.

    (b) There may be psychological trauma were the child to discover that it had been unexpected and 'unwanted'.

    (c) That the floodgates may be opened to all sorts of financial claims related to the child.

    (d) The more wealthy the couple the higher the award of damages that could be claimed.

McFarlane represents an anomalous view of the realities facing a couple who have a child 'out of the blue' and was thankfully overturned on appeal (see *The Times*, 6 May 1998). The case still has importance as it is apparent that not all members of the judiciary have an englightened view of the economic cost of a child (for a more realistic consideration of the damages issue in Canada see *Kealey* v *Berezowski* (1996) 136 DLR (4th) 708).

8.4   WRONGFUL BIRTH OF A HANDICAPPED CHILD

8.4.1   Introduction

The factual circumstances will be varied. The child may have been damaged *in* or *ex utero* (if conception were achieved by the use of *in vitro* fertilisation (IVF) for example). There may have been negligent treatment of the mother during the course of pregnancy which has damaged the child. There could have been a negligent failure to diagnose the handicap of the unborn child, therefore depriving the woman of the opportunity of an abortion. Point (e) of Brooke J's analysis of the damages issue in wrongful conception (see 8.3.5) clearly notes that substantial damages are potentially available.

8.4.2   A damages injustice

In *Salih* v *Enfield Health Authority* [1991] 3 All ER 400, a child was born with congenital defects as a result of rubella. The defendant had negligently failed to warn the mother of the possibility of this condition in the unborn child, so depriving her of the opportunity of an abortion. The parents had planned to have another child after this, but abandoned the plan, considering that their energies would be sufficiently taxed with this child. Surprisingly, the Court of Appeal reversed the trial judge in finding that the money they saved through not having the fourth child would be deducted from the damages awarded for the upkeep of the handicapped child. Charles Lewis (*Medical Negligence*, 2nd ed. (Croydon: Tolley, 1992), p. 308) expresses the dissatisfaction with the award:

> It is really odd to think that, having forced the parents by their negligence to give up their plan for another child, the defendants should derive a financial advantage from that.

8.4.3   Causation and the legality of the abortion

In *Rance* v *Mid-Downs Health Authority* [1991] 1 QB 587 the failure of the defendants to diagnose a congenital defect was found not to be a cause of the damaged existence of the child because at the time when it would have been possible to discover the defect, any abortion would have been unlawful under the abortion legislation as it then stood (for further discussion of this in the context of abortion law, see 12.5.1).

8.4.4   Child's claim for a handicapped existence

While the claim of the parents will proceed along the broad path of medical negligence actions generally, the more complex medical law issue is whether the child can claim for the handicapped, as opposed to a healthy, existence. The problem is that the child, as a matter of common law, is claiming that the negligently caused injuries occurred before the child had a legal existence. There is a fair amount of authority to suggest that the child, as a matter of law, has no legal existence, at least until it is born (see 12.10 and the cases of *St George's Healthcare National Health Servide Trust* v *S* (1998) *The Times*, 8 May 1998; *Winnipeg Child and Family Services (Northwest Area)* v *G* (1998) 3 BHRC 611, Can SC)'. The doctor will argue that a legal non-entity cannot be owed a duty of care at law. While the common law issues have essentially been resolved by the passing of the Congenital Disabilities (Civil Liability) Act 1976, there are still residual issues. In *Burton* v *Islington Health Authority* [1993] QB 204, the Court of Appeal considered the following issue defined by Dillon LJ:

> can a child who is born alive, but suffering from disabilities occasioned by negligence on the part of the proposed defendant at the time when the child was en ventre and unborn, maintain an action for damages for negligence against the defendant.

The Court of Appeal was forced to recognise the fact that English common law had on a number of occasions clearly enunciated the view that the child cannot have a legal status until it is born alive (see, for example, *Paton* v *British Pregnancy Advisory Service Trustees* [1979] QB 276). As a matter of common law, at the same time, there have been expressions of the opinion that the unborn child will be deemed to be born when its interests require it. A good example is *Montreal Tramways* v *Leveille* [1933] 4 DLR 337 in which Lamont J explained the problem:

> If a child after birth has no right of action for pre-natal injuries, we have a wrong inflicted for which there is no remedy, for, although the father may be entitled to compensation for the loss he has incurred and the mother for what she has suffered, yet there is a residuum of injury for which compensation cannot be had save at the suit of the child. If a right of action be denied to the child it will be compelled, without any fault on its part, to go through life carrying the seal of another's fault and bearing a very heavy burden of infirmity and inconvenience without any compensation therefore. To my mind it is but natural justice that a child, if born alive and viable, should be allowed to maintain an action in the courts for injuries wrongfully committed upon its person while in the womb of its mother.

The 1976 Act established a legislative form of action for the child injured en ventre sa mère, but was enacted after the birth of the children in *Burton* v *Islington Health Authority* and so did not apply to them. Therefore the court sought a common law justification for a duty of care, and found it in *Watt* v *Rama* [1972] VR 353. This case found that a negligent driver owed a duty to an unborn child injured through injury to the mother. Such circumstances 'constitute a potential relationship capable of imposing a duty on the defendant in relation to the child as and when born. On the birth the relationship crystallises.' Whatever justification is sought, it has to be regarded as somewhat fictitious of the law to talk of a potential duty existing, which becomes a fully fledged duty on the birth of the child. If the breach of duty takes place at the factual time of negligence, the child has no legal status, if the breach takes place at the point of birth this is a construct of law, isolated from the factual time of injury. The practical recognition that justice requires damages, despite the separation of duty and breach, evident in the decision in *Montreal Tramways* v *Leveille* [1933] 4 DLR 337, is the most appropriate view.

Recently, there appears to be an expansion of judicial recognition of the rights of the unborn which assist in confirming the changes apparent in *Burton* v *Islington Health Authority*. It has already been noted that the decision in *Re S (Adult: Refusal of Treatment)* [1993] Fam 123 ('forcing' the born-again Christian woman to have a caesarian section; see 6.2.1.1) was partially based on the interest in saving the life of the child. In addition the criminal law of murder has recognised the duty to the unborn child. *Attorney–General's Reference (No. 3 of 1994)* [1996] QB 581 (see 12.10) held that it can be manslaughter, but not murder, where a pregnant woman was stabbed, and recovered, but the child died soon after birth.

8.5 CONGENITAL DISABILITIES (CIVIL LIABILITY) ACT 1976

8.5.1 Introduction

This is a major piece of legislation as far as the ability of the disabled child claiming for pre-natal injuries is concerned. It resulted from the Law Commission's *Report on Injuries to Unborn Children* (Law Com. No. 60, Cmnd 5709) (London: HMSO, 1974). The Act is wide, in that it legislates for occurrences prior to the child's conception, as well as negligence during the process of its *in utero* development.

8.5.2 Grounds for a claim

The negligent occurrences on which the child born has a cause of action are those which either affected the ability of either parent to have a normal healthy child (s. 1(2)(a)) or affected the mother during the process of pregnancy (s. 1(2)(b)). The child has to be born to maintain an action – it needs to have an existence 'separate from the mother' (s. 4(1)). Anyone apart from the mother of the child is a potential defendant (s. 1(1)). The defendant will be liable if there was a breach of duty to the mother, even if the mother suffered no damage (s. 1(3)). The defendant will not be liable for an occurrence which took place before conception, affecting either parent's ability to have a healthy child, if either parent knew of the risk to any future child's health. This does not apply if the father is the defendant and knew of the risk but the mother did not (s. 1(4)). The Act also provides, by way of s. 1(5) for a legislative '*Bolam*' defence for the medical profession. It states:

The defendant is not answerable to the child, for anything he omitted to do when responsible in a professional capacity for treating or advising the parent, if he took reasonable care having due regard to then received professional opinion applicable to the particular class of case; but this does not mean that he is answerable only because he departed from received opinion.

The developments which have taken place in reproductive technology (see chapter 10) may mean that the negligent 'occurrence' might take place *ex utero*, in the Petri dish. With this in mind the Human Fertilisation and Embryology Act 1990 inserted s. 1A into the 1976 Act. Where a child born as a result of certain infertility treatment is born disabled, and this disability results from negligence in the selection, keeping or use outside the body of the embryo or gametes, this disability is to be regarded as damage resulting from this act or omission.

The 1976 Act can apply in a vast array of factual circumstances, and obviously applies outside the medical sphere. A defective drug may have been given to the woman as a fertility treatment, but causes congenital defect in a child later conceived. The mother may have been given a negligent blood transfusion some years before conception, which made her rhesus incompatible with her husband, with the result that the child suffers from haemolytic (foetal blood contamination) disease (as happened in *Roberts* v *Johnstone* [1989] QB 878).

Concern has been voiced that a legislative policy which recognises liability for pre-conception torts is to imply into the law an interest in not being conceived. The doctor, theoretically, should terminate a damaged existence to escape liability for the disabled birth and subsequent life (see P. J. Pace 'Civil Liability for Pre-natal Injuries' (1977) 40 MLR 141). A more profound difficulty exists for medical law: Is there an action, either under common law or the 1976 Act, for a wrongful existence?

8.6 WRONGFUL LIFE

The debate on wrongful life has been analysed mainly from the perspective of whether 'the child would have been better off not born at all' (Kennedy and Grubb, *Medical Law*, 2nd ed. (London: Butterworths, 1994), p. 954). Angela Holder ('Is Existence Ever Injury?' in Spicker et al. (eds), *The Law–Medicine Relation* (Dordrecht: Reidel, 1978, p. 225) regards the better approach as being whether life is something someone should have monetary compensation for. Nevertheless the common claim of the wrongful life plaintiff is that there is a fundamental right to be born healthy, or not to be born at all. An important US case, *Curlender* v *Bio-Science Laboratories* (1980) 165 Cal Rptr 477, which debated the action before the English courts, considered the unquantifiability of the damages and the other public policy objections to the action. This was followed in English medical law.

The factual allegation of wrongful life as a matter of English medical law is typified by the leading case of *McKay* v *Essex Area Health Authority* [1982]

QB 1166. The plaintiff here was damaged in the womb, having been infected with rubella. The allegation was not that the doctor had caused the injuries, but that the doctor should have warned the mother of the damage that may have been caused, and thus informed her about the desirability of an abortion. The mother, according to the evidence, would have accepted this 'offer'. The claim therefore was that there should be liability for the child's 'entry into a life in which her injuries are highly debilitating'. Put even more simply the child alleged: If you had not been negligent I would not have been born at all.

There were both public policy and common law grounds for the rejection of this claim given by Ackner and Stephenson LJJ which reflected the views expressed by the Chief Justice of Quebec in *Cataford* v *Moreau* (1978) 114 DLR (3d) 585 at p. 596:

> It is clearly impossible to compare the situation of the infant after his birth with the situation in which he would have been if he were not born. Merely to state the problem shows its illogicality.

Ackner LJ in *McKay* v *Essex Area Health Authority* could not find it acceptable for the common law to impose a duty to terminate existence.

The plaintiffs had sought support for such a duty from *Re B (A Minor) (Wardship: Medical Treatment)* [1981] 1 WLR 1421 (see 14.4) where it was suggested that there might be a duty to withdraw treatment from a severely handicapped child whose life was 'bound to be so full of pain as to be not worth living'. Ackner LJ in *McKay* v *Essex Area Health Authority* found this wardship decision irrelevant for the purposes of the case at hand. There should have been a rather more acute analysis of the neonaticide cases. More recently medical law has moved toward implying that there may be a duty not to treat the severely disabled patient (see the debate on *Airedale NHS Trust* v *Bland* [1993] AC 789 in 15.5.2). One can surely extrapolate from this that there may be a duty not to allow the commencement of what is known will be an intolerable existence. Negligently to fail to make a timely pre-natal diagnosis of that future existence would then be a breach of duty.

The plaintiff's argument was conceded as leading to the possibility of liability for not advising an abortion on discovering a minor handicap. In addition the possibility would exist of a further extension to the liability of the mother for refusing an abortion when informed of handicap. The absurdity of framing damages on the difference between a handicapped existence and no existence at all was arguably the major stumbling block for the plaintiffs. Nevertheless the argument could have been made that the assessment of damages in negligence generally is something of a fiction. How can the court, for example, put a price on the negligent amputation of a leg to the amateur sports enthusiast? The dissenting voices in *Gleitman* v *Cosgrove* (1967) 227 A 2d 689 argued that one should not deny a remedy because of the difficulties of calculation. It would be like the court arguing that there is no negligence for performing an amputation instead of a minor knee operation because the calculation of damages is impossible.

In *Curlender* v *Bio-Science Laboratories* (1980) 165 Cal Rptr 477 the California Court of Appeal considered these wrongful life actions from a perspective allowed by the US Constitution, which has a certain logical attraction. It was found that the decision of *Roe* v *Wade* (1973) 410 US 113, giving the woman a constitutional right to abortion without interference for the first three months of pregnancy would impact on the wrongful life action. Included by implication in abolishing State criminalisation of abortion was the right of parents not to have children. That right will exist where there is a high possibility that the child will be born with a deformity. Extrapolating from *Roe* v *Wade* further, it may be that a breach of this right through the negligence of the doctor may also be the breach of a fundamental right of a child to be born healthy.

The court in *Curlender* v *Bio-Science Laboratories*, having considered the history of the wrongful life action in the USA, argued that there were different sorts of wrongful life case. Claims that illegitimacy is a form of impairment, for example, should not be allowed, because that status is not injury. The court recognised the progression of other US States from a position of barring all such claims to a stance of at least allowing the parents' claims in negligence. Public policy has been used to stop such claims proceeding, but the metaphysical or religious objections to the action have not gone unchallenged. There are also those who have argued that it is the law that matters, not religious objection. Legal public policy might begin to recognise that the advances in medical science make the pre-natal discovery of defect easier. Medical law might, through the development of the wrongful life action, encourage such developments in genetic research and counselling to occur in a more 'careful' way. It has already been argued that medical law is slow to react to change and at best a reactive rather than a proactive tool of medicine. This would be an opportunity for 'good' medical law to shape the development of 'good' medical practice.

The real difficulty for medical law here is not breach of duty, it is the nature of injury. It was argued in *Curlender* that the basis of the wrongful life action is that the child exists and it suffers. This is due to someone's negligence. The court argued forcefully that:

It is neither necessary nor just to retreat into meditation on the mysteries of life. We need not be concerned with the fact that had defendants not been negligent, the plaintiff might not have come into existence at all. The certainty of genetic impairment is no longer a mystery. In addition a reverent appreciation of life compels recognition that plaintiff, however impaired she may be, has come into existence as a living person with certain rights. (per Jefferson J)

Subsequent US cases have modified this approach, but have still been 'forward looking' rather than 'backward looking' decisions, such as *MacKay* v *Essex Area Health Authority*, which talk of public policy and the intangible nature of non-existence. US cases concern themselves not with the difference between impaired and non-existence. Instead they approach the matter from a rights-based medical law perspective which emphasises the damages which should be paid for the rest of the child's life (see, for example, *Turpin* v *Sortini* (1982) 643 P 2d 954).

The Law Commission explicitly excluded the wrongful life action from its recommendations, which became the Congenital Disabilities (Civil Liability) Act 1976. The Commission rehearsed the same objections to the action in terms of the duty to terminate life, the unquantifiability of the damage and the invisibility of the nature of the damage itself. As it confirmed (*Report on Injuries to Unborn Children* (Law Com. No. 60, Cmnd 5709) para. 89):

> Such a cause of action, if it existed, would place an almost intolerable burden on medical advisers in their socially and morally exacting role. The danger that doctors would be under subconscious pressures to advise abortions in doubtful cases through fear of action of damages is, we think, a real one.

It thus appears something of a mystery that the Act does not make this antipathy to the cause of action explicit. Ackner LJ had to argue that s. 1(2)(b) 'imports' the assumption that the action does not exist. Nevertheless this is a clear reading of the statute; that the occurrence causes a disabled rather than a healthy existence. It says nothing about an occurrence which causes existence as opposed to non-existence (note now that attempts at a 'wrongful life' claim are invariably abandoned and proceed as 'wrongful birth' claims; *Arnolt* v *Smith* (1996) 7 Med LR 35).

8.7 CONCLUSION

The law is in a state of flux. The parents of a child born as the result of negligence can claim for its upkeep, whether it is born healthy or 'damaged'. The child born handicapped as a result of negligence on the part of the doctor can claim for the difference between a damaged and a healthy existence. The child cannot claim that it should never have existed. Arguably there is a 'cost' which can be attached to a painful and debilitated existence. The fact that it may be a metaphysically uncomfortable equation should not blind the courts to the injustice of demarcated situations of liability and damage.

Medical law, in the area of wrongful conception, birth and life actions does have the moral dilemma that to encourage claims creates an atmosphere where the doctor can see only one saving point; to advise on an abortion. This will reduce damages. The counter-argument is that the doctor can only advise, not force, the patient to have a termination of pregnancy. As indicated earlier, however, doctors can couch advice in a number of ways. The doctor, in the face of a potentially substantial claim for damages for the upkeep of a child, perhaps in private education, to the age of majority, may find these factors influence the force and direction of that 'advice'.

Further reading

Brahams, D., 'Damages for Unplanned Babies – A Trend to be Discouraged?' (1983) 133 NLJ 643.

Grubb, A., 'Medical Law – Failure of Sterilisation – Damages for "Wrongful Conception"' [1985] CLJ 30.
Fortin, J., 'Is the "Wrongful Life" Action Really Dead?' [1987] JSWL 306.
Mullis, A., 'Wrongful Conception Unravelled' (1993) 1 Med L Rev 320.
Slade, M., 'The Death of Wrongful Life: A Case for Resuscitation?' (1982) 132 NLJ 874.
Teff, H., 'The Action for "Wrongful Life" in England and the United States' (1985) 34 ICLQ 423.

NINE
Mental health and the law

9.1 INTRODUCTION

The mental health of an individual can impact on any number of aspects of that individual's life, but is a crucial determinant in the medical treatment decision-making process (see chapter 6 on the ethical and legal basis of consent, which is of some importance here). The issue of the mental health of the patient is complex and value-laden. Paternalism and autonomy interests confront difficulties of definition, diagnosis and the impact of labelling. Treatment of the mentally handicapped for this often debilitating 'disability' is required, but the patient, by the very fact of the condition, may be unaware of the problem, or unable to make treatment decisions that would help the condition. Paternalism thus dictates intervention, and that the human right of autonomy be minimalist.

The acute difficulty one immediately perceives is the difficulty of definition. To label an individual as 'mentally ill' can have a drastic impact on his or her life, but unlike a physical illness such as a fractured leg, diagnosis can be difficult, based on more intangible considerations than a more obvious physiological infirmity. The difficulty turns on the fact that one person's eccentric may be another person's mentally ill. It has been closely questioned whether the forms of 'aberrant' behaviour that have been designated a form of mental illness deserve such a label, given that it can act as a key to non-consensual detention and even treatment (see the famous work by T.S. Szasz, *The Myth of Mental Illness*, new ed. (London: Paladin, 1972)). The utilitarian concept of compulsion is itself minimalist. Remember that to John Stuart Mill law should limit freedom as little as possible. The individual whose actions do not adversely affect anyone else (called 'self-regarding actions') should be left alone. When this is applied to those who do not fit within some societal norm, then arguably those whose behaviour is perceived as bizarre should be left alone. The difficulty is that the utilitarian calculus of the free action is only supposed to apply to those who are 'in the maturity of their faculties'. If people with alternative conceptions of normality are held by society as not in this category then decisions can be taken on their behalf, because they are not autonomous rationalising individuals who can live a free life. Historically, Britain has taken that lack of right to freedom to heart, and controlled those deemed mentally ill by incarcerating them. Many authors have written of the horror and injustice of this sort of regime, and of the blinkered legal and political system which promoted the 'out of sight out of mind' or rather the 'out of mind out of my sight' attitude. Mason and McCall Smith (*Law and Medical Ethics*, 4th ed. (London: Butterworths, 1994), p. 386), among others, noted the problems the system was setting up for itself with large numbers of patients who had spent the greater part of their lives in hospital and could never be able to cope with any new world offered to them outside the small world of incarceration they had grown used to. The current clamour for care in the community to be more responsibly handled, to stop those who are not ready to step back into society harming others, is a potent reminder of the very real cost of the original decision to isolate from the community. As a matter of fact, and as a matter of medical law, the issue once again is one of *balance* in the regulation of mental health.

The doctor has a number of balancing issues to consider where the mentally disturbed patient is concerned. That patient, like any other, has rights, but the doctor too has duties which extend beyond the patient. Chapter 2 showed the importance of confidentiality, and the possible and very real dangers of a blanket mainenance of patient confidence (in respectively *W* v *Egdell* [1990] Ch 359 (see 2.5) and *Tarasoff* v *Regents of the University of California* (1976) 551 P 2d 334 (see 2.5)).

The Mental Health Act 1959 was a small revolution in that it attempted legislatively to demystify and desegregate mental illness as far as possible from other forms of illness. The concerns of civil libertarians that the term 'mental illness' opened the door to compulsion in treatment and lifestyle in general were partly met, with more informal procedures for the reception and treatment of the ill patient. This was combined with the beginnings of a realisation, that to term a person mentally ill did not make the consent of that individual an insignificant matter to be sought, before treatment for that condition or some other infirmity could begin. The technical debates and refinements on mental illness that took place after the Act, combined with an accelerating shift from viewing those so labelled as dangerous and potentially violent criminals, to a view that they were more often than not a vulnerable group ripe for exploitation and indignity. With this, and a number of other reformist considerations in mind, the Mental Health Act 1983 was passed.

While the 1983 Act itself (and the Code of Practice issued under it) was considered to be a further liberalising treatment measure with formal admission to be considered something of a last resort, recent figures indicate that there has been a considerable rise in the number of such admissions for assessment and treatment. Between 1989/90 and 1994/95 admissions rose significantly from 17,400 to 27,100 (a 55 per cent increase). This increase may be due to a number of reasons; there may be simply more people in society in need of protection and treatment under the regime of the Mental

Health Act 1983. The publicity surrounding violence on members of the public by those discharged from the controlled environment of treatment and assessment could well have encouraged those involved in mental health to adopt the attitude 'when in doubt, section' to protect the public or even to protect themselves from public criticism or perhaps legal action (see, for example, *Clunis* v *Islington and Camden Health Authority* (1996) *The Times*, 27 December 1996). It has also become apparent that there has been a 'liberalisation' of attitude to the provisions of the Mental Health Act 1983 itself. There is concrete evidence that compulsory treatment of patients, while it should be *for* the mental disorder from which they suffer, is now being undertaken where it is at best allied to their mental disorder (see *Tameside and Glossop Acute Services Trust* v *CH* [1996] 1 FLR 762; *B* v *Croydon Health Authority* [1995] Fam 133; *St George's Healthcare National Health Service Trust* v *S* (1998) *The Times*, 8 May 1998).

Recently the issue of the policy of informal treatment has been fundamentally questioned but thankfully resolved by the House of Lords. An attempt to interpret informal treatment as an illegitimate policy under the Act has been refuffed by the House of Lords (see *R* v *Bournewood Community and Mental Health NHS Trust ex parte L* [1998] 3 All ER 289).

9.2 MATTERS OF DEFINITION

9.2.1 Significance of definitions

One of the most effective writers on mental health law, Brenda Hoggett, has made a comprehensive and neat encapsulation of the crux of the importance of definitions, and the distinctions underlying them (*Mental Health Law*, 3rd ed. (London: Sweet & Maxwell, 1990), p. 43). Bear them in mind when considering the admissions and treatment regimes created by the 1983 Act.

The Act makes two vital distinctions. First, for admission for assessment (ss. 2 or 4) or removal to a place of safety (ss. 135 or 136) the patient need only be suffering from some 'mental disorder'. For longer-term admission for treatment (s. 3), or reception into guardianship (s. 7), or for a court hospital or guardianship order (s. 37), interim hospital order (s. 38), or transfer during sentence (s. 47), he must have one of the four specific forms of mental disorder: 'mental illness', 'severe mental impairment', 'psychopathic disorder', or 'mental impairment'. Secondly, admission for treatment, hospital orders (but not interim hospital orders), and transfers during sentence all distinguish between *major* disorders of mental illness and severe mental impairment, which justify admission even if hospital treatment is unlikely to do the patient any good, and the *minor* disorders of psychopathic disorder or mental impairment, which only justify admission if treatment is likely to make him better, or at least prevent his getting worse. Similarly, remands to hospital for treatment (s. 36) and transfers of unsentenced prisoners (s. 48) can only happen where the patient is suffering from a major disorder.

The Act then makes an explicit categorisation, with significant implications for the patient (arguably in an area where the definition of whether any mental disorder exists is difficult enough) without many important refinements. Does the Act help with the definitions of 'mental illness', 'severe mental impairment', 'mental impairment', 'mental disorder' or 'psychopathic disorder'?

9.2.2   Sexual deviance

A first level of refinement, which is policy based, is contained in s. 1(3). This essentially states that a person is not to be regarded as being in any of the above categories where the actions of that person are by reason only of sexual deviance, dependence on drugs or alcohol, promiscuity or some other immoral conduct. This subsection fell to be considered in the case of *R* v *Mental Health Review Tribunal, ex parte Clatworthy* [1985] 3 All ER 699.

The applicant had been convicted of indecent assault, and was given a hospital order and a restriction order on the ground that there was psychopathic disorder sufficient to warrant detention. Some time later an application was made to a mental health review tribunal with the responsible medical officer stating that there was no evidence of psychopathy. The applicant's main problem was one of sexual deviance, and according to s. 1(3) was not a mental disorder. The tribunal rejected this. The applicant successfully sought judicial review of the nature and extent of the tribunal's reasons, and Mann J found that sexual deviancy meant indulgence in it rather than a propensity to it. Section 1(3) required sexual deviancy to be discounted from diagnosis of mental disorder. The argument of the tribunal that there was sexual deviancy which had the features of mental disorder was an incorrect application of the law.

While this de-categorisation has echoes of a liberal policy, there still appears from cases such as *R* v *Mental Health Tribunal, ex parte W* (1988) *The Times*, 27 May 1988 (see 9.5.2 for a consideration of the case) to be a desire on the part of mental health professionals to introduce sexual deviants to a treatment regime by way of alternative diagnosis (see the analysis of the case in the useful article by Peter Fennell, 'Sexual Suppressants and the Mental Health Act' [1988] Crim LR 660).

9.2.3   Mental illness

The Act itself does not seek to define 'mental illness' despite the variant opinions that have been expressed about its precise meaning and scope. The folly of this failure was clearly demonstrated when the judiciary made an attempt at definition in *W* v *L* [1974] QB 711.

Soon after marriage a wife began to note that her husband was exhibiting more and more extreme symptoms of mental disorder. It began with the mutilation of pets, and reached its most serious when he threatened violence against his wife. He went into a mental hospital on a voluntary basis, but soon after discharged himself. Matters came to a head when he threatened to push his wife down the stairs, as a way of getting rid of the baby she was carrying. He was taken to hospital as an emergency under the Mental Health Act 1959, s. 29. Such an order expired after 72 hours and application for a longer period was made under s. 27 of the same Act. This required the permission of the 'nearest relative'. The wife objected, stating that she could cope with her husband at home. There was a need to establish that the man was suffering from mental illness to make application under the 1959 Act without her consent. Lawton LJ described 'mental illness' (at p. 719) as:

> ordinary words of the English language . . . [which] should be construed in the way that ordinary sensible people would construe them. . . . what would the ordinary sensible person have said about the patient's condition in this case if he had been informed of his behaviour to the dogs, the cat and the wife? In my judgment such a person would have said: 'Well, the fellow is obviously mentally ill'.

Hoggett (*Mental Health Law*, 3rd ed., p. 48) critically describes this as the 'man must be mad test'. It is a societal rather than a psychiatric assessment. It attempts to use a societal deviation test: that if a person does not correspond to the vision the man on the Clapham omnibus has of normality, then he or she can be described as suffering from 'mental illness'.

9.2.4 Mental disorder

The Act does provide definitions of the other terms, with varying degrees of success. 'Mental disorder' is defined to mean 'mental illness, arrested or incomplete development of mind, psychopathic disorder or any other disorder or disability of mind' (s. 1(2)). This is obviously a wide term, with an underlying fluidity that can be utilised in a number of factual settings. The term, while broad, only entitles assessment, not the right to impose any sort of treatment. For that to take place there needs to be one of the four specific forms of disorder in existence. 'Mental illness' has been noted in 9.2.3 as legislatively undefined, with the judicial version untenable. It does not include instances defined in s. 1(3), but otherwise has eluded a consistency of definition.

9.2.5 Mental impairment and severe mental impairment

'Severe mental impairment' is a major disorder under the Act and 'mental impairment' a minor one. They describe, according to s. 1(2) 'a state of arrested or incomplete development of mind'. The former includes severe intelligence impairment and lack of social functioning, and the latter the same, obviously without the 'severity' requirement. Both are associated with abnormally aggressive or seriously irresponsible conduct. Once more this is a wide definition which, on an initial reading, can fit a number of characteristics of individuals which, as with all definitions, depend on the perspective of the viewer. To some there is an unwelcome conflation of those with subnormal intellect or intellectual handicap and those with mental disorder. Arguably this is further exacerbated by the use of the phrase 'arrested or incomplete development of mind'. It has to be questioned whether such individuals should be placed within a legislative regime that is treatment oriented. One might attempt curative intervention where the patient is suffering from a psychopathic disorder, for example, but there can be no such intervention in the case of the handicapped. While there have been IQ-based attempts to define mental and severe mental impairment, the definition really looks as much to the manifestations of the handicap, as the handicap itself.

The Mental Health Act 1983 could be interpreted as having a protective function. Those who are mentally impaired (or severely so) may well be prone to exploitation by the unscrupulous. To place such persons in a controlled environment would assist in that protection. To writers such as Larry Gostin, however, incarceration is a strange form of protection, while the exploiters have the freedom (see *The Great Debate: MIND's Comments on the White Paper on the Review of the Mental Health Act 1959* (London: MIND, 1978) cited in Hoggett, *Mental Health Law*, 3rd ed., p. 378).

9.2.6 Psychopathic disorder

'Psychopathic disorder' is a minor disorder under the Act. It describes a 'persistent disorder or disability of mind (whether or not including significant impairment of intelligence) which results in abnormally aggressive or seriously irresponsible conduct'. Again there appears to be a predominance in the definition on the manifestation rather than the underlying pathology. To concentrate on this factor could be to risk labelling the persistent criminal of limited intelligence as suffering from a form of mental disorder. This danger is exacerbated by the fact that the public's perception, fuelled by inaccurate labelling in popular media fiction, is that a psychopath is automatically a potential or actual serial killer. Labels stick whether they are accurate or not. 'Any other disorder or disability of mind' is simply a residual legislative catch-all for those that are felt not to fit in the other category of minor mental disorder.

9.3 ADMISSION FOR ASSESSMENT AND TREATMENT

9.3.1 Policy of the Act

The Mental Health Act 1959 had proceeded on the basis that wherever possible there should be an informal process of treatment, and compulsion should only be an option where the informal process was regarded as inappropriate. Gostin had questioned whether the 1959 Act as a matter of practical interpretation had achieved this desire (see *A Human Condition*, vol. 2, ch. 3 (London: MIND, 1977)). Section 131 of the Mental Health Act 1983 makes the desirability of informal treatment, where possible, explicit. This important section indicates the policy underlying the whole Act:

Nothing in this Act shall be construed as preventing a patient who requires treatment for mental disorder from being admitted to any hospital or mental nursing home in pursuance of arrangements made in that behalf and without any application, order or direction rendering him liable to be detained under this Act, or from remaining in any hospital or mental nursing home in pursuance of such arrangements after he has ceased to be so liable to be detained.

The patient treated informally is in the same position as any other person receiving medical treatment, and can refuse consent to treatment. (For more detail on the current operation of s. 131 see the significant House of Lords decision in *R v Bournewood Community and Mental Health NHS Trust, ex parte L (Secretary of State for Health and Others Intervening)* [1998] 3 All ER 289, HL.)The situation of the patient here may change, or the informal nature might be deemed no longer an appropriate format for treatment or assessment. Under s. 5(1) the patient can be detained if 'it appears to the registered medical practitioner in charge that an application ought to be made'. This expires after 72 hours. An emergency power is given to nurses by virtue of s. 5(4) but this only lasts for six hours, or until the registered medical practitioner is able to attend.

9.3.2 Treatment and care without admission

In line with the overall policy of the Mental Health Act 1983 itself detailed above there are several options (in addition to the non-statutory care programme approach and supervision register system) whereby treatment and care can take place short of formal admission. It is even the case that the patients have entitlements by reason of s. 117 of the Act to have treatment *after* they have been discharged from hospital. The requirement that the health authority continue this after care lasts as long as the patient needs it (see *R v Ealing District Health Authority, ex parte Fox* [1993] 1 WLR 373). Under ss. 7–10 of the Mental Health Act 1983 a patient can be made the subject of a guardianship order. According to s. 8 of the Act a person named as guardian has the power to require the patient to reside at a specified place, to attend at specific times and places for treatment, occupation, education or training. There is also a power that access be given for a doctor or approved social worker to see the patient. According to s. 7 a patient can only be the subject of guardianship where the patient is suffering from a mental disorder of a nature and degree which warrants the use of guardianship. Even a patient who is no longer formally detained under the 1983 Act can be the subject of guardianship. The Mental Health (Patients in the Community) Act 1995 inserted ss. 25A–25J into the 1983 Act, which deal with supervision and aftercare. To be subject to the supervised discharge regime, however, the patient still needs to be suffering from 'mental disorder (including mental illness, severe mental impairment, psychopathic disorder and mental impairment)'. In addition there needs to be a substantial risk that the patient will harm himself or others, or the patient is in danger of serious exploitation and such danger will be real if the patient does not receive the aftercare services required by s. 117. A further option for those treating the patient is to give a leave of absence under s. 17 of the Act. This has the advantage of enabling the treaters to recall patients who do not cooperate with the conditions of their leave. The patient though still needs to be liable to be detained under the Act, so treatment without consent can take place (for further debate on this section see 9.3.4 and 9.3.5 and *R* v *Hallstrom, ex parte W* [1986] QB 1090).

9.3.3 Formal admission

The formal admissions process is contained in part II of the 1983 Act. Section 6(1) is important in that it requires that an application be 'duly completed' before compulsion is used to admit for assessment or treatment. The practical difficulties facing those involved with the admissions process, and the consequences of non-compliance with the formal application process, are clearly indicated by the facts and judgment in *Townley* v *Rushworth* (1963) 62 LGR 95. The Mental Health Act 1959, s. 29(2) provided that an emergency application for admission of a patient to hospital for observation might be made by either a mental welfare officer or any relative of the patient, and s. 29(3) provided that such application should be sufficient in the first instance if founded on one medical recommendation. Section 31(1) noted that 'an application duly completed' would be a sufficient authority to take the patient away and convey him or her to hospital.

The defendant's wife had signed an emergency application form and handed it to the defendant's doctor for medical recommendation according to s. 29. The doctor refused to sign it until the defendant had been seen. The defendant, when approached by the doctor and two policemen, made it clear that they were not welcome in the house and he went into the bedroom. He was followed in by the officers and the doctor, who told the defendant that he needed to go to hospital and had to have an injection. While this was being prepared the defendant was restrained by one of the officers. The other thought that there was a scuffle and intervened, whereupon he was punched by the defendant. The defendant was then injected. The defendant was charged with assault occasioning actual bodily harm. Significantly, the medical recommendation was only signed after the scuffle had taken place. In allowing the appeal of the defendant against conviction for the assault, the Divisional Court found that since the form had not been duly completed, there was no authority under s. 31 to restrain the defendant. They were therefore trespassers, one of whom had become the subject of reasonable force in self-defence.

Brenda Hoggett, (*Mental Health Law*, 3rd ed.), notes that there are situations where a form of detention of a mentally disordered person may be required where the Mental Health Act 1983 does not seem applicable. The medical lawyer must then look to the common law to see if there is a legal right of detention. There appears to be some historical precedent which allows that 'a private person may without an express warrant confine a person disordered in his mind who seems disposed to do mischief to himself or any other person' (Bacon, cited by Hoggett at p. 115). Is it really, as a matter of practicality, a question of the common law right to enter private premises? It appears unlikely in relation to the mentally disordered, but has not been fully tested by the courts in this context.

9.3.3.1 Admission for assessment Section 2 of the Mental Health Act 1983 provides the prerequisites for formal admission to hospital for assessment. The grounds for such an application are that:

(a) the patient is suffering from a mental disorder which is of a nature and degree which warrants detention for assessment (or assessment followed by treatment); and
(b) the detention is in the interests of the protection of other persons or for the patient's own health or safety.

The application is to be made on the written recommendations of two registered medical practitioners (s. 2(3)), and the assessment period lasts 28 days (s. 2(4)). The application can be made either by the patient's 'nearest relative', a person given the power to act on the patient's behalf, or an approved social worker.

Where there is an urgent need to admit the patient for assessment, an application can be made by either an approved social worker or by a nearest relative of the patient (s. 4(2)). There only needs to be one medical recommendation. The effect of the application lasts only 72 hours, and after that if further assessment or treatment is still required, there needs to be a second medical recommendation, as under s. 2 (s. 4(4)(a)).

9.3.3.2 Admission for treatment Section 3 of the Mental Health Act 1983 controls applications for the compulsory treatment of patients. The grounds for an application are that the patient:

(a) is suffering from mental illness, severe mental impairment, psychopathic disorder or mental impairment (in other words either a major or minor form of mental disorder) of a nature and degree which makes it appropriate to receive treatment, and
(b) where there is psychopathic disorder or mental impairment, the treatment is likely to alleviate or prevent deterioration of the condition, and
(c) the treatment is necessary for the health and safety of the patient or others.

There must be two medical recommendations. If the application is to be made by a social worker, the nearest relative has to be consulted. If that nearest relative objects, the authority of the court is required (see s. 11(4)). A list of those described as 'nearest relative' is to be found in s. 26.

The effect of a duly completed application for admission for treatment is to allow the patient to be detained for up to six months. This can be initially renewed for another six months, and thereafter for one-year periods. Where such a renewal application is made, s. 20(4) requires that the treatment be to alleviate or prevent deterioration of the condition or be for the safety of the patient or others. But where the condition is one of severe mental impairment or mental illness, then as well as to alleviate or prevent deterioration, the renewal can be for reasons of the likely inability of the patient to take care of himself, or protection from the dangers of exploitation.

In practice patients who are incapable of giving assent have been informally admitted. There would appear on the surface to be no problem, as the justification could be necessity or implied consent. In chapter 6 the weakness of these justifications was noted; so should a doctor in this situation make an assessment for treatment under the Mental Health Act 1983, s. 2? One commentator felt that this should not be necessary (see (1998) NLJ 249). The Court of Appeal appeared to take a different view. In *R v Bournewood Community and Mental Health NHS Trust, ex parte L* [1998] 2 WLR 764 the appellant was severely handicapped, being autistic as well as unable to speak and needing constant care. For a considerable period of life he was an in-patient in hospital and after that had lived with carers and attended a day centre. On one occasion he became agitated at the day centre and a doctor admitted him to hospital. He never tried to leave, so the hospital thought it was all right to keep him informally detained. While he was there his carers were refused admission to see him, as there was felt to be a risk that he might want to leave with them. The decision was that he remain until there had been time to make a reassessment of his condition. There was an application for a declaration that this was an unlawful detention. At first instance the application for judicial review was denied as there could be no restraint where the patient could leave at any time, but chose not to. Lord Woolf MR considered that the hospital (and a number of others utilising the same practice) were approaching the issue from a false premise that treatment of this in-patient without consent was legitimate provided there was no dissent. Where this is the case what actually should happen is that the incompetent patient should be formally admitted under s. 3 of the Mental Health Act 1983. This statutory protection is important for the patient as the Act itself provides the means for such patients to make challenges and applications where an aspect of their care or treatment regime is in dispute. Leave to appeal was granted, but the reasoning of Lord Woolf MR on the false premise is clear and could have impacted on a common practice of informally treating such patients that had existed for some time. There seems little doubt that given the ethical significance of consent and the protection it affords to the autonomy of the individual one cannot assume coercion. Nevertheless, the House of Lords ([1998] 3 All ER 289) took a diametrically opposed view. Section 131 only applied to patients who consented to admission; this patient could not. Therefore informal treatment was justified on the basis of the common law doctrine of necessity. The patient was not detained as he had made no attempt to leave and had been kept in an unlocked ward. One could not therefore say that there was a deprivation of liberty.

9.3.4 Admission and treatment in the community

Two important questions arise out of the existence of part II of the Mental Health Act 1983. What is the true ambit of s. 3? What is the disgruntled patient to do if there is suspicion that the admission process has been abused?

A trend that has been something of a political and media football has been the desire to treat the mentally ill in as non-coercive an environment as possible. It has long been thought that the treatment process would be greatly aided by the ability of the doctor to allow the patient freedom within the community, while retaining a 'legal leash' to maintain compulsory treatment.

The preliminary issue which needs to be resolved, however, is the existence and extent of the patient's right to question the grounds and ambit of his or her detention. A number of authors have noted that there was a widespread fear that the court could be swamped by patients making spurious allegations with regard to both admission and treatment. Unpalatable as it may seem, the mental condition of the patient might create feelings of paranoia and injustice toward those treating. Section 139 of the 1983 Act has cognisance of this:

> No person shall be liable, whether on the ground of want of jurisdiction or on any other ground, to any civil or criminal proceedings to which he would have been liable apart from this section in respect of any act purporting to be done in pursuance of this Act or any regulations or rules made under this Act, or in, or in pursuance of anything done in, the discharge of functions conferred by any other enactment on the authority having jurisdiction under part VII of this Act, unless the act was done in bad faith or without reasonable care.

Section 139(2) provides that a patient requires the leave of the High Court before issuing civil proceedings. For more detail on the history and application of this section see J and A Jaconelli, 'Tort Liability under the Mental Health Act 1983' (1998) JSWFL 151.)

The Court of Appeal in *Ex parte Waldron* [1986] QB 824 and *R v Hallstrom, ex parte W* [1986] QB 1090 decided that the protection afforded the medical profession by s. 139 did not include an application for judicial review because such an application was not a civil proceeding. Parliament must have intended there to be a way for a patient to question the actions of those purporting to treat under the 1983 Act, and gain the protection of the courts where necessary. The applicant for judicial review thus does not have to show that the act was done in bad faith or without reasonable care. This has significant implications for the treatment of the patient as well as the admissions process itself.

In *Ex parte Waldron* the issue was whether it was lawful to use the admissions process in s. 3 to enable 'long leash' treatment to be given in the community. The existence of habeas corpus is a vital means by which the civil liberties of the patient can be secured, but judicial review has an arguably equal significance here. In this case the legality of the decision to use s. 3 in combination with the leave of absence provisions of s. 17 was questioned. Section 3 was not enacted with community-based care in mind. Section 3 is to enable the patient to be *admitted* for treatment. This is supported by s. 3(2), which states that the mental disorder has to be of a nature and degree which makes it appropriate to receive treatment *in hospital*. One cannot use s. 3 to initiate treatment, then allow the patient out of hospital for treatment in the community.

9.3.5 Challenging decisions

There is still an inadequacy inherent in both habeas corpus and judicial review, which is identified by M.J. Gunn in 'Judicial Review of Hospital Admissions and Treatment in the Community under the Mental Health Act 1983' [1986] JSWL 290 at p. 293:

> Although judicial review and habeas corpus do permit consideration of the original admission decision neither provide a form of appeal on the merits of the decision: neither can question whether the decision was right or wrong. Instead they concentrate on whether the doctors, social workers and nearest relatives had the legal power to admit the patient; they consider whether the discretion that the professionals have was exercised in proper manner, for example, did they take all the relevant factors into account?

The other case which proves significant in considering the existence and scope of the power of the patient to question activities undertaken in the name of the Mental Health Act 1983 is that of *L*, which is reported with *R* v *Hallstrom, ex parte W* [1986] QB 1090. The somewhat convoluted facts of the case were that the patient, Mr L, had been admitted under s. 3 of the Act for treatment and was granted a s. 17 leave of absence some months later. Mr L agreed to go back to the hospital so that a second opinion could be gained according to s. 58(3)(b) for the medication to continue to be administered without consent. A further problem was that the s. 3 admission was due to expire. Dr Gardner examined the patient for the purposes of a detention renewal (s. 20(4)). The patient questioned whether the report completed outside hospital was lawful. If it was found to be lawful, there would be a question mark over the validity of the leave of absence. The doctor's report was made with a renewal of an 'admission'. Dr Gardner was under the impression that when Mr L had gone back to the hospital for the second opinion to be obtained, that ended the initial leave of absence, and another one had taken its place. Mr L was asked to return to the hospital some time later because that second leave of absence was coming to an end. Section 17(5) states that if a leave of absence lasts more than six months, the patient ceases to be under the control of the Act. This would not be the case if the patient returned to the hospital. Mr L considered that either there had been one continuous leave of absence which had run out some time ago; or, if the recall was correct, it was an abuse of the law. One night's stay was being used as a device to keep the leave of absence running.

Section 20, the court decided, could renew a s. 3 admission for treatment. The important point, however, was that the renewal must be because the patient needs to receive treatment *in hospital*. Therefore the examination outside the hospital was invalid, and there was no lawful authority to detain or treat after that time.

There have also been applications for judicial review where the policies underlying the Mental Health Act 1983 have been questioned. In *R* v *Broadmoor Special Hospital Authority, ex parte S* (1998) *The Times*, 17 February 1998, patients challenged the legitimacy of the policy of random searches of patients detained under the Act. The policy was initiated in 1997 when a patient was found to have hidden a heavy drinking mug which had been used to attack the hospital priest. Previously the only time a search took place was where there was a specific reason to do so. It was considered after this violent incident that the old policy did not satisfactorily protect patients, staff and visitors. The Act itself contains no power to search patients, but the Secretary of State has power by virtue of s. 118 to revise the Mental Health Code of Practice. At first instance it was held that the policy was not *Wednesbury* unreasonable, and there was a general implied power to search. There was an appeal on the basis that the random use of this power was irrational. Auld LJ considered that this policy was not irrational as there was a 'self-evident and pressing need' for it (*R* v *Secretary of State for the Home Department, ex parte Leech* [1994] QB 198). There had to be times where the general interest in protecting from violence had to take precedence over an individual interest.

9.4 ALLEGATION OF WANT OF CARE BY THE PATIENT AGAINST THE DOCTOR

The difficult question about the Mental Health Act 1983, s. 139, is the position of the patient alleging that there has been an action in bad faith or without reasonable cause. The leave of the High Court is required for such a patient to commence proceedings, but when, if ever, will it be granted? This has been considered in relation to the forerunner to s. 139 of the 1983 Act, namely, the Mental Health Act 1959, s. 141.

The type of circumstance which can confront the courts is exemplified by *Buxton* v *Jayne* [1960] 1 WLR 783. Mrs B had become emotionally upset and her doctor called in a duly designated officer under the legislation then in force. This person attempted to get Mrs B to go to hospital voluntarily, but she refused. The officer then had Mrs B removed to a mental hospital having satisfied herself, as required by the law, that there were reasonable grounds for believing that Mrs B was a person of unsound mind and a proper person to be sent to a mental hospital. Mrs B was released some days later and sought to initiate proceedings against the individual who had removed her to the hospital. The legislation stated that the matter could not proceed unless the High Court was first satisfied that there were substantial grounds for the contention. Leave was granted to proceed with the action on the basis that there needed to be reasonable grounds for the removal of Mrs B, but this did not appear to have been the case on the affidavit evidence before the court.

In *Carter* v *Commissioner of Police for the Metropolis* [1975] 1 WLR 507, application was made to proceed under s. 141 of the 1959 Act by a person who had been detained under s. 136 of that Act and taken to hospital by police officers. The applicant was examined by a doctor and released. She brought an action against the Police Commisioner for false imprisonment because the officers had acted without reasonable cause and in bad faith. There was a distinct conflict of evidence, with the police stating that they thought the woman was mentally unstable, and her deposing that she had remained courteous and quiet. There was, however, no medical evidence that went towards showing that the applicant was mentally ill. In refusing the application to proceed, the Court of Appeal confirmed that the applicant had to satisfy the judge that there was *substantial ground* for the contention of bad faith or lack of reasonable care. It would not be sufficient merely to indicate that there was a conflict of evidence. In considering the 'inherent probabilities' of the matter there seemed to be no rational explanation why officers would take away a woman they had never met before, and who was calm and collected, into custody. There would thus be no leave to proceed in the matter.

A variant of the application under s. 141 of the 1959 Act was seen in the House of Lords case of *Pountney* v *Griffiths* [1976] AC 314. The appellant, who was a patient, alleged that the respondent, a male nurse, had punched him on the arm at the end of a visit by the appellant's family. The nurse had been convicted of a criminal offence and received a conditional discharge. The conviction was quashed in the Divisional Court on application for certiorari. The reason was that the appellant had failed to obtain leave of the High Court to proceed. The appellant tried to argue that this was not needed as the assault was not an act done in pursuance of the 1959 Act, as it was done in the everyday work of the hospital staff. The appeal failed on the ground that the nurses in the mental hospital were discharging control and treatment functions under the 1959 Act as a whole. This was the case when the alleged incident occurred. Therefore leave of the High Court should have been sought before pursuing the allegation of assault. A different result was reached with regard to an alleged assault on an informal patient in *R* v *Moonsami Runighlan* [1977] Crim LR 361. The acts done to the victim were not done in pursuance of the Act, due to the informal nature of the patient's presence. The defendant, however, was acquitted of the alleged assault.

The 1983 Act has retained the essential wording of its predecessors, but the circumstances where the court will grant leave to proceed appear now to be interpreted differently. In *Winch* v *Jones* [1986] QB 296 the applicant had been remanded to a centre as a result of a contempt of court, and was thereafter committed to a mental hospital under the provisions of the 1959 Act. Application was made for leave to proceed in a negligence action against the doctors who had performed the treatment, under s. 139 of the 1983 Act, which was in force when the applicant left hospital. The judge ruled that the test to be applied under that section was whether the applicant had established a prima facie case against the doctors. Leave to proceed was refused on the basis that the applicant had failed to so establish. Lord Donaldson MR formulated what one may regard as a test which more fairly balances the risks of a frivolous claim against the right of the patient to make an allegation of a breach of duty by those treating:

> In striking such a balance, the issue is not whether the applicant has established a prima facie case or even whether there is a serious issue to be tried, although that comes close to it. The issue is whether, on the material immediately available to the court, which, of course, can include material furnished by the proposed defendant, the applicant's complaint appears to be such that it deserves the fuller investigation which will be possible if the intended applicant is allowed to proceed. (p. 305)

In *Albert* v *Lavin* [1982] AC 546 the important point of law was made that, while the Mental Health Act makes lawful the detention of a citizen which might otherwise be a serious and unlawful interference with the liberty of the subject, there is also a right to detain a person against his or her will where there is an actual or reasonably foreseeable breach of the peace. It would be unlawful to resist a restraint imposed because of a breach of the peace. The implication of this is that there are grounds for the detention of a mentally ill person, as long as there is an apprehended or actual breach of the peace, regardless of the provisions of the Mental Health Act 1983. The key point to be considered where this was in issue would be the reasonableness of the claim that there was or was about to be, a breach of the peace.

In *Furber* v *Kratter* (1988) *The Times*, 21 July 1988 an application to proceed under s. 139 of the 1983 Act was successful where there was an allegation of negligence. The patient was found to have an arguable case that a lawful regime could become unlawful where it went beyond a particular degree of severity. After a violent attack on a ward sister of a special hospital the plaintiff was placed in seclusion for 16 days. The plaintiff alleged that she had been denied clothes or reading and writing material. There was a dispute, which had to wait for the trial of the action, whether these things had been offered and refused by the patient, or denied by the staff.

9.5   TREATMENT FOR MENTAL ILLNESS

9.5.1   Introduction: common law justification

Potentially this is the most significant area of the legislation as far as this book is concerned, and the focus of political as well as legal controversy. Treatment can be justified as a matter of common law on the grounds that it is necessary in the best interests of the patient (see *Re F (Mental Patient: Sterilisation)* [1990] 2 AC 1 and 13.4.2; see also *R v Bournewood Community and Mental Health NHS Trust, ex parte L (Secretary of State for Health and others intervening)* [1998] 3 All ER 289). Treatment in such circumstances can take place where the patient is either incompetent to consent because of unconsciousness, or lacks the capacity to understand the nature and implications of treatment because, for example, of the existence of the mental illness.

The Law Commission has now clarified the way it is anticipated that the law will move forward with regard to those with a mental disorder who require treatment for an allied or separate physical illness (see 6.6). Here the main concern is with the statutory framework for the treatment of the mental disorder itself.

9.5.2 Statutory framework

Treatment and consent provisions are found in part IV of the Mental Health Act 1983. Section 57 specifies treatment which requires patient consent *and* a second opinion. The treatment to which s. 57 applies is treatment either for destroying brain tissue or to destroy the functioning of brain tissue. The Secretary of State is authorised to extend the coverage of s. 57. Regulation 16 of the Mental Health (Hospital, Guardianship and Consent to Treatment) Regulations 1983 (SI 1983/893) has added surgical implantation of hormones for the purpose of reducing male sexual drive.

Apart from the circumstances detailed in s. 62, in addition to patient consent, there needs to be a medical practitioner and two other persons appointed for the purpose, but not registered medical practitioners, who have certified that the patient is capable of understanding the nature, purpose and likely effects of the treatment in question. In addition the registered medical practitioner needs to be satisfied that the operation is to alleviate or prevent deterioration of the patient's condition.

Section 58 specifies treatments which require *either* consent *or* a second opinion. The only limitation in s. 58 on the type of treatment to which it applies is the administration of medicine for the treatment of mental disorder. However, s. 58 applies only if the medicine is administered 'at any time during a period for which [the patient] is liable to be detained as a patient to whom this part of this Act applies if three months or more have elapsed since the first occasion in that period when medicine was administered to him by any means for his mental disorder'. The same regulation as that specified in relation to hormone treatment has added treatment by way of electroconvulsive therapy to the treatment covered by s. 58.

Section 58(3) allows for treatment *without* consent, where a registered medical practitioner has certified in writing that the patient is incapable of understanding the nature and effects of the treatment, but this treatment should be given because of the likelihood of it alleviating or preventing a deterioration of the patient's condition.

Section 60 allows the patient required and/or capable of consenting to treatment to withdraw that consent at any time.

The main derogation from the principle of the Act, that as far as possible the patient should be allowed to exercise autonomous decision-making, is contained in s. 62. It states that the provisions of ss. 57 and 58 will not apply where the treatment:

(a) is necessary to save the patient's life, or

(b)   while not irreversible, is immediately necessary to prevent a serious deterioration in the condition, or

(c)   while not irreversible or hazardous, is immediately necessary and is the minimum interference necessary to stop the patient behaving violently or being a danger to himself or others.

The significance of this part of the Act is obvious. If the preconditions are satisfied, the medical practitioner's action in treating the patient's mental illness is not predicated on the consent of the patient. This is a major inroad into patient autonomy, and so needs to have in place with it well-considered guidelines. The need for a second opinion and certification of reasons assists in this respect. The two major treatments that are of concern are so-called 'psychosurgery' and hormone treatment to reduce male sex drive. An important case on the treatment provisions of the 1983 Act, which indicates the modern judicial approach to the issues, is *R* v *Mental Health Act Commission, ex parte W* (1988) *The Times*, 27 May 1988.

The Mental Health Act 1983 sends conflicting signals to mental health professionals. On the one hand it seeks to exclude the possibility that a person will be treated as mentally disordered solely on account of sexual deviancy (s. 1(3)), whilst on the other regulations made under the Act purport to include the surgical implantation of hormones for the reduction of male sexual drive as treatments for mental disorder. (P. Fennell, 'Sexual Suppressants and the Mental Health Act' [1988] Crim LR 660 at p. 661)

The case concerned a compulsorily detained paedophile who had been convicted of numerous offences involving young boys. The evidence was that, at the end of the sentence of imprisonment, the man sought help through a consultant psychiatrist. The first prescription of drugs did not decrease the patient's sexual drive. There was thus a fear that the patient might re-offend, or be damaged by the high dose of the drug originally prescribed, if it was to have any appreciable affect.

The doctor then prescribed a drug known as Goserelin. The drug, says Fennell, 'reduces testosterone to castrate levels' (at p. 664). The patient had the effects and delivery of the drug explained, and was keen to proceed. A matter of fact which was to gain importance in the case was that the drug was delivered by way of the subcutaneous implant of a slow-release cylinder. The doctor felt obliged to contact the Mental Health Act Commission to review the treatment method. The Commission concluded that this treatment was within s. 57 of the Act, and that the issues had been fully explained to the patient to gain proper consent as required.

The doctor had a problem, however, in that there needed to be certification that the treatment was needed by two others professionally concerned with the patient, but they could not be contacted. The doctor was advised that without this there could be no more treatment. Application was therefore made by the patient that in fact such certification was not required because the treatment fell outside the 1983 Act altogether.

Two issues were concerned here. The first was whether Goserelin was a hormone. If it was, the argument that the Act *applied* would be at least partially successful. If, however, this was combined with a decision that the delivery of the implant was not a surgical implant then s. 57 could *not* apply.

The court decided Goserelin was not a hormone. In a somewhat exotic avoidance of the effects of s. 57 it was stated that 'Goserelin is a synthetic analogue of a hormone , and it would be more accurate to describe it as a hormone analogue'. Stuart-Smith LJ said:

> I do not think there is any warrant for including in the term 'hormone' hormone analogues which are separate substances well known at the time the regulations were made. If Parliament passes legislation on the control of leopards, it is not to be presumed that leopards include tigers on the basis that they are larger and fiercer.

With regard to the nature of the implant, Stuart-Smith LJ continued that the means of implanting by way of large-bore syringe was different from that commonly used to deliver hormones to mentally ill (and other) patients. It was:

> simply a device for placing the implant in position without using the fingers. It has no cutting edge; the bore is at least five times that of the needle used with Goserelin, and it is used again and again. It requires a surgical incision and subsequent suturing; it can in no way be likened to or described as an injection.

Therefore the implant was not surgical, and was regarded by the court as the implant of something not quite a hormone.

A wider question fell for the court's consideration. Was the treatment that was being received even for mental disorder? Section 1(3) of the Mental Health Act 1983 explicitly excludes sexual deviancy from the definition of mental disorder. The 'patient' here was a paedophile, and so was apparently suffering from a form of sexual deviancy. If this were the case then part IV of the Act relating to treatment for mental disorder would not apply. According to Fennel:

> This argument was dropped in the course of the proceedings. The reasons why it was not pursued remain obscure. Stuart-Smith LJ states that it was because it became clear in the course of the hearing that the applicant's psychiatrist took the view that the treatment was for his mental disorder as well as his sexual deviancy.

This really has to be doubted. It appeared that the court 'conflated the two questions into one and glossed over the whole issue'. Stuart-Smith LJ came to a wary conclusion:

> . . . where the mental disorder is quite distinct from the sexual deviancy or other matter referred to in s. 1(3) . . . and the proposed treatment is solely

for the purpose of dealing with the sexual deviancy or other s. 1(3) condition, it is difficult to see how this can be treatment for mental disorder. In practice, however, it seems likely that the sexual problem will be inextricably linked with mental disorder, so that treatment for the one is treatment for the other as in this case.

The case, then, as well as controversially applying a 'broad terms' concept of consent, decided that Goserelin was not governed by the provisions of s. 57 of the 1983 Act.

More recently there has been considerable controversy over what can be covered by the term treatment *for* mental disorder. It is obvious that a formally admitted patient may require treatment for other illnesses aside from the mental disorder. What of the patient who refuses this 'other' treatment? Can there be treatment without consent? The question has been controversially answered by the courts in the following two cases, which deserve some detailed consideration.

In *Tameside and Glossop Acute Services Trust* v *CH* [1996] 1 FLR 762 a 41-year-old woman was suffering from paranoid schizophrenia. She was detained under s. 3 of the 1983 Act. She became pregnant and this pregnancy was such that it was felt that the best way of saving the life or health of the child was to have the option of performing a Caesarean section. There were fears that the patient would either not understand the need for this operation or would resist. The hospital sought a court declaration that the operation could be performed without the patient's consent if she were to refuse and that she could be reasonably restrained for the purpose of the operation. Under s. 63 of the Mental Health Act 1983 the consent of the patient is not required for any emergency treatment *for* the mental disorder. The court considered that the Caesarean section did come within s. 63 as it was treatment ancillary to her mental health. It was felt that the patient's mental health would suffer were she to have a stillborn child, and therefore the operation was to prevent deterioration in mental health.

The scope of s. 63 was also extended considerably in the Court of Appeal decision in *B* v *Croydon Health Authority* [1995] Fam 133. The patient here was also detained under s. 3 of the Mental Health Act 1983, suffering from a borderline personality disorder coupled with post-traumatic stress disorder. These problems lead to a compulsion for self-harm due to an irrationally low regard for herself. During her detention she refused to eat as a means of self-harm and punishment. At times she accepted food but only under threat of being force-fed by nasogastric tube. At first instance it was held that the patient did not lack the capacity to consent (or obviously refuse) but declared that she could be lawfully fed without her consent under s. 63 as treatment for mental disorder. The patient appealed, contending that that this nasogastric feeding was not treatment for mental disorder because it did not prevent or alleviate a deterioration in her condition (s. 3(2)(b)). It was further argued that even if it were such treatment then it fell within one of the exceptions to s. 63, in that it was a 'medicine' by virtue of s. 58. Nevertheless, it was the first point which was the main focus of appeal.

Hoffmann LJ, at pp. 138–9, seemed clearly to regard the nasogastric feeding as falling within the term 'treatment for mental disorder':

Nursing and care concurrent with the core treatment or as a necessary prerequisite to such treatment or to prevent the patient from causing harm to himself or to alleviate the consequences of the disorder are in my view all capable of being ancillary to a treatment calculated to alleviate or prevent a deterioration of the psychopathic disorder. It would seem to me strange if a hospital could, without the patient's consent, give him treatment directed to alleviating a psychopathic disorder showing itself in suicidal tendencies, but not without such consent be able to treat the consequences of a suicide attempt. In my judgment the term 'medical treatment . . . for the mental disorder' in s. 63 includes such ancillary acts.

Hoffmann LJ went on to approve of the approach in the similar case of *Re KB (Adult) (Mental Patient: Medical Treatment)* (1994) 19 BMLR 144 that the tube-feeding of an anorexic is aimed at 'relieving symptoms and is just as much a part of treatment as relieving the underlying cause'.

The main criticism of these cases is that they have simply gone against the core notion that a patient may lack competence in relation to some matters, but that should not necessarily be taken as a signal for a declaration of blanket incompetence and thereafter compulsion. It has also been suggested that the common law has developed ways of answering the kinds of questions raised by the facts of the above two cases, and the Mental Health Act 1983 should not be stretched beyond its logical wording. The Mental Health Act 1983 has, as the discussion on consent and incompetent adults in chapter 6 indicates, replaced the common law powers over the mentally handicapped, and so the Act is the proper tool to use (although according to *R v Bournewood Community and Mental Health NHS Trust, ex parte L* [1998] 3 All ER 289, the fact that the Act remains silent on necessity means that the common law doctrine can be used to justify treatment even while a patient is informally detained). Such a broad interpretation of s. 63 seems to represent a slippery slope that could lead to formally detained patients losing the right to say no to certain forms of treatment.

9.6 CONCLUSION

The mental health care regime is much wider than this admissions and treatment analysis suggests. The other issues, however, stray into much broader areas of criminal law and criminal justice, which have themselves had considerable analysis in numerous works. Nevertheless the above aspects of mental health law provide the essential 'nuts and bolts' of mental health knowledge for the purposes of a medical law text.

The definitional, admissions and treatment parts of the Mental Health Act 1983 all suffer from the perhaps inevitable limitations of legislation in making provision for the wide variety of conditions and factual situations that have been seen. The Mental Health Act 1983, as well as containing specific provisions later in the Act, which are themselves important, has attempted to give form to a less Draconian, blanket and patronising notion of mental illness, although it may appear that recent case law and policy are beginning to reverse that trend. The existence of a legal culture aware of the sentiments expressed in s. 131 is to be welcomed. The combination of this Act and the common law concept of 'best interests' of the patient (if more effectively utilised) may well place medical law on the road to a regime that protects the patient, treats, but at the same time acknowledges the significance of personal autonomy and the need, where at all possible, to gain consent before there is any violation of that personal right. The Law Commission recommendations detailed in chapter 6 are a further and welcome addition to this more enlightened medical law debate.

Further reading

Alexander, M., et al. 'Should a Sexual Offender Be Allowed Castration' (1993) 307 BMJ 790.
Fennell, P., 'Sexual Suppressants and the Mental Health Act' [1988] Crim LR 660.
Fennell, P., 'Arrest or Injection?' (1993) 143 NLJ 395.
Gunn, M., 'Judicial Review of Hospital Admissions and Treatment in the Community under the Mental Health Act 1983' [1986] JSWL 290.
Jaconelli, J. and A., 'Tort Liabiity under the Mental Health Act 1983' (1998) JSWFL 151.

TEN
Embryo research

10.1 INTRODUCTION

Technological developments in the area of assisted reproductive technology are significant and accelerating. A review of recent scientific literature or even popular science on television indicates the massive potential of this aspect of medical research. The debate has always been polarised. After *in vitro* fertilisation (IVF) – literally fertilisation in glass – was developed by Steptoe and Edwards at the Bourn Clinic in Cambridgeshire, and the birth of Louise Brown in 1978 using the technique, many infertile couples saw a new chance to found a family. It was not long before scientists were considering the wider possibilities:

(a) To conduct research on the excess of embryos produced as an inevitable result of the technique.

(b) To go one stage further and actually create *in vitro* embryos for the explicit purpose of conducting research on them.

The ensuing debate on the morality of such research was signified by dramatic images. Proponents of research invoked the scientific imperative of the 'right to know', while opponents used the memory of research undertaken under the Third Reich, and a vision of the future of a 'Brave New World' of genetically engineered clones, to stop what was seen as a pernicious development. Recently the debate has resurfaced with the cloning of Dolly, the sheep. To scientists this made the cloning of humans a realistic possibility within a couple of years. It has nevertheless been condemned by opponents as the slippery slope to harvesting the organs of clones to replace the 'tired' organs of an ageing population. In addition there has been strong speculation that were the same technique applied to humans then the current legislative ban on cloning would not apply (see 10.3.2).

While the current debate has developed a more sophisticated terminology, the ethically polarised arguments have stayed the same. In no other area of medical law has an understanding of the strands of moral philosophy, competing human rights and clinical intuition been so important. In terms of the Hart–Devlin debate it may be questioned whether embryo research is a proper subject for the intervention of the medical law at all (for an introduction to all these issues, see chapter 1).

The current Chair of the Human Fertilisation and Embryology Authority (set up under the Human Fertilisation and Embryology Act 1990), Ruth Deech, has recently sought to justify the intervention of medical law regulation in the light of increasing opposition to any form of regulation on embryo research and infertility treatment. In a recent international conference (10th World Congress on IVF and Assisted Reproduction, May 1997) Deech notes that there was distinct opposition from the medical profession to any form of control, whether on infertility treatment (see chapter 11) or research. The reasons appeared to be an amalgam of rights, ethics and the nature of State intervention itself. It was argued that every man and woman has a right to be able to found a family, whatever their physical circumstances might be; therefore intervention and regulation would place, and indeed has placed, a limit on that right. The medical profession further argued that ethically there should be no limit on what techniques should be used to achieve this rights-based objective – safety taking second place to efficacy. More widely it was stated that State interference in using these developments in reproductive technology was the calling card of an overly authoritarian State rather than a liberal democratic one.

Ruth Deech responds that regulation is necessary and justified by the fact that many aspects of family life are already the subject of extensive regulation. As issues in reproductive technology are a modern facet of family life, society should govern it with rules of law. (For further debate on this see Ruth Deech, 'Infertility and Ethics' [1997] CFLQ 337.) Given the dynamics of this debate, it seems a little strange that the current editions of medical law texts appear to be devoting less and less time to the wider issues of reproductive technology. After the Warnock Report (Department of Health and Social Security, *Report of the Committee of Inquiry into Human Fertilisation and Embryology* (Cmnd 9314) (London: HMSO, 1984)) there was a spate of literature on the moral and ethical status of the human embryo, the human right to reproduce and the place of the law in controlling such potentially powerful technology. Now there seems to be more of an assumption that there has to be legal regulation and less devoted to the debate on these wider issues. The fact that a law exists does not preclude ethical debate. It is difficult, if not impossible, for the medical lawyer to discuss the regulation of embryo research fully without an ethical consideration of the subject matter. This debate has importance not only for the future of embryo research, but also for the possibility of human-assisted reproduction, surrogacy arrangements and experimentation on the more developed foetus.

Morgan and Nielsen ('Dangerous Liaisons? Law, Technology, Reproduction and European Ethics' in McVeigh and Wheeler (eds), *Law, Health and Medical Regulation* (Dartmouth, 1992) bolster the importance of the debate:

Technology has hastened our notion of self-conception to the brink of an evolutionary surge; the notions of value and worth which we attach to individuals and social groups, the nature and meaning of fertility, and the concept of the family are all implicated. The ensuing debate cuts into fundamental values and increasingly the very institutions of maternity, paternity, motherhood and fatherhood are subject to examination and re-evaluation. New demons and chimeras and spirits are conjured to haunt the new families which technological and personal upheavals have introduced. The 'reproduction revolution' brings in its wake many new and difficult choices. This gives rise to the dilemma that 'for every complex problem there is a solution that is neat, plausible and wrong'. (p. 53)

The first element of the ethical debate is the status of the subject matter. Right and law cannot be considered without designation of status. How can you discuss something when you do not know what 'it' is? As Kennedy and Grubb argue in the first edition of their *Medical Law* (London: Butterworths, 1989) (written prior to the Human Fertilisation and Embryology Act 1990):

The claims to protection that an embryo may make upon us clearly condition how we should respond to problems such as embryo donation, storage, disposition and the use of embryos for research purposes. If there be no law at present which clearly stipulates the status of an embryo, and if there be a need for such law, any proposed law should reflect the conclusions of the ethical analysis of the status of the embryo. (p. 655)

10.2 THE ETHICAL DEBATE

10.2.1 Moments of human development

There are a number of potentially factually significant stages in the development of the human that can impact on the moral debate, and therefore possibly affect the existence or extent of legal regulation of many aspects of reproductive technology. Both the proponents of and those opposed to research place a great deal of emphasis on the moral or physiological importance of a particular stage of development. To give any phase of development of the human a particular 'designation' is immediately to invoke a notion of status, and therefore the intricacies of language are of primary concern. Even the use of the term 'human' is of some import, given that:

Human beings protect themselves with a thicket of rights they do not grant other beings, and some of these rights are said to be human rights – rights which one has by virtue of simply being human. (L. Becker, 'Human Beings: Boundaries of the Concept' in *Medicine and Modern Philosophy: A Reader in Philosophy and Public Affairs*, p. 23)

A simple preliminary question to consider: Is the fertilised egg and sperm in a Petri dish 'human'?

It will be seen that those who support research use relatively precise (if nonetheless controversial) definitional categories. Those opposed, while not denying the general accuracy of the definitions of the stages of development attach very different values to them. To many of the authors on the complex moral debate on the status of the human embryo the key issue is when human life comes into existence.

Legally, *birth* itself has been regarded as important. The laws relating to homicide generally, and civil actions in relation to pre-natal negligent activity which harms the unborn specifically (whether through misconduct of the medical profession or through the mother's conduct which could be potentially damaging to the developing foetus (see, for example, *Winnipeg Child and Family Services (Northwest Area)* v *G* (1998) 3 BHRC 611 Can SC), all turn on the birth of the child; what some have termed the child's 'entry' into civil society (see also *Attorney-General's Reference (No. 3 of 1994)* [1997] 3 WLR 421). *Physiologically,* it is also a significant event. After birth the child is no longer dependent on the mother for its oxygen supply. Writers such as Fletcher argue that the point of birth is the moment at which there should be accorded the status of 'humanness' (see Walters and Singer (eds), *Test-tube Babies: A Guide to Moral Questions, Present Techniques and Future Possibilities* (Oxford: Oxford University Press, 1982), p. 52). The limited amount of case law which has considered the status of the unborn has clearly stated that there is no legal status until birth (see for example *Paton* v *British Pregnancy Advisory Service Trustees* [1979] QB 276). The recent House of Lords decision in *Attorney-General's Reference (No. 3 of 1994)* [1998] AC 245 has, however, indicated an uneasy acknowledgement that the unborn could be given a retrospective status, at least as far as the criminal law of manslaughter is concerned. During the course of the fairly wide-ranging judgment (for more detail on this see 12.10) Lord Mustill pointed out that the Court of Appeal had been incorrect in considering the unborn to be a part of the mother, just as a leg or an arm. Lord Mustill found this untenable for the following reason, which is useful to note as an attempt at invoking some sort of independent status for the unborn, based on *genetic uniqueness*:

> The reason for the uniqueness of S [the unborn child] was that the development of her own special characteristics had been enabled and bounded by the collection of genes handed down not only by M [the mother] but also by the natural father. This collection was different from the genes which had enabled and bounded the development of M, for these had been handed down by her own mother and natural father. S and her mother were closely related but, even apart from differing environmental influences, they were not, had not been, and in the future never would be 'the same'. There was, of course, an intimate bond between the foetus and the mother, created by the total dependence of the foetus on the protective physical environment furnished by the mother, and on the supply by the mother through the physical linkage between them of the nutrients, oxygen and other substances essential to foetal life. . . . But the relationship was one of bond, not of identity. (at p. 255)

Nevertheless their lordships were clear that there had to be live birth (of however brief a time) to maintain a charge of homicide where there was criminal injury to the unborn.

Legislation, such as the Congenital Disabilities (Civil Liability) Act 1976 (see 8.5), has also given retrospective status to the unborn in respect of prenatal negligence The success of a claim is once more, however, dependent on live birth.

The point at which the unborn is regarded as *viable*, arguably the stage at which the child is not just capable of being born alive, but also of having a reasonable prospect of remaining alive with or without the support of medical science, can have significance to some writers. The main difficulty with utilising this notion morally and/or legally is that it is indeterminate and can be heavily dependent on variable environmental factors. To have a standard of protection based on this factor would mean that where technology was more sophisticated, the point of viability would move backwards. Simply the better the technology, the earlier the point of viability is reached. This would be further evidence of its indeterminacy. In reply, it may be said that while it might move backwards, there will inevitably be a point at which technology could not perform all the functions of something that was physiologically and neurologically simply not ready.

The time of *quickening*, the first perceptible movement of the unborn in the womb, is now more of historical interest, but it still forms an influence on rabbinical law. In England, before 1861, there was a more serious offence of abortion when the woman was 'quick with child' than earlier in the pregnancy. Ethically, the link was with Aristotle's theory of a sudden 'ensoulment' that takes place, therefore morally animating the unborn.

Conception or *fertilisation* has great significance ethically, and is one of the main features of the opposition to embryo research and abortion. The Roman Catholic church, in particular, maintains that a human 'person' comes into existence at the moment of fertilisation. This has also been termed the theory of immediate animation. The mortal soul enters the body when egg and sperm combine. There is now a morally valuable human individual in existence. The legal protective regime should, according to this view, begin at this point. This is a clear example of the acquisition of a moral status culminating in a proposed legal and 'human' right to life.

Implantation of the embryo in the womb has been argued as having importance too. It would appear though to be a point rather more of convenience than due to an ethical model. Nevertheless, as chapter 12 will show, certain proponents of this phase of development argue that legislation could be interpreted with implantation in mind as a cut-off point for certain procedures under the abortion regulatory mechanism.

Ability to feel pain has recently been strongly suggested as the key determining factor relevant to status. In 1996 a report by the organisation CARE noted that there were a number of stages of development where the unborn appeared to react in certain ways to stimuli such as external light shined on the mother's womb. There was also a video publicised by anti-abortion groups purporting to show a foetus writhing in agony during the termination.

The issue of pain is an emotive one, and has been used to develop a current drive to inhibit research as well as abortion access. The difficulty with this new style of argument is that there are different views on pain itself. The foetus may be reacting to a stimulus very early on in gestation, but is this reaction one of pain? The real focus of the argument, one suspects, is the idea that when there is pain there is sentience – the ability to think – and this is one of the hallmarks of 'humanness'. The likelihood appears to be, however, that the issue of pain will continue to be a focus of attack, but more relevant to those opposed to the current abortion legislation than research on the 'primitive' embryo.

10.2.2 Ethical dilemmas

The current ethical debate on embryo research is typified by the confrontation between those who regard fertilisation or conception as morally relevant and those who consider moral relevance to attach to later developmental events. One might attach moral significance to any one of the above moments or none at all. That really is the problem (and to some the frustration) of this ethical debate (see, for example, M. Brody, 'On the Humanity of the Fetus' in Goodman (ed.), *What is a Person?* (Clifton NJ: Humana Press, 1988)). All of the above physiological or moral stages of development have been at one time or another persuasively argued as when 'life' comes into existence. Thereafter this 'life' should become protected in a legal framework.

While such a moral debate is extensive, an understanding of the views of the major camps in the debate is important for a great deal of medical law, impacting as the debate does not only on the area of embryo research, but foetal research, infertility treatment techniques, and abortion.

10.2.2.1 Rejection of destructive embryo research
Those who accept the theory of immediate animation believe that any discussion of destructive research is a discussion about destroying an embodied human soul. The researcher here may be seen as guilty of murder. The researcher has killed. Member of Parliament Michael Alison stated in the House of Commons debate on the regulation of such research that 'the embryonic human individual . . . has been imperceptible, invisible and not in evidence but essentially, logically and potentially there from the moment of fertilisation'. It has to be admitted that as a matter of medical fact, there is here a specific point to which one may give the term 'life'. The other terms and events, such as viability, personhood or quickening are all variable in timing and can to some be difficult to regard as an identifiable single moment when life comes into existence (see, for example, Samuels, 'Embryo Research: The Significance of the New Law' (1991) 31 Med Sci Law 115).

A more recent sophistication of the argument that life begins at conception has it that at this point the 'entity' becomes a member of the human species. That, of itself, warrants protection born of that classification. To be a member of the human species is to be accorded human rights. Further, it is a less hazardous definition than the complexities that surround differences between 'pre-embryo' and 'embryo' with the latter's definition being predicated on the existence of the primitive streak (see 10.2.4) (Holland, 'A Fortnight of My Life is Missing: A Discussion of the Status of the Human Pre-Embryo' (1990) J App Phil 25). Once an entity is granted the status of member of the human species, all rights that exist for the adult exist for the fertilised egg. This entity then has to be regarded as special by the mere fact of the species it belongs to. To this those who reject embryo research would add that at the point of fertilisation a genetically unique individual is created. Authors have noted that the rejection of destructive embryo research can be based on a perception that human reproductive material has a special nature, and it is this uniqueness that has a moral significance. To destroy this special material then, is to demean respect for that part of us which is unique (see the quotation from Lord Mustill's speech in *Attorney-General's Reference (No. 3 of 1994)* [1997] 3 WLR 421 in 10.2.1).

For the moral philosopher of the deontological school, to term the embryo human means that there can be no destructive research. This is not based on any religious conviction, but on the main plank of deontological philosophy itself: 'Do unto others'. The morally correct action (the one which the law will invoke where human nature tends against it) it will be recalled, is one that treats people never as a means to an end but an end in themselves. There is no point in the researcher confronting deontology with arguments about the benefits of the research. The researcher cannot use a person to gain something. Further, the reply would be that if an embryo can be destroyed, then the researcher could equally be destroyed. The morally right action is one that treats both embryo and researcher equally. The deontological medical law would make the researcher do the right thing.

Even if one is not convinced by the above analysis of the status of the human embryo, those who reject embryo research emphasise that if a moment when 'life' comes into existence cannot be proved, then logic and caution dictate that, given the destructive nature of what will happen to the embryo at any time after fertilisation, protection should exist from the earliest discernible point, which is fertilisation (see M. Brazier, 'Embryos' "Rights": Abortion and Research' in M. Freeman (ed.), *Medicine, Ethics and the Law* (London: Stevens, 1988)).

One of the dominant arguments against embryo research is based on the potentiality argument. The embryo is alive and developing. The destructive research on it destroys its chance to become fully fledged. As Meyer says:

> Our intuition tells us that a human fertilised egg or embryo should not be regarded as if it were a hamster. . . . The reason may well lie in the fact that it has the potential to be human, regardless of whether it can or will realise it.

The fertilised egg *in utero* can be argued to have a self-initiating potential. It has within it the capacity to develop from the moment of fertilisation. It might be an 'intuitively' disagreeable notion, but all that is required is a suitable environment for development. Consider though the fear of Gena

Corea (*The Mother Machine* (London: Women's Press, 1988)) that '[when] reproductive engineers have developed an artificial womb, they might place the cultured embryo directly into the mother machine'.

There is some support for the view, however, that it is difficult to describe the potential as self-initiating, as it is dependent on circumstances beyond the control of that entity. With the fertilisation process taking place *in vitro*, the potential is dependent on transfer into the uterus of a woman. The general thrust of the potentiality argument is that there is no point after fertilisation where the potential for life is any greater. There is the potential for the fertilised egg to suffer from a destructive defect, as there is such a danger for the mature foetus.

The recent speech of Lord Mustill in *Attorney-General's Reference (No. 3 of 1994)* [1998] AC 245 could also be used by those opposed to embryo research. His lordship had found that the unborn was not another 'limb' of the mother, but then proceeded to argue tentatively what a foetus is:

> Eschewing all religious and political debate I would say that the foetus is neither [person nor adjunct of mother]. It is a unique organism. (at p. 256)

From this it could be argued that rules of law or morality which are designed to respect persons may not be applied, but neither should there be no rules applied to this genetically unique entity. Any discussion and subsequent ban, regulation or allowance of research should be based on an acknowledgement that this organism is *sui generis*. It requires a new language and a new form of debate. Merely to consider such 'uniqueness', though, conjures up images of a single personality; again the process of individuation and identification leads towards value, and protection from destruction.

10.2.3 Support for embryo research

It is generally agreed by most philosophers in this area that the point at which a human life exists is not necessarily the same as when a human 'person' comes into existence. This view arguably leads to a more realistic assessment of the issues. One may indeed accept that human life begins at fertilisation, but this does not automatically lead to a declaration that a human person is in existence, and therefore deserving of protection. In response it could be argued that the point at which a person comes into existence is indeterminate, and value-laden to the point of being impossible of consensual resolution. Nevertheless, many writers have tried to establish what they regard as the relevant criteria necessary to be a person. To be called a 'person' implies the ownership of personal (or human) rights that can be morally and legally demanded. Most obviously here the right not to be researched upon and destroyed.

Those who support embryo research obviously are confronted by the ethical objections noted earlier. They respond to the view that the law should protect at fertilisation by arguing that while fertilisation creates genetic 'uniqueness' this is different to stating that a person exists. Colourfully, it has

been said that 'such an egg is no more a person than an acorn is an oak tree
or a bowl of unbaked ingredients is a cake' (J. Glover, *Causing Death and
Saving Lives* (Harmondsworth: Penguin, 1977), p. 124). Added to this
refutation is the point that, to talk of the fertilised egg as a genetically unique
individual is to ignore the fact that not all of the material will form part of
the embryo (some of it has to form the placenta, for example) and the
possibility that the individual may in fact be twins.

On a simpler level, there has been the argument that it is simply unrealistic
to expect society to accept that a microscopic conglomeration of cells is a
human being. Allied to this 'intuitive' support for research is that it is equally
unrealistic to conclude that something that has no notion of its species status
and has nothing approaching human form can be a human being.

It has already been seen that some theological theories hold that the
relevant criterion is ensoulment. To writers such as Lockwood, Tooley and
Fortin, the essential reference points are complex combinations of physical
and mental properties.

Michael Lockwood makes three main physiological points of discrimination; human *organisms*, human *beings* and human *persons*. The theory of a
protective regime is developmentalist as a result. A human organism is
deemed to have none of the qualities which merit protection, whereas
development into a human being means that some of the protective qualities
exist. The main candidate for this development stage is regarded as being the
development of memory and personality – also known as the 'brain development criterion'. (For references to all the main authors in this part of the
debate, see Jane Fortin, 'Legal Protection for the Unborn Child' (1988) 51
MLR 54.) When, the argument goes, the being can 'sustain distinctively
mental processes it deserves certain protection'. To Lockwood the significance of the term human being, and the fact that protective measures should
flow from it, is that it denotes: 'what you and I are essentially, what we can
neither become nor cease to be, without ceasing to exist' (Lockwood (ed.),
Moral Dilemmas in Modern Medicine (Oxford: Oxford University Press, 1986),
p. 13).

As discontinuity or 'dis-integration' of the functions of the brain tends to
be part of a definition of death (see chapter 16), symmetry of argument holds
that the continuity or 'integration of brain function' will denote the existence
of human life.

It might be argued, as an extension, that protection will only be accorded
to a human *person*, and until that stage arrives the being is not worthy of the
full moral and legal protection every other person has. This is an extensive
and controversial area, once more dependent on moral conviction and the
very basic question of what one values in one's own existence. To writers such
as Harris the term 'person' describes 'any being capable of valuing its own
existence' (J. Harris, *The Value of Life: An Introduction to Medical Ethics*
(London: Routledge, 1985), p. 18). One may approach it from the opposite
way, in deciding when a person comes into existence, by asking when it would
be intrinsically wrong to destroy something. The answer would itself be a
description of a person. The status of a 'person' would be accorded to

something with those capacities enunciated, which might include (amongst many other potential candidates) sentience and rationality, the ability for independent action or the ability to communicate, or feel pain.

A significant ethical argument in favour of destructive embryo research is the utilitarian argument (see 1.3.3). Although this ethical theory has a number of complex internal issues, the main tenet can be simply stated. The researcher will argue that while the research is destructive of whatever is described, this is justified on the basis that it is for the greater good of society. While one may die, it is posited, many in the future may be saved by the products (the 'consequences') of this research.

Such a utilitarian argument may support a wider proposition. Society will benefit from the knowledge gained from the destructive research that is performed on the 'spare' embryos which chance to result from the inexactitude of IVF. Society would be able to benefit even more from the wider use of embryos if it were possible to create them with the explicit purpose of doing this destructive research. If developments in IVF continue, the number of accidental 'spare' embryos will decrease, and this would have a debilitating effect on research programmes.

In response it should be noted that some writers do perceive a moral difference between *chance* and *purpose*. The failure of a 'spare' embryo to implant is different to the wrong done to an embryo created to be destroyed in a research programme (see the debate surrounding the Warnock Report below).

The utilitarian argument depends for its force partially on societal recognition that the products of research are not immediate, as well as the basic acceptance that destroying embryos is 'good' because of its consequences generally. Before the scientific application of knowledge to specific areas of medicine there needs to be an understanding of the pure science. The researcher on embryos would no doubt support the view that:

> When we bear in mind that . . . we are extremely likely to be able to use what we learn from such embryos to save many lives and ameliorate many conditions which make life miserable, we would not only be crazy, but wicked to cut ourselves off from these benefits unless there are the most compelling of moral reasons so to do. (J. Harris, 'Embryos and Hedgehogs: on the Moral Status of the Embryo' in A. Dyson and J. Harris (eds), *Experiments on Embryos* (London: Routledge, 1990), p. 80)

As the later legislative debate indicated, there were still those who were very strongly of the opinion that there were indeed compelling moral reasons not to research in this manner. Nevertheless, the main specific argument put by supporters of allowing embryo research was the fact that it could assist in gaining knowledge and treating the causes of infertility. It could be of assistance in discovering the causative mechanisms in, and creating greater diagnostic ability to cure, some congenital defects. It could further be used to investigate the development of new and more effective forms of contraceptive. To some there is a perverse irony with such research programmes, as 'the

procedure becomes sacrificing the few to learn how to sacrifice the many'
(M. Brazier, *Medicine, Patients and the Law*, 2nd ed. (London: Penguin,
1992)).

10.2.4 The Warnock Report

The *Report of the Committee of Inquiry into Human Fertilisation and Embryology*
(Cmnd 9314) (the Warnock Report) was published in 1984, and has been the
focus of fervent debate from that time on. The general remit of the committee
was described as being:

> To consider recent and potential developments in medicine and science
> related to human fertilisation and embryology; to consider what policies
> and safeguards should be applied, including considerations of the social,
> ethical and legal implications of these developments; and to make recom-
> mendations. (para. 1.2)

The members of the committee clearly recognised that they were entering
an ethical minefield. In para. 2 of the foreword to the report it was stated that
they were 'reluctant to dictate on matters of morals to the public at large'.
They felt that what they should do was to make recommendations which
accorded with their perception of the public good. The report admitted that
a strict utilitarian approach to the matters under discussion would lead one
to be able to calculate 'future advantages, therapeutic or scientific [which]
should be weighed against future harm'. The problem the committee saw was
that this could not answer the more fundamental question of whether it was
right that such procedures should be carried out. The report, very early on
then, failed to note that utilitarianism is a form of moral questioning to
discover what is 'right'. If the consequences of research outweigh the burdens
of destruction, then it is right.

The introduction to the report revealed a common view that people
generally wanted some principle or other to govern the development and use
of the new artificial reproductive techniques. The committee did argue,
however, that 'There must be some barriers that are not to be crossed, some
limits fixed, beyond which people must not be allowed to go' (Introduction,
para. 5).

It has to be said that the criticisms of the ethical reasoning behind the
Warnock Report's recommendations (which, as will be seen, are now largely
enshrined in legislation) have appeared to bring the polarised camps in the
debate together, at least to the extent of accusing the report of 'fudging the
issues'. The commentary on the Warnock Report by the Life organisation,
found that it was a 'betrayal of human life at its earliest stages' (Commentary,
p. 3). They went on to say in their introduction that at critical moments the
report merely asserts its views without offering any reasoned support for
them. At the start of the report's consideration of the issue of embryo research
(para. 11.9) it appears that the specifics of the debate on the status of the
embryo are ignored and the conclusion enunciated:

Although the questions of when life or personhood begin appear to be questions of fact susceptible to straightforward answers, we hold that the answers to such questions in fact are complex amalgams of factual and moral judgments. Instead of trying to answer these questions directly we have therefore gone straight to the question of *how it is right to treat the human embryo.*

The report confirmed that the human embryo per se did not have any legal status. This was the position at common law. There were, however, legislative protective measures involving the legality of the termination of pregnancy (see chapter 12). The Congenital Disabilities (Civil Liability) Act 1976 provided the unborn child with retrospective rights to damages for pre-natal injuries negligently caused (see 8.5). The next error of the report followed on from this. The argument was that these protections meant that any law on embryo research should be based on the idea that 'the embryo of the human species should be accorded a special status which should be enshrined in law' (para. 11.17).

The major failing of the Warnock Report, however, was that it did not indicate the arguments that resulted in the according of such 'special' status, or indeed really what that status was (see A. Parkin, 'Research on Embryos: A Search for Principle' (1985) 1 PN 164).

When considering the matter of the development of the embryo, the report stated that once fertilisation has occurred, there is no particular point of development that is more important than another; all are part of a continuous process (para. 11.19). Nevertheless the report went on to set a 14-day limit on experimentation on embryos. The initial justification was that it was 'necessary to allay public anxiety' (para. 11.19). Strangely, immediately afterwards, the report found another rationale for the existence of this limit: the existence at this stage of the 'primitive streak'. This term denotes a 'heaping up' of cells within the growing embryo at 14–15 days (para. 11.22). The report, however, seemed unsure of the true significance of this stage of development. At one point the argument was put that at 14 days the embryo is recognisable as such for the first time. It went on to say, however, that the primitive streak is merely 'the first of several identifiable features which develop', but does mark the development of the individual embryo. The report justified this last comment by stating that 14 days is the last time at which twinning can occur.

Subsequently there have been rather better attempts to justify the formation of the primitive streak as a key physiological, ethical and therefore legal point. Morgan and Lee (*Blackstone's Guide to the Human Fertilisation and Embryology Act 1990* (London: Blackstone, 1991)) have pointed out that it is a key developmental point in time: '. . . if the primitive streak does not form, embryonic development does not progress'. In addition there is a form of identification attaching to this stage. As well as the formation of the primitive streak being the last moment at which twinning can occur, it is also the time when one can identify what one may term an integrated form. It is possible to state accurately the left, right, top and bottom of the embryo. The processes of identification and individuation can be regarded as distinct features to which moral weight and therefore legal protection can attach.

The Warnock Report had a further aspect of the ethical debate to consider in the context of embryo research; whether there was a moral difference between chance and purpose. Should the report and any resultant law distinguish between the utilisation of embryos that are 'spare' as a result of the inexact nature of IVF treatment, and the development of an embryo by the research scientist with the express purpose of using it for research and then discarding it? A significant minority of the committee saw a distinct separation between chance and purpose, the latter being seen as morally repugnant. Such research went against the 'special status' accorded the embryo by the committee itself. This opposition to deliberate creation was also supported by an oft utilised intuitive theory in medical law debate – the 'slippery slope' argument. Once it is thought permissible to allow embryos to come into being with the sole intention that they be used for research, this would open the way for an ever-increasing use of human embryos for routine and less valid research. The majority, nevertheless, argued that if research on embryos were to be permitted at all, it would make no difference whether these embryos happen to be available or were brought into existence for the sake of research. In neither case would they have the potential for life, because in neither case would they be transferred into the uterus of a woman. The report recommended that any legislation should provide that research may be carried out on any embryo resulting from IVF, whatever its source, up to the 14th day after fertilisation, but subject to all other restrictions that may be imposed by the licensing body to be set up as part of the proposals (para. 11.22).

The committee had a strong predisposition to make it clear that embryos were not to be treated as mere chattels that could be used and abused casually. The committee appeared also to feel that if they were to be too forthright in this view, this would undermine their aim of supporting to some extent the use of embryos for research. The difficulties of compromise, in an area where there is no consensus to the moral debate, have proved to many to undermine a major part of the report. The committee made it clear that there should be no right of ownership in an embryo (para. 10.11). Later on, though, the committee state that a couple who have stored an embryo for their own use may have 'rights to use and dispose of the embryo' (para. 10.11). According to para. 11.17 of the report, 'We were agreed that the embryo of the human species ought to have a special status', then para. 11.18 sanctions embryo research. The confusion is recognised by numerous authors, who argue that if a couple have the right to control, use or order destruction of an embryo, then that power exhibits all the features of a property right (on the argument that the embryo has resulted in a *sui generis* concept which exhibits some property concepts see *Davis* v *Davis* (1992) 842 SW 2d 588).

Ultimately many regard the Warnock Report as having failed to answer Margaret Brazier's two questions: of the position one should take on the embryo in pure theory and whether one can create effective and enforceable legal rules on the same ethical basis (M. Brazier, 'Embryos' "Rights": Abortion and Research' in Freeman (ed.), *Medicine, Ethics and the Law* (London: Stevens, 1988)). The report has been viewed by some as suffering from perhaps the inevitable weakness of seeking to propose regulation on the basis of a consensus approach where none could exist. Both pro- and anti-research lobbies have argued that they gained nothing from the report. The pro-life lobby certainly abhorred the existence of a 14-day period, which, if legislated for, would allow what to them was a 'killing zone' of 14 days. Researchers would obviously gain a period to conduct investigation, but many of them were already agreed that most meaningful research could only occur after this time.

10.2.5   The dissenting view

The members of the Warnock Committee were deeply divided on virtually every aspect of their remit. This resulted in the publication of the 'Expression of Dissent' which was indicative of the permanence of the debate in society, and an indication that legislation would never be capable of compromise, even were that to be thought valuable in itself.

The essence of the Dissent was to express the essential 'wrongness' in creating something only to destroy it (Dissent B, para. 3). There was explicit support for the potentiality argument. It was felt that research on infertility could proceed by alternative means (for example, animal experiments: para. 6). The anguish of infertility for the couple unable to have children does not permit the destruction of an embryo. The limited idea that there should only be experimentation on the 'spare' embryos was rejected on the basis that this would merely tempt doctors to create more of these spares, effectively bypassing the prohibition.

10.3   HUMAN FERTILISATION AND EMBRYOLOGY ACT 1990

10.3.1   Introduction

When the legislation was introduced in the House of Commons, by the then Secretary of State, Kenneth Clarke, it was argued as being 'one of the most significant measures to be brought forward by a Government in the last 20 years' (Hansard HC, 2 April 1990, col. 914). The main matters for the legislation to cover were:

(a)   The regulation of research on embryos.

(b)   The protection of the integrity of reproductive medicine.

(c)   The protection of scientists and clinicians from legal action and sanction.

It was essential to provide precise measures of control to alleviate tensions aroused by fears that reproductive medicine might develop in some sort of sinister, covert manner.

Morgan and Lee (*Blackstone's Guide to the Human Fertilisation and Embryology Act 1990* (London: Blackstone, 1991)) have noted that, until the amendments to the abortion legislation were placed in the Act, embryo research was by far the most controversial element of the legislation proposed. When both Houses debated the issues, the melodramatic language increased, and was a stark illustration of the fervency of the views held on embryo research and the rights and status of the unborn in general. Lord Rawlinson of Ewell vocalised the confusion of many over the recommendation to limit embryo research to 14 days by exclaiming, 'Fourteen days after what?' (Hansard HL, 8 February 1990, col. 954).

The White Paper itself gave two opposed options for legislative direction in the free vote. Paragraph 30(a) stated that it would be a criminal offence to carry out any procedures on a human embryo, other than those aimed at preparing the embryo for transfer to the uterus of a woman; or those carried out to ascertain the suitability of that embryo for the intended transfer. Paragraph 30(b) allowed for research to be permitted as part of a project specifically licensed by a statutory licensing authority. The latter has become the favoured option.

10.3.2 Legislative scheme

The broad objectives of the 1990 Act are as follows:

(a) To provide a statutory framework for the supervision and control of human embryo research.

(b) To allow for the licensing of certain forms of what are termed 'assisted conception' practices.

(c) To effect changes to the Abortion Act 1967 (see chapter 12 on this element).

The 1990 Act set up the powerful Human Fertilisation and Embryology Authority. Some activities are only permitted under a licence from this Authority. These cover:

(a) Treatment.
(b) Research.
(c) Storage.

The research licence allows for the creation and use of *in vitro* embryos for certain specified projects. Paragraph 3 of sch. 2 to the Act sets out the type of projects for which these licences may be granted:

(a) The promotion of advances in the treatment of infertility.
(b) Increasing knowledge about the causes of congenital disease.
(c) Increasing knowledge about the causes of miscarriage.
(d) Developing more effective contraception techniques.
(e) Developing methods of detecting the presence or absence of gene or chromosome abnormalities before the implantation of an embryo.

While the general recommendations of the Warnock Report were followed, there appears to have been a little confusion over the definition of the 'embryo' . In s. 1(1)(a) it is regarded as being 'a live human embryo where fertilisation is complete'. In s. 1(1)(b) it is considered to include 'an egg in the process of fertilisation', but then refers immediately to 'the appearance of a two-cell zygote'. These provisions do not make it clear whether the Act covers embryos before, during or after fertilisation.

Section 3 of the Act defines the parameters of activity allowed in relation to embryos, as determined by the Authority. The Authority may not authorise the use or retention of a live human embryo after the appearance of the 'primitive streak' (s. 3(3)(a)). This is taken to be not later than 14 days beginning with the day when the gametes are mixed (s. 3(4)). This will be so unless the embryo is stored by freezing. This is a clear recognition of the recommendation of the Warnock Report. The Authority may not authorise the placing of a human embryo in any animal (apart from the so-called 'hamster test' to check the fertility of sperm, and then not beyond the two-cell stage). Also prohibited is the development of the practice of nucleic substitution (better known as cloning). The spectre of the repoduction of genetically identical humans was felt to outweigh the prospects for work with genetically inherited diseases and the production of immunologically identical organs for transplantation purposes. The cloning of Dolly, the sheep (see *The Times*, 7 March 1997), has raised the concrete possibility that human cloning could take place within the next two years (according to one of those involved in the Dolly cloning, Dr Ian Wilmut of the Roslin Institute). There appears though to be some doubt whether the particular technique used in the sheep cloning experiment, if applied to human material, would be caught by the prohibition of the 1990 Act. It will be recalled that there are two definitions of the term 'embryo' in the legislation, and it does seem to be the case that this new technique is outside such a definition. The dilemma is clearly revealed by Sharon Korek in 'Following "Dolly"' (1997) 147 NLJ 428:

[The Human Fertilisation and Embryology Act (HFEA)] 1990, s. 1(1)(a) states that 'embryo' means a live human embryo where *fertilisation* is complete. Section 1(1)(b) says references to an embryo include an egg *in the process of fertilisation* (emphasis added). The cell that developed into Dolly was not a gamete (i.e. a sperm or an egg) and it did not undergo fertilisation (i.e. fusion of an egg with a sperm). Thus it is not within the meaning of 'embryo' as defined and used in HFEA 1990. Rather it was an artificially created cell, the genetic material of which is more akin to that of any other adult body cell.

While there would seem to be a loophole here (the result of the 1990 Act being based on the Warnock Report, which only had 1984 technology to work on) there is little difficulty in solving the problem, if that were thought necessary. There could either be a suitable redefinition of 'embryo' to include such genetically designed material, or the Secretary of State could use the powers in s. 45 of the Act to make regulations to stop or control the practice.

In a recent debate involving bodies such as the Human Fertilisation and Embryology Authority and the House of Commons Science and Technology Committee there now appears to be a move towards what has been termed 'therapeutic cloning'. One example of such a practice would be to produce a genetically identical foetus to provide skin for burn victims which would not be rejected by the accident victim.

More broadly, the Authority, by virtue of s. 8(a), is under a duty to monitor and review information about embryos as well as of the treatment services being provided by reason of the granting of a licence. With regard to cloning, for example, the Authority might consider treatment licences which involve the use of cloning techniques, but this would have to be combined with a suitable redefinition of embryo. One which has been suggested is: 'embryo means a live human embryo where fertilisation is complete or where a cell has been modified, created or altered such that it has the potential to develop into an embryo or foetus' (Sharon Korek, 'Following "Dolly"' (1997) 147 NLJ 428 at p. 429).

10.4 CONCLUSION

In international terms the Human Fertilisation and Embryology Act 1990 is a permissive but reasonably well structured piece of legislation in terms of embryo research. The form of regulation is predicated on issues of consent by the parties ultimately involved in the creation of the embryo, as well as the licensing of projects. It appears to meet the wishes of those who accept the moral significance of the development of the primitive streak. The research scientist is thus able, under relatively strict guidelines concerning subject matter and degree, to perform a limited amount of research. The opponents of destructive use of embryos to forward science have gained nothing from the legislation apart from some knowledge that there is a limitation on the time within which the research can be done, the scope of that research and the monitoring of it.

The limitations of the licensing scheme have become apparent. As Morgan and Nielsen confirm:

Where a clinic performs AID [artificial insemination by donor] using gametes from the couple alone, or where it undertakes a procedure such as GIFT – gamete intrafallopian transfer – using the couple's own gametes, then the licensing conditions of the legislation do not apply. (p. 57)

One can do little better than conclude by quoting Jonathan Montgomery's view of the 1990 Act as:

the first attempt in English law to provide a comprehensive framework for making medical science democratically accountable. Its interest therefore arises both from the solutions it adopts for particular issues and from the model of regulation on which it builds. ('Rights, Restraints and Pragmatism' (1991) 54 MLR 524)

Further reading

Brownsword, R., 'Dolly, Dignity and the Genetics Debate' (1998) 148 NLJ 413.
Fortin, J., 'Legal Protection for the Unborn Child' (1988) 51 MLR 54.
Holland, A., 'A Fortnight of My Life is Missing: A Discussion of the Status of the Human Pre-embryo' (1990) J App Phil 25.
Korek, S., 'Following "Dolly"' (1997) 147 NLJ 428.
Montgomery, J., 'Rights, Restraints and Pragmatism' (1991) 54 MLR 524.
Samuels, A., 'Embryo Research: The Significance of the New Law' (1991) 31 Med Sci Law 115.

ELEVEN
Legal and ethical issues in human reproduction

11.1 INTRODUCTION

Both the Warnock Report and the Human Fertilisation and Embryology Act 1990 cover a much wider area than embryo research (see the remit of the Warnock Committee quoted in 10.3.4). There were a number of other important implications of the development of modern reproductive technology that could be prone to legal regulation. The legal and ethical issues are based primarily around the following matters of controversy:

(a) The question of whether such reproductive techniques are artificial and 'unnatural' and should be criminalised.
(b) The anonymity of the donor of reproductive material.
(c) Privacy and treatment.
(d) Consent and infertility treatment.
(e) Issues of legitimacy of the child.
(f) Eligibility for infertility treatment.
(g) Freedom to receive treatment abroad.

The latter part of the chapter will deal with another difficult ethical issue, the availability and legality of surrogacy.

Before one considers these issues of debate there needs to be an understanding of the fact of infertility and the processes available to overcome it.

11.2 INFERTILITY AND THE OPTIONS FOR TREATMENT

The fact that a couple (or individual) cannot have children should not be underestimated. There is evidence that inability to have children can lead to the breakdown of relationships and even, tragically, suicide (see M. Hull,

Human Embryo Research: Yes or No? (CIBA Foundation, 1990)). There is some debate whether the anguish and frustration is an indication of a societal, physiological or psychological compulsion to reproduce. Whatever the reason for infertility, its existence (and it may be that 10 per cent of marriages are infertile) was one of the factors which led to scientific developments to realise the possibility of having children, despite an underlying physical inability to do so (see Gillian Douglas, *Law, Fertility and Reproduction* (London: Sweet & Maxwell, 1991)). Historically, the Warnock Report noted, the fact of infertility was not understood by society. There was little discussion of what was felt to be something which stigmatised a couple, and in less enlightened times made the woman feel 'less than whole'. Ignorance and lack of discussion meant there was no knowledge of the ways infertility could be overcome. Some of them (most notably artificial insemination of the woman by donor – AID, or surrogacy) had been available for a considerable amount of time. Infertility was not thought of as a malfunctioning of the human body, but the 'will of God'; or otherwise was considered not a medical condition but an absence of something. Adoption was available, but opportunities have become less and less and the infertile still might feel the genetic gap between adoptive parent and adopted child.

Now arguably the language of health care rights has lead to an opening up of issues such as the right to found a family (European Convention on Human Rights, art. 12), and the demand to be treated to be able to do so. There is now available a whole gallery of possibilities. As Morgan and Nielsen point out:

> The development of reproductive technology presents contradictory choices, especially for women. Technically, some of the developments have increased the capacity of women to take control of their own bodies; with some versions of cloning and parthenogenesis [the development of a gamete without the need for fertilisation] it has even been argued that the notion that reproduction belongs to women would take on a new dynamic with the ability to reproduce without the need for the patriarchal genetic. (McVeigh and Wheeler (eds), *Law, Health and Medical Regulation* (Dartmouth, 1992), p. 53)

The traditional notions of relationship, family, reproduction, illness, treatment are all being reformulated by reproductive technology. Whether medical law is doing the right thing in regulation, permission or prohibition depends on one's acceptance of those traditional ideas. How are medical law and society to react to the fact that a homosexual female couple can (and do) have a child, by one of them being inseminated artificially with semen donated by an anonymous man? Whether the reaction is permission, regulation or prohibition depends on the moral view of the pluralist society in existence at present. Consider how the philosophies of utilitarianism and deontology would weigh the moral 'rightness' or 'wrongness' of the situation. Consider whether you think the above example is morally 'right', then consider, if it is felt to be wrong, whether medical law should be invoked to stop it. If the assistance of the medical profession is needed to facilitate conception, what does clinical intuition point towards? Does the human right to found a family encompass the above rights-based demand?

A number of techniques have developed; and while the wider research implications of the treatment options available were considered by the Warnock Committee, the mere existence of these forms of medical intervention has also been considered important.

Infertility can affect either the man or the woman. It may be due to a myriad of causes. The situation can possibly be remedied by one of the following methods:

(a)   Artificial insemination by the husband (AIH). This can take place without the licence that is required for the other forms of infertility treatment.

(b)   Artificial insemination by, or donation of, sperm (AID) or ovum. This is appropriate where the problem is the infertility of the male partner, or the risk of that partner passing on a congenital defect.

(c)   Gamete intrafallopian transfer (GIFT). This is not regulated by the Act as it involves the transfer of gametes between a couple. As far as the 1990 Act is concerned, in general, where there is no donation there is no regulation.

(d)   *In vitro* fertilisation (IVF), where the ovum is fertilised outside the woman's body and thereafter transferred into the uterus of the recipient woman. It is this technique which has given rise to the possibility of embryo research. The main reason for the use of IVF is where the woman, while able to produce ova, has other difficulties with the fallopian tubes, which necessitate fertilisation outside the body. The technique is still inexact, and the medical team require the woman to go through a difficult process, including superovulation, stimulated by drugs. The failure rate is going down, and the success of the programme is increased by the multiple transfer of embryos to the uterus of the woman to increase the chances of success. The First Report of the Human Fertilisation and Embryology Authority in 1992 noted that the success rate was 7 per cent on single embryo transfer, but 27 per cent on multiple transfer. This is still not a particularly high figure to quote when the doctor is counselling couples on the proposed treatment. By 1995-6, however, there were over 1,500 births from IVF and other forms of infertility treatment from almost 6,000 incidents of donor insemination. The spare embryos that have been transferred, should more than one or two succeed in beginning to develop, can create hazards for the pregnancy as a whole, and where this is thought to be the case these embryos are 'reduced' and absorbed into the woman's body. The legality of this technique is a matter for the law relating to abortion (see chapter 12), and has been of considerable, if ill-informed, media interest in the latter part of 1996 (see 12.1).

11.3   CONTROL OF REPRODUCTIVE TECHNOLOGY

The Human Fertilisation and Embryology Act 1990 had a fine balance to strike between the paternalist regulation of the developing methods of avoiding or overcoming infertility, and the freedom of individuals or couples to have children by whatever means are available. Allied to this was the fact that the Act needed to come to a view on whether applications to use resources in the treatment of the infertile and applications for use in other medical services were to be judges by different criteria. If infertility is treatment, how important is it when compared with other people's medical requirements?

The Warnock Report had recommended regulation rather than prohibition, and the 1990 Act provides a regulatory scheme for selective licensing of treatment services.

The Human Fertilisation and Embryology Authority (set up by s. 5 of the 1990 Act) is charged with the task of supervising treatment services, and informing the Secretary of State of the availability of services covered by the Act. The services which come under the regulatory framework of the Act are broadly those which involve the use of material (egg, sperm or embryos) which has been donated. Informal or 'do-it-yourself' infertility treatments, such as AIH, are not licensed because there is no donation. It has already been noted in chapter 10 that the functions of the Authority cover the licensing of treatment, storage and research (s. 11). The Authority also has a Licence Committee to oversee particular aspects of the criteria for the granting of such licences, which cannot combine treatment and research.

So far this chapter has given a general introduction to the regulatory framework of the 1990 Act. Specific aspects of importance are revealed by analysing the problems that have been considered major stumbling blocks in the development and use of artificial infertility treatment techniques. Even the fact of artificiality has been attacked, which of itself shows that there are strong ethical objections to the practices that have developed.

11.4 PROBLEMS OF REPRODUCTIVE TECHNOLOGY

11.4.1 Unnaturalness

Objectors to the whole notion of artificial reproduction techniques set great store in the existence of the natural order of biological processes. Naturalness has here been equated with something that is untainted with modern human intervention. The unnaturalness may also be seen as stemming from the introduction of a third party into what is considered an intimate relationship. AID can be considered a form of adultery. As Pope Pius XII argued, 'To reduce the shared life of a married couple and the act of marital love to a mere organic activity would be like turning the domestic home into a laboratory'.

Before it is considered that this argument is straying outside the legal realm and into the realms of theology, consider the case of *Maclennan v Maclennan* (1958) SC 105, which considered such a 'third-party' objection. It was held that a woman who goes through a process of AID does not commit adultery, because there has been no sexual contact between the woman and the male sperm donor. What many have argued, however, is that a married woman's decision to undergo AID without the consent of her husband could be regarded as constituting unreasonable behaviour for the purposes of divorce proceedings (see, for example, Mason and McCall Smith, *Law and Medical Ethics*, 4th ed. (London: Butterworths, 1994), p. 53).

The Human Fertilisation and Embryology Act 1990 recognises the possibility of conflict between partners and makes AID illegal without a licence, unless it is performed through mutual agreement between the partners.

The objection really resolves itself into one about the morality of artificial forms of infertility treatment per se. It also questions the selection of the 'best' embryos for implantation with some of the techniques. It is wrong to 'make' children, the argument goes (see LIFE Report, *Warnock Dissected*, p. 7). 'IVF is a form of domination over another human life, whereas in authentic parenthood the child is a partner in the common life expressed in the procreative act of married union.'

This view has been regarded by some as a little flippant. It is agreed that such views are no doubt strongly held and are sincere. Therefore, those who object have every right to refuse to use such technology or even, where appropriate, to conscientiously object to involvement in such procedures. The 1990 Act does provide for such a conscientious objection. Section 38 states:

(1)   No person who has a conscientious objection to participating in any activity governed by this Act shall be under a duty, however arising, to do so.

(2)   In any legal proceedings the burden of conscientious objection shall rest on the person claiming to rely on it.

A rather more pertinent response than that of Warnock might be that the availability of technology in medicine as a whole creates a massive amount of artificial activities in life, even to sustain life. If these were thought to tend toward the unnatural, then artificial respiration should not be undertaken as part of medical practice, artificial heart valves should not be placed in dying patients and there should be no artificial hip replacement. Technology, it could be further argued, is natural, in that it is a product of natural tendencies to act in an inquisitive and acquisitive manner, which form part of human make-up. The altruistic use of technological development is the gift of a species which asserts its imperative of advancement. Clinical intuition is to use available technology to treat.

11.4.2   Anonymity of the donor

In the USA, some clinics have been offering AID services which include detailed descriptions of donors, allowing the 'purchaser' of such services to exercise choice of donor. Early in 1998 *The Times* reported the development of an illicit market in sperm, available through the Internet. The Human Fertilisation and Embryology Authority noted that these catalogues of apparently physically attractive donors were resulting in charges of about £280 for each sperm sample. What is seen as most disturbing is the fact that these donors seem prepared to forgo at least some of their anonymity; a number will forgo anonymity completely, but others will allow a video of themselves to be shown to the child when it reaches 18. The Chair of the Human Fertilisation and Embryology Authority, Ruth Deech, is quoted as warning that in addition the rigorous screening requirements of the 1990 Act will not be guaranteed, and may lead to the spread of a number of serious diseases, even HIV (see 'Warning; Don't Buy Sperm on the Internet' *The Times*, 28 January 1998, p. 4). The dangers of allowing unfettered access to donor information are numerous, but are all based around the premise that any form of identification introduces the donor as a specific individual, with possibly extensive legal consequences.

The Warnock Report had been somewhat ambivalent about this matter. The committee concluded overall that the couple would need enough information on the donor to be reassured. With regard to the child born as the result of AID, the report recommended that on reaching the age of 18, the child should have access to basic information about the donor's genetic health and ethnic origin. The contrary view has it that any successful AID programme must have anonymity as its mainstay. Potential donors would be reluctant to come forward if there was a perceived threat of legal, parental or some other form of responsibility attaching to donation. Earlier AID programmes were thought to have been unsuccessful because of the danger of paternity attaching to the donor. Under the 1990 Act that can no longer be the case (s. 28(6)(a)).

That does not resolve the general issue of anonymity. Section 31(2) requires the Authority to keep a register of 'identifiable individuals whose gametes have been treated, whose gametes have been stored or used and who were, or may have been, born as a result of treatment services'. This register of information is then given to the Authority. Thereafter, according to s. 31(3):

A person who has attained the age of 18 ('the applicant') may by notice to the Authority require the Authority to comply with a request under subsection (4) below, and the Authority shall do so if—

(a)   the information contained in the register shows that the applicant was, or may have been, born in consequence of treatment services, and

(b)   the applicant has been given suitable notice to receive proper counselling about the implications of compliance with the request.

As yet no regulations have been made to specify the level of information disclosure to an individual. It seems likely, however, that any regulations will follow the Warnock Report and restrict the information to basic genetic and ethnic information.

One should be aware of the potential importance of art. 8 of the European Convention for the Protection of Human Rights and Fundamental Freedoms, 1950, which states that 'everyone should be able to establish details of their identity as individual human beings'. This may well confer a right to demand person-specific information. (On the general application of art. 8 to medical information disclosure see *Gaskin* v *UK* (1990) 12 EHRR 36.)

The Act does already provide for information disclosure in specific circumstances, including the following:

(a)   Under s. 34 a court can require the Authority to disclose information where there is a parentage dispute.

(b)   Under s. 35 a court may also require the Authority to divulge information where there is to be a claim by the child under s. 1 of the Congenital Disabilities (Civil Liability) Act 1976.

(c)   Under s. 33(6B)–(6D) the consent of the patient who underwent the infertility treatment will allow for disclosure, but only as long as the implications of that disclosure have been explained.

11.4.3   Infertility treatment and privacy

One of the difficult balancing acts in relation to infertility treatment is to consider the conflict between the need to maintain the privacy of the couple involved in the treatment and the need to improve information flow and protect the welfare of children who are the products of such techniques. It was noted above that the child may well want to know of its genetic origins, but the parents who have brought it up may well want to keep the fact of donation from it. Added to this it is argued that to gauge the success or otherwise of infertility treatment regimes there needs to be empirical research on the children of this reproductive revolution. What of the parents who do not wish this information to become available for risk of alerting the child to its origins or the fact that one or both of them were infertile? There is also a serious potential conflict between infertility clinics and the couple's own doctor. The Human Fertilisation and Embryology Authority Code of Practice demands that infertility treatment clinics satisfy themselves that the couple would be suitable for treatment, which includes being satisfied about the welfare of any child that might be born as a result of the proposed treatment. What of the couple's doctor who is asked about their suitability? There may be a fear that to give this sort of information out might breach medical confidence or lead to other legal or medical disciplinary consequences. As yet there have been no clear answers to these dilemmas of privacy and access to information. It is a difficult balance of welfare and rights.

11.4.4   Legal status of the child born as a result of donation

The Warnock Committee were faced with the inevitable conclusion that the child born as a result of AID was illegitimate at law. The potential seriousness of this conclusion was that the husband of the woman who bears the AID child would have no parental rights and duties with regard to the child so produced, though, as a matter of general family law, the label of illegitmacy now carries with it fewer implications than it once did. The report recommended that the child should be treated at law as the child of the mother and her husband where they have both consented to the treatment. Legislation on what must be regarded as an urgent matter was delayed until the passing of the Family Law Reform Act 1987, which was itself supplemented by ss. 27 to 30 of the 1990 Act.

Section 28(2) of the 1990 Act covers the situation of the married woman. It is basically a repeat of the Warnock Report recommendation; that where the husband has consented to the treatment he will be treated as the father of the child. This rule is voided if the husband can prove he did not consent.

There was, though, some disquiet about the registration of the birth of the child. It was argued by Lord Denning that any legislation would be doubtful as a matter of legal ethics, as it would condone what amounted to aiding and abetting a perjury. Section 29(1) has clarified all areas where the legitimacy of the child may be in issue. This was done by the simple expedient of providing that the consenting husband is now to be regarded as the father of the child 'for all purposes'.

11.4.5 Potential liability of the donor

What of the situation of the AID child who suffers from a genetic defect passed on from the donor male? Can the donor be found responsible for a failure to communicate his knowledge of the defect, or can the law find the donor negligent for a failure to discover the existence of the defect before becoming a donor, or the doctor in doing the treatment?

Section 1 of the Congenital Disabilities (Civil Liability) Act 1976 provides that if a child is born disabled because of an occurrence which pre-dated birth, and someone is answerable for the existence of that disability, then that person can be found liable at the suit of the child. The occurrence needs to be one which:

(a) affected either parent's ability to have a normal healthy child, or
(b) affected the mother during the pregnancy.

Section 1A was inserted to deal with a situation not covered by the Act as originally drafted, namely, that disability could be caused by 'negligent donation':

In any case where—
(a) a child carried by a woman as the result of the placing in her of an embryo or of sperm and eggs or her artificial insemination is born disabled,
(b) the disability results from an act or omission in the course of the selection, or the keeping or use outside the body, of the embryo carried by her or of the gametes used to bring about the creation of the embryo, and
(c) a person is under this section answerable to the child in respect of the act or omission,
the child's disabilities are to be regarded as damage resulting from the wrongful act of that person and actionable accordingly at the suit of the child.

(2)   Subject to subsection (3) below . . . a person . . . is answerable to the child if he was liable in tort to one or both of the parents . . . or would, if sued in due time, have been so; and it is no answer that there could not have been such liability because the parent or parents concerned suffered no actionable injury, if there was a breach of legal duty which, accompanied by injury, would have given rise to the liability.

(3)   The defendant is not under this section answerable to the child if at the time the embryo, or the sperm and eggs, are placed in the woman or the time of her insemination (as the case may be) either or both of the parents knew the risk of their child being born disabled (that is to say, the particular risk created by the act or omission).

11.4.6   Availability of infertility treatment

Infertility treatment, particularly IVF, is costly, time consuming, still not particularly effective, but nevertheless subject to increasing demand. Should infertility treatment be available to all or should it be regarded as a form of elective medical intervention and therefore of limited availability? Those opposed to treatment for infertility point to the fact that while there is an ageing population and a growing one, the health-care system will be under financial pressure. To give infertility priority is a form of double jeopardy; the treatment devotes resources better spent saving life, and if successful increases the population. Alternatively:

> . . . the announcement by the UK government in late 1991 that they would fund the new regulatory authority HFEA to only 50 per cent of its total operating costs led to renewed charges that 'the infertile' [were] being unfairly, even unlawfully, discriminated against, and that charges raised for private infertility treatments amount to a 'tax upon the infertile'. (Morgan and Nielsen in McVeigh and Wheeler (eds), *Law, Health and Medical Regulation* (Dartmouth, 1992), p. 54 citing Hansard 17.7.91, col. 194)

The Warnock Report placed what it regarded as a moral limit on access to infertility treatment, stating that, 'In discussing treatment for infertility, this report takes the term couple to mean a heterosexual couple living together in a stable relationship, whether married or not' (para. 2.6). This is a major bone of contention as a matter of ethics and law. While the broad issue of anti-discrimination law is beyond the scope of this book, there appear to be very real problems in legally applying the Warnock Report view to the scenario at the start of the chapter. Whatever view one takes of the morality, there appears barely hidden discrimination.

The current trend is for applications to undergo assisted reproductive treatment to be considered by ethical committees. Such bodies have wide remits to deal with the variety of applications that may materialise. Whether there is an internal pluralism to focus debate correctly, in a rights-based medical law system, is another matter.

Section 13(5) of the 1990 Act states that a woman shall not be provided with treatment unless account has been taken of the welfare of any child born as a result of the treatment and of any other child who may be affected by the birth. It is argued by Gillian Douglas that it impliedly contemplates a social, if not a legal role for a 'father'. This section is of such potential breadth as to be largely unhelpful. It may be prudent rather to consider a case in the realm of public law and access to infertility treatment, *R v Ethical Committee of St Mary's Hospital (Manchester), ex parte Harriott* [1988] 1 FLR 512. The applicant for judicial review had already been turned down as an applicant to be a foster or adoptive parent. The reasons for refusal being a criminal record and a history of involvement in prostitution. She therefore applied to be placed on a waiting list for IVF treatment, but the hospital removed her from the list when it too discovered her background. Gillian Douglas, *Law, Fertility and Reproduction* (London: Sweet & Maxwell, 1991), pp. 119–22, reproduces the criteria for applicants at the hospital:

> [Couples] must, in the ordinary course of events, satisfy the general criteria established by adoption societies in assessing suitability for adoption . . . [and there] must be no medical, psychiatric or psychosexual problems which would indicate an increased probability of a couple not being able to provide satisfactory parenting to the offspring or endanger the mother's life or health if she became pregnant.

Schiemann J refused her application for judicial review, on the basis that the opportunity for her to answer the refusal indicated that there had been no procedural unfairness. On a wider front it was stated that while a blanket policy of refusal may be illegitimate, that was not the case here.

The attempted policy underlying the Warnock committee's view of availability linked to heterosexuality and cohabitation was not the only one apparent:

> Attempts during the passage of the Act through Parliament to limit treatment to the married, or at least to members of a heterosexual cohabiting couple were unsuccessful . . . this requirement [of s. 13(5)] was put in as an amendment expressly to prevent the creation of one-parent families through assisted reproduction (and implicitly to prevent lesbian women from receiving treatment). (Gillian Douglas, op. cit., p. 122)

There is arguably little logic in limiting access to infertility treatment in such a way. The point has been made many times that children of one-parent families do not necessarily suffer disadvantage. There seems even less of a 'welfare worry' where the single parent seeks infertility treatment. The likelihood is of a stable lifestyle and an emotional and economic readiness for the child. Similarly there has been no evidence put forward that a child would suffer some psychological trauma or 'sexuality crisis' just because the parents happen to be homosexual. Nevertheless there are those who argue that these possibilities only stress the unnaturalness of artificial reproduction and the need to legislate against it for the 'Devlin-esque' protection of the moral fabric of society.

11.4.7   Treatment together and treatment abroad

11.4.7.1   Recently two key cases have concerned themselves with the core policies that underpin the 1990 Act. The well-publicised case of Diane Blood's wish to have a child by using the sperm of her dead husband brought many of the emotional and legal dilemmas of modern infertility treatment to public attention, and brought the workings of the Human Fertilisation and Embryology Authority to judicial attention. The case needs to be considered in some detail as it is an indication that medical law will always be likely to lag behind controversial technology, and is increasingly going to be susceptible to rights-based demands for access to treatment in other jurisdictions.

11.4.7.2   *R* v *Human Fertilisation and Embryology Authority, ex parte Blood* [1997] 2 WLR 806   Towards the end of 1994 Diane Blood and her husband started trying to have a child. Sadly in early 1995 the husband was diagnosed with meningitis. It was decided, after the husband had lapsed into unconsciousness, that sperm samples would be taken from him and placed with the Infertility Research Trust, for storage with a view to Diane Blood being impregnated at a later stage. Shortly after the samples were taken Mr Blood was certified dead. He had never regained consciousness. Diane Blood wanted to use the sperm in this country, notwithstanding the fact that there had never been any consent from her husband to its use. It was also contended that if the use of the sperm was not lawful in this country due to lack of consent then she should be allowed to export it to another EC country where the use would not contravene national law.

The Human Fertilisation and Embryology Authority considered that the treatment proposed for Diane Blood would be contrary to the 1990 Act. The Authority refused permission for it, giving the following reasons:

(a)   The Act required written and effective consent from the man. This needs to have been after counselling and time to consider the idea of posthumous birth. The fact of her husband's unconsciousness when the sperm was taken meant this could not have happened.

(b)   Diane Blood should not be allowed to export the sperm for treatment abroad in order to avoid the requirements which mean that she cannot receive the treatment in this country. Such export could only take place if there was a personal link with another country and an intention to remain there. Diane Blood had neither connection nor intention.

(c)   There has to be consent *from* the man, and not through the evidence given from another person. Diane Blood had contended that she and her husband had discussed the notion of posthumous birth, and he had expressed his consent to that taking place.

When the matter of judicial review of the reasons for refusal came before the Court of Appeal, Lord Woolf MR took the opportunity to survey the structure of the 1990 Act. The key underpinning concepts of the Act are licensing, counselling and consent. The Act in general terms allows nothing to happen where there is no licence. In addition the Authority has the responsibility to keep such licences under review, and for licensees to accord with the Code of Conduct which emphasises the same key concepts. The Act itself expands usefully on the nature of consent. Schedule 3 to the Act is headed 'Consents to the use of gametes or embryos'. Within that there are a number of paragraphs which emphasise the nature of a consent regarded as valid. According to paras 1 and 2.

1. A consent under this Schedule must be given in writing and, in this Schedule, 'effective consent' means a consent . . . which has not been withdrawn.

2. . . . (2) A consent to the storage of any gametes . . . must—
    (a) specify the maximum period of storage . . . and
    (b) state what is to be done with the gametes or embryo if the person who gave the consent dies or is unable because of incapacity to vary the terms of the consent or to revoke it.

Building on this, para. 3 states that before someone can give consent under sche. 3 there needs to be proper counselling in relation to what is proposed, and such counselling should be the result of the provision of proper information. Paragraph 5 is one of the central planks of the refusal:

(1) A person's gametes must not be used for the purpose of treatment services unless there is an effective consent by that person to their being so used and they are used in accordance with the terms of the consent.

(2) A person's gametes must not be received for use for those purposes unless there is an effective consent by that person to their being so used.

(3) This paragraph does not apply to the use of a person's gametes for the purpose of that person, or that person and another together, receiving treatment services.

Obviously, because Mr Blood was unconscious when the sperm was taken and stored, there was no effective consent under the Act. While the Act discusses this notion of effective consent, there is in addition the issue of whether there can be import or export of reproductive material. Under s. 24 the Authority has power to make directions which authorise a licence holder to send gametes or embryos outside the UK. The Authority may, however, make these directions subject to any conditions, such as the need for export to be in accordance with the aspirations needed to he a licence holder. One of the most obvious aspirations is that there be effective, informed consent. Diane Blood could have been helped by the fact that such directions can be revoked or varied to suit the justice of the individual case. Diane Blood was seeking an individual direction which allowed her to export.

If one recalls the facts, there appears to have been treatment to recover the sperm and storage of the sperm without effective consent. Storage under s. 4(1) of the 1990 Act can only be undertaken pursuant to a licence, and sch. 3 requires that licensed storage be pursuant to consent. Therefore the

Infertility Research Trust should not have stored the sperm and were guilty of an offence under the Act. Lord Woolf MR recognised that the treatment and storage had taken place pending the resolution of this legal dispute, and therefore there was no question of any prosecution being mounted.

Next, Lord Woolf had to consider the original taking of the sperm – the treatment. The situation confronting the court here was not specifically covered by the 1990 Act. Section 4(1)(b) states that treatment services need not be in pursuance of a licence (and therefore require matters such as effective consent) where the provision of such services is 'for the woman and the man together'. Diane Blood's tentative argument was that one should take a broad view of this term, and as a matter of fact she and her husband were still being treated together notwithstanding the fact that he was unconscious. In considering the idea of 'treatment together' counsel for Diane Blood sought assistance from the case of Re B (Parentage) [1996] 2 FLR 15. Here the man had donated sperm which was to inseminate the woman. Prior to the insemination taking place their relationship had broken down and his consent was not sought before the insemination took place. The issue for Bracewell J was whether, at the time of the insemination, they were being 'treated together'. If this were so, it would be an exception to the need for effective consent. The court, on the facts of the case, decided that they were being so treated as the man had not withdrawn consent. While one can see this as a robust interpretation of the term 'treatment together', with the fundamental factual differences between the two cases it did not really help Diane Blood. The 1990 Act itself clearly foresaw the significance of the donor dying as it provided in para. 2(2)(b) of sch. 3 that any consent must state what is going to happen if the donor dies. There is no part of the Act which envisages the idea of the dead sperm donor being 'treated together' with someone else. Therefore both the storage and the original treatment were unlawful.

As already noted s. 24(4) gives the Authority discretion to allow export. Diane Blood wanted such a direction. In the Court of Appeal the Authority were forced to concede that arts 59 and 60 of the EC Treaty gave Diane Blood a directly enforceable right to receive medical treatment in another member State. The Authority's prohibition was contended as being a prohibition on such a freedom. It is obvious that the Authority were infringing such a right. Counsel for the Authority had sought to argue that Diane Blood had the freedom to receive medical treatment in another State, it was just the export of the sperm that was being restricted. The Court of Appeal gave this short shrift, as without the export of the sperm Diane Blood was being denied the only form of treatment that she wanted.

There was a further element in the restriction of the freedom provided by the EC Treaty for the Court of Appeal to consider. Even where there is a restriction on the freedom it is possible for it to be justified by the legitimate requirements of the State whose actions are challenged. Parliament, by the 1990 Act, left issues of public policy on export to be determined by the Authority. Therefore it is the decision of the Authority which has to be justified in relation to art. 59. Consent is the justificatory mechanism to be balanced against Community rights. The problem with the decision of the Authority was that it never really considered cross-border rights. The Authority only mentioned that Diane Blood had no connection with the country she sought treatment in. The Court of Appeal considered the failure to consider the impact of art. 59 a serious flaw in the decision-making process of the Authority. The Authority argued that they were worried that to allow export in this case would create a serious precedent. In response the Court of Appeal succinctly pointed out that the issue would never arise again because technically the sperm should never have been taken or stored in the first place (so any future taking or storage without consent would, by implication, result in a criminal prosecution). The decision then was that the Authority were correct on their view of consent, but had failed to consider the impact of EC law. The Authority should reconsider the idea of export.

11.4.7.3 *U* v *W* *(Attorney-General Intervening)* [1997] 3 WLR 739

The decision had been made that this case not be heard before the Court of Appeal delivered its judgment in the *Blood* case. The opportunity to consider further the issues of 'treatment together' and the effect of art. 59 of the EC Treaty appears to have been used effectively, as this case is again a broad analysis of the core areas of the 1990 Act as they relate to access to and the consequences of treatment outside the UK.

At the time of the hearing U had twin boys born as a result of infertility treatment abroad (in Rome). She was seeking a maintenance order against W. Under s. 27 of the Child Support Act 1991 U wanted a declaration that W was the father. The Attorney-General supported W's denial of paternity. U and W had what one might term a 'stormy' relationship for a number of years. They had discussed having a child together, but it was soon discovered that W's sperm was of poor quality. After a number of attempts to use the latest reproductive technology had failed to result in pregnancy, the couple heard of a Dr A in Rome who had developed a new technique of direct laser implantation of the *in vitro* embryo into the uterus. During the course of consultations with Dr A (through an interpreter) it became apparent that donor sperm might have to be used. W clearly was ill at ease with the prospect. There was some conflict of evidence about the discussion which took place before the actual treatment, but eventually donor sperm had to be used. Later on the relationship soured and the couple split up.

U claimed that W was the father of the twins because of the existence of s. 28(3). As already noted this subsection states that where an embryo has been placed in a woman in the course of treatment services provided to her and the man together by a person to whom a licence applies and the creation of the embryo carried by her was not lawfully brought about with the sperm of the man, then that man shall be treated as the father of the child. The initial problem was that Dr A was not 'a person to whom a licence applies'. If the 1990 Act were construed without reference to Community law, then s. 28(3) does not apply so as to attach paternity. U sought to invoke EC law and argued that the requirement of a licence in s. 28(3) constituted a restriction on the freedom under art. 59 to provide services within the EC.

U's desire therefore was either to gain a generous construction of s. 28(3) so it applied to her situation or to disapply the requirement as a breach of art. 59.

To begin with the High Court was not impressed with W's argument that U and W were not actually treated together in Italy. The reality of the evidence was that while W may not have been particularly enthusiastic about the idea of the use of donor sperm, they had discussed the matter together the night before the actual treatment, and indeed after he had sought reassurances in relation to the donor sperm being tested for AIDS and so forth, even signed an admittedly vague and ill-explained declaration of paternity.

The importance of the case lies in the first place in the focus it places on licensing of treatment sevices. Many strict conditions apply to the granting of a licence. These include:

(a) the need to maintain confidential records;
(b) that such records be available at all reasonable times for inspection;
(c) a regulated procedure for obtaining the consent of donors;
(d) where a donor has been used, the man (who is not the donor) should have the opportunity to receive counselling.

In fact, under the 1990 Act there is no express prohibition on the granting of licences for treatment abroad, but no such licence has been or would be granted. The main reason for this is that the 1990 Act itself is buttressed by the national criminal law (s. 41).

Nevertheless the most important issue to arise from *U* v *W* is the matter of the art. 59 restriction. Wilson J in considering whether there was such a restriction, gave a hypothetical case:

. . . a reasonable couple, infertile and unmarried, are contemplating treatment with donor sperm and, in that connection, are considering the effects of s. 28(3). . . . the effects are carefully explained to the couple and . . . they are given a proper opportunity to reflect on them. My conclusion is that s. 28(3) would substantially incline most such couples to seek treatment under licence in the United Kingdom rather than in another member State. I consider that most such men would want to be the legal father of any resultant child; that most such women, concerned . . . less with the financial responsibility of the man for the child following any breakdown of their relationship than with the creation of a fully integrated family life, would want him to be the legal father; and that, in reaching those conclusions, both of them would in particular consider that it was in the child's interests that the man, rather than an anonymous donor, should be his father.

Therefore s. 28(3) is a restriction on the freedom to provide services under art. 59. However, as EC lawyers will no doubt be aware, there can be reasons which justify the restriction on an article freedom. The rationalisation for the process of justification is best explained in the case of *Säger* v *Dennemeyer & Co. Ltd* (case C-76/90) [1991] ECR I-4221, para. 15:

> ... the freedom to provide services may be limited only by rules which are justified by imperative reasons relating to the public interest and which apply to all persons or undertakings pursuing an activity in the State [making the rules], in so far as that interest is not protected by the rules to which the person providing the services is subject in the member State in which he is established. In particular, those requirements must be objectively necessary in order to ensure compliance with professional rules and to guarantee the protection of the recipient of services and they must not exceed what is necessary to attain those objectives.

It should be noted here that where paternity is ascribed under s. 28(3) the man acquires substantial obligations with regard to the child, but only rather shadowy rights in respect of that child. Therefore it is important that this man is warned of such consequences and is able to make an informed consent. This is exactly what the UK licensing system achieves. The Act is bolstered by the Code of Practice, which itself devotes a great deal to the need for counselling and consent. It is here then that one can find a strand of justification for the restriction on the art. 59 freedom. No such justification would exist, however, where the other member State protects such interests through comparable legislation. In such circumstances there can be no restriction on the freedom. In the EC there are great disparities in the licensing and control of infertility treatment. There is, effectively, no other jurisdiction with comparable legislation. The justification therefore remains.

In the end then U's application was dismissed. While it was certainly the case that the couple had been 'treated together', they had not been so treated by a licence holder, therefore s. 28(3) did not apply to ascribe paternity to W.

11.4.7.4 Significance of the decisions What then is one to make of these two recent decisions of the courts? There are both narrow and broad matters of significance arising out of them. A narrow significance is that there is now precedent on the scope of the term 'treatment together' which can act as a guide for future practice. It may even be that the medical profession could use the examples of these two cases to indicate the need for the couple about to undergo treatment to consider carefully and reflect on the ramifications of treatment involving donors. The cases also reveal that the central blocks of the 1990 Act are accepted as being the need for a licensed regime, for that regime to be based on consent and for that consent to be based on sufficient information and counselling. On the broad front the cases reveal that the judiciary apparently feel no qualms about criticising the deliberations of the Human Fertilisation and Embryology Authority. It might be suggested that this will not be the last time the decisions of the Authority are challenged. Equally significant for medical law is the dawning realisation of the impact of EC law on medical practice, particularly infertility treatment. To talk of equal rights to infertility treatment is to talk too of free access to the fruits of reproductive technology in other jurisdictions. The current conflict for the law stems from the fact that the UK appears to have strict yet well-defined parameters for access to and the need to understand the legal consequences of treatment. The facts of *U* v *W* indicate that other jurisdictions may still see counselling and consent as taking second place to money and scant apparent agreement. How much longer the justification for the restriction on the freedom afforded by article 59 will remain must be doubted as other States see the value of structure and licence.

11.5 SURROGACY ARRANGEMENTS

11.5.1 Introduction

A child born in 1985 to a woman called Kim Cotton, which was then given away to a couple who had 'commissioned' the pregnancy, brought the issue of surrogacy arrangements to public attention. Later that same year the main legislation – the Surrogacy Arrangements Act 1985 – was passed, evidently to assuage public anxiety at what was perceived by sectors of society as a pernicious development.

To many this was also their first encounter with the concept of surrogacy, yet numerous authors have pointed out the historical recognition of the practice (see Singer and Wells, *New Ways of Making Babies: The Reproductive Revolution* (1984), pp. 107–8, describing the story in Genesis of Abraham impregnating a slave girl because his wife Sarah could have no children, and Sarah subsequently taking the child as her own).

The issue of surrogacy taxed the Warnock committee, which had to decide on the moral status of the practice, and then whether to propose that medical law be used to control or prohibit the practice (see 1.4). The committee used the form of debate on legal regulation of moral issues suggested by Hart.

Before considering the arguments for and against surrogacy, the possible reactions the law could have had to modern evidence of the continued practice and its commercialisation, and what medical law has actually done, one needs to understand what surrogacy is, and the different forms it can take.

11.5.2 Nature of surrogacy

There are different forms of surrogacy and different reasons why one technique may be used over another. One of the most common reasons for surrogacy is the infertility of the woman, sometimes due to damage to the uterus, or even having no uterus at all. Here the *in vitro* fertilised embryo of the 'commissioning couple' will be placed in the uterus of the surrogate mother who will go through the process of pregnancy, give birth to the child and hand it to the commissioning couple. One may term this a 'full' surrogacy, with the surrogate mother having no genetic relationship to the child. Another form of surrogacy is where the male of the commissioning couple impregnates the surrogate woman, who then goes through the same physiological process. This could be termed 'partial' surrogacy, as the surrogate woman has a genetic relationship with the child, whereas the woman of the commissioning couple has none. Rather more rarely, the genetic father may be an anonymous donor so that the commissioning couple would have no genetic link to the child.

The arguments and subsequent legislation make it clear that there are three key points to be aware of:

(a) The genetic constitution of the child.
(b) Where the best interests of the child lie.
(c) Whether the arrangement is altruistic or commercially motivated.

11.5.3 Objections to surrogacy

According to Singer and Wells (*New Ways of Making Babies: The Reproduction Revolution* (OUP 1984)) there is an international antipathy to the whole concept of surrogacy. This has been evidenced by opinion polls. In both Australia and Britain public opinion was firmly against it. There does appear to be a great emotional intensity surrounding the scenes of surrogacy. Singer and Wells noted that different forms of question provoked considerably different responses. Where the question involved the concept of the surrogate 'giving back' a baby, there was a more negative response than where the emphasis was that the procedure was to 'give the couple a child'. We will return to the issue of where society's focus lies in a moment. Consider at this stage whether you approach the morality of surrogacy from the perspective of the childless couple or the surrogate woman.

Opponents of surrogacy, as with other artificial conception techniques, see it as unnatural, potentially exploitative, damaging to the child and to society as a whole.

Before the *Cotton* case the Warnock Report gave a central place to considering the issue of surrogacy. As the relevant paragraphs illustrate, there were strong objections to the practice. It is worth quoting in full, given medical law's tendency to follow where Warnock leads:

8.10 There are strongly held objections to the concept of surrogacy, and it seems from the evidence submitted to us that the weight of public opinion is against the practice. The objections turn essentially on the view that to introduce a third party into a process of procreation which should be confined to the loving partnership between two people is an attack on the value of the marital relationship. . . . Further, the intrusion is worse than in the case of AID, since the contribution of the carrying mother is greater, more intimate and more personal, than the contribution of the semen donor. It is also argued that it is inconsistent with human dignity that a woman should use her uterus for financial profit and treat it as an incubator for someone else's child. The objection is not diminished, indeed it is strengthened, where the woman entered an agreement to conceive a child, with the sole purpose of handing the child over to the commissioning couple after birth.

8.11 . . . it is argued that the relationship between mother and child is itself distorted by surrogacy. It is . . . potentially damaging to the child, whose bonds with the carrying mother, regardless of genetic connections, are held to be strong, and whose welfare must be considered to be of paramount importance. Further, it is felt that a surrogacy arrangement is degrading to the child who is to be the outcome of it, since, for all practical purposes, the child will have been bought for money.

8.12 It is also argued that since there are some risks attached to pregnancy no woman ought to be asked to undertake pregnancy for another, in order to earn money. Nor, it is argued, should a woman be forced by legal sanctions to part with a child, to which she has given birth, against her will.

There is a strong line of both utilitarian and deontological objection to the practice here. For example, the objection is partly based on the fact that the surrogate woman is being treated as a means to an end rather than as an end in herself – a distinctly Kantian view of morality, bolstered by the reciprocal idea of 'Do unto others'. Do not exploit others as you would not wish to be exploited. Later on the Warnock Report (para. 8.17) takes a consequentialist stance in declaring that 'even in compelling medical circumstances the danger of exploitation of one human being by another appears to the majority of us to *outweigh* the potential benefits, in almost every case'.

While those supporting surrogacy will be seen to make a plea based on autonomy, those objecting also point to the psychological pressures that the potential surrogate woman can face. The pressures that may be faced by one sister being begged by the other to have a child 'for her' can cast doubt on whether the decision to become a surrogate is a genuinely autonomous one.

Ultimately the report came out against commercial arrangements for surrogacy. It was felt that to criminalise the commissioning couple and the altruistic surrogate mother would cause further potential harm to the child through parental stigma of criminality. As noted in chapter 1, the intrusion of the law into freedom was a price too high for society to pay for its perceived objection to surrogate arrangements. The report recommended, however, that agencies who advertise, recruit and offer surrogacy services should be liable to criminal prosecution. The price of prohibiting this practice in terms of the curtailment of individual freedom was though to be worth paying.

It is clear from the tenor of the argument that the focus was on the exploitation of the woman and the potential psychological damage to the child. The argument that the existence of surrogacy and its legitimisation through law would be exploitative of women is an extensive and crucial one. Briefly put, the numerous authors against the practice of surrogacy argue that it is a form of prostitution. The surrogate woman is 'selling her body for profit' and this degrades that woman and women as a whole. It is another form of the image of woman as object rather than person. The exploitation is arguably another example of the inherent economic disadvantages that women have within society (see L. M. Harding, 'The Debate on Surrogate Motherhood: The Current Situation, Some Arguments and Issues: Questions Facing Law and Policy [1987] JSWL 59).

A further difficulty, and one which will be seen to have become a thorny problem for medical law courts here and in the USA, is the potential 'tug of love' (the commissioning couple wanting the child and the surrogate woman wanting to keep the same child) or 'push of hate' (neither party wanting the resultant child). If surrogacy arrangements were allowed, what would the law do in the following apparently simple situation?

Helen has agreed to become a surrogate for Brian and Sally, because Sally carries a genetic defect that would be passed on to any child with her genes. Helen is artificially inseminated with Brian's semen, and becomes pregnant. When the child is born, Helen decides that she does not want to hand over the child. Brian and Sally want to enforce the agreement.

Opponents of surrogacy place great store in the possibility of such an impasse. To allow surrogacy to take place in society would invariably lead to this happening. The issue of who should have the child would be no issue to those opposed to surrogacy, because, at least as a matter of moral theory, the criminalisation of such arrangements would stop them occurring. Singer and Wells point to a number of cases in the USA where precisely this problem has been in the courtroom. Opponents to surrogacy invariably use them as examples of the fact that allowing any surrogate arrangement does more harm than good. One slightly different example from Singer and Wells's analysis indicates the very real dangers for medical law in this country.

They describe the case of a Michigan housewife, Judy Stiver, who saw an advertisement for potential surrogate mothers to be paid for their services. Judy Stiver decided to approach the agent, because she, her husband and two-year-old daughter needed some extra money to pay bills and go on a holiday. The agent agreed a surrogacy arrangement between Judy and Mr and Mrs Malahoff. She agreed to be impregnated with Mr Malahoff's sperm and to abstain from sexual intercourse until the baby was conceived. She was to get $10,000 and in return Mr Malahoff would get the child. When the child was born it was discovered to have a condition called microcephaly. The child was not expected to live, but pulled through. The baby had an abnormally small head and was mentally handicapped. Mr Malahoff suggested that the child was not his because of blood tests on the baby, and refused to accept the baby or pay the fee. The Stivers did not want the baby. They said they had geared themselves up to giving it away and had not wanted any more children. The blood test revealed that the child was not Malahoff's. The Stivers kept the baby.

Singer and Wells note that, whatever view one takes of moral philosophy, ethics or law, there is little doubt that the only outcome in cases such as this is anguish for both couples and potential profound distress for the child. Opponents of surrogacy point to sad events such as this to argue that the Warnock Report did not go far enough. The report should have recommended that criminalisation of all concerned would be the only way to avoid repetition (whether it would do so in reality is considered below).

11.5.4 In support of surrogacy

One might feel safe in stating that generally it is accepted that circumventing infertility is a good thing (aside from those who see it as unnatural and unnecessarily increasing the population). To some, this would be impossible without surrogacy. The only other option is the notoriously difficult path of adoption, which itself would mean that neither parent would have a genetic relationship to the child adopted. In addition there are few children available for adoption these days. In strictly medical terms it can be the case that, due to the dangers of passing on congenital defect, it would be unwise for a woman to become pregnant. It is argued that it would be unfair to deny such women the possibility of being involved in the development of a child which will at least be genetically related to the partner.

Somewhat more radical is the suggestion that surrogacy, whether total or partial, may be a convenience to the woman who does not wish to be burdened with the incapacitating effects of pregnancy. Allied to this is the argument that it can be economically valuable to the surrogate woman. Kim Cotton herself admitted that her main motivation was money. Many people, the argument continues, provide services for money. Some do also involve forms of physical danger. Proponents of surrogacy along these lines of argument ask why there should be a differentiation between types of service offered and undertaken for money.

A wider argument in favour of surrogacy, which to some extent encapsulates the above points, is that the willingness to be a surrogate mother, whatever the motivation, is an expression of the autonomy of the woman, and the right to treat her body in any way that she sees fit. A rights-based medical law should respect the autonomy of the woman and allow surrogacy to take place.

In the whole realm of the debate in the Warnock Report there is an arguably rather blinkered notion of feminism, which will be seen to be repeated in the courtroom. There is sympathy with the 'commissioning woman' for desperately wanting a child, but not with the surrogate woman who is seen as having an 'unnatural' desire to give birth to a child and then give it up. The former is seen as normal and the latter abnormal: it is all right for women to want to have children, but not for someone else.

There is also the argument that women who have acted as surrogates have balked at the label of 'exploited woman'. It has been forcefully argued in the context of surrogacy arrangements in the USA (see L. A. Bitner, 'Womb for Rent' (1985) 90 Dick L Rev 227 at p. 253) that psychological pressure and exploitation is a myth:

> A baby born as the result of a surrogate gestation transaction is hardly unplanned, nor does it create an unexpected financial burden for the surrogate mother. On the contrary, the baby is conceived after careful planning. The surrogate mother has agreed to terminate her parental interests before the baby is conceived. . . . Unlike the typical baby-selling transaction, there is no opportunity for the adopting couple to pressure the

surrogate mother because the decision to become pregnant by artificial insemination rests solely with the surrogate mother.

11.5.5 Potential legal regulation of the surrogacy arrangement

In practical terms, is a total prohibition on surrogacy arrangements, of whatever origin and motivation, altruistic or commercial, possible? If it were felt to be morally wrong, and that legal prohibition were needed then Shelley Roberts ('Warnock and Surrogate Motherhood: Sentiment or Argument' in P. Byrne (ed.), *Rights and Wrongs in Medicine* (1986)) notes that there would be 'tremendous practical difficulties'. As with the argument on abortion there may be some who are so desperate to have a child that they will be willing to flout the law. The Warnock Report had pointed out that there would be very real problems of detecting and enforcing these 'crimes'. To prohibit actions sometimes drives them underground, and makes those involved vulnerable to exploitation and danger from the unscrupulous. The images of a '1984' style of surveillance of intimate family life would come closer with the snooping necessary to prohibit and enforce. What would the law do to a couple it detected seeking a surrogate woman? Shelley Roberts considers that a fine would be useless, as those who want a child are evidently quite willing to part with large sums of money to have a child. If a completed surrogacy arrangement were detected and prosecuted, what would happen to the child while the commissioning couple and surrogate were in prison? Other options for the law within a regime of prohibition could be to 'make' the surrogate keep the child. The potential psychological damage to the child living with a 'parent' who does not want it should be obvious.

If then, one accepts the Warnock Report's view that, at least as far as non-commercial arrangements are concerned, legal prohibition is too costly a curtailment of freedom and, as Shelley Roberts notes, practically impossible, why not regulate it? There could be a licensing scheme set up which would control all surrogate arrangements. This would have the advantage of first making the practice open rather than dangerously hidden. Professional advisers, medical and psychological, could be used to make sure that all parties are aware of the potential emotional minefield they are entering. The licensing scheme could make patently obvious, before the arrangement is entered into, the consequences of particular outcomes; for example, the Helen, Sally and Brian situation above, or the events surrounding the Stivers and the Malahoffs. On the negative side, Roberts notes that to set up a regulatory scheme would be to proclaim the activity to be a legitimate one. This would be likely to make it more common. It really comes back to one's moral stance. In Britain there appears to be a bare tolerance of the practice, but no desire to encourage it.

Roberts, having noted the difficulty of these two options, moves on to the only other option left. To discriminate morally and legally between different forms of the practice. The Warnock Report (and in a less than clear fashion the medical law which succeeded it) made a clear demarcation between altruism and commercialism. The limitation of this approach is that taking the middle ground tends unfortunately to satisfy no one and to have profound internal problems. To outlaw commercial surrogacy stops expert medical, psychological and legal counselling and investigation. The outlawing of commercial agencies is a tacit legitimisation of the practice of altruistic surrogacy. The law does not attack what the Warnock Report sees as the emotional and societal harm of surrogacy. Roberts makes the useful point that the law would best serve society if, instead of attacking the commercial middleman, it prohibited payment to the surrogate mother. This would limit surrogacy to its more traditional state; the private arrangement between relatives and friends.

One might also make the tentative point that a surrogacy arrangement could be a conspiracy to corrupt public morals, or outrage public decency. While it seems unlikely, given the Warnock Report's recognition of the intrusiveness any criminal law would have on the private lives of the individuals intimately involved in the surrogacy arrangement, this common law crime has a fickle and unpredictable history. It is probably best left with Lord Devlin, in the moral outrage of the 1950s and early 60s.

11.5.6 Current legal regulation

11.5.6.1 Illegal payment for adoption One of the initial questions for medical law and the legality of surrogacy arrangements, is whether in the handing over of the child there has been a criminal offence contrary to the Adoption Act 1976. This fell to be considered in *Re Adoption Application (Payment for Adoption)* [1987] Fam 81.

In this case the parties involved met casually, the surrogate being motivated by the desire to help a childless couple. She was, as agreed, impregnated by the man. They had agreed a figure of £10,000, but the surrogate returned half because she had sold her lucrative story to a national newspaper. All parties were content with the arrangement. The couple were handed the baby at birth, but it was not until two years later that the couple applied to adopt the child. The question was whether the element of 'payment or reward' invalidated the adoption applied for, because the baby had been 'bought'. Despite the case proceeding on the forerunner of the Adoption Act 1976 (namely the Adoption Act 1958, s. 50), it is convenient to consider the case as one under the present Act. Section 57 states as follows:

> (1) Subject to the provisions of this section, it shall *not be lawful* to make or give to any person any payment or reward for or in consideration of—
>   (a) the adoption by that person of a child;
>   (b) the grant by that person of any agreement or consent required in connection with the adoption of a child;
>   (c) the handing over of a child by that person with a view to the adoption of the child; or
>   (d) the making by that person of any arrangements for the adoption of a child. (emphasis added)

Latey J found that in the circumstances of the case a surrogacy arrangement would not contravene the Act, because, perhaps surprisingly, it was considered that the payments made did not constitute an element of profit or financial reward. The payments made did no more than compensate for the inconveniences of pregnancy. Even more liberally, Latey J said that, if necessary he would apply powers given under the legislation (now s. 57(3) of the Adoption Act 1976) to allow some profit or reward retrospectively in the interests of the child if that were ever felt to be necessary. This has to be seen as a decision which may have accorded with Latey J's sense of justice in the case, but as regards the first part of the decision, is a rather wide reading of that particular section.

In the USA courts there is evidence of a more realistic assessment of such payments. In relation to the issue of reward or expenses, which should really be applied in medical law in England and Wales, if the matters Latey J had to consider occurred again. *Re Baby M* (1988) 537 A 2d 1227 raised a number of the issues that confront medical law courts in this country that have considered surrogacy. The New Jersey Supreme Court noted that US law prohibits payment for adoption except for the reasonable expense of an agency, or the costs associated with the birth of the child. The surrogacy arrangement purported to pay the surrogate for 'services' as opposed to the subsequent adoption by the commissioning couple. Mrs Stern, who adopted the child had legally been no part of the surrogacy arrangement, which had been between her husband and the surrogate woman. The court clearly saw the payments to the surrogate, and of $7,500 to the agency (said to be for legal and administrative services) for what it was, money to give up parental rights to the child, and money paid in connection with an adoption.

Mr Stern knew he was paying for the adoption of a child; [the surrogate] knew she was accepting money so that a child might be adopted; [the agents] knew that it was being paid for assisting in the adoption of a child. The actions of all three worked to frustrate the goals of the statute. It strains credulity to claim that these arrangements, touted by those in the surrogacy business as an attractive alternative to the usual route leading to an adoption, really amount to something other than a private placement adoption for money. (p. 1241)

11.5.6.2 The surrogacy 'contract' The terms 'arrangement', agreement' and so forth have been used in relation to surrogacy. These are obvious clues to the fact that a major issue is the 'contract' of whatever form which exists between surrogate and commissioner, surrogate and agent, and commissioner and agent. It may be that a traditional contractual analysis will point the way to resolution, but English medical law has disproved the general law of contract's inability to deal with this difficult matter of medical law. The US decision of *Re Baby M* (1988) 537 A 2d 1227 is a comprehensive analysis of how the US courts approach such contracts, and provides a legal template which might be followed in medical law in Britain. Wilentz CJ provides a useful reminder of the essential issues for medical law:

In this matter the court is asked to determine the validity of a contract that purports to provide a new way of bringing children into a family. For a fee of $10,000, a woman agrees to be artificially inseminated with the semen of another woman's husband; she is to conceive a child, carry it to term, and after its birth surrender it to the natural father and his wife. The intent of the contract is that the child's natural mother will thereafter be forever separated from her child. The wife is to adopt the child, and she and the natural father are to be regarded as its parents for all purposes. The contract providing for this is called a 'surrogacy contract', the natural mother inappropriately called the 'surrogate mother'. (p. 1234)

Mr Stern had such a contract with the surrogate, Mrs Whitehead. He also had a contract with an agency which had brokered the arrangement, the Infertility Center of New York. It was an uneventful pregnancy and birth (if any could be called that). The New Jersey Supreme Court found (as noted earlier) that the arrangement breached legislation on payment for adoption and the contracts were therefore invalid and unenforceable.

The key matters for the court to consider were the public policy aspects of such contracts. The contract, it was noted, was predicated on the fact that before conception a contractual decision was made on who should adopt the child, when the whole idea of adoption is that the placement of the child is dependent on where the child's 'best interests' lie at the time of application. It was the view of the court that the surrogacy contract was against the policy of the State to give equal weight to the rights of both natural parents. The contract itself expressly made provision for the destruction of the rights of one of those natural parents, namely, the natural mother. The rights of a parent should not be easily destroyed, at least not without some provision for counselling on the consequences. The surrogate mother here received no counselling. The only information that she was given was in relation to the provisions of the contract, not the potential emotional cost. There had been a psychological assessment by the agency of her suitability as a surrogate, but no reliance seems to have been placed on it by anyone. There is suspicion in the judgment of Wilentz CJ that it was regarded by all as something of a formality. Lip service had been paid to good practice, while an eye was toward the fast buck, in the opinion of the court. The general dangers of the arrangement were shown by the comments of Wilentz CJ that:

> Under the contract, the natural mother is irrevocably committed before she knows the strength of her bond with her child. She never makes a totally voluntary, informed decision, for quite clearly any decision prior to the baby's birth is, in the most important sense, uninformed, and any decision after that, compelled by a pre-existing contractual commitment, the threat of a lawsuit, and the inducement of a $10,000 payment, is less than totally voluntary. Her interests are of little concern to those who controlled this transaction. (p. 1248)

Dominating criticism of this contract the court saw the dual issues of the failure of the contract to recognise the best interests of the child and the selling of a child, or at least the selling of a mother's rights to the child, as crucial in public policy terms. It was felt that the prohibitions on payment for adoption were needed to protect against every aspect of this case. In conclusion, the court forcefully pointed out all the potential and real problems of commercial surrogacy:

> It guarantees the separation of a child from its mother; it looks to adoption regardless of suitability; it totally ignores the child; it takes the child from the mother regardless of her wishes and her maternal fitness; and it does all of this, it accomplishes all of its goals, through the use of money. (p. 1250)

The central issue of public policy in relation to surrogacy contracts has also been a consideration by the civil courts in England. Consider whether English or US medical law is 'good' and 'does the right thing'.

A v *C* [1985] FLR 445 was originally concerned with the debate surrounding the custody of the child born as a result of AID, but is obviously applicable, given the nature of the arrangement. A man and his cohabitant made an agreement with a prostitute that, in return for a fee of £3,000, she would be artificially inseminated and subsequently hand over the child. As has always been a well-recognised risk with such arrangements, at birth the carrying mother refused to hand over the baby to the couple. At first instance Comyn J held that the agreement was a pernicious one for the sale of a child and would be unenforceable. Comyn J did, however, grant access to the man, who was the genetic father.

On appeal Ormrod LJ described the arrangement as 'most extraordinary and irresponsible, bizarre and unnatural. . . . a sordid commercial bargain'. Similarly Cumming-Bruce LJ described it as 'a kind of baby farming of a wholly distasteful and lamentable kind'. The genetic father was refused access.

Another case where the surrogacy arrangement was not the ideal that was anticipated between the parties was that of *Re P (Minors)(Wardship) (Surrogacy)* [1987] 2 FLR 421. A woman offered her services as a surrogate to a married man, who agreed to pay a lump sum to adopt the resultant child. During the course of the pregnancy the surrogate began to have misgivings over handing the child to the commissioning couple. When she gave birth to twins her disinclination grew. While regretting disappointing the couple she decided to keep the children.

Sir John Arnold P made it plain that the overriding issue was the welfare of the twins. Every consideration would be subordinate to that 'golden thread' which runs through the jurisprudence of the court in the exercise of its wardship jurisdiction. The fascinating aspect of the case, however, lies in his articulation of the factors which led him to his decision.

Heavily in her favour was the matter of the surrogate mother's maternity. As he said, 'she bore the children and carried them for the term of their gestation and ever since has conferred upon them the maternal care which they have enjoyed, and has done so successfully'.

His lordship did reveal what were considered by the courts to be weighty counter arguments deserving of consideration. They are obviously controversial, and may make one question once more whether the judge is in the best position to make decisions on issues of surrogacy arrangements and where the best interests of children lie. First, the court recognised that the 'shape' of the commissioning family was a better one in which to bring up these children 'because it contains a father and a mother'. The court continued by stating that the commissioning family were more affluent. In addition the intellectual environment would be more stimulating. Despite these counter considerations the court came to the firm conclusion that the predominant consideration was the existence of the maternal bond the carrying mother had.

A more notorious case, but one which effectively considered the 'best interests of the child' issue, was the Kim Cotton case itself, *Re C (A Minor) (Wardship: Surrogacy)* [1985] FLR 846. The facts were that the commissioning woman had a congenital defect, which prevented her from having a child. The commissioning couple were resident in the USA. In 1983 the commissioning man contacted an agency in the USA, and entered into a contract whereby he paid a sum of money and the agency undertook to find a surrogate to bear a child that would be genetically related to him, but not his wife. The resultant insemination of the woman (in the UK) was successful. When the child was born, the local authority (Barnet) obtained a place of safety order in relation to the child. Immediately after this the genetic father issued a wardship summons. It was soon established that the biological mother had voluntarily relinquished all rights in relation to the child. The local authority itself fully supported the application by the father that the child be given into the care of the commissioning couple.

Latey J forcefully stated that the morality, ethics and legality of surrogacy were not the court's main concern. Due to the very specific and basic nature of wardship proceedings, 'all that matters is what is best for her now that she is here and not how she arrived' (p. 848). As a result of the agreement between all concerned, it was held that it was in the best interests of the child to be placed with the commissioning couple.

The case law overall reveals an antipathy to surrogacy arrangements that has become more pronounced over time. The arguments against surrogacy, which were so clearly indicated in *Re Baby M* (1988) 537 A 2d 1227, have been obscured by the very specific wardship jurisdiction of the English courts. There have been broad pronouncements that surrogacy is sordid, but medical common law in England needs to reflect more closely the very clear and considered articulation of issues apparent in US decisions. It is difficult to state that there is a clear public policy element in judicial decisions at present, because the arguments on the benefits and burdens of commercial surrogacy have not yet been aired fully in the courtroom.

11.5.6.3 Surrogacy Arrangements Act 1985 The Act has limited aims; basically to rid society of what Parliament saw was the evil of commercial surrogacy. The Act does not consider the legal nature of surrogacy or the effects of recent reproductive technological developments. The legislation seems to have been a stopgap measure, or rather a Parliamentary knee-jerk reaction to a widely debated issue as a result of the Kim Cotton case.

At the outset one should note that the legislation does not cover the activities of charitable organisations in respect of surrogacy. Altruistic private surrogacy arrangements are also not covered. This type of arrangement usually takes place in an intimate family setting, so apart from the intrusiveness of any criminal sanction, there would be difficulties of detection.

The Act prohibits the recruitment of women as surrogates (s. 1) and the negotiation of surrogacy arrangements by agencies acting on a commercial basis (s. 2). The Act also prohibits the advertising of or for surrogacy services (s. 3). Surrogates themselves are exempt from criminal liability (s. 2(2)(a)). The commissioning couple are also exempt from criminal liability (s.2(2)(b)).

A man who negotiates directly with a potential surrogate and offers her a fee does not commit a crime. He cannot, however, avail himself of professional advice from lawyers or doctors because any professional who becomes involved and charges for the advice will be guilty of taking part in negotiations for a surrogacy arrangement on a commercial basis.

As originally enacted, the 1985 Act did not specifically state that a surrogacy contract was an illegal one. It also did not state that such contracts were unenforceable in the courts. But s. 1A, which was inserted into the 1985 Act by the Human Fertilisation and Embryology Act 1990, explicitly makes such contracts unenforceable.

There continues to be some doubt whether the 1985 Act applies to total surrogacy (where the surrogate mother has no genetic link with the child). A great deal depends on who is legally regarded as the mother. Could it be the woman who provides the egg, or the woman who carries the child and subsequently gives birth? The previous discussion of the case law appears to confirm the view of the Warnock Report that the carrying mother should be regarded as mother at law. The problem arises out of the fact that if the woman who gives birth is the mother, the child is illegitimate and the mother alone has parental rights and duties in respect of the child (although one could well imagine the courts not maintaining such a restrictive attitude where the welfare of the child was in issue). The surrogacy arrangement, if it has a commercial aspect, will be in breach of the Act. If, in the alternative, the genetic mother is regarded as the legal mother of the child that is born, then a strong argument could be put that the child is not a surrogate one. Section 1(2)(b) states that a surrogate mother means a woman who carries a child as part of an arrangement 'made with a view to any child carried in pursuance of it being handed over to, and parental responsibility being met (as far as is practicable) by, another person or other persons'. So, if the mother is the commissioning woman then the handing over of the child will not mean that the legal responsibility passes.

The Human Fertilisation and Embryology Act 1990, s. 27 provides that 'The woman who is carrying or has carried a child as a result of the placing in her of an embryo or of sperm and eggs, and no other woman, is to be treated as the mother of the child'. Gillian Douglas ('The Intention to be a Parent and the Making of Others' (1994) 57 MLR 637) recognises the underlying legislative policy as being one to discourage surrogacy. There seems little encouragement for the woman to be a surrogate where the law makes the assumption that she wants the child.

The presumptive fatherhood indicated by s. 28 of the 1990 Act applies here, as does the rebuttal where the woman has been treated in the absence of his consent. The possibility exists that where the surrogate mother has been impregnated by the commissioning man he may be treated as the father by reason of s. 28(3). After all there is ground to suggest that where the insemination is artificial they have actually received 'treatment together' and are unmarried. The judiciary have clearly moved against this. In *Re Q (Parental Order)* [1996] 1 FLR 369 the facts of the case pointed away from this.

The confusion over parental status was resolved by s. 30 of the 1990 Act. This section allows the commissioning couple to acquire parental status and rights. There are a number of conditions which need to be satisfied for such rights to be acquired:

(a)   The applicants must be married, with one of them being genetically related to the child (s. 30(1)).

(b)   The application must be made within six months of the birth of the child (s. 30(2)).

(c)   The child must be living with the couple at the time the application or the order is made (s. 30(3)).

(d)   Both applicants have attained the age of 18 (s. 30(4)).

(e)   The court needs to be satisfied that the couple and the surrogate mother have freely consented to the parental order being made (s. 30(5)).

(f)   No money or other benefit, apart from expenses, must have passed to or from the applicants, unless the court has authorised otherwise (s. 30(7)).

On the application of s. 30, including the fact that retrospective payment may be allowed, at least in terms of reasonable expenses, see *Re Q (Parental Order)* [1996] 1 FLR 369, where Johnson J authorised loss of earnings payment of £5,000.

11.6   CONCLUSION

Developments in reproductive technology which have enabled embryo research to take place have caught medical law and ethics in England unprepared. The familiar images that society had of the 'nuclear family' – husband, wife and 2.4 children – were now challenged. Theories of the family, relationships and parentage were all changed as the language of rights in medical law was used to demand access to the treatment available. The right of the individual to express autonomy through procreative freedom confronted medical law still entrenched in well-worn notions of 'father', 'mother' and 'parent'.

English medical law has been forced to expand the idea of legal rights and legal duties into a new area. This has been done with mixed success. The duty of the donor of reproductive material to be aware of genetic health has been melded on to the common law of duty with relative ease. The arguably most long-standing way of overcoming infertility, surrogacy, has not been well dealt with. The Warnock Report was perhaps typical in showing, if not an ambivalence to the practice then an unwillingness to let words of moral disapproval manifest themselves in prohibitive legal deeds. Societal intuition is arguably uncomfortable with the practice; to many there is something 'wrong' with it. That is not to say that many would have sought the incarceration of Kim Cotton.

Overall, the fact that the common law and rushed legislation are cumbersome tools to use when considering the moral, ethical and human rights impacts of rapid technological change is once more revealed.

Further reading

Blyth, E., 'Section 30 – The Acceptable Face of Surrogacy?' [1993] JSWL 248.

Douglas, G., 'The Human Fertilisation and Embryology Act' [1991] Fam Law 110.

Douglas, G., 'The Intention to Be a Parent and the Making of Mothers' (1994) 57 MLR 636.

Freeman, M. D. A., 'After Warnock – Whither the Law?' [1986] CLP 33.

Hogg, J. G., 'Surrogacy – Nobody's Child' [1991] Fam Law 276.

Morgan, D., and Lee, R., 'In the Name of the Father? Ex parte Blood: Dealing with Novelty and Anomaly' (1997) 60 MLR 840.

O'Donovan, K., 'A Right to Know One's Parentage?' (1988) 2 Int J Law & Fam 27.

TWELVE
Abortion and the law

12.1 INTRODUCTION

It is the intention of this chapter to explain briefly the major ethical arguments in favour of abortion and those against the practice. This will lead on to an analysis of the development of the law, which, until the major changes introduced by the Human Fertilisation and Embryology Act 1990, was described by Jane Fortin as 'an astonishing hotchpotch of overlapping legislative provisions' ('Legal Protection for the Unborn Child' (1988) 51 MLR 54 at p. 62). Modern abortion law in England can be fairly described as creating a liberal regime for the practice, while still retaining a significant level of ambiguity as to the preconditions for the performance of a lawful abortion. There is in addition still debate about whether others have the right to control the abortion decision of the woman, the legality of new abortion techniques and the selective reduction of the multiple pregnancies which are a by-product of new infertility treatments (see chapter 10). Abortion law will be seen to reflect accurately Margaret Brazier's concern that it 'represents in many respects an attempt to reach a compromise in a debate in which there is no consensus' (*Medicine, Patients and the Law*, 2nd ed. (London: Penguin, 1992), p. 287).

Few areas of medical law have aroused such emotions and raised such profound moral issues as abortion. Recently in Ireland the Supreme Court decided to lift an injunction which had prevented a 14-year-old rape victim, made pregnant by her attacker, from travelling to England to get an abortion (*Attorney-General* v *X* [1992] 1 IR 1). This was one of the factors that led to a national referendum on access to abortion information which was in favour of the practice, yet defeated on procedural grounds when proposed for legislation. In the USA in 1994 a number of workers at an abortion clinic were killed by a gunman alleged to have been a member of a militant pro-life group. In England the debate may have been less violent, but has nevertheless been fervent. The High Court recently upheld the convictions for public order offences of pro-life lobbyists who had demonstrated outside the clinic run by the British Pregnancy Advisory Service. The pressure group had argued in their defence that they believed that illegal abortions were being carried out (see *Morrow* v *Director of Public Prosecutions* [1994] Crim LR 58). In August 1996 there was a widely publicised case of a woman who required the 'selective reduction' of twins to one child, because the other would have been too expensive to bring up. When the doctor revealed the existence of the anonymous case, the hospital was flooded with offers of financial support if the child was kept (although the offer was never communicated to the woman, and the reduction had taken place before the doctor had even been interviewed about the case).

12.2   THE ABORTION DEBATE

The abortion debate is immensely wide-ranging, embracing numerous concepts, such as the beginning of human life, the differential perspectives of when a 'person' comes into existence, the theological theory of the ensoulment of the human, the developmentalist idea of the human being and the theory that life is a gift from God and therefore sacrosanct. Confronting these views is the assertion of the moral, ethical and legal right of the woman to choose what shall happen to her body (the concept of autonomy). These are just a sample of the ethical dilemmas confronting society in this arena. Numerous books have been written on the ethical abortion debate, and one should not deny the importance of it. The law as it stands is a result of a continuously polarised argument between those who believe that abortion is morally and practically justified and those who see it as sinful or wasteful of human life.

The essence of the ethical arguments surrounding the practice of abortion can be seen in the famous US case of *Roe* v *Wade* (1973) 410 US 113. This case, concerning the right generally of a woman to have an abortion, decided that it would be an invasion of a woman's constitutional right to privacy to be refused or limited in her access to abortion by statute. While *Roe* v *Wade* has obvious significance for the whole abortion debate, there is some difficulty in using it as a tool for consideration of English medical law and human rights. The case was based on an interpretation of an element of a written constitution guaranteeing the right to privacy. In addition to the option of constitutional debate not yet being possible in England, there is the very clear political dimension and make-up of the US Supreme Court. The development of the legal debate on abortion since *Roe* v *Wade* indicates swings of law consonant with swings in political fortune. The US debate should not be ignored, however, because of a simple fact, which is important for this and many medical law debates. While having no written constitution, England is developing the language of human rights in the context of medicine. As the WHO document, *Promotion of the Rights of Patients in Europe*, indicated, one of the broad rights of a patient is the right of privacy. There thus seems scope for arguing that the form of medico-legal debate that has happened in the USA can happen here.

The fundamental recognition of *Roe* v *Wade* is of the woman's right to choose what shall happen to her body. As the law relating to battery is a legal recognition of the ethical importance of bodily integrity (see chapter 7) so the woman's right to choose or refuse an abortion is a legal recognition of that right too. There have constantly, in many countries, been demands for more liberal abortion laws, or at least to maintain a level of freedom to have an abortion. The most strident variant on the claim of the right to choose is grounded on the notion of self-defence. If the unborn child's existence is inconsistent with the wishes of the woman, then abortion is permissible in order for the woman to protect herself against an invader. Further still, feminist writers have noted the possible conflict between woman and foetus in wider terms. As Benschoff argues:

> The increasing tendency to view the foetus as an independent patient or person occurs at the cost of reducing the woman to the status of little more than a maternal environment. . . . The need is to reform the right to abortion as one not to be defined by the foetus or by technological advances, but one that is tied to women's constitutional rights to privacy, autonomy and bodily integrity. ('Reasserting Women's Rights' in *Late Abortion and Technological Advances in Foetal Viability* (Fam Planning Perspec) (1985), p. 162).

The feminist argument has currently been given fresh impetus by developments in medical technology. As Calliope Farsides argues: 'Advances in pre-natal sceening and the ability to see the foetus *in utero* have contributed to the increasingly common representation of "foetus as patient"' ('Body Ownership' in McVeigh and Wheeler (eds), *Law, Health and Medical Regulation* (Dartmouth, 1992), p. 44). This has been combined with the view of the woman requesting an abortion being 'the bad girl' and the foetus 'the innocent'.

The decision in *Roe* v *Wade* also recognises that while the rights of the foetus may exist, these rights are subordinate to those of the woman. This utilitarian view of balancing harms is complex, in that it depends for its force on the ethical significance of a number of factors, such as when a human person worthy of protection comes into existence. *Roe* v *Wade* decided that the woman had a largely unfettered right to an abortion in the first three months (trimester) of pregnancy. There was, however, recognition by the Supreme Court that as the foetus develops, so its rights increase. The court decided that in the second trimester the judiciary may intervene to reinforce maternal rights. The focus thus remains on the ethical dominance of the woman when considering the rights of the unborn. In the third trimester, when the foetus is viable, the State has a compelling interest in maintaining that life, but not to the detriment of the life of the woman. The Supreme Court did recognise that the foetus, while not being a fully fledged individual, was nevertheless deserving of some protection, so the freedom of the mother to have an abortion would be subject to restrictions based on an ethical recognition that it was valued, although even at the stage of viability there is no recognition of the notion of maternal sacrifice.

The suggestion was made that in the first trimester there is the right to an abortion on demand, notwithstanding the fact that the woman is in no physical or mental danger. The decision was that 'preserve life or health' does not include convenience abortions. The debate here rests on the differing ideas of the freedom of a woman to make choices about her body. A consistent point put in favour of unfettered access to abortion is that the foetus is not an independent ethical individual (and as will be seen later, at law not recognised as an individual), merely part of the woman. The counter to this is that there is an ethically recognised individual, even though unborn, and that individual is deserving of protection at law against being sacrificed for mere convenience. English law will be seen to allow for what may be termed abortions on social grounds (see Abortion Act 1967, s. 1(2)). There is even a possibility that legislation in England allows for abortions to be performed on demand (see 12.6.1)

The other arguments voiced in and around *Roe* v *Wade* against abortion raise the most profound issues possible. One of these fundamental arguments is that life is a gift from God and therefore no one but God has authority to end that life. To some there are no exceptions to this rule, while others feel that some tragic circumstances such as rape or incest could, in extreme situations, justify such a taking of life. In somewhat wider terms Margaret Brazier has said:

An individual woman who believes on religious or other grounds that human life as such, the human organism, commands respect necessarily must accept that an embryo within her enjoys a status equal to her own. ('Embryo "Rights" Abortion and Research' in M. Freeman (ed.), *Medicine, Ethics and the Law* (London: Stevens, 1988))

A strand of feminist argument that has been raised is that liberal abortion laws are in the interest of men and indeed may be against the public interest, because such laws allow them the pleasure of sexual intercourse without the responsibilities resulting from a completed pregnancy. Denning LJ, in the case of *Bravery* v *Bravery* [1954] 1 WLR 1169, argued similarly in relation to the sterilisation of men for convenience only, rather than to alleviate a medical condition (see chapter 13).

There is a perception that a liberal regime of abortion could lead to foetuses being aborted on minor medical grounds, even at a stage when they may have been capable of living. A further implication is that such a situation may lead to abortion on the ground of trivial handicap, thereby placing society in a position of being able to value life in terms of its approximation to an illusory goal of perfection. A comment by David Alton MP during the course of the most recent abortion legislation, the Human Fertilisation and Embryology Act 1990, indicates further the concerns of those opposed to abortion to what they see as the killing of a human:

. . . the unborn child at 18 weeks is complete in organs and sensitive to touch and sound, the foetus can feel pain and the sensory neurones are more sensitive than those of an adult or a newborn.

The arguments between those opposed to abortion and those who support the current system, or would like to see a further liberalisation, remain as dramatic and emotional as ever. The question now is, to what extent has English law followed a restrictive or liberal path?

12.3 DEVELOPMENT OF THE LAW

At common law it was established that legal protection of human life extended to the unborn child. Professor Bernard Dickens, in his book *Abortion and the Law* (London: MacGibbon & Kee, 1966) stated that as early as the thirteenth century, ecclesiastical legal authorities were debating whether counselling an abortion or providing poison or using violence on the pregnant woman would be homicide. Later, Coke's definition of homicide being the killing of a creature '*in rerum natura*' was interpreted as applying only to those born alive (for more detail see 12.10), though there seemed to be no consensus on this aspect of the law.

Prior to the first intervention in this area by the legislature, abortion was generally regarded as a common law misdemeanour which could be committed by the pregnant woman or others. Ethical and therefore legal significance was attached to the first perceptible movement of the foetus in the womb, so an offence would only be committed where the foetus had 'quickened' (for an explanation of the various stages of foetal development which may be significant for medical law see 10.2.1).

In 1803 Lord Ellenborough's Act (43 Geo 3, c. 58) was passed. Section 1 provided that those who counselled, aided or abetted the abortion of a 'quick' child would, on conviction, be sentenced to death. Section 2 of the Act recognised that the pre-quick foetus was deserving of protection and so criminalised those involved in its abortion, although the punishment was not as Draconian as under s. 1, the maximum sentence being transportation for up to 14 years. Lord Lansdowne's Act of 1828 (9 Geo 4, c. 31) replaced the 1803 legislation. The Offences against the Person Act 1837 (7 Wil 4 & 1 Vict, c. 85) extinguished the legal distinction between the pre-quick and quick foetus, and replaced the death penalty as punishment with transportation or imprisonment.

These pieces of legislation were curious in that they nowhere referred to the woman's involvement, or acquiescence, in the performance of the abortion. References were to those who counselled or procured the offence. Dickens suggests that even though not expressly mentioned, it was generally accepted that the woman would be liable to the same punishment in the unlikely event of detection and prosecution.

12.4 OFFENCES AGAINST THE PERSON ACT 1861

The Offences against the Person Act 1861, despite being over 130 years old, is still an essential element in the criminalisation and regulation of abortion. The Act is couched in the language of the nineteenth century and therefore suffers from some ambiguity. Terms encountered are unfamiliar and recently have shown themselves open to a number of interpretations. The two relevant sections are as follows:

58. Every woman, being with child, who, with intent to procure her own miscarriage, shall unlawfully administer to herself any poison or other noxious thing, or shall unlawfully use any instrument or other means whatsoever with the like intent, and whosoever, with intent to procure the miscarriage of any woman, whether she be or be not with child, shall unlawfully administer to her or cause to be taken by her any poison or other noxious thing, or shall unlawfully use any instrument or other means whatsoever with the like intent, shall be guilty of [an offence], and being convicted thereof shall be liable to [imprisonment] for life.

59. Whosoever shall unlawfully supply or procure any poison or other noxious thing, or any instrument or thing whatsoever, knowing that the same is intended to be unlawfully used or employed with intent to procure the miscarriage of any woman, whether she be or be not with child, shall be guilty of [an offence], and being convicted thereof shall be liable to [imprisonment for a term not exceeding five years].

The sections apply to 'every woman being with child' so that the unborn are protected at whatever stage of development they have reached. The Act nowhere points to a specific stage of foetal development where the law will intervene. It has to be accepted, however, that any abortion which takes place soon after the moment of conception would be difficult to prove. The term 'miscarriage' was preferred in this legislation, and generally during the nineteenth century, to the term 'abortion', but recently the term has provoked debate on its exact meaning, particularly with the development of new abortion techniques and the increase in the variety of contraceptive methods available (see 12.11). However, it is still incorrect to talk of 'unlawful abortion'. An abortionist who breaches the law will be liable for the unlawful procuring of a miscarriage under the 1861 Act.

Section 58 makes the activities of the pregnant woman criminal. It also makes the involvement of others in the process criminal, even if it is subsequently proved that the woman was not in fact pregnant. The same applies to the person supplying the abortifacient under s. 59.

Glanville Williams (*Textbook of Criminal Law*, 2nd ed. (London: Stevens, 1983) at pp. 293–4) has recognised that although s. 58 (as it relates to the pregnant woman's activities) is still on the statute book, it would be extremely unlikely that a woman would be convicted by a jury, which would no doubt feel that the act must have been done under conditions of extreme despair. It is also the case that the rare conviction under s. 58 would only attract a nominal sentence. Williams cites the unreported case in 1977 of a 13-year-old girl receiving a free pardon and an apology. The term 'using means with intent' absolves the prosecution from having to prove that the abortionist actually caused the abortion.

12.5 INFANT LIFE (PRESERVATION) ACT 1929

The Infant Life (Preservation) Act 1929 was introduced to deal with a significant gap in the law not envisaged by the drafters of the Offences against the Person Act 1861. The common law, prior to 1861, had distinguished between a foetus and a child born alive. The 1861 Act had failed to deal with the killing of a child during the process of birth. There would, in such a situation, be no artificial facilitation of a miscarriage so it would be outside the ambit of the 1861 Act. The common law crimes of murder and manslaughter (see 12.10) would not apply because the child was not born alive, in that it did not have an existence independent of the mother. As Jane Fortin observed: 'The 1929 Act reflected a concern that the criminal law was unable to deal . . . with women who strangled their babies at birth' ('Legal Protection for the Unborn Child' (1988) 51 MLR 54 at p. 63). The Act filled this lacuna in the law in the following terms:

1.   (1)   Subject as hereinafter in this subsection provided, any person who, with intent to destroy the life of a child capable of being born alive, by any wilful act causes a child to die before it has an existence independent of its mother, shall be guilty of [an offence], to wit, of child destruction, and shall be liable on conviction thereof on indictment to [imprisonment] for life:
       Provided that no person shall be found guilty of an offence under this section unless it is proved that the act which caused the death of the child was not done in good faith for the purpose only of preserving the life of the mother.
       (2)   For the purposes of this Act, evidence that a woman had at any time been pregnant for a period of 28 weeks or more shall be prima facie proof that she was at that time pregnant of a child capable of being born alive.

The important case which resolved many issues in relation to the meaning of the terms contained in s. 1(1) and established that there was an interrelationship between the 1861 and 1929 Acts was *R v Bourne* [1939] 1 KB 687.

On 27 April 1938 a 14-year-old girl had been the victim of horrific rape (as if there could be any other). As a consequence of the attack she became pregnant. The defendant surgeon, Mr Aleck Bourne, upon being consulted, performed an abortion on the girl with the consent of her parents. At the time Mr Bourne stated publicly, 'I have done this [therapeutic abortion] before and have not the slightest hesitation in doing it again. I have said that the next time I have such an opportunity I will write to the Attorney-General and invite him to take action.' He was taken at his word. Mr Bourne was prosecuted under the Offences against the Person Act 1861, s. 58.

The key to the decision comes from two linked elements of Macnaghten J's summing up to the jury. First the meaning to be attached to the word 'unlawfully' in s. 58. Secondly the breadth of the term 'to preserve the life of the mother' in s. 1(1) of the 1929 Act. The judge set the tone of his summing up by reiterating that while at common law the killing of the unborn was a grave crime there could be legal justifications for such acts in certain circumstances. The term 'unlawfully' was not a meaningless one. There were circumstances where the procuring of a miscarriage would not be unlawful. His lordship then went on to link the two Acts by stating that it would not be unlawful where the abortion was performed 'in good faith for the purpose of preserving the life of the mother' as stated in the proviso to s. 1(1) of the 1929 Act. On the evidence, there was no immediate danger to the girl's life if the pregnancy continued, but Mr Bourne had performed the abortion on the ground that if it continued the girl would suffer psychologically. Another witness, Dr Rees, confirmed that the pregnancy, if it continued, would make her a 'mental wreck' (at p. 695). Macnaghten J felt that 'preserving the life of the mother' extended beyond acts to save her physical existence. He declared that a woman's life depended on both physical and mental health. In this view he was tacitly rewording the statute to read 'to save life or preserve health'. Mr Bourne was found not guilty of the offence.

Glanville Williams has noted that the impact of Mr Bourne's acquittal on the medical profession was not what might have been expected. There was an expectation that doctors would find in Mr Bourne's acquittal a justification for the performance of abortions where none had existed before. In an unreported case (Williams, *Textbook of Criminal Law*, 2nd ed. (London: Stevens, 1983), p. 296) a 12-year-old girl made pregnant by her father was refused an abortion. This strictness of approach appeared widespread and the back-street abortionist seemed able to continue in a profitable trade. It may be something of an exaggeration but there was evidence that 'the only people effectively deterred by the law were the doctors' (ibid., loc. cit.).

12.5.1 Time limit for abortions under the 1929 Act

An amendment made to the Abortion Act 1967, s. 5(1), by the Human Fertilisation and Embryology Act 1990 appears to have made the provisions of the 1929 Act irrelevant to registered medical practitioners. The Abortion Act 1967, s. 5(1), now provides that a registered medical practitioner who terminates a pregnancy in accordance with the provisions of the 1967 Act does not commit any offence under the 1929 Act. However, the term 'capable of being born alive' could still be relevant in relation to:

> . . . a civil action brought by a mother whose pregnancy pre-dated the . . . amendments [which came into effect in 1991] and who has given birth to a disabled child. She claims that she was negligently not given the opportunity to choose an abortion. In such a case, a defendant might argue that the disability was only discovered (or discoverable) at a time when an abortion would have been illegal under the 1929 Act. (Kennedy and Grubb, *Medical Law*, 2nd ed. (London: Butterworths, 1994), p. 878)

The major question to resolve in such a situation would be what is meant by the term 'capable of being born alive'. Section 1(2) of the 1929 Act provides that a 28-week-old foetus is prima facie capable of being born alive. This is only a presumptive rule, and it could be argued that a foetus is viable below this gestational age. Tunkel ('Abortion: How Early, How Late, and How Legal?' [1979] 2 BMJ 253) argues that under the law of homicide generally, the child does not have to be capable of staying alive, as long as it is just capable of being born alive (see 12.10). There has been some debate about whether a child, incapable of breathing without the help of a respirator can be 'capable of being born alive'. Margaret Brazier has argued that the child is so capable if it can 'survive with the support of medical science'. In the case of C v S [1988] QB 135 (for a further analysis see 12.9), a husband was trying to stop his wife from having an abortion on the ground that the child was 'capable of being born alive' and therefore any abortion at this stage would be in breach of the 1929 Act. The conclusion of the Court of Appeal, after a deal of conflicting medical testimony, equated capability with viability. Therefore it would not be enough if the child could be supposed to be able to live for however short a time, it had to have a prognosis which supported future survival.

More recently in *Rance v Mid-Downs Health Authority* [1991] 1 QB 587 a woman was 26 weeks pregnant, when a negligent doctor failed to spot the fact that the child had spina bifida. This negligence meant that the woman was deprived of the opportunity to have an abortion. In their defence the health authority argued that a foetus of this maturity would be 'capable of being born alive'. It would therefore be against public policy for the court to award damages for the failure to carry out an unlawful act. Brooke J, finding that the child was capable of being born alive stated that:

> Once the foetus has reached a state of development in the womb that it is capable, if born, of possessing those attributes [breathing through its own lungs and having no connection to the mother] it is capable of being born within the meaning of the 1929 Act.

This would appear to move the legal concept of capability away from viability and towards the fact of independent life, however short that may be.

12.6 ABORTION ACT 1967

This was the most hotly debated issue of medical law, as indicated by the fervency of debate both during the passage of the Act in the 1960s and also more recently when changes to the Act were debated and subsequently made as part of the reforms introduced by the Human Fertilisation and Embryology Act 1990 (see s. 37). Before these amendments the 1967 Act had to be read alongside the Infant Life (Preservation) Act 1929 and the Offences against the Person Act 1861. It was this complexity which caused criticism of the regulation of abortion (for more detail see Fortin (1988) 51 MLR 54). If the requirements of the Abortion Act 1967 were not met, and the foetus was below 28 weeks, the charge would be under the Offences against the Person Act 1861. If the foetus was of 28 weeks age or above, the presumption at law was that it was capable of being born alive and, unless that presumption was

rebutted by the defence, the charge would be under the Infant Life (Preservation) Act 1929.
The amendments made three important changes:

(a) The Abortion Act 1967 as originally enacted did not introduce any protection for a doctor who aborted a 'child capable of being born alive' other than in circumstances such as R v Bourne [1939] 1 KB 687 (see 12.5). The old s. 5(1) maintained the provisions of the 1929 Act, which was described as 'protecting the life of the viable foetus'. The new s. 5(1) substituted by the 1990 Act does not. It states:

No offence under the Infant Life (Preservation) Act 1929 shall be committed by a registered medical practitioner who terminates a pregnancy in accordance with the provisions of this Act.

(b) The amended 1967 Act introduces the possibility of an abortion being performed without time limit and on a new ground of substantial foetal handicap.
(c) There is now a time limit for many abortions of 24 weeks.

The amended 1967 Act provides that no offence will be committed under the law relating to abortion (this being defined by the Abortion Act 1967, s. 6 as ss. 58 and 59 of the Offences against the Person Act 1861) where a pregnancy is terminated by a registered medical practitioner in circumstances where two such practitioners have formed an opinion in good faith that one of the following conditions is in existence:

(a) That the pregnancy has not exceeded 24 weeks and that continuance would involve risk, greater than if the pregnancy were terminated, of injury to the physical or mental health of the pregnant woman or any existing children of her family (s. 1(1)(a)).
(b) That the termination is deemed to be necessary to prevent grave permanent injury to the physical or mental health of the pregnant woman (s. 1(1)(b)).
(c) That continuance of the pregnancy would involve risk to the life of the woman, greater than if the pregnancy were terminated (s. 1(1)(c)).
(d) That there is a substantial risk that the child if born would suffer from such severe physical or mental abnormalities as to be seriously handicapped (s. 1(1)(d)).

Whereas two medical practitioners would normally be required to form an opinion in relation to the above, this will not apply where one medical practitioner forms an opinion in good faith that termination is necessary to save the life or prevent grave permanent injury to the pregnant woman. This is legislative recognition of the possibility of an emergency.
Few of these preconditions have proved uncontroversial, and the courts have been called on to clarify some of the terminology used. Ethical criticism

has focused on the grounds for abortion, particularly the ground of serious foetal handicap. In general terms the amended Act suffers from the same uncertainties and has attracted similar criticism to the original Act.

12.6.1 The limited ground: s. 1(1)(a)

The insertion of a specific time limit of 24 weeks under this ground is a recognition of both the physiological development of the foetus and the perceived ethical significance of this stage of development. A number of MPs and pressure groups had attempted to lobby Parliament during the passage of the 1990 Act with either more restrictive or more liberal abortion regime proposals. Aside from those who demanded an outright ban on abortions, the time limits suggested varied significantly. Calls were for no time limit at all, the retention of the 28-week presumptive rule, all the way down to an 18-week limit. The reduction to 24 weeks was approved by Parliament in recognition of the fact that modern medical technology allows for far more effective intervention in support of the less mature foetus than has ever been the case before. The contemporary special baby care unit would be well equipped to deal with the foetus born at 24 weeks, and to a limited extent less mature than that.

Debate on this ground has tended to focus on the hypothesis that with modern non-surgical abortion techniques it is invariably the case that the continuance of a pregnancy (at least in the early stages) will be more hazardous to health than the performance of the abortion. Therefore the inference is clear: there may be first-trimester abortion on demand under the law.

Would it be legitimate for a medical practitioner to invoke national maternal mortality statistics to support this abortion on demand theory? Such statistics tend to indicate that risk within the general population supports first-trimester abortion. If a statistical analysis were disallowed, the practitioner is forced back to a speculative consideration of the woman's current physical and mental health and a potentially wide-ranging theorising of what the future may hold in those terms.

The statistical argument is based on the view that early abortions are a matter of medical discretion based on general mortality rate for first-trimester abortion compared to general maternal mortality. The problem with the statistical argument is that there are too many socio-economic, demographic and physiological variables to make such a calculation reliable. The practitioner will be able to find a form of analysis to justify what is really an ethical or clinically intuitive decision based on the individual patient. Further, the Act nowhere states that pregnancies may be terminated where there is a general risk that childbirth is more hazardous to the woman. It has been argued that the doctor who looks to statistics rather than the individual patient may be breaching the Act by failing to act in good faith (see T.G.A. Bowles and M.N.M Bell, 'Abortion on Demand or Request: Is it Legal?' (1980) 77 LS Gaz 34 at 938). In practical terms the medical practitioner will act in the same way with this patient as with other patients in the assessment of risk. Nevertheless the ambiguity of the Act may act as a cloak for the doctor to perform an abortion on the basis of it being the woman's right to choose (see 12.2). Whatever the moral support that may be felt for such an action, the doctor articulating such a view would not be acting in good faith, and would arguably place him- or herself outside the ambit of the Act.

The courts have only been called on once to consider the issue of good faith in abortion procedure, in *R* v *Smith* [1973] 1 WLR 1510, and this was in the very specific area of certification of the abortion. Nevertheless the case is of general interest as being one of the rare convictions under modern abortion legislation. This case also points away from the validity of the statistical argument, in that the judgment indicates the necessity for the doctor to consider the mental and physical impact of pregnancy on the *individual* patient.

Dr Smith, in performing an abortion on a patient, was accused of breaching the 1967 Act. The claim was that he had not properly examined the patient to ascertain the necessity of an abortion and had not acted in good faith by asking his anaesthetist for the required second opinion when the patient was in the theatre. Evidence indicated that the woman was young and healthy and practitioners called to give evidence themselves commented that normally careful enquiries would be made before proceeding. Dr Smith was charged under the Offences against the Person Act 1861, s. 58. Those representing Dr Smith argued amongst other things that he had formed what was termed an 'honest' opinion of the need for an abortion. Upon this and a number of other matters (including the doctor's contention that certification documents, which declared that the patient had been reviewed by the anaesthetist as well as Dr Smith, were not forgeries completed after the event) he was disbelieved by the jury and convicted. During the course of the doctor's failed appeal, Scarman LJ made the important comment that under the law of abortion 'a great social responsibility is firmly placed upon the shoulders of the medical profession', in that, along with the patient, the medical practitioner is the central decision-making figure under the legislation. In going on to reject the appeal there was an acknowledgement that the Act was open to abuse and the courts would not shy away from the opportunity to interpret the abortion legislation in relatively strict terms.

The existence of the 24-week limit, and the potentially wide interpretation of the precondition for such an abortion, make it important to gauge accurately how long there has been a pregnancy. Current medical opinion favours measuring the time from the first day of the woman's last period. This is convenient and simpler to ascertain than the alternative, which is to calculate from the moment of implantation of the fertilised egg. It does have to be conceded that implantation has been the key element underlying the mischief of the Offences against the Person Act 1861, s. 58 (see 12.11.1), and so legislative consistency would tend to favour such an interpretation, notwithstanding the difficulties of working out precisely when implantation takes place.

The Abortion Act 1967, s. 1(2), states that account may be taken of the woman's actual or reasonably foreseeable environment. Again this would appear to open the opportunity for the doctor to undertake a far-reaching consideration of factors when deciding upon the abortion request. It has been asserted a number of times that some ethnic groups value the birth of a son more highly. Should a woman, on discovering that she carries a female, be allowed to use this section, and s. 1(1)(a) to secure an abortion?

Again the question would come back to the good faith of the doctor in making the assessment of the future.

12.6.2 The unlimited grounds

12.6.2.1 Necessary to prevent grave permanent injury to physical or mental health: s. 1(1)(b)   Section 1(1)(b) was introduced in 1990. The motivation behind it differs from s. 1(1)(a) in that it is meant to cover emergency situations. The use of the term 'necessary' indicates that a doctor, in order to be acting in good faith, and therefore within the law, needs to consider whether an alternative form of treatment, falling short of an abortion, could achieve the same medical end, namely, preventing grave permanent injury to physical or mental health. 'Grave permanent injury' should be given its ordinary meaning. The Lord Chancellor, Lord Mackay of Clashfern, in a House of Lords debate on the 1990 Bill argued:

> The use of the words 'grave' and 'permanent' suggest[s] that there is a stiff legal test to cover special situations where termination might be contemplated primarily in the interests of the pregnant woman. (Hansard HL, 18 October 1990, col. 1039)

He went on to give the example of the pregnant woman with severe hypertension where a continuance of the pregnancy might well result in permanent kidney, brain or heart damage.

Given the continued existence of s. 1(4) to cover the situation of an immediate threat to life or health, 'grave permanent' injury here envisages a scenario which falls short of being an immediate threat to life or health. Section 1(1)(b) provides for the type of patient encountered in *R v Bourne* [1939] 1 KB 687 (see 12.5).

12.6.2.2 Risk to the life of the pregnant woman: s. 1(1)(c)   To provide symmetry with s. 1(1)(a) and (b) the interpretation placed on 'preserving life' by McNaghten J in *R v Bourne* [1939] 1 KB 687 cannot be used. Section 1(1)(c) is more restrictive in scope. There has to be a risk of death before it can be invoked. If this were not so, and the liberal interpretation of *R v Bourne* were used, then this would nullify the effect of s. 1(1)(b).

12.6.2.3 Serious foetal handicap: s. 1(1)(d)   Arguably this is the most controversial element of the abortion legislation. An abortion can now take place where 'there is substantial risk that if the child were born it would suffer from such physical and mental abnormalities as to be seriously handicapped'.

It was this provision which caused the MP David Alton to describe the Act as '. . . . the refuge of a society that has grown uneasy with disability' (Hansard

HC, 24 April 1990, col. 251). His reference was to the potential for the Act being used as a cover for the development of a policy of eugenics. The House of Lords committee considering amendments to the Act took the provision to cover situations where the foetus suffered gross abnormality and would be unable to lead any meaningful life. Glanville Williams has preferred the view that the welfare of the parents is the key issue, with a secondary consideration being the expense put upon the State in having to provide care for the severely handicapped. This is a liberal interpretation of the provision which is difficult to sustain.

Given the factual and moral significance of this law it is vital to consider the meaning of the terms 'substantial risk' and 'seriously handicapped'. In reality the situation, as it presents itself to the doctor, will necessitate a link between the two phrases in an assessment of risk and level of handicap. Glanville Williams has suggested that:

[The medical practitioner] may, of course, take the view that a relatively low risk justifies termination if the risk is of relatively serious handicap; in common sense, the two factors are inversely related. Even when the doctor thinks that the 'foetal indication' is not sufficiently present, the fact that the patient is extremely depressed by worry that the child may be affected can itself be a reason for termination on the health ground.

This is not what the legislation says. There has to be a substantial risk. Anything short of that would be insufficient to invoke s. 1(1)(d).

Another form of analysis suggests that 'substantial risk' may assume that the serious handicap was more likely than not (A.J.C. Hoggett 'The Abortion Act 1967' [1968] Crim LR 247). This is a reading of the word 'substantial' which takes it away from its ordinary and natural meaning. The Act does not say 'on the balance of probabilities'.

Overall the term 'seriously handicapped' is potentially vague. There appears no consensus on what degree of mental or physical damage can justify abortion up to term under s. 1(1)(d). The possibility of a wide interpretation and the creation of a liberal regime of abortion for relatively minor handicap (such as cleft lip) means that the courts may well be called on in the future to make a determination of what 'seriously handicapped' encompasses. A possible means to gauge the level of handicap has been suggested (D. Morgan [1990] Crim LR 690). An analogy could be made with the growing body of case law which considers levels of handicap justifying the withdrawing or non-treatment of the seriously handicapped newborn (see chapter 14). There would, however, need to be an awareness of the differential legal status accorded to the foetus and the neonate. The latter has been accorded full legal status by virtue of having an existence independent of the mother.

12.7 CONSCIENTIOUS OBJECTION TO ABORTION

The Abortion Act 1967 makes provision for health-care workers to object on moral grounds to participating in an abortion. Section 4 of the Act provides that '. . . no person shall be under any duty, whether by contract or by any statutory or other legal requirement, to participate in any treatment authorised by this Act to which he has a conscientious objection'. The section goes on to state that, in legal proceedings, the person claiming to object has the burden of showing a conscientious objection. The section also makes it clear that it does not affect the duty of practitioners to participate in treatment which would be necessary to save life or prevent grave permanent injury to the physical or mental health of the pregnant woman. A refusal thereafter to perform an abortion in such circumstances would lead to criminal liability. This may even be an indictment for manslaughter, where the doctor is aware of the potentially fatal consequences of his refusal to the pregnant woman, yet still refuses to treat. The practical result of a refusal in non-emergency situations is that the medical practitioner would be under a duty to advise, even if this was merely to refer the patient to another practitioner willing to carry out the procedure.

The only issue so far to come before the courts on this section considered the ambit of the phrase 'participate in any treatment' (*Janaway* v *Salford Area Health Authority* [1989] AC 537, HL). Given the complexity of structure of the modern hospital or clinic, involvement in the process of abortion can take a number of forms, from the person on the reception desk to the nurse and medical practitioner who are more intimately involved.

Mrs Janaway was employed as a secretary/receptionist at a health centre. She was asked by a doctor to type a letter referring a patient to a consultant for advice on a possible abortion. Mrs Janaway was a practising Roman Catholic, and had a moral objection to the performance of abortion. She therefore refused to type the letter. Her refusal to give a reassurance that there would be no similar incident in the future led to her dismissal on the grounds of misconduct. There was an attempt to rely on s. 4. In court the assertion made was that the words should be given a wide interpretation to include preliminary arrangements for an abortion. The justification for such a view was that:

> . . . the acts attracting the protection afforded by s. 4(1) are intended to be coextensive with those which are authorised by s. 1(1) and which in the absence of that provision would be criminal. The criminal law about accessories treats one who aids and abets, counsels or procures a criminal act as liable to the same extent as a principal actor. In the absence of s. 1(1) the applicant by typing a letter of referral would be counselling or procuring an abortion, or at least helping to do so, and subject to a possible defence on the principle of *R* v *Bourne* [1939] 1 KB 687 would be criminally liable. Therefore any requirement to type such a letter is relieved, in the face of conscientious objection, by s. 4(1). (p. 570)

The House of Lords rejected the contention that the typing of the letter would be potentially criminal if the abortion legislation was not complied with. The House stated that the term 'participate in any treatment' held its ordinary meaning: participation in the medical process of abortion itself. Mrs Janaway was not involved in the process.

12.8 PARTICIPATION IN THE ABORTION PROCESS

A lawful abortion may only be carried out by a registered medical practitioner. Modern abortion techniques do not necessitate the continuous presence of the doctor with the patient. The legality of the involvement of nurses in the present-day process of abortion was considered extensively by the House of Lords in *Royal College of Nursing of the United Kingdom* v *Department of Health and Social Security* [1981] AC 800.

Aside from the initial surgical intervention of the doctor in the abortion by prostaglandin (a drug which stimulates the muscles to contract and premature labour to begin) the practitioner has little involvement in the rest of the process compared to nursing staff. Nursing staff, through the RCN, began this action because they were anxious about the danger of acting contrary to the 1967 Act, in that they were unsure whether they came within the term 'medical practitioner'. If they did not, they would be acting outside the Act, and their liability insurance would thereby be nullified, in addition to the obvious potential criminal liability under s. 58 of the Offences against the Person Act 1861.

Lord Diplock argued that the Abortion Act 1967 was designed both to state the broad grounds for a legal abortion, and of particular relevance here, to ensure that such abortions were carried out with the necessary skill and in hygienic conditions. He then went on to recognise modern abortion practice as a team effort. The interpretation to be placed on the Act should therefore take that practicality into account, with the registered medical practitioner retaining general control and responsibility. If medical practice commonly demands a particular physical act be undertaken by a medical practitioner, that must be done. Similarly, where it is common ground that doctors routinely instruct others to perform particular acts as part of the abortion process then that too should be done. In essence, the practitioner or that person's substitute should be available throughout the abortion process. If these guidelines are followed then the pregnancy is terminated by a registered medical practitioner and lawful provided the other requirements of the law are satisfied.

12.9 PREVENTING AN ABORTION

In a series of cases, fathers (or putative fathers) of the unborn have attempted to prevent a partner from having an abortion. The essence of the claims in each case have varied somewhat, but the fundamental grounds for making a claim have been that:

(a) The father has *locus standi* to mount a challenge to the abortion. The attempt is to have the words 'with the consent of the father' inserted into the Abortion Act 1967.

(b) The unborn child has a legal right to be recognised and protected. The father here is acting as a next friend of the unborn child and invoking the rights of that child.

(c)   The abortion itself would be a breach of the 1967 Act.

(d)   The father is a protector of the public interest in preventing the abortion.

In the cases which have considered these matters, none of the claims to stop an abortion has been successful.

The seminal case which, either overtly or covertly, considers many of the above claims is *Paton v British Pregnancy Advisory Service Trustees* [1979] QB 276. The husband sought an injunction against the BPAS and his wife, to prevent an abortion taking place without his consent. Immediately, the judge in this case, Sir George Baker P, spotted the difficulty of the claim for an injunction. As he questioned, 'If an injunction were ordered, what could be the remedy?' The answer appeared obvious: '. . . no judge could even consider sending a . . . wife to prison for breaking such an order'. The court was equally swift in recognising the importance to be attached to the fact that the abortion, if it took place, would not be in breach of the 1967 Act. The requirement of the husband's consent was nowhere to be found in the legislation, and it would not be the place of the judiciary to insert such a requirement. That would be a matter for Parliament.

The basis of the judgment is to be found in the now well-known statement that: 'The foetus cannot, in English law, in my view, have a right of its own at least until it is born and has a separate existence from its mother'. Ultimately Sir George Baker could see no *locus standi* to mount the action and concluded, '. . . this claim for an injunction is completely misconceived and must be dismissed'.

This view is supported by the recent case of *St George's Healthcare National Health Service Trust v S; R v Collins and others ex parte S* (1998) *The Times*, 8 May 1998. This, although not an abortion case, is another example of the reluctance of the courts to recognise and protect the legal rights of the unborn. In this case it was held that the right of a pregnant woman to refuse treatment is not diminished merely because her decision to exercise this right will result in the death of her unborn child, notwithstanding the fact that her decision might appear morally repugnant. Their Lordships' judgment in this case once again emphasises that an unborn child is not a separate person from its mother.

Furthermore, an equally recent decision of the Supreme Court of Canada supports the position of the English courts. In *Winnipeg Child and Family Services (Northwest Area) v G* (1998) 3 BHRC 611 Can SC the legal status of the unborn child was not recognised. In this case the respondent was five months pregnant and addicted to glue sniffing, which was known to be potentially damaging to the nervous system of the developing foetus. The appellants sought an order to place the respondent in the custody of the Director of Child and Family Services with a view to her detention in a health centre for treatment until the birth. A superior court judge made the order, but it was struck down on Appeal. The appellant accordingly appealed to the Supreme Court asking for the restoration of the detention order. It was held that the law does not recognise the unborn child as a legal or juridical person possessing any rights but has always treated the mother and the unborn child as one legal entity.

Ian Kennedy (1979) 42 MLR 324 has argued that other theoretical grounds could have been attempted to prevent termination of pregnancy. Some of them rather exotic. The husband in *Paton* could have invoked the wide notion of the unborn child's right to life. Such a declaration would have been analogous to Heilbron J's statement in the context of the sterilisation of the mentally handicapped that there exists a fundamental right to reproduce (see *Re D (A Minor) (Wardship; Sterilisation)* [1976] Fam 185). There are, however, two main problems with this approach. First it would be difficult to phrase the right in such a way as to make it justiciable in the courts. Secondly, Heilbron J was invoking the rights-based notion in relation to a legal person, whereas here the unborn has been declared on numerous occasions, *Paton v British Pregnancy Advisory Service Trustees* being just one example, to be a legal non-entity.

Another option might have been to frame the action as one for custody of the unborn child. Kennedy must be right when he states that this would only be the result of a bold act of judicial creativity; one which would appear unlikely given the limitations it would invariably place on the freedom of the pregnant woman.

An exotic legal argument could have based an action on the notion of property. Once more Kennedy admits the unusual nature of the argument, but it is, in a sense, the most factual reflection of the husband's claim: 'That child is half mine'. Nevertheless one can predict a level of judicial unease with such an approach.

The husband in *Paton* then took the case to the European Commission of Human Rights. The Commission needed to consider the applicability of art. 2 of the European Convention of Human Rights that 'Everyone's right to life shall be protected by law'. The Commission felt that the term 'Everyone' only applied postnatally. The husband's right to family life, and the unborn child's right to life must be subordinate to the rights of the mother where the abortion takes place on medical grounds.

In *C v S* [1988] QB 135, *Paton v British Pregnancy Advisory Service Trustees* was applied, but the basis of the action was somewhat different. The applicant, to stop the partner's abortion, contended that the doctor, in performing the abortion, would be in breach of the Infant Life Preservation Act 1929. As stated earlier (see 12.5.1), the contention was that the child had a gestational age of 18 weeks and therefore was 'capable of being born alive'. As has already been seen, there was considerable debate on whether such a foetus was so capable, as well as what the phrase itself meant. Heilbron J admitted the uncertainty of the phrase, indicating that interpretation based on potentiality, viability or mere live birth depended as much on moral as legal interpretation.

While dismissing the plaintiff's application on grounds substantially the same as *Paton v British Pregnancy Advisory Service Trustees*, Donaldson MR, in the Court of Appeal, concluded that the foetus of 18 weeks' development would still be incapable of breathing, so not 'capable of being born alive'. Therefore the termination would not be contrary to the 1967 Act as it then stood.

The debate on the right of the foetus to be protected was further considered in the case of *Re F (in utero)* [1988] Fam 122 (CA). This was a claim by a local authority to make an unborn child a ward of court to protect it from injury, due to the aberrant behaviour of the nomadic mother. May LJ concluded, as had the courts in *Paton v British Pregnancy Advisory Service Trustees* and *C v S*, that the court had no jurisdiction to entertain the application. There was a recognition that in providing legal protection for the unborn child the situation would invariably lead to conflict with the legal interests of the woman. The only way to make the wardship effective would have been physically to control the activities of the mother.

Although yet to be considered by the UK courts, the possibility exists that the father could frame the action as a protector of the public interest in preventing abortions. This has been considered by the Canadian courts in the significant case of *League for Life in Manitoba Inc. v Morgentaler* (1985) 19 DLR (4th) 703. The contention by the pro-life lobby was that Dr Morgentaler and the clinic he worked in were procuring unlawful miscarriages. The court after lengthy and heated debate found that the League had no *locus standi* to seek injunctive relief as protectors of the public interest, given the legality of the abortions taking place.

12.10 ABORTION AND THE LAW OF HOMICIDE

Murder is a common law offence. The definition still considered the most authoritative is that of Coke:

> Murder is when a man of sound memory, and of the age of discretion, unlawfully killeth within any county of the realm any reasonable creature *in rerum natura* under the king's peace, with malice aforethought, either expressed by the party or implied by law, so as the party wounded, or hurt etc., die within a year and a day after the same. (3 Inst 47)

The question is when life has begun as far as this common law definition is concerned. Life may be seen as beginning at conception, at various stages up to birth and after the moment of birth. The decision of the common law can be seen through three nineteenth-century cases which considered deaths that had occurred around the moment of birth.

In *R v Poulton* (1832) 5 Car & P 329, an illegitimate child was strangled by its mother at the point of birth. While finding insufficient evidence that the child had ever been fully born, Littledale J directed the jury that they would be required to find under the law of homicide: 'With respect to the birth, the being born must mean that the whole body is brought into the world; it is not sufficient that the child respires in the process of birth'. *R v Brain* (1834) 6 Car & P 349 was slightly less conservative in its approach, declaring that the child, while needing to be 'wholly in the world' need not have breathed.

The case of *R v Senior* (1832) 1 Mood CC 346 shows that an act which causes the death of a child born alive but which preceded the birth itself may constitute murder. A midwife, negligent in carrying out the birth, had compressed the skull of the child, causing its later death. The midwife was convicted of manslaughter, notwithstanding counsel's contention that the injuries were caused while the child was still en ventre sa mère, and therefore not a legally recognised person.

McCluskey v *HM Advocate* 1989 SLT 175, was a case of reckless driving which injured a pregnant woman, causing the death of the child after it had been born. The Road Traffic Act 1972, s. 1 (as substituted by the Criminal Law Act 1977, s. 50(1)) states: 'A person who causes the death of another person by driving a motor vehicle on a road recklessly shall be guilty of an offence'. The court, dismissing the driver's appeal, argued that it was irrelevant that the injuries had been caused while the child was *in utero*.

In *Kwok Chak Ming* v *The Queen* [1963] HKLR 349, the Hong Kong Court of Appeal decided that a man who had stabbed a nine-months pregnant woman in the abdomen was guilty of the manslaughter of the baby who had died three days later (having been delivered by emergency caesarian section) from the injuries received *in utero*. The decision neatly sidestepped the fact that it appeared to rest on the legal recognition of the child before it was born by arguing in terms of transferred malice. This countered the contention that the defendant could not form *mens rea* in relation to the unborn.

Now there is the potentially crucial *Attorney-General's Reference (No. 3 of 1994)* [1996] QB 581, which appears to create criminal liability on the part of a defendant who injures a pregnant woman, whose child dies after birth from the injuries, for the manslaughter, but not murder, of the child.

12.11 LEGALITY OF SPECIAL ABORTION PROCEDURES

12.11.1 Morning-after pills and intrauterine devices

These forms of post-coital birth control have the potential to cause particular legal problems under the law of abortion, because they are what are known as 'contragestive' or 'interceptive' rather than 'contraceptive'. The first issue is whether the use of the morning-after pill or its prescription would be an offence under ss. 58 or 59 of the 1861 Act unless complying with the provisions of the Abortion Act 1967. The issue of medical law here is the interpretation to be placed on ss. 58 and 59, particularly the phrase 'with intent to procure a miscarriage'.

The argument advanced that there would be a miscarriage under the legislation, and therefore potential criminal liability comes from John Keown ('Miscarriage: A Medico-Legal Analysis' [1984] Crim LR 608). Keown seeks to persuade that the construction of the term 'miscarriage' has been raised in several cases. He cites authority from the USA, India and Victoria to suggest that their tone considers the term to apply at any moment after conception irrespective of implantation in the uterus.

Support for Keown's view comes from Victor Tunkel [1974] Crim LR 461, who himself relies on a statement by Glanville Williams in '*Sanctity of Life and the Criminal Law*' (London: Faber & Faber, 1958):

At present both English law and the law of the great majority of the United States regard any interference with pregnancy, however early it may take place, as criminal, unless for therapeutic reasons. The foetus is a human life to be protected by the criminal law from the moment when the ovum is fertilised. (p. 141)

Tunkel refines this by stating:

To hold otherwise would, in effect, give a sort of free-for-all moratorium of a week or more during which every sort of abortionist could ply his craft with impunity. ([1974] Crim LR 461 at p. 465)

Glanville Williams, in his more recent *Textbook of Criminal Law*, 2nd ed. (London: Stevens, 1983) appears to change his mind on the interpretation to be given to the term 'miscarriage' as it applies to the IUD and morning-after pill. The preference now is for legal recognition of miscarriage dating from the point of implantation onwards.

There is, therefore, nothing to prevent the courts interpreting the word 'miscarriage' in a way that takes account of customary and approved birth control practices. (p. 294)

Williams's new interpretation was accepted by the Attorney-General (Hansard HC, 18 May 1983, col. 239).

In practical terms Kennedy and Grubb must be correct when they argue that the common-sense view of the term 'miscarriage' presupposes that something has actually been carried, at least in the sense of implantation in the uterus. Section 2(3) of the Human Fertilisation and Embryology Act 1990 ends doubt on the matter, because it states that 'For the purposes of this Act, a woman is not to be treated as carrying a child until the embryo has become implanted'.

12.11.2 Selective reduction of multiple pregnancy

The most accurate general description of selective reduction was made by the Voluntary Licensing Authority (the forerunner to the Human Fertilisation and Embryology Authority) in 1988:

. . . one or more embryos in a multiple pregnancy are selectively killed to allow others to develop. In multiple pregnancies resulting from infertility treatment the procedure is used to avoid large multiple births though the technique was originated to stop the development of abnormal embryos in a multiple pregnancy where the remainder were normal.

The key distinguishing feature between selective reduction and other forms of abortion is that selective reduction leads to the destroyed foetus being absorbed into the mother's body. The fact that it is not expelled may mean that there is no termination of a pregnancy. If this is the case then it is not within the ambit of the Abortion Act 1967, and therefore not regulated. The question thus becomes, is selective reduction covered by the Offences against the Person Act 1861, s. 58? If it is, would compliance with the terms of the 1967 Act make it lawful?

John Keown's view is that selective reduction is caught by s. 58, because:

> . . . it has long been accepted by both medical and legal authorities that 'miscarriage' pertains not to the destination of the foetal remains but to the failure of gestation. ('Selective Reduction of Multiple Pregnancy' (1987) 137 NLJ 1165)

If Keown is correct, it becomes important to decide whether the pregnancy has been 'terminated', given the fact that this is a requirement of the 1967 Act. D.P.T. Price has argued that termination of a pregnancy does encompass selective reduction, so it must be performed under the requirements of the 1967 Act.

To some extent this is now only of academic interest following the insertion of a new s. 5(2) into the Abortion Act 1967 by the Human Fertilisation and Embryology Act 1990:

> For the purposes of the law relating to abortion, anything done with intent to procure a woman's miscarriage (or, in the case of a woman carrying more than one foetus, her miscarriage of any foetus) is unlawfully done unless authorised by section 1 of this Act and, in the case of a woman carrying more than one foetus, anything done with intent to procure the miscarriage of any foetus is authorised by that section if—
>
> (a) the ground for termination of the pregnancy specified in subsection (1)(d) of that section applies in relation to any foetus and the thing is done for the purpose of procuring the miscarriage of that foetus, or
>
> (b) any of the other grounds for termination of the pregnancy specified in that section applies.

This means that selective reductions can take place on the ground of foetal abnormality or that the multiple pregnancy creates the amount of risk to the mother for s. 1(1)(a), (b), or (c) to be satisfied.

12.11.3 Abortion pills

The development of the drug Mifepristone (RU 486) means that effectively an abortion can take place without surgery or anaesthetic. RU 486 complicates the Keown–Tunkel debate about modern post-coital birth control methods. This drug can dislodge the implanted fertilised egg at a later stage than other methods. The argument is that a doctor who administers RU 486, knowing that a woman is pregnant, with intent to end the pregnancy, clearly intends to procure a miscarriage under the Offences against the Person Act 1861, s. 58, and will do so only if the terms of the 1967 Act are complied

with. The abortion pill was perceived as a late way of avoiding an inconven-
ient pregnancy, rather than being predominantly a means of therapeutic
abortion. As yet the legislature has not considered this matter apart from
inserting s. 1(3A) into the 1967 Act. This enables the Secretary of State to
limit approval for abortion to a class of places, where the treatment consists
of specified medicinal treatment. Approval also may require that the termination be carried out in a specified manner. This is clear anticipation of the
possible development of the abortion pill, which could potentially be sold at
pharmacies and therefore be used in a relatively unregulated manner.

12.12 CONCLUSION

Abortion poses numerous moral, ethical, human rights and legal dilemmas.
The deontological argument of the sanctity of life, if applied to the unborn,
would lead to a legal regime morally opposed to abortion and prohibiting the
doctor from performing it. Even where the doctor's clinical intuition inclines
towards the performance of an abortion, the moral superiority of law in
forwarding the concept of the categorical imperative – the moral theory of
'Do unto others', would control the inclinations of the doctor. There would
be no abortion in a regime based on this view of how medical law can do the
right thing. The utilitarian tradition equally is hampered in being an effective
moral agent for doing the right thing. The calculation of the consequences,
good or bad, depends fundamentally on the moral existence of the unborn.
If there is a moral weight to be placed on the unborn, then the second-order
difficulty is to compare the consequences for the mother with those for the
child in considering the moral character of proposed action, which is no easy
task.

There appears to have been some judicial unease at getting the law involved
in this area of medicine. There is the question whether regulation, in that it
necessarily hampers freedom, does more good than the harm of limiting
freedom of action. The law of abortion at present is indicative of that unease.
There is regulation, but it is so open-textured in the way it is worded that
there has to be a suspicion that there is a distinct element of our pluralist
society that feels that the law has no real place here. The matter revolves
around clinical intuiton and patient rights.

The development of legal demands framed in human rights phraseology
takes English medical law towards a more mature analysis of the rights and
duties of patient and doctor. The tension which remains becomes re-focused
with the development of medical, particularly diagnostic, technology. While
at once indicating that the foetus is there and can be seen and is thereby
'person-alised', it gives the option of safe termination for the woman at a
much earlier stage, with greater knowledge of the qualities of the unborn.
Society and thereafter the law are embroiled in a debate based on image,
language and perspective. There seems to be no possibility of medical law
creating compromise where there is no consensus, but any decision that is
made by society should be more clearly articulated in medical law legislation
than exists at present.

Further reading

Bowles, T. G. A., and Bell, N. M. N., 'Abortion on Demand or Request: Is it Legal?' (1980) LS Gaz 24 September.
Fortin, J., 'Legal Protection for the Unborn Child' (1988) 51 MLR 54.
Hoggett, A. J. C., 'The Abortion Act 1967' [1968] Crim LR 247.
Keown, I. J. K., 'Miscarriage: A Medico-Legal Analysis' [1984] Crim LR 608.
Tunkel, V., 'Abortion: How Early, How Late, and How Legal?' [1979] 2 BMJ 253.

THIRTEEN
Sterilisation and the mentally handicapped

13.1 INTRODUCTION

There are several reasons why it may be necessary or desired that a sterilisation operation take place. First, it may be that a couple no longer want to have any (or more) children. Sterilising the man or woman here is simply an all but permanent form of contraception. Secondly, there may be therapeutic reasons why a woman requires a sterilisation. A common reason being, for example, the fact that the woman suffers from heavy periods, which can be painful, anxious, and in certain situations a hazard to general health. The reason that will form the focus of this chapter is the situation where a mentally handicapped woman is thought by those caring for her to be at risk of becoming pregnant, and would be incapable of looking after a child, or perhaps unable to form a maternal bond through a lack of understanding of the concept of reproduction. Further it may be that the carers fear that the woman would not be able to cope with the physical fact of pregnancy and birth. This latter reason for performing a sterilisation has been rightly been described as 'a minefield of powerful objections' (see Mason and McCall Smith, *Law and Medical Ethics*, 4th ed. (London: Butterworths, 1994), p. 83).

In the very important work *On Liberty*, the utilitarian John Stuart Mill argued that:

> . . . the only purpose for which power can be rightfully exercised over any member of a civilised community, against his will, is to prevent harm to others. His own good, whether physical or moral, is not a sufficient warrant. . . . It is, perhaps, hardly necessary to say that the doctrine is meant to apply only to human beings in the maturity of their faculties.

Consider how a utilitarian or deontological medical law would react to the following situation.

Ann is 17 years old, but mentally handicapped since birth. Her level of intellect is that of a six-year-old. She lives with her mother and housebound father. Sue, the mother, has noticed that Ann has been talking to some local boys of her age in the local park, when Sue has been helping her husband. Ann has been holding hands with one of them, and they have been seen kissing. Sue consults the local care worker, saying, 'I'm terrified she's going to get pregnant. I can just about cope with her and my husband. I'll never manage a new born baby as well.' When Ann is asked about being sterilised she clearly does not know what it means, and becomes distressed when sexual intercourse, pregnancy and birth are explained to her. She calms down when asked if she wants a baby, and replies, 'I would love to cuddle a real doll from my tummy'. All parties concerned agree she could not be trusted to take oral contraceptives. Any other contraceptive measure would react badly with drugs she is already taking to help with the occasional fits she gets. The mother, doctor and care worker all wish Ann to be sterilised.

The issue of non-consensual sterilisation has been fiercely debated for some time in this country, and, as will be seen, has been perceived as a shadowy element of US medico-legal and civil libertarian legal history. English academic legal writers have not stinted themselves in their criticisms of the development of English medical law. The general but important ethical, human rights and legal issues are set out by Josephine Shaw:

> One of the most problematic interactions between law and sexuality lies at the point where a medical device for preventing conception – sterilisation – emerges as an ostensibly convenient solution to the difficulties thrown up by the exercise of sexual autonomy on the part of a group of people for whom conception is by and large seen as socially undesirable: those suffering from a mental disorder or handicap. Sterilisation challenges the law, since it represents an interference in bodily integrity and reproductive autonomy which, in the absence of the consent of the subject to the sterilisation, would be seen in liberal terms as a human rights violation, attracting the sanction of penalties under the law. ('Regulating Sexuality: A Legislative Framework for Non-Consensual Sterilisation' in McVeigh and Wheeler (eds), *Law, Health and Medical Regulation* (Dartmouth, 1992), at p. 75)

Once more the case law development reveals a shifting balance between patient rights, patient welfare and medical and judicial paternalism. Again, the decisions slowly fashion a rights-based medical law perspective, only for the judiciary to retreat from that to the comfort of a test of best interests of the mentally handicapped predicated on the *Bolam* standard of decision-making.

13.2 CONSENSUAL STERILISATION

Before considering the debate on sterilisation and the mentally handicapped, it is important to be aware that there has been voiced a wider objection to sterilisation per se. In *Bravery* v *Bravery* [1954] 1 WLR 1169, there was an allegation of cruelty as a ground for a woman's divorce from her husband. The cruelty was said to have come from the fact that he underwent a sterilisation operation without her consent. During the course of his dissenting judgment Denning LJ voiced this general objection:

> When [a sterilisation operation] is done with the man's consent for a just cause, it is quite lawful; as, for instance, when it is done to prevent the transmission of a hereditary disease. But when it is done without just cause or excuse, it is unlawful, even though the man consents to it. Take a case where a sterilisation operation is done so as to enable a man to have the pleasure of sexual intercourse, without shouldering the responsibilities attaching to it. The operation then is plainly injurious to the public interest. It is degrading to the man himself. It is injurious to his wife and to any woman whom he may marry, to say nothing of the way it opens to licentiousness; and, unlike contraceptives, it allows no room for a change of mind on either side. It is illegal, even though the man consents to it.

This view does not now hold sway, given that the National Health Service (Family Planning) Amendment Act 1972 (now superseded by the National Health Service Act 1977) made provision for voluntary vasectomy services on the same basis as other contraception services.

13.3 NON-CONSENSUAL STERILISATION

13.3.1 Historical development of sterilisation

The debate on sterilising the mentally handicapped has been a long, and as the case law will show, a vociferous one. The debate has as its emotive backdrop the history of late nineteenth and early twentieth centuries. The case law will show that the judiciary of a number of common law jurisdictions are aware of the dark side of this history. Sterilisation for eugenic purposes was not a product of Nazi Germany, although that regime was the most horrific expression of the perversion of the concept of eugenics. The theory that the species could be improved or perfected by a cleansing of the gene pool through selective breeding was introduced by Sir Francis Galton at University College London in 1869. It was not long before a number of US state reformatories were using the concept to justify the sterilisation of what were deemed to be those carrying undesirable traits within society. By the 1920s, 28 States had followed Indiana's 1907 lead and enacted compulsory sterilisation statutes (see M. Freeman, 'Sterilising the Mentally Handicapped' in Freeman (ed.), *Medicine, Ethics and the Law* (London: Stevens, 1988)). One of the best known, and to some most frightening, judicial justifications for the performance of these irreversible operations was found in *Buck* v *Bell* (1927) 274 US 200. Carrie Buck was described as the 'feeble-minded' daughter of a mother who was herself described (among other things) as 'feeble-minded'. Her proposed sterilisation was challenged on 'due process' and 'cruel and unusual punishment' grounds under the US Constitution. The Supreme Court's view was that it was not going to be done as a punishment, but as a means to facilitate her freedom within the community. One of the most chilling quotes comes from Mr Justice Oliver Wendell Holmes (at p. 207):

> We have seen more than once that the public welfare may call upon the best citizens for their lives. It would be strange if it could not call upon those who already sap the strength of the State for these lesser sacrifices, often not felt to be such by those concerned, in order to prevent our being swamped with incompetents. It is better for all the world, if instead of waiting to execute degenerate offspring for crime, or to let them starve for their imbecility, society can prevent those who are manifestly unfit from continuing their kind. The principle that sustains compulsory vaccination is broad enough to cover cutting the fallopian tubes. Three generations of imbeciles are enough.

The Nazi compulsory sterilisation law came about in 1933, with the formation of what were known as 'hereditary health courts'. The law which brought about this savage development was known as the law on 'the prevention of hereditary diseases in future generations'. Enforced sterilisation took place openly after this time. The grounds for enforced sterilisations were: (a) hereditary blindness or deafness, (b) alcoholism, (c) being a Gypsy, (d) children, known as 'Rhineland bastards', who had been fathered after the First World War by French North African occupation troops.

Other races and cultures were included, and the policy became even more radical than sterilisation and certainly more horrific.

13.3.2 Potential areas of ethical and legal debate

Many of the aspects of the debate surrounding the sterilisation of the mentally handicapped will be familiar, having been encountered in the areas of medical law that have already been considered. While the debate itself encompasses many concepts, the essential point of the legality and scope of non-consensual sterilisation will be seen in the development of the case law. The matter revolves around the relative weight given to the following:

(a)   The right of the individual to bodily integrity and autonomy.
(b)   The right of the individual to reproduce.
(c)   The concept, as a matter of ethics and law, of consent.
(d)   The concept of the 'best interests' of the individual concerned.
(e)   The differentiation between 'therapeutic' and 'non-therapeutic' concepts of the sterilisation procedure for the mentally handicapped individual.
(f)   The existence of a policy of eugenic sterilisation and societal interests in the practice.

13.3.3   The right to reproduce: *Re D (A Minor) (Wardship: Sterilisation)* [1976] Fam 185

Child D suffered from a condition known as Sotos syndrome. The relevant characteristics of this condition were that B suffered accelerated growth, epilepsy, clumsiness, behavioural problems including emotional instability and aggressive outbursts, and mental impairment described as leading to dull intelligence or possibly more serious retardation. D had not settled well in her original school so was moved to a school more equipped to deal with her particular traits. D was assessed there as having the intelligence of a child about nine years of age. There was some evidence that D might improve further over time. Nevertheless, D's mother was unconvinced of the actual or possible improvement and remained convinced that she would be unable to look after herself or any children she might give birth to. A medical expert agreed with this latter theory despite acknowledging that, in time, she would have the mental capacity to marry. There was thus debate on the social and behavioural reasons for the proposed sterilisation. Application was made to make the child a ward of court to prevent the sterilisation being carried out.

Heilbron J, in giving judgment, had a number of issues to consider, not least of which was the appropriateness of using the wardship procedure. Heilbron J was swayed by the fact that the wardship jurisdiction

> is founded on the obvious necessity that the law should place somewhere the care of individuals who cannot take care of themselves, particularly in cases where it is clear that some care should be thrown around them. (*Wellesley* v *Duke of Beaufort* (1827) 2 Russ 1 at p. 20 per Lord Eldon LC)

Heilbron J was of the view that this was such a case due to the fact that the proposed sterilisation would involve 'the deprivation of a basic human right, namely, the right of a woman to reproduce, and, therefore it would be, if performed on a woman for non-therapeutic reasons and without her consent, a violation of such right' (at p. 193).

As to the necessity of performing the operation, the court heard evidence from a doctor who argued forcefully that such an operation would not be of any therapeutic value in treating the syndrome from which D suffered. In addition, the evidence indicated that the future was uncertain, and it could be that D might be able to understand the implications of such an operation and be able to make her own informed choice at some future date.

With regard to the involvement of the wardship court in such decisions, a majority of the consultants agreed, and found support from Heilbron J, that to perform a sterilisation operation not for the treatment of some disease or illness can never be within the sole clinical judgment of the medical profession.

Heilbron J concluded:

> A review of the whole of the evidence leads me to the conclusion that in a case of a child of 11 years of age, where the evidence shows that her mental

and physical condition and attainments have already improved, and where her future prospects are as yet unpredictable, where the evidence also shows that she is unable as yet to understand and appreciate the implications of this operation and could not give a valid or informed consent, but the likelihood is that in later years she will be able to make her own choice, where, I believe, the frustration and resentment of realising (as she would one day) what had happened could be devastating, an operation of this nature is, in my view contra-indicated. (p. 196)

It is possible that, aside from the importance attached to the right to reproduce, the court may have been influenced by the non-therapeutic nature of the proposed sterilisation, the irreversible nature of the operation and the uncertainties surrounding D's capacity to improve and thereby give valid consent (or refusal!) later on. Heilbron J may have also feared that allowing D to be sterilised would open the door to sterilisation for the convenience of carers and possibly society, rather than for the therapy of the mentally handicapped patient.

Bainham ('Handicapped Girls and Judicial Parents' (1987) 103 LQR 334) has criticised Heilbron J for having failed to address sufficiently the issues that were introduced by the case. It was felt that to indicate potentially relevant issues was not comprehensive enough. Whatever the force of this criticism it was not long before another common law jurisdiction, Canada, provided such a comprehensive analysis, while substantially agreeing with the sentiments expressed in Re D.

Arguably a good medical law is one which respects human rights. It will be recalled from 1.5 that human rights are based on society's promise to aid and guarantee the liberty and freedom from exploitation of the weaker members of society. There is no doubt that children (or adults) in the situation of child D are prime candidates for exploitation and therefore need the protection of society's human rights promises. Human rights law contains within it a certain tension, apparent in the issue of non-consensual sterilisation, between the protection of individual autonomy and the right of the mentally handicapped to be protected. Human rights law contains, as well as an autonomy principle, a welfare principle. In assessing the scope and applicability of human rights here, there are three rights to be considered. First there is the right to procreative freedom (the right to reproduce). Secondly, there is the right to sexual freedom (the right of sexual choice). If child D had been sterilised, she would arguable have lost the former, but not the latter. As will be repeated in cases of non-consensual sterilisation, one has to be clear of the implications of the particular sterilisation on D. Some criticism of subsequent cases on non-consensual sterilisation seems to adopt a vision of rights which is a blinkered or utopian rather than placing them in their correct medical law context. The third aspect of rights is the welfare aspect. Human rights, and medical law, have a place for a limited, strictly demarcated and arguably legislative system of non-consensual sterilisation, based primarily on protecting sexual freedom, denying procreative freedom, but protecting from physical and mental suffering (see, for example, F. Scroggie, 'Why Do Parents

Want Their Children Sterilised?' (1990) 2 JCL 25). Therefore Bainham may well be right. There is a great deal for medical law to consider in non-consensual sterilisation.

13.3.4 Best interests and the therapeutic–non-therapeutic divide: *Re Eve* (1986) 31 DLR (4th) 1

At the time in question Eve was 24 years of age, and suffered from a condition which has as a feature mild to moderate retardation. Learning skills were described as limited, but Eve was attracted to and attractive to men. Eve was further described as capable of carrying out the mechanical functions of a mother, but only under supervision. A feature of the condition, which proved important in this, and certainly in later cases in England, was that Eve had some notion of the nature of a family unit, but could have no concept of the relationship between intercourse, pregnancy and birth.

La Forest J, in giving the judgment of the Supreme Court of Canada, recognised that Eve's proposed sterilisation was not intended to treat any existing medical condition, so the operation, if performed, would be non-therapeutic. Eve's underlying mental handicap would not be cured or even treated by the sterilisation operation.

Before this issue was discussed in detail, the court had to illuminate the essential issues of the case. These were:

(a)   Whether, in the absence of statutory authority, the court's inherent *parens patriae* jurisdiction allows it to consent to the sterilisation of an adult who is mentally incompetent.

(b)   What standard of proof is to be applied where application is made to the court for its substituted consent to a non-therapeutic procedure on behalf of a mentally incompetent adult?

(c)   Does the court have a duty to protect an individual against sterilisation without consent?

(d)   If the court has a duty to so protect, when, if ever, will it permit the sterilisation of a mental incompetent who is incapable of giving consent?

(e)   Does the individual have the right to choose not to procreate, and, if so, does the court have jurisdiction to make that choice on behalf of an individual who is unable to do so?

La Forest J held that there was an inherent jurisdiction of the court to look after those who cannot look after themselves. There needed to be a symmetry between the care afforded to minors under the *parens patriae* jurisdiction and the care the courts should afford to those who, while adult in years, are as incapable of making decisions as minors. It was recognised that the jurisdiction, while seeming potentially unlimited (see *Re X (A Minor) (Wardship: Jurisdiction)* [1975] Fam 47), was subject to an important factual qualification: 'The jurisdiction must be exercised in accordance with the underlying principle that it be exercised for the protection of the person for whose benefit it is exercised'.

The precise nature of the exercise the courts were to undertake in such situations was something which taxed La Forest J. Through an analysis of US decisions there was discerned two clear lines of approach to the issue: the *best interests* test and the *substituted judgment* test (see also in relation to the selective non-treatment of the handicapped neonate, in chapter 14). Having reviewed the development of authority, La Forest J recognised that either test would inevitably lead to uncertainties (*Re Guardianship of Hayes* (1980) 608 P 2d 635). Nevertheless US courts had sought to provide a list of guidelines to help decision-makers in deciding whether the particular circumstances warranted a sterilisation in the best interests of the patient. However, they were themselves prone to wide interpretation. The US case of *Re Guardianship of Hayes* had indicated the breadth of the test proposed.

The substituted judgment test was applied in the US case of *Re Grady* (1981) 426 A 2d 467. The decision whether to sterilise an adult with Down's syndrome focused primarily on the rights of the handicapped individual. The right particularly focused on was the right to procreate, which was seen as a fundamental one. With this in mind, La Forest J introduced the substituted judgment test as a test to:

> attempt to determine what decision the mental incompetent would make, if she was reviewing her situation as a competent person, but taking account of her mental incapacity as one factor in her decision. It allows the court to consider a number of factors bearing directly upon the condition of the mental incompetent. (p. 27)

What the substituted judgment test also allowed, as indicated by US legal authority, was that in focusing on what the actual patient would want (albeit a necessarily fictitious exercise), the court could take account of the rights of that person.

La Forest J held that the practical and logical difficulties of the test did not mean that it should not be used. It was a test which made 'good' medical law because it was as subjective to the patient as possible, and respected individual rights. Overall, La Forest J felt that the best interests test was not sufficiently stringent or workable. The main thrust to the objection was that it is not an objective, rights-based test at all, but one dependent on the subjective prejudices of the decision-maker. La Forest J continued that sterilisation applications have to be looked upon carefully. There is judicial recognition here that while there are complex values, benefits, rights and interests involved, there is also the danger that the dark history of the development of the practice of sterilisation might cloud the vision of the decision-makers, at the cost of patient welfare or human rights. In addition, to ignore history may also be to ignore the fact that there is still a tendency to see the mentally handicapped as rather less than fully human, and therefore less deserving of the protective mechanisms that the law can offer.

La Forest J referred in considerable detail, in coming to his decision, to the Canadian Law Reform Commission, *Sterilisation*, Working Paper 24 (1979) which revealed a number of important perspectives on the reality of non-consensual sterilisation. These guided the court strongly, yet appeared to have been largely ignored elsewhere. In their introduction to the report, the Commission make a point that should be borne in mind throughout discussion of non-consensual sterilisation:

> Sterilisation as a medical procedure is distinct, because except in rare cases, if the operation is not performed, the physical health of the person involved is not in danger, necessity or emergency not normally being factors in the decision to undertake the procedure. In addition to its being elective it is for all intents and purposes irreversible. (p. 3)

Later on the paper notes evidence it received that indicated the profound psychological impact sterilisation can have on the individual. It was found that attitudes to sex and parenthood vary as widely amongst the mentally handicapped as the competent. The report goes on to confirm the suspicion that the mentally handicapped who are told of their sterilisations sometime later feel themselves to be worth less than others. They perceive themselves as something less than normal.

Some of the reasons put forward for sterilisation in *Re Eve*, and other applications that have followed, have rested on rather more shaky ground than would at first sight appear. It was stated that Eve would suffer unduly from the trauma of birth. In response La Forest J observed that the Commission Working Paper itself argued something different:

> For this argument to be held valid would require that it could be demonstrated that the stress of delivery was greater in the case of mentally handicapped persons than it is for others. Considering the generally known wide range of post-partum response would likely render this a difficult case to prove. (p. 60)

La Forest J was not convinced by the assertion that there would be no maternal bond. The Working Paper again concludes that the mentally handicapped can show a marked affection for their children. It has to be admitted that the mentally handicapped might have difficulty coping, but this is a social question, which La Forest J observed 'is not limited to incompetents'. Further such a social difficulty does not provide grounds for the invocation of the *parens patriae* jurisdiction of the court.

Having considered in detail the arguments and questions raised above, La Forest J resolved them into a relatively simple statement of principle:

> The grave intrusion on a person's rights and the certain physical damage that ensues from non-therapeutic sterilisation without consent, when compared to the highly questionable advantages that can result from it, have persuaded me that it can never safely be determined that such a procedure is for the benefit of that person. Accordingly, the procedure should never be authorised for non-therapeutic purposes under the *parens patriae* jurisdiction. (p. 32)

La Forest J admitted the difficulties of precision where concepts such as 'therapeutic against non-therapeutic' and 'best interests' were concerned. By their very nature these were both subjective and to an extent value-judgmental. It was' this inherent vagueness and even inapplicability that the Law Lords were to seize on in the leading, and arguably most controversial, case in this area of medical law, which will be considered next.

13.3.5 An alternative best interests test: *Re B (A Minor) (Wardship: Sterilisation)* [1988] AC 199

Child B was 17 years old at the time of the hearing. She was an epileptic who had a mental age of five or six. The evidence indicated that the child had no basic understanding of the connection between sexual intercourse, pregnancy and birth. The evidence further showed that the concept of birth itself would be alien and alarming to her, and she would be unable to care for any child born. Nevertheless, B was exhibiting the normal sexual drives of a person of her physical age, and there was concern that she might be seduced and become pregnant. The obvious option of placing her on a course of contraceptive drugs was not possible because they would react with the drugs she was prescribed for her handicapped condition. Further, her condition meant that she could not be trusted to take contraceptive pills. The local authority was not in favour of sending B to an institution, so applied that she be made a ward of court with a view to a sterilisation operation taking place. B's mother supported this application.

Lord Hailsham of St Marylebone LC immediately recognised that the paramount consideration of the wardship court was the 'best interests' of the ward. Obviously aware of the public attention and outcry over the lower courts' decision to approve the sterilisation, Lord Hailsham was forthright in his comment that:

> . . . there is no issue of public policy other than the application of the above principle which can conceivably be taken into account, least of all (since the opposite appears to have been considered in some quarters) any question of eugenics. (p. 202)

Lord Hailsham was aware of the difficulties of wardship if the case were delayed, and anticipated difficulties which occurred in later cases where the party whose sterilisation was in issue was of the age of majority. Lest public criticism were that the decision had thus been rushed by the House of Lords, Lord Hailsham again sought to defend himself by stating:

> We should be no wiser in 12 months' time than we are now and it would be doubtful then what legal courses would be open in the circumstances. (p. 203)

The House was referred to the judgment of the Supreme Court of Canada in *Re Eve* (1986) 31 DLR (4th) 1. Lord Hailsham replied to the notion that there could never be a sterilisation for non-therapeutic purposes in an important, but extensively questioned, statement of judicial attitude to mental handicap and human rights in medical law. His lordship said that it was:

> . . . totally unconvincing and in startling contradiction to the welfare principle which should be the first and paramount consideration in wardship cases. Moreover, for the purposes of the present appeal I find the distinction they purport to draw between 'therapeutic' and 'non-therapeutic' purposes of this operation in relation to the facts of the present case . . . as totally meaningless, and, if meaningful, quite irrelevant to the correct application of the welfare principle. To talk of the 'basic right' to reproduce of an individual who is not capable of knowing the causal connection between intercourse and childbirth, the nature of pregnancy, what is involved in delivery, unable to form maternal instincts or to care for a child appears to me wholly to part company with reality. (p. 203–4)

The House of Lords, while criticising La Forest J in *Re Eve*, sought to distinguish *Re D (A Minor) (Wardship: Sterilisation)* [1976] Fam 185 factually, in that the child in *Re D* did appear to have the possibility of improvement. The child in *Re B*, on the other hand, would never have the opportunity of an understanding of the most basic issues, let alone gain the capacity to give informed consent. The decision in *Re B* was that where the best interests of the law require it, the court would be willing, as guardian of the child, to authorise sterilisation, notwithstanding the absence of the patient's consent.

In concluding, Lord Oliver of Aylmerton sought to reassure that the case was not about eugenics: 'it is not about the convenience of those whose task it is to care for the ward or the anxieties of her family; and it involves no general principle of public policy ' (p. 212).

One of the most effective critics of the decision in *Re B*, Freeman ('Sterilising the Mentally Handicapped' in M. Freeman (ed.), *Medicine, Ethics and the Law* (London: Stevens, 1988) has argued that *Re B* was decided wrongly for a number of reasons.

First, it is contended that B's best interests were both inadequately defined and inadequately considered. Freeman describes the concept as both value-laden and indeterminate. This indeterminacy is shown by the fact that the courts in both *Re Eve* and *Re B* said they were acting in the best interests of the ward, yet they reached opposite conclusions. One is forced into a dual notion of best interests, which may be dependent on the particular case presented before the court or, as in *Re Eve*, a global term capable of being expressed identically whatever the merits of the proposed sterilisation. English law appears to individualise best interests to the case before the court; other jurisdictions appear to state simply that it can never be in the best interests to perform non-therapeutic sterilisation.

Freeman argues that, despite the difficulties of definition, there are some factual matters which the court should have taken account of in *Re B* in deciding if the sterilisation were truly in B's best interests. It is a fact that the likelihood of B being fertile was low. Most members of the population who are mentally handicapped are incapable of having children as a physiological fact. Concern was also expressed about making predictions about future development. The manifest inability to foretell future events accurately in this area should be an indication that sterilisation should be a last resort. The simple point is: given that prediction is notoriously difficult, one should be wary of undertaking an irreversible procedure.

A further line of attack can be based on the acknowledgement in *Re D* and implicit in the judgment of the House of Lords in *Re B* that there does exist a right to reproduce. While *Re D* appeared not to qualify this right in any way, in *Re B* their lordships sought to conflate it with cognisance and recognition. Lord Hailsham said that the concept of a right to reproduce meant nothing to B. The House went on to utilise this to argue that in addition B could not exercise this right to reproduce (a manifestly dubious notion!). Overall, the tenor of the judgments was that the right only existed if a valid choice could be made whether to and in what way to exercise it. What needs to be borne in mind when debating the relative weight to be given to this right to reproduce is whether such a right is considered from a subjective or an objective viewpoint. In *Re D* and *Re Eve* there appeared to be an objective recognition of the right, notwithstanding that the mentally handicapped person might not have been aware of it. In *Re B* there had to be subjective knowledge of and appreciation of its existence. Overall Freeman's criticisms of *Re B* are:

(a)   The House of Lords put what it thought of as B's best interests before her rights.

(b)   There was a refusal to accept that best interests should really mean 'best medical interests'.

(c)   The case, as a whole, gave too little consideration to rights, and did not take them seriously.

There have been numerous other criticisms of the decision in *Re B* (see the reading list at the end of this chapter), but many of them revolve around the 'slippery slope' argument. This can often be invoked, and is difficult to deny, in many branches of medical law (consider its use in the debate about the scope of s. 1(1)(d) of the amended Abortion Act 1967 – see 12.6.2.3, or in relation to the growth of voluntary euthanasia in the Netherlands – see chapter 15). Here it might be said that the weight of historical evidence points towards the existence of the slope of abuse.

There is difficulty from these early cases in defining terms such as 'best interests' and 'therapeutic–non-therapeutic', but these have remained the central terms for consideration in England and other Commonwealth jurisdictions that have, at least to some extent, developed a more sophisticated notion of what circumstances are encompassed by such phrases. The cases after *Re B* had other issues to confront in addition to those considered above, and in general terms indicate that in English medical law at least, there has been a liberalisation of the policy of sterilising the mentally handicapped.

The slippery slope does appear to have been constructed by the House of Lords in *Re B*. It is based strangely on the ambivalence of their lordships. It is the first example of what will clearly be seen as:

> The apparent ease with which the courts have reached their decisions, dealing, seemingly in passing, with some of the most intractable moral issues of our time, such as the conflict between sexual and procreative freedom, the conflict between paternalism and autonomy and the continuing influence of eugenicist and discriminatory thinking, allowing simple assertion to become the substitute for argument. (Shaw, in McVeigh and Wheeler (eds), *Law, Health and Medical Regulation* (Dartmouth, 1992), p. 81)

13.3.6   A therapeutic–non-therapeutic test: *Secretary, Department of Health and Community Services* v *JWB and SMB* (1992) 175 CLR 218

While this is a decision from Australia, it has persuasive significance for English medical law for a number of reasons. It was a comprehensive consideration of the development of the case law and concepts in a number of jurisdictions, and went beyond the perceived procedural mandate of where the power to authorise a sterilisation operation lies. It also sought to point the way in which the law relating to the sterilisation of the mentally handicapped should develop, more in line with a rights-based approach to medical law and the diminishing dominance of the medical profession in the decision-making process.

Natasha Cica ('Sterilising the Intellectually Disabled' (1993) 1 Med L Rev 186) considered the three major areas of concern of the Australian High Court as:

(a)   the usefulness of attempts to distinguish between therapeutic and non-therapeutic sterilisations;

(b)   the respective roles of the court and of parents; and

(c)   the adequacy of the 'best interests' test in determining the lawfulness of a proposed non-therapeutic sterilisation.

The factual background to the various discussions was the proposed sterilisation of a 'mentally handicapped' 14-year-old girl (although one should note that the High Court was aware of the value judgments involved in defining the individual in these terms, and therefore preferred the phrase 'intellectually disabled'). While one admits the wide-ranging nature of the debate, the issue resolved around the simple procedural question: Who could authorise the sterilisation on the child's behalf?

Evidently, in considering the first issue, the court was confronted with two lines of case law. *Re D (A Minor) (Wardship: Sterilisation)* [1976] Fam 185 and (more directly) *Re Eve* (1986) 31 DLR (4th) 1 had sought to distinguish strongly between the terms 'therapeutic' and 'non-therapeutic', but without any notable success in seeking to accurately define what the terms meant.

Re B (A Minor) (Wardship: Sterilisation) [1988] AC 199 and *Re F (Mental Patient: Sterilisation)* [1990] 2 AC 1 (see 13.4.1 for a consideration of the latter case) pounced on that lack of specificity and found that the terms were 'meaningless' or 'irrelevant' to the issues at hand, and based the decision on 'best interests'.

13.3.6.1 Therapeutic medical treatment In *JWB and SMB* Brennan J, while dissenting, sought to define therapeutic and non-therapeutic:

> I would define treatment (including surgery) as therapeutic when it is administered for the chief purpose of preventing, removing or ameliorating a cosmetic deformity, a pathological condition or a psychiatric disorder, provided the treatment is appropriate for and proportionate to the purpose for which it is administered. 'Non-therapeutic' medical treatment is descriptive of treatment which is inappropriate or disproportionate having regard to the cosmetic deformity, pathological condition or psychiatric disorder for which the treatment is administered and of treatment which is administered chiefly for other purposes. (p. 269)

The court went on to regard the boundary between the two as significant as a protector of human dignity here and one that was more in accordance with legal principle than the 'best interests' test, which was regarded as crude. Brennan J quoted with wholehearted approval Ian Kennedy's view that such a banal best interests test in transforming complex moral and social questions into a question of fact, leaves the courts in the hands of 'experts' who assemble a dossier of fact and opinion on matters which they deem relevant without reference to any checklist of legal requirements (at pp. 272–3). The contention once more is that the judiciary have handed the legal questions back to the medical profession. The House of Lords, in *Re B (A Minor) (Wardship: Sterilisation)* [1988] AC 199, by deciding that the therapeutic–non-therapeutic divide was irrelevant, left themselves with a test that was meaningless. There were no legal guidelines that could be utilised from case to case other than the amorphous concept of 'best interests'. As Brennan J in *JWB and SMB* appreciated, 'Absent any rule or guideline, that approach simply creates an unexaminable discretion in the repository of the power' (at p. 271). This is supported by Ian Kennedy, who says that the truth is that the 'best interests' test is no test at all, merely a conclusion 'of social policy' ('Patients, Doctors and Human Rights' in Blackburn and Taylor (eds), *Human Rights for the 1990s* (1991) at pp. 91–2).

The court's criticism of the best interests test is thus based on the conception that it is overly pragmatic, particularly given the human rights perspective of the decisions being taken by the court, and that it is insufficiently stringent given the irreversibility of the operation.

The best interests test has been subject to sustained criticism since its articulation in *Re B*. Freeman described the decision in *Re B* as 'Nazi-like'. Other commentators felt that the inadequacies of this test meant that the situation was similar to neutering pet animals. *Re B* had focused on the need to establish what would be in the best interests of the patient. The House of Lords, it could be argued, articulated the conclusion of a debate without any reasoned notion of how that conclusion was arrived at. The third issue raised by Natasha Cica is resolved by the decision in *JWB and SMB*. The best interests test as it is currently understood in English medical law is patently inadequate for such a potentially Draconian task. While rejecting such a test the court had to be aware that there would always be difficulties of the border between therapeutic and non-therapeutic. That to the court did not mean that this test was a meaningless one:

> *Proportionality* and *purpose* are the legal factors which determine the therapeutic nature of medical treatment. Proportionality is determined as a question of medical fact. Purpose is ascertained by reference to all the circumstances but especially to the physical or mental condition which the treatment is appropriate to affect.

Where the court in *Re Eve* (1986) 31 DLR (4th) 1 had considered that there could never be an authorisation of a sterilisation designated as 'non-therapeutic', the majority of the Australian High Court found that one could be performed, but only with the court's authorisation. One now sees the significance of declaring a sterilisation to be for one or the other purpose but also how elusive the terms remain.

Natasha Cica concludes correctly that the court was attempting as far as possible to make a differentiation between best social interests and best medical interests, with the former being considered non-therapeutic and the latter therapeutic (see (1993) 1 Med L Rev 186 at p. 195). So it was perhaps inevitable that the court had overtly to consider the grey areas created by the utilisation of this distinction. This was perceived to be most difficult of resolution where the psychiatric illness of the patient was in issue. Deane J was rather unnecessarily mournful, however, where he argued that the borderline 'is far from precise and, particularly where psychiatric illness is involved, may be all but meaningless' (at p. 296).

One must appreciate that in cases such as *Re E (A Minor) (Medical Treatment)* [1991] 2 FLR 585 (see 13.5) it may appear that sterilisation is medically indicated, but for the maintenance or improvement of a *social* as opposed to a medically therapeutic interest, either of the patient herself, or others involved in the care of the patient. Cica also notes the word game that can be played where, for example, the sterilisation proposed is defined as necessary for the patient to integrate into the community more successfully. If it is described as of psychological benefit, that term 'medicalises' the process and makes it in the patient's best medical interests and thereby therapeutic.

13.3.6.2 Consent of parents to sterilisation   The majority of the court in *JWB and SMB* considered that there were a number of factors which led to the view that a sterilisation operation 'should not come within the ordinary scope of *parental* power to consent to medical treatment' (at p. 249, emphasis added). The involvement of the court was felt to be necessary as a procedural safeguard in such cases. It was made clear that, while the judges remained somewhat uncomfortable with the terms 'therapeutic' and 'non-therapeutic', they were not considering that courts should be involved in sterilisations that were a by-product of surgery to treat some other malfunction or disease.

Generally, the factors the court wished to take into account in justifying judicial involvement were based around the dangers of a wrong decision being made without the 'security' of such judicial involvement. The court felt that this was a significant risk for a number of reasons:

(a) The complexity of the question of consent. There was a realisation, which one feels had been lacking in the earlier case law, that incompetence to make decisions about some things did not necessarily lead to incompetence to make decisions about anything, including whether or not a steriiisation operation should take place (see chapters 6 and 9). The mere fact of disability should not lead to such a blanket conclusion. One might point to the case of *Re D (A Minor) (Wardship: Sterilisation)* [1976] Fam 185 where this danger almost became reality.

(b) While the medical profession play a central role in deciding on and performing sterilisation, there is a danger that a condition can all too easily become medicalised. The court in *JWB and SMB* appeared to feel that wholehearted support of, and trust in, the medical profession was not always warranted. Some may act in an inappropriate manner, or may make their decisions with 'limited terms of reference' – an obvious allusion to the fact that doctors may tend to see a social problem in a clinical light.

(c) The decision of parents may not always be made on the basis of the mentally disabled person's interests. There may be concern that the numerous other interests of parents and other family members are harmed by the condition of the handicapped person.

This point is illustrated by the recent case of *Re S (Adult Sterilisation) (Family Division)* (1988) May Fam Law 291. In this case S was aged 22 but mentally incapable of looking after herself. Her parents sought the court's approval for her sterilisation in view of her vulnerability to sexual exploitation. An important consideration is that S had no understanding of sexuality. The issue for the court to decide was whether the risk of pregnancy outweighed the risks of such an invasive procedure. Johnson J held that although it might seem unfair that the law should not give effect to the wishes of the parents, the risk of pregnancy in this case did not justify sterilisation. It so happened that S was very rarely away from parental supervision and there had been no identifiable occasion when S had been at risk. If, therefore, the court had declared sterilisation to be lawful in this case, it would have been difficult to envisage any factual situation in which the relief would be refused. The judgment of Johnson J makes it clear that a real risk of pregnancy should be shown in order to justify sterilisation notwithstanding the wishes of the parents. His lordship considered that the facts of *Re S* were indistinguishable from those in *Re LC (Medical Treatment: Sterilisation)* [1997] 2 FLR 258, where the application for sterilisation was refused for the same reasons.

The court realised that the burden on family and other carers is a factor to be taken into account but felt that it should be placed in a proper context. As in relation to consent and minors (see chapter 7) it may even be that the parents are the last people to have the power of decision-making. There is potent danger of a conflict of interest.

The English decisions in relation to the sterilisation of minors appear to be once again dominated by the medical profession (in *JWB and SMB*). There is little doubt that with the significant admission that the *Bolam* test is the overriding prerequisite in working out where the 'best interests' of the minor patient lie, it is the responsible body of medical opinion which holds sway. This becomes even more clear when the courts were required to look at proposed sterilisations of mentally handicapped adults.

13.4   STERILISATION OF MENTALLY HANDICAPPED ADULTS

13.4.1   Difficulties of jurisdiction

In *T* v *T* [1988] Fam 52, the court was confronted with an incompetent adult who was actually pregnant. There was consistent medical opinion which suggested that a lawful abortion should take place under the terms of the Abortion Act 1967. T's mother was also in favour of the court giving leave for a sterilisation to take place at the same time to stop the risk of another pregnancy.

Wood J could find no assistance in the terms of treatment under the Mental Health Act 1983, because that legislation only governed treatment aimed directly at the psychiatric condition (see 9.5). There is a part of the Mental Health Act (part VIII) which deals with others who may consent to matters which concern the 'management of property and affairs of patients'. Part IV of the Act refers to 'consent to treatment' but is only applicable to treatment *for* the mental disorder and so did not apply. The court could not be assisted by part VIII because it referred to issues other than those related to 'the management or care of the patient's person' (*Re W* [1971] Ch 123 at p. 143 per Ungoed-Thomas J).

There was also no one who could give consent on T's behalf, as T was an adult. Doubt was expressed over utilising the *parens patriae* jurisdiction of the court, which is now entirely governed by statute. The power of consent was given to a guardian under the Mental Health Act 1959, but this was excluded from the 1983 legislation. The existence of statute giving power of consent over an adult means that the common law power of consent no longer exists.

The court was placed in even more difficulty by its opinion (see 7.2) that the performance of the operation, in the absence of any consent, would be tortious, notwithstanding that it would be done without hostile intent. The court then found that it would not be possible to rely on the concept of implied consent. The fact of T's incompetence meant that she could never consent. Implied consent, if it is a realistic doctrine at all (see chapter 14 and the decision in *Re J (A Minor) (Wardship: Medical Treatment)* [1991] Fam

33), should be reserved for patients in an emergency situation who are temporarily incompetent. As if all these indicators against the performance of the sterilisation were not enough, Wood J also rejected the defence of necessity for the performance of the operation. The reason for this was, as is typical of many of the discussions of defence in criminal law, that the nature of the defence itself was uncertain. Despite all these hurdles, Wood J decided that the court had power under its jurisdiction to make an *anticipatory declaration* that the operation would not be unlawful (Rules of the Supreme Court 1965, ord. 15, r. 16). Wood J made this decision, despite all the apparent barriers, for the same reason as given by Lord Bridge of Harwich in *Re B (A Minor) (Wardship: Sterilisation)* [1988] AC 199 at p. 205:

I find it difficult to understand how anybody examining the facts humanely, compassionately and objectively could reach any other conclusion.

Nevertheless the utilisation of the anticipatory declaration was clumsy and Wood J acknowledged the fact that many of these cases needed to be decided as a matter of urgency. Indeed, he received evidence during the course of the hearing that similar cases occurred every month. With that in mind, the court expressed its desire to return to the prerogative jurisdiction of *parens patriae*.

13.4.2 A best interests test from negligence

T v T [1988] Fam 52 was a bold decision, but *Re F (Mental Patient: Sterilisation)* [1990] 2 AC 1 gave the House of Lords the opportunity to debate once more many of the crucial issues of non-consensual sterilisation, but in the context of the mentally handicapped adult.

F was a 36-year-old woman who suffered from serious mental incompetence. Her verbal capacity was of a child of two years of age. Her overall mental capacity was of a child of four to five years of age. While a voluntary in-patient at a mental hospital, she formed a sexual relationship with a male patient. The considerable psychiatric evidence presented indicated that it would be a disaster if she became pregnant. Available contraceptives were unsuitable to her situation, even to the extent of being a danger to her physical health. The medical staff involved with F felt that it would be best if she were sterilised. F's mother sought the same declaration that had been successful in *T v T* [1988] Fam 52, namely, a declaration from the court that sterilising F without her consent, would not be unlawful.

In effect the Law Lords were reconsidering the issues encountered in *Re B (A Minor) (Wardship: Sterilisation)* [1988] AC 199, the only real difference being that here the mentally handicapped individual was an adult.

All parties (save F, who could not express an opinion on the matter) were in agreement that it would be F's best interests that there be a sterilisation operation:

It might have been supposed that, with such complete agreement that it was in F's best interests that she should be sterilised, no difficulty about giving effect to that agreement would have arisen. Difficulty, however, has arisen because of doubts about three questions of law and legal procedure. (Lord Brandon of Oakbrook at p. 54)

The first question the House sought to answer was whether it had any place in the decision-making process at all. The Law Lords recognised the basic issue of consent to medical treatment of the mentally competent and the difficulties that arise due to incompetence to consent. The common law had facilitated the treatment of those unable, for whatever reason, to decide for themselves by means of the concept of acting in the best interests of the patient. Indeed, the argument was strengthened by the theory that the doctor may be under a *duty* to act in the patient's best interests. From this Lord Brandon made something of a leap to the statement that:

> . . . the lawfulness of a doctor operating on, or giving other treatment to, an adult patient disabled from giving consent, will depend not on any approval or sanction of a court, but on the question whether the operation or other treatment is in the best interests of the patient concerned. (p. 56)

Nevertheless Lord Brandon was of the opinion that while the decision will be a matter for the medical profession, the involvement of the courts would be desirable 'as a matter of good practice'.

The second question was the jurisdictional basis of the court being involved in the decision. As in *T* v *T* the inapplicability of the Mental Health Act 1983 to this kind of operation on the mentally handicapped was confirmed. Having considered in some detail the lack of jurisdiction to approve or disapprove the operation on an adult incompetent, the House of Lords approved the applicability of the advance declaration. Objections had been that this was inappropriate because, *inter alia*, the public interest in such serious medical procedures required an express approval rather than a declaration. Lord Brandon swept aside this fear by regarding it as largely a matter of semantic debate rather than substantive law.

The most significant part of the decision in *Re F* is the analysis of how the 'best interests' of the patient should be measured. All were agreed that the clinical nature of such decisions meant that the medical profession were to be the dominant force in the decision-making process. The matters that the House of Lords took into account were summarised in an important passage in the speech of Lord Goff of Chieveley:

> . . . in making decisions about treatment, the doctor must act in accordance with a responsible and competent body of professional opinion, on the principles set down in *Bolam* v *Friern Hospital Management Committee* [1957] 1 WLR 582. No doubt, in practice, a decision may involve others besides the doctor. It must surely be good practice to consult relatives and others who are concerned with the care of the patient. Sometimes, of course, consultation with a specialist or specialists will be required; and in others, especially where the decision involves more than a purely medical

opinion, an inter-disciplinary team will in practice participate in the decision. It is very difficult, and would be unwise, for a court to do more than to stress that, for those who are involved in these important and sometimes difficult decisions, the overriding consideration is that they should act in the best interests of the person who suffers from the misfortune of being prevented by incapacity from deciding for himself what should be done to his own body, in his own best interests. (p. 78)

The House of Lords went on to reiterate that the decisions being made were serious, and used *Re D (A Minor) (Wardship: Sterilisation)* [1976] Fam 185 as an example of where there was widespread support by doctors and relatives that a sterilisation operation be performed, but a closer examination of the actual capacities, present and future, of the patient were against the operation. With this in mind, Lord Goff felt, as had been the case in *Re B* that the courtroom was the best forum for deciding such matters.

A number of criticisms could be made of Lord Goff's analysis of the ideal decision-making process. In the Court of Appeal, Lord Donaldson of Lymington MR and Neill LJ felt that the *Bolam* test would be an inadequate safeguard here. Lord Donaldson significantly argued:

Just as the law and the courts rightly pay great, but not decisive, regard to accepted professional wisdom in relation to the duty of care in the law of medical negligence (see *Bolam* v *Friern Hospital Management Committee* [1957] 1 WLR 582), so they equally would have regard to such wisdom in relation to decisions whether or not and how to treat incompetent patients in the context of the law of trespass to the person. However, both the medical profession and the courts have to keep the special status of such a patient in the forefront of their minds. (pp. 18–19).

His lordship went on to argue that the court, in considering such a serious issue, could regard the existence of a significant minority view as sufficient to indicate that an operation should not take place. The *Bolam* test, as it is traditionally understood, would not allow the court to favour one body of opinion over another.

Neill LJ focused more on the fact that the first point of consideration is the necessity of the operation. In deciding necessity one could have regard for the responsible body of medical opinion (the *Bolam* test) or one could be more refined and declare it to be: '. . . that which the general body of medical opinion in the particular specialty would consider to be in the best interests of the patient in order to maintain the health and to secure the well-being of the patient.'

Neill LJ went on to pose what was thought to be the real question for the courts in these situations: 'What action does the patient's health and welfare require?' The focus appears here to move toward the idea of substituted judgment, canvassed by La Forest J in *Re Eve* (1986) 31 DLR (4th) 1.

The House of Lords utilised the *Bolam* test, and disagreed with the sentiments of Lord Donaldson in the Court of Appeal. One needs, however, to look a little more closely at the words of Lord Goff. Apparently while approving the *Bolam* test, there is a recognition that others may need to be consulted about the advisability of the operation being performed. If the matter is not exclusively one of clinical judgment, who should be involved in the decision-making process? Relatives? Ethics committees? Social workers? Society? That there is no answer to these questions raises once more the perceived danger that sterilisations could take place on the basis of less laudable motives than the true best medical and psychological interests of the patient.

The Law Lords, in exclusively considering the parameters of the 'best interests' test have also been criticised for their ignorance of the 'therapeutic–non-therapeutic debate so relied upon in *Re Eve*. One should note the difference between the language of the House of Lords in *Re F* and the courts in *Re D* and *Re Eve*. It is apparent from the decision in *Re F* that there is discomfort in a comprehensive recognition and articulation of human rights and reproduction. As in an increasing number of spheres of medical law, the applicability of a test of the standard of medical care in the context of negligent treatment, diagnosis or advice has to be questioned in an area studded with patient rights.

In cases of sterilisation the argument is that the issues are not simply ones of the clinical necessity of the procedure being carried out. Issues of the social, human rights, emotional value and even the economic may enter into the equation. There seems no good reason why doctors should be any better equipped to make decisions when weight is given to the wider questions of sterilisation. This is a persistent theme in the development of modern case law in this area of medical law. Once more the allegation is made that the judiciary have handed over power to clinicians.

The judiciary seem to be profoundly confused about the relative influence of the court and the medical profession in making the non-consensual sterilisation decision. While the decision in *Re F* is authority for the fact that it is desirable to receive the declaration of the court that such an operation would not be unlawful, the House of Lords, at the same time, handed the decision-making power back to the doctors by utilising the *Bolam* test as the test of 'best interests':

> The *Bolam* 'responsible body of medical opinion' test is concerned less with the process of seeking the reconciliation of possibly competing individual rights to procreative and sexual freedom in the light of the perceived best interests of the patient, and more with the operation of interprofessional solidarity between the medical and legal professions and the willingness of the English judiciary to accept, largely at face value, assertions of professional competence by the doctors. (Shaw in McVeigh and Wheeler (eds), *Law, Health and Medical Regulation* (Dartmouth, 1992), pp. 81–2)

Such a distortion of medical and legal roles is even more evident in the recent activities of the judiciary in non-consensual sterilisation of the mentally handicapped. (See also *Re W (Mental Patient) (Sterilisation)* [1993] 1 FLR 381, where the risk of pregnancy was slight, but nevertheless a 'responsible body of medical opinion' was in favour of sterilisation. This opinion held sway and the 18-year-old was sterilised.) To some extent this trend is in the process of reversal, evidenced by the first instance decisions of *Re LC (Medical Treatment: Sterilisation)* [1997] 2 FLR 258 and *Re S (Medical Treatment: Adult Sterilisation) (Family Division)* [1998] June FLR 325.

13.5 MEDICALISATION OF THE STERILISATION DECISION

In a series of cases the courts have decided that where an operation is carried out to alleviate a 'medical' condition, and the sterilisation of the mentally handicapped person is a side-effect of that operation being performed, then the courts will not intervene.

In *Re E (A Minor) (Medical Treatment)* [1991] 2 FLR 585, it was held that parents were able to give valid consent to a proposed hysterectomy to be performed for therapeutic reasons on their mentally handicapped daughter aged 17, notwithstanding that the incidental result would be sterilisation. Sir Stephen Brown P found that the operation was necessary due to a menstrual disorder, leading to episodes which E could not understand, and therefore caused considerable anxiety. The President of the Family Division held that the declaration of the High Court was not necessary as, 'A clear distinction is to be made between an operation to be performed for a genuine therapeutic reason and one to achieve sterilisation' (at p. 587).

This was supplemented by another decision of Sir Stephen Brown P in *Re GF (Mental Patient: Medical Treatment)* [1992] 1 FLR 293, where it was decided that the declaration of the Court would not be required as long as two gynaecologists were satisfied:

(a)   that the operation was therapeutically indicated;
(b)   that the operation was in the best interests of the patient; and
(c)   that there was no other form of less drastic treatment that could accomplish that end.

No doubt some would argue that the High Court should be involved in all sterilisation decisions, and that cases such as *Re B (A Minor) (Wardship: Sterilisation)* [1988] AC 199 and *Re F (Mental Patient: Sterilisation)* [1990] 2 AC 1 should in addition have these prerequisites as a common determinant of such operations.

The Australian High Court has considered such 'medicalised' sterilisations as one of the grey areas between therapeutic and non-therapeutic sterilisation. One might argue that such operations, while focusing on the psychological trauma of dealing with the process of menstruation in the mentally handicapped, in actual fact may be a disguise for a social sterilisation, in terms of being 'performed largely for the convenience of institutions or other caregivers' (Cica, 'Sterilising the Intellectually Disabled' (1993) 1 Med L Rev 186 at p. 198).

It has been proposed that sterilisation should be considered in the light of the following broad principles:

(a) The sterilisation is therapeutic if it is performed to prevent or otherwise treat a clinical condition, with the focus being on the term 'clinical'. This would allow for the existence of psychological disturbance, without a carte blanche where emotional upset is claimed as a factor in the decision to sterilise.

(b) There needs to be a real, as opposed to fanciful, possibility that the clinical condition (if it has not done so) will arise. The keys to this principle are the notions of a *substantial risk* and *imminence*.

(c) The sterilisation or hysterectomy will only be permissible where no less drastic and intrusive measure can achieve the same clinical objective, so that the sterilisation is in the best medical interests of the patient. The operation must be one of last resort.

(d) Expert advice must be presented which indicates that these preconditions have been satisfied.

Although not strictly what one may term a 'medicalised' sterilisation, the case of *Re HG* [1993] 1 FLR 587 is a further indication of the judiciary distancing themselves from the true objectives of a 'best interests' sterilisation. The court here permitted a girl to be sterilised even though there was no evidence adduced that she was, in fact, sexually active. It was clear from the judgment that the court was influenced by medical opinion, but particularly the fact that the interests of other parties (here the parents and other carers) were influential. Therefore it appears that overtly the courts are looking to the medical profession for opinion, but are then also looking to the parties that in previous case law they had sought to assure should not and would not become part of the decision-making process.

13.6 BEST INTERESTS AND REVERSIBILITY OF STERILISATION

13.6.1 Development of case law

The inherent vagueness of the 'best interests' test as enunciated by the House of Lords in *Re F (Mental Patient: Sterilisation)* [1990] 2 AC 1 has been evident in the expansion of cases in this area, both in terms of the medicalisation of the procedure, and, perhaps most disturbing of all, in the notion of the reversible nature of certain sterilisation procedures, namely tubal ligation. Two cases deserve particular attention, and have been the subject of forthright criticism (see M. Brazier, 'Sterilisation: Down the Slippery Slope?' (1990) 6 PN 25).

In *Re M (A Minor) (Wardship: Sterilisation)* [1988] 2 FLR 497, the court was concerned with a 17-year-old girl. The evidence indicated a mental age of five or six, and an apparent lack of maternal instinct. When the sterilisation proposal was put before the court it was supported by expert gynaecological evidence that there was, due to improvements in medical science, a possibility in the region of 50 to 75 per cent that the sterilisation could be reversed, if in the future the mental handicap of the patient improved. As Brazier points out:

Bush J stated very firmly that eugenic considerations were in themselves irrelevant but then did appear to take into account evidence that if M should become pregnant an abortion on the ground of foetal handicap might be recommended.

It is clear too that Bush J was heavily persuaded by the percentage chance of reversibility.

The true implications of this development can be seen in the subsequent case of *Re P (A Minor) (Wardship: Sterilisation)* [1989] 1 FLR 182. The case again concerned a 17-year-old girl described as of normal and attractive appearance. Her mental age was assessed as six years. Brazier notes that, unlike the child in *Re B (A Minor) (Wardship: Sterilisation)* [1988] AC 199, P's verbal communication skills were of an effective six-year-old. There was some debate about her skills development, but it was felt that, while not likely to improve intellectually, training would improve her general skills in a social environment. Evidence also indicated a danger of her being seduced, but also of having some maternal instincts. Significantly, there was a fear expressed by the mother that while there was limited mental capacity, P might, upon becoming pregnant, refuse an abortion. In addition it was felt that it would be a traumatic event if the child born were taken away from P.

Despite all this, Eastham J decided that the sterilisation operation should go ahead. Additional evidence might lead one to be more suspicious of such an authorisation. It was felt that while at present P did not have the capacity to marry, that might well change in the future. It was also found that P considered intercourse painful and thus there was no current risk of pregnancy. Brazier also notes that P was regarded specifically by the court as:

quite clearly a young woman with greater understanding of human relationships and maternity than B. The 'right' to reproduce, to bear a child and give birth appeared to be something P might well value.

What then led the court to authorise what was regarded by the courts in the development of the law on sterilisation to be a last resort? Eastham J felt that the evidence of reversal success statistics meant that it would no longer be strictly correct to regard the operation as one of last resort. The obvious question is: Can the possibility, even probability, of successful reversal justify no longer treating sterilisation as a last resort, but rather as a convenient method of contraception? The answer has to be that this is now the case.

13.6.2 Objections to the case law

It might be argued that P (*Re P (A Minor) (Wardship: Sterilisation)* [1989] 1 FLR 182) was prone to seduction by men. The sterilisation will not stop that possibility, only a possible consequence, a pregnancy. It might be argued that the pregnancy and birth of a child would have been a disaster for P. Pregnancy and birth can be disasters for many women, dependent on a number of factors not necessarily related to mental health. There has been no suggestion that there should be enforced sterilisation in such cases.

13.7 CURRENT LAW AND PRACTICE

The *Practice Note (Sterilisation: Minors and Mental Health Patients)* [1993] 3 All ER 222 is a potentially significant recent development in the decision-making process where the mentally handicapped are concerned. The cases of *Re B (A Minor) (Wardship: Sterilisation)* [1988] AC 199 and *Re F (Mental Patient: Sterilisation)* [1990] 2 AC 1 eschewed the notion that a list of factors could be taken into account in deciding the best interests of a patient. Nevertheless the Official Solicitor sought to provide a list of suggestions, which, while useful, have one should note, no legal force.

The general points made in the *Practice Note* are as follows:

(a) The sterilisation of the mentally handicapped individual will in almost all circumstances require the sanction of a High Court judge.

(b) It is preferable in the case of a minor that the court invoke its inherent *parens patriae* jurisdiction when an application is made.

(c) The purpose of the proceedings will be to establish whether or not the sterilisation is in the best interests of the patient. The judge needs to be satisfied that the application for the sterilisation is made in good faith. The paramount concern of those applying should be for the best interests of that patient, rather than their own or the public's convenience.

(d) Although not an exhaustive list, the judge should have evidence to establish the following:

(i) The patient is incapable of making his or her own decision about sterilisation.

(ii) The patient is unlikely to develop sufficiently to make an informed judgment in the foreseeable future. It must be borne in mind, however, that the fact that a person is legally incompetent for some purposes does not mean that such a person is incompetent for the purposes of the sterilisation decision. Matters such as youth and potential development may mean that the future is impossible to predict with any degree of accuracy.

(iii) The condition the sterilisation is aimed at avoiding will actually occur if it is not performed. This relates to the likelihood of the patient engaging in sexual activity. There needs to be a real danger that pregnancy may occur rather than a mere chance that pregnancy will result. This is also obviously itself dependent on the establishment of the fact that the patient is capable of procreation.

(iv) The patient will experience substantial trauma or psychological damage greater than that resulting from the sterilisation itself.

(v) If the sterilisation were not performed, and the patient became pregnant, the patient would be incapable of caring for the child.

(vi) There is no other form of contraception that can be used to alleviate the current condition or perceived danger.

One has some cause to doubt whether the recent decisions of the court, particularly *Re P (A Minor) (Wardship: Sterilisation)* [1989] 1 FLR 182 and

Re M (A Minor) (Wardship: Sterilisation) [1988] 2 FLR 497 can be reconciled with the tenor of the *Practice Note.*

13.8 CONCLUSION

In general terms, Brazier confirms the suspicions earlier expressed by Freeman in relation to *Re B (A Minor) (Wardship: Sterilisation)* [1988] AC 199, that the label 'mentally handicapped' has been insufficiently explored in relation to the individual patient, despite the serious consequences of being a woman so labelled in the context of sterilisation. While one needs to be wary of presuming the ability to consent, one may nevertheless have sympathy with the view that:

It must . . . follow that to be competent to give a valid consent, the patient need only be able to understand in broad terms the nature and purpose of treatment. In the context of sterilisation that means she should understand that she will be put to sleep while a doctor operates on her tummy to ensure that she is never able to have babies. Most six-year-olds who have learned something of how babies are born would comprehend that information. (Brazier, 'Sterilisation: Down the Slippery Slope?' (1990) 6 PN 25)

Where the consequences, and indeed the procedure itself, are so serious, and an interference with the right to reproduce (whatever weight is given to that concept), there is scope for the court to require more than the application of the *Bolam* formulation and, as was suggested in the Court of Appeal in *Re F (Mental Patient: Sterilisation)* [1990] 2 AC 1, to utilise a wider decision-making base than the clinician. Brazier also supports this idea of the inapplicability of *Bolam,* which is regarded as merely protecting the potential plaintiff in a medical negligence action 'from the complete maverick whom none of his colleagues would back in his decision to sterilise her'.

It may be that the development of decisions in the area of sterilisation has now moved the focus away from the consideration of the best interests of the individual patient to the interests of others concerned with the patient's welfare or perhaps their own convenience. There is an urgent need for legislation to control the practice of sterilisation. It would need to note that it should still be regarded as an operation of last resort. The factors to be taken into account in reaching the sterilisation decision need to be clearly articulated. Perhaps most important of all there needs to be an explicit realisation that the medical professon are not always in the best position to make the decision. The prerequisites apparent in the Australian High Court in *Secretary, Department of Health and Community Services v JWB and SMB* (1992) 175 CLR 218 should be repeated as a matter of English medico-legal legislation. Once more the current law appears to pay lip service to the dictates of arriving at a 'good' medical law: moral analysis, ethical correctness and respect for human rights.

Further reading

Bainham, A., 'Handicapped Girls and Judicial Parents' (1987) 103 LQR 334.
de Cruz, S.P., 'Sterilisation, Wardship and Human Rights' (1988) 18 Fam Law 6.
Fortin, J., 'Sterilisation, the Mentally Ill and Consent to Treatment' (1986) 51 MLR 634.
Grubb, A., and Pearl, D., 'Sterilisation and the Courts' [1987] CLJ 439.
Lee, R., and Morgan, D., 'Sterilisation and Mental Handicap: Sapping the Strength of the State?' (1988) 15 J Law & Soc 229.
Shaw, J., 'Sterilisation of Mentally Handicapped People: Judges Rule OK?' (1990) 53 MLR 91.

FOURTEEN
Neonaticide

14.1 INTRODUCTION

Previous chapters have indicated that while there are protective mechanisms by which medical law shields to some extent the unborn, whether it is in terms of the regulation of pre-natal research or the law relating to abortion, these have all been governed by the overriding concept identified by Sir George Baker P in *Paton v British Pregnancy Advisory Service Trustees* [1979] QB 276 that the unborn child does not gain legal status until it enters civil society, that is, until it is born. Now there is a growing realisation by the judiciary that the interests of the unborn have a moral and therefore legal value, and deserve protection, though, at present, these developments have taken place in specifically articulated circumstances (see, for example, *Attorney-General's Reference (No. 3 of 1994)* [1996] QB 581) rather than in a general framework of medico-moral and medico-legal theory. This chapter is concerned with the newborn child, who has entered into the realm of legal protection. To what extent does there exist effective protection for those who are still at the stage where they are unable to look after themselves? The issues raised in relation to the neonate revolve around the handicapped newborn, and should be seen as a separate issue for medical law and ethics, although sharing a number of common points that will be encountered in relation to the broader euthanasia debate.

Much of the current focus of the debate has been given its initial impetus by the trial of Dr Leonard Arthur at Leicester Crown Court, on a charge of the attempted murder of a neonate. The publicity surrounding the trial meant that there was renewed focus on what may have been a matter of clinical decision-making for some time before the trial, as some of the evidence itself very clearly revealed.

Gillon ('An Introduction to Philosophical Medical Ethics: The *Arthur Case*' (1985) 290 BMJ 1117) has argued that there are few issues of medical ethics (indeed one would suggest of criminal law in the medical context as a whole) that *R* v *Arthur* (1981) 12 BMLR 1 does not raise. Issues of autonomy, respect for the sanctity of life, the quality of handicapped existence and the place of medical law in clinical decision-making were all encountered. Other authors have regarded the case as aberrant and with little precedential value, and therefore to be consigned to the legal history books. This is not correct. While the trial of Leonard Arthur resulted in what some might perceive to be a perverse jury verdict, that verdict was given after hearing a considerable amount of evidence which indicated that neonaticide, if certainly not a standard practice, was an activity with well-established covert clinical guidelines. Knowledge of the case, and the legal and ethical debate which followed it, is vital to an understanding of the development of this aspect of medical law and an indication that the law and ethics of this area are still far from being 'now relatively stabilised' as claimed by Mason and McCall Smith, *Law and Medical Ethics*, 4th ed. (London: Butterworths, 1994), at p. 147. Before going any further, the following important point needs to be understood as correct:

> Passive euthanasia of defective newborns through selective non-treatment is now widely practised in England and the USA. Many persons defend the practice as a morally and socially justifiable way to prevent suffering. However, a practice of withholding necessary medical care from defective infants to cause their death does not square easily with basic norms of liberal democratic society that accord equal respect to the life of all persons whatever their physical, mental or social characteristics. (John Robertson, 'Substantive Criteria and Procedures in Withholding Care from Defective Newborns' in Spicker et al. (eds), *The Law–Medicine Relation* (Dordrecht: Reidel, 1978), p. 217)

14.2 THE ISSUES IN NEONATICIDE: A FORM OF EUTHANASIA

When considering the case of *R* v *Arthur* (1981) 12 BMLR 1 and, indeed, the other significant cases in this area, the following points should be borne in mind as relevant to whether the handicapped neonate should live or be left to die.

Gillon ('Introduction to Philosophical Medical Ethics: The *Arthur* Case' (1985) 290 BMJ 1117) has argued that there needs to be a search for an element of symmetry when considering neonatal rights. By this is meant that a comparison must be made between a handicapped neonate and a handicapped adult. If the two are regarded as morally identical, if sharing the same general level of handicap, the same legal status should be accorded to both. If there is a difference, so that it is legitimate to let a handicapped newborn child die, then what characteristics does the neonate lack, compared to the the adult, that allow the child to die, but the adult to live?

Obviously one could argue that there are no moral differences between the two, and therefore the law must treat the two in the same way. This is the case whether that legal reaction to a moral judgment leads to the practice of euthanasia or not. Gillon argues against symmetry here, mainly it seems on the basis of an ethical slippery slope. If the terminal management of certain handicapped adults and neonates is allowed, then what is the essential moral difference between the handicapped neonate and the handicapped foetus? In separating out issues of euthanasia, it could be tentatively suggested that the child has had no opportunity to express lifestyle preferences, but this equally may apply to more mature members of the population. It may be safest to admit that the separation of neonaticide and euthanasia may be based either on intuitive values or even the convenience of debate.

When considering whether medical law as it relates to the neonate is a 'good' law, look at the following situation, and consider the questions raised. How should medical law react?

Joan has just been rushed into hospital in premature labour. After a difficult delivery she gives birth to a son. He is grossly underweight and evidently has a number of severe physical handicaps, including withered limbs and an abnormally large head, which the child would never be able to support unaided. Tests reveal that the child is blind and has severely limited electrical brain activity. An urgent operation is required to ease the pressure of fluid on the brain. Joan is told of the situation, and replies, 'Please don't operate, let my baby die'.

The questions for medical law to consider here are:

(a) What is the morally 'right' thing to do?
(b) How can the law respect patient rights and welfare most effectively?
(c) Is the decision one for the parents, the doctor or the court?
(d) Does medical law have a place here at all?

Moral philosophy points in starkly different directions here. Basic morality and the Hippocratic tradition hold that the doctor should do good, or at least not do harm. There is thus scope for arguing that letting the handicapped newborn die does not violate a moral right of the patient if it prevents the child from suffering. The case law will reveal that there are judicial pronouncements which pay lip-service to the dictates of deontology (the doctor can *never* accelerate the death of a handicapped neonate), but perform a utilitarian moral calculation of the right thing to do (where the quality of the life of the neonate will be below a certain threshhold, it is permissible for the doctor to 'let' the child die). There are difficult questions of rights here too. Autonomy is not quite as simple a notion to articulate here. The child, by reason of both age and handicap, is unable to express that moral and human right of self-determination through consent to, or refusal of, treatment. There is still a legally and morally relevant individual here, though, so there has to be someone to consent or refuse on that child's behalf (see chapter 6 for a discussion of who can consent for the minor lacking capacity to consent). This is a significant point for the intervention of human rights into medical law. Those who argue that human rights do not really exist as an enforceable aspect of law should pause to consider the usefulness of utilising them here. Both John Rawls and Ronald Dworkin (see 1.5) emphasised that human rights are valuable to protect the worst-off and weakest members of society.

Ronald Dworkin particularly emphasised that rights law 'is crucial, because it represents the majority's promise to the minorities that their dignity and equality will be respected'. The two crucial 'rights' terms to remember during the course of looking at neonaticide are *dignity* and *equality*. Always bear in mind that the neonate is a patient, and has patient rights. English cases involving the handicapped newborn have found this all too easy to forget.

The WHO document, *Promotion of the Rights of Patients in Europe* (Kluwer, 1995) is a useful tool to have when considering neonatal rights. It will be recalled (from 1.5) that its general principles include the right to be respected as a human being, to self-determination. The views of Lord Donaldson in the more recent cases considering neonatal patients appears to be slowly moving into the language of medico-legal rights. There still appears, though, to be a dominant position for clinical decision-making, through medical law's acceptance of the *Bolam* test of a patient's best interests.

Glanville Williams, appearing to pay homage to Lord Devlin, has argued that medical law has no place in controlling the decision-making of patients and doctors: '. . . where the good order of society is not at stake the criminal law should stay its hand. The decision of the parents should prevail' ('Life of a Child' (1981) *The Times*, 13 August 1981). In response to this one can do little better than quote William Bartholomew:

> Some have argued that parents should have the right to make medical decisions on behalf of their children since they must live with the consequences of the decision. But, it has also been pointed out that having to live with the consequences is also an excellent basis for arguing that parents should not have the right to decide; i.e. there is a conflict of interest. ('The Child-Patient: Do Parents Have the "Right to Decide"?' in Spicker et al. (eds), *The Law–Medicine Relation* (Dordrecht: Reidel, 1978), p. 272)

The argument of what rights are held by the neonate patient and the duties incumbent upon the doctor appears difficult to resolve. It might be suggested that one is forced back into the largely pragmatic world of clinical intuition and public opinion. Clinical intuition, if it is to have guidelines which make medical decision-making that is coherent, justifiable and open to scrutiny, will have to articulate that while there has to be a libertarian aspect to that intuition, the fact of the neonate's vulnerability and inability to communicate preferences as to treatment necessitates paternalism. There is some suspicion, however, of where clinical intuition takes us:

> . . . many anecdotal reports from doctors and nurses confirm that selection for non-treatment occurs on a large-scale, willy-nilly fashion, without careful attention to morally justifiable criteria for non-treatment. (John Robertson, 'Substantive Criteria and Procedures in Withholding Care from Defective Newborns' in Spicker et al. (eds), *The Law–Medicine Relation* (Dordrecht: Reidel, 1978), p. 222)

Other matters that will prove important in the development of the debate, which itself develops with the cases themselves, really turn around the dilemma of whether there is an acceptance of the absolute sanctity of human life, or that there are qualities of life that can be demarcated. Does there thus exist a threshold level where life is simply no longer of sufficient quality to be sustained? The importance of this should be obvious. There appears to be evidence that the practice in England and the USA has yet to be properly justified as a matter of morals or medical law and medical practice. It is also the case that both regimes appear to be over-inclusive. The utilitarian calculation of benefits and burdens of treatment is crucial. Medical law, to be good law will need to do the following:

If bright lines that do not encroach too much on the concept of equal respect for the lives of all persons can be drawn, we may expect the courts, when faced with such a case, to identify in effect a class of infants from whom necessary care may be withheld, on the ground that the resulting benefits to them do not justify the costs of treatment. (Robertson, op. cit., p. 221)

The Hippocratic oath states 'To please no one will I prescribe a deadly drug, nor give advice which may cause his death'. It has equally been long recognised that there are circumstances where the doctor may not be acting faithfully to his profession where treatment is undertaken which will only prolong suffering and merely delay an inevitable death.

This acceptance of the existence of the quality threshold itself creates dilemmas that the cases will need to resolve:

(a)   When considering the quality of life of the handicapped neonate, will it only be that child's quality of life and interests that will be considered?

(b)   If not, should the quality of life, interests and views of the parents be taken into account?

(c)   Should the law go wider and consider the interests of society as a whole, whether in terms of economic impact of protecting the handicapped neonate, or the more extreme notion of a perceived societal interest in the perfectibility of the human species?

There are two further questions which could be addressed, the latter having proved to be a major point of controversy in relation to the practice of neonaticide and in the wider realm of euthanasia.

(a)   Is it actually the case that, as stated earlier, and repeated once more by Glanville Williams 'There is a strong argument for keeping the law out of these cases. . . . when the good order of society in general is not at stake, the criminal law should stay its hand.' (G. Williams, *Textbook of Criminal Law*, 2nd ed. (London: Stevens, 1983)).

(b)   Is there a moral or legal difference between allowing the handicapped neonate to die and actively accelerating death?

14.3 NON-TREATMENT OF THE NEONATE AND THE CRIMINAL LAW

As already mentioned (in 14.1) Dr Arthur was tried for the attempted murder of a newborn baby named before his death as John Pearson. The original charge was one of murder, but this was reduced to the attempt charge after argument about evidence.

The child was born and almost immediately diagnosed as suffering from what was described as 'uncomplicated' Down's syndrome. Aside from this handicap it appeared that the child was healthy, and had a good chance of survival. The mother was told of the Down's syndrome and rejected the child. In addition the parents did not want the child to survive with such a handicap. After a meeting with the parents, Dr Arthur wrote in the case notes, 'Parents do not wish the child to survive. Nursing care only', and prescribed an appetite suppressant. Some hours later the child's condition began to deteriorate. Later on that same evening the child's condition was described as critical and arrangements were made for the child to be baptised. Some 69 hours after the child was born, it died.

The prosecution sought to rely on the preparation of the case notes and the treatment chart as evidence of an attempt to kill. These actions, it was alleged, combined with the prescription of the appetite suppressant, 'Set into train the course of events which could only have resulted in the child's death' (per Farquharson J).

The defence on the other hand contended, *inter alia*, that there was no positive act on the part of Dr Arthur, 'he was simply prescribing a treatment which involved the creation of a set of circumstances whereby the child would peacefully die, and that there is all the difference in the world between the one and the other' (ibid.).

In summing up, Farquharson J informed the jury that the case 'really revolves round the question of what is the duty of the doctor when prescribing treatment for a severely handicapped child suffering from a handicap of an irrevocable nature where parents do not wish the child to survive'. It can be argued that even on this basic point the judge was mistaken. The duty of a doctor is a matter of law not a matter of fact. Matters of law are the domain of the judge, matters of fact are the domain of the jury.

The main plank of the defence was the difference between activity and passivity. Between killing and letting the child die. A number of different forms of words were used, but they all resolved into this dilemma. Does the law distinguish between the two?

The case of *R v Gibbins* (1918) 13 Cr App R 134 established that on a charge of murder, 'It is enough if you [the jury] find that he or she intended to set up such a set of facts by withholding food or anything as would in the ordinary course of nature lead gradually but surely to her death' (per Roche J). It would seem plain that Dr Arthur fulfilled this definition.

Even if this were not the case, there seems to be some difficulty over the use of the term 'nursing care only' in the medical notes that Dr Arthur wrote. One nurse who gave evidence in the case described the meaning:

'Nursing care' – if it appears on the sheet of the mother and the baby, the baby goes to a different ward. The nurses would cherish him and remain in the ward until he died. If 'nursing care only' is prescribed it depends on the context whether the patient survives, but in the case of the severely malformed child this has never happened in this hospital.

There may be some scope for arguing that the activities involved in nursing care could amount to acts designed to hasten death.

In terms of the doctor's duty in the context of the neonate, this duty would appear to be unequivocal, and certainly not dependent on the handicap of the child. Farquharson J was apparently aware of such a duty when he stated forcefully:

> However serious a case may be; however much the disadvantage of a mongol or, indeed, any other handicapped child, no doctor has the right to kill it.
>
> There is no special law in this country that places doctors in a separate category and gives them extra protection over the rest of us. It is undoubtedly the case that doctors are, of course, the only profession who have to deal with these terrible problems. But notwithstanding that they are given no special power . . . to commit an act which causes death, which is another way of saying killing. Neither in law is there any special power, facility or licence to kill children who are handicapped or seriously disadvantaged in an irreversible way.

In essence the part of Farquharson J's summing up which has attracted most criticism has been the insistence upon a positive act as opposed to the setting up of a regime whereby a child would die. The defence described the procedure adopted in relation to John Pearson as a 'holding operation' which allowed for a change of heart on the part of the mother. There is a strong argument that there is no difference in law between actively killing and setting up circumstances which result in what was intended: the death of the child. It is arguable that Farquharson J, in repeating evidence that there was a strong difference between killing and letting die, was seeking to elevate a moral comment by the practitioners giving evidence into a statement of law. In the end the jury acquitted Dr Arthur.

It has been suggested, by authors too numerous to mention, that the doctor could have been more accurately charged under the Children and Young Persons Act 1933, s. 1:

> If any person who has attained the age of 16 years and has responsibility for any child or young person under that age, wilfully assaults, ill-treats, neglects, abandons or exposes him, or causes or procures him to be assaulted, ill-treated, neglected, abandoned, or exposed, in a manner likely to cause him unnecessary suffering or injury to health (including injury to or loss of sight, or hearing, or limb, or organ of the body, and any mental derangement), that person shall be guilty of [an offence].

There is thus the possibility that if the actions of Dr Arthur were to be repeated, the criminal law could be involved in setting the parameters of future conduct by using this section. One can see a clear argument that the actions of such a clinician would fall within the category of 'wilful neglect', but does the doctor have 'custody, charge or care'? It would appear that the doctor does, but consider the view of Kennedy and Grubb (*Medical Law*, 2nd ed. (London: Butterworths, 1994), p. 1249) that:

> A doctor cannot be liable under the Act since he would not in law be regarded as 'ha[ving] responsibility [for the child]', since the section is limited to those with 'parental responsibility'.

While this interpretation can be doubted, one can be more convinced of the view that the term 'wilful neglect' may not sit comfortably as a term accurately encompassing a decision on the clinical management of a patient. This may, however, be a matter of semantics to move the focus away from the reality of the overall activities and intentions of the doctor.

As indicated earlier the case of *R* v *Arthur* is a useful staging post in considering the applicable legal arena where such decisions should be made. It is also of continuing importance, in that the case recognised that Dr Arthur was not the first, and no doubt would not be the last, to selectively non-treat the defective neonate. His statement to the police read as follows:

> If a non-treatment course of conduct with mongol children is adopted, it is in accordance with my own practice, which is accepted by modern paediatric thought. If non-treatment is elected it means it would be wrong to treat infection with antibiotics. The withholding of food is accepted as part of non-treatment. Some lay people feel that this is distasteful. Sometimes we do feed babies, even if non-treatment is decided upon, if the parents or nurses wish it. But our major aim is to relieve distress in the child. The baby will take water or water and sugar. If it is fed milk it may be that it will inhale it and suffer a distressing condition. Paediatricians may use any of these foods or water. It really contributes little to the overall outcome. When non-treatment is decided upon the paediatrician may hope that the parents will change their minds after the immediate shock of birth. If they do not do so the course is continued in the hope that the baby will die peacefully from infection.

From this quote, and the tenor of the arguments in *R* v *Arthur* as a whole, there appears, at least as far as the criminal court and the clinicians who gave evidence are concerned, a policy not based on the best interests or quality of life of the neonate, but the best interests and quality of life of the parents of the child. The doctor here is clearly influenced by the wishes of the parents. The implication could not be more clear. If the parents want the child it will be fed and treated to protect it from infection. If the child is unwanted by the parents then it will not be fed and will remain unprotected from the infection which it is hoped will kill it. Therefore the case cannot 'be consigned to legal history for the oddity it is' (Kennedy and Grubb at p. 1251). Recent case law has also given primacy to the decision of the parents of the handicapped child. Later in the discussion of the development of the law it will be seen that the case of Re T (A Minor) (Wardship: Medical Treatment) [1997] 1 WLR 242 appeared to base the decision not to treat the child almost exclusively on the views of the parents.

There was a considerable public outcry at the decision in R v Arthur. The Attorney-General was called upon to exercise powers to refer the matter to the Court of Appeal as the case had raised issues of law of general concern. This the Attorney-General refused to do. The decision in the case was felt not to have changed any principles in relation to murder which had preceded it. One can only express surprise where the grounds for refusal included the reason that, 'I am satisfied that a person who has a duty of care may be guilty of murder or attempted murder by omitting to fulfil that duty, as much as by committing any positive act' (Hansard HC, 9 March 1982, written answers, coll. 348–9)

14.4 BEST INTERESTS, WARDSHIP AND THE DEFECTIVE NEONATE

Two decisions of the Court of Appeal (Re B (A Minor) (Wardship: Medical Treatment) [1981] 1 WLR 1421; and Re J (A Minor) (Child in Care: Medical Treatment) [1993] Fam 15 have considered the issue of the non-treatment of the defective neonate in the context of a wardship hearing, where the 'best interests' of the ward is the golden thread which runs through the exercise of the court's jurisdiction.

Before one considers the development of the case law, a few points need to be borne in mind when considering the judgments, as well as those mentioned earlier:

(a) Can non-existence – death – ever be regarded as being in the best interests of the ward?

(b) If death can be in the best interests of the ward, what should be taken into account in the decision?

(c) If death is the 'preferred option' according to the best interests test, then who should make the decision?

The 'best interests' or 'quality of life' argument is the core of this medical law issue. The phrases, without some further refinement, some more flesh, could justify any number of actions (or inactions) in relation to patients. These phrases need to be seen in the context of the overall objectives of medical law here:

If selection for non-treatment is to be morally and socially acceptable, two conditions must be met. The first is that the decision be made according to criteria that are authoritatively articulated and publicly announced. The criteria cannot be whatever individual doctors and families decide, for the question is which of their decisions are morally and socially defensible. Rather, they should be developed by an authoritative body that is representative of the community as a whole, such as a legislature, a national commission or some other publicly constituted body that reflects a wide range of societal views. (John Robertson, 'Substantive Criteria and Procedures in Withholding Care from Defective Newborns' in Spicker et al. (eds), *The Law–Medicine Relation* (Dordrecht: Reidel, 1978), p. 223)

Has medical law authoritatively articulated the relevant criteria? The case which effectively still represents the law on this matter, that of *Re B (A Minor) (Wardship: Medical Treatment)* [1981] 1 WLR 1421, CA, was rightly described as 'a very poignantly sad case' (per Templeman LJ at p. 1423). The child was born suffering from Down's syndrome, but what made the case different from *R v Arthur* was that the child also suffered from an intestinal blockage. This would prove fatal unless an operation were performed to remove it. The parents refused their consent to the operation. The basis of that refusal was that they felt it would be kinder if the child were allowed to die. The child was made a ward of court after the hospital informed the local authority of the parents' refusal. The intention was to gain a judicial order that the operation be immediately performed. There was some disagreement amongst clinicians whether the operation should be carried out, particularly when they were informed that the parents had objected. One doctor contacted them personally and then stated:

> I decided therefore to respect the wishes of the parents and not to perform the operation, a decision which would, I believe (after about 20 years in the medical profession), be taken by the great majority of surgeons faced with a similar situation.

Another doctor, however, was willing to carry out the operation.

Templeman LJ was clear at the outset that he felt sympathy with the plight of the parents, but the parental concept of the best interests of the child, while being taken into account, could not be the sole determining factor in deciding whether or not to perform the operation. In this there seemed to be an acknowledgement that the parents might not have the objectivity or dispassionate position of the court in making such decisions.

The central question put by the Court of Appeal was, at least on the surface, a simple one:

> . . . whether it is in the interests of this child to be allowed to die within the next week or to have the operation in which case if she lives she will be a mongoloid child, but no one can say to what extent her mental and physical defects will be apparent.

The question is similar to that encountered in relation to the sterilisation of the mentally handicapped. There the question was whether the child would be so mentally handicapped as to have no notion of the concepts of procreation, pregnancy and birth. The threat was of the destruction of the right and ability to reproduce. Here the stakes are higher: the threat is of death.

The Court of Appeal seemed acutely aware that there was no certainty about what the future held for child B. There seemed to be an acceptance that while there was every probability that B would be severely mentally and physically handicapped, the child would not be a 'cabbage' (as Templeman LJ so delicately put it).

Although it must now be regarded as somewhat tentative, Templeman LJ recognised that:

> . . . it devolves on this court in this particular instance to decide whether the life of this child is demonstrably going to be so awful that in effect the child must be condemned to die, or whether the life of this child is still so imponderable that it would be wrong for her to be condemned to die. There may be cases, I know not, of severe proved damage where the future is so certain and where the life of the child is so bound to be full of pain and suffering that the court might be driven to a different conclusion.

It was decided that there was too much doubt about what the future might hold for the child for it to be allowed to die without the opportunity to realise one of those possible futures.

The test proposed by Templeman LJ is one which is perhaps inevitably inexact. It is rightly termed a best interests test, but there is some difficulty in accurately discerning what factors are to be taken into account. There was a concrete prospect of the child surviving with the operation for 20 to 30 years, or only two to three months. Against this possibility had to be weighed the level of handicap the child would suffer from even if the operation were successful. Logic dictates that with the seriousness of the conclusion not to operate, the case could have been decided no other way.

Against this must be the argument that there are wider implications in marginalising the views of the parents in such cases. There is some uncertainty whether parents would wish to care for such children. There would no doubt be some significant anguish where a court decides against the parents' decision and allows the child to live. The parents may perceive that they have acted against the child's interests and are in some way 'in the wrong'. This may be compounded where the parents feel unable to look after such a child, but have the agony of knowing that the handicapped child still lives. That this is speculative when compared with the reality that any other decision in *Re B* would effectively have consigned the child to death, tends to seriously undermine these arguably intuitive views.

14.5 WHAT IS AN UNACCEPTABLE QUALITY OF LIFE?

The phrase 'quality of life' is so vague on its own as to be virtually meaningless, but both US and English medical law courts have considered it crucial. The difficulty involved with the whole debate about best interests and the quality of life is that one all-encompassing definition is impossible to find. Most people, if asked what should happen to Joan's child (at the start of the chapter), would answer either 'I would find a life like that intolerable' or 'I would want to be treated'. The debate for medical law is as much about perspective as anything else. The answer will depend at whom the law directs the question.

Attempts at refinement have been tried, and at the very least the debate, which has been rather more comprehensive in the USA and Canada, might show the need for a body to look at the issues afresh in England.

The quality of life issue can be considered from the medical or the social aspects of a case. An example of a medical analysis of quality of life – one based on the *medical* benefits and risks of a particular form of neonatal treatment – can be seen in the US case of *Re Hofbauer* (1978) 411 NYS 2d 416. The parents of a child who had a serious condition known as Hodgkin's disease decided not to accept a doctor's advice that their child receive chemotherapy and radiation treatment. Instead they decided on an 'alternative' dietary-based therapy. The allegation that the parents were neglecting their child was refuted by the judge. It was a justifiable concern that chemotherapy and radiation were distressing, that the alternative was helping and the parents would return to the conventional treatment if the child's condition required it. The best interests of the child were therefore considered the sole determinant. This medical test is one based on narrow criteria affecting the child at the time. Another line of authority considers the best interests and quality of life test on a wider basis. These look at the longer term medical *and social* implications of the treatment decision. The example given by Gostin ('A Moment in Human Development: Legal Protection, Ethical Standards and Social Policy on the Selective Non-Treatment of Handicapped Neonates' (1985) 11 Am J L & Med 32) comes from *Re Phillip B* (1979) 156 Cal Rptr 48. The court refused to order that a life-prolonging heart operation take place. The judge made the decision on the basis that the child's chances of surviving the operation were good, but the child had Down's syndrome. Gostin notes that, at first instance, the judge 'commented that he personally could not handle it, "if it happened to me"'. The decision not to authorise treatment was based on the judge's subjective view of what the future of the 'whole' child was, not just the medical necessity of the immediate operation. Whichever one is regarded as more appropriate, both views operate on a theory of patient quality, which itself is based on welfare. We shall see in a moment whether a definition of best interests, and quality of life can be considered by medical law from a more concrete human rights basis.

The English cases so far considered in this chapter appear to take the same line as *Re Phillip B*. Templeman LJ in *Re B (A Minor) (Wardship: Medical Treatment)* [1981] 1 WLR 1421 considered the necessity and possibilities for the operation in wide terms, while stressing a legal intuition which would accord with clinical intuition that when you cannot predict the future, you treat. The overriding concept for clinical intuition is to save the life of the patient. Neither the doctor nor the judge in *R v Arthur* (1981) 12 BMLR 1 appeared to have the same intuition, yet the decision was obviously reached on a view of the quality of life of a Down's syndrome child from a perspective of intellectual and social functioning. This was allied of course to the view of the prospective quality of the parents' life with a Down's syndrome child.

The USA also had the advantage (at least for a time; see 1.4) of an appropriate body to consider the best interests and quality of life issues. The President's Commission Report, *Deciding to Forgo Life-Sustaining Treatment* (1983), considered there would be more clarity and consistency of decision-making were attempts made to consider which of three situations was in existence:

(a)   treatment would be of clear benefit to the patient;
(b)   treatment would be futile;
(c)   the results of treatment would be uncertain.

Obviously there then needs to be further refinement of what is meant by 'benefit', 'futility' and 'uncertainty'. Look again at the situation of Joan at the start of the chapter. An operation would relieve pressure on the child's brain, but still leave the serious physical (and easily diagnosed) and mental (but not easily diagnosed) handicaps. Is the operation 'beneficial', 'futile' or 'uncertain'? In terms of 'benefit':

> The Commission has concluded that a very restrictive standard is appropriate: . . . permanent handicaps justify a decision not to provide life-sustaining treatment only when they are so severe that continued existence would not be a net benefit to the infant. (quoted in Kennedy and Grubb, *Medical Law*, 2nd ed. (London: Butterworths, 1994), p. 1243)

This would be decided by a reasonable decision-maker ariving at a subjective decision. If a reasonable decision-maker decided that he or she would not have that treatment then it would not happen. The obvious difficulty of this approach will be seen in a moment (see the comment of Glanville Williams below), but the Commission felt that this 'reasonable' decision-maker should attempt to look at matters of benefit from the perspective of the child.

The Commission recognised that some treatments are 'futile':

> Such therapies do not help the child, are sometimes painful for the infant (and probably distressing for the parents), and offer no reasonable probability of saving life for a substantial period. (loc. cit.)

The Commission's view on 'uncertainty' accords with that of Templeman LJ. It is difficult to tell the future severity of Down's syndrome when it is first diagnosed. There is uncertainty over improvements that may or may not occur over time. The longer the child lives, the easier prediction becomes. If life-saving treatment is needed, then it should take place so that a decision on the condition can be made later on with more certainty.

There needs to be further debate in medical law and ethics of the scope of the quality of life issue after *Re B*. Templeman LJ did conceive that there may be cases in the future where the quality of life would be so low that a different decision would have to be reached. That he was not able to posit a factual scenario as an illustration is an indication of the imprecision of the terms 'best interests' and 'quality of life'.

Other writers have attempted, with some limited success, to give some substance to these terms. Gostin is not alone in referring quite rightly to the fact that to use either term without elucidation makes them inevitably devoid of meaning.

The word 'quality' can invoke numerous images, based on an individual's perception, itself based on personal experience. There is difficulty in attempting to quantify *quality* of life objectively. It has been seen in the President's Commission Report and US jurisprudence that the term may be given meaning by utilising clinical theory. The quality of life is low when a particular operative procedure has little chance of success, and even were there to be success a longer term prognosis would also appear poor. Here the focus is on the physical suffering of the individual and the potential medical benefit of a particular procedure. This view appears to narrow the issue and thereby to increase the level of clinical as opposed to legal or ethical involvement. There could, Gostin noted, be a further level of sophistication in the articulation of a handicapped neonate's quality of life were the clinical assessment to be related to the possibility of an improved state of intellectual development and quality levels of social interaction. This would obviously be dependent on an assessment of the acceptability of the pre-treatment state of the neonate in 'quality' terms.

There is another form of calculation available. The best interests of the patient are served by an assessment of his or her welfare needs and human rights. The rights-based reform of medical law would point towards treatment as opposed to non-treatment regimes. It would stress benefits over burdens:

> One is the benefit to the treated infant who now will be able to live. A second benefit is the respect for all human life that treatment of the most severely disabled necessarily entails. Protecting all human life, regardless of social worth and potential, reinforces the general societal commitment to equal respect for all lives, which ultimately benefits eveyone. (John Robertson, 'Substantive Criteria and Procedures in Witholding Care from Defective Newborns' in Spicker et al. (eds), *The Law–Medicine Relation* (Dordrecht: Reidel, 1978), p. 220)

Blind alliegance to this one-sided idea of human rights in health care would create difficulties. The child here is seen, not solely as an individual, but a symbol of some higher societal ideal. This has dangers of loss of perspective. It would be difficult to extol such virtues to the parents of child J (see 14.6).

Human rights and medical law cannot exist outside the domain of welfare, and they have not done so. The WHO makes pleas to respect various human rights, one of which is dignity. There are times when one has to see welfare in not treating. One can respect the right to dignity and welfare by ending suffering.

That all of the above ideas of best interests and quality of life may themselves be less than precise does not make such quality assessments valueless. They are useful as staging posts on the path of considering the individual case under the umbrella term 'best interests'.

One should be aware of a more sinister potential involved in the general desire to see a wider articulation of the quality threshold. It may be argued that the quality of life calculation should extend beyond the individual to consider the wider interests of society as a whole, whether in economic terms or in terms of the level of handicap in society itself. One such view holds it desirable as a matter of 'societal' quality of life that the handicapped are not treated at birth. The sinister implications of this have been seen as a matter of historical reality in relation to the sterilisation of the mentally handicapped. There is overwhelming judicial and academic opinion that the quality of life calculation should be patient-specific.

How does the court consider a neonate's quality of life? Is it in terms of the benefits and burdens of treatment as a matter of medical improvement, or is it a wider calculation of aspirations of intellectual attainment and social functioning? In *Re J (A Minor) (Wardship: Medical Treatment)* [1991] Fam 33 (see 14.6), the Court of Appeal articulated a test which at first blush appeared to be different from the 'best interests' test, and seemed to be more like the transatlantic test of 'substituted judgment'.

14.6 THE SUBSTITUTED JUDGMENT TEST IN THE COURT OF APPEAL

The Court of Appeal in *Re J (A Minor) (Wardship: Medical Treatment)* [1991] Fam 33 was faced with another heart-rending case. A child had been born 13 weeks prematurely. The child was not breathing at birth, and was immediately placed on a ventilator and given antibiotics to fight an infection. For the first 10 days it seemed unlikely that the child would survive. The episodes the child suffered from that time onward were extreme, painful and on a number of occasions life-threatening. The evidence was clear that the child had suffered severe brain damage at birth and would as a result suffer from severe spastic quadriplegia. In addition the child would be blind and deaf, and unlikely ever to gain the ability to speak. Also the child would not be able to sit or hold his head up. What was significantly raised as a matter of fact was that the child would nevertheless have the ability to feel pain as a basic response.

The matter came before the court because there was the likelihood that the child, as had happened in the past, would need to be re-ventilated if another episode of breathing difficulty overcame him.

At first instance, Scott Baker J ordered that the child be given antibiotics to fight infection, but declared that it would not be in the *best interests* of the child to be re-ventilated if breathing stopped unless those involved in his care felt that it was clinically appropriate at that time.

At this stage of the decision it is useful to note that there is a clear separation between some activities in relation to the patient and others. While

Scott Baker J was clear that there need not be re-ventilation, there should be procedures in place to suck out the child's airway if it became blocked. Those treating had also to continue to supply oxygen by face mask. If infection developed the doctors were to administer antibiotics and maintain hydration to stave it off.

The Official Solicitor appealed against this decision, which made the parents re-evaluate their decision that their child should be left to die if another critical episode occurred. As one might expect, parents can suffer the anguish of wondering if they have done the right thing in such a situation. This point illustrates why the court is the most appropriate forum to decide a neonate's future, rather than the parental home or the doctor's surgery.

The main submission to the Court of Appeal was based on an absolutist approach – the sanctity of human life. The Official Solicitor argued that the court could never be justified in withholding life-saving treatment, whatever the quality of life that would persist as a result of its success. An alternative line of argument put was that the requirement of Templeman LJ in *Re B (A Minor) (Wardship: Medical Treatment)* [1981] 1 WLR 1421 that the future of the child 'be so demonstrably awful' as to not be worth living was not satisfied here.

Lord Donaldson MR's response to the sanctity of life argument had to confront a line of decisions from other jurisdictions that supported this deontological absolutism in fairly strident terms.

In *Re Superintendent of Family and Child Service and Dawson* (1983) 145 DLR (3d) 610 McKenzie J in the British Columbia Supreme Court supported a US decision in *Re Weberlist* (1974) 360 NYS 2d 783, in which Asch J, at p. 787, had argued that it could never be the place of court or parents to judge what quality threshold a child's life has achieved, though this was expressed in a slightly different way to that which the Official Solicitor in *Re J* sought to convey, and one which was certainly not absolutist:

> There is a strident cry in America to terminate the lives of *other* people – deemed physically or mentally defective. . . . Assuredly, one test of a civilisation is its concern with the survival of the 'unfittest', a reversal of Darwin's formulation. . . . In this case, the court must decide what its ward would choose, if he were in a position to make a sound judgment.

Asch J's point is that while it can never be the place of the court or parents to impose their views of the quality of life of the child, given that they are external decision-makers, the court can 'don the mantle' of the child and ask itself what the disabled child would choose for itself. The point is *not*, as Glanville Williams put it:

> If a wicked fairy told me she was about to transform me into a Down's baby and would I prefer to die I should certainly answer yes. ('Down's Syndrome and the Duty to Preserve Life' (1981) 131 NLJ 1020)

The question cannot be put and answered from the perspective of the normal neonate, for the simple reason that the handicapped child has no knowledge of normality, and the healthy child (or other decision-maker, the parents for example) has no conception of the relevant handicap by which to make a 'quality' comparative judgment.

This alternative guesstimate of what *this* child would want was to become the 'substituted judgment' test. This test, while seemingly attractive as a general proposition, has to be recognised as hard to sustain as a matter of logic. Nevertheless the test is justified by Stuart Hornett, who states:

> The subjective test assumes and indeed finds justification in the idea that a patient has the right to self-determination and can himself choose whether or not to be treated. If a competent patient has such a right, so the argument runs, an incompetent patient should not be deprived of it merely because of his physical condition. The patient's autonomy should be recognised and respected by proxy decision-makers, who, in so far as is possible, should act according to the patient's wishes. ('The Sanctity of Life and Substituted Judgment: The Case of Baby J' (1991) Ethics and Medicine 2 at p. 4)

It can be argued that this is not a subjective test or even a test at all. The decision-maker may attempt to have the aspirations and interests of the handicapped newborn child in mind when making a quality of life calculation, but that will be coloured by the prejudices of that decision-maker. This would appear to be a problem which is incapable of resolution, and strongly suggests that it is merely a different way of explaining the best interests test which exists in the wardship court, and in the many other branches of medical law where it is required.

An alternative view is that while it has an internal illogicality, the substituted judgment test is rather a plea for a human rights analysis of medical law. The focus of the test swings it away from deontology and utilitarianism, and certainly away from the paternalist model of modern medical practice, and refocuses it on the neonate as a separate individual with the rights that we all share in medicine. The rights are to life, respect, self-determination and dignity, without the need to calculate which right trumps the others. All are of an importance dependent on the choices of the individual.

Lord Donaldson agreed that the court could never sanction steps that would accelerate death, even where there was the most horrendous handicap, therefore re-emphasising the unlawfulness of direct activities. Lord Donaldson proceeded from that view to endorse the fictional legality of *R v Arthur* (1981) 12 BMLR 1, that there is a difference between such activity and 'choosing a course of action which would fail to avert death'.

In finally rejecting the sanctity of life argument Lord Donaldson emphasised:

> In real life there are presumptions, strong presumptions and almost overwhelming presumptions, but there are few, if any, absolutes.

The second submission was that, as a result of *Re B*, there had to be a child whose 'condition was demonstrably so awful' that the child should be left to die, and that J had not reached that threshold. Lord Donaldson felt that *Re B* was virtually binding authority to the effect that a balancing exercise must be performed when deciding where the best interests of the child lie. While this might well be the case, there was also a recognition in *Re J* that a calculation could never be done with any mathematical exactitude. The presumption in favour of life, while not being absolute, is regarded by the Court of Appeal here as a strong one, which will weigh heavily when the balancing exercise takes place.

In seeking to formulate where the best interests of J lay, the Court of Appeal sought to elucidate what factors should be taken into account. A consideration of the judgment indicates, as perhaps was inevitable with English medical law, that the factors are extremely varied and internally vague.

Lord Donaldson emphasised that the court was concerned with the concepts of pain and prospects for development. The pain and general quality of life of the child in the future had to be considered as well as the pain and suffering that would be an inevitable part of the treatment process itself. For J, the ventilation process itself would be invasive, complex and obviously distressing. Even if this was felt to be tolerable, the longevity of the child's life might be improved but not the quality of that life. Therefore the appeal of the Official Solicitor was dismissed.

Taylor LJ also sought to be more specific about the factors that would weigh in this difficult balancing exercise. An example given of a circumstance where the neonate should be allowed to die would be where a child was damaged to the extent that it had 'minimal use of most of its faculties' and in addition could only be preserved by 'extremely painful treatment' which would effectively lead to a life of continuous pain.

Taylor LJ also endorsed the substituted judgment test which was felt to be a test which would recognise the strong will to live that may exist in the individual, even were it to appear intolerable to an outside observer. Once more, however, it has to be conceded that where the child has never and can never exercise rational judgment, it seems impossible to attribute that ability of reflection to it.

Ultimately the Court of Appeal was left with a difficult task. Any precision about what goes into the melting pot of 'best interests' could be regarded as exclusionary of other factors. Any emphasis on one particular aspect of neonatal existence might begin a process of giving more weight to some factors than others. The fact that pain is mentioned in the case law may mean that those neonates who are insensate and therefore incapable of feeling pain (or anything else for that matter) might not come within the notion of the intolerable existence. That this has been a problem for the judiciary is emphasised by Handler J in the US case of *Re Conroy* (1985) 486 A 2d 1209:

> While the basic standard purports to account for several concerns, it ultimately focuses on pain as the critical factor. The presence of significant pain in effect becomes the sole measure of such a person's best interests. 'Pain' thus eclipses a whole cluster of other human values that have a

proper place in the subtle weighting that will ultimately determine how life should end. (p. 1247)

The undesirability of considering pain as the crucial determinant was also to find support in the Court of Appeal in *Airedale NHS Trust* v *Bland* [1993] AC 789 (see chapter 15).

The best interests test has to be regarded as something of a protective mechanism. The development of the wardship jurisdiction has been marked by relatively consistent pronouncements that the court should focus on the individual patient and not be side-tracked by extraneous considerations. It may be that whether the test is described as one of 'best interests' or 'substituted judgment' is once more a matter of semantics, and the courts, while being forced into a form of 'ad-hockery' may, as a result of *Re J*, have more cognisance of the independent rights of the neonate. This might avoid allegations of decision-making from the perspective of others affected by the handicapped condition of the neonate or of an overly paternalistic mechanism which values sanctity without reference to quality.

It is now apparent that the test remains one of 'best interests', without the need to embellish it (or rather to change the perspective) with notions of substituted judgment. Fairly recently, the High court has once more had to consider a truly tragic case under the mantle of best interests and decide whether there is any need to add content to this phrase, or even to consider the state of the law in any detail: Sir Stephen Brown P took the latter view in *Re C (A Baby)* [1996] 2 FLR 43.

The child in this case was three months old at the time of the hearing. She had been born eight weeks premature and suffered from a number of difficulties associated with such an early birth. Most significantly, however, she developed meningitis which led to serious brain damage. The result of this damage itself was that she suffered continuous convulsions and could not survive without the aid of artificial ventilation. An attempt had been made to see if she could survive without this support but her condition soon deteriorated. It was clear that the child was suffering pain and distress and that this would only increase as time went on. Further evidence indicated that this child had a limited life expectancy, perhaps two years. Having heard such tragic evidence one would expect the court to give leave that the life support regime be discontinued; this it did. What it did not do was to go into any real detail on how previous case law gave guidance here. There seemed to be more an acceptance that this was the right course of action without a need to articulate in any detail the factors which led to this conclusion. As Ian Kennedy comments, after the carefully considered cases of *Re B* and *Re J* 'by the time we reach the instant case, the sadness and regret are still there, but the court no longer felt the need to explore the law' ((1997) 5 Med L Rev 102). One could argue once more that where such profound decisions are being made there needs to be a more comprehensive articulation of factors than is apparent here. Ian Kennedy notes the fact in his commentary on the case that there can be perceived to be a 'coarsening' of the law here. There were certainly factual circumstances which needed to be explored utilising the case law available, particularly *Airedale NHS Trust* v *Bland*. There is the issue, for instance, of which of the particular factors weighed most heavily in the balance in deciding where the best interests of the child lay. There was clear evidence that this child was in what was termed a 'low awareness state'. This meant that the child was not in the persistent vegetative state that Anthony Bland was in. There was evidence of increasing levels of pain; how did this weigh in the balance? What was the significance for the law that the child was tragically ill, but not terminally so? While the vast majority would agree that this was the only conclusion the High court could have reached, there are sufficiently complex and important questions for a rather more mature reflection on the medico-legal concepts involved.

14.7 THE POSITION OF THE PARENTS IN DECIDING BEST INTERESTS

At the beginning of the chapter the fact that Leonard Arthur was guided in his actions by the wishes of the parents of John Pearson was noted (see 14.3). Recently the Court of Appeal has apparently given judicial approval of the dominance of parental views in deciding whether the child should live or die. The case of *Re T (A Minor) (Wardship: Medical Treatment)* [1997] 1 WLR 242 is a significant one for medical law, for a number of reasons which will become apparent when considering it in some detail.

Child C had been born suffering from a serious condition of the liver known as biliary atresia. There had been an attempt to correct the defect by surgery when the child was three and a half weeks old, but it had not worked. There was only one option left, a full liver transplant. When the parents, themselves experienced in the care of severely handicapped newborns, were informed, they refused to give permission for the operation to take place. The prognosis was that without the operation the child would live in relative comfort for some two years. The operation itself would be a gruelling one for the child and require a substantial period of post-operative support from the mother. What marked this case out from others that confronted the courts was revealed by one of the medical teams which gave evidence. Dr A (at p. 246) stated that:

I would consider an excellent result of transplantation to be many years of life with normal growth with no treatment necessary other than immuno-suppression, and there is certainty that such an outcome could be achieved.

It was this significant factor, that the life of the child, on successful completion of the operation, would be of a high quality that has marked this case out from the others, like *Re B (A Minor) (Wardship: Medical Treatment)* [1981] 1 WLR 1421 and *Re J (A Minor) (Wardship: Medical Treatment)* [1991] Fam 33, that have confronted the courts.

At the time the parents were resident outside the jurisdiction, and an opportunity to use an available liver had been lost because they could not be contacted. The local authority made a decision that proceedings should be brought under s. 100(3) of the Children Act 1989. The application to commence proceedings under this section was granted and the Official Solicitor was appointed guardian *ad litem*. At first instance Connell J held that it was in the child's best interests to have the operation notwithstanding the refusal of the mother to consent. The core of Connell J's reasoning was that the mother was acting as an unreasonable parent as she could not accept the reality of the situation which was evidenced by unanimous medical opinion on the chances of success and longer-term prospects. The mother appealed, contending that she was not an unreasonable parent as professional literature suggested that it was good practice in the situation of liver transplants to have regard to the wishes of the parents. The mother further declared that she was a loving and dedicated parent who had acted in good faith.

In opening analysis of the appeal Butler-Sloss LJ accepted that the core was that the mother had not been unreasonable as the medical profession felt it was correct to accede to parental wishes. Counsel for the mother sought to go slightly further in arguing that 'the consequence of the decision to operate was to commit the mother to a lifetime of care of the child with a lifetime commitment to the treatment'. In contrast counsel for the respondents sought to argue that the best interest test was a test of the interests of the child not the reasonableness of the decision of the parents. It was accepted that parental views should be taken into account, but these views should not be determinative of the issue. The Court of Appeal accepted from *Re B* that its task was indeed one of weighing best interests, and that the court, in invoking its *parens patriae* jurisdiction, takes over from the parents. Butler-Sloss LJ considered that Connell J had erred in focusing on the medical evidence rather than looking too at the broader arguments against treatment.

The main controversial points were revealed by the judgment, which has been considered to be 'the nadir of the best interests test'. Already it has been noted that the child would have had a 'normal' life other than immuno-suppression. This child would not be one of those tragic newborns like baby J. Butler-Sloss LJ considered that because of the level of post-operative care required from the mother, mother and child should be considered one for the purpose of consent. It was therefore decided that it would not be in the best interests of the child to have the operation.

In *Re T* the clinical factors pointed toward successful treatment for the child. The 'social' factors pointed towards an extended period of extensive support from the mother and the difficulties of the fact that the parents were resident abroad. Surprisingly Butler-Sloss LJ decided that it was not in the best interests of the child to be treated despite being uncertain of a great many factors. The following quote (at p. 252) reveals that there were a number of issues which could not be answered, yet the Court of Appeal felt able to come to the certain conclusion that the child should be allowed to die:

Will the father stay in country AB and work or come with her [the mother] to England, giving up his job and having to seek another job? If he does not come she will have to manage unaided. How will the mother cope? Can her professionalism overcome her view that her son should not be subjected to this distressing procedure? Will she break down? How will the child be affected by the conflict with which the mother may have to cope? What happens if the treatment is partially successful and another transplant is needed? The mother may not wish to consent to the further surgery. Is the court to be asked again for consent to the next operation?

It seems now that where the medical situation is uncertain it is parental views which will hold sway. Waite LJ compounded this error by making the frankly stunning comment in an area of medical law where the weak need to be protected that 'the rights of the child are not in issue'. There is a disturbing tone of distrust of human rights in the analysis of Waite LJ. Instead the Court of Appeal fall back on the apparently empty rhetoric of best interests. Earlier in this chapter the danger of parents having a conflict of interest was noted as a reason why there needs to be judicial involvement. It appears that the independent rights of the newborn now take second place to the judicial recognition that it is the parents who have the power to decide. This fact is confirmed by the conclusion of Butler-Sloss LJ, at p. 253:

> Once the pressure of this litigation is over it may be the parents will reconsider whether they should remain in country AB or should return to this country and attend at hospital Y with a view to a further assessment for the purpose of carrying out the operation. That, however, will be a matter for them and not for this court.

More recently, however, the courts have rejected parental views and acceded to the request of the medical profession. In *Re C (Medical Treatment)* [1998] 1 FLR 384 a 16-month-old child was suffering from spinal muscular atrophy, a fatal disease. Her life expectancy was both short and one of serious disability. At the time of the hearing the child was on a ventilator. Despite the wishes of the parents, the hospital authority sought the approval of the court that there should be withdrawal of artificial ventilation and non-resuscitation were there to be heart failure. In addition approval was sought for palliative care to be given to make the end of the child's life as dignified and comfortable as possible. Due to their religious convictions the parents genuinely believed that life should always be preserved, even here where the medical opinion was unanimous. Sir Stephen Brown P granted the leave to withdraw treatment. According to the headnote in [1998] Fam Law 135 it was held that:

> (1)   The paramount consideration governing the exercise of the court's inherent jurisdiction was the best interests of the child and not the sanctity of life.
> (2)   The proposed treatment was in the child's best interests. It was supported in these circumstances not only by all the individual experts but also by the publication . . . *Withholding or Withdrawing Lifesaving Treatment in Children: A Framework of Practice* (Royal College of Paediatrics and Child Health, 1997).

(3)   The court's power is limited to authorising a proposed course of treatment when the person or body whose consent is requisite is unwilling or unable to do so. The court will not make an order requiring a medical practitioner to treat a child in a manner contrary to his clinical judgment.

14.8   TREATMENT OF THE TERMINALLY ILL NEONATE

The cases encountered so far in this chapter have considered the plight of the handicapped neonate requiring treatment to survive for an indeterminate period. The courts have also been called upon to consider the tragic situation of the child whose handicaps are such that the child is terminally ill. Here any procedure adopted will have more limited effectiveness even if fully successful, for the child is dying. The question for the courts has been whether the 'best interests' or 'substituted judgment' tests are appropriate to this situation.

Looking at the best interests of such a patient from the perspective adopted by the US President's Commission Report of 1983 (see 14.5), any treatment is 'futile'. As far as there can be certainty in medical science it exists here.

The child in *Re C (A Minor) (Wardship: Medical Treatment)* [1990] Fam 26 was found at birth to be suffering from a severe form of hydrocephalus (fluid on the brain). The brain structure itself was described in evidence as badly formed. The child suffered from pressure on the brain itself, which needed to be alleviated by an operation. This operation was performed, and something called a shunt was inserted to relieve the pressure of the fluid that had built up in the brain cavity. That further episodes requiring surgical intervention would occur was not without doubt, so the true question was whether such treatment would be in the best interests of C. In addition, the medical evidence clearly showed that C was dying. It thus might appear a little strange to consider the matter in terms of 'best interests' as understood in *R v Arthur* (1981) 12 BMLR 1, *Re B (A Minor) (Wardship: Medical Treatment)* [1989] 1 WLR 1421 and *Re J (A Minor) (Wardship: Medical Treatment)* [1991] Fam 33. Nevertheless the court was acting in its capacity as a wardship court and the best interests test was to be applied, but taking the factual issues of C's condition into account in arriving at a decision.

C's condition was most alarming and pointed clearly to the existence of what, on any reading of the facts as reported by the paediatrician, was a massive and terminal handicap. Poignantly this expert concluded:

> In the event of her acquiring a serious infection, or being unable to take feeds normally by mouth I do not think it would be correct to give antibiotics, to set up intravenous fusions or nasal-gastric feeding regimes. Such action would be prolonging a life which has no future and which appears to be unhappy for her.

Balcombe LJ recognised the comment of Templeman LJ in *Re B* that there may be cases severe enough that the court would authorise that the treatment be such as to allow a child to die with dignity, relieved of pain, distress and suffering, and that this was indeed one of those cases.

Balcombe LJ did appear to wish to distance the court from the situation outlined in the Canadian case of *Re Superintendent of Family and Child Service and Dawson* (1983) 145 DLR (3d) 610, where the court had been concerned with a severely handicapped child with severe brain damage who required a shunt. The question of whether to operate on the child in future was based on the fact that the boy might not necessarily die, but live for months or years. Balcombe LJ sought to distinguish that case from the one before him on the basis that the Canadian case did not involve a 'right to die':

> The evidence in the present case shows . . . that this is the case of a child terminally ill since, as the professor says in his report: 'I do not believe that there is any treatment which will alter the ultimate prognosis, which appears to be hopeless'.

It was accepted in *Re J* that *Re B* and *Re C* give similar guidance, but should they? *Re B* was concerned with the future prospects of the neonate if treatment were undertaken and successful. To a large extent, the Court of Appeal in *Re C* was concerned with the nature of the death of the child, which appeared inevitable, and with the quality of that process of dying rather than the quality of living. The articulation of the best interests test here is concerned with the best interest in maintaining dignity and the relief of suffering at the end of life. *Re C* is important in that it further indicates that there can never be a fixed set of interests worthy of consideration in every case concerning the neonate. The court took the only real option open to it on the particular facts of this case. That others might push medical law into new areas seems not to be in doubt. Consider this final situation.

Susan has just given birth to a severely handicapped child. The confident prognosis of the doctor is that a heart operation will give the child a maximum life span of three years. During that time the child will require a large amount of surgery and other invasive and painful forms of treatment to slow the inevitable deterioration of the constantly painful condition.

Having considered how the medical law has developed, what would the court decide?

14.9 CONCLUSION

Medical law is one of the only areas of law that confronts the stark and most human of dilemmas described in this chapter. Life and death issues are not new to the courts, but advances in medical technology and the massive improvement in surgery have meant that medical law now has to confront them more and more. The English courts have not been assisted by legislation upon which to base their extremely difficult decisions. Any evaluation of this aspect of medical law shows clearly that there are more than purely clinical issues at stake. A doctor could have a decent attempt at assessing on a scale of 1 to 10 how painful a neonate's day-to-day existence is, but there is more to measuring the quality of life than that. There are intangible notions of respect for dignity and the cost of life as well as the right to it. There is an urgent need for the courts to be able to articulate principles of guidance that have been the result of the sort of comprehensive debate that has happened in the USA. At present the typical response of medical law, when dealing with the selective non-treatment of the neonate, and numerous other crucial legal and ethical issues, is that the doctor looks to the judge to sanction a step, the judge looks to Parliament, Parliament turns away, so the judge shrugs his shoulders and leaves it all to the doctor. Now it may well be that the law and the medical profession are leaving the decision to the parents, who may not have the impartiality and objectivity required in this crucial area. Whether the power should remain here is open to question. What is clear is that recent case law reveals that this is not a 'good' way to make 'good' medical law.

The fact that hard cases make bad law has been stated often. In the decision of the Court of Appeal in *Re T (A Minor) (Wardship: Medical Treatment)* [1997] 1 WLR 242 there is concrete recognition that the parents hold the reins of decision-making. While one must have the deepest sympathy with the parents of all the tragically ill children encountered in this chapter, there is very real danger in leaving the decision in the hands of the parents. While one may baulk at the notion, there may be circumstances where the parents look at broader issues than the pain of the operation for the child, the prospects of that operation's success and the future handicap of the child. There may be considerations of the cost of keeping the child, effects it may have on career prospects or even existing children. It may simply be that the anguish of discovering one's child to be seriously ill or having a profound handicap makes it difficult to see the options clearly (or as is apparent from *Re C (Medical Treatment)* [1998] 1 FLR 384 a religious conviction that life should be saved whatever the level of handicap). There needs to be concrete guidance for the court, beyond intoning best interests as a catch-all concept. When one combines the emptiness of best interests with the Court of Appeal openly declaring the rights of the child to be a non-issue, then one can see very real dangers for medical law leaving the decision on when to stop treating the newborn to any other body than Parliament.

Further reading

Brahams, D., '*Arthur's* Case (2) Putting *Arthur's* Case in Perspective' [1986] Crim LR 387.
Davies, M., 'Selective Non-Treatment of the New-Born: In Whose Best Interests? In Whose Judgment?' [1998] 49 NILQ 1 at 82.
Freeman, M.D.A., 'Using Wardship to Save a Child from its Parents' (1982) 12 Fam Law 73.
Gillon, R., 'An introduction to Philosophical Medical Ethics: The *Arthur* Case' (1985) 290 BMJ 1117.
Gunn, M.J., and Smith, J.C., '*Arthur's* Case and the Right to Life of a Down's Syndrome Child' [1985] Crim LR 705.
Poole, D., '*Arthur's* Case (1) A Comment' [1986] Crim LR 383.
Williams, G., 'Down's Syndrome and the Doctor's Responsibility' (1981) 131 NLJ 1040.

FIFTEEN
Euthanasia

15.1 INTRODUCTION

15.1.1 Breadth of the issue

Ronald Dworkin in his work *Life's Dominion* (London: HarperCollins, 1993) notes that even where issues concerning the end of life arise, there are common concerns of medical law and ethics. Chapter 14 showed how medical law deals with the handicapped newborn, and other chapters confront what can generally be perceived as being life or death issues, and the considerations that go to make up a legal response to these most profound of legal and ethical questions. Dworkin's introduction indicates the dramatic nature of events:

> Abortion is a waste of the start of human life. Death intervenes before life in earnest has even begun. Now we turn to decisions that people must make about death at the other end of life, after life in earnest has ended. We shall find that the same issues recur, that the moral questions we ask about the two edges of life have much in common. (p. 179)

It may now be that the issue of euthanasia – decisions at and concerning the end of life – is the main focus of public, academic and legal debate on the moral issues of the sanctity of life, the quality of life, the paternalism of the medical profession and the State, autonomy and consent to medical treatment and even the proper limits of the criminal law. Euthanasia is a hotly debated issue in almost every country, and even those States with reasonably well settled constitutions find them tested by medico-legal decision-making at the end of life. Even the medical profession can find no consistency of clinical intuition to aid in answering the question of where the doctor's duty and the patient's right lie. The medical profession includes both proponents of euthanasia and those opposed to it. Fervent advocacy of a duty to end a suffering patient's life as an act of medico-moral compassion will be met with an equally strong call for the medical profession to maintain the sanctity of life, and the tenet of the Hippocratic oath, which states: 'To please no one will I prescribe a deadly drug, nor give advice which may cause his death'.

Case law, which came after the decision to remove ventilation and hydration to Anthony Bland (*Airedale NHS Trust v Bland* [1993] AC 789) has had to confront a number of aspects of medical practice at the end of life. It will be seen during the course of this chapter that, like selective non-treatment of the newborn, there has been a widening of the circumstances where the courts have been willing to declare the non-treatment decision to be a lawful one (see, for example, the case of *Re R (Adult: Medical Treatment)* [1996] 2 FLR 99; *Re D* (1997) 5 Med LR 225). This expansion of circumstances is in part a recognition by the medical profession that their vocation is sometimes as much about easing suffering at the end of life as it is about saving life, even where the patient has some awareness, albeit low, of his or her surroundings and the people there. In contrast to this there have been several decisions where the courts have gone against the express wishes of patients demanding that they be left alone, whether this refusal is for an operation or force-feeding by the medical profession. This pronouncement of lawfulness of 'forced' treatment has most often been made following a declaration by the medical profession and thereafter the court that the patient is not competent to make the decision whether to live or die. Although obviously a matter which concerns chapters 6 and 7 on the law of consent, it is of obvious significance here in revealing the constant conflict between autonomy and medico-legal paternalism where life-and-death decisions fall to be made (see, for example, *B v Croydon Health Authority* [1995] Fam 133; *Re MB (Medical Treatment)* [1997] 2 FLR 426).

15.1.2 Definitional problems

Despite its emotive backdrop in the activities of the Third Reich in relation to the selective termination of both young and old on various perverse grounds, the initial problem with the debate on euthanasia is one of definition. This definitional difficulty appears, one might suggest, from the different perspectives from which euthanasia may be defined. A proponent of the power of the individual to make decisions about when his or her death should occur could regard the term 'euthanasia' in a positive light. The word 'euthanasia' may be seen as an enabler and have a wide definitional base which encompasses and legitimises active or passive ending of life. An advocate of the 'right to die' might equally be considered an advocate of the 'right to euthanasia'. Alternatively, the word might be used in the negative sense, and indeed appears to have been so used by the judiciary in relation to the non-treatment of the neonate (see the comments in 14.3) or even the patient in a persistent vegetative state. For example, in the Court of Appeal, in the focal case of *Airedale NHS Trust v Bland* [1993] AC 789, Bingham MR stated unequivocally that the issue of the removal of life support from a patient in a persistent vegetative state:

is not about euthanasia, if by that is meant the taking of positive action to cause death. It is not about putting down the old and infirm, the mentally defective or the physically imperfect. It has nothing to do with the eugenic practices associated with fascist Germany. (p. 808)

The term 'euthanasia' here has been given a taint of criminality and immorality; 'euthanasia' means a positive act which causes death.

Mason and McCall Smith (*Law and Medical Ethics*, 4th ed. (London: Butterworths, 1994), p. 316) consider two definitions. First a medical one, '1. A quiet, painless death. 2. The intentional putting to death by artificial means of persons with incurable or painful disease' (*Stedman's Medical Dictionary*, 20th ed.). Secondly a general one: 'the act of killing someone painlessly, especially to relieve suffering from an incurable illness' (*Collins English Dictionary*, 2nd ed.). The common feature is the notion of a pain*less* end to a pain*ful* or incurable illness. There is also some common ground that a form of activity is involved. Activity and passivity have become the main focal points for judicial intervention concerning decisions at the end of life (see also the medico-legal significance of this debate in relation to the selective non-treatment of the neonate in chapter 14).

That one may not find a consensual or comprehensive definition of euthanasia does not mean that the term is useless. It may best be described as an umbrella term connoting decisions made in relation to the ending of the life of the patient. Thus the focus moves away from the heated moral debate somewhat, and toward the key issue of the legality or illegality of forms of euthanasia. Nevertheless to blind oneself to the sweep of this ethical as well as legal minefield is to ignore the dilemmas the doctor, the relative and the judge are faced with.

The factual issues that can impact on the legal regulation of euthanasia are fairly wide, but in essence centre on the difference between *voluntary* and *involuntary* forms of euthanasia and a debate encountered in chapter 14 of whether there is a moral and/or legal difference between *actively* terminating life and creating circumstances where other causes of death will occur, the latter being commonly called *passive* euthanasia. Before moving on, consider, as well as what law might do in the following situations, which of them most easily fits with your idea of 'euthanasia':

(a)   Steven has just been diagnosed as having terminal cancer. It has been further diagnosed as being inoperable. The doctor informs Steven that while there will be little pain, he will lose a great deal of weight and mobility. He asks the doctor, 'Please give me something to stop the worry of dying'. The doctor leaves a bottle of tablets on the bedside cabinet and says, 'These are very strong painkillers. If you take more than 10 they could prove fatal.' Steven takes 20 tablets and is found dead by a nurse two hours later.

(b)   Kevin has been rushed to hospital after a car accident and is unconscious. When looking for his identity, a nurse finds a card in his wallet which says, 'NO BLOOD TRANSFUSION. It is a mortal sin and the path to everlasting damnation. If this card is found obey its instructions.' Kevin requires a blood transfusion. His wife pleads with the doctor to perform it, but cannot deny that he was a devout member of his faith. The doctor does not give Kevin a transfusion and he dies.

(c)   Debbie is in the final stages of an illness, a feature of which is that in the final days before death the patient becomes hypersensitive to pain. Painkillers at this stage have the opposite effect. When she is lucid she begs the doctor to end her life. One evening the doctor injects a massive dose of an opiate, knowing that this dose will prove fatal, and while normally a painkiller, here can only be effective in ending the life of the patient. Debbie dies a few minutes later.

In considering these issues consider the pathway that medical law needs to follow. What is the moral status of the act? If it is morally wrong to do one, both or all of the things in these situations, is it necessarily the place of the law to prohibit or regulate such action? What human rights are in issue, and do they conflict? What do you think a 'good' medical law would do (if anything) in these situations?

15.1.3   General fears

The debate in this area, as with the treatment of neonates in chapter 14, is dominated by emotion and vociferous calls for liberalisation answered by equally dramatic entreaties that society has embarked on the termination of those deemed to be unwanted and a burden on relatives, carers and society. The legal issues which flow from that debate concern a wide range of matters that permeate medical law and have been addressed in earlier chapters: issues of consent, autonomy, and the place of the medical and legal professions in the decision-making process. It is not too dramatic to say that the courts will be seen to be concerned at times with the fundamental concepts of human existence: worth, pain, dignity and autonomy at the end of life.

15.1.4   Technology at the end of life

Another dominating feature of the legal and ethical debate is the existence of high-technology medicine to sustain life, which, only a few years ago, would have ended at a much earlier stage. In the relatively recent past, patients died at home. Technology was limited to the hospital setting and was used to treat emergencies, as opposed to those seen as coming to the end of life as a natural result of the ageing process or the ravages of illness.

Medicine has developed its own technology with the underlying theme of sustaining life. The Hippocratic oath is predicated on good faith and the saving of life. There is some evidence, though, that this leap in technology has led to an inevitable distortion in the true aims of medicine itself. It could be alleged that doctors no longer always extend the life of the patient, but can prolong death. Margaret Brazier puts the matter more starkly: 'High technology medicine can sometimes be as cruel as the illness itself' (*Medicine, Patients and the Law*, 2nd ed. (London: Penguin, 1992), chapter 3) Nowhere will this be seen to be more significant than in the key case to an understanding of the legal and ethical concepts surrounding the end of life than the case of Anthony Bland, placed on a respirator after being crushed in the Hillsborough stadium disaster of 1989 (*Airedale NHS Trust v Bland* [1993] AC 789). This case will be referred to throughout the consideration of the debate on euthanasia. The report runs to some 110 pages and during the passage of the case through the courts there seems to be little of the legal and ethical debate that remains untouched.

15.2 TERMINATING THE LIFE OF THE COMPETENT PATIENT

15.2.1 Mercy killing and assisted suicide

The moving story of the end of Janet Adkins's life, detailed by Ronald Dworkin in *Life's Dominion* (London: HarperCollins, 1993) gives an example of the type of scenario that the medical law courts can be called upon to consider.

Janet Adkins was aware that she was in the early stages of Alzheimer's disease. Her awareness came from the fact that she should beat her son at tennis, but had difficulty keeping the score. She was also aware that matters would not get better. She read about a Dr Jack Kervorkian, who had developed a machine whereby people could give themselves lethal injections. She arranged to meet Dr Kervorkian, who was eventually satisfied, having had a long discussion with her, that she was competent and had reflected sufficiently to make the decision to end her own life. Two days later they entered the back of Dr Kervorkian's modified van where he inserted the needle and instructed her on what to do next. She pressed the relevant button, the poison was injected and she died. This may seem an overly dramatic way to introduce the subject of the legality of actively terminating the life of the competent individual, but this is precisely the type of situations the courts have to attempt to rationalise within the existing structure of medicine, ethics and the law. The emotional intensity of these situations has impacted on the English criminal courts, which have had to consider whether to judge these cases according to the criminal law as it is commonly understood, or to create a distinct branch of criminal law to apply to doctors involved. While there can be no definite answer to this, two notorious cases in this country appear to indicate that the latter approach is developing. *R v Arthur* (1981) 12 BMLR 1 appeared to distort the traditional conceptions of intention and causation in criminal law, as, arguably, has *Airedale NHS Trust v Bland* [1993] AC 789. While the criminality of doctors as a new matter for medical law has been struggling to assert itself, it has been forced recently to give way to a limited extent to the former traditional notions of causation and criminal intention (see *R v Cox* (1992) 12 BMLR 38 discussed in 15.2.1.1). These cases all indicate the somewhat confused judicial attitude to the 'mercy killer' of a terminally ill patient who may well be in agony.

15.2.1.1 'Double effect', intent and causation   *R v Adams* [1957] Crim LR 365 was a murder trial in which it was alleged that Dr Adams injected an

incurably (not terminally) ill patient with increasing doses of opiates. In summing up to the jury, Devlin J created the notion of the 'double effect' as it has been described subsequently. Prior to that Devlin J summed up according to traditional conceptions of causation and intent at the time:

> If the acts done were intended to kill and did, in fact, kill, it did not matter if a life were cut short by weeks or months, it was just as much murder as if it were cut short by years.

But the following part of the summing up appears to contradict this sentiment:

> If the first purpose of medicine, the restoration of health, can no longer be achieved there is still much for a doctor to do, and he is entitled to do all that is proper and necessary to relieve pain and suffering, even if the measures he takes may *incidentally* shorten life. (emphasis added)

Nevertheless Devlin J concluded his summing up by stating:

> But it remains the fact, and it remains the law, that no doctor, nor any man, no more in the case of a dying man than a healthy, has the right deliberately to cut the thread of life.

Dr Adams was acquitted of murder on the ground that the ending of life was incidental to the relief of pain.

The concept of 'double effect' is significant, for it appears to establish the fact that if the doctor gives pain-relieving drugs in the knowledge that as well as acting in their primary role as pain relievers these same drugs will shorten life, then that is not seen as a legal cause of death or alternatively is not proof of intention to kill. A dual principle of intention is being enunciated as a part of criminal law. Where there are two effects of an action, and only the 'good one' is desired, while the 'bad one' is not, then the latter is not intended. This is not a test of intention which fits within the criminal law. An effect can be intended as a matter of law without being desired. Cases such as *R v Moloney* [1985] AC 905 and *R v Nedrick* [1986] 1 WLR 1025, establish that intention can be inferred from conduct which the defendant perceives will have a virtually certain result, even though the defendant may fervently hope that this virtual certainty does not become reality.

An alternative route to justifying this summing up might rest on the contention that Dr Adams did not, as a matter of law, cause the death of the patient. One can do little better than quote Glanville Williams's reply to this contention:

> While I am reluctant to criticise a legal doctrine that gives a beneficial result, the use of the language of causation seems here to conceal rather than to reveal the valuation that is being made. To take an example, suppose that it were shown that the administration of morphine in regular

medical practice caused a patient to die of respiratory failure or pneumonia. Medically speaking, this death would not be caused by the disease: it would be caused by the administration of morphine. There seems to be some difficulty in asserting that for legal purposes the causation is precisely the opposite. (*The Sanctity of Life and the Criminal Law* (London: Faber & Faber, 1958), pp. 289–90)

This compassionate, yet legally distorting decision, needs now to be read in the light of the successful prosecution of Dr Cox (*R* v *Cox* (1992) 12 BMLR 38) for the attempted murder of Lillian Boyes. Mrs Boyes was suffering from an incurable and increasingly distressing form of arthritis which made her hypersensitive to touch and this could not be eased by painkillers in its latter stages. Prior to the onset of the latter manifestations, Dr Cox and Mrs Boyes, who had known each other for a considerable period, had talked of such events, and she had extracted a promise from him that he would not let her suffer. As the hypersensitivity to pain increased at the end of her life, Mrs Boyes and her sons repeatedly requested that the doctors in attendance end her life. Dr Cox administered a clearly lethal dose of potassium chloride and Mrs Boyes died within minutes.

It appears that Dr Cox was tried on indictment alleging attempted murder because it could not be proved that the injection ended Mrs Boyes' life. Evidence was given that Mrs Boyes was perhaps only minutes away from death when the injection was given. It appeared in the summing up that both prosecution and judge were aware of the near certainty that the potassium chloride was the cause of the death. The main issue for the jury was one of intent to kill. The issue for the jury was set out by Ognall J in the following way, at times reminiscent of *R* v *Adams*:

It was plainly Dr Cox's duty to do all that was medically possible to alleviate her pain and suffering even if the course adopted carried with it an obvious risk that as a side-effect . . . of that treatment her death would be rendered likely or even certain.

There can be no doubt that the use of drugs to reduce pain and suffering will often be fully justified notwithstanding that it will, in fact, hasten the moment of death, but . . . what can never be lawful is the use of drugs with the primary purpose of hastening the moment of death.

The evidence indicated clearly that the injection of potassium chloride could have no pain-relieving effect and the jury convicted.

In sentencing Dr Cox to one year in prison, suspended, Ognall J regarded the act of injecting as a breach of an 'unequivocal duty' toward a patient. In *Airedale NHS Trust* v *Bland* [1993] AC 789 Lord Goff considered that to take such action was to 'cross the Rubicon which runs between on the one hand the care of the living patient and on the other hand euthanasia'.

The decision to prosecute at all in *R* v *Cox* has been roundly criticised, as well as the legal analysis which, while convicting, still perpetuated the dual legal myths of 'double effect' causation and intention introduced in *R* v

Adams in relation to the activities of the doctor in ending the life of the terminally ill patient. For example, Helme and Padfield ('Safeguarding Euthanasia' (1992) 142 NLJ 1335) regarded the prosecution as 'disproportionate' to any perceived wrong in the actions of the doctor, and an example of the relative invisibility of the DPP's use of discretion to initiate a prosecution. They implied that the traditional guidelines on the decision to mount a criminal prosecution may not be appropriate to such a situation. Critics of the decision in *R* v *Cox* also point to the charge itself. There is a suspicion that the charge of attempted murder (with a flexible sentencing power on the court upon conviction) was manufactured rather than the obvious full charge of murder because the latter carries with it an automatic life sentence upon conviction. In addition, the defence of diminished responsibility would appear wholly inappropriate to such a situation. The significance of these factors is that there appears to be a mixture of public policy in preventing the active termination of the life of the competent patient according to request (the conviction), and sympathy for the actions of the doctor when that action is undertaken (the sentence).

R v *Adams* and *R* v *Cox* are clear examples of the legally indefensible medical law interpretation of double effect and intention, and the fiction of causation. The decisions allow the doctor to escape criminal liability if use is made of analgesic drugs in large doses even where it is known that the dosage will accelerate death. If the doctor indicates that the primary purpose is pain relief then there will be no criminal liability for the death. The traditional legal notions of criminal law intention and causation have not been used here. Consider how the law would react to the following non-medical situation.

Tim has been nursing his wife through the latter stages of arthritis, at home. At times she begs him to kill her. He always refuses. One night she is clearly distressed. Tim takes a bottle of painkillers provided by the doctor, and gives her the whole of the bottle with a large glass of whisky. His wife drifts off to an apparently restful sleep, but is found dead by their son the next morning.

While of course there would be scope for utilising the defence of diminished responsibility to reduce the conviction to one of manslaughter, one would be surprised if there were an acquittal in the absence of such a defence (see, however, *R* v *Johnson* (1961) 1 Med Sci Law 192, where a plea of diminished responsibility appears to be rubber-stamped on such 'domestic' cases). A medical practitioner could rarely claim diminished responsibility so the patchwork garment of medical law has distorted the criminal law to secure policy acquittals or reductions of charge.

That the courts have started to worry about the dubious demarcation between primary and secondary purposes, and more directly between killing and allowing the patient to die, is revealed by the comment of Lord Goff of Chieveley in *Airedale NHS Trust* v *Bland* [1993] AC 789 that:

> It is true that the drawing of this distinction may lead to a charge of hypocrisy; because it can be asked why, if the doctor, by discontinuing treatment, is entitled in consequence to let his patient die, it should not be

lawful to put him out of his misery straight away, in a more humane manner, by a lethal injection, rather than let him linger on in pain until he dies. But the law does not feel able to authorise euthanasia, even in circumstances such as these; for once euthanasia is recognised as lawful in these circumstances, it is difficult to see any logical basis for excluding it in others. (p. 865)

It will be seen that in *Airedale NHS Trust* v *Bland*, the Law Lords had to confront directly the ethical and legal difference between activity and passivity.

Where one is considering the refusal of the patient to undergo treatment that is necessary to save his or her life there is also the key concept of competence and consent which determines the actions (or inactions) of the medical profession where a patient in effect wishes to commit suicide, for example, by starving to death. There have been a number of examples over the years of prisoners wishing to starve themselves to death for political or other reasons. How should medical law react when a patient staunchly refuses food? This was considered in *Secretary of State for the Home Department* v *Robb* [1995] Fam 127. The respondent prisoner, who had been diagnosed as having a personality disorder and other problems associated with criminal behaviour, went on hunger strike. Having been told of the consequences of refusing to eat the patient maintained the stance, and was declared to be of sound mind and understanding in coming to that decision. The Home Secretary sought declarations that members of the prison service could lawfully accede to these refusals without invoking a criminal sanction. Once more the High court ruled that the overrriding consideration was autonomy, and that a person of sound mind has an absolute right to determine what shall happen to his or her body. Therefore the Home Secretary was under no duty to provide feeding and hydration as there was no evidence to rebut the presumption that the patient had the capacity to refuse.

Recently there have been a number of cases which have had to consider the ability of the patient to make a competent decision to refuse life-saving treatment. As with a number of aspects of the medical law of consent, there appears to be a judicial practice which seeks to make the declaration that the treatment be given in circumstances where it may be seriously questioned whether the presumption of competence has truly been rebutted. It may be suspected that the courts are once more guided by paternalistic notions from the medical profession. It may also be that where there are interests at stake other than those of the patient then these may influence whether the court makes a declaration of competence or not. One example already referred to in relation to the test of competence in the chapter on the ethical and legal basis of consent and the later discussion on the status of the unborn is the significant and wide-ranging decision of the Court of Appeal in *Re MB (Medical Treatment)* [1997] 2 FLR 426. While the danger to the mother was low, but the danger to the unborn high if the operation were not performed, and therefore not strictly an issue of euthanasia, nevertheless the threat to the life of the unborn was sufficient to persuade the Court of Appeal that the mother's needle phobia meant that she was incapable of making competent decisions about treatment. Nevertheless there are circumstances where the refusal of the mother to have this operation might well prove fatal to mother and child, and the courts feel willing to make the declaration that enables the medical profession to save both even in the face of a refusal by the mother (see *Rochdale Healthcare (NHS) Trust* v *C* (3 July 1996 unreported). Equally there is a small suspicion that the courts have been willing to give a broad interpretation to legislation in order to declare force-feeding to be lawful in the case of someone compulsorily detained under the Mental Health Act 1983 (see *B* v *Croydon Health Authority* [1995] Fam 133; see also section of chapter 9 on mental health).

15.2.1.2 Possible defences Outside the medical arena, it has already been noted, the criminal law provides defences which might avail the 'mercy killer'. In *R* v *Johnson* (1961) 1 Med Sci Law 192, for example, the prosecution accepted a plea of diminished responsibility. If a partial defence proves successful, the judge can reflect the circumstances of the offence of manslaughter in the sentence (see *R* v *Taylor* [1979] CLY 570). There is even the possibility of the more sympathetic utilisation of the discretion of the DPP not to initiate a prosecution. There have been attempts to develop a specific offence of mercy killing, with the sentence reflecting a societal view of the offence. While this could aid individuals like Dr Cox, it has been perceived as politically rather too hot to handle for a number of years (see Roger Leng, 'Mercy Killing and the CLRC' (1982) 132 NLJ 76).

15.2.1.3 Assisting suicide Another possibility for medical law to consider with regard to the competent patient is where there is a request that the doctor provide the means by which the competent terminally ill or incurable patient might commit suicide. It was precisely such means that Janet Adkins requested and Dr Kervorkian supplied, but how would English law react?

In 1961 the Suicide Act was passed with s. 1 decriminalising the ending of life by suicide. What the Act did not do was decriminalise the activities of those who assisted a person to end his or her life. Section 2(1) states:

A person who aids, abets, counsels or procures the suicide of another, or an attempt by another to commit suicide, shall be liable on conviction on indictment to imprisonment for a term not exceeding 14 years.

Some doubt has been expressed as to the likelihood of a successful prosecution (see, for example, Mason and McCall Smith, *Law and Medical Ethics*, 4th ed. (London: Butterworths, 1994), p. 328). But in any number of scenarios one might consider there would, if the facts were proved, be every likelihood of a successful prosecution. It might be rather safer to suggest that it would be unlikely that a prosecution would be *mounted*. This, however, does not place the doctor who leaves a bottle of pills by the bedside with the words '10 or more of these will prove fatal' uttered to the terminally ill patient on safe legal ground. To extrapolate from the judgment of Woolf J in one of the only cases that have concerned the scope of s. 2(1), *Attorney-General* v *Able* [1984] QB 795 (a case concerning the distribution of published material indicating ways of committing suicide), one would need to prove:

(a)   That the doctor had the necessary intent that the pills would be used by someone who was contemplating suicide, and the patient would be assisted in doing so by the use of the pills.

(b)   That the pills were given to the patient while the doctor had that intent.

(c)   That the patient was actually assisted by the pills to take or attempt to take his or her own life.

The argument in favour of changing this law has been based on the autonomy of the patient who wishes to end his or her own suffering, but either through the physical impact of the illness or fear of pain at death or even failure to 'succeed', is unable to act in a *physically* autonomous way. Such patients would argue that they need help to die, and the doctor is the most appropriate individual to give that help. Doctors themselves might argue that while their predominant ethical and professional role is to save life, there is also a role to alleviate the suffering of the patient, as well as possibly those who are suffering the anguish of seeing a loved one die a painful or increasingly debilitating death. Against this one has to weigh the fact (effectively detailed by R. Weir, 'The Morality of Physician Assisted Suicide' (1992) Law, Medicine and Health Care 116) that this would be a major realignment of the activities of the medical profession. In addition it would place an arguably intolerable ethical burden and conflict on the shoulders of the doctor. The major argument, which permeates the whole debate on euthanasia, not just the issue of assisted suicide, is the oft-utilised 'slippery slope' argument that doctors would assist suicides in ever more equivocal circumstances. For example, the patient suffering from pain may make the request of the doctor as an expression of that pain or a crisis of self-worth which often results from highly debilitating or terminal illness. This request may be transient, but if the doctor accedes then it is too late for a change of mind. The publicity surrounding the activities of Dr Kervorkian in the USA is a stark illustration of this fear.

15.3   ACTIVE EUTHANASIA IN THE NETHERLANDS

15.3.1   Introduction

The slippery slope from voluntary to involuntary euthanasia is typical of a slippery slope argument: easy to invoke, difficult to refute. Those who oppose the active termination of the competent patient requesting death, pointed originally to the dark part of the twentieth century, and now also to the law and practice of euthanasia in the Netherlands. This overseas development is significant for English medical law, in that it indicates a way forward that has been proposed by proponents of physician-assisted suicide. It is also a thought-provoking example of the development of a law and practice which has moved a distinct distance from its original motivation and scope.

15.3.2 The general law

John Keown has analysed the development of the law and has considered the existence of the slippery slope in a comprehensive article entitled 'The Law and Practice of Euthanasia in the Netherlands' (1992) 108 LQR 51. The significance of the debate on the experience of the Netherlands is further indicated by the vast array of recent literature in the medical press. In 1984, the Netherlands Supreme Court in *Alkmaar* (Nederlandse Jurisprudentie 1985 No. 106) interpreted art. 293 of the Dutch Penal Code (the *offence* of taking another's life at that other's 'express and serious request') and art. 294 (the *offence* of assisting suicide, in effect the same as s. 2(1) of the Suicide Act 1961) as susceptible to the *defence* of necessity contained in art. 40 of the Penal Code. In acquitting a doctor upon reversion of the case to the Court of Appeals from the Dutch Supreme Court (with the direction that the Court of Appeals were able to consider the applicability of the defence in the circumstances of the case) it was decided that the defence would apply where the doctor acted according to 'reasonable' medical opinion.

The conviction of a medical practitioner who had killed a friend suffering from multiple sclerosis in 1986 revealed the parameters that appeared to exist for lawful euthanasia to take place. They have been interpreted as including the following factors:

(a)   The request must come from the patient. It must, in addition, be free and voluntary.

(b)   This request must have been a considered and persistent one.

(c)   The patient should be suffering intolerably (although not necessarily physically) and there should be no prospect for improvement.

(d)   The decision to end the patient's life must be one of last resort, having considered whether there is any less drastic alternative.

(e)   The euthanasia must be performed by a doctor who has beforehand consulted with an independent doctor who has experience in the area of euthanasia.

Having been obviously aware of the existence of this medical practice, the Dutch version of the BMA, the KNMG, set out guidelines which considered that the decision needed to be voluntary, well-considered, durable and made in a situation of unacceptable suffering.

With these differential legal and professional guidelines, there obviously needed to be some form of resolution. Between the mid 1980s and the passing of legislation in 1993 there appears to have been an expansion and an acceptance of the practice of euthanasia. The title of the article by Hellema – 'Euthanasia – 2 per cent of Dutch Deaths' (1991) 303 BMJ 877 – makes the point. The slippery slope is evidenced by the advocacy of the termination of life of those who have not specifically consented to it. As Mason and McCall Smith confirm, by 1993:

. . . the concept of life-terminating acts without the specific request of the patient was clearly being accepted as a normal part of medical practice. (*Law and Medical Ethics*, 4th ed. (London: Butterworths, 1994), p. 319, referring to the work of L. Pijnenborg et al. 'Life-terminating Acts without Explicit Request of Patient' (1993) 341 Lancet 1196)

The 1993 legislation confirms that strict guidelines, including establishing the competence of the patient, need to be adhered to. There thus appears to be evidence that where the law opens the door to the practice of euthanasia it can lead to the practice in broader and broader circumstances. Where does this motivation come from – the patient, the doctor or society as a whole? There appears to be no direct evidence to point to a single motivating force. The Remmelink Committee, set up in the Netherlands, reports the practice in a number of factual circumstances. Whether that is abuse depends on the predilections of the reader, and the interpretation of the statistical information of the practice of euthanasia in the Netherlands, where it has been openly acceptable for some time (see M. Battin, 'Voluntary Euthanasia and the Risk of Abuse: Can We Learn Anything from the Netherlands?' (1992) 20 Law, Medicine and Health Care 133).

15.3.3 Current law and practice in the Netherlands: the conviction in *Chabot*

Office of Public Prosecutions v *Chabot* (1994) Nederlandse Jurisprudentie 1994 No. 656 is a fascinating example of the law and practice of euthanasia in the Netherlands and an equally effective example of both the existence of the 'slippery slope' argument and the fact that its invocation can be rather indiscriminate and in ignorance of many facts. The usefulness of the case is increased by its translation and analysis by John Griffiths ('Assisted Suicide in the Netherlands: The *Chabot* Case' (1995) 58 MLR 232).

This was another case in which the Dutch Supreme Court considered the the defence of necessity. The defendant psychiatrist had supplied lethal drugs to Mrs B after she had requested them. He had also been present when she took them and died some 30 minutes later. As required the doctor then reported to the coroner that there had been a suicide in which he had assisted. The facts of the case take one away from the scenarios that have been encountered so far in English medical law. The deceased had been suicidal for some time, and had actually attempted suicide through storing up prescription drugs for that purpose. The key point, as far as the present discussion is concerned, was that the deceased was suffering from no painful or terminal physical condition as in *R* v *Adams* [1957] Crim LR 365 or *R* v *Cox* (1992) 12 BMLR 38. The deceased had become depressed after a series of tragic family events. Therefore:

In considering the question 'whether Mrs B was suffering from any illness', the Court of Appeals concluded that there was no indication of any somatic condition which might have been the source of Mrs B's wish to die. From the beginning of the defendant's contacts with her, it was clear that she was suffering from psychic traumas which in principle lent themselves to psychiatric treatment so that the defendant was justified in entering into a doctor–patient relationship with her, even though that might ultimately expose him to a conflict of duties. (Griffiths (1995) 58 MLR 232 at p. 234)

The defendant decided that she was suffering from what is described as an 'adjustment disorder consisting of a depressed mood, . . . [but] experiencing intense, long-term psychic suffering that, for her, was unbearable and without prospect of improvement'. The Court of Appeals found on the evidence that her decision to die was well-considered, the suffering had been and was likely to be long-term. Sadly, it was also revealed that if the actions of the doctor had not taken place it was highly likely that she would have tried increasingly violent methods to end her life.

The general issues confirmed on appeal were that:

Particularly over the past decade there has been a public debate concerning the prohibition of euthanasia and assistance with suicide, which has included the question whether art. 294 of the Criminal Code should be revised. (translation of the Supreme Court's judgment in Griffiths op. cit., at p. 236)

The fact that necessity was the crucial determinant of the legality of the actions of the doctor was once more in issue. Here it concerned what was termed 'non-somatic suffering', and was held to apply to such conditions as well as physical suffering through pain:

In answering the question whether in a particular case a person's suffering must be regarded as so unbearable and lacking in any prospect of improvement that an act which violates art. 294 must be considered justified because performed in a situation of necessity, the suffering must be distinguished from its cause, in the sense that the cause of the suffering does not detract from the extent to which suffering is experienced. But the fact remains that when the suffering of a patient does not demonstrably follow from a somatic illness or condition, consisting simply of the experience of pain and loss of bodily functions, it is more difficult objectively to establish the fact of suffering and in particular its seriousness and lack of prospect of improvement. For this reason, the trial judge must in such cases approach the question whether there was a situation of necessity with exceptional care. (ibid., p. 237)

In the particular circumstances of the case the Supreme Court held that the Court of Appeals should have consulted with independent colleagues who have seen and examined the patient, and so the defence of necessity should have been rejected.

Griffiths provides an analysis of the decision which appears to cast doubt on the expansiveness of the reasoning in the case, yet defends the practice.

The criticism comes from the fact that the Supreme Court appeared to enunciate the inherent flexibility of the concept of necessity, which, Griffiths argues, thus has the appearance of a piece of judicial legislation which can guide in the future in unpredictable ways. While necessity needs to have flexibility, it needs to be utilised in a regulatory, or rather prohibitory, framework. The wider implications of the case are that:

> Assistance with suicide in the case of non-somatic suffering is only in a residual sense 'medical'. The fundamental basis for Dutch euthanasia law therefore seems, with the decision in the *Chabot* case, to have taken a decisive step away from the doctor-centred approach which has dominated legal development up to now (euthanasia and assistance with suicide being justified as a special empowerment of doctors, subject to the request of the patient) toward patient self-determination. (Griffiths (1995) 58 MLR 232 at p. 246)

Opponents of the decision see it as an assertion of the slippery slope towards involuntary euthanasia. Griffiths responds to authors such as Hendin ('Seduced by Death; Doctors, Patients and the Dutch Cure' (1994) 10 Issues in Law and Medicine 123) by arguing that such fears are simply not borne out by the facts. For example, there is a strong indication that psychiatrists in a number of jurisdictions, as a matter of professional fact, turn a blind eye to the fact that their patients are storing up medicines for a suicide attempt, or refer them to organisations such as the Hemlock Society or to books on DIY suicide. Dutch law does not represent a departure from practice, but recognises that it exists.

15.4 REFUSAL OF A COMPETENT PATIENT TO BE TREATED

15.4.1 Introduction

The timing and circumstances of a refusal of a terminally ill or incurable (or for that matter any, as shown in chapter 6) patient to be treated is of importance to medical law. A patient may refuse when directly confronting the doctor wishing to treat, or the refusal may have taken place before the present condition arose. A patient may have made it known that if certain conditions were to arise, and the patient was unable to make his or her feelings clear the patient would not wish to receive life-sustaining treatment.

15.4.2 Contemporaneous refusal

Contemporaneous refusal is when a patient who is confronted with a treatment option, refuses to allow it, effectively saying, 'Leave me alone, I wish to die'. What is the doctor to do?

In chapters 6 and 7 it was indicated that the law regards the individual patient's body as inviolate, and that any treatment of 'an adult person of sound mind' in the face of a refusal would be an assault (see the judgment of

Cardozo J in *Schloendorff* v *Society of New York Hospital* (1914) 105 NE 92 quoted in 6.1). In *R* v *Cox* (1992) 12 BMLR 38, for example, Ognall J referred to the latter stages of the life of Lillian Boyes:

> . . . Lillian Boyes was fully entitled to decline any further active medical treatment and to specify that thereafter she should only receive painkillers. . . . That was her . . . absolute right and doctors and nursing staff were obliged to respect her wishes.

Chapter 6 also revealed that medical law appears to be developing exceptions to this 'absolute right'. In *Re W (A Minor) (Medical Treatment: Court's Jurisdiction)* [1993] Fam 64, for example, it was decided that the court or the parents maintained the right to consent on a child's behalf, even where the child is regarded as *Gillick*-competent and thus has the capacity to understand the nature and implications of the treatment, and by logical extension, a refusal. The alternative view of *Re W* and the other judicial overrriding of a refusal, *Re R (A Minor) (Wardship: Consent to Treatment)* [1992] Fam 11, is that the exclusive right of the competent minor to consent, whether as a matter of common or statute law, does not include with it a right to refuse treatment.

Earlier in the chapter cases such as *Secretary of State for the Home Department* v *Robb* [1995] Fam 127 and *B* v *Croydon Health Authority* [1995] Fam 133 have indicated that competence and consent in these tragic circumstances are fluid concepts, which may be prone to some manipulation where the legal and medical professions combine in their paternalistic attitude to a patient refusing to have his or her life saved.

As far back as 1976, Ian Kennedy ('The Legal Effect of Requests by the Terminally Ill and Aged Not to Receive Treatment' [1976] Crim LR 217) noted that while the ethic of self-determination as reflected in the crime and tort of battery had been judicially recognised on a number of occasions, paternalism as a matter of clinical intuition also existed as a force for acting in the best interests of the competent patient refusing life-saving treatment. One can be less tentative in making such a comment on the existence of this force for treatment after the judgments in *Re W* and *Re R*.

15.4.2.1 Possible defences   In addition to the fact that consent powers of the *Gillick*-competent minor might be wider than refusal powers, enabling the court or the parents to exercise paternalist treatment powers, there might be other justificatory mechanisms by which the paternalist might treat any competent patient who refuses, whether adult or minor. The doctor can claim that initiating or continuing treatment in the face of a refusal was a necessity. The impossibility of combining self-determination and necessity should be apparent. The doctor who states, 'I had to treat the patient to save his life' is being paternalist. A doctor can only use the justificatory defence of necessity where the patient is either temporarily or permanently incompetent according to the tests enunciated judicially in *Gillick* v *West Norfolk and Wisbech Area Health Authority* [1986] AC 112 or *Re C (Adult: Refusal of Treatment)* [1994]

1 WLR 290 (see 6.3). As a practical matter it could only be based on a form of 'therapeutic lie' by the doctor that the patient refusing to be treated was not competent to act autonomously when in fact the patient was competent. This would be a legally and professionally hazardous course of conduct.

Kennedy notes the possibility of the doctor justifying treatment in the face of a competent refusal as a defence to the charge that the doctor has otherwise neglected the patient. Both question and answer are obvious:

> Is there any legal foundation for this concern? Is the doctor in breach of his duty to his patient if he discontinues treatment? Provided that the doctor is satisfied that the patient when forbidding further treatment was aware of what he was saying, the short answer must be that he is not in breach of his duty. ([1976] Crim LR 217 at p. 229)

15.4.3 Advance refusal

As the decision in *Airedale NHS Trust* v *Bland* [1993] AC 789 has now clearly established, the right of self-determination is of a higher order than the right to life. The duty of the doctor is to respect patient rights in that order. *Re F (Mental Patient: Sterilisation)* [1990] 2 AC 1 is a persistent reminder of that. In supporting the sentiments expressed in that case, Lord Keith in *Airedale NHS Trust* v *Bland* (at p. 857) saw a natural extension of this right in that:

> This extends to the situation where the person, in anticipation of his, through one cause or another, entering into a condition such as PVS, gives clear instructions that in such event he is not to be given medical care, including artificial feeding, designed to keep him alive.

What is the justification for such an extension? The answer once more lies in the breadth of the concept of autonomy, which transcends the ability to articulate it at the time of treatment, as long as a competent decision has been made at some previous point. In practical terms it has to be recognised as part of everyday medicine that, whenever a consent is given in relation to medical treatment (written consent to surgery for example), it is made in advance of that treatment. All consents are to a future event, the only matter is how far in advance the competent choice is made.

While Lord Keith found support for the potential legitimacy of an advance declaration of refusal of treatment in the cases of *Re F* and *Re T (Adult: Refusal of Treatment)* [1993] Fam 95, there are still issues which may affect whether such a directive will apply to or bind those who may be considering treatment in the future.

(a) Was the directive made while competent?
(b) Was it meant to apply in the situation which has arisen?
(c) Was it an autonomous, freely made decision?

All three matters can confront the courts in the future, but an indication of the pressures on decision-makers when faced with an advance refusal can be seen in the important case of *Re T*, which concerned a pregnant woman who refused a blood transfusion on religious grounds having had private discussions with her mother when the option of blood transfusion was put to her (see 6.2.11).

Lord Donaldson of Lymington MR made it clear that while prudence and good medical practice might well give the views of patients' relatives important moral value, relatives had no legal right to make decisions for a competent adult patient. Prudence nevertheless dictates contacting relatives where possible, because it might actually reveal that the patient had made an anticipatory refusal, either oral or written, relating specifically or generally to the proposed treatment regime. The contact with relatives might equally reveal that, for example, a written refusal found in an accident victim's wallet no longer represents that person's religious views on certain treatment (but given a parent's natural anxiety to save a Jehovah's Witness son or daughter such family insights must be carefully looked at). In deciding thereafter what the scope of such a decision actually is, Lord Donaldson enunciated a factor which could be interpreted in a way which assumes the overriding autonomy of the patient, or in a restrictive way so as to encourage treatment. The patient cannot be questioned about the nature and scope of the anticipatory refusal for obvious reasons, and the next of kin have no legal right of interpretation, so:

. . . what the doctors cannot do is to conclude that if the patient still had the necessary capacity in the changed situation he would have reversed his decision. This would be simply to deny his right of decision. What they *can* [original emphasis] do is to consider whether at the time the decision was made *it was intended by the patient to apply in the changed situation* [emphasis added]. (p. 114)

This will be primarily a matter of fact, but also a decision which will be invariably based on the underlying professional clinical intuition. As Lord Donaldson went on to point out, the simple anticipatory directive which states, 'I am a Jehovah's Witness; I refuse a blood transfusion', may result, as one would imagine, in the doctor not treating. The doctor may justify treatment, however, on the basis of a *limiting* interpretation of the directive. For example, it could be read as 'I refuse a blood transfusion, so long as there is an effective alternative', or 'I refuse a blood transfusion unless that refusal endangers my life', or any number of other ways which open the door to treatment. Another option for the doctor wishing to treat would be to regard such a blanket ban on treatment as based on incorrect, insufficient or misunderstood medical information, to the extent that the patient would have been unable to understand the nature and effects of a refusal or a particular form of treatment. The doctor wishing to treat can attempt to circumvent the anticipatory refusal through interpretation (or manipulation) of its phraseology, or the circumstances in which it was made. Once more, however, there is no secure legal footing upon which this can take place. The doctor undertaking such an exercise still risks liability for battery.

With such potential difficulties, those who support the advance expression of autonomy have encouraged the development of detailed 'advance directives' as to treatment, and, at least to a limited extent, there appears to be a societal culture which is increasingly aware of rights and therefore predisposed to such a development.

The Law Commission consultation paper, *Mentally Incapacitated Adults and Decision-Making. Medical Treatment and Research* (No. 129) (London: HMSO, 1993), has recommended the development, through legislation, of legally binding anticipatory declarations as to treatment. The British Medical Association (*Statement on Advance Directives*, 1992) argued that such declarations were to be generally welcomed, without necessarily agreeing that legislation was necessary, or that they be legally binding. The statutory option was recommended by the Law Commission because:

> If a statutory framework for decision-making for incapacitated adults of the sort proposed in this paper were introduced, it would be difficult to avoid consideration of the extent to which courts and other decision-makers, including doctors, should be bound by relevant decisions made by a patient prior to his incapacity. Legislation could clarify the position. (para. 3.11)

Anticipatory decisions could conceivably take a number of forms, being general or specific, oral or written. The danger with allowing the patient an oral power to make an anticipatory refusal is that it might be an expression of transient anxiety. Whatever view one takes of the practical likelihood of this danger, the Law Commission recommended that:

> There should be a rebuttable presumption that an anticipatory decision is clearly established if it is in writing, signed by the maker [with appropriate provision for signing at his direction], and witnessed by [one] person who is not the maker's medical treatment attorney. (para. 3.19)

Since decisions such as *Airedale NHS Trust* v *Bland* there has been a considerable debate on the morality, legality and form of such advance declarations. The Law Commission, the Lord Chancellor and others have all reflected on this issue on a number of occasions. The Law Commission, in its more recent report (*Mental Incapacity* (Law Com No. 231) has gone into some detail on many of the aspects of concern to the medical lawyer. While it maintains its stance on giving statutory authority to advance directives as to treatment there appears now to be a stronger tone that a directive which endangers the life of that patient should be presumed not to apply. Of course this presumption is a rebuttable one. It is proposed in cl. 9(5) of the draft Bill in the Law Commission report that there should be a rebuttable presumption that one applies where the formalities suggested in para. 3.19 of their previous report have been complied with.

It can be suggested that the court, if it encounters a specific form of anticipatory refusal, will decide that the medical profession should comply with it or face an action for damages for battery. In the Canadian case of

Malette v *Schulman* (1990) 67 DLR (4th) 321, the advance directive read as follows:

NO BLOOD TRANSFUSION!
As one of Jehovah's Witnesses with firm religious convictions, I request that no blood or blood products be administered to me under any circumstances. I fully realise the implications of this position, but I have resolutely decided to obey the Bible command: 'Keep abstaining . . . from blood' (Acts 15:28, 29). However, I have no religious objection to use the non-blood alternatives . . .

The doctor who administered a blood transfusion in the face of this written refusal was found liable in battery. The court also emphasised that it was not the place of the judiciary or the medical profession to question the reasons for the objection to treatment. The action succeeded despite attempts by the doctor to argue that:

. . . he was not satisfied that the card signed by Mrs Malette expressed her current instructions because, on the information he then had, he did not know whether she might have changed her religious beliefs before the accident; whether the card may have been signed because of family or peer pressure; whether at the time she signed the card she was fully informed of the risks of refusal of blood transfusions; or whether, if conscious, she might have changed her mind in the face of medical advice as to her perhaps imminent but avoidable death.

The crucial legal question still remains whether the patient was competent at the time that the decision to refuse was made (see the central importance of this for the whole of medical law in chapter 6).

15.5 TERMINATING THE LIFE OF THE INCOMPETENT PATIENT

15.5.1 Introduction

The fact that at the end of life a patient may be incompetent should be no bar to the treatment or non-treatment options that are available to the competent. As with consent in general, the right of a patient to dignity demands that such a form of discrimination does not take place. Medical law needs to deal with the following situations that may arise, each having its own legal problems:

(a)   The patient in a persistent vegetative state, whose cognitive functions have been destroyed and who is being maintained with the assistance of medical technology to 'live' in that state without hope of improvement.
(b)   The patient who is incompetent but in need of treatment to survive his or her current medical condition. If treatment takes place, the overall condition of the patient will still remain extremely severe and permanent.

The former situation is typified by the condition of Anthony Bland and the second by the condition of the physically and mentally defective newborn child (considered in chapter 14).

There needs to be a forum where the condition of the patient is considered together with the ability of the patient or others to consent. The crux of the matter, however, is that, while literally life and death decisions are going to be made with regard to the patient, the only person not able to articulate the treatment preference is the patient him- or herself.

15.5.2 Terminating the treatment of the incompetent patient: the *Bland* case

15.5.2.1 Significance of the case
To a large extent *Airedale NHS Trust* v *Bland* [1993] AC 789 clarifies the nature of the ethical and legal debate on euthanasia in Britain. It indicates that there is a certain symmetry between a number of jurisdictions on these ethical and legal issues, and that the law cannot ignore the ethical debate taking place. The decision also reveals an element of unease in the application of the current medical law to this as yet relatively novel, but increasingly common situation confronting the medical profession. The desire of the House of Lords to see an informed Parliamentary debate and action, and the formation of a House of Lords select committee as a result of the decision, indicated unease about the judicial forum being thrust into applying the common law to this ethical powder keg. It would not be an exaggeration to say that the case is a microcosm of the whole of modern medical law. It reveals the moral dilemmas of medical practice, the unsteady and uncertain growth of legal intervention in medicine, the growing legal voice of human rights, the conflicts of clinical intuition and the residual yet still powerful place of the medical profession in setting the tone of medical law. Perhaps most negative of all, the pleading voices of many of the judges involved that Parliament do something about this hottest of ethico-legal potatoes still remain unheard.

15.5.2.2 The facts of *Bland*
Anthony Bland was one of the many who suffered in the crush that took place at the Hillsborough football stadium in 1989. As a result of the crushing injury he suffered, his brain was starved of oxygen. He suffered from hypoxic brain damage. After emergency treatment had taken place to stabilise his condition it was found that Bland was in a persistent vegetative state. This meant that his cerebral cortex had been destroyed by the lack of oxygen. In this part of the brain are located what are known as the 'higher-brain' functions of communication, consciousness and the ability to make voluntary, directed as opposed to reflex movements. The brain stem, which among other things maintains spontaneous breathing, was still functioning. As indicated in chapter 16, he was not legally dead. The emotional intensity of the day-to-day situation of Bland which had to be dealt with by medical staff was known by the parents and had to be dealt with head on by the courts. It was starkly revealed by Hoffmann LJ (at pp. 824–5):

He lies in Airedale General Hospital in Keighley, fed liquid food by a pump through a tube passing through his nose and down the back of his throat into the stomach. His bladder is emptied through a catheter inserted through his penis, which from time to time has caused infections requiring dressing and antibiotic treatment. His stiffened joints have caused his limbs to be rigidly contracted so that his arms are tightly flexed across his chest and his legs unnaturally contorted. Reflex movements in his throat cause him to vomit and dribble. Of all of this, and the presence of members of his family who take turns to visit him, Anthony Bland has no consciousness at all . . . .The darkness and oblivion which descended at Hillsborough will never depart.

15.5.2.3 The legal questions The doctors were of one mind that the condition would never improve, but might persist for a considerable period of time. They required legal sanction to withdraw the artificial feeding and hydration regime, ventilation and the prescription of antibiotics to treat infection, but otherwise to treat the patient so that death would be dignified and with the least suffering and anguish. The NHS Trust therefore applied to the court for declarations which would state that these withdrawals would not be unlawful.

The Official Solicitor appealed to both the Court of Appeal and House of Lords that to withdraw this treatment would be a breach of the duty of the doctor to the patient and a criminal offence.

15.5.2.4 The ethical questions The condition of Bland, the level of public interest the case had generated and the 'finality' of what was proposed, led Hoffmann LJ to recognise explicitly that there were wider questions which pervaded the legal issues involved. While their lordships generally referred to the major ethical debating points, Hoffmann LJ articulated the intuition that led him to support the proposed withdrawal of treatment, though he said (at p. 825) that 'To argue from moral rather than purely legal principles is a somewhat unusual enterprise for a judge to undertake'. This is an indication, I would suggest, that there is a strong judicial realisation that the judicial forum is not always the most appropriate to deal with medical law matters.

The first ethical question felt worthy of consideration sounds deceptively simple: Why would we think that it would be a tragedy to allow Anthony Bland to die? The answer suggested is that there is in society a consensus that human life has an intrinsic value. This, Hoffmann LJ suggested, is not necessarily based on religious views, but is part of an intuitive respect for the value of life and why, for example, the criminal law punishes those who kill.

There may well be respect for the sanctity of life combined with a respect for the dignity of that life, which is expressed in the idea of autonomy.

Hoffmann LJ confirmed that these two notions, sanctity and autonomy, are not always complementary, and can indeed conflict. A number of other areas of medicine have already revealed this conflict. The expression of self-determination by refusing life-saving treatment directly confronts the principle of the sanctity of life. It may be that the decriminalisation of suicide by

s. 1 of the Suicide Act 1961 reveals the relative weight that the law gives to these ethical principles. From this Hoffmann LJ considered that the law's approach should be:

> that there is no morally correct solution which can be deduced from a single ethical principle like the sanctity of life or the right of self-determination. There must be an accommodation between principles, both of which seem rational and good, but which have come into conflict with each other. (p. 827)

Counsel for the Official Solicitor, opposing the application, considered that there was no ethical or corresponding legal right to assume, in the absence of information to the contrary, that Bland would choose to die. The fact that he was unaware of the surroundings, or even of his life at all, was argued to mean that there was no interest which could be balanced against the intrinsic right to life. In response Hoffmann LJ once more argued that, intuitively, there are more interests at stake than the inherent interest in life. His lordship pointed, for example, to the existence of dignity, and how one would wish to be perceived by others. Respect for the dead means that relatives carry out wishes made while alive. There may be an interest in being remembered as one would wish to be remembered.

The answer to this ethical conundrum typifies the response of English medical law. While one should have cognisance of the sanctity of life, this should not be regarded as an absolute and can give way to other rights, particularly when the situation is such that life itself 'has almost become empty of any real content'.

An ethical question which also was a central issue in the legal consideration of the case of the PVS patient, indeed the whole debate about euthanasia, was whether there is a moral difference between acts which cause death and the withdrawal of treatment – between act and omission. Arguably, in seeking to differentiate between the two as an ethical matter which the law should pursue, Hoffmann LJ enunciated an ethical to legal process of debate that has proved less than universally popular. The controversy comes from the view that:

> most of us would be appalled if he was given a lethal injection. It is, I think, connected with our view that the sanctity of life entails its inviolability by an outsider. (p. 831)

It is argued that this ethical notion should be translated into law. For example, as already mentioned, to commit suicide is not a crime, but aiding and abetting a suicide is (Suicide Act 1961, s. 2(1)). Hoffmann LJ extended this idea of 'inviolability' by arguing that there is a moral difference between 'an act or omission which allows an existing cause to operate and the introduction of an external agency of death' (p. 831). It is this distinction which led to the conviction in R v Cox (1992) 12 BMLR 38.

15.6   THE DECISION OF THE HOUSE OF LORDS IN THE *BLAND* CASE

15.6.1   Introduction

While all agreed that the life of Anthony Bland should be brought to an end, their lordships were not of one mind on the approach to answering the legal questions. There was unanimous appreciation of the existence of the sanctity of human life as well as a recognition of the right of self-determination, but there was suspicion in some quarters that the common law had been incorrectly understood and applied by previous cases and in the academic treatment of the central issues.

The main aspects of the House of Lords decision can, for convenience, be divided into the following:

(a)   The legal recognition of the sanctity of life, and its application in English law.

(b)   The 'best interests' of the insensate patient. Who judges and on what basis?

(c)   The legal difference between actively accelerating death and allowing death to occur.

(d)   The cause of death.

15.6.2   The sanctity of life in law

While Hoffmann LJ indicated the moral, if not absolute, force of the right to life, Lord Goff of Chieveley noted that there was international recognition of the right through art. 2 of the European Convention on Human Rights and the International Covenant on Civil and Political Rights. These documents also make it clear that as a matter of law this right is not to be regarded as an absolute. If it were, then there would be no lawful right to kill another in self-defence. The case of the PVS patient raises the issue of the extent to which the law should respect this sanctity where other interests are at stake. The right of self-determination as recognised in *Re F (Mental Patient: Sterilisation)* [1990] 2 AC 1 has noted the legal supremacy of the right to determine whether or not one's life should end over an absolute right to life. The problem with Anthony Bland was that he never explicitly expressed what he would wish to happen if PVS were to overtake him, and could obviously not express his autonomous decision at the time of the judicial hearing. The law has regarded the competent refusal of the patient to treatment as (in general terms) legally binding, whether expressed at the time of the proposed treatment or before (see *Re T (Adult: Refusal of Treatment)* [1993] Fam 95; *B v Hôtel-Dieu de Québec* (1992) 86 DLR (4th) 385).

From this starting point the House of Lords had to consider how and on what basis the decision about the treatment of Bland could be taken in the absence of consent.

15.6.3 Best interests of the patient

The decision in *Re F (Mental Patient Sterilisation)* [1990] 2 AC 1 provided the rationale for the treatment legal and ethical to take place. In *Re F* the decision to sterilise a mentally handicapped woman was declared to be lawful in the absence of the patient's consent on the basis that it would be the duty of the doctor to act in the best interests of that patient as understood by a responsible body of medical opinion (utilising the test in *Bolam* v *Friern Hospital Management Committee* [1957] 1 WLR 582). Could the withdrawal of life support be in the best interests of Anthony Bland?

Lord Goff supported what was said in *Re F* about the duty to act in the patient's best interests, and showed how this duty applied to Anthony Bland by quoting the Massachusetts Supreme Court in *Superintendent of Belchertown State School* v *Saikewicz* (1977) 370 NE 2d 417:

> To presume that the incompetent person must always be subjected to what many rational and intelligent persons may decline is to downgrade the status of the incompetent person by placing a lesser value on his intrinsic human worth and vitality.

If 'best *interests*' of the insensate patient are to be the axis point of consideration, did Bland have any interests at all? Hoffmann LJ in the Court of Appeal obviously considered that there were such potential moral interests in the balance. What all the courts had to consider was the simple fact that was recognised by all their lordships, that in reality Anthony Bland had no interests at all. Lord Goff felt that despite the insensate condition one needed to consider the invasiveness of the treatment and anguish and stress to others that was graphically relayed by Hoffmann LJ. Lord Mustill (at p. 897) (and also Lord Keith of Kinkel at p. 859) made his discomfort with the talk of competing interests clear where he argued:

> . . . it seems to me to be stretching the concept of personal rights beyond breaking point to say that Anthony Bland has an interest in ending these sources of others' distress. Unlike the conscious patient he does not know what is happening to his body. . . . The distressing truth which must not be shirked is that the proposed conduct is not in the best interests of Anthony Bland, for he has no best interests of any kind.

While this may factually be the case, to translate this lack of interest into law would have one of two effects. First, the law could react by then stating that it was not exclusively concerned with the subjective (or purely personal) interests of the PVS patient, such as relief from pain and intrusive treatment, but with the wider societal interests of the maintenance of dignity and respect for memory that are interests which relate to some extent with the objective relationship between patient and others. To this Lord Mustill responded that such broad issues would certainly be ones for Parliament and not the courts to consider. Secondly, Lord Mustill in essence endorsed a best interests test, then sought to avoid it by saying that Anthony Bland had no interest in the continuation of life, and therefore there were no best interests to be served in continuing treatment. The justification for treatment has gone and there is no longer a duty to provide nutrition and hydration.

While there has never been an explicit trend as a matter of medical law to espouse societal or State interests, Lord Mustill appeared to be drawing himself closer to an analysis which had 'constitutionalist' reflections reminiscent of the Canadian and US courts. The insistence of the US Supreme Court in *Cruzan* v *Director, Missouri Department of Health* (1990) 110 S Ct 2841 on clear evidence of patient desire to have feeding and hydration withdrawn, was predicated on the articulated State interest in the preservation of life. The decision to switch off the life support machine of Karen Quinlan (*Re Quinlan* (1976) 355 A 2d 647) was made after debate about whether the State has an interest in preserving the life of its citizens, which, while absolute, could on occasion sanction 'terminal' treatment. Cases almost too numerous to mention (see, for example, *Satz* v *Perlmutter* (1978) 362 So 2d 160 at p. 162; *Superintendent of Belchertown State School* v *Saikewicz* (1970) 370 NE 2d 417 and *Re Conroy* (1985) 486 A 2d 1209) have articulated the existence of State interests also in the prevention of suicide, safeguarding the integrity of the medical profession and the protection of dependent third parties.

While Lord Mustill might eschew such a notion as inapplicable in a State without a written constitution or bill of rights upon which to make such articulations, there was a realisation of the potential legitimacy of Parliament legislating to the effect that there was a State interest in the effective distribution of health care resources under the banner of the 'best interests of the community' (see p. 896):

> The large resources of skill, labour and money now being devoted to Anthony Bland might in the opinion of many be more fruitfully employed in improving the condition of other patients, who if treated may have useful, healthy and enjoyable lives for years to come.

The majority, however, appeared to support a 'best interests of the patient' test (see the judgments of Lords Goff, Browne-Wilkinson and Lowry). The pre-eminence of the medical profession in judging best interests was endorsed by the House of Lords, but there appeared to be a lack of enthusiasm about applying *Bolam* v *Friern Hospital Management Committee* [1957] 1 WLR 582. Lord Mustill most strongly expressed this suspicion (at p. 898), which has a broader application than just the situation of the PVS patient and could apply to many other areas of medical law:

> . . . I venture to feel some reservations about the application of the principle of civil liability in negligence laid down in *Bolam* v *Friern Hospital Management Committee* [1957] 1 WLR 582 to decisions on 'best interests' in a field dominated by the criminal law. I accept without difficulty that this principle applies to the ascertainment of the medical raw material such as diagnosis,

prognosis and appraisal of the patient's cognitive functions. Beyond this point, however, it may be said that the decision is ethical, not medical, and that there is no reason in logic why on such a decision the opinions of doctors should be decisive.

Nevertheless the majority adopted the utilisation of *Bolam*, while Lord Mustill felt it was irrelevant because of the lack of interests.

The Law Lords then had to answer the question of whether it can be in the best interests of the patient to stop feeding and hydrating him? Even if it might be in the best interests of the patient as recognised and endorsed by a responsible body of medical opinion to withdraw medical treatment, withdrawal of food and water could be of a different order altogether, and therefore outside the medical realm. The Law Lords were in agreement that the medical treatment of the patient included artificial feeding and hydration. Such technological interventions to treat were part of the clinical regime within which the patients lived and the doctors operated.

This point has some significance. To term feeding and hydration the 'essentials of life' or 'basic necessities' takes them further outside the clinical realm, so that providing them is not a medical matter at all, but may be termed a basic human right.

15.6.4 Acts, omissions and causes

Airedale NHS Trust v Bland [1993] AC 789 concerned a declaration that the withdrawal of treatment would not be contrary to the criminal law. This required consideration of two linked issues of criminal law in the medical context that had appeared in the cases of *R v Arthur* (1981) 12 BMLR 1, *R v Adams* [1957] Crim LR 365 and *R v Cox* (1992) 12 BMLR 38: the differentiation between act and omission and the legal cause of death. The *actus reus* for murder is broadly the act of killing with the intent to kill or virtual certainty that the act will kill. The criminal law also imposes liability for an omission to act in circumstances where there is a duty on the defendant to care for the deceased. *Airedale NHS Trust v Bland* appears to have been the opportunity for the majority of those who sat in judgment to consolidate the policy underlying previous criminal law decisions surrounding the termination of life. However, as with other aspects of the case, there are differences of emphasis, and blatant discomfort with many of those common law concepts in the judgment of Lord Mustill.

The Official Solicitor argued that the proposed 'terminal regime' (to attempt to use a neutral term!) in withdrawing the naso-gastric tube, would:

(a)   inevitably cause and would be intended to cause, Anthony Bland's death and would, necessarily be unlawful and criminal;

(b)   be a breach of the doctor's duty to care for and feed Anthony.

Lord Goff rehearsed and followed the common law established in *R v Adams* and *R v Cox*. It would be unlawful to administer drugs to a patient with the object of bringing about death, however laudable the motive. Where the withdrawal of life support is in issue, Lord Goff asked himself the question, Why is it that the doctor who does so withdraw, and allows the patient to die, does not act unlawfully if there is no breach of duty to the patient? The answer lies in the fact, according to Lord Goff, that the doctor's conduct is an omission. The doctor is simply allowing nature to take its course and the patient to die from the pre-existing condition. An omission can still lead to criminal liability, but only if it is a breach of the doctor's duty. From that is established the rule, according to his lordship (at p. 867) that:

> . . . a doctor may, when caring for a patient who is, for example, dying of cancer, lawfully administer painkilling drugs despite the fact that he knows that the incidental effect of that application will be to abbreviate the patient's life. Such a decision may properly be made as part of the care of the living patient, in his best interests; and, on this basis, the treatment will be lawful. Moreover, where the doctor's treatment of his patient is lawful, the patient's death will be regarded in law as exclusively caused by the injury or disease to which his condition is attributable.

Lord Browne-Wilkinson's opinion was that withdrawal of feeding would not be an act but an omission to treat, and this would of itself not be a cause of death. The removal of the naso-gastric tube would not have causative significance because on its own it did not keep Bland alive.

The doctors were clearly under a duty to care for Anthony Bland, so the omission to act would be a criminal breach of that duty. This duty, particularly evident from the decision in *Re F (Mental Patient: Sterilisation)* [1990] 2 AC 1, is to act in the best interests of the patient, and, to a majority of their lordships, this meant that the crucial question was not whether it was in the patient's best interests to die, but whether it was in his best interests to continue with the artificial regime.

This still does not answer the issue of the cause of death. Lord Mustill found that the sentiments on causation typified by Lord Browne-Wilkinson were unhelpful, or, as was rather charitably put, it 'depends upon a very special application of the doctrine of causation' (at p. 895). Lord Mustill openly criticised the stance of Skegg (*Law, Ethics and Medicine* (Oxford: Clarendon Press 1988)), who had anyway admitted that to find the withdrawal of life support non-causative requires a manipulation of the traditional criminal law. Lord Mustill preferred a rather more realistic conclusion that the withdrawal of life support is factually causative, but because of the legal characterisation of the 'terminal regime' as acting in the best interests of the patient, that causative action has no legal consequence.

While in the minority in his discomfort over the application of many traditional common law concepts, Lord Mustill's judgment is arguably the most accurate justification for the removal of hydration and nutrition, which was declared lawful (see pp. 897–8) despite the controversial utilisation of the concept of omission and the effective abandonment of the best interests test. The steps in Lord Mustill's reasoning are:

(a)   The withdrawal of nutrition and hydration is an omission rather than an act.

(b)   Therefore this withdrawal will not be unlawful unless there was a duty owed to the patient.

(c)   'All hope of recovery has now been abandoned. Thus, although the termination of his life is not in the best interests of Anthony Bland, his best interests in being kept alive have also disappeared, taking with them the justification for the non-consensual regime and the co-relative duty to keep it in being.'

(d)   Without the existence of this duty, the withdrawal of feeding and hydration is not a criminal offence.

While Lord Mustill was aware of the fact that the distinction between act and omission may be difficult to draw in future cases. However, there is unlikely to be such a problem in the medical context, because even if (as in Anthony Bland's case) the proposed course of treatment were regarded as an omission, there would still be a duty not to fail to act in the interests of the patient.

15.7   DEVELOPMENTS SINCE *BLAND*

It would be going too far to suggest that the decision of the House of Lords in *Airedale NHS Trust* v *Bland* [1993] AC 789 opened the floodgates of euthanasia. What can be said with certainty is that the decision itself opened a floodgate of consideration of the parameters of the decision. The matter has been considered by a House of Lords Select Committee, it has been covertly part of the Law Commission's considerations on incapacity and medical treatment. In addition there have been several cases concerned with other patients in a persistent vegetative state, and perhaps more controversially those who are not in a persistent vegetative state, but are in a low awareness state and in addition may be totally dependent on high-level medical technology to keep them alive in this state. We have already encountered these difficult issues in relation to the handicapped neonate, but the courts have also had to consider the plight of physically more mature members of the population.

In *Frenchay Healthcare NHS Trust* v *S* [1994] 1 WLR 601, as well as an application of specific aspects of the decision in *Bland* there was some consideration (albeit rather unclear) of the position of the medical profession in deciding whether treatment should come to an end, whether the medical factors used to determine that the patient was in fact in PVS were merely guidelines or were diagnostic rules which had to be strictly adhered to. In terms of the decision-making structure there seemed to be a difference of opinion in the Court of Appeal. Waite LJ emphasised the dominance of the judge in determining where the best interests of the patient lay, and expressed the view that the court could overrule the opinion of the medical profession where that was considered necessary in such patient interests. Contrary to that, Bingham MR would defer to the medical profession, or at least consider the reasonableness of medical opinion in preference to substituting judicial views.

In terms of the diagnosis of PVS the guidelines issued by the British Medical Association were revealed in *Frenchay Healthcare NHS Trust v S* to be just that, guidelines. A number of the diagnostic tools for determining PVS were not strictly used. For example, the BMA advised that the diagnosis of PVS should be reserved for 12 months, yet in *Frenchay* the diagnosis was made after four months. It was this aspect, among others, that lead the Official Solicitor to issue *Practice Note (Persistent Vegetative State: Withdrawal of Treatment)* [1996] 4 All ER 766 (which has no legal force). The Official Solicitor suggested that indeed PVS should not be diagnosed for 12 months, in line with both the guidelines of the BMA and also the Royal College of Physicians ((1996) J R Coll Phys 119–21). While there was a clear statement in the *Practice Note* that the parents or other next of kin should be consulted and their views made known to the court, there has already been a case where the judge has declared the final decision to be that of the court not the relatives. In *Re G* [1995] 2 FLR 46 the judge showed willingness to authorise non-treatment even where the mother objected to the withdrawal (although one should note that the patient's wife did not object). It seems then that one of the effects of *Bland* is to have respect for the views of the spouses and parents, but not to give them a determinative status. This indicates a significant departure from the situation of the handicapped newborn, where the views of the parents do appear to hold sway, despite the protestations of the Court of Appeal.

Recently the High Court has considered its tenth PVS case since *Bland*, and, if not exactly comfortable with its role, at least seems to have a view on the status of the medical profession and the legal profession in the power structure of decision-making, as well as reviewing the status of the BMA and RCP guidelines on PVS. The patient here had suffered serious head injuries in a road accident. These did not lead immediately to PVS but to a state of depression regarding the patient's perceived quality of life. Some time later the patient suffered a mysterious collapse, and was thereafter declared to be in PVS. Some 15 months after the collapse the patient was declared to be in a permanent vegetative state. Three months after that her gastrostomy tube became detached and the declaration was sought that it would be lawful to discontinue all life-support measures. This declaration was granted as there was evidence from three experts that the patient was unaware of her surroundings: she could not see, hear or feel. The problem was (once more) that she did not come strictly within the RCP guidelines as she was able to perform some activities, such as tracking moving objects, and reacting to menacing and other stimuli. The decision appears to confirm once more that medicine is not an exact science and there has to be some flexibility in clinical diagnosis. The RCP and BMA guidelines may appear to some to be compulsory, but not to the judiciary. It seems safest to state that this patient was 'effectively' in PVS.

A patient who certainly did not appear to be in PVS was considered in *Re R (Adult: Medical Treatment)* [1996] 2 FLR 99 (see also *Re H (A Patient)*

[1998] June, Fam Law 370). R was 23 years old and had numerous profound learning and physical disabilities. The evidence indicated that he was operating at the level of a newborn baby. There was an ability to respond basically, but there appeared to be no thought process. The patient had been in and out of hospital and had suffered a number of serious conditions. This patient was truly in a tragic condition, and, unpleasant as it may be, one needs to be aware of his everyday existence to consider the possible response of medical law:

> He is spastic and is unable to walk or to sit upright unaided or indeed to reach for objects. It is believed that he is blind although it is possible he may perceive light. He is probably deaf although it is possible that he showed some reaction to a buzzer when recently examined by a medical expert. . . . He cannot chew, and food has to be syringed to the back of his mouth. . . . The only response to touch appears to be when he is cuddled when he gives an indication of pleasure. (at p. 100)

Nevertheless staff at the day centre which R attended expressed some opposition to the parents' and consultant's view that were he to face another life-threatening situation and suffer a cardiac arrest then he should not be resuscitated. The staff sought an order of certiorari to quash the decision to invoke a 'do not resuscitate' (DNR) policy in relation to R. The High Court appeared to approach the matter from two rather exclusive ends. It was stated that the issue was the quality of life of the patient (as considered in *Re J (A Minor) (Wardship: Medical Treatment)* [1991] Fam 33). To withhold treatment would be justified where the life of the patient would be 'so afflicted as to be intolerable'. The High Court then went on to note that there were three situations where it would be permissible to invoke a DNR policy. Only one of these applied to a patient who could not consent (and R obviously could not). This would be where the DNR was unlikely to be successful. The fact that he was likely to suffer a collapse in a residential home setting made the chances of failure greater, as did the frailty of R. The slight problem with the reasoning of Stephen Brown P here is that if the DNR decision is on the basis that one of the accepted guidelines is in existence then this is a medical question. If it is the quality of life of the patient then this is a question of a different order altogether. If the former were recognised as the sole basis for the decision then it is really the case that the court has no place at all.

The courts have, since *Bland*, been confronted with patients who, while on any reading of the cases are in a desperate state, are not within the definition of PVS. The question has been for the courts then, does the same process of reasoning apply to such patients? In *Bland* itself two significant members of the House of Lords, Lords Mustill and Browne-Wilkinson were uncomfortable with the idea that the *Bland* criteria should extend beyond cases of PVS. The answer appears to be that the courts are using a mix of criteria gleaned from *Bland* and the quality of life neonate, cases of *Re B (A Minor) (Wardship: Medical Treatment)* [1981] 1 WLR 1421 and *Re J*.

The patient in the persistent vegetative state then is not the only one to confront medical law and practice in relation to non-treatment. There may be occasions where there is a more acute test of best interests that needs to be considered. In chapter 14 it was seen that in addition to considering whether the quality of a patient's life would fall below a tolerable level, even if a proposed treatment were carried out and was successful to an extent, other less tangible interests of the patient would hold sway as a matter of responsible medical opinion. *Airedale NHS Trust v Bland* [1993] AC 789 is useful in that it considered the less tangible interests of dignity and respect that could influence a decision not to treat. To those one could add a calculation of what the future of the defective neonate (or adult for that matter) might hold in terms of the pain and intrusiveness of the treatment and the prospects of an improvement in the quality of the patient's life to a level regarded as 'worth living'. While there still appears to be some discomfort with the fictional nature of the substituted judgment apparent with regard to the neonate, it might be suggested that the adult patient who has become severely physically and mentally incapacitated needs treatment to survive, but without the prospect of any improvement in the quality of that life may be a more amenable subject for the importation of the transatlantic concept of substituted judgment. Kennedy and Grubb (*Medical Law*, 2nd ed. (London: Butterworths, 1994), p. 1265) rightly regard *Re Spring* (1980) 405 NE 2d 115 as an example of a case in which substituted judgment is applicable. The adult patient in *Re Spring* was suffering from 'end stage' kidney disease requiring frequent periods of dialysis. He was also in the advanced stages of senility which led to confusion, made him disoriented and was, like the kidney ailment, incurable. It was increasingly difficult to perform dialysis because of his aberrant behaviour and the side effects of the dialysis itself. He would die without the dialysis, but would not have suffered any discomfort. He had never expressed an opinion on what should happen in such circumstances, but his wife and son were of the opinion that withdrawal of dialysis would have been preferred. There appeared to be sound evidence that both wife and son had the patient's best interests at heart, and would be in the best position to know what the patient's decision would have been.

While one may agree with Kennedy and Grubb that this would appear a case for the exercise of substituted judgment, it would be an uncomfortable situation for an English court. If the decision to terminate dialysis were thought to be just in England, then one would be confident that the courts would once more emphasise that the best interests of the patient are to be appraised according to a responsible body of opinion, which would no doubt regard as good practice taking account of evidence of previously articulated desires or treatment options from the next of kin. In other words, the substituted judgment test is just part of considering the best interests of the patient. (But now see the hint of introducing substituted judgment in *Re D (Adult: Medical Treatment)* [1996] 2 FLR 99 at 108–9 per Stephen Brown P.)

15.8 CONCLUSION

Throughout the journey of *Airedale NHS Trust v Bland* [1993] AC 789 through the courts, the judges showed awareness of the onerous nature of the task that had been given to the medical profession and then the courts by the development of the technology used to keep PVS patients alive. The subsequent utilisation of the views of the House of Lords in another PVS case, that of *Frenchay Healthcare NHS Trust* v *S* [1994] 1 WLR 601, and the support for *Bland* evident in the House of Lords select committee report of 1995 (House of Lords Select Committee Report on Medical Ethics, HL Paper 21, 1993–4), indicate both that the issue is going to be encountered repeatedly by the medical profession and the courts, and that the law as applied in *Bland* is a cloak ill-fitted to protect either the rights of the patient or the doctor from the fear of liability without recourse to the judiciary.

Airedale NHS Trust v *Bland* has led both the medical profession and the judiciary into something of a trap. By utilising (admittedly less than wholeheartedly) the *Bolam* test to decide where the best interests of the PVS patient lie, the courts are delegating responsibility to a medical profession which is still seeking judicial guidance.

It appears that medical law here is once more making pronouncements, particularly with regard to those regarded as competent, that are more closely allied to a rights-based view of medical law. The decision in *Re C (Adult: Refusal of Treatment)* [1994] 1 WLR 290 in relation to the patient with gangrene who refused a potentially life-saving amputation (see 6.2.1.1 for further discussion on this) was predicated on the fact that the competent patient can refuse to have his or her life saved by the application of medical science. Whether as a matter of medical or judicial practice there will be an accurate assessment of competence where the patient's life is at stake is another matter. Judicial pronouncements also seem to allow the patient to issue a directive refusing such life-saving treatment in advance, which would force the doctor to abstain from treatment with threat of sanction through an action for battery. Whether the directive will be read literally, or with the fatal consequences of refusal in the medical and judicial mind, is less obvious.

Euthanasia as a medical and ethical debating point has been with us for some time now. There are patients in PVS throughout the world. There are those for whom the agony of life should be replaced by the peace of death. There are those whose cultures and religions demand abstention from some or all forms of medical intervention. Medical law will have to decide by legislation what should happen. Does medical law respect rights or welfare? In regulating euthanasia, is it possible to do both?

Further reading

Finnis, J. M., '*Bland*: Crossing the Rubicon?' (1993) 109 LQR 329.
Griffiths, J., 'Assisted Suicide in the Netherlands: The *Chabot* Case' (1995) 58 MLR 232.
Lanham, D., 'The Right to Choose to Die with Dignity' (1990) 14 Crim LJ 401.
Leng, R., 'Mercy Killing and the CLRC' (1982) 132 NLJ 76.
Kennedy, I., 'Switching off Life Support Machines: The Legal Implications' [1977] Crim LR 443.

Kennedy, I., 'The Legal Effect of Requests by the Terminally Ill and Aged Not to Receive Further Treatment from Doctors' [1976] Crim LR 217.
Keown, J., 'The Law and Practice of Euthanasia in the Netherlands' (1992) 108 LQR 51.

SIXTEEN
Death and transplantation

16.1 INTRODUCTION

Definitions of death have changed over time to encompass the massive developments in medical technology and diagnostic ability. The medico-legal definition of death has had an impact on the law and practice of transplantation in England. As Pallis has usefully pointed out, the changes in the definition are considerable and challenge the preconceptions and fears of many members of society:

> A dead brain in a body whose heart is still beating is one of the more macabre products of modern technology. During the last 30 years techniques have developed that can artificially maintain ventilation, circulation and elimination of waste products of metabolism in a body whose brain has irreversibly ceased to function. (C. Pallis, *ABC of Brain Stem Death* (London: British Medical Journal, 1983), p. 2)

When considering the death of the individual it might appear a little strange to consider human rights, but there is an argument that human rights include the right to dignity at the end of life, the right to die as one may wish, the right to be remembered as an individual or even the allied rights of those who survive the deceased. The 'good' medical law is one which links the two issues of death and transplantation in a rights-based framework and is based on the right to do with one's body as one wishes at the end of, as well as during, life. The final act of donation (or prior refusal to do so) after death is arguably the last expression of the autonomy of the individual.

16.2 DEFINITION OF DEATH

The discussion of what constitutes death is often regarded as an unpalatable one. People do not like to be reminded of the fact that their lives are finite.

There is a deeper fear surrounding this unwillingness. Members of society have long held a fear, which is described in horror films and stories, rather than originating there, that they will be declared dead when they are really alive. This fear is often combined with the image of the person on an operating table having organs removed while incapable of communicating vitality. To some this may sound mildly amusing, but one only has to consider the shortfall in the number of cadaver organs for transplantation, and the low number of people who have filled in and carry donor cards, to recognise that even those who scoff at such a fear, may in fact find it exists not too far below the surface of their own consciousness.

In the late nineteenth century this fear led a certain Count Karnice-Karnicki to patent a coffin with some interesting optional extras. If the buried person were to regain consciousness then there existed in the coffin a system of bells and flags which could be utilised to attract attention.

Cases encountered, such as those of the tragic anencephalic or hydro-cephalic child (respectively, the child with little or no real brain material in the skull cavity, and the child with poor brain formation and instead a large percentage of fluid in the cavity) or the patient in the persistent vegetative state, indicate the very real difficulty in deciding the margins of life and death. The importance of a definition lies not only in enabling a transplant procedure to begin, but also to make decisions with regard to the criminal law and the distribution of resources in treatment. If the law were to declare that in the case of the anencephalic child, or the PVS patient, what was being ventilated was legally a corpse, then that designation would allow the expensive and unproductive apparatus to be removed and utilised elsewhere. One cannot, then, avoid a discussion of what is death.

As a starting point it is worth turning again to Pallis for an initial optional definition:

> I conceive of human death as a state in which there is irreversible loss of the capacity for consciousness combined with irreversible loss of the capacity to breathe (and hence to maintain a heartbeat). Alone, neither would be sufficient.

This dual idea of death combines absence of *cognition* and absence of *respiration*. Combined with these two is the unifying matter of the *brain stem*. This is the key part of the triangle of biological and cognitive existence. The heart and the lungs as a team supply oxygen to the brain, therefore the brain cannot function without the operation of the heart and the lungs. Respiration itself is controlled by the brain stem, which in general terms performs the basic or 'vegetative" functions. For present purposes the significance of modern medical technology is that the activities of the heart and the lungs can be artificially maintained, but not those of the brain stem. If the brain stem has irreversibly ceased to function then there can never be (as tech-nology currently stands) spontaneous heartbeat or respiration, and this has long been the popular conception that death has occurred. There is further significance in the focus being on the functioning of the brain stem. The cerebral hemispheres of the brain control thought, feelings and the ability to rationalise. These are only 'activated' (to use Pallis's terminology) by the functioning brain stem. There has been further semantic debate on the fact that there is no point of death; death has been described as a process rather than an event. Whatever the correctness of this viewpoint, the true importance of the definition of death is as much to do with the permanent absence of valued capacities as it is about physiological events.

Robert Veatch in his work, *Death, Dying and the Biological Revolution* (Yale UP, 1989), considered the available options of what could amount to a definition of death, and felt that because of the breadth of philosophical, biological, religious and evolutionary features of humanity there could be definitions which focused on widely varying concepts.

First, the definition of death could be approached from what one may term a traditional perspective. This accords with the Western cultural notion of death as the irreversible cessation of respiration and heartbeat. However, there may be difficulty in maintaining that a person is dead if technology were available to reproduce mechanically the activities of the heart and the lung. Would society consider a person to be dead who is rational and communicative, yet unable to oxygenate and circulate his or her own blood? Veatch does admit that there may be those who regard the man–machine concept as an affront to human dignity, and that the available technology should not be used to this end, but nevertheless would find difficulty in regarding the person who utilised that technology as 'dead'.

An argument which has symmetry with concepts of the start of life is that the definition of death can be predicated on the theory of the desoulment of the spiritual individual. As it has been argued that human life begins when the soul enters the body, so life has ended when the soul departs. That this may be vague and prone to determination dependent on the particular strand of religious conviction may weaken it in the eyes of those who do not share the particular conviction. Nevertheless it is a view that is held by some members of society.

The idea which, despite its apparent complexity, Veatch finds the most compelling as an underpinning for the definition of death is described by him as 'the irreversible loss of the capacity for bodily integration'. It is based on an acceptance that there are parts of the human body that no longer function, while others are maintained artificially.

> Humans are more than the flowing of fluids. They are complex, integrated organisms with capacities for internal regulation. With and only with these integrating mechanisms is *Homo sapiens* really human.

When this process of continuous integration, in terms of internal bodily interreaction, and integration with society through consciousness, no longer takes place, persons lose the values that go to make up life, and thereafter are deemed to be dead, with all that entails. A tentative analogy may be made with the biodegradation of materials. When a paper cup is dropped on the floor it is clear what it is. Over time its constituent parts lose the capacity to integrate. Eventually the cup loses integration and form, until a time comes when it ceases to be 'a cup'. The human body is a complex and integrated machine, that toward the end of life starts to lose its ability to maintain itself as an integrated whole. The lungs may lose the ability to integrate productively with the heart, or vice versa. The time will come when the process of disintegration is at a stage where a person is no longer alive.

The concept of the loss of the ability to interact socially with others through consciousness has arguably become more prominent with the development of technology such as the ventilator. Does the fact that a person is unable to relate or react to his or her environment mean that there is an irreversible loss of that which goes to make up life? This may appear to be opening the way to considering those who do not have the ability to communicate effectively or rationally and who are no longer part of the living. That this would be unacceptable goes without saying. But what if one were to expand on the values that would need to be absent before a person is considered to be dead? Is an individual who has no personality, memory, reason or communicative ability alive or dead? That there may be the retort that there is insufficient information here to make a decision, might mean that this 'test' of life, in concentrating on the intellectual to the exclusion of the biological and physiological, lacks a dimension.

It may be that ultimately David Lamb is correct in his assertion that:

. . . whilst it is important to separate the sphere of the philosophical from the medical, it is equally important to stress that in any discussion of death neither party can afford to ignore the contributions of the other. (*Death, Brain Death and Ethics* (London: Croom Helm, 1985).

These available concepts of death comprise a wide range of values and demands, but all really are attempts to provide an explanation and definition for what is essentially a person-specific concept which is therefore intuitive. An individual (the author, for example) may regard the relevant criteria for the determination of death to encompass a variety of the matters raised above, but with particular weight put on communication, consciousness and rationality. That others may disagree only goes to indicate that one's true definition of death may well be as individual as a fingerprint.

16.3 THE MEDICAL PROFESSION'S DEFINITION OF DEATH

Whatever view is taken of the values to be utilised, there has long been a need for a definition which is based on medical practice, but not solely determined by it. The medical profession require a definition which is aligned to the public's perceptions, fears and interests. The definition may also have a role to fill in providing an explanation of current medical activity and the values underpinning it. The medical lawyer will be assisted by a definition in directing the medical profession on the legality of turning off life-support machines, and the potential issues of causation in homicide which may arise.

The 'medical' definition in England is based on the brain stem function itself (the physiological significance of which has already been noted). It is generally noted that the current definition came from the recognition in the late 1950s of a condition known as 'coma dépassé' or 'a state beyond coma' (defined by P. Mollard and M. Goulon, 'Le Coma Dépassé' (1959) 101 Rev Neurol 3). After that the criteria for determining that the brain stem was permanently incapable of functioning became more sophisticated. There was some worry over the development of terminology, with the Harvard Medical School defining what was in effect a test for brain stem death in terms of 'irreversible coma', thus evoking images of the PVS patient being seen as clinically dead (see 'A Definition of Irreversible Coma: Report of the ad hoc Committee of the Harvard Medical School to Examine the Definition of Brain Death' (1968) 202 J Am Med Ass 337).

Now the medical profession in England has decided on the definition and tests to be performed in determining death. It should be noted that this test and definition will not be used in a vast array of cases. Most deaths will be to a large extent a systematic and swift bodily disintegration. The heart will stop, there will thus be no oxygenated blood flowing through the body, and that lack of oxygenated blood will lead to the brain cells being starved of oxygen, and themselves dying.

The Conference of Royal Medical Colleges' memorandum 'Diagnosis of Death' [1979] 1 BMJ 332 referred to the fact that 'the permanent functional death of the brain stem constitutes brain death'. The tests required to determine that the brain stem had irreversibly ceased to function were enunciated in *R v Malcherek* [1981] 1 WLR 690 (see 16.4), and are comprehensive. The important modern case of *Re A* (1992) 3 Med LR 303, however, is an indication of the current scope of the test that takes place on the relatively rare occasions when it it necessary to perform it. A child was placed on a ventilator having arrived at hospital not breathing. Having noted some gasping activity when turning off the ventilator for a sample period, the next day the doctor carried out the following tests detailed in the judgment of Johnson J:

A's pupils were fixed and dilated. On movement of the head his eyes moved with his head. What is called the 'doll's eyes' response was absent. On his eye being touched with a piece of cotton wool there was no response. On cold water being passed into his ear there was no eye movement in response. On steps being taken, in effect to cause him to 'gag' there was no reflex reaction, neither was there reaction to pain being applied to his central nervous system. Finally, on his temporary removal from the ventilator to enable the carbon dioxide level of his body to increase there was no respiratory response. . . . The consultant was satisfied that A was brain stem dead.

16.4 LEGAL IMPACT OF THE BRAIN STEM DEFINITION

While as yet there is no statute which explicitly defines what amounts to death, the common law has had to confront issues which have required a recognition of the medical profession's definition of death and the need of that profession to have a notion that the law concurs with its perception.

A case considered by David Meyers (*The Human Body and the Law* (Edinburgh: Edinburgh UP, 1970)) illustrates the need for the criminal law to adopt a consistent definition of when life comes to an end, given that the traditional definition of death being the cessation of respiration and heartbeat, if used in a criminal court, could (and arguably did) lead to unjust results. In *R v Potter* (1963) *The Times*, 26 July 1963, the victim of a violent assault was taken to hospital suffering from severe head injuries. After 14 hours his breathing stopped, so he was placed on a respirator. After 24 hours a kidney was removed for transplantation purposes and then the respirator was turned off. After that there were no spontaneous signs of life. Meyer acknowledges that under the 'traditional' definition of death the doctor could have been found liable for malicious wounding or at the very least a battery. That this line of prosecution was not followed has not been explained, but there would have been great difficulty in the court (or the doctor for that matter) declaring that the removal was performed on a corpse. The argument for the court to consider was that the defendant was no longer a substantial and operative cause of the victim's death as the actions of the doctor in switching off the respirator broke the chain of causation. Meyer reports that 'It would seem that the judge agreed, for the defendant was committed for trial by the coroner after a jury's finding of manslaughter, yet was convicted only of common assault by the court'. Such a decision could have serious implications. The court might have to consider the activities of the doctor in switching off the life-support machine of the victim of criminal violence. Will the doctor be found to have broken the chain of causation? If the court were to regard the chain of causation broken by the doctor switching the machine off, it would be apparent that the law regards the doctor's actions as legally and factually significant. Is the doctor guilty of some form of homicide? This is a logical consequence of stating that the victim of violence placed on the life-support machine is not dead. While the courts have confronted the issue of causation, there may still be some unease with the concept of the switching off the life-support machine having no legal significance whatsoever (see *Airedale NHS Trust v Bland* [1993] AC 789, which is discussed in chapter 15).

The key to an understanding of how the law deals with such difficulties, and an example of judicial recognition of the brain stem death definition and tests are to be found in *R v Malcherek; R v Steel* [1981] 1 WLR 690, where appeals in two criminal cases were heard together.

In *Steel*, a woman had been the victim of a severe beating. She was found suffering from multiple injuries and unconscious. She was rushed to hospital and was found to be incapable of breathing unaided, and was therefore placed on a ventilator. The doctors concerned noted that she was deeply unconscious, her eyes while open were fixed. There appeared to be no electrical brain activity, and a follow-up test showed that there was no blood flowing through the brain. Subsequently the patient was taken off the ventilator. When a post mortem was carried out about an hour later, the brain was found to be already in the process of decomposition.

In *Malcherek* the victim had been stabbed a number of times, one being a deep stab wound to the abdomen. While appearing to recover after some days in hospital, she collapsed with what proved to be a massive blood clot in the heart, which had stopped, and spontaneously started again only when the clot was removed some 30 minutes later. It was suspected that the fact that there had been no oxygen supply to the brain for that amount of time would have meant damage. On returning to the ward, the victim was placed on a ventilator. It was not clear how much brain damage had occurred as her pupils were reacting to light stimulus. The decision was made to see if she could do without the machine. She managed to breath spontaneously for some time, but her condition deteriorated and she was placed back on the ventilator. Successive monitoring of her electrical brain activity showed it to be decreasing. A decision was thereafter made to disconnect the ventilator. Oxygen was fed into the lungs to assist if spontaneous efforts were made to breathe, but there were none. She was then certified dead.

At trial the judge ruled that the issue of causation should not be left to the jury. Lord Lane CJ noted that the traditional definitions of death were out of step with the advances in medical technology. There was recognition too that the medical profession were *ad idem* that the test of death was the irreversible cessation of brain stem function. Given the fact that the doctors were not on trial, Lord Lane CJ felt that it was not a case where the court was required to give a definition of death at law. The decision, however, comes as close as one arguably needs to come, although in unfortunately vague terms:

> Where a medical practitioner adopting methods which are generally accepted comes bona fide and conscientiously to the conclusion that the patient is for practical purposes dead, and that such vital functions as exist – for example, circulation – are being maintained solely by mechanical means, and therefore discontinues treatment, that does not prevent the person who inflicted the initial injury from being responsible for the victim's death. Putting it in another way, the discontinuance of treatment in those circumstances does not break the chain of causation between the initial injury and the death.

While there is nothing to suggest that this is other than an accurate statement of the law on causation, one pauses to wonder why Lord Lane CJ, while eschewing the opportunity to make what would admittedly have been an *obiter* statement on the legal definition of death, muddied the waters somewhat by using the phrase 'for all practical purposes dead'. While again that may be correct, there is a notable absence of the phrase 'for all legal purposes dead'. This absence indicates the need for Parliament to provide a statutory definition.

Re A (1992) 3 Med LR 303 may have solved the debate about whether Lord Lane CJ's decision not to consider legal death means that it is regarded as separate from 'practical' or 'clinical' death.

A baby was taken to hospital suffering from injuries apparently as a result of a fall at home. The child was found not have a heartbeat on arrival at the accident and emergency department. The child was transferred to another hospital where a number of attempts were made to resuscitate. The child was later placed on a ventilator, and the tests detailed by the Royal Medical Colleges memoranda carried out. The parents sought to have the child left on the ventilator, even though the consultant paediatric neurologist considered the child to be brain stem dead. There appeared to be some suspicion that the child may have met with a non-accidental death while at home. Johnson J, in a strongly worded speech, declared that the child was dead for legal as well as for medical purposes. In addition, the court made the significant points that the doctor was not acting unlawfully because the child was already dead, and, even while being ventilated, the court had no standing to consider the issue of wardship for the best interests of the child, because obviously that jurisdiction ended with the death of the child.

From the common law consideration of these end of life issues one begins to see a definition in the case law that conforms to the medical definition of brain stem death. The fact that the child in *Re A* was dead, and therefore the actions of the doctor not legally significant, can be combined with the very clear statement of all Law Lords in *Airedale NHS Trust* v *Bland* that the PVS patient with the functioning brain stem is alive and the actions of the doctors potentially legally significant, to indicate that the common law may have no need to exhort Parliament to provide a statutory definition of death.

16.5   A STATUTORY DEFINITION OF DEATH?

In their 14th Report, the Criminal Law Revision Committee (1980), while acknowledging the existence of the brain stem definition of the Conference of Medical Royal Colleges in 1979, felt that to place this definition in a statute would be too restrictive. The Committee were of the opinion that future developments in medicine may mean that this definition may not remain the majority view of the medical profession. It was further felt that, in terms of transplantation, the medical profession themselves might be hindered by the adoption of a statutory definition. In addition any definition was regarded as having to apply to the civil law.

Skegg has argued that there is a need for a statutory definition ('The Case for a Statutory Definition of Death' (1976) 2 J Med Ethics 190) on the basis that there is sufficient unanimity in the medical profession of the stage at which the patient is regarded as dead to provide a single definition which will be applicable to all circumstances and which can be explained to the anxious public.

Kennedy on the other hand does not support such a definition ('The Definition of Death' (1977) 3 J Med Ethics 5). His article seeks to argue that the enactment of legislation would be geared to transplant concerns, and would promote distrust rather than trust in the motivations and parameters of the legislation. Kennedy may be more to the point when he refers to the difficulties of the style used in legislation rather than the motivation behind it. There needs to be public education and debate about the motivations of the current definition, and legislation should reflect public conclusions. Criticisms that legislation might be seen as a cloak for an expansion in the circumstances in which organs would be removed for transplantation would be equally if not more pertinent to a code of practice or some other non-statutory protocol.

16.6 TRANSPLANTATION

Recently the debate surrounding transplantation has resurfaced. There is now the possibility, in addition to cadaver transplantation and live donor transplantation, of what is known as 'transgenic' transplantation. Recent reports indicate that developments in genetic engineering have resulted in the development of mammals (pigs being the 'best' so to speak) that can be 'harvested' for major organs to transplant into human beings. Recently the development of transgenic pig hearts and kidneys by Imutran has been considered by the Nuffield Council on Bioethics. The Council's report accepted that there were on average in any given year around 5,000 people waiting for kidneys, and 300 plus waiting for new hearts. The report recommended that the development of transgenic organs was a way to alleviate the anguish of the shortfall of organs for those patients, but 'in the context of a careful regulatory framework' (Mark Wolpert quoted in 'Pig transplants win ethical backing', *New Scientist*, 9 March 1996, p. 4).

In the USA the level of transplant experimentation has increased substantially. Recently, an AIDS victim was given a bone marrow transplant from a baboon, which failed to take. As far as medical law is concerned, the danger has been expressed that a virus or other undetected infectious agent might infect a pig heart, which as well as leading to potential liability on the part of those who performed the procedure and the monitoring of organ selection, could also lead to the release of a novel virus into the population at large.

As early as 1964 there was evidence that attempts were being made to utilise mammalian organs. A now routine operation in England to transplant a pig heart valve was developed. Baby Fae was given a baboon's heart in 1984 (see L. L. Hubard, 'The Baby Fae Case' (1987) 6 Med Law 385) in a doomed attempt to save her life. The fervency of opposition was not unexpected. The development proposed by (amongst others) James ('Transplants with Transgenic Pig Organs?' (1993) 342 *The Lancet* 45) has now become a reality.

Recently an advisory group set up by the Department of Health reviewed many aspects of xenotransplantation. While the group had to confront the various opponents, it has recommended that in principle intra-species transplants should be allowed. Nevertheless there were sufficient concerns about the transfer of disease from animals into the human population that such transplantation is not yet allowed in practice. The advisory group considered that there had not yet been enough research and safeguards. It was aware that there was vociferous opposition to the practice from animal rights activists. It was accepted that there were such things as animal rights but at present these were certainly extremely limited. The central animal right recognised was the avoidance of suffering. It was this concept which underpinned legislation controlling animal experiments (see the Animals (Scientific Procedures) Act 1986, which appears to take a utilitarian stance that the amount of pain the animal is permitted to suffer must depend on the purpose of the project s. 5(4)). The advisory group then went on to distinguish between animals and primates. It was contended that it would be ca to use primates as donors as they were of a higher intellectual order than other animals. The government has accepted these recommendations, and has approved in addition the setting up of the Xenotransplantation Interim Regulatory Authority to monitor the progress of inter-species disease transfer, and other issues raised by this medical development.

The debate is likely to continue to be a vociferous one and will need to consider allegations of speciesism on the part of those breeding animals for the sole purpose of providing transplant material. Against this is likely to be the response that there is a need to save life, and the public would support the scientist developing, or the transplant surgeon utilising, this scientific advance. Opponents of the development may well point out their perception of the public disquiet that the correct focus of debate, which should be on the finite resources available to society and the problems (including the economic impact) of the ageing of the population, militates against the utilisation of ethically contentious techniques to prolong life. The debate is too broad for an analysis here, but that should not detract from the fact that it is an important one, as much in terms of the future of the population as the welfare of other life forms.

In addition to the profound philosophical, ethical and legal debate that arises from this development, the advances in immunosupressant drugs have increased the chances of any type of organ transplantation being successful. Recently a cancer patient was given a triple transplant of liver, pancreas and bowel to attempt to save his life (*The Times*, 6 March 1996, p. 5). To some these developments are exciting, to some life-saving, but to some worrying or even immoral. The ageing of the population will mean that there will be an ever-increasing need to replace what one might term 'tired' or diseased organs as well as society requiring transplants to correct birth defects or the onset of cancer.

There are three main ways that transplant organs can be made available:

(a) Through transgenic transplants (considered briefly above).
(b) Through live donor transplants.
(c) Through donation from the deceased.

The latter two will be analysed in detail. They raise a central problem of medical law, that of the limits of consent. It will become apparent that common and statute law have proved somewhat unwieldy in dealing with the subject of transplantation.

16.6.1 Live donor transplants

The first 'candidates' for involvement in transplantation are the competent potential donor. In the press there is often the human interest story of the father or mother willing to 'give up' a kidney to save the life of a loved one.

To the vast majority of people this would be greeted with praise, but there are more issues at stake than appear from such a simple scenario:

(a)   Can a competent person ever consent to an operation that is non-therapeutic to him or her?

(b)   Can a competent person consent to a transplant operation which will prove fatal to him or her?

(c)   Can a competent person sell an organ of his or her body for money?

(d)   Can a child, regarded as *Gillick* competent, consent to donating tissue or an organ?

(e)   Can anyone consent to the donation of an organ from a person regarded as legally incompetent to make a decision regarding his or her own welfare?

16.6.1.1   The competent, common law and donation   It has already been seen that in a great many areas of medical law the fact of consent to treatment is crucial. Where the donation of organs from the competent patient to another is concerned there are difficulties from the vague historical precedents of the common law and its exact parameters. It has been observed on a number of occasions that the closest the common law has come to a consideration of the issue of consent to a non-therapeutic activity was with the crime of maim. Dworkin ('The Law Relating to Organ Transplantation in England' (1970) 33 MLR 353) uses the example of the Victorian soldier who requested that a dentist remove his teeth so that he did not have to bite gun cartridges as part of his training. That this was one of the best examples that could be found illustrates the paucity of relevant precedent. The general issues of common law that would appear relevant turn on the fact that the consent can be accurately perceived as being for something non-therapeutic for the donor, and, in certain circumstances, could be regarded as being against public policy. Recently the case of *R* v *Brown* [1994] 1 AC 212 concerned the legality of consent to sadomasochistic sexual activity. While the decision was made essentially on the basis of the undesirability of the law regarding consent to cruelty as valid, one could suggest that *Brown* was also decided as an issue of societal morality, which can also be termed public policy. In relation to the altruistic donation of an organ by a competent person, one would perceive there to be very real difficulties in regarding such a laudable offer as against public policy. The Victorian court might have regarded the pulling of teeth as depriving the country of a fighting man, but that is far removed from the altruistic donor.

As a basic issue it will be recalled that the individual's body is inviolate. Any touching of a person without his or her consent is unlawful, and liability can thereafter be founded on the criminal or the civil law of battery. If any touching without consent is prima facie unlawful, then consent justifies and makes lawful such a touching. A less firmly established general principle of law, derived from public policy perceptions, is that there may be times when the individual, as a matter of social welfare or paternalism, needs to be protected from him or herself. It is the conflict between these two concepts that the common law has to resolve in relation to live donor transplants from a competent person. The key to legitimising what would otherwise be an unlawful touching is consent. Dworkin therefore identifies this as the first condition that needs to be satisfied before a transplant operation can take place:

(a) 'The patient must give a full, free and informed consent.'

The matter of testing the competence of the patient and the levels of disclosure to the patient have all been dealt with in earlier chapters on consent. While the principles are of relevance here, one needs to be aware of the need for careful counselling to lead to a fully informed consent, and also as an opportunity to test the freedom of the consent. The psychological pressure that may be placed on a family member to donate a kidney to a brother or sister, for example, may place intolerable burdens on the potential donor and mean that consent is not freely given.

(b) 'The operation must be therapeutic: it must be expressly for the patient's benefit.'

Arguably strict adherence to this concept would mean that there would be very few (if any!) organ donations. It is extremely difficult to regard the competent patient who goes into hospital with two kidneys and comes out with one, the other having been donated to his brother, as therapeutic for the donor. The answer to this question relies on a broad determination of what the term 'therapeutic' encompasses. As well as physical benefits from various forms of medical treatment, patients can find psychological benefits. There may be instances where the benefit of seeing a family member healthy as a result of the donation may offset the loss of a kidney and thereby benefit the donor (see *Strunk* v *Strunk* (1969) 445 SW 2d 145). That this is something of a weak argument has to be admitted, if attempted as a general justification for all such transplants. Dworkin suggests that a donor who is left with one kidney is not really harmed as the remaining one compensates for the absence of the 'partner' organ. There is an admission, however, that there has to be an increased risk of any damage to the remaining kidney having much more serious consequences. It would thus appear that the donation of a kidney, for example, cannot be regarded as therapeutic as far as the donor is concerned.

(c) 'There must be lawful justification.'

This, it also has to be admitted, is a potentially broad theory. It may be more accurate to ask the question: Can there be a lawful justification for the non-therapeutic surgical procedure? The single most powerful argument in terms of justification is that the donor is in a position of altruism and sacrifice. As a rescuer is treated generously by the law, so should the donor. Allied to this is the extra-judicial comment of Edmund Davies LJ quoted in Dworkin's article, that he would:

. . . be surprised if a surgeon were successfully sued for trespass to the person or convicted of causing bodily harm to one of full age and intelligence who freely consented to act as donor – always provided that the operation did not present unreasonable risk to that donor's life or health.

That proviso is essential. A man may declare himself ready to die for another, but the surgeon must not take him at his word. ((1969) 62 Proc Roy Soc Med 633 at p. 634)

This is a tentative statement at best and indicates that there is still no firm judicial footing which consistently justifies the donation of organs from the competent donor. His lordship appears to make a number of differentiations here. There is the recognition that there can be valid consent to a donation operation, as long as the risk is within acceptable limits. The comment appears to be a conclusion to a debate which justifies donation, but not the argument in support of that conclusion. Is the basis public policy in donation? The pre-eminence of the concept of consent? Altruism within limits?

Weaker attempts than these have been used to justify the activity. It has been suggested that while the operation cannot really be regarded as in the best interest of the donor, 'interests' can be given a broad definition to encompass activities that are at least not harmful to the patient. Skegg (*Law, Ethics and Medicine,* at p. 36) tends toward this view, arguing that the operation would not amount to the offence of battery, and then moving on to a broad justification that the operation will not attract the attention of the courts, because there is 'just cause or excuse' or a 'good reason' for it.

The matter has now fallen to be considered by English medical law and appears to follow the idea that the interests of the donor can be social and psychological as well as medical benefit. In *Re Y (Mental Patient: Bone Marrow Donation)* [1997] Fam 10 Connell J made a declaration that it would be lawful to make preliminary blood tests and a 'conventional' bone marrow harvesting operation under a general anaesthetic. This was declared to be lawful notwithstanding the fact that the donor was a severely mentally disabled 25-year-old. The situation was that the plaintiff, who was 36 years old, had developed myelodispestic syndrome, a pre-leukaemic bone marrow disorder, which would without a transplant develop into an even more serious condition. The plaintiff had three sisters, but only Y was compatible. There was evidence that the defendant (the intended donor) was close to her mother, who herself was suffering increasing medical problems made worse by the condition of her seriously ill daughter.

In making the declarations that the operations could take place, the High Court recognised that taking without consent would have been a crime and a tort. Connell J went on therefore to focus on the term 'best interests'. The operation could take place without patient consent where that patient was not competent but the operation was in her best interests. Here it was accepted that the taking of blood samples and the bone marrow under general anaesthetic could not be for Y's medical benefit in any traditional sense, i.e., treatment for Y's illness. Nevertheless Connell J stated that since donation by the defendant to the plaintiff would help to prolong the life of her ill and anxious mother, the defendant would receive an 'emotional, psychological and social benefit from the operation and suffer minimal detriment'. Therefore it was in her best interests.

It may appear that this sets a powerful precedent for families and medical practitioners seeking decalarations which would allow a sibling to donate a kidney, for example, even where the potential donor is handicapped and unable to consent or refuse. This possibility was noted by Connell J who sounded a warning (at p. 116):

> It is doubtful that this case would act as a useful precedent in cases where the surgery involved is more intrusive than in this case, where the evidence shows that the bone marrow harvested is speedily regenerated and that a healthy individual can donate as much as two pints with no long-term consequences at all.

In general, the issue is still without satisfactory resolution. It would appear likely that this will remain the case, as it would be difficult to foresee the donor raising an allegation of battery, or an observer of the procedure contacting the relevant authorities.

What might well attract the attention of the courts would be a transplantation which proved fatal to the donor. In 1996 there was an unreported case of a Leicester man who wished to donate both kidneys, one to each son, to correct a congenital defect. The local hospital refused to allow the father to take this course of action. In the case of single kidney donation, terms such as 'altruism' and 'rescuer' are used. A term which is not used as much, but one which may be relevant is the idea of 'sacrifice'. The profound difficulty the potential 'double donor' faces is that any operation undertaken by a surgeon would amount to murder, and that surgeon would not (save in the most extreme circumstances) have any criminal law defence.

16.6.1.2 Selling organs Although it appears to rest on less than settled legal ground, a competent donor may consent to the removal of a non-vital organ to save or improve the life of another. A central justification may be a return to the fundamental notion of the autonomy of the individual and the right to do with one's body as one wishes. Can this, or any other form of justification allow for the agreement to donate an organ for money?

In the late 1980s a scandal erupted over evidence that there were donors selling kidneys for transplantation into those who had no genetic or other relation to the donor. Indeed the evidence came from advertisements inviting Turks (among others) to come to England to make such donations. It was apparent that this activity exhibited all the features of a commercial enterprise. The three doctors who were found to have been involved in these matters were found guilty of serious professional misconduct by the GMC. One of these doctors had his name erased from the medical register and the activities of the other two were only slightly less severely curtailed (see C. Dyer, 'GMC's Decision on "Kidneys for Sale"' (1990) 300 BMJ 961).

The reaction of the government was no less swift and severe. The Human Organ Transplants Act 1989 was rushed through Parliament. Section 1 of the Act provides:

> (1)   A person is guilty of an offence if in Great Britain he—
>   (a)   makes or receives any payment for the supply of, or for an offer to supply, an organ which has been or is to be removed from a dead or

living person and is intended to be transplanted into another person whether in Great Britain or elsewhere;

(b)   seeks to find a person willing to supply for payment such an organ as is mentioned in paragraph (a) above or offers to supply such an organ for payment;

(c)   initiates or negotiates any arrangement involving the making of any payment for the supply of, or for an offer to supply, such an organ; or

(d)   takes part in the management or control of a body of persons corporate or unincorporate whose activities consist of or include the initiation or negotiation of such arrangements.

(2)   Without prejudice to paragraph (b) of subsection (1) above, a person is guilty of an offence if he causes to be published or distributed, or knowingly publishes or distributes, in Great Britain an advertisement—

(a)   inviting persons to supply for payment any such organs as are mentioned in paragraph (a) of that subsection or offering to supply any such organs for payment; or

(b)   indicating that the advertiser is willing to initiate or negotiate any such arrangement as is mentioned in paragraph (c) of that subsection.

Before considering the scope of this section, one needs to be aware of s. 1(3)(b) of the Act, which considers payment to have been made if done in money or money's worth, but not including the payment of expenses or other disbursements of the donor's which are directly attributable to the supplying of an organ from that donor's body. As with the attempts to portray the payment to a surrogate mother as expenses as opposed to the illegal money for adoption in the USA, it would seem likely that any attempt to get around the legislation by making inordinate expenses claims would be dealt with severely by the courts in England.

Potentially a wide range of those involved in a 'commercial' transplantation procedure can come within the scope of s. 1 of the Act. The organ donor is guilty under s. 1(1)(a) as there is payment for supply. Is it the case that those doctors, nurses and surgeons involved in the transplantation, either removal or transplant, are involved in receiving 'payment for supply' as indicated in s. 1(1)(a).

The answer on first inspection of the law appears to be plainly that they do. Both surgeons in this circumstance are part of the chain of supply. There need not be exclusivity of supply, i.e., the donor being the only supplier. It should be remembered that the Act aims to prohibit commercial dealings in organs. The mischief at which the Act is aimed is therefore those who profit from the whole enterprise. Against this view of s. 1(1)(a) is the problem that any surgeon in the private sector could be convicted, as there is payment for the transplant operation. To this needs to be added, however, s. 1(3)(a). This excludes those who receive 'the cost of removing, transporting or preserving the organ to be supplied'.

Whatever the cogency of the debate on who falls to be criminalised under the Act, the general intention of the legislation is clear: the commercialisation of live donor transplantation is unlawful. The argument in favour of the enactment of the 1989 Act is that the underprivileged and poor of other countries (and potentially this country) will be pressurised into selling parts of their bodies for money. There was evidence in the Humana Hospital scandal, which led to the passing of the 1989 Act, that one of the donors intended to use the money gained from the donation to fund his daughter's medical treatment. This can be viewed as an indication of the exploitative risks associated with commercialisation. It can also be seen as a benefit of the practice for those who would be unable to fund such treatment any other way. The Act is another example of the pressure of arguments which range from autonomy to paternalism. As with the argument surrounding surrogacy, the potential commercial donor can regard the decision to sell an organ as an expression of the ethical view that one can do with one's body what one wishes. Opponents can point out that financial pressures on the potential donor mean that the consent, which is still an essential part of any donation, will never truly be free.

Overall one would suggest that professional medical practice approves of the GMC's guidance that:

> In no circumstances may doctors participate in or encourage in any way the trade in human organs from live donors. They must not advertise for donors nor make financial or medical arrangements for people who wish to sell or buy organs. . . . Doctors must also satisfy themselves that consent to a donation has been given without undue influence of any kind, including the offer of financial or material benefit. (General Medical Council, 'Guidance for Doctors on Transplantation of Organs from Live Donors' (1992) News Review, December.

16.6.1.3 Transplantation and genetic relationship   As well as the prohibition on commercial dealings in organs, the Human Organ Transplants Act 1989 restricts the altruistic donation of parts of the body considered by the law to be 'organs' to those 'genetically related' to the donor. Section 7(2) defines the former:

> Organ means any part of a human body consisting of a structured arrangement of tissues which, if wholly removed, cannot be replicated by the body.

Of central importance then is the fact that this 'structured arrangement of tissues' is incapable of being reproduced upon its removal. Heart, lungs, kidneys etc. would all comfortably fit within this definition. The Act, though, does not apply to such things as hair, blood or bone marrow, which are reproduced by the body. Kennedy and Grubb have argued that the definition leaves something to be desired, in that it refers to parts of the body 'which, if wholly removed . . . '. Where one is concerned with the transplantation of the lobe of a liver, for example, is this a part of the body wholly removed? If not, then it does not come within the regulatory framework of the Act. It is a part of the body, it does consist of a structured arrangement of tissues, but even if a lobe is regarded as a wholly removed part, it can regenerate. There are arguments to suggest that the legislature intended the Act to regulate partial organ transplants, but the Act does not make it clear. If the lobe removal and transplant is not of an organ as the term is understood, then arguably there can be a commercial arrangement with regard to such a procedure.

An 'organ' can (subject to regulations that will be detailed in a moment) only be transplanted to someone 'genetically related' to the donor. The offence and the breadth of the relationship allowed are clear from s. 2:

(1)   Subject to subsection (3) below, a person is guilty of an offence if in Great Britain he—
(a)   removes from a living person an organ intended to be transplanted into another person; or
(b)   transplants an organ removed from a living person into another person,
unless the person into whom the organ is to be or, as the case may be, is transplanted is genetically related to the person from whom the organ is removed.
(2)   For the purposes of this section a person is genetically related to—
(a)   his natural parents and children;
(b)   his brothers and sisters of the whole or half blood;
(c)   the brothers and sisters of the whole or half blood of either of his natural parents; and
(d)   the natural children of his brothers and sisters of the whole or half blood or of the brothers and sisters of the whole or half blood of either of his natural parents;
but persons shall not in any particular case be treated as related in any of those ways unless the fact of the relationship has been established by such means as are specified by regulations made by the Secretary of State.

The testing under s. 2(2) is by means of DNA profiling (as detailed in reg. 2 of the Human Organ Transplants (Establishment of Relationship) Regulations 1989 (SI 1989/2107)).

This is not to say that any transplantation involving live donors who are unrelated will be offences under the Human Organ Transplants Act 1989. Section 2(3) of the Act empowers the Secretary of State to make regulations which allow for unrelated donations. Under the provision the Secretary of State made the Human Organ Transplants (Unrelated Persons) Regulations 1989 (SI 1989/2480), which set up the Unrelated Live Transplant Regulatory Authority (ULTRA). Regulation 3 allows for transplants between the genetically unrelated to take place where the following conditions are satisfied:

(a)   That no payment has been made.
(b)   That the registered medical practitioner who referred the matter to ULTRA has clinical responsibility for the patient.
(c)   That this practitioner has explained the nature of the medical procedure to the donor.

(d) That the donor understands this explanation, including the risks of the operation.

(e) That the consent of the donor was not obtained through some form of duress or offer of some form of payment (of whatever form).

(f) That the donor has been made aware of the right to a change of mind, and no change of mind has occurred.

(g) That both the donor and the recipient have been interviewed by somebody suitably qualified to do so, who has been satisfied that all the above conditions have been complied with.

The overall effect of the legislation appears to allow for a wide range of transplant arrangements, which nonetheless have to have one thing in common: that there is no commercial aspect to them.

16.6.1.4 Minors, consent and transplantation The legal and ethical issues surrounding consent and the minor having been already considered in some detail, one needs now to decide whether the same legal responses to that debate are suitable here. The typical scenario will involve a brother or sister (and not uncommonly and for obvious medical reasons concerning rejection of organs, twins), one of whom has some organ defect that can only be alleviated in the long term by a transplantation.

It has already been indicated that the law has not undertaken a particularly effective analysis of the issue of consent where the rational adult donor is concerned, and therefore the same uncertainties apply here. In addition, where what one might call 'sibling' organ transplantation is in issue, there needs to be a consideration of the tests of competence which have been utilised, particularly the concept of the *Gillick*-competent child.

It will be recalled that the Family Law Reform Act 1969, s. 8(1), is predicated on the fact that there is 'treatment' involved (see chapter 6). Unless one takes an extremely broad view of the donation by a sibling as treatment for the donor, the question whether the child can consent will depend on whether he or she is legally capable of understanding the fact and implications of the operation.

In *Re W (A Minor) (Medical Treatment: Court's Jurisdiction)* [1993] Fam 64, Lord Donaldson of Lymington MR stated that, unlike other forms of medical intervention:

> Organ transplants are quite different and, as a matter of law, doctors would have to secure the consent of someone with the right to consent on behalf of a donor under the age of 18 or, if they relied upon the consent of the minor himself or herself, be satisfied that the minor was '*Gillick* competent' in the context of so serious a procedure which could not benefit the minor. (p. 78)

Despite some confusion over the application of the common law to the 18-year-old (his Lordship must have meant 16), Lord Donaldson went on to explain that the reliance on *Gillick* competence would be highly unlikely without parental consent, and then only with court approval. This, it is suggested, is to begin to chip away at the breadth of application of *Gillick* competence as a test of medical law in the context of transplantation, as has been seen in refusals of consent as a whole (see 6.3 on the cases of *Re R (A Minor) (Wardship: Consent to Treatment)* [1992] Fam 11 and *Re W)*. The right of the mature minor to consent to or refuse treatment should depend on the competence of the minor, not the implications and seriousness of the operation.

Concern, however, has been expressed that the psychological pressures on an adult to become a donor may be multiplied where the parents of one ill child, knowing that the chances of improvement depend on the other child donating a kidney, raise the issue of transplantation. A minor might find it difficult to rationalise the benefits and burdens of the operation under such emotional pressure, and there may thus be no free consent.

A potential justification for transplantation involving the minor as donor can be illustrated by the approach of the US courts in *Strunk* v *Strunk* (1969) 445 SW 2d 145 and *Re Y (Mental Patient: Bone Marrow Donation)* [1997] Fam 10. In the former case the elder son was dying of a kidney disease. The artificial mechanism which substituted for the kidney was only of short-term benefit. His brother was 27 years old, but with a mental age of around six years. When tested the brother was found to be a highly medically acceptable donor. It was held that the donation could take place notwithstanding the lack of consent of the brother, because the operation would be in the donor's interests. There was evidence of a deep devotion to the other brother and evidence also that the death of this ill brother might well have a devastating emotional effect on the prospective donor.

Debate, as well as concerning the capacity of the minor to consent and the position and power of any proxy decision-maker, in relation to transplantation and minors, has veered once more between the autonomy of the child and society's interests in protecting children. Attempts have been made to rationalise a wholesale ban on the use of minors (or for that matter the permanently legally incompetent) as donors. In Canada this latter pathway has been taken. The Ontario Human Tissue Gift Act 1990 does so prohibit.

16.7   CADAVER TRANSPLANTATION

16.7.1   Introduction

The difficulties of transgenic transplants at present, and the obvious legal and moral arguments surrounding live donor transplants, whether for money or not, mean that all countries have still to rely heavily on the supply of organs from those who have died. Recently, the well-publicised shortfall of resources in the National Health Service has led to, amongst other things, a reappraisal of the costly long-term use of high-technology medicine to assist patients who have a less than fully functioning organ. Transplants for such patients would mean the reallocation of the funds needed for such intensive treatment, as well as giving the patient relatively more freedom and a higher quality of life.

The shortage of organs is still acute in this country, and hospitals have been forced to adopt cut-off age points of those eligible for transplantation treatment, in seeking to maximise the possibilities of success of those cadaver organs that are transplanted. The advantages of cadaver transplantation are obvious. The dead donor encounters no risk in the performance of the transplantation operation. The removal of organs, which would prove fatal to the live donor (the heart, for example) can be effected on the cadaver. At present this is the only way that a vital organ can be replaced. All is not as positive as may seem, however. The cadaver organs have to be removed and stored or transplanted within a relatively short time, before they become useless, or even hazardous to the donee. There is the problem of the donee body rejecting the organ, although this has become less of a hazard as imunosuppressant drugs have become more sophisticated. On a more emotional level, relatives may be horrified at the thought of a loved one who has just died being 'cut up' and the body parts harvested to keep others alive. There may still be those terrified by the thought that unscrupulous doctors are willing to remove organs from those who are not dead. A 1980 'Panorama' programme, entitled 'Organ Transplants: Are the Donors Really Dead?', disputed the validity of the definition of death as it stood. Public anxiety after the programme was such that there was evidence of a 65 per cent reduction in the number of donors, arguably attributable to the programme itself. Many people when asked state that they would like to donate some or all of their organs after death, yet only a small (but admittedly increasing) number actually carry donor cards. In this area of medicine, public opinion is obviously highly volatile. Any legislation in relation to cadaver transplantation would need to be well drafted to reassure the public, and clearly spell out the parameters within which the transplant doctor may lawfully act.

16.7.2 Current law

Cadaver transplantation is governed by the Human Tissue Act 1961, which expanded on the obviously limited provisions of the Corneal Grafting Act 1954. It should be evident on any reading of the 1961 Act that it is vague and open to a wide variety of interpretations. In addition, far from facilitating the supply of organs, which the legislation aimed to do while giving the public reassurance, it may have had the opposite effect.

Section 1(1) of the Act may be termed the 'donor authorisation' subsection:

> If any person, either in writing at any time or orally in the presence of two or more witnesses during his last illness, has expressed a request that his body or any specified part of his body be used after his death for therapeutic purposes or for purposes of medical education or research, the person lawfully in possession of his body after his death may, unless he has reason to believe that the request was subsequently withdrawn, authorise the removal from the body of any part or, as the case may be, the specified part, for use in accordance with the request.

The innate vagueness of many of the preconditions for the invocation of s. 1(1) of the Act is exacerbated by the fact that there is still no directly applicable case law that can be utilised. One has therefore to proceed carefully by way of legal analogy.

The main culprit as far as this vagueness is concerned is also the key concept underlying the legislation, namely, authorisation by a person 'lawfully in possession' of the body. This is the *only* person who can legally authorise. It should be noted that a corpse at law can never be the subject of ownership. One should briefly note, though, the case of *Dobson* v *North Tyneside Health Authority* [1997] 1 WLR 596, in which it was held that there is no property in a body unless it has undergone a process or application of human skill, such as stuffing or embalming (see also *R* v *Kelly* (1998) unreported, which concerned the theft of body parts). Here the preservation of a brain in paraffin was found not to be such an application of skill, so parents who required their deceased daughter's brain to support a claim of medical negligence against those who treated their daughter could not recover damages for conversion of it from persons who had disposed of it. An individual cannot decide what shall happen to his or her body after death (although usually as a matter of respect for the deceased the next of kin will comply with any request that had been made during life). This person 'in lawful possession' is therefore an important figure; but who are the available candidates?

According to Lanham ('Transplants and the Human Tissues Act 1961' (1971) 11 Med Sci Law 16) the nineteenth-century authority of *Williams* v *Williams* (1882) 20 ChD 659 indicates that the executors of the deceased were the ones lawfully 'entitled' to possession. If the deceased died intestate then the administrators were the ones so entitled. During the passage of the Bill through Parliament it was argued that the most likely candidate would be the hospital where the deceased was taken. Authority may be used to bolster such an argument. In *R* v *Feist* (1858) Dears & B 590 it was held that the master of the workhouse where the deceased pauper lay was the person having lawful possession of the body and could permit anatomical examination in accordance with the Anatomy Act 1832. The Parliamentary debate also involved attempts, which were resisted, to put the matter beyond any doubt and make the hospital authority the party in lawful possession. According to Lanham, Parliament resisted this on the ground that it might be seen as ousting the superior rights of the executors (643 HC Deb, 5th ser. col. 836). Despite continued debate the matter seems to be resolved by the intention underlying s. 1(7) which states:

> In the case of a body lying in a hospital, nursing home or other institution, any authority under this section may be given on behalf of the person having the control and management thereof by any officer or person designated for that purpose by the first-mentioned person.

While this gives the right of lawful possession to the hospital authority this is not to be read as an exclusive right. Where, for example, the parents or next of kin demand possession, that demand is based on a superior right of possession and arguably has to be acceded to. While the body may still be at the hospital, the possessory right of the relevant authority is limited by conditions imposed on it by the party with the superior right of possession (namely the next of kin).

Further significance comes from the fact that the 'person in lawful possession' *may* authorise. There is no compulsion on that party to accord with the wishes of the deceased. It may thus be the case that whoever is so designated may refuse removal, even where the deceased had expressed an oral or written wish that organ(s) be donated.

Section 1(1) makes provision for a change of mind on the part of the potential donor, whose withdrawal of request must be complied with. Such withdrawal of request will be effective, whatever form, written or oral, it takes.

Section 1(2) may be termed the 'possessor authorisation' subsection:

Without prejudice to the foregoing subsection, the person lawfully in possession of the body of a deceased person may authorise the removal of any part from the body for use for the said purposes if, having made such reasonable enquiry as may be practicable, he has no reason to believe—

(a)   that the deceased had expressed an objection to his body being so dealt with after his death, and had not withdrawn it; or

(b)   that the surviving spouse or any surviving relative of the deceased objects to the body being so dealt with.

The vaguely defined 'person lawfully in possession of the body' appears in this subsection, and there are other less than satisfactory elements.

(a)   '. . . having made such reasonable enquiry as may be practicable'.

The obvious question is how reasonable is enough to satisfy the requirement of the legislation. Allied to this is 'practicable' in relation to what? According to Skegg ('Human Tissues Act 1961' (1976) 16 Med Sci Law 197):

In determining whether the person lawfully in possession of the body has made reasonable enquiries, some weight must clearly be given to the resources – both in terms of finance and manpower – available to him, and to the other claims on those resources.

It seems self-evident that the hospital could not grind to a halt while all available staff carry out an extensive inquiry into whether the deceased ever expressed an objection, or the surviving spouse or relatives object to the removal.

In making a determination about what is 'practicable', one has to consider the motivations behind the legislation itself. The Act was designed to facilitate the availability of transplant organs, but within a structure that protected those close to the deceased from any more anguish than was necessary, and secured public confidence about the practice, arguably in that order of priority. Practicability, then, would appear on such a reading to be based on the time within which it would be possible to make enquiry without jeopardising any possible transplant operation which could utilise the body part. Parliament could not have envisaged extensive inquiry of all relatives, nor could it have considered desirable that no transplantation should take place where a relative is out of the range of immediate contact (on a walking holiday, for example).

The legislation does not provide for who comes within the term 'surviving relative'. In keeping with the objectives of the legislation as a whole, the best interpretation would be any relative who could be contacted within the time during which the organ is viable for transplantation. That this may appear a rather open-textured interpretation reveals the vague articulation of factors throughout the subsection.

Of importance is the point that the current definition of death allows for the 'beating heart' donor. The 'deceased' may still be connected to a ventilator even where the brain stem has irreversibly ceased to function (this is known as 'elective ventilation'). Section 1(4) provides for the transplant surgeon to satisfy himself that 'life is extinct'. The advantage of transplants here would be that removal and transplant could be effected as part of one procedure, therefore the donated organ would be transplanted before the process of deterioration had begun in earnest. While this is valuable, where it is proposed that this take place, it might well impact on the reasonableness of the enquiry under s. 1(2). The ventilator could be kept on until a relative was contacted. However, the ventilator could also be kept on for a considerably longer period. Does this then mean that all relatives need to be contacted? This may be extending matters too far, but is another indication of the vagueness inherent in the legislation itself.

Perhaps the most surprising thing about the Human Tissue Act 1961 is not so much the vagueness of what it does say as what it fails to say at all. A consideration of the Act as a whole reveals that there appears to be no sanction for failing to observe the preconditions for the removal of an organ from the deceased. One again has to attempt to proceed by way of analogy in the absence of a specific sanction in the legislation itself.

Skegg ('Liability for the Unauthorised Removal of Cadaveric Transplant Material' (1974) 14 Med Sci Law 53) examines the common law alternatives. He indicated that there has long been recognised the common law crime of preventing the disposal of a corpse. Skegg argues that if the transplant team were to retain the whole body when it was demanded by the spouse or other person with a superior right to possession, then there might be liability under this common law crime. Skegg's response, based on the reality of contemporary medical practice, is that where the body is returned to the person with a right to lawful possession in a recognisable form then liability would be unlikely.

Skegg considers an even more 'exotic' common law crime, that of the 'indecent interference with the bodies of the dead'. He admits the unlikeliness of a prosecution given that the aim of the common law was the unnecessary mutilation of the dead or post mortem sexual interference (necrophilia). One can safely say that the common practice of cadaver transplant surgery involves neither of these activities!

Kennedy and Grubb note (*Medical Law*, 2nd ed. (London: Butterworths, 1994), p. 1157) that failure to comply with the 1961 Act may be perceived as a common law crime of disobedience of a statute. This, it is noted, is an ancient crime. The case of *R v Lennox-Wright* [1973] Crim LR 529 surprisingly actually concerned an alleged breach of the Human Tissue Act 1961. The allegation was that the defendant, who was unqualified, removed eyes from a dead body. He was charged with 'Doing an act in disobedience of a statute by removing parts of a body, contrary to s. 1(4) of the Human Tissure Act 1961'. This subsection allows only 'registered medical practitioners' to perform cadaveric organ removal. An attempt was made to quash the indictment because the statute was only regulatory. This attempt failed and there was found to be a common law crime of disobedience of the 1961 Act. One would suppose that, at least with the modern drafting of legislation, if there is to be a sanction imposed then one would be spelled out in the body of that (or related and referred to) legislation. Kennedy and Grubb (p. 1158) have further argued that, even if there is such a common law crime in existence (highly doubtful after the decision in *R v Horseferry Road Justices, ex parte Independent Broadcasting Authorities* [1987] QB 54), it does not apply because of the Human Tissue Act 1961, s. 1(8):

> Nothing in this section shall be construed as rendering unlawful any dealing with, or with any part of, the body of a deceased person which is lawful apart from this Act.

While there seems no realistic possibility of a criminal prosecution there is a chance (still slim) that there might be grounds for a civil action in negligence for nervous shock. Subject to all the policy-based limitations developed to stop the floodgates of litigation in nervous shock claims (see, for example, *Alcock v Chief Constable of South Yorkshire Police* [1992] 1 AC 310), there still exists the possibility that the distressed mother of a child killed in a car crash, informed that the child's organs had been removed without consulting her or considering the child's wishes, who then sees the deceased child with that knowledge of the organ removal and suffers a recognised psychiatric illness as a result, may recover for nervous shock. While one needs to note the policy limitations in nervous shock cases (see Skegg, 'Liability for the Unauthorised Removal of Cadaveric Transplant Material: Some Further Comments' (1977) 17 Med Sci Law 123), these are limitations not blanket exclusions. Therefore the possibility of liability being incurred still exists.

16.8   FOETAL TISSUE TRANSPLANTS

The changes in abortion practice wrought by the 1990 reforms to the Abortion Act 1967, s. 1(1)(d) set up a regime of liberal abortion up to term provided the foetus was likely to suffer from serious abnormality. While such a situation occurring must be seen as a tragic event for foetus and parents, one cannot be blind to the opportunities in terms of transplant surgery such an abortion would bring.

Recently foetal neural tissue has been implanted into those suffering from Parkinson's disease. As Mason and McCall Smith indicate (*Law and Medical Ehtics*, 4th ed. (London: Butterworths, 1994), p. 310):

> Normal adult nerve cells cannot replicate whereas foetal cells are actively growing and multiplying; theoretically, therefore, an implanted foetal cell will grow and provide a source of important cellular metabolites that are often deficient in the aged.

There appears to be clear recognition of two matters concerning removal and transplant of cadaver foetal brain tissue. First, aside from the spontaneous miscarriage which may occur, the supply of such tissue is dependent on abortion. Allied to this is the second point that there seems to be agreement that an abortion should not be undertaken to provide such tissue where such abortion would not have been undertaken if that were not a consideration (see, for example, Nolan, 'The Use of Embryo or Foetus in Transplantation: What There Is to Lose' (1990) 22 Transplant Proc 1029).

In addition to this essentially moral issue, one must also consider the possible utilisation of the organs of the anencephalic neonate. The Human Tissue Act 1961 will apply, and therefore there will need to be a determination of when 'life is extinct'.

Mason and McCall Smith (p. 308) acknowledge that while there appears a restatement that life needs to be extinct by the Working Party of the Royal Medical Colleges (*Organ Transplantation in Neonates* (1988)) this may well be derived from a notion that there is something 'different' about the issue of neonatal donation, and public reassurance that 'spontaneous respiration has ceased' is needed.

16.9 CONCLUSION

One of the main candidates for reform in this area of medical law has to be the Human Tissue Act 1961 itself. One of the most voiced reforms of this legislation has been to remove totally the 'opt-in' system which exists at the moment and replace it with an 'opt-out' system. This simple reform could have a profound effect. Any legislation would indicate that everyone is assumed to wish to donate all their suitable organs after death unless they indicate otherwise. Rather than those wishing to donate carrying donor cards as at present, there would be a central register of those who had voiced an objection to their organs being used after death. This register would be available to all hospitals who carried out transplant surgery. It might be that the legislation would make it a requirement that this register be consulted by a registered medical practitioner before any removal of organs took place. The further advantage of this is that it would not be necessary for a doctor or nurse to confront those grieving for the dead with the additional anguish of deciding whether the organs should be donated. Not expressed as often, but nonetheless important, would be that the medical profession would be relieved of this onerous duty.

Before one becomes too enamoured of the prospect, one should note the comments of Ruth Redmond-Cooper ('Transplants Opting Out or In – The Implications' (1984) 134 NLJ 648) in relation to France. There the contracting-out system has been in place since 1976. However:

> In practice . . . French doctors prefer to obtain the consent of the next of kin . . . possibly since the majority of French people would seem to be unaware of the provisions of the Law of 1976. The result of this is that the number of transplants performed in France is lower than in the UK.

It would appear, therefore, that any legislation along the lines of an opt-out system would need to be combined with a process of public consultation and education, particularly, as mentioned earlier, concerning the definition of death. Of course, one could be more authoritarian and give the next of kin no power of veto over what should happen to the deceased. Once more one would anticipate that such a development might well lead to an increase in suspicion and fear surrounding the process of transplantation.

Despite the attractiveness of the opt-out system, the Working Party on the Supply of Donor Organs for Transplantation chaired by Sir Raymond Hoffenberg (1987) decided that:

> We do not recommend this. There would be a risk that organs might be removed when this had not been the wish of the person or their relatives. It does not in itself enlist the cooperation of doctors. We would prefer organ donation to be seen as a positive gift with the consent of relatives who in practice would always be approached. (p. 6)

The Hoffenberg Report was rather more helpful in illuminating the underlying problems of cadaver donation and transplantation, which, if correctly addressed, could create a culture more attuned to the donation of organs, although some of the observations are a little naive. The report indicated that part of the reason for the shortfall was that many doctors have little awareness of the requirements for brain stem death to be diagnosed, and also are practically inexperienced in the process of organ donation requests. The report reveals that 'Some hospitals seldom provide organs for transplantation, yet when a sympathetic and experienced person talks with the relatives, permission is likely to be granted. Some hospitals have obtained 90 per cent agreement to donation.' In addition the report noted evidence of doubts about the success of transplant programmes, and stated firmly that 'This should no longer be entertained since the benefits of transplantation to the majority of recipients are proven'. The report confirmed the continued ignorance and suspicions that surround the determination of death. Rather than confronting this suspicion with education with regard to brain stem death the report argues that 'We accept that a small minority of doctors and some members of the public have reservations about that concept of brain stem death despite full explanation, and that patients and their relatives must always be free to decline consent to organ donation'.

Further reading

Bumford, S.E., 'Bone Marrow Donation: The Law in Context' (1998) 10 CFLQ 2135.

Dworkin, G., 'The Law Relating to Organ Transplantation in England' (1970) 33 MLR 353.

Lanham, D., 'Transplants and the Human Tissues Act 1961' (1971) 11 Med Sci Law 16.

Price, D., and Mackay, R., 'The Trade in Human Organs' (1991) 141 NLJ 1272.

Skegg, P., 'Human Tissue Act 1961' (1976) 16 Med Sci Law 197.

Skegg, P., 'Liability for the Unauthorised Removal of Cadaveric Transplant Material' (1974) 14 Med Sci Law 53.

Spencer, J., 'Tissue Donors: Are They Rescuers, or Merely Volunteers?' [1979] CLJ 45.

Index

DR M.D. MACLEOD MBChB MRCGP
The Health Centre
Wellington Avenue
Aldershot
Hants
GU11 1PA
Tel: 01252 324577
Fax: 01252 324861
e.mail:mdmacleod@librykim.demon.co.uk